C000179823

STREE

Bristol
and Bath

Clevedon, Portishead, Thornbury, Weston-super-Mare, Yate

www.philips-maps.co.uk

First published in 1995 as 'Bristol and Avon' by

Philip's, a division of
Octopus Publishing Group Ltd
www.octopusbooks.co.uk
2-4 Heron Quays, London E14 4JP
An Hachette Livre UK Company

Third colour edition 2007
First impression 2007
BABCA

ISBN-10   0-540-09188-X (pocket)
ISBN-13   978-0-540-09188-1 (pocket)

© Philip's 2007

Ordnance Survey®

This product includes mapping data licensed from
Ordnance Survey® with the permission of the
Controller of Her Majesty's Stationery Office.
© Crown copyright 2007. All rights reserved.
Licence number 100011710.

No part of this publication may be reproduced,
stored in a retrieval system or transmitted in any
form or by any means, electronic, mechanical,
photocopying, recording or otherwise, without the
permission of the Publishers and the copyright
owner.

To the best of the Publishers' knowledge, the
information in this atlas was correct at the time of
going to press. No responsibility can be accepted
for any errors or their consequences.

The representation in this atlas of a road, track or
path is no evidence of the existence of a right
of way.

Data for the speed cameras provided by
PocketGPSWorld.com Ltd.

Ordnance Survey and the OS Symbol are
registered trademarks of Ordnance Survey, the
national mapping agency of Great Britain

Printed by Toppan, China

Contents

II   **List of mobile speed cameras**

III   **Key to map symbols**

IV   **Key to map pages**

VI   **Route planning**

VIII   **Administrative and Postcode boundaries**

1   **Street maps** at 2⅔ inches to 1 mile

141   **Street maps of Bath and Bristol city centres** at 5⅓ inches to 1 mile

144   **Index** of towns, villages, streets, hospitals, industrial estates, railway stations, schools, shopping centres, universities and places of interest

Digital Data

The exceptionally high-quality mapping found in this atlas is available as digital data in TIFF format, which is easily convertible to other bitmapped (raster) image formats.

The index is also available in digital form as a standard database table. It contains all the details found in the printed index together with the National Grid reference for the map square in which each entry is named.

For further information and to discuss your requirements, please contact james.mann@philips-maps.co.uk

Mobile speed cameras

The vast majority of speed cameras used on Britain's roads are operated by safety camera partnerships. These comprise local authorities, the police, Her Majesty's Court Service (HMCS) and the Highways Agency.

This table lists the sites where each safety camera partnership may enforce speed limits through the use of mobile cameras or detectors. These are usually set up on the roadside or a bridge spanning the road and operated by a police or civilian enforcement officer. The speed limit at each site (if available) is shown in red type, followed by the approximate location in black type.

Mike Harrington / Alamy

M32
60 Bristol Stadium

A4
30 Bath, Newbridge Rd
30 Bristol, Anchor Rd
30 Bristol, Totterdown Bridge
50 Nr Keynsham, Keynsham Bypass jct A4175 Durley Hill
50 Portway
30 Portway, nr A4176 Bridge Valley Rd

A4/B4054
30 Bristol, Avonmouth Rd

A37
30 Bristol, Wells Rd (nr jct Airport Rd)
30 Bristol, Wells Rd (nr St Johns La)

A38
40 Aztec West, nr Bradley Stoke Way
30 Bathpool
40 Bedminster Down, Bridgwater Rd
40 Bristol, Bedminster Down Rd nr Bishopsworth Rd
30 Bristol, Bedminster Down Rd/West St
30 Bristol, Cheltenham Rd/Gloucester Rd, nr Cranbrook Rd
30 Bristol, Gloucester Rd nr B4052 Ashley Down Rd
30 Bristol, Stokes Croft nr Bond St
40 Churchill – Langford
40 Cross
40 Filton, Gloucester Rd (north) nr B4057 Gypsy Patch Lane

40 Patchway, Gloucester Rd nr Highwood Rd
50 Redhill

A46
60 Bath to Wickwar Rd
40 Dunkirk

A367
30 Bath, Green Park Rd
30 Bath, Bear Flat
30 Radstock, Wells Rd

A369
40 Abbots Leigh
60 Easton-in-Gordano, Martcombe Rd nr M5 jct 19

A370
30 Backwell, West Town
30 Cleeve Village
30 Congresbury, Station Rd, Bristol Rd
30 Flax Bourton nr B3130
40 Long Ashton Bypass, Bristol End
50 West Wick, Somerset Avenue, west of M5 jct 21
30 Weston-super-Mare, Beach Rd
50 Weston-super-Mare, Herluin Way nr Winterstoke Rd
50 Weston-super-Mare, Somerset Avenue (central reservation)
50 Weston-super-Mare, Somerset Avenue, jct Moor Lane
30 Weston-super-Mare, Winterstoke Rd

A371
30 Winscombe, Sidcot Lane nr jct A38,

A403
40 Avonmouth Docks

A420
30 Bristol, Lawrence Hill
30 Kingswood, Two Mile Hill Rd, Regent St
30 Old Market, nr Temple Way/Bond St
30 Redfield, Church Rd
30 St George, Clouds Hill Rd/Bell Hill Rd
30 Warmley, High St London Rd nr A4175 Bath Rd
60 Wick, Tog Hill

A431
30 Longwell Green, Bath Rd

A432
30 Bristol, Fishponds Rd nr B4048 Lodge Causeway
30 Bristol, Fishponds Rd nr B4469 Royate Hill
30 Bristol, Fishponds Rd with B4469 Muller Rd
30 Bristol, Stapleton Rd nr jct A4320 Easton Way
40 Badminton Rd nr A4174 Avon Ring Rd
40 Kendleshire
30 Yate, Station Rd/B4059 Stover Rd

A3029
40 Bristol, Avon Bridge

A3039
30 Devonshire Rd

A4018
30 Bristol, Black Boy Hill/Whiteladies Rd
30 Bristol, Cribbs Causeway jct 17 M5
30 Bristol, Westbury Rd nr B4054 North View
30 Bristol, Whiteladies Rd into Queens Rd
30 Westbury on Trym, Falcondale Rd

A4044
30 Bristol, Temple Way/Redcliffe Way

A4081
40 Catbrain

A4162
30 Bristol, Sylvan Way/Dingle Rd/Canford Lane

A4174
50 Avon Ring Rd nr jct 1 M32
30 Bristol, Hartcliffe Way
40 Bristol, Hengrove Way/Airport Rd nr Creswicke Rd
50 Bromley Heath
50 Filton, Filton Rd/Avon Ring Rd nr Coldharbour Lane
40 Filton, Station Rd, nr Great Stoke Way

A4320
30 Bristol, at A4 Bath Rd nr Sandy Park Rd

B3124
30 Clevedon, Walton Rd

B3130
30 Nailsea, Stockway (north)/Chapel Avenue
30,40 Wraxall

B3133
30 Clevedon, Central Way

B3440
30 Weston-super-Mare, Locking Rd/Regent St/Alexandra Parade

B4051
30 Bristol, Park Row/Perry Rd

B4054
30 Sea Mills, Shirehampton Rd

B4056
30 Bristol, Northumbria Drive/Linden Rd/Westbury Park
30 Bristol, Southmead Rd nr Pen Park Rd
30 Bristol, Southmead Rd nr Wellington Hill

B4057
30 Bristol, Crow Lane nr A4018 Passage Rd
30 Gypsy Patch Lane nr Hatchet Rd
50 Winterbourne Rd nr B4427 Gloucester Rd

B4058
30 Bristol, Frenchay Park Rd
30 Winterbourne, Winterbourne Hill/High St

B4059
30 Yate, Goose Green Way

B4060
30 Yate, Station Rd/Bowling Hill/Rounceval St

B4061
30 Thornbury, Bristol Rd

B4465
30 Mangotsfield, Broad St
30 Staple Hill, Staple Hill Rd/High St nr Forest Rd

UNCLASSIFIED
30 Bristol, Bishopsworth, Whitchurch/Hareclive Rd
30 Bristol, Bishport Avenue
30 Knowle Bristol, Broadwalk
30 Bristol, Hengrove, Hawkfield Rd nr A4174 Hartcliffe Way
30 Bristol, Kingsway
30 Bristol, Long Cross, Lawrence Weston
30 Bristol, Stoke Hill/Stoke Rd nr Saville Rd, Clifton
30 Bristol, Sturminster Rd
30 Bristol, Whitchurch Lane nr Dundry Rd

Key to map symbols

III

Motorway with junction number (22a)	
Primary route – dual/single carriageway	
A road – dual/single carriageway	
B road – dual/single carriageway	
Minor road – dual/single carriageway	
Other minor road – dual/single carriageway	
Road under construction	
Tunnel, covered road	
Speed cameras - single, multiple	
Rural track, private road or narrow road in urban area	
Gate or obstruction to traffic (restrictions may not apply at all times or to all vehicles)	
Path, bridleway, byway open to all traffic, road used as a public path	
Pedestrianised area	
DY7 Postcode boundaries	
County and unitary authority boundaries	
Railway, tunnel, railway under construction	
Tramway, tramway under construction	
Miniature railway	
Railway station	
Private railway station	
Metro station	
Tram stop, tram stop under construction	
Bus, coach station	

- ◆ Ambulance station
- ◆ Coastguard station
- ◆ Fire station
- ◆ Police station
- ✚ Accident and Emergency entrance to hospital
- Ⓗ Hospital
- ✛ Place of worship
- ⓘ Information Centre (open all year)
- Shopping Centre
- P P&R Parking, Park and Ride
- PO Post Office
- ⋏ ⛟ Camping site, caravan site
- ▶ ✕ Golf course, picnic site
- Prim Sch Important buildings, schools, colleges, universities and hospitals
- Built up area
- Woods
- River Medway Water name
- River, weir, stream
- Canal, lock, tunnel
- Water
- Tidal water
- Church Non-Roman antiquity
- ROMAN FORT Roman antiquity

87 Adjoining page indicators and overlap bands
The colour of the arrow and the band
237 indicates the scale of the adjoining or overlapping page (see scales below)

Enlarged mapping only

- Railway or bus station building
- Place of interest
- Parkland

Acad	Academy	Inst	Institute	Recn Gd	Recreation Ground
Allot Gdns	Allotments	Ct	Law Court		
Cemy	Cemetery	L Ctr	Leisure Centre	Resr	Reservoir
C Ctr	Civic Centre	LC	Level Crossing	Ret Pk	Retail Park
CH	Club House	Liby	Library	Sch	School
Coll	College	Mkt	Market	Sh Ctr	Shopping Centre
Crem	Crematorium	Meml	Memorial	TH	Town Hall/House
Ent	Enterprise	Mon	Monument	Trad Est	Trading Estate
Ex H	Exhibition Hall	Mus	Museum	Univ	University
Ind Est	Industrial Estate	Obsy	Observatory	W Twr	Water Tower
IRB Sta	Inshore Rescue Boat Station	Pal	Royal Palace	Wks	Works
		PH	Public House	YH	Youth Hostel

■ The small numbers around the edges of the maps identify the 1 kilometre National Grid lines

■ The dark grey border on the inside edge of some pages indicates that the mapping does not continue onto the adjacent page

The scale of the maps on the pages numbered in blue is 4.2 cm to 1 km • 2⅔ inches to 1 mile • 1: 23810

0	¼	½	¾	1 mile
0	250 m	500 m	750 m	1 kilometre

The scale of the maps on pages numbered in red is 8.4 cm to 1 km • 5⅓ inches to 1 mile • 1: 11900

0	220 yards	440 yards	660 yards	½ mile
0	125 m	250 m	375 m	½ kilometre

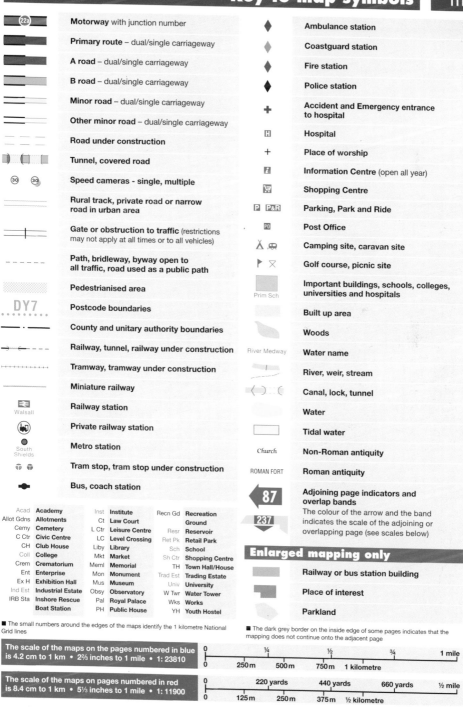

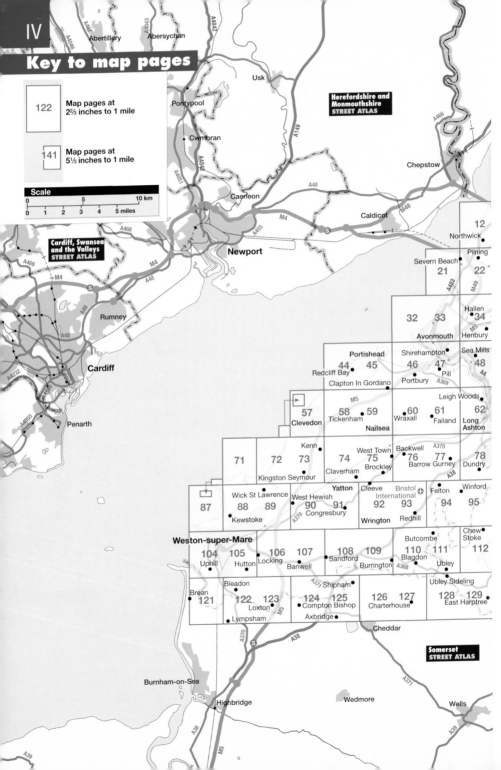

IV

Key to map pages

122	Map pages at 2⅔ inches to 1 mile
141	Map pages at 5⅓ inches to 1 mile

Scale

0 _____ 5 _____ 10 km

0 __ 1 __ 2 __ 3 __ 4 __ 5 miles

Abertillery   Abersychan

Usk

Pontypool

Herefordshire and Monmouthshire STREET ATLAS

Cwmbran

Chepstow

Caerleon

A48

Caldicot

M4

Newport

Severn Beach   **21**   **22**

12
Northwick

Pilning

Cardiff, Swansea and the Valleys STREET ATLAS

Rumney

Hallen
32   **33**   **34**

Avonmouth   Henbury

Cardiff

Portishead   Shirehampton   Sea Mills
44   **45**   **46**   **47**   **48**
Redcliff Bay   Pill
Clapton In Gordano   Portbury   A369

Penarth

Leigh Woods
57   **58**   **59**   **60**   **61**   **62**
Clevedon   Tickenham   Wraxall   Failand   Long Ashton
Nailsea

Kenn
71   **72**   **73**   **74**   West Town **75**   Backwell **76**   **77**   **78**
Kingston Seymour   Claverham   Brockley   Barrow Gurney   Dundry

Yatton   Cleeve   Bristol   Felton   Winford
Wick St Lawrence   West Hewish   International
87   **88**   **89**   **90**   **91**   **92**   **93**   **94**   **95**
Kewstoke   Congresbury   Wrington   Redhill

Chew Stoke
Butcombe
Weston-super-Mare   **104**   **105**   **106**   **107**   **108**   **109**   Blagdon **110**   **111**   **112**
Uphill   Hutton   Locking   Banwell   Sandford   Burrington   Ubley

Bleadon   Shipham   Ubley Sideling
Brean   **121**   **122**   **123**   **124**   **125**   **126**   **127**   **128**   **129**
Loxton   Compton Bishop   Charterhouse   East Harptree
Lympsham   Axbridge
Cheddar

Somerset STREET ATLAS

Burnham-on-Sea

Wedmore   Wells

Highbridge

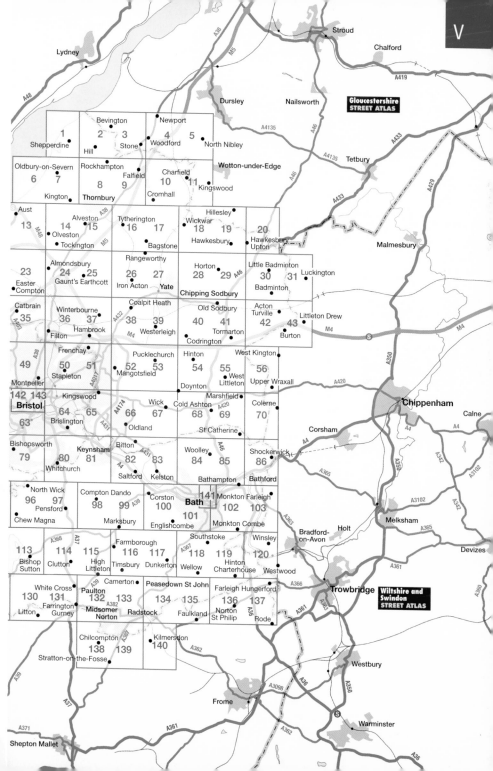

V

Stroud
Chalford
Lydney
A419
Dursley
Nailsworth
Gloucestershire STREET ATLAS
A4135
Bevington
Newport
Tetbury
A4135
A46
A433
1
2   3
4   5
North Nibley
Shepperdine
Hill
Stone
Woodford
A429
Oldbury-on-Severn
Rockhampton
Charfield
Wotton-under-Edge
A433
6   7
Falfield
Kingswood
8   9
10 11
Malmesbury
Kington
Thornbury
Cromhall
Aust
Hillesley
13
14   Alveston
Tytherington
Wickwar
18 19
20
15
16   17
Olveston
Bagstone
Hawkesbury
Hawkesbury Upton
Tockington
M5
Rangeworthy
Horton
Little Badminton
Luckington
23
24   25
26   27
28   29
30 31
Easter Compton
Gaunt's Earthcott
Iron Acton   Yate
Badminton
Catbrain
Coalpit Heath
Old Sodbury
Acton Turville
Littleton Drew
35
36   37
38   39
40   41
42 43
M4
Winterbourne
Westerleigh
Tormarton
Burton
Filton
Hambrook
Codrington
M4
Frenchay
Pucklechurch
Hinton
West Kington
49
50   51
52   53
54   55
56
Montpelier
Stapleton
Mangotsfield
West Littleton
Upper Wraxall
A420
Chippenham
Doynton
142 143
Kingswood
Wick
Marshfield
Colerne
Bristol
64   65
66   67
68   69
70
Calne
63
Brislington
Oldland
St Catherine
A4
Corsham
Bishopsworth
Bitton
Woolley
Shockerwick
A4
A342
79
80   81
82   83
84   85
86
A3102
Whitchurch
Keynsham
Saltford   Kelston
Bathampton
Bathford
Melksham
North Wick
Compton Dando
Corston
141
Monkton Farleigh
A3102
96   97
98
99 100
Bath
102 103
Pensford
101
Bradford-on-Avon
Holt
Chew Magna
Marksbury
Englishcombe
Monkton Combe
Devizes
Farmborough
Southstoke
Winsley
113
114 115
116 117
118 119 120
Bishop Sutton
High Littleton
Timsbury   Dunkerton
Hinton Charterhouse
Westwood
Clutton
Wellow
Trowbridge
White Cross
Camerton
Peasedown St John
Farleigh Hungerford
130 131
Paulton
132 133
134 135
136 137
Wiltshire and Swindon STREET ATLAS
Litton
Farrington Gurney
Midsomer Norton
Radstock
Faulkland
Norton St Philip
Rode
Chilcompton
Kilmersdon
138 139
140
Westbury
Stratton-on-the-Fosse
Frome
A371
A361
Warminster
Shepton Mallet

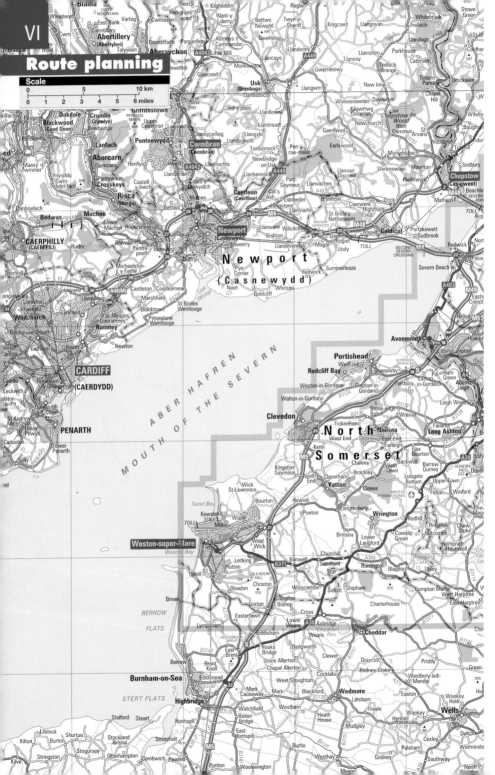

Route planning

Scale

0   5   10 km
0 1 2 3 4 5   6 miles

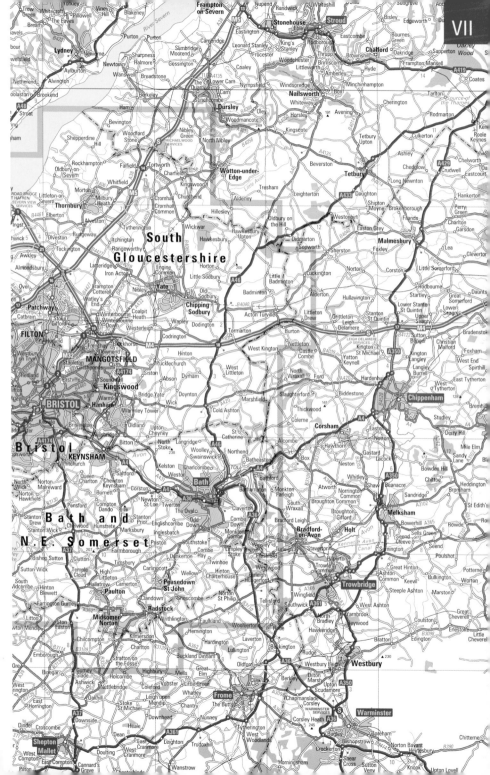

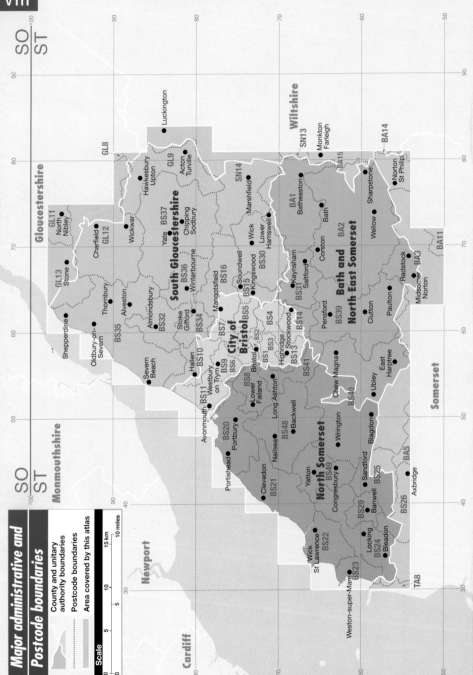

Major administrative and Postcode boundaries

Scale
0   5   10   15 km
0   5   10 miles

County and unitary authority boundaries
Postcode boundaries
Area covered by this atlas

A   B   C   D   E   F

Gloucestershire STREET ATLAS

8

7

97

GL13

6

River Severn

White House

Severn Way

Chapel House

Manor Farm

+

The Laurels

5

NUPDOWN RD

PH

Shepperdine Farm

96

North Ham Corner

Shepperdine Farm

4

Shepperdine

Brickhouse Farm

Shepperdine Withybed

BS35

3

GL13

95

Harestreet La

Jobscreen Farm

SHEPPERDINE RD

Lowgoods Farm

2

Oldbury Power Station

Knight's Farm

Mast

HILL

1

60   A   B   61   C   D   62   E   F   94

Gloucestershire STREET ATLAS

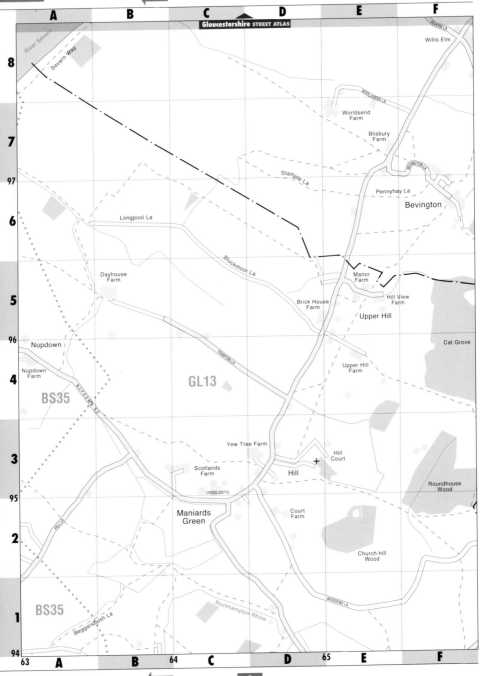

Gloucestershire STREET ATLAS

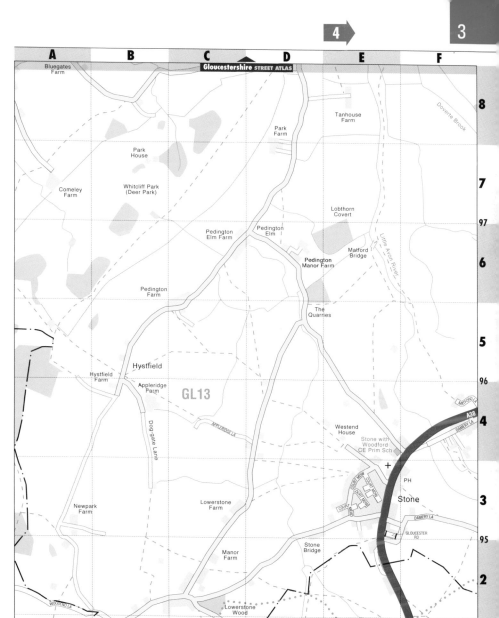

Gloucestershire STREET ATLAS

Bluegates
Farm

Doverte Brook

8

Park
House

Park
Farm

Tanhouse
Farm

7

Comeley
Farm

Whitcliff Park
(Deer Park)

Lobthorn
Covert

97

Pedington
Elm Farm

Pedington
Elm

Matford
Bridge

Little Avon River

6

Pedington
Manor Farm

Pedington
Farm

The
Quarries

5

Hystfield

GL13

Hystfield
Farm

96

Appleridge
Farm

APPLERIDGE LA

Westend
House

Stone with
Woodford
CE Prim Sch

MATFORD LA

A38

DAMERY LA

4

Dog-gate Lane

COURT VIEW

COLT WOOD

PH

COURT
MEAD

Stone

3

Newpark
Farm

Lowerstone
Farm

DAMERY LA

Manor
Farm

Stone
Bridge

GLOUCESTER
RD

95

WOODFORD LA

Lowerstone
Wood

2

Lower
Stone

MOORSLADE LA

Green
Farm

Glen
Farm

The
Mount

1

GL12

Moorslade

A38

Chestnut
Farm

94

66   A   B   67   C   D   68   E   F

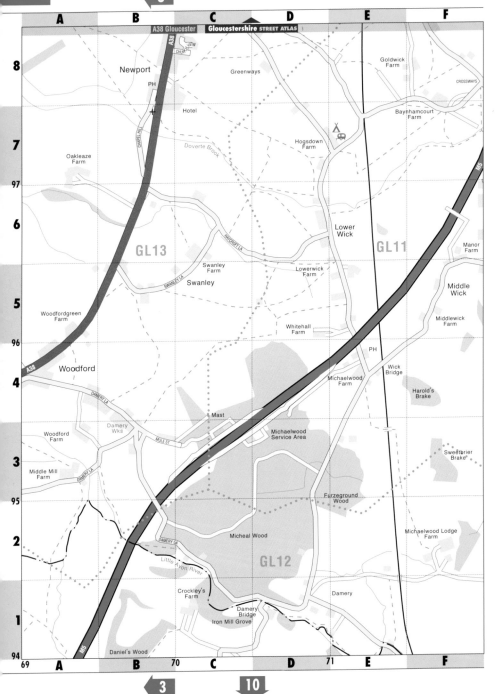

A38 Gloucester Gloucestershire STREET ATLAS

A **B** **C** **D** **E** **F**

8

Newport

PH

Hotel

Greenways

Goldwick
Farm

CROSSWAYS

Baynhamcourt
Farm

7

Oakleaze
Farm

Doverte Brook

Hogsdown
Farm

97

6

Lower
Wick

GL13

GL11

MAYCROFT LA

Manor
Farm

Swanley
Farm

Swanley

Lowerwick
Farm

Middle
Wick

5

Woodfordgreen
Farm

Middlewick
Farm

Whitehall
Farm

96

PH

A38

Wick
Bridge

Woodford

Michaelwood
Farm

Harold's
Brake

4

DAMERY LA

Mast

Sweetbrier
Brake

Damery
Wks

MULE ST

Michaelwood
Service Area

Woodford
Farm

3

Middle Mill
Farm

DAMERY LA

Furzeground
Wood

95

Michaelwood Lodge
Farm

2

DAMERY LA

Micheal Wood

GL12

Little Avon River

Crockley's
Farm

Damery

1

Damery
Bridge
Iron Mill Grove

Daniel's Wood

94

69   **A**   **B**   70   **C**   **D**   71   **E**   **F**

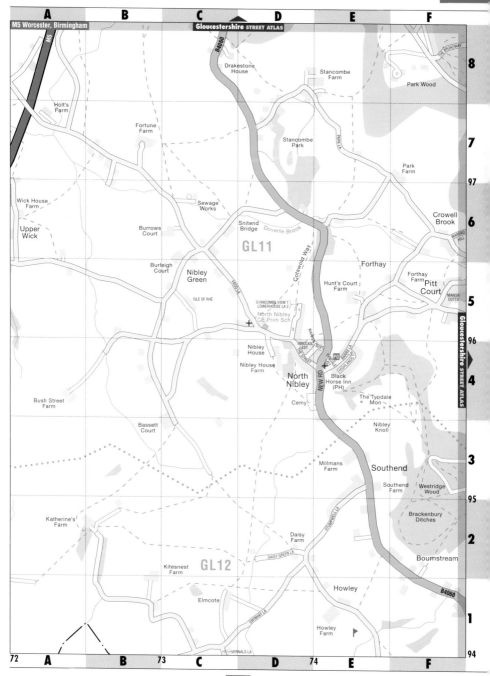

M5 Worcester, Birmingham

A   B   C   D   E   F

8

7

97

6

97

5

96

4

3

95

2

1

94

Drakestone House
Stancombe Farm
THE BROADWAY
Park Wood
Holt's Farm
Fortune Farm
Stancombe Park
PARK LA
Park Farm
Wick House Farm
Sewage Works
Crowell Brook
WAEND HILL
Upper Wick
Burrows Court
Snitend Bridge
Doverte Brook
GL11
Forthay
Forthay Farm
Pitt Court
MANOR COTTS
Burleigh Court
Nibley Green
Hunt's Court Farm
ISLE OF RHÉ
Cotswold Way
STANCOMBE VIEW 1
LOWER HOUSE LA 2
North Nibley CE Prim Sch
TYNDALE LA
Nibley House
WAEND CROFT
INNOCKS DROVE
HIGHLANDS LA
Nibley House Farm
North Nibley
THE STREET
NEW RD
Black Horse Inn (PH)
Bush Street Farm
Cemy
The Tyndale Mon
Bassett Court
Nibley Knoll
Millmans Farm
Southend
Southend Farm
Westridge Wood
Katherine's Farm
STANCOMBE LA
Brackenbury Ditches
Daisy Farm
GL12
Bournstream
Kitesnest Farm
DAISY GREEN LA
Howley
B4060
Elmcote
SWINNART LA
Howley Farm
VERNALS LA

72   A   B   73   C   D   74   E   F

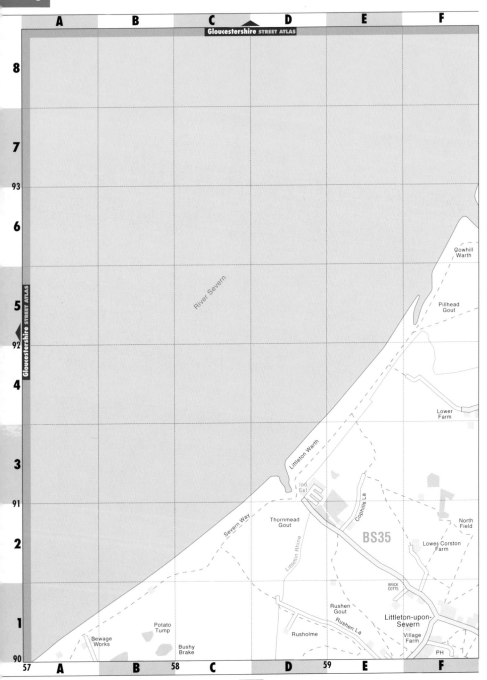

A B C D E F

8

7

93

6

Cowhill
Warth

5

River Severn

Pillhead
Gout

92

4

Lower
Farm

3

Littleton Warth

91

Ind
Est

Cophills La

Severn Way

Thornmead
Gout

North
Field

BS35

2

Littleton Rhine

Lower Corston
Farm

BRICK
CDTTS

1

Rushen
Gout

Littleton-upon-
Severn

Potato
Tump

Rusholme

Rushen La

Village
Farm

Sewage
Works

Bushy
Brake

PH

90

57 A B 58 C D 59 E F

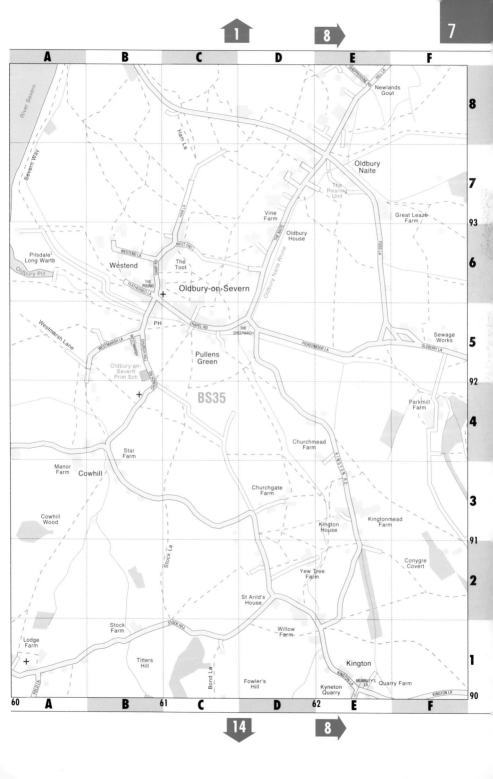

A B C D E F

8

Northfields

Northfield Lane

GL13

The Old Rectory

7

Lodge Farm

The Hollies

CHURCH VIEW

Rockhampton

Court Farm

93

Henridge Hill

Pennywell Farm

The Firs

6

Yew Tree Farm

Newton

Luce's Farm

Pound Mill Farm

Groves Tully

5

Pound Mill Bsns Ctr

Maypole Farm

HORSE LA

Duckhole

Longman's Grove

Oak Farm

92

OLDBURY LA

Spring Farm

Lower Morton

BS35

4

MORTON RD

Manor Farm

Morton House

Upper Morton

Park Farm

GLOUCESTER RD

Mile End Farm

Morton

Yewtree Farm

B4061

The Knapp

3

Knapp Farm

Mahorbrook Prim Sch

The Castle Sch

THORNBURY

91

CROSSWAYS LA

Sheiling Sch

Thornbury Castle

Crossways

2

St Mary's CE Prim Sch

Crossways House

MORTON WAY

WHITEWALL LA

Christ the King RC Prim Sch

New Siblands Sch

GL12

1

Cerny

KINGTON LA

The Castle Sch Sixth Form Ctr

Thornbury

Crossways Jun & Inf Schs

HACKET LA

B4061 HIGH ST

THE PLAIN

90

63 A B 64 C D 65 E F

B1
1 QUAKER CT
2 ST JOHN ST
3 PULLINS GN
4 CRISPIN LA
5 SAW MILL LA
6 ST MARYS WAY
7 SILVER ST
8 ST MARY ST
9 ROCKLEASE
10 GROVESEND RD
11 BUCKINGHAM PAR
12 GLOUCESTER TERR

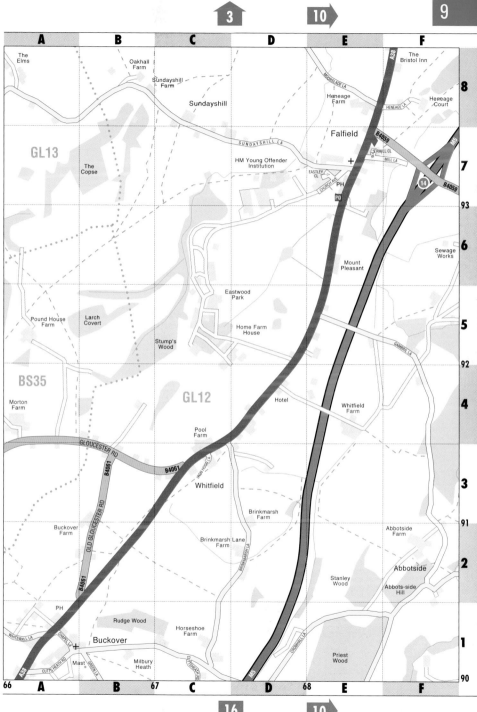

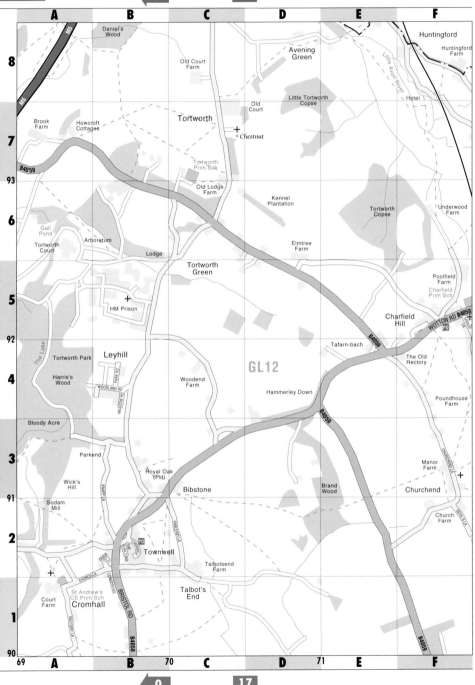

A   **B**   **C**   **D**   **E**   **F**

Huntingford

Huntingford Farm

Daniel's Wood

Avening Green

8

Old Court Farm

Little Tortworth Copse

Old Court

Hotel

Tortworth

+ Chestnut

7

Brook Farm

Howcroft Cottages

B4059

93

Tortworth Prim Sch

Old Lodge Farm

Kennel Plantation

Tortworth Copse

Underwood Farm

6

Gall Pond

Arboretum

Lodge

Tortworth Court

Tortworth Green

Elmtree Farm

Poolfield Farm

Charfield Prim Sch

5

HM Prison +

Charfield Hill

WOTTON RD B4058

PO

92

The Lake

Tafarn-bach

B4059

The Old Rectory

Tortworth Park

Leyhill

4

Harris's Wood

PARK RD

WOODLAND RD

MEADOW RD

Woodend Farm

Hammerley Down

GL12

B4059

Poundhouse Farm

Bloody Acre

3

Parkend

KNAPP LA

Royal Oak (PH)

Brand Wood

Manor Farm +

Churchend

Wick's Hill

Bibstone

91

Sodam Mill

HARLEIGH LA

Church Farm

2

PO

CHURCH BUILDINGS

Townwell

DUDLE

LONGCROSS

BRISTOL RD

CHURCH LA

Talbotsend Farm

+

St Andrew's CE Prim Sch

Cromhall

Court Farm

Talbot's End

1

RECTORY LA

B4058

B4059

90

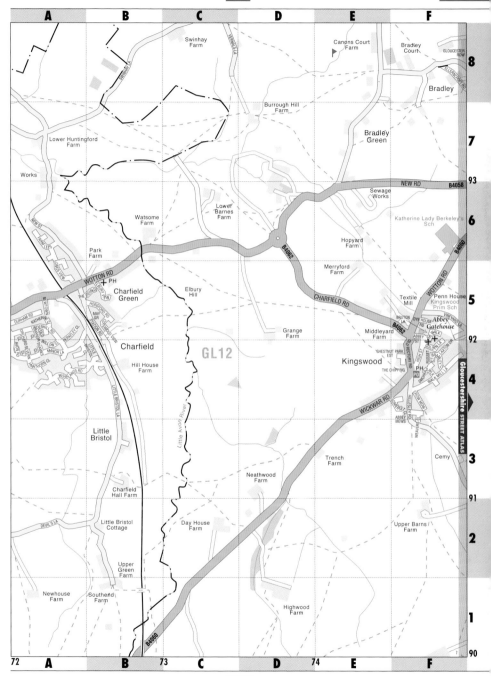

A   B   C   D   E   F

Swinhay
Farm

Canons Court
Farm

Bradley
Court

GLOUCESTER
ROW

8

Bradley

Burrough Hill
Farm

Bradley
Green

7

Lower Huntingford
Farm

NEW RD   B4058   93

Works

Sewage
Works

Watsome
Farm

Lower
Barnes
Farm

Katherine Lady Berkeley's
Sch

6

Park
Farm

Hopyard
Farm

WOTTON RD   PH

Charfield
Green

Elbury
Hill

Merryford
Farm

Textile
Mill

Penn House
Kingswood
Prim Sch

5

CHARFIELD RD

Charfield

Grange
Farm

Middleyard
Farm

Abbey
Gatehouse

92

GL12

Hill House
Farm

CHESTNUT PARK
EST

Kingswood

PH

THE CHIPPING   PO

Little
Bristol

Little Avon River

4

WICKWAR RD

Abbey
Mews

Cemy

3

Charfield
Hall Farm

Neathwood
Farm

Trench
Farm

91

DEVIL'S LA

Little Bristol
Cottage

Day House
Farm

Upper Barns
Farm

2

Upper
Green
Farm

Newhouse
Farm

Southend
Farm

Highwood
Farm

1

B4090

72   A   B   73   C   D   74   E   F   90

Gloucestershire STREET ATLAS

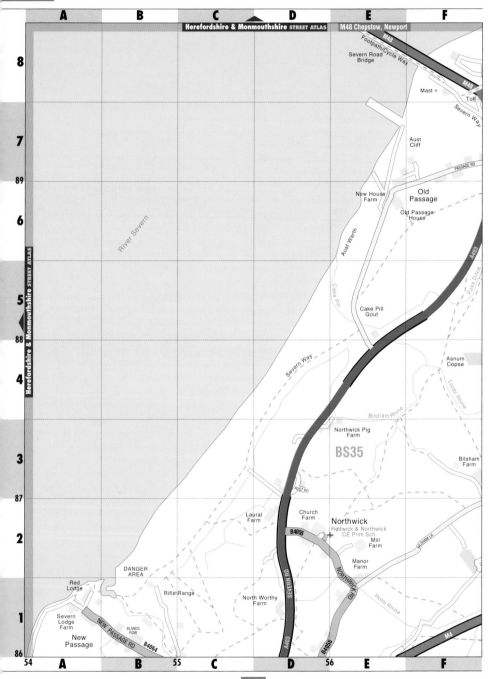

8

7

89

6

5

88

4

3

87

2

1

86

Footpath/Cycle Way

M48

Severn Road Bridge

Mast

Toll

Severn Way

Aust Cliff

PASSAGE RD

New House Farm

Old Passage

Old Passage House

Aust Warth

A403

Foss Ditch

Cake Pill

Cake Pill Gout

River Severn

Asnum Copse

Severn Way

Lords Rhine

Bilsham Rhine

Northwick Pig Farm

Bilsham Farm

BS35

AUST RD

Laural Farm

Church Farm

Northwick

Redwick & Northwick CE Prim Sch

Mill Farm

B4055

Manor Farm

BILSHAM LA

SEVERN RD

A403

NORTHWICK RD

Holm Rhine

DANGER AREA

Red Lodge

Rifle Range

North Worthy Farm

Severn Lodge Farm

NEW PASSAGE RD

BLANDS ROW

B4064

New Passage

B4055

M4

54 A B **55** C D **56** E F

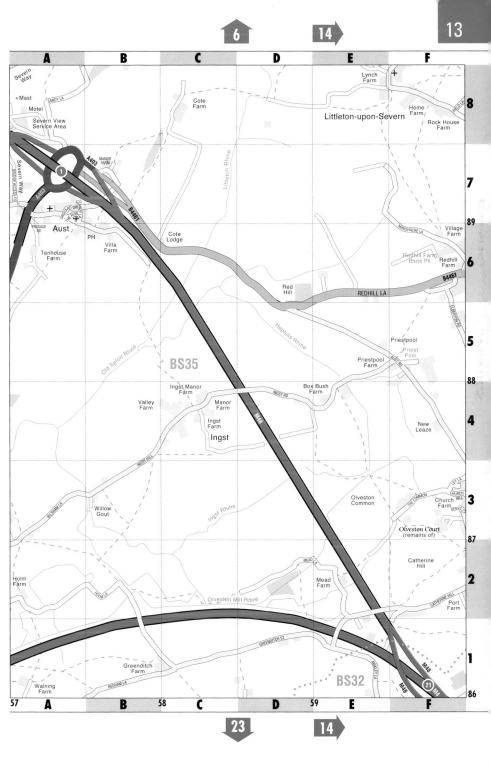

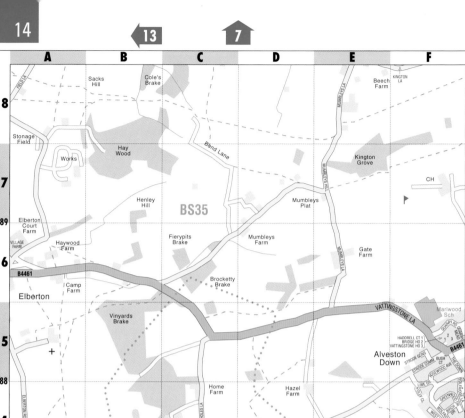

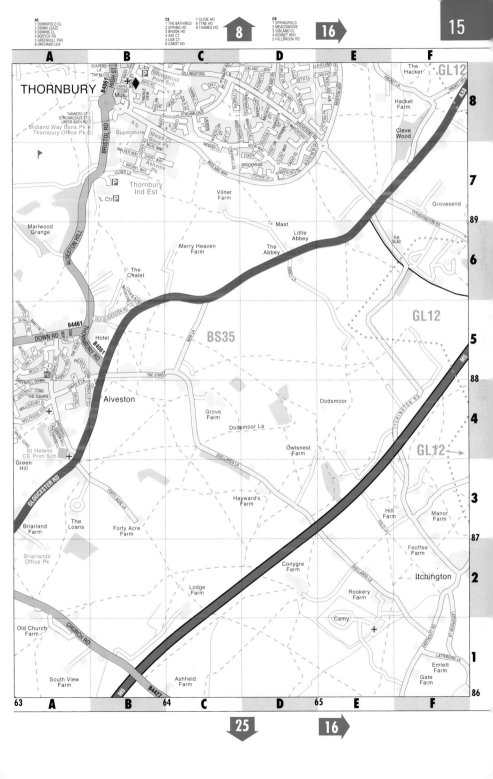

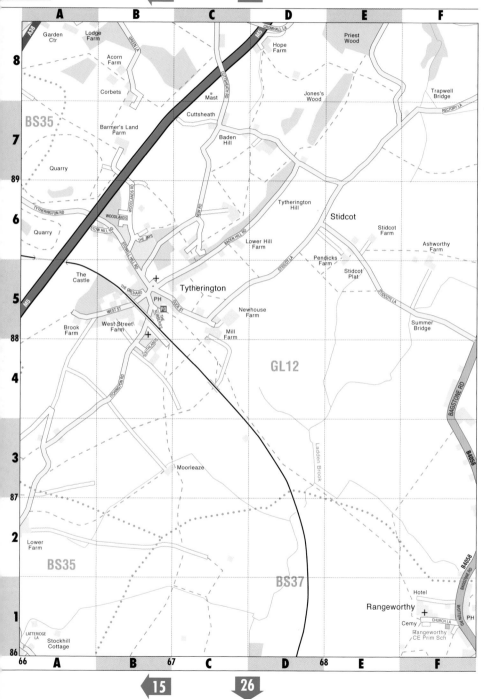

15
9

A **B** **C** **D** **E** **F**

A38

Garden Ctr

Lodge Farm

CROMHALL LA

Hope Farm

Priest Wood

8

Acorn Farm

GREEN LA

Corbets

Mast

Jones's Wood

Trapwell Bridge

RECTORY LA

BS35

Cuttsheath

CUTTSHEATH RD

Barmer's Land Farm

7

Baden Hill

Quarry

89

Tytherington Hill

Tytherington RD

WOODLANDS RD

NEW RD

Stidcot

6

WOODLANDS

Quarry

STOW HILL RD

THE JAYS

BADEN HILL RD

Lower Hill Farm

Stidcot Farm

Ashworthy Farm

STIDCOT LA

Pendicks Farm

Stidcot Plat

STIDCOTE LA

The Castle

THE ORCHARD

Tytherington

5

DUCK ST

PH

PO

WEST ST

THE TURNPIKE

Newhouse Farm

Summer Bridge

M5

Brook Farm

West Street Farm

SOUTHLANDS

88

Mill Farm

GL12

BAGSTONE RD

4

ITCHINGTON RD

B4058

Moorleaze

3

Ladden Brook

87

Lower Farm

2

BS35

BS37

B4058

Hotel

Rangeworthy

1

Cemy

CHURCH LA

PH

WOTTON RD

BAGSTONE RD

LATTERIDGE LA

Stockhill Cottage

Rangeworthy CE Prim Sch

86

66 **A** **B** 67 **C** **D** 68 **E** **F**

15
26

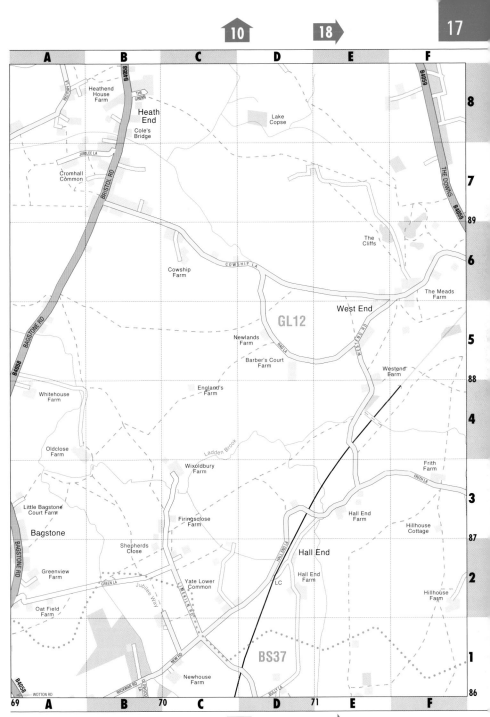

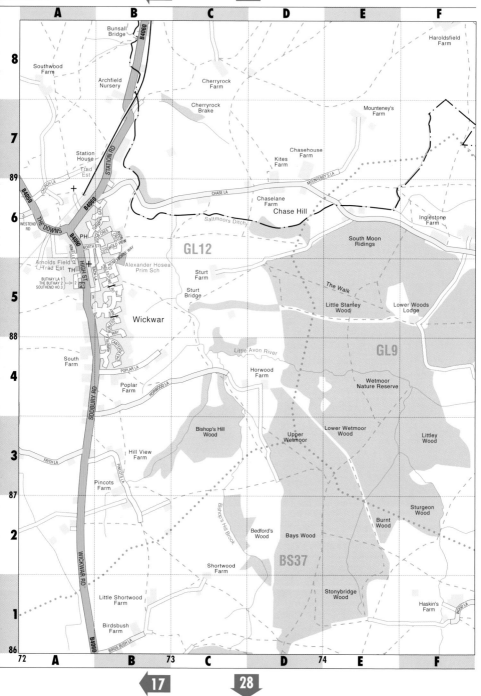

17
11

A   B   C   D   E   F

8

Southwood
Farm

Bunsall
Bridge

Archfield
Nursery

Cherryrock
Farm

Cherryrock
Brake

Haroldsfield
Farm

Mounteney's
Farm

7

Station
House

Trad Est

Chasehouse
Farm

Kites
Farm

89

CROUCH LA

CHASE LA

MOUNTENEY'S LA

Chaselane
Farm

Chase Hill

Inglestone
Farm

6

B4058

THE DOWNS

B4060

B4060

STATION RD

PH

WESTEND
RD

NORTH ST

CHESTNUT CRES

COTSWOLD VIEW

HOME FARMING WAY

Saltmoors Ditch

GL12

South Moon
Ridings

Arnolds Field
Trad Est

TH

HIGH ST

BUTHAY LA 1
THE BUTHAY 2
SOUTHEND HO 3

Alexander Hosea
Prim Sch

Sturt
Farm

Sturt
Bridge

The Walk

Little Stanley
Wood

Lower Woods
Lodge

5

Wickwar

CARTER'S CL

SODBURY RD

88

POPLAR LA

Little Avon River

GL9

South
Farm

HORWOOD LA

Poplar
Farm

Horwood
Farm

Wetmoor
Nature Reserve

4

FRITH LA

Hill View
Farm

PINCOTS LA

Bishop's Hill
Wood

Upper
Wetmoor

Lower Wetmoor
Wood

Littley
Wood

3

Pincots
Farm

87

Bishop's Hill Brook

Sturgeon
Wood

2

WICKWAR RD

Bedford's
Wood

Bays Wood

Burnt
Wood

BS37

Shortwood
Farm

1

Little Shortwood
Farm

Stonybridge
Wood

Haskin's
Farm

A4060 LA

Birdsbush
Farm

B4060

BIRDS BUSH LA

86

72   A   B   73   C   D   74   E   F

17
28

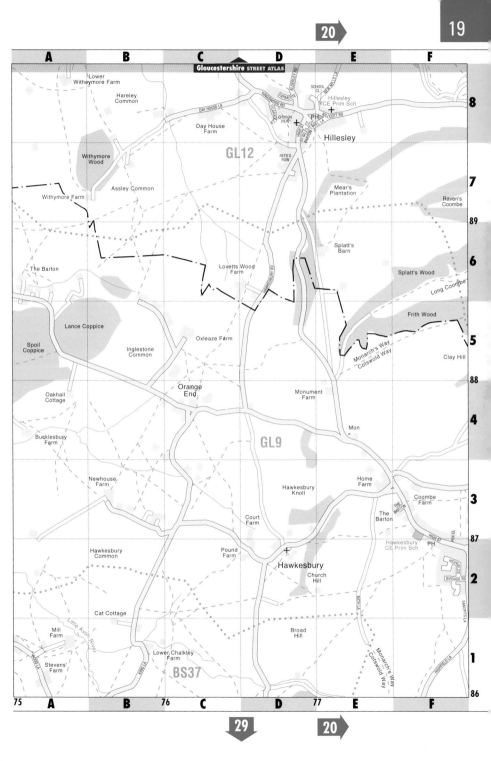

Gloucestershire STREET ATLAS

A B C D E F

8
7
89
6
5
88
4
3
87
2
1
86

Lower
Witheymore Farm

Hareley
Common

Day House La

Day House
Farm

SCHOOL
CL

Hillesley
VCE Prim Sch

Hillesley

PH

REED'S
ROW

GL12

Withymore
Wood

Assley Common

Withymore Farm

Mear's
Plantation

Raven's
Coombe

The Barton

Lovetts Wood
Farm

Splatt's
Barn

Splatt's Wood

Long Coombe

Frith Wood

Lance Coppice

Oxleaze Farm

Spoil
Coppice

Inglestone
Common

Monarch's Way
Cotswold Way

Clay Hill

Oakhall
Cottage

Orange
End

Monument
Farm

GL9

Mon

Bucklesbury
Farm

Newhouse
Farm

Hawkesbury
Knoll

Home
Farm

Coombe
Farm

The
Barton

Court
Farm

The
Barton

Hawkesbury
CE Prim Sch

PH

Hawkesbury
Common

Pound
Farm

Hawkesbury

Church
Hill

BIRGAGE RD

Cat Cottage

Mill
Farm

Little Avon River

Broad
Hill

Monarch's Way
Cotswold Way

Stevens'
Farm

Lower Chalkley
Farm

BS37

KINGSWOOD RD
HAWKESBURY RD
KINGS LA
MIDGER LA
HILLESLEY RD
WICKWAR RD
HIGH ST
BARTON LA
KILCOTT RD
NEW MILLS LA
ALDERLEY RD
LAHARMOTE
CHURCH
VIEW
BATH LA
HIGH ST
HIGH FIELDS
SANDPITS LA
HIGHFIELD LA
RIDE CL

75 76 77

A B C D E F

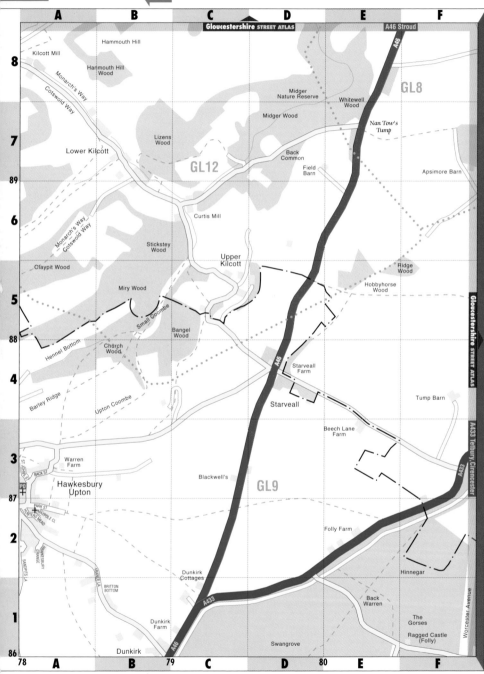

Herefordshire & Monmouthshire STREET ATLAS M4 Newport, Cardiff

Second Severn Crossing

The Binn Wall

Severn
Beach

BEACH AVE

RUSTIC
PK
STATION RD

RIVERSIDE PK

BS35

River Severn

Severn Way

Severn
View
Ind Pk

CENTRAL AVE

BS10

New Pill
Gout

SEVERN RD

Works

Red Rhine

Chittening Warth

Power
Station

BS11

Stup Pill

Crook's Marsh

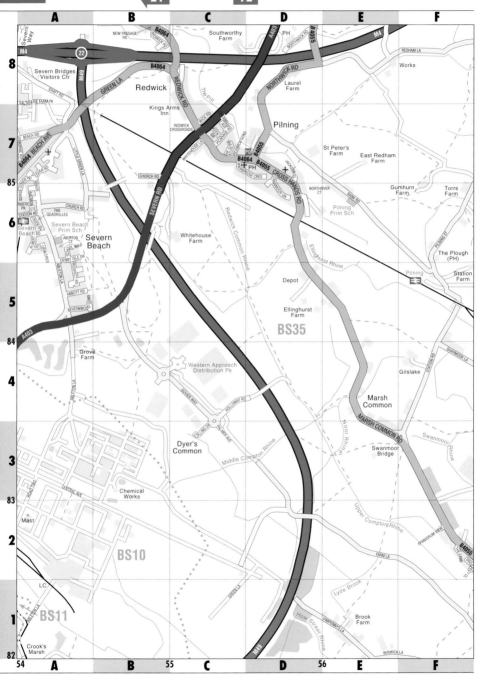

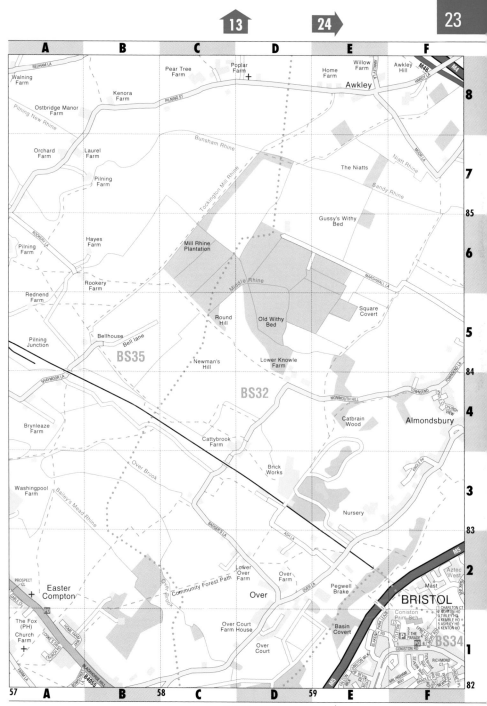

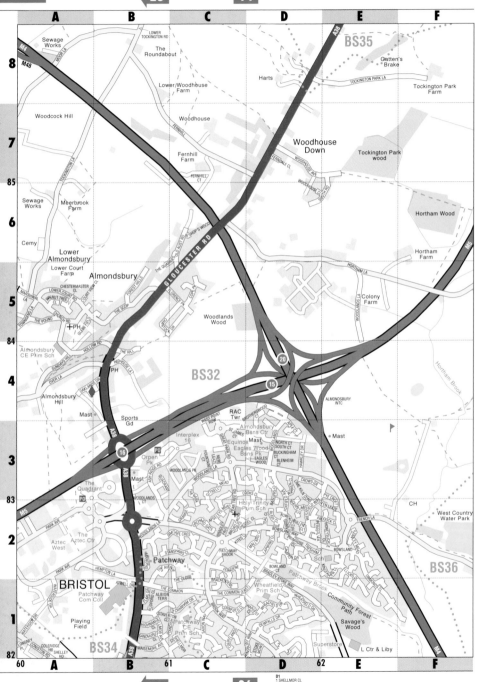

D1
1 SHELLMOR CL
2 HEDGEROWS
3 SHEPHERDS WLK

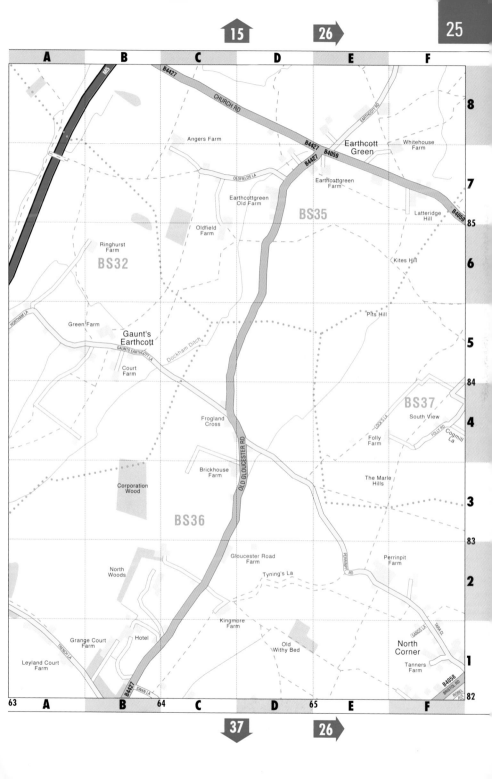

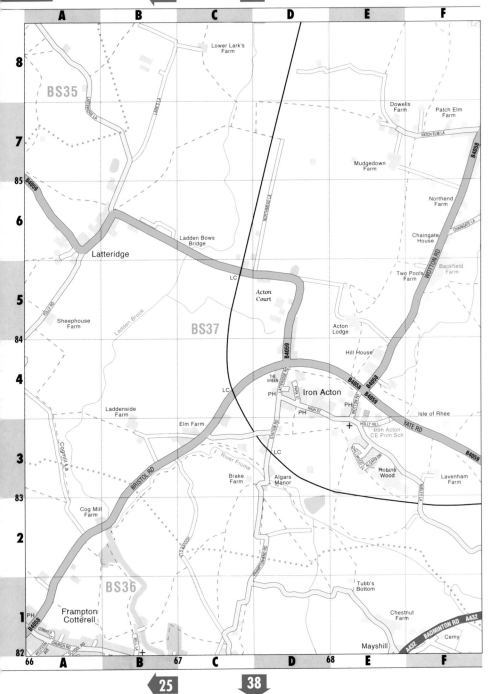

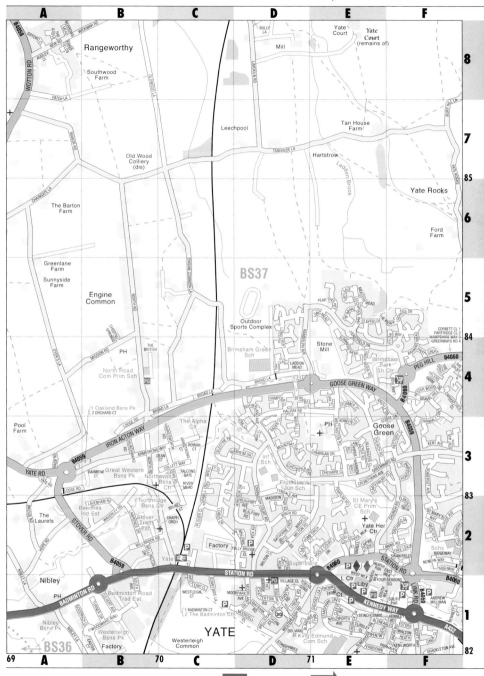

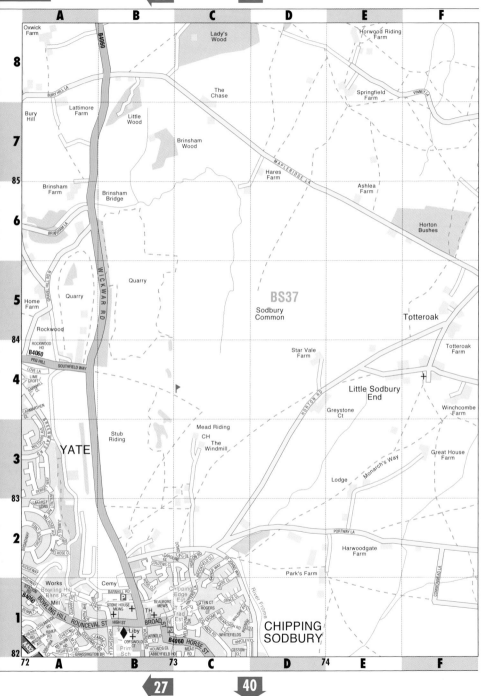

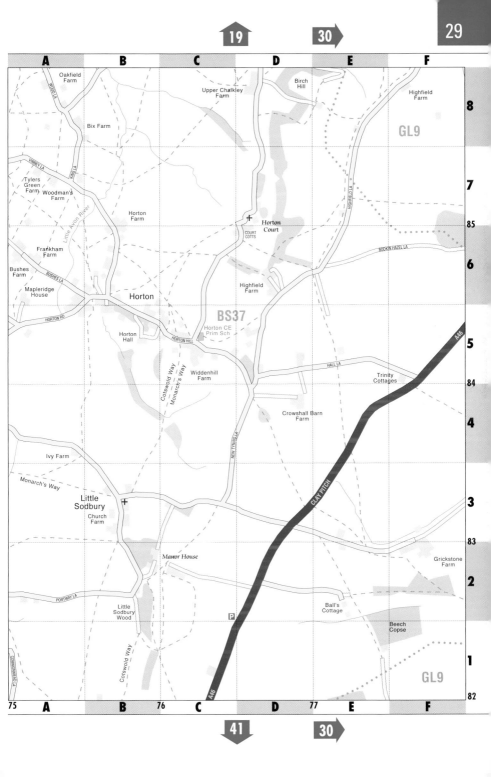

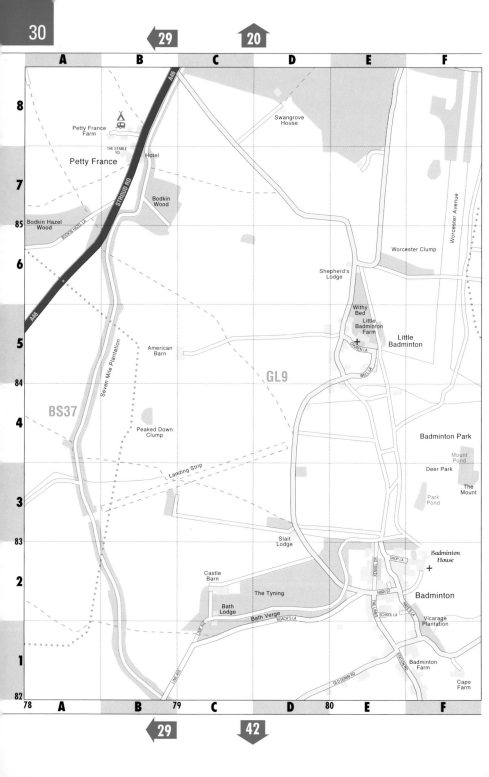

A   B   C   D   E   F

8

Petty France
Farm

THE STABLE
YD

Hotel

Petty France

7

Bodkin
Wood

85

Bodkin Hazel
Wood

BODKIN HAZEL LA

STROUD RD

A46

A46

6

Swangrove
House

Worcester Clump

Shepherd's
Lodge

Worcester Avenue

Withy
Bed

Little
Badminton
Farm

Little
Badminton

5

American
Barn

CHURCH LA

WELL LA

84

GL9

BS37

Seven Mile Plantation

Peaked Down
Clump

4

Badminton Park

Mount
Pond

Deer Park

Park
Pond

The
Mount

Landing Strip

3

Slait
Lodge

83

Castle
Barn

SHOP LA

Badminton
House

KENNEL LA

2

The Tyning

HIGH ST

THE LINES

SCHOOL LA

BAKES LA

Badminton

Bath
Lodge

Bath Verge

ROACH'S LA

Vicarage
Plantation

LUCKINGTON RD

1

LIME AVE

LINE AVE

Badminton
Farm

Cape
Farm

82

OLD DOWN RD

78   A   B   79   C   D   80   E   F

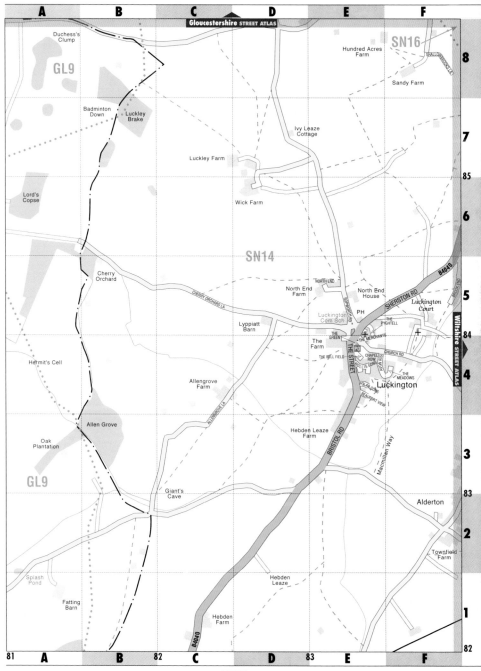

A B C D E F

SN16

GL9

Duchess's Clump

Hundred Acres Farm

Sandy Farm

8

Badminton Down

Luckley Brake

Ivy Leaze Cottage

7

85

Luckley Farm

Lord's Copse

Wick Farm

6

SN14

Cherry Orchard

CHERRY ORCHARD LA

North End Farm

NORTH END

North End House

North End

SHERSTON RD

Luckington Court

B4040

WINDMILL RD

5

Lyppiatt Barn

Luckington Com Sch

PH

THE PYGHTELL

Wiltshire STREET ATLAS

84

The Farm

THE GREEN

THE MERCHANTS

CHURCH RD

Hermit's Cell

THE BELL FIELD

THE STREET

CHAPEL ROW

THE MEADOWS

4

Allengrove Farm

POLAR GDNS

Luckington

Allen Grove

ALLENGROVE LA

BEAUFORT VIEW

Hebden Leaze Farm

Macmillan Way

Oak Plantation

BRISTOL RD

3

GL9

Giant's Cave

Alderton

83

Townfield Farm

2

Splash Pond

Fatting Barn

Hebden Leaze

1

Hebden Farm

B4040

82

81 A B 82 C D 83 E F

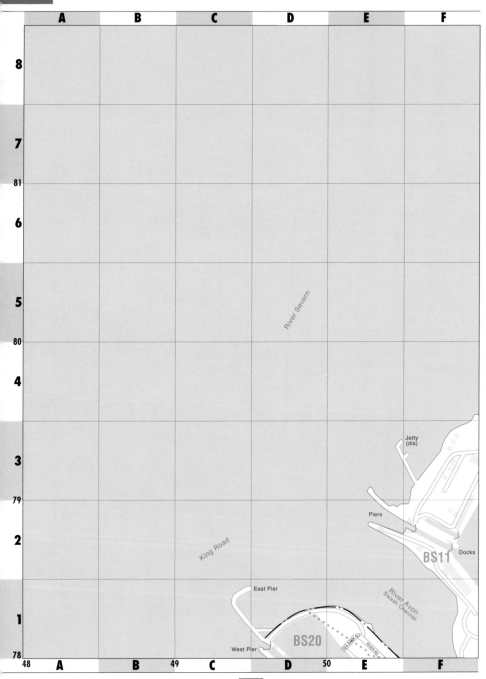

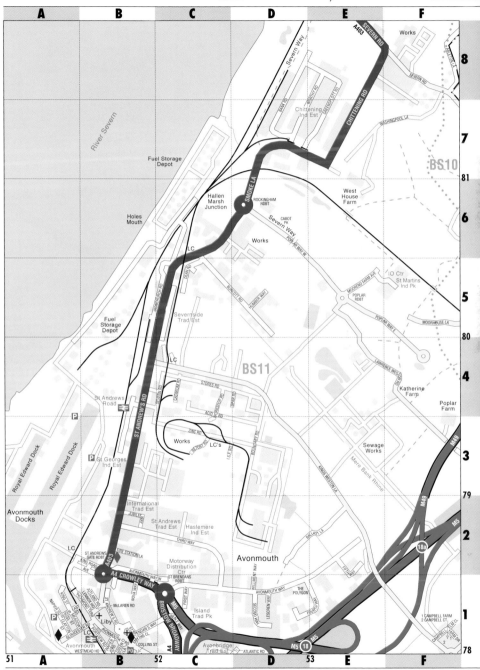

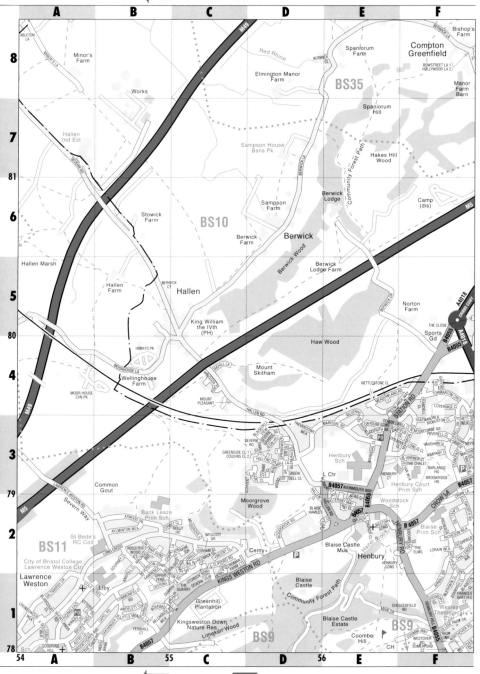

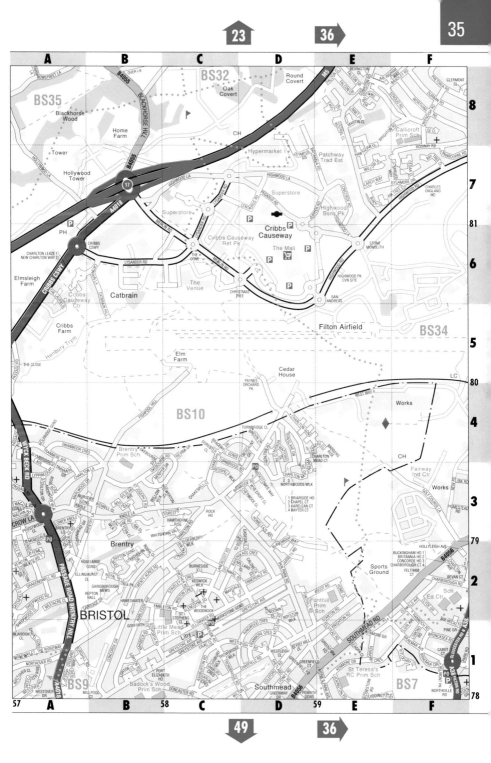

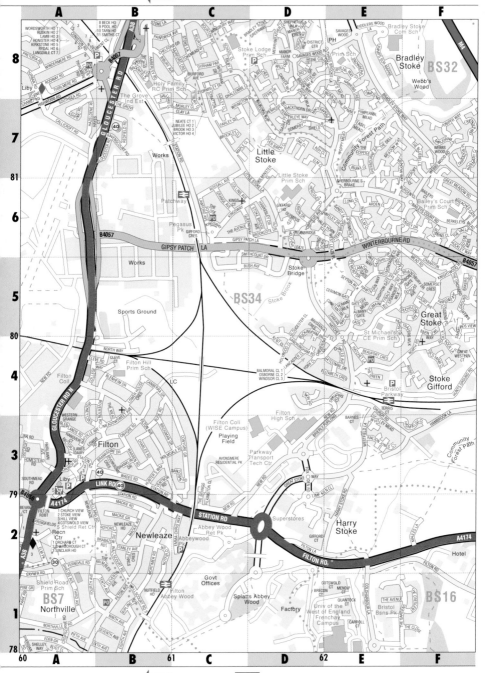

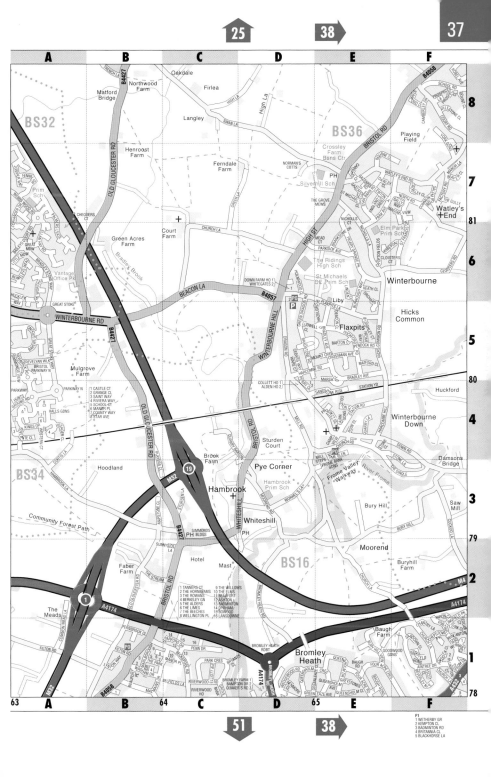

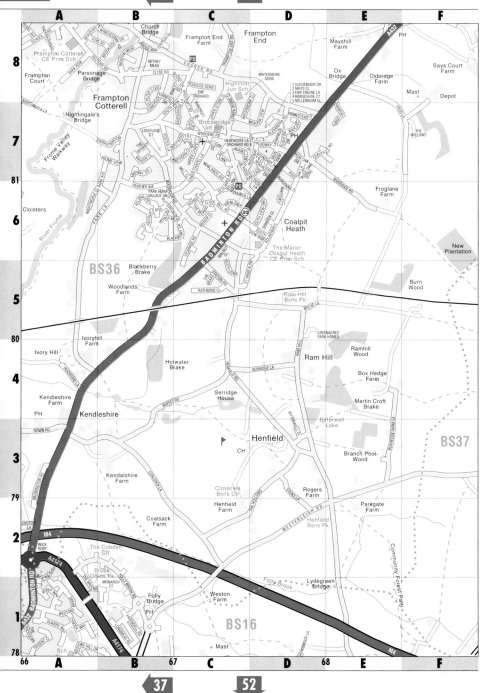

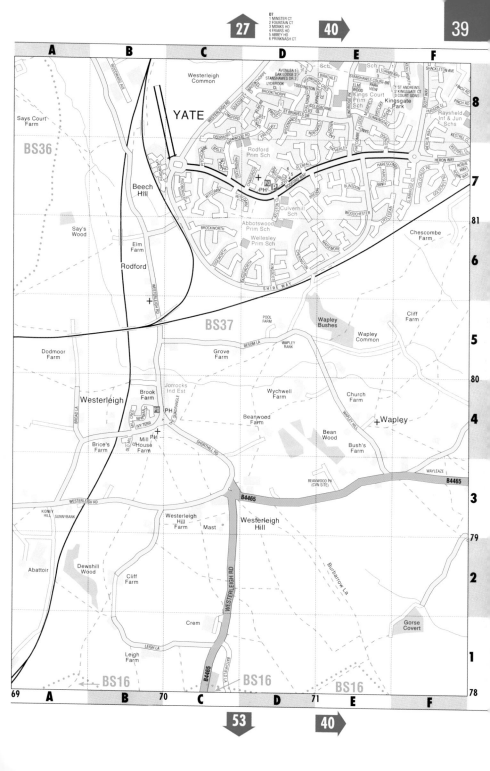

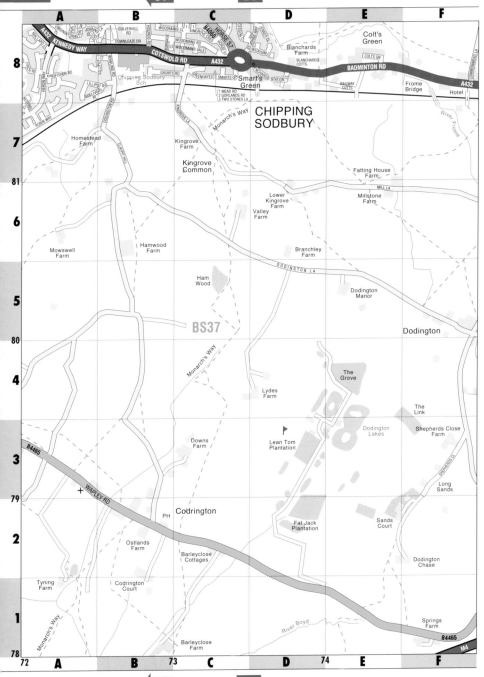

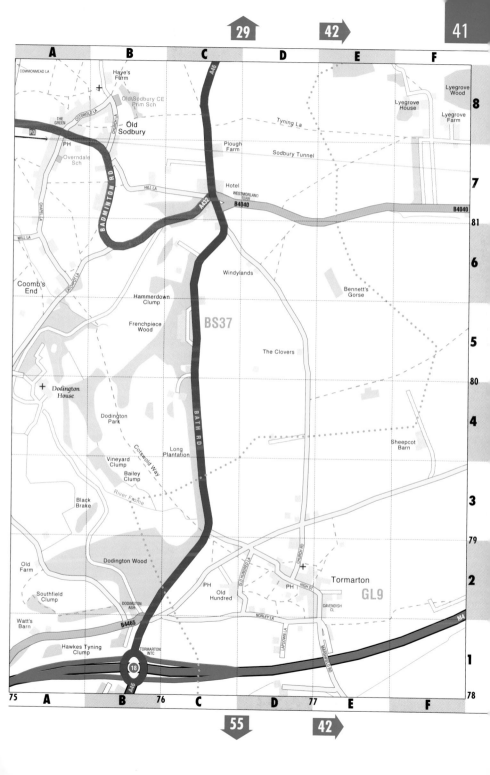

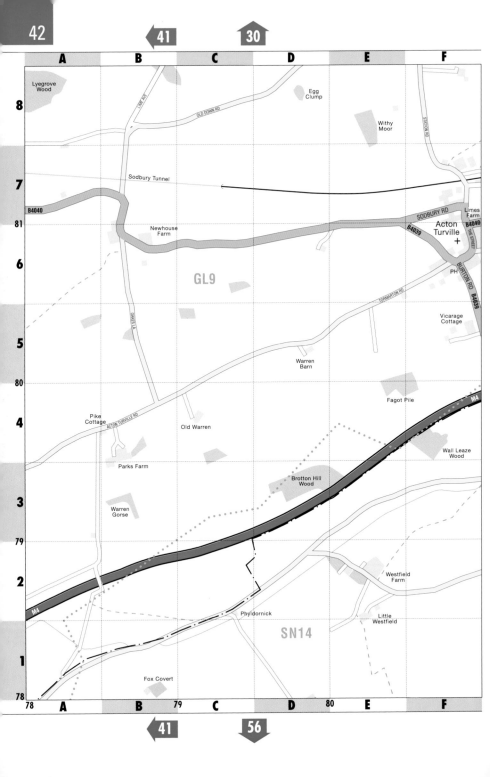

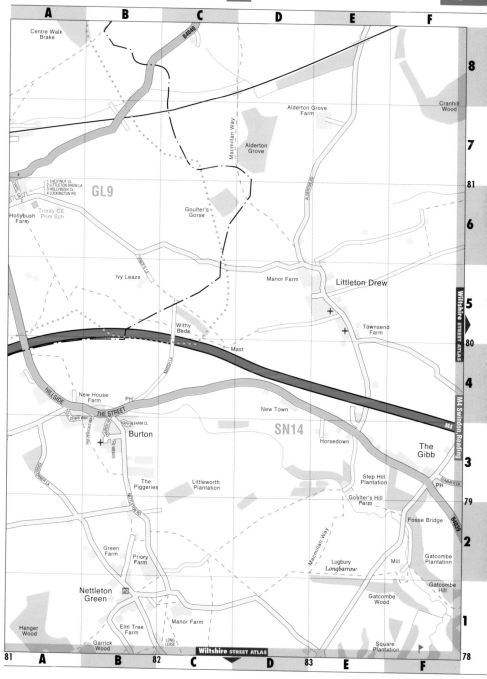

A B C D E F

8

7

81

6

5

80

4

3

79

2

1

78

Centre Walk
Brake

B4040

Cranhill
Wood

Macmillan Way

Alderton Grove
Farm

Alderton
Grove

ALDERTON RD

GL9

1 CHESTNUT CL
2 LITTLETON DREW LA
3 HOLLYBUSH CL
4 LUCKINGTON RD

CHAPEL LA

Trinity CE
Prim Sch

Hollybush
Farm

Goulter's
Gorse

INNER LA

Ivy Leaze

Manor Farm

Littleton Drew

Townsend
Farm

Withy
Beds

MARSH LA

Mast

HILLSIDE

New House
Farm

PH

New Town

SN14

Horsedown

The
Gibb

SUMMER LA

PH

THE STREET

DOWN WAY

BURTON FARM CL

FOXGLOVE WAY

CHURCHILL DR

Burton

THE MEADS

The
Piggeries

Littleworth
Plantation

Step Hill
Plantation

Goulter's Hill
Farm

Fosse Bridge

B4039

Gatcombe
Plantation

NETTLETON RD

COSSHAM LA

Green
Farm

Priory
Farm

Macmillan Way

Lugbury
Longbarrow

Mill

Gatcombe
Wood

Gatcombe
Hill

Nettleton
Green

PO

Elm Tree
Farm

Manor Farm

LONG
LEASE

Square
Plantation

Hanger
Wood

Garrick
Wood

81 A B 82 C D 83 E F

Wiltshire STREET ATLAS
M4 Swindon, Reading

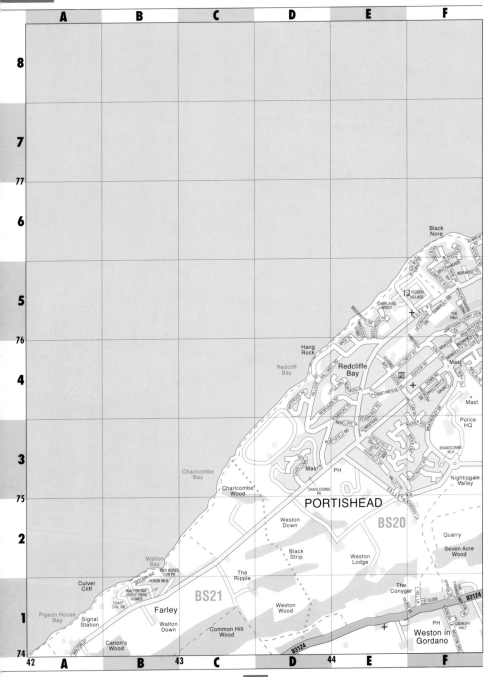

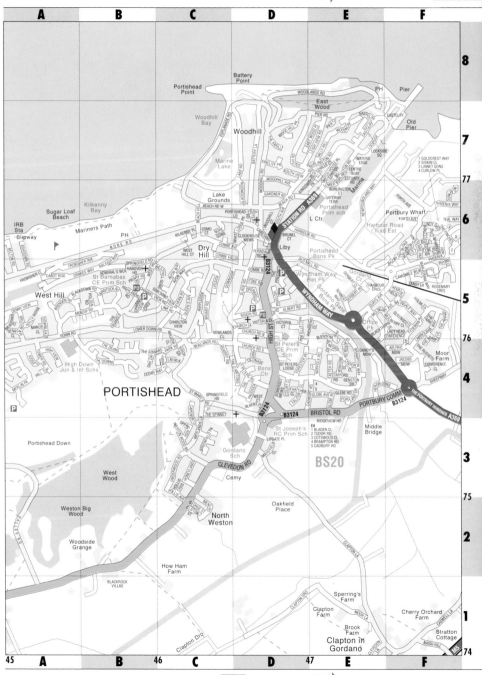

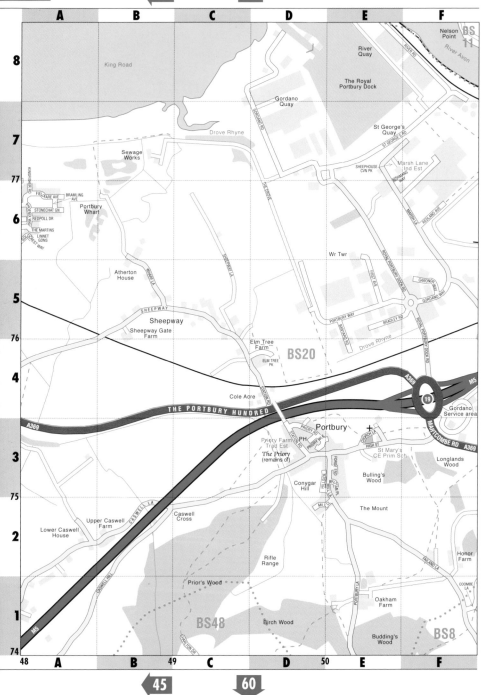

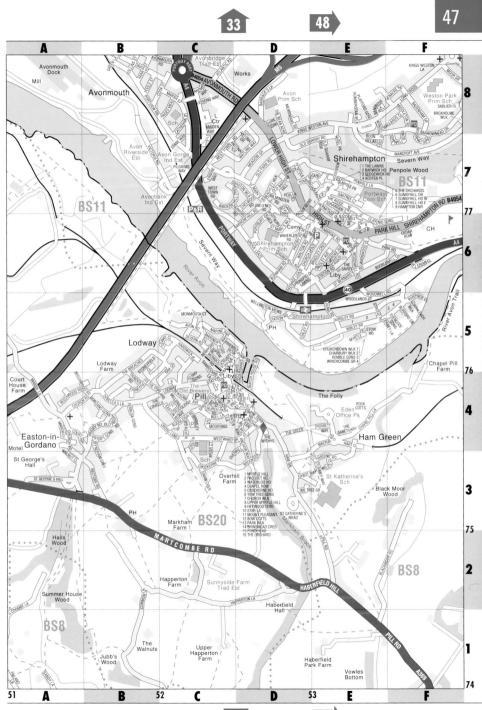

Avonmouth Dock

Mill

Avonmouth

Avon Riverside Est

Avon Gorge Ind Est

PILGRIMS WAY

WEST TOWN RD

Avonbank Ind Est

BS11

Works

Avon Prim Sch

KINGS WESTON LA

Weston Park Prim Sch

SADLIER CI

BROXHOLME WLK

8

Shirehampton

Severn Way

BS11

7

Penpole Wood

1 THE LAWNS
2 BARWICK HO
3 SEDGEWICK HO
4 AUSTEN PL

5 THE ORCHARDS
6 SUNNYHILL DR
7 SUNNYHILL HO W
8 SUNNYHILL HO E
9 HAMPTON CNR

SHIREHAMPTON RD B4054

77

P&R

Severn Way

River Avon

PORTWAY

MONMOUTH CT

Shirehampton Prim Sch

Portway Com Sch

HIGH ST

Cemy

P

PO

Liby

Sch

THE SAVOY

BUCKLEWELL CI

A4

CEDAR ROW

CH

6

Lodway

Lodway Farm

The Breaches

STOREYFIELD

Liby

PO

The Old Brewery

Pill

MOORINGS

The Withys

WELLINGTON MEWS

STATION

PH

Shirehampton

DURSLEY RD

NIBLEY RD

STOW HO

CHURCHOWN WLK 2
CHARBURY WLK 2
KEMBLE GDNS 2
WINCHCOMBE GR 4

The Folly

ROCK COTTS

Eden Office Pk

Chapel Pill Farm

76

5

Court House Farm

Easton-in-Gordano

Motel

St George's Hall

ST GEORGE'S HILL

PH

RECTORY RD

Sch

Overhill Farm

1 MYRTLE HILL
2 PADQUET HO
3 WATERLOO HO
4 CHAPEL ROW
5 CROCKERNE HO
6 YEW TREE GDNS
7 CHURCH WLK
8 UPPER MYRTLE HILL
9 HEYWOOD TERR
10 STAR LA
11 MOUNT PLEASANT
12 BOW COTTS
13 PARK WLK
14 BRINSMEAD CRES
15 POND HEAD
16 THE ORCHARD

THE GREEN

PERRETT WAY

The Sanctuary

MACRAE

CABOT WAY

LIME TREE GR

St Catherine's Mead

Ham Green

St Katherine's Sch

Black Moor Wood

75

4

3

Hails Wood

Markham Farm

BS20

MARTCOMBE RD

Markham Brook

PH

Happerton Farm

HAPPERTON LA

Sunnyside Farm Trad Est

HABERFIELD HILL

Haberfield Hall

PILL RD

BS8

2

Summer House Wood

BS8

Jubb's Wood

The Walnuts

Upper Happerton Farm

Haberfield Park Farm

Vowles Bottom

A369

1

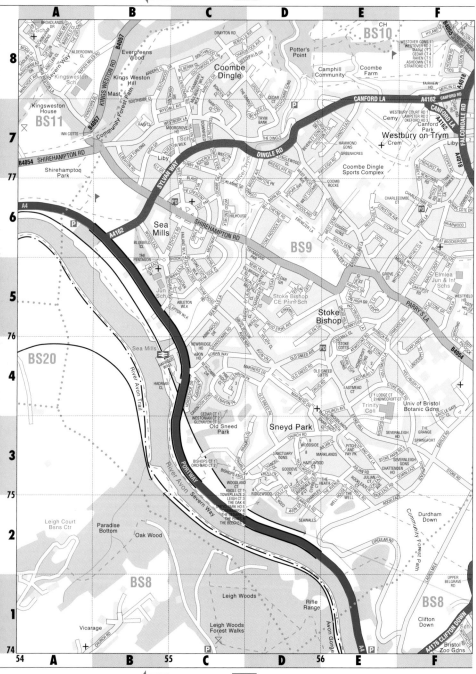

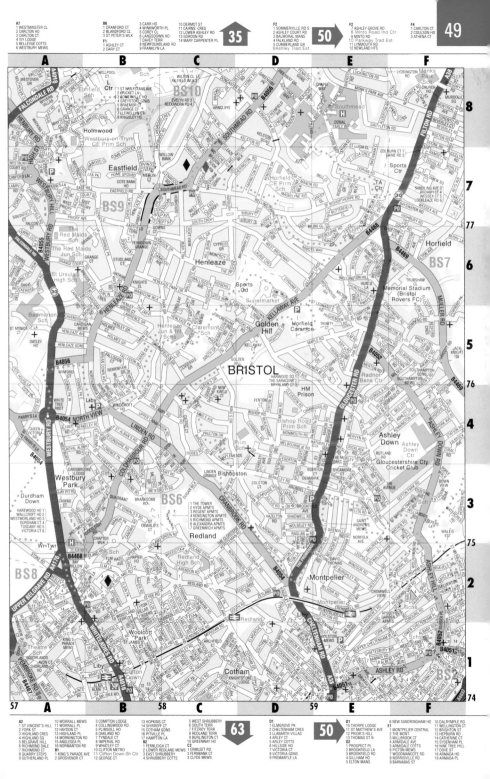

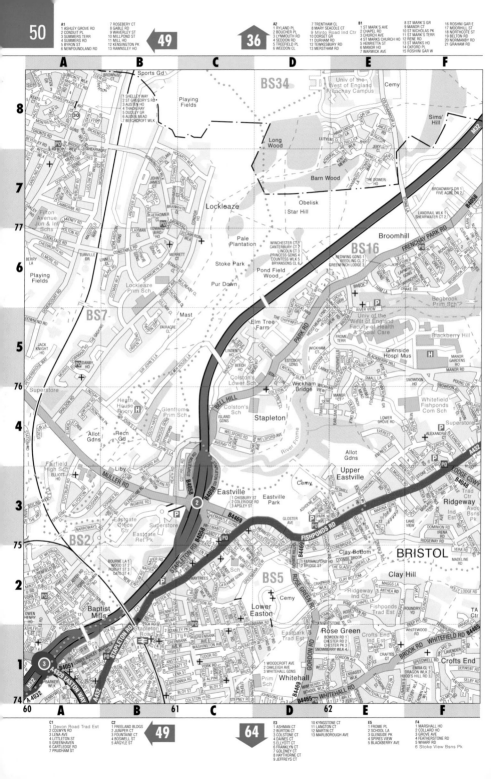

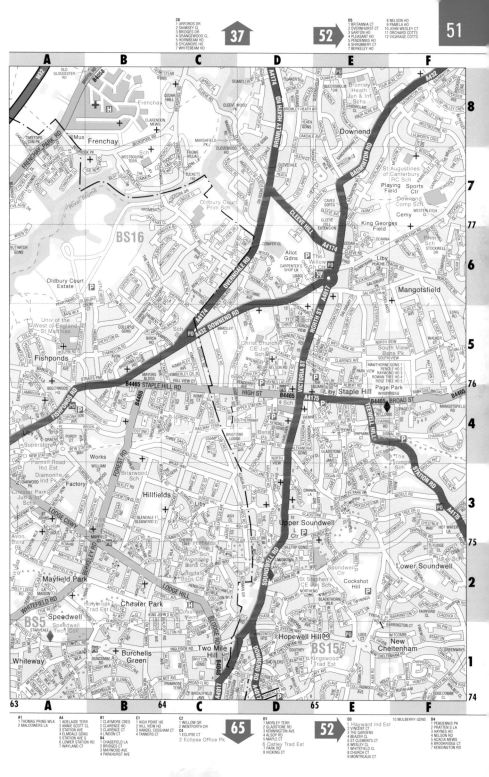

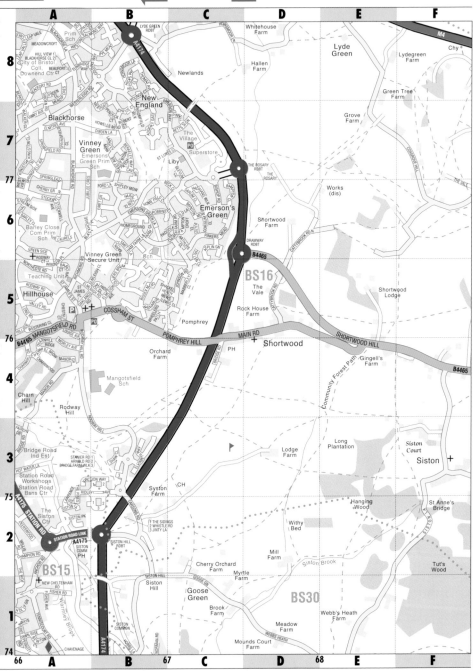

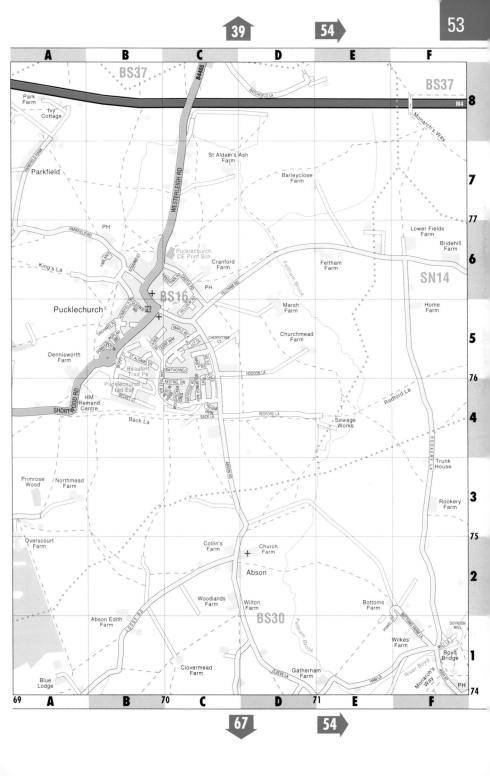

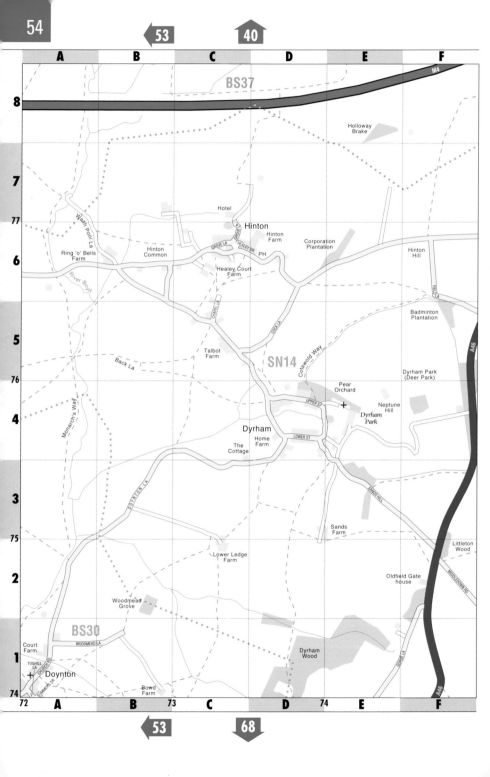

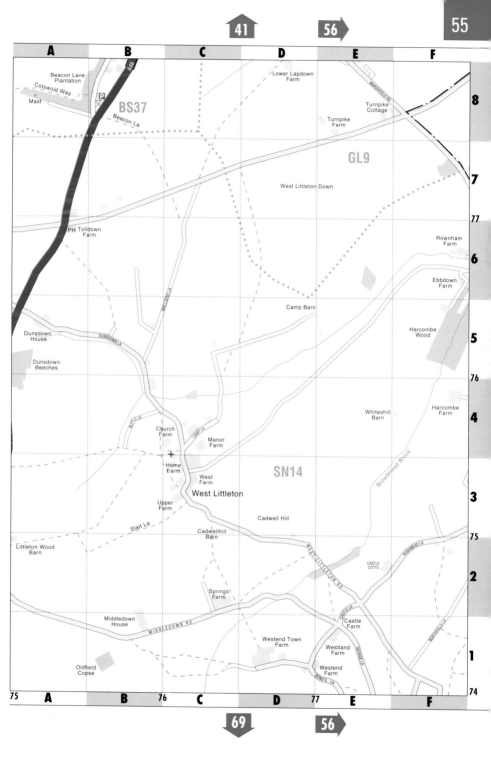

A   B   C   D   E   F

Beacon Lane Plantation

Cotswold Way

Mast

BS37

Beacon La

Lower Lapdown Farm

Turnpike Cottage

Turnpike Farm

8

GL9

West Littleton Down

7

77

PH Tolldown Farm

Rownham Farm

6

Ebbdown Farm

Camp Barn

Dunsdown House

DUNSDOWN LA

Harcombe Wood

5

Dunsdown Beeches

76

Whiteshill Barn

Harcombe Farm

4

BUTT'S LA

Church Farm

CAMP LA

Manor Farm

WALLSEN LA

Broadmead Brook

Home Farm

West Farm

SN14

West Littleton

3

Upper Farm

Cadwell Hill

Slait La

Cadwellhill Barn

75

Littleton Wood Barn

WEST LITTLETON RD

BUSHMEAD LA

CASTLE COTTS

2

Springs Farm

Middledown House

MIDDLEDOWN RD

CASTLE LA

Castle Farm

NORTHEND LA

Oldfield Copse

Westend Town Farm

Westland Farm

GEORGE LA

Westend Farm

BOND'S LA

1

74

75   A   B   76   C   D   77   E   F

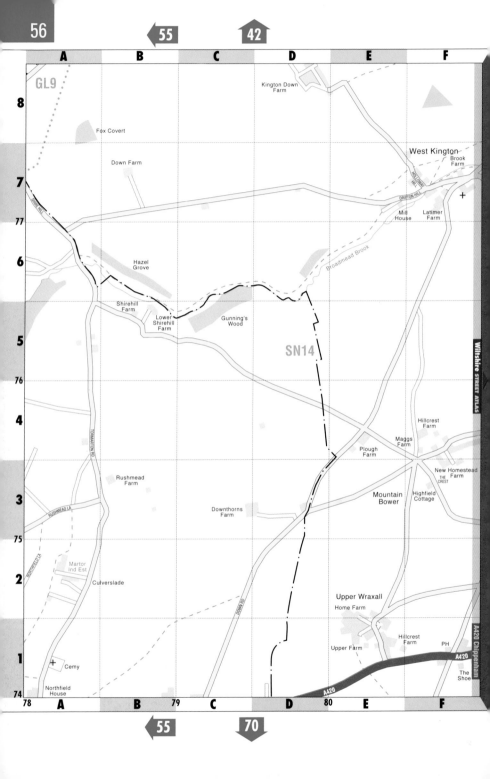

A   B   C   D   E   F

GL9

8

Fox Covert

Kington Down Farm

West Kington
Brook Farm

Down Farm

7

77

Mill House
Latimer Farm

Hazel Grove

6

Broadmead Brook

Shirehill Farm

Lower Shirehill Farm

Gunning's Wood

SN14

5

76

Hillcrest Farm

4

Maggs Farm

Plough Farm

New Homestead Farm
THE CREST

Rushmead Farm

Mountain Bower

Highfield Cottage

3

75

Downthorns Farm

Martor Ind Est

2

Culverslade

Upper Wraxall
Home Farm

Hillcrest Farm

PH

Upper Farm

A420

1

Cemy

A420

The Shoe

74

Northfield House

78   A   B   79   C   D   80   E   F

Wiltshire STREET ATLAS

A420 Chippenham

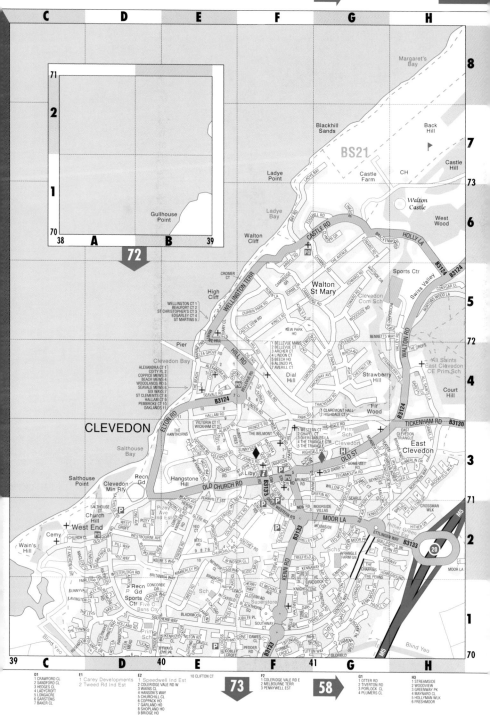

C D E F G H

8

71

2

Margaret's Bay

Blackhill Sands

Back Hill

7

BS21

Ladye Point

Castle Farm

CH

Walton Castle

Castle Hill

73

Walton St Mary

Sports Ctr

Swiss Valley

West Wood

6

B3124

B3124

1

70

38

A

B

39

72

Gullhouse Point

Walton Cliff

Ladye Bay

CASTLE RD

PO

Clevedon Com Sch

WALTON RD

5

72

CROMER CT

Clevedon Bay

WELLINGTON CT 1
BEAUFORT CT 2
ST CHRISTOPHER'S CT 3
EDGARLEY CT 4
ST MARTINS 5

High Cliff

WELLINGTON TERR

HILL RD

1 BELLEVUE MANS
2 BELLEVUE CT
3 ARCHER CT
4 LINDON CT
5 BEECH HO
6 ALONZO PL
7 AVERILL CT

New Park Ho

Dial Hill

Strawberry Hill

All Saints East Clevedon CE Prim Sch

Court Hill

4

Pier

ALEXANDRA CT 1
COITY PL 2
COPPICE MEWS 3
BEACH MEWS 4
WOODLANDS RD 5
SEAVALE MEWS 6
SIX WAYS 7
ST CLEMENTS CT 8
HALLAM CT 9
PEMBROKE CT 10
OAKLANDS 11

B3124

HALLAM RD

Fir Wood

B3124

CLEVEDON

FELTON RD

VICTORIA CT 1
WICKHAM CT 2

The Hawthorns

1 CLAREMONT HALL
2 HIGHDALE CT

1 WESTERN CT
2 CHAPEL CT
3 OVERISVABLES LA
4 THE TRIANGLE CTR
5 THE TRIANGLE

Prim Sch

East Clevedon Triangle

TICKENHAM RD

B3130

East Clevedon

3

Salthouse Bay

THE BELMONT

Clevedon Min Rly

HANGSTONE HILL

Hangstone Hill

OLD CHURCH RD

OLD ST

HIGH ST

OLD DAIRY

B3133

71

Salthouse Point

Clevedon Min Rly

Recn Gd

SALTHOUSE CT

Church Field

P

West End

Cemy

Wain's Hill

FELTON RD

MOOR LA

P

B3133

MOOR LA

2

20

B3133

MOOR LA

Recn Gd Sports Ctr

Five O Bsns Ctr

Superstore

The Chaffins

The Pennel

M5

1

Blind Yeo

Prim Sch

Jubilee Pl

B3133

Blind Yeo

70

39

C

D

40

E

F

73

41

G

58

H

D1
1 CRAWFORD CL
2 SANDFORD CL
3 HEDGES CL
4 LADYCROFT
5 LONGACRE
6 GARSTONS
7 BAKER CL

E1
1 Carey Developments
2 Tweed Rd Ind Est

E2
1 Speedwell Ind Est
2 COLERIDGE VALE RD W
3 WAINS CL
4 HANSON'S WAY
5 CHURCHILL CL
6 COPPACK HO
7 GARLAND HO
8 SHOPLAND HO
9 BRIDGE HO

10 CLIFTON CT

F2
1 COLERIDGE VALE RD E
2 MELBOURNE TERR
3 PENNYWELL CL

G1
1 OTTER RD
2 TIVERTON RD
3 PORLOCK CL
4 PLUMERS CL

H3
1 STREAMSIDE
2 WOODVIEW
3 GREENWAY PK
4 MAYNARD CL
5 HOLLYMAN WLK
6 FRESHMOOR

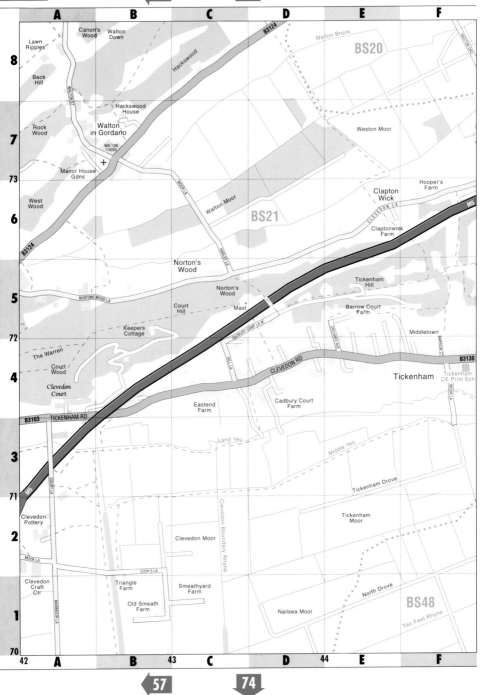

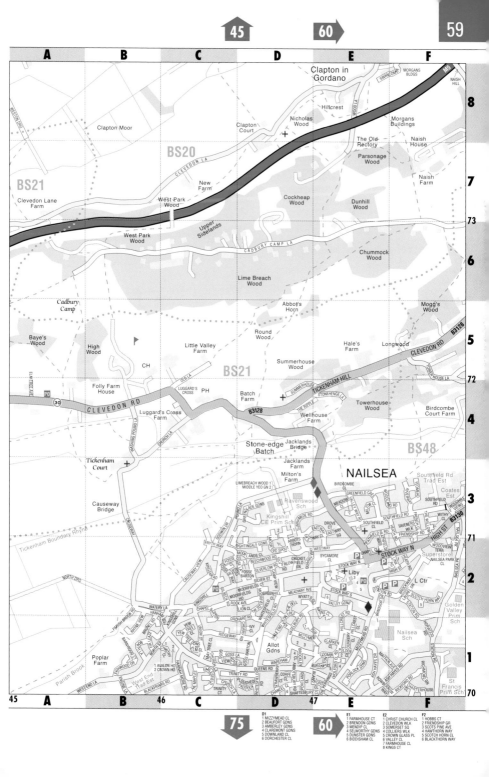

A   B   C   D   E   F

8

Clapton in
Gordano

SWANCOMBE   MORGANS
BLDGS   NAISH
HILL

Hillcrest   M5

Clapton Moor   Nicholas
Wood   WOOD LA   Morgans
Buildings

Clapton
Court   Naish
House

BS20   The Old
Rectory

Naish
House

CLEVEDON LA   Parsonage
Wood   **7**

BS21   New
Farm'   Naish
Farm

Clevedon Lane
Farm   West Park
Wood   Cockheap
Wood   Dunhill
Wood   **73**

West Park
Wood   Upper
Sidelands   Chummock
Wood   **6**

CADBURY CAMP LA

Lime Breach
Wood

Cadbury
Camp   Abbot's
Horn   Mogg's
Wood

Baye's
Wood   High
Wood   Little Valley
Farm   Round
Wood   Hale's
Farm   Longwood   CLEVEDON RD   B3128   **5**

CH   BS21   Summerhouse
Wood   TICKENHAM HILL   **72**

Folly Farm
House   LUGGARD'S
CROSS   PH   Batch
Farm   SUMMERHOUSE   STONEHENGE   Towerhouse
Wood   Birdcombe
Court Farm

CLEVEDON RD   30   B3128   THE TEMPLE   **4**

Luggard's Cross
Farm   CHURCH LA   Wellhouse
Farm   BS48

Tickenham
Court   Stone-edge
Batch   Jacklands
Bridge

Causeway
Bridge   Jacklands
Farm   **NAILSEA**   **3**

LIMEBREACH WOOD 1   Milton's
Farm   BIRDCOMBE
CL   Southfield Rd
Trad Est

Tickenham Boundary Rhyne   Ravenswood
Sch   Coates
Est   B3130

Kingshill
CE Prim Sch   SOUTHFIELD   **71**

NORTH DRO   STOCK WAY N.   Superstore!
NAILSEA PARK
CL   **2**

Liby   L Ctr   Golden
Valley
Prim
Sch

Poplar
Farm   Nailsea
Sch   **1**

Allot
Gdns

1 AVALON HO
2 CROWN HO   Nailsea
Sch   St
Francis
Prim Sch   **70**

West End
Trad Est   Queens Rd   Trinity Rd

Parish Brook   Trinity Rd

45   A   B   46   C   D   47   E   F

D1
1 MIZZYMEAD CL
2 BRENDON GDNS
3 AMBERLEY GDNS
4 CLAREMONT GDNS
5 DOWNLAND CL
6 DORCHESTER CL

E1
1 FARMHOUSE CT
2 BRENDON GDNS
3 MENDIP CL
4 SELWORTHY GDNS
5 DUNSTER GDNS
6 BIDDISHAM CL

E2
1 CHRIST CHURCH CL
2 CLEVEDON WLK
3 SOMERSET SQ
4 COLLIERS WLK
5 CROWN GLASS PL
6 VALLEY CL
7 FARMHOUSE CL
8 KINGS CT

F2
1 HOBBS CT
2 FRIENDSHIP GR
3 SCOTS PINE AVE
4 HAWTHORN WAY
5 SCOTCH HORN CL
6 BLACKTHORN WAY

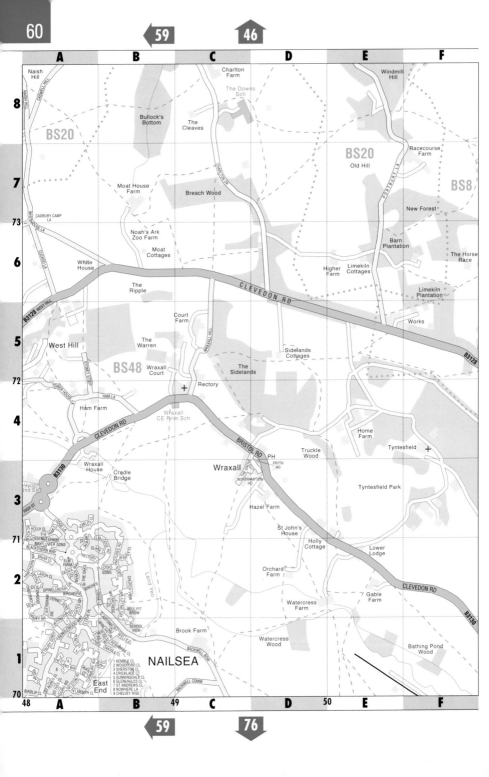

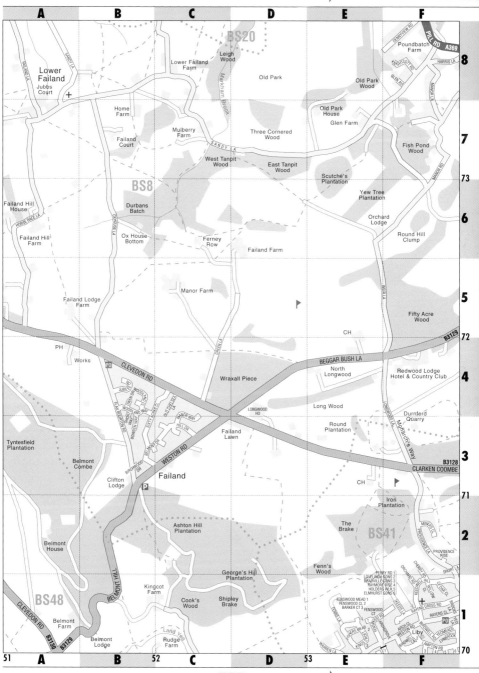

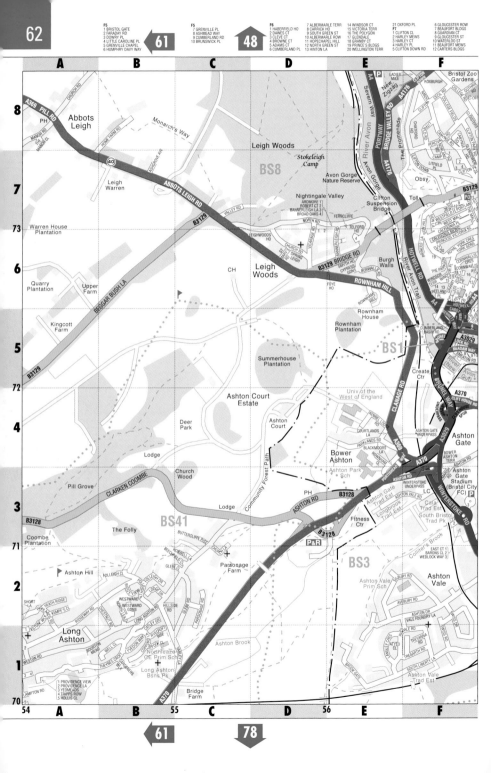

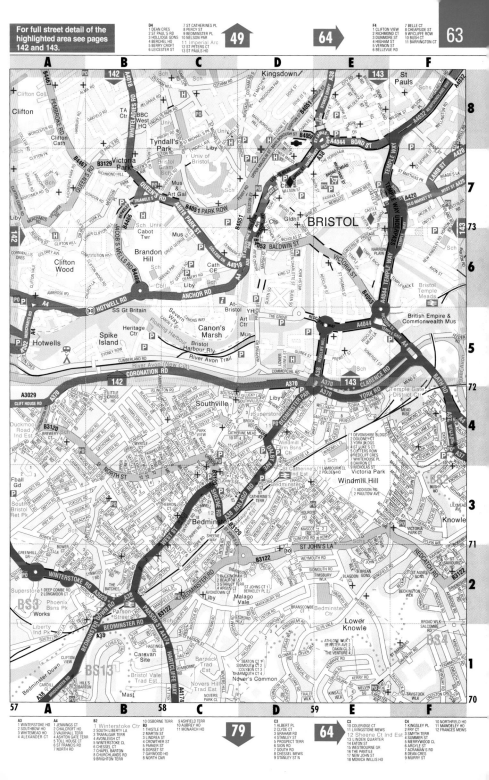

For full street detail of the highlighted area see pages 142 and 143.

63

D4
1 DEAN CRES
2 ST PAUL'S RD
3 HOLLIDGE GDNS
4 BERCHEL RD
5 BERRY CROFT
6 LEICESTER ST

7 ST CATHERINES PL
8 PERCY ST
9 BEDMINSTER PL
10 NELSON PAR
11 Imperial Arc
12 ST PETERS CT
13 ST PAULS HO

→ 49

→ 64

F4
1 CLIFTON VIEW
2 RICHMOND CT
3 DUNMORE ST
4 HIGHAM ST
5 VERNON ST
6 BELLEVUE RD

7 BELLE CT
8 CHEAPSIDE ST
9 WYCLIFFE ROW
10 BUSH CT
11 BARRINGTON CT

BRISTOL

Kingsdown

St Pauls

Clifton

Victoria Park

Tyndall's Park

Univ of Bristol

Clifton Wood

Brandon Hill

Hotwells

Spike Island

Canon's Marsh

Southville

Bedminster

Windmill Hill

Victoria Park

Knowle

Malago Vale

Lower Knowle

Nover's Common

British Empire & Commonwealth Mus

Bristol Temple Meads

A3
1 WINTERSTOKE RD
2 SOUTHBOW HO
3 WHITEMEAD HO
4 ALEXANDER CT

A4
1 JENNINGS CT
2 CHALCROFT HO
3 VAUXHALL TERR
4 ASHTON GATE TERR
5 TOLL HOUSE CT
6 ST FRANCIS RD
7 NORTH RD

B2
1 Winterstoke Ctr

B3
1 THISTLE ST
2 MARTIN ST
3 LINDREA ST
4 CROWTHER ST
5 PARKER ST
6 DORSET ST
7 GAYWOOD HO
8 NORTH CNR

10 OSBORNE TERR

1 SOUTH LIBERTY LA
2 TRAFALGAR TERR
3 AVONLEIGH CT
4 WINTERSTOKE CL
5 CHESSEL CT
6 CHAPEL BARTON
7 CHURCHLANDS RD
8 BRIGHTON TERR

9 ASHFIELD TERR
10 AUBREY HO
11 MONARCH ST

C3
1 ALBERT PL
2 CLYDE CT
3 GRAHAM RD
4 STANLEY ST
5 PROSPECT TERR
6 SION RD
7 SOUTH RD
8 CHESSEL MEWS
9 STANLEY ST N

C3
10 COLERIDGE CT
11 LIVINGSTONE MEWS
12 Sheene Ct Ind Est
13 LINDEN QUARTER
14 EATON ST
15 WESTBOURNE GR
16 THE PANTILE
17 NEW JOHN ST
18 MONICA WILLIS HO

C4
1 KINGSLEY PL
2 FRY CT
3 SMYTH TERR
4 SUMMER ST
5 MERRYWOOD CT
6 ARGYLE ST
7 ACRAMAN S RD
8 DEAN CRES
9 MURRY ST

10 NORTHFIELD HO
11 MAWDELEY HO
12 FRANCES MEWS

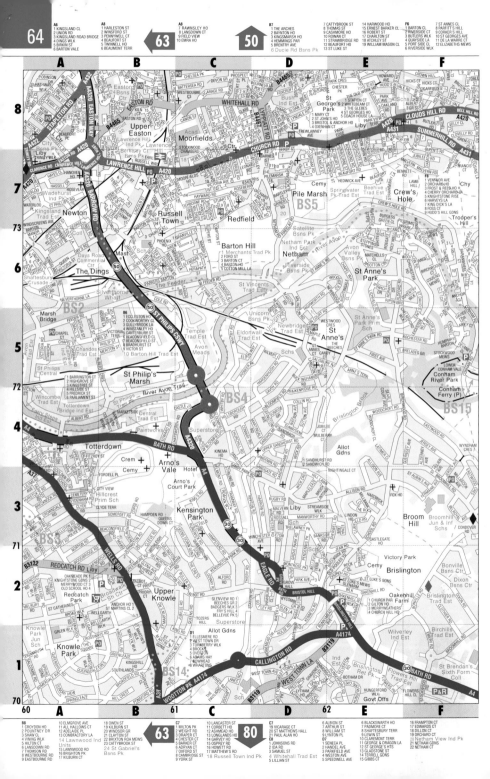

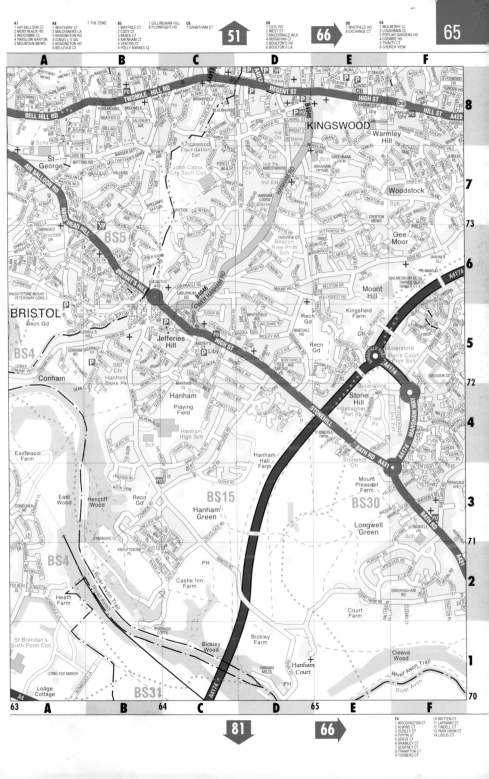

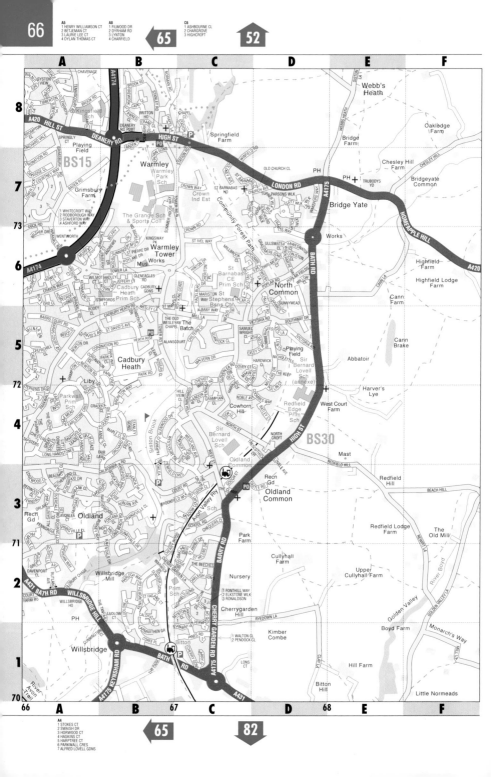

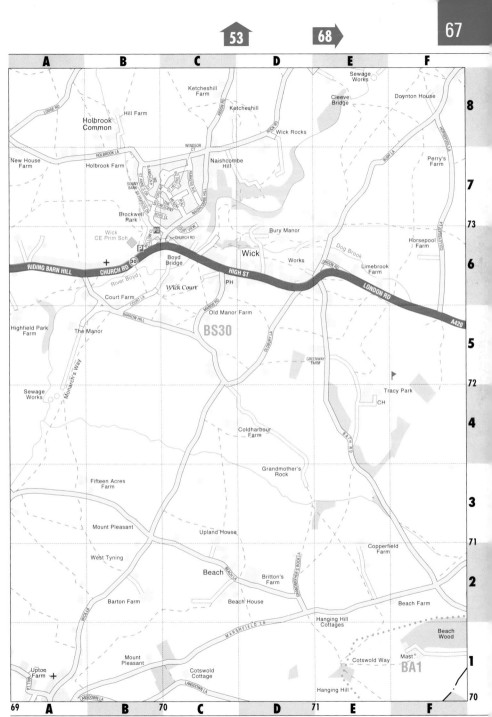

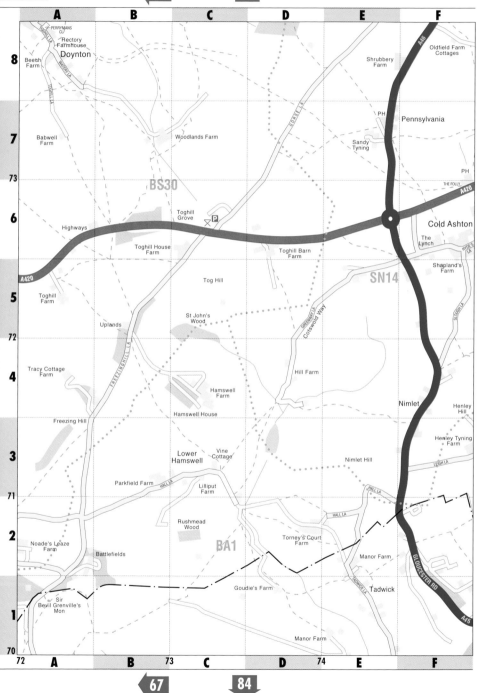

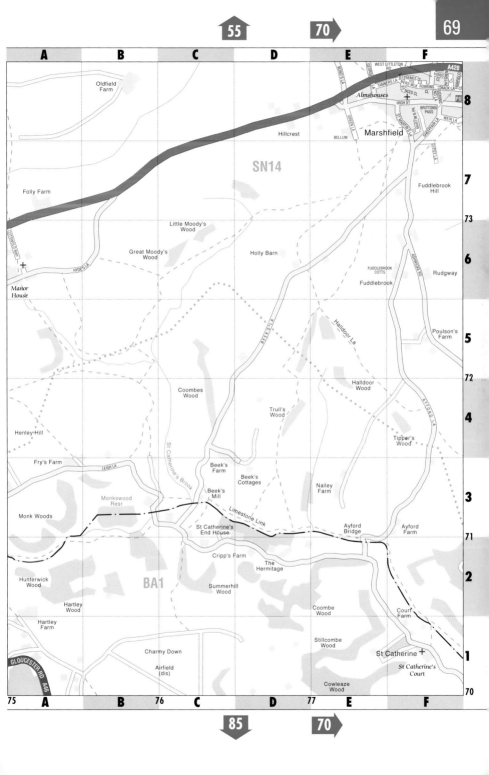

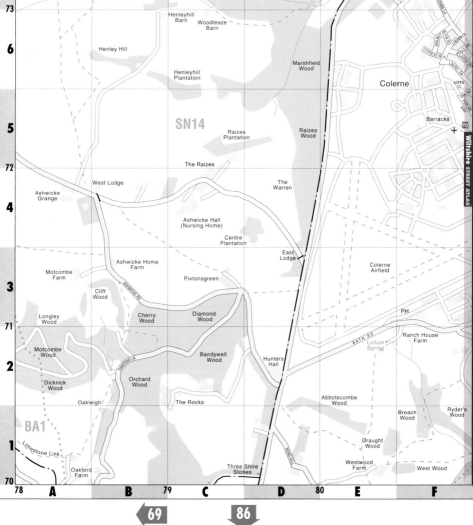

| A | B | C | D | E | F |

Wiltshire STREET ATLAS

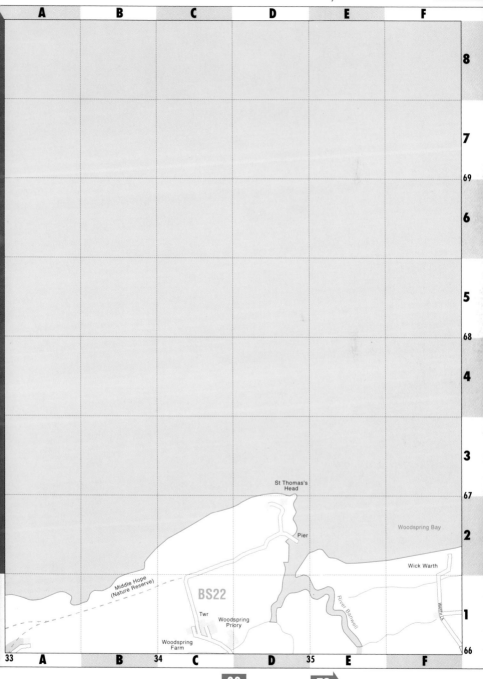

St Thomas's Head

Pier

Woodspring Bay

Wick Warth

Middle Hope
(Nature Reserve)

BS22

Twr   Woodspring
Priory

River Banwell

WARTH LA

Woodspring
Farm

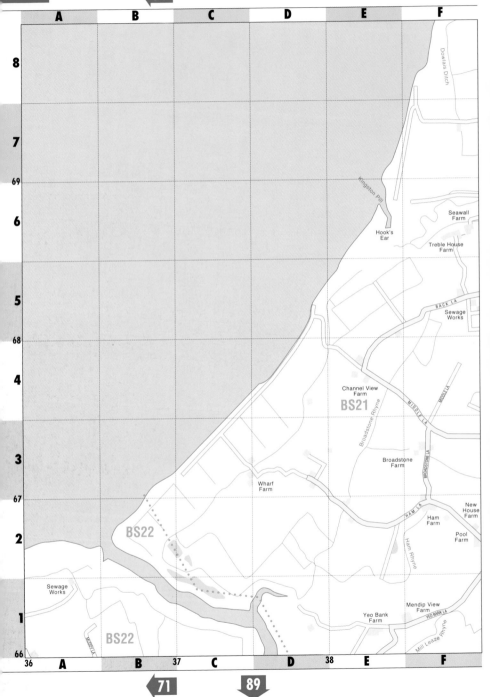

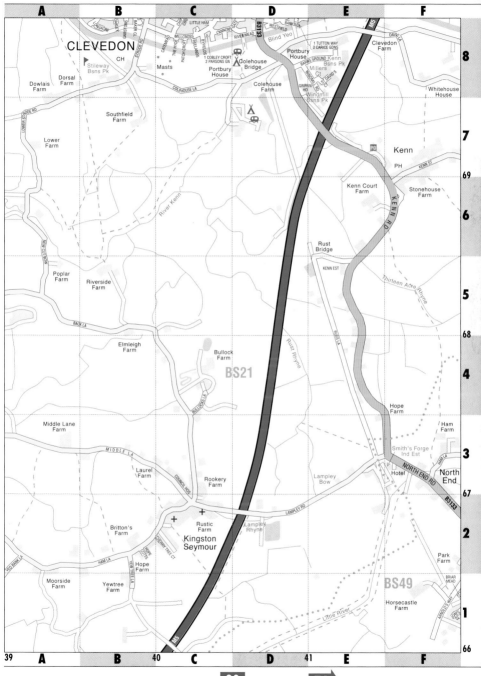

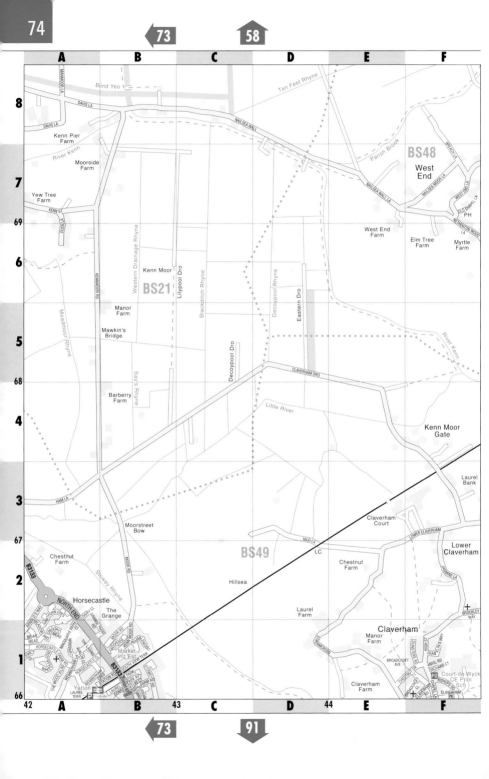

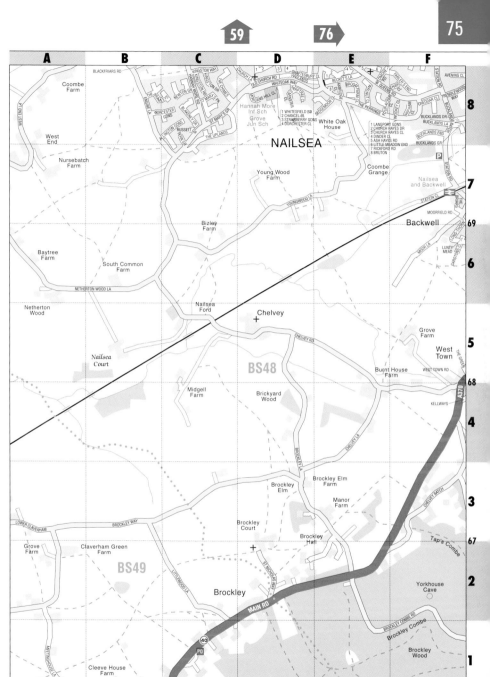

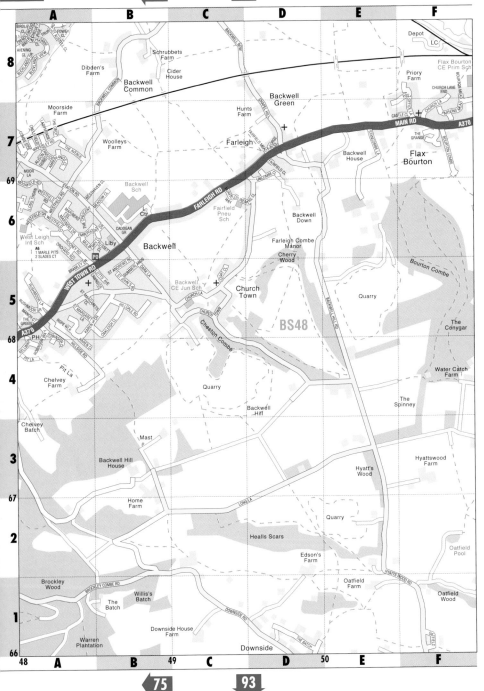

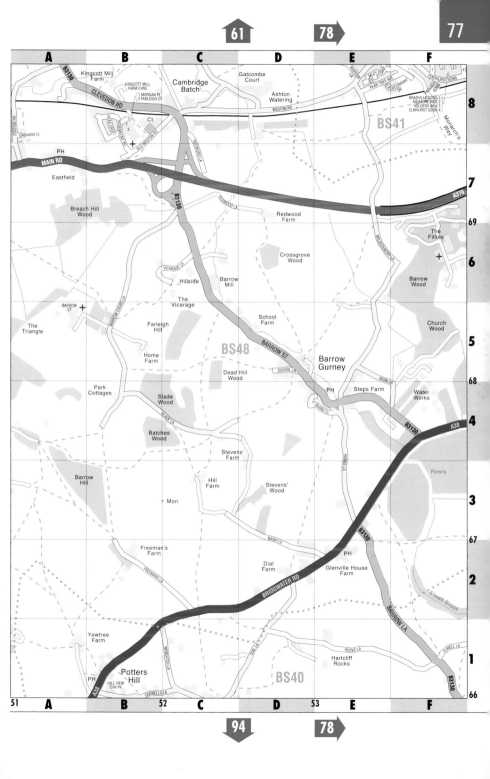

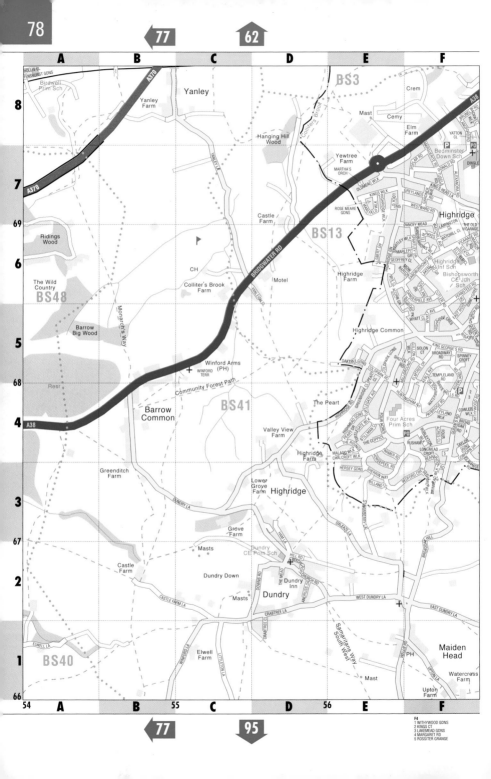

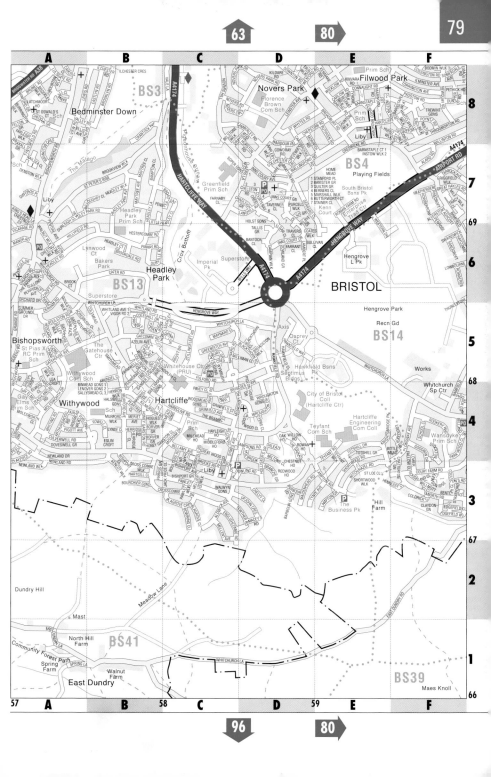

79 **64**

BS4

BROADFIELD
GILMINSTER RD
PONSFORD RD
A4174 AIRPORT RD
A37

Sports Gd
WEST TOWN LA
B3119 WEST TOWN LA
B110
Sports Gd

8

BS4

Brislington Ent Coll
Flowers Hill Trad Est
P&R

Scotland Farm

Flowers Hill

WELLS RD

BRISTOL
7

1 FIRST AVE
2 SIXTH AVE
3 SEVENTH AVE
4 EIGHTH AVE
5 THIRD AVE
6 SECOND AVE
7 FOURTH AVE
8 FIFTH AVE

Hengrove Com Arts Coll

New Oak Prim Sch

69

Hengrove

The Coots

Ilsyngrove SWALLOW

NEW MEADS
NEW FOSSEWAY RD

St Bernadette RC Prim Sch

St Bernadette RC Sch

Hollyridge

CAITLIN CT

DUTTON CL
DUTTON WLK

6

Perry Court Jun & Inf Schs

Whitchurch District Ctr

1 CHARTER WLK
2 PYRACANTHA WLK
3 KING EDWARD CL

1 OAK CT
2 PINKHAMS TWIST
3 BEECH CT

COPELAND DR 1
WEDGWOOD CL 2
EXTON CL 3
CURLAND GR 4
BLACKDOWN CT 5
WANSDYKE CT 6
SHIPHAM CL 7
ALDER CT 8

Superstore

BURGIS RD

Burnbush Prim Sch

Stockwood

LIBY
Waycroft Prim Sch

ROBIN

STORMINSTER LODGE

KNIGHTSTONE SQ

THE DRIVE
RIDGE
RIDGEWAY LA

5

RIDGEWAY

RIDGEMOUNT GDNS

SALTWELL AVE

DENE RD

OLD VICARAGE CT

CRAYDON RD
CRAYDON GR

Langdown
MATERMAN CT
WOOLLEY
GOSLET RD

68

MOORETON CL

Whitchurch Prim Sch

BS14

Stockwood Green Prim Sch

4

WHITCHURCH LA

Whitchurch

MAGGS LA

CHURCH RD

CHURCH MDWS

Manor Farm
ORCHARD PK
STAUNTON WAY

Horse World

Newlands

3

Dundry Hill

LITTLEWOOD
ELTON CROFT

BRISTOL RD

Cemy

QUEEN CHARLTON LA

2

Whitewood Farm

The Cot

Nursery

BS31

1

BS39

A37

BLACKROCK LA
GIBBET LA
HURSLEY LA

MAPLEWOOD
GIBBET LA

CHARLTON RD

66

79 **97**

60 61 62
A B C D E F

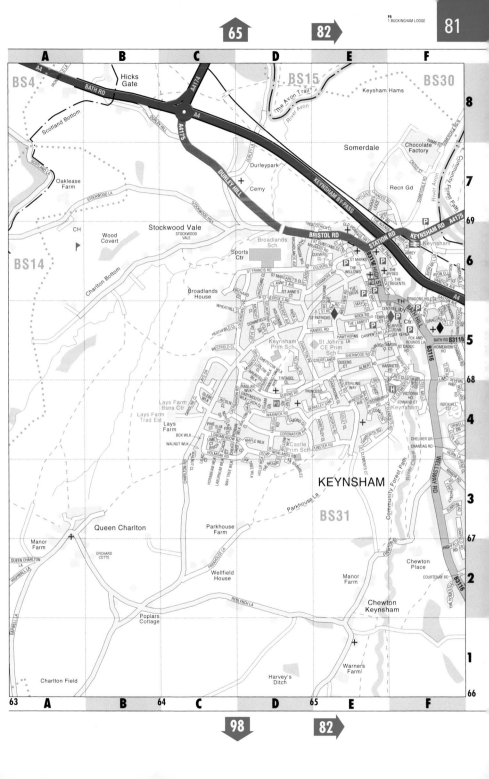

A B C D E F

8

Londonderry Farm
Londonderry Farm
Community Forest Path
KEYNSHAM RD
A4175
Nursery
Field Grove Farm
A431 BATH RD
The Meadows Prim Sch
Works
Mfl
Nursery
Barrow Hill
PH
PO
HIGH ST
Bitton
BREWERY HILL
Monarch's Way

7

BS30
Avon Valley Rly
River Boyd
BATH RD
A431
Nursery
A4175
Broad Mead
Broadmead Lane Ind Est
River Avon
Holm Mead
Mickle Mead

69

6

Sewage Works
Wansdyke Workshops
Mill
The River Avon Trail
Avon Valley Country Park
Avon Riverside
Bristol & Bath Rly Path
Avon Farm

A4
KEYNSHAM BY-PASS
Unity Ct
Superstore
CONSTABLE CL
Ashmead Bsns Pk
Ashmead Road Ind Est
Avon Valley Farm Bsns Pk
TA Ctr
BROADMEAD
Coll
Pixash Bsns Ctr
Pixash Works
WORLD'S END LA

5

B3116 BATH RD B3116
1 NASH CL
2 RUBENS CL
3 CHELSEA CL
4 HILLS CL
5 REYNOLDS CL
6 TURNER CL
HARDING PL

68

Wellsway Sch
Chandag Jun & Inf Schs
KEYNSHAM
Nurseries
LONGREACH
Glenavon Farm
WEDMORE RD
STRATTON
CALMERTON
PH

4

BS31
COLNE GN
BATH RD
IFORD CL
JENA CT
Liby
PO
THE BATCH
P
River Avon

3

Playing Field
Eastover Farm
Keynsham Manor
MANOR RD
Saltford CE Prim Sch
Collingwood
CLAVERTON RD
Weir
MILL COTTS

67

2

B3116
Saltford
THE FOLLY
A4

1

WELLSWAY
B3116
Uplands
Burnett Bsns Pk
BA2
Folly Wood
CH
THE GLEN

66

66 A B 67 C D 68 E F

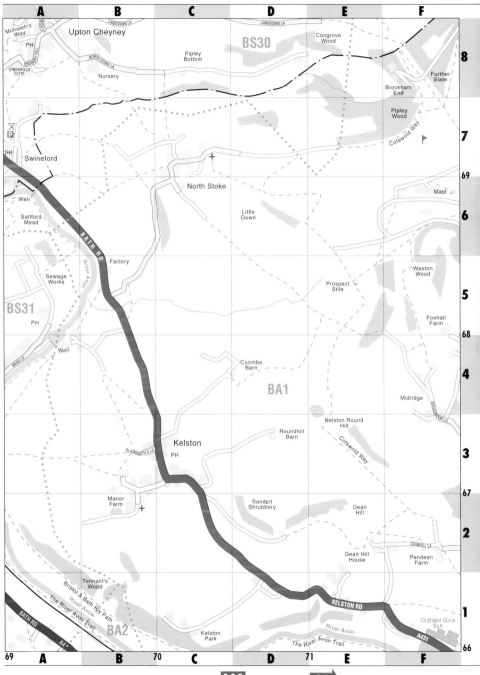

8

Midfields
The Grove
Court Farm
Langridge House
Langridge La
Upper Langridge
Ashcombe Farm
Ashcombe House

7
Upper Farm
Hall
Aldermoor Wood
Horwick La
Lam Brook

69

Lansdown Hill
CH
Bath Race Course
PH
Lansdown
Upper Langridge Farm
Mill Farm

6
Woolley
CHURCH
HIGH ST
WOOLLEY LA

Heather Cottage
Charlcombe Grove Farm
Ravenswell House

5
Soper's Wood

68
Aldermead
P&R
BA1
Govt Offices
View Point Farm
COLLIERS LA

4
Heather Farm
Beckford's Twr & Mus
Cemy
Charlcombe
GRANVILLE RD

NAPIER RD
DUNCAN GDNS
BERESFORD GDNS
LEGG...
Mount Haviland
Upper Weston Farm
Hamilton Ho
Stoneleigh Ct
CAM PK
LANSDOWN RD

3
Upper Weston
BROADMOOR LA
HAVILAND GR
THE GLADE
BROOKSIDE DR

67
Weston All Saints CE Prim Sch
Dean Hill
Nursery
DEANHILL LA
LANSDOWN VIEW
BROADMOOR PK
SIX STREAMS
EAST TERR
Rotrannon Farm
FONTHILL RD
VAN DIEMEN'S LA

2
MICHAELS MEAD
WESTON LODGE
HOLCOMBE GN
WEST TERR
BLIND LA
THE ELMS
HOLCOMBE LA
WESTMEAD GDNS
WESTON PK
HARCOURT GDNS
WELLINGTON BLDGS
Kingswood Sch
HAMILTON RD
Royal High Sch
FAIRFIELD PARK RD
NORTHFIELDS
RICHMOND

1 BROOKSIDE HO
2 KNIGHTSTONE PL
3 SHEPPARDS GDNS
4 THE OLD BREWHOUSE
5 GAINSBOROUGH CT
6 CHELSCOMBE
7 EDGECOMBE MEWS
8 PROSPECT PL

BATH
Primrose Hill
Summerhill Park
Kingswood Prep Sch
Lansdown
Laggan Ho
BEAUMONT
CHARLCOTTE
HERMITAGE RD
SOMERSET
Prim Sch
Beacon Hill

1
Weston
Cotswold Way
Penn Hill
St Mary's RC Prim Sch
ANCHOR RD
BELTON CT
BIBURY CT
SOUTHDEAN
Liby
P
PO
Weston Park
HOOLEY CT
ST CLEMENTS
LUCKLEY RD
THE GRANGE
THE ELMS
MULBERRY MEWS
SCAMMELL
SION HILL PL
FONTHILL
Sion Hill
Univ
SOMERSET
RICHMOND
ST STEPHENS

66
Sch
Royal United
H
THE GROVE
MANOR VILLAS
MONTROSE COTTS
Threeways Sch
Summerfield Site

F1
1 LANDSDOWN PL W
2 LANDSDOWN CRES
3 MOUNT BEACON PL

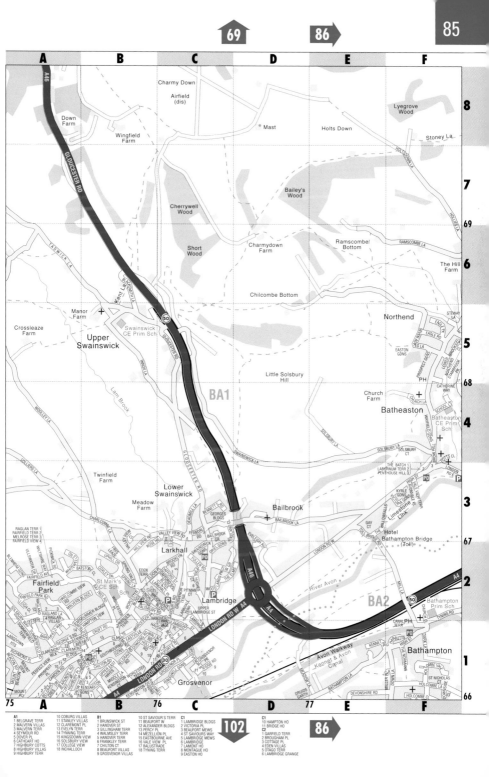

A1
1 BELGRAVE TERR
2 MALVERN VILLAS
3 MALVERN RD
4 SEYMOUR RD
5 DOVER PL
6 CATHCART HO
7 HIGHBURY COTTS
8 HIGHBURY VILLAS
9 HIGHBURY TERR

10 COBURG VILLAS
11 STANLEY VILLAS
12 CLAREMONT PL
13 EVELYN TERR
14 TYNING TERR
15 KINGSDOWN VIEW
16 SOLSBURY VIEW
17 COLLEGE VIEW
18 INCHALLOCH

B1
1 BRUNSWICK ST
2 HANOVER ST
3 GILLINGHAM TERR
4 WALMSLEY TERR
5 HANOVER TERR
6 FRANKLEY TERR
7 CHILTON CT
8 BEAUFORT TERR
9 GROSVENOR VILLAS

10 ST SAVIOUR'S TERR
11 BEAUFORT W
12 ALEXANDER BLDGS
13 PERCY PL
14 MEZELLION PL
15 EASTBOURNE AVE
16 VALE VIEW PL
17 BALUSTRADE
18 TYNING TERR

C1
1 LAMBRIDGE BLDGS
2 VICTORIA PL
3 BEAUFORT MEWS
4 ST SAVIOURS WAY
5 LAMBRIDGE MEWS
6 LAMBRIDGE
7 LAMONT HO
8 MONTAGUE HO
9 EASTON HO

C1
10 HAMPTON HO
11 BRIDGE HO
C2
1 GARFIELD TERR
2 BROUGHAM PL
3 COTTAGE PL
4 EDEN VILLAS
5 OTAGO TERR
6 LAMBRIDGE GRANGE

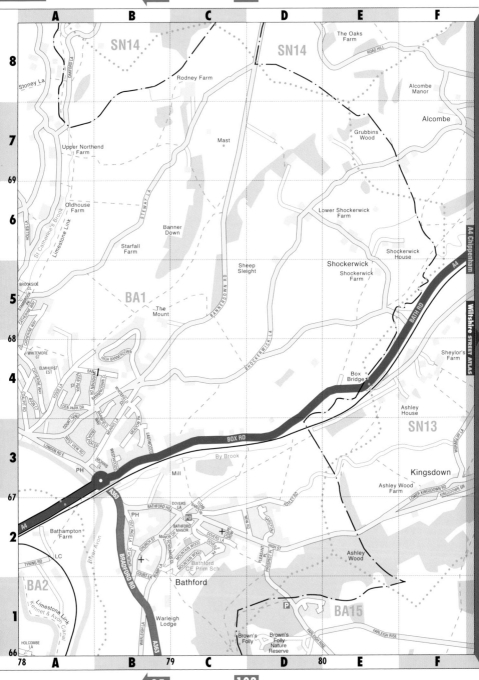

SN14

SN14

The Oaks Farm

ROAD HILL

Alcombe Manor

Alcombe

Rodney Farm

Stoney La

Mast

Grubbins Wood

A4 Chippenham

Upper Northend Farm

Lower Shockerwick Farm

St Catherine's Brook

Oldhouse Farm

STEWAY LA

Banner Down

Shockerwick House

Limestone Link

Shockerwick

A4

BANNERDOWN RD

Starfall Farm

Sheep Sleight

Shockerwick Farm

BA1

BROOKSIDE CL

The Mount

SHOCKERWICK LA

BATH RD

Sheylor's Farm

Wiltshire STREET ATLAS

WHITEMORE CT

ELMHURST EST

Box Bridge

Ashley House

SN13

Ashley Wood Farm

Kingsdown

BOX RD

By Brook

PH

Mill

Ashley Wood

KINGSDOWN RD

LOWER KINGSDOWN RD

KINGSDOWN DR

A363

Bathampton Farm

PH

BATHFORD HILL

DOVERS LA

Bathford Manor

MILL LA

ASHLEY RD

HIGH ST

LC

TYNING RD

River Avon

BRADFORD RD

CHURCH LA

COURT LA

MOUNTAIN WOOD

Bathford CE Prim Sch

DOVERS LA

PROSPECT PL

PLEASANT PL

BA15

FARLEIGH RISE

BA2

Limestone Link
Kennet & Avon Canal

Bathford

P

P

Ashley Wood

FARLEIGH RISE

HOLCOMBE LA

A363

WARLEIGH LA

Warleigh Lodge

Brown's Folly

Brown's Folly Nature Reserve

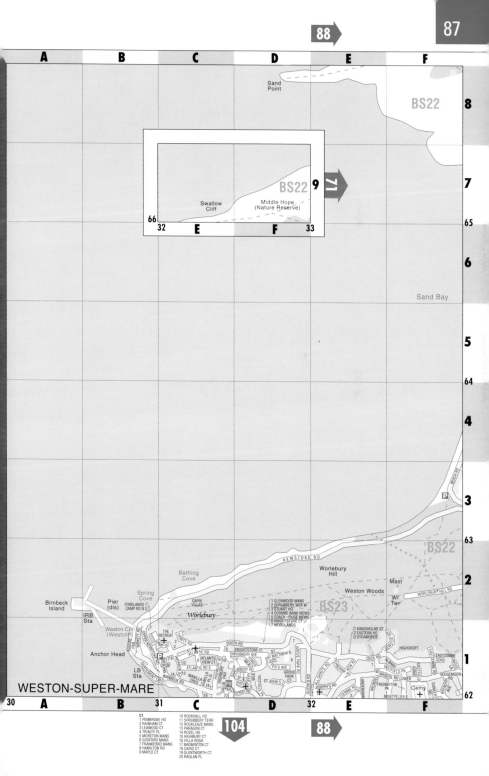

BS22

8

BS22 9

71

Sand
Point

Swallow
Cliff

Middle Hope
(Nature Reserve)

66

32 E F 33

7

65

6

Sand Bay

5

64

4

3

63

BS22

2

KEWSTOKE RD

Worlebury
Hill

Weston Woods

Mast

Wr
Twr

WORLEBURY HILL RD

Bathing
Cove

CAPRI
VILLAS

1 GLENWOOD MANS
2 SHRUBBERY, WCK W
3 STUART HO
4 COOMBE BANK MEWS
5 COACH HOUSE MEWS
6 KNIGHTSTONE CT
7 WOODLANDS

BS23

Birnbeck
Island

Pier
(dis)

Spring
Cove

FORELANDS 1
CAMP RD N 2

Worlebury

1 KINGSHOLME CT
2 EASTERN HO
3 SYCAMORES

HIGHCROFT

IRB
Sta

Weston Coll
(Westcliff)

THE 1
RETREAT

EASTCOMBE
GDNS

Anchor Head

ATLANTIC RD

SOUTH RD

ST
MATTHEW'S

GROVE PARK RD

CECIL RD

HIGHCROFT

ATLANTIC
VIEW CT

KNIGHTSTONE C1

SHRUBBERY AVE

DATFIELD PK

LB
Sta

MANILLA CRES

ATLANTIC RD S

SHRUBBERY RD

ST JOHN'S C

GROVE
PARK

SEDGEMOOR

BIRNBECK RD

UPPER CHURCH RD

ST JOSEPH'S RD

TREWARTHA
PK

Cemy

62

WESTON-SUPER-MARE

30

A

31

B

C

104

D

32

E

88

F

62

C1
1 PEMBROKE HO
2 RAINHAM CT
3 LEAWOOD CT
4 TRINITY PL
5 MORETON MANS
6 GOSFORD MANS
7 FRANKFORD MANS
8 HAMILTON RD
9 MAPLE CT
10 ROCKHALL HO
11 SHRUBBERY TERR
12 ROCKLEAZE MANS
13 PARAGON CT
14 ROZEL HO
15 HIGHBURY CT
16 VILLA ROSA
17 BADMINTON CT
18 CAIRO CT
19 GLENTWORTH CT
20 RAGLAN PL

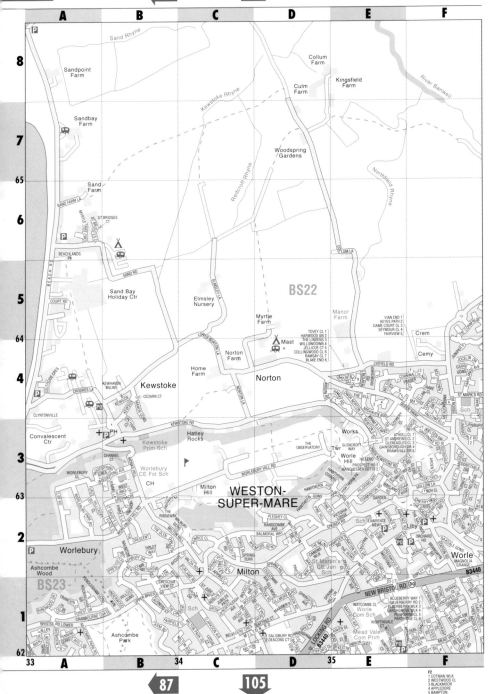

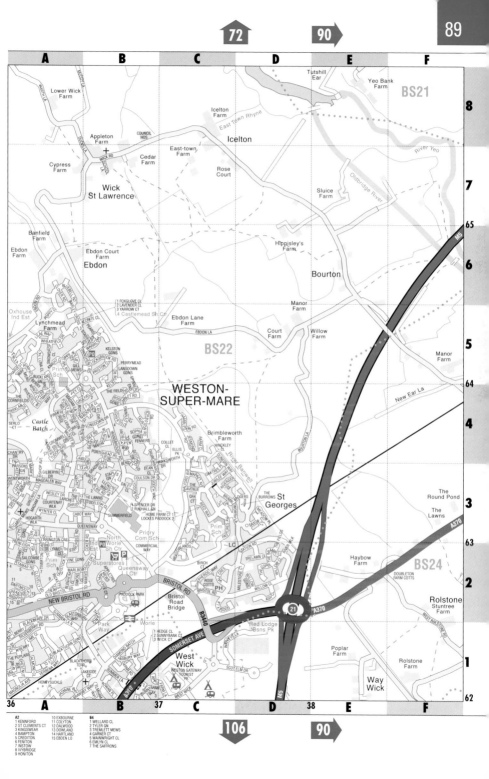

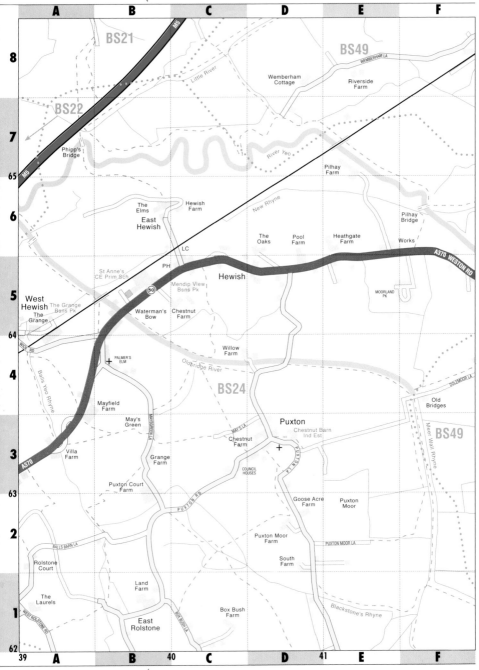

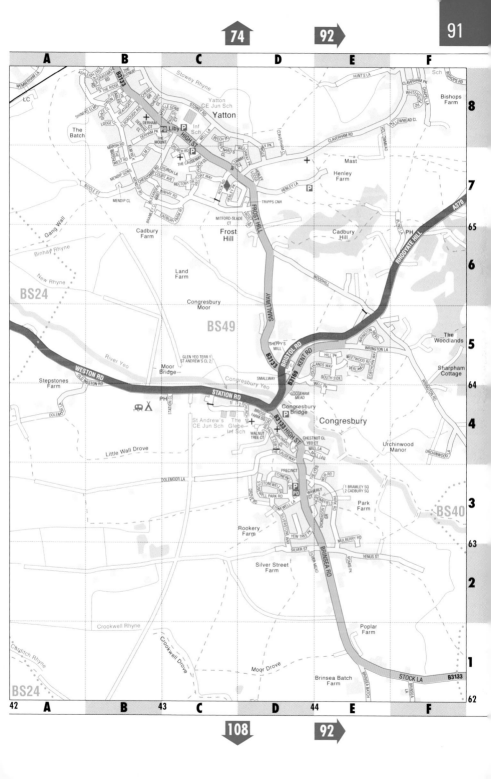

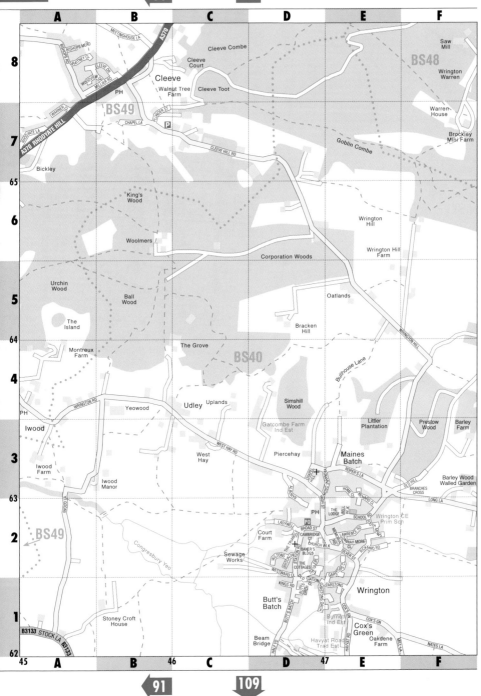

8

7

65

6

5

64

4

3

63

2

1

62

A B C D E F

BS48

Saw Mill

Wrington Warren

Warren House

Brockley Mini Farm

Cleeve Combe

Cleeve Court

Cleeve

Walnut Tree Farm

Cleeve Toot

MEETINGHOUSE LA

A370

BISHOPS MEAD

GRAFFNEY CL

BISHOPS LA

CLEEVE DR

WOODVIEW

MILLER RD

PH

CLEEVE GDNS

BS49

CHAPEL LA

PLUNDER ST

P

CLEEVE HILL RD

A370 RHODYATE HILL

HOSPITAL LA

WEBBER RD

Bickley

Goblin Combe

King's Wood

Woolmers

Corporation Woods

Wrington Hill

Wrington Hill Farm

Urchin Wood

Ball Wood

The Island

Oatlands

Bracken Hill

Montreux Farm

The Grove

BS40

Bullhouse Lane

WRINGTON HILL

Udley

Uplands

Simshill Wood

Littler Plantation

Prestow Wood

Barley Farm

WRINGTON RD

Yeowood

Gatcombe Farm Ind Est

PH

Iwood

West Hay

WEST HAY RD

Piercehay

Maines Batch

ROPER'S LA

Barley Wood Walled Garden

BRANCHES CROSS

OLD HILL

LONG LA

Iwood Farm

Iwood Manor

CHAMS RD

ROMANS RD

PLAYS RYE

ROPERS RD

ORCHARD CL

HOME CL

SCHOOL RD

Wrington CE Prim Sch

Congresbury Yeo

BS49

PH

PO

Court Farm

CAMBRIDGE

LADYWELL

BROAD ST

THE LODGE

CHURCH WLK

HANNAH MORE RD

LAWRENCE RD

SOUTH

RD

STOCK LA

THE TYNINGS

Sewage Works

WESTWARD DR

THE COTTAGES

GARDENS

SILVER ST

Butt's Batch

KINGS RD

STATION RD

GARSTONS

BUTTS BATCH

CARRS RD

Wrington

BURNETT CL

Cox's Green

Oakdene Farm

COX'S GDN

B3133 STOCK LA B3133

Stoney Croft House

Beam Bridge

Havyat Road Trad Est

Burnett Ind Est

HAVYAT RD

NATES LA

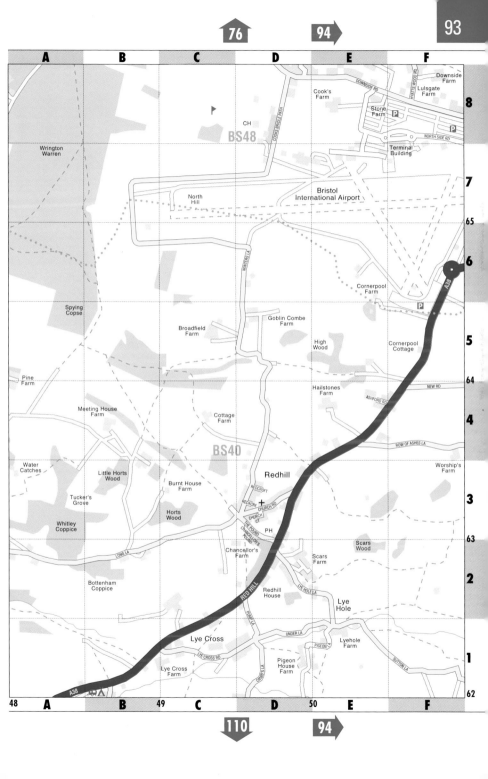

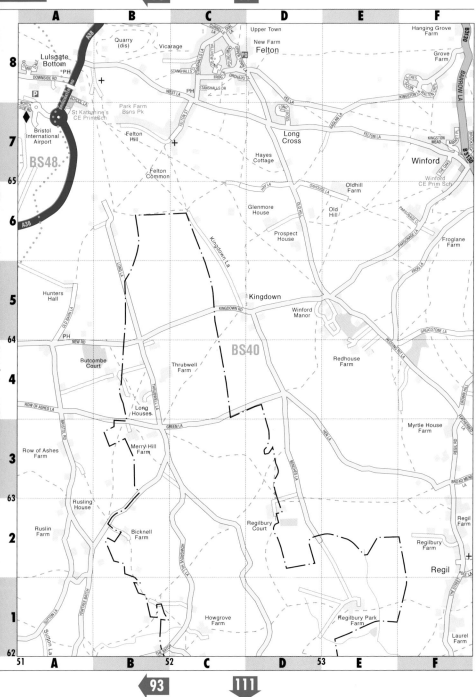

A   B   C   D   E   F

8   Lulsgate Bottom   Quarry (dis)   Vicarage   Upper Town   New Farm   Felton   Hanging Grove Farm   Grove Farm

DOWNSIDE RD   STANGHALLS   WEST LA   PH   STANGHALLS DR   FROG   ORCHARD CL   CRES   KINGSTON CL   FULTON

7   Bristol International Airport   Park Farm Bsns Pk   Felton Hill   Felton Common   Long Cross   Felton La   Kingston Mead   Winford

BS48   St Katharine's CE Prim Sch

65   Hayes Cottage   HAY LA   OXHOUSE LA   Oldhill Farm   OLD HILL   Old Hill   Winford CE Prim Sch

6   A38   Glenmore House   Prospect House   PARSONAGE LA   Froglane Farm   FROG LA

Kingdown La

5   Hunters Hall   OLD BARN LA   LONG LA   Kingdown   KINGDOWN RD   Winford Manor   GREATSTONE LA

64   PH   NEW RD   Butcombe Court   Thrubwell Farm   BS40   Redhouse Farm   BECKNELL LA   THE WOOD

4   ROW OF ASHES LA   THRUBWELL LA   Long Houses   GREEN LA   FELT LA   Myrtle House Farm   FIELDGROVE LA   DRI RISH

3   Row of Ashes Farm   Merry Hill Farm   BENCHELL LA   BROAD MEAD LA

63   Rusling House   Regil Farm

2   Ruslin Farm   Bicknell Farm   HOWGROVE HILL LA   Regilbury Court   Regilbury Farm   Regil   POOL HSE RD

1   BUTTLA LA   SUTTON LA   PEWTREE BATCH   THE BATCH   Howgrove Farm   Regilbury Park Farm   Laurel Farm

62   51   A   B   52   C   D   53   E   F

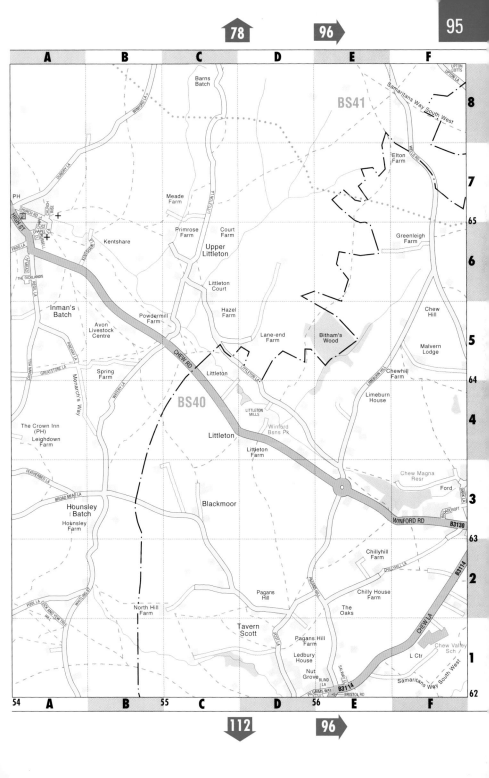

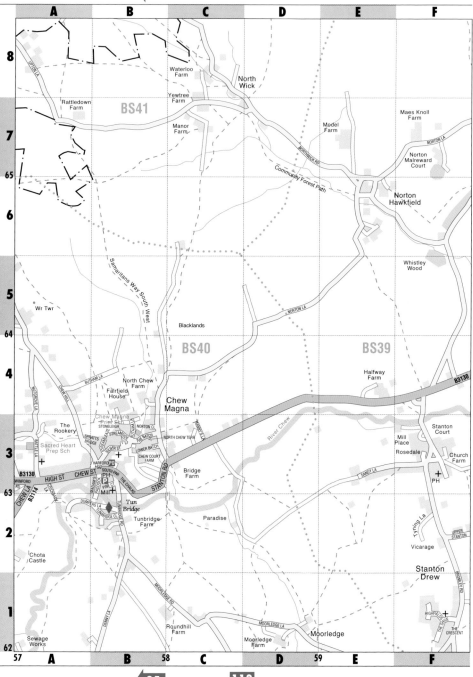

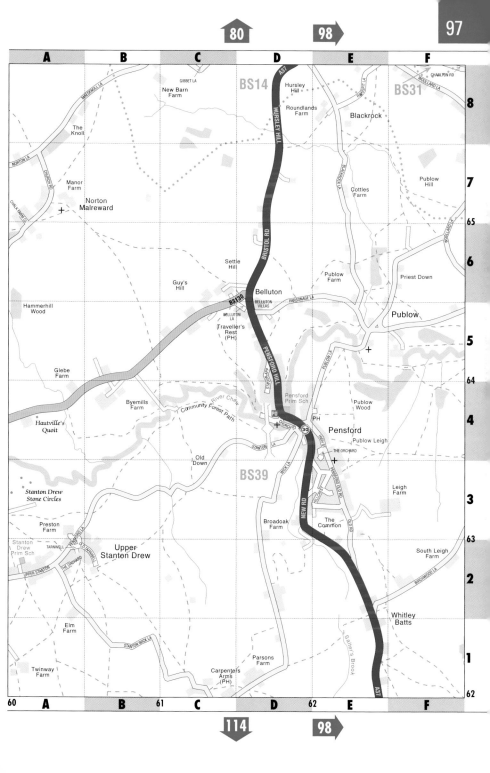

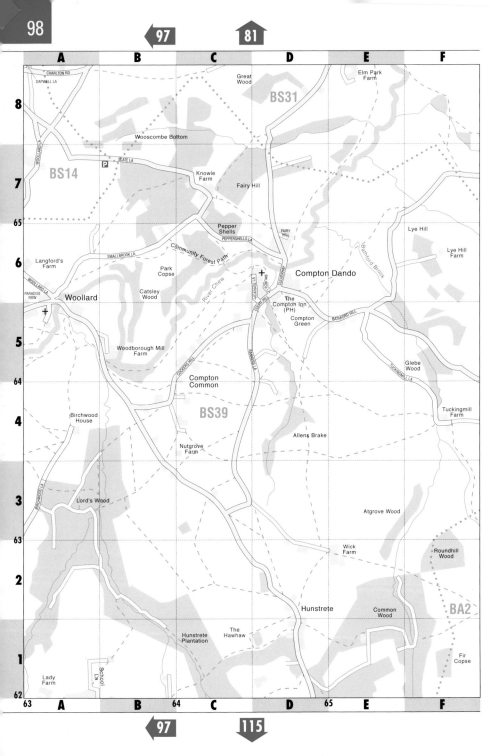

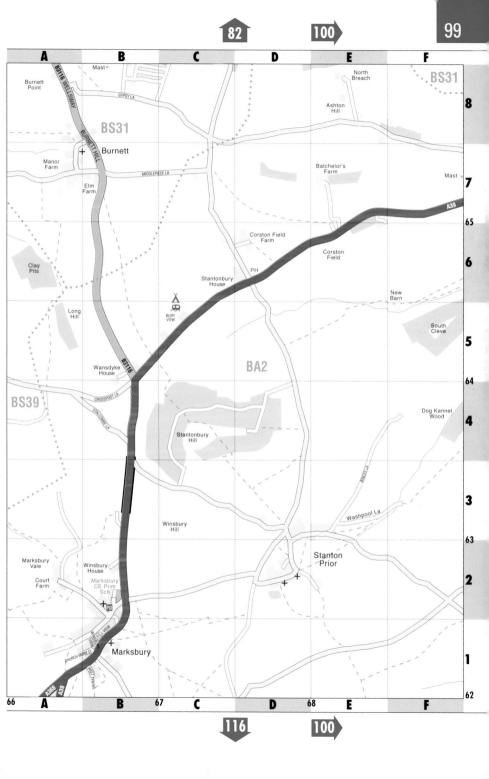

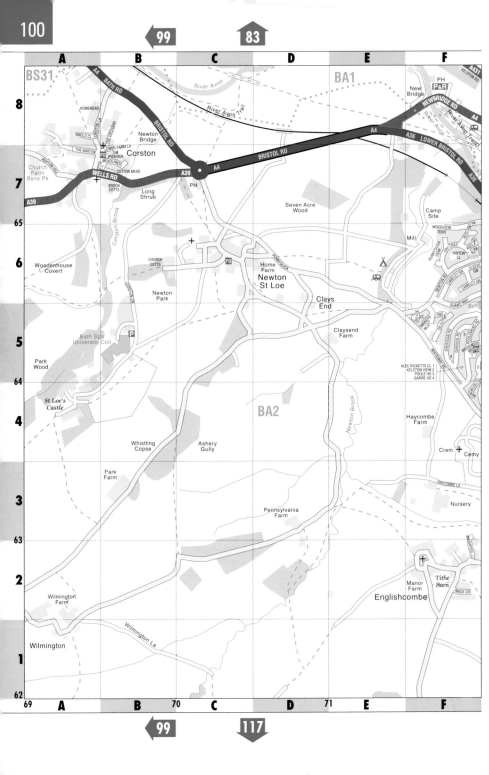

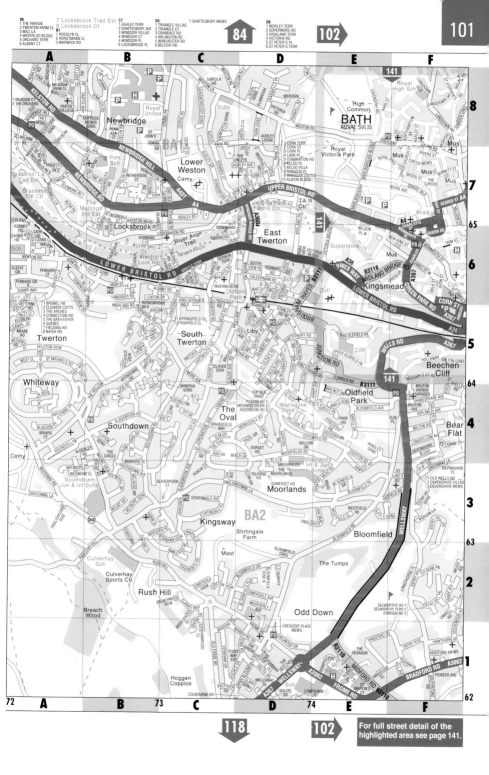

B6
1 THE PARADE
2 TWERTON FARM CL
3 MILL LA
4 WATERLOO BLDGS
5 ORCHARD TERR
6 ALBANY CT

7 Locksbrook Trad Est
8 Locksbrook Ct

B7
1 ROSSLYN CL
2 HORSTMANN CL
3 WARWICK RD

C7
1 ASHLEY TERR
2 SHAFTESBURY AVE
3 WINDSOR VILLAS
4 WINDSOR CT
5 WINDSOR PL
6 LOCKSBROOK PL

D5
1 TRIANGLE VILLAS
2 TRIANGLE CT
3 DRANDALE RD
4 ARLINGTON RD
5 WINCHESTER CT
6 BELVOIR RD

7 SHAFTESBURY MEWS

D6
1 MORLEY TERR
2 GOVERNORS HO
3 HIGHLAND TERR
4 VICTORIA RD
5 ST PETER'S PL
6 ST PETER'S TERR

BATH
AQVAE SVLIS

For full street detail of the highlighted area see page 141.

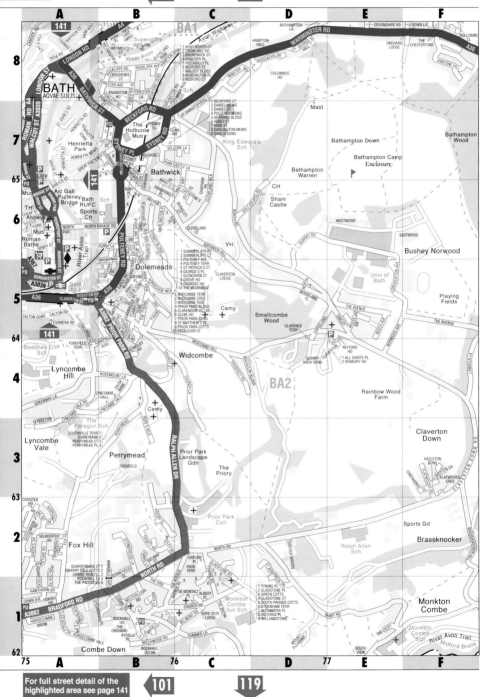

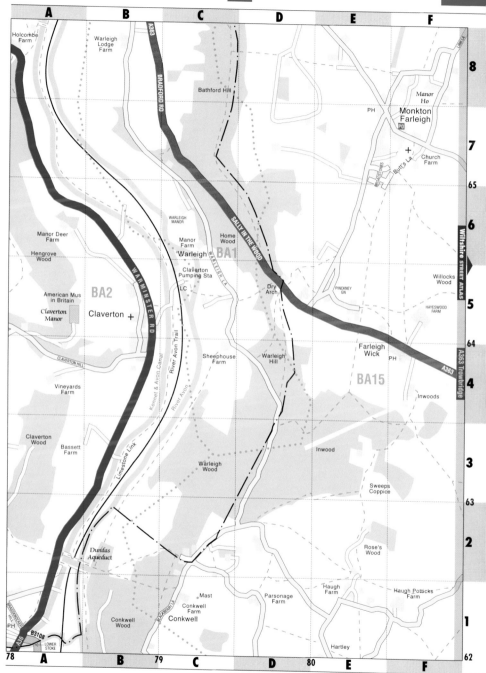

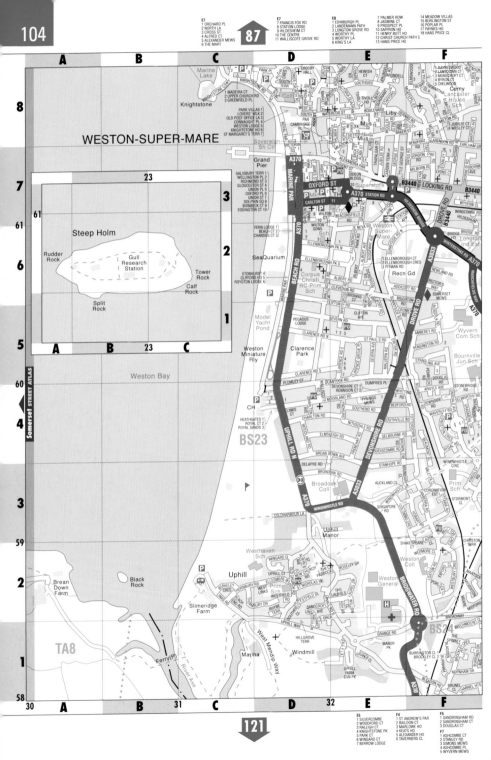

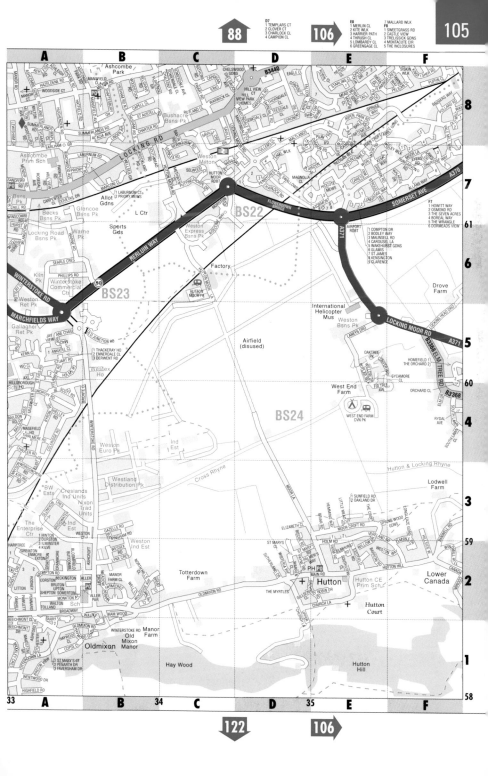

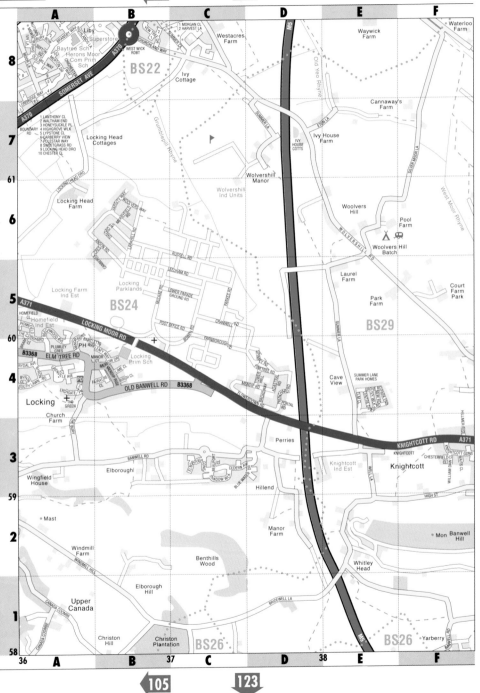

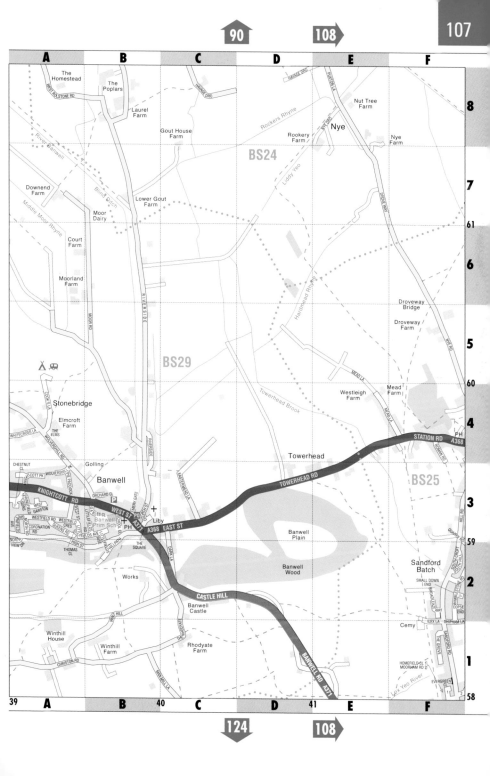

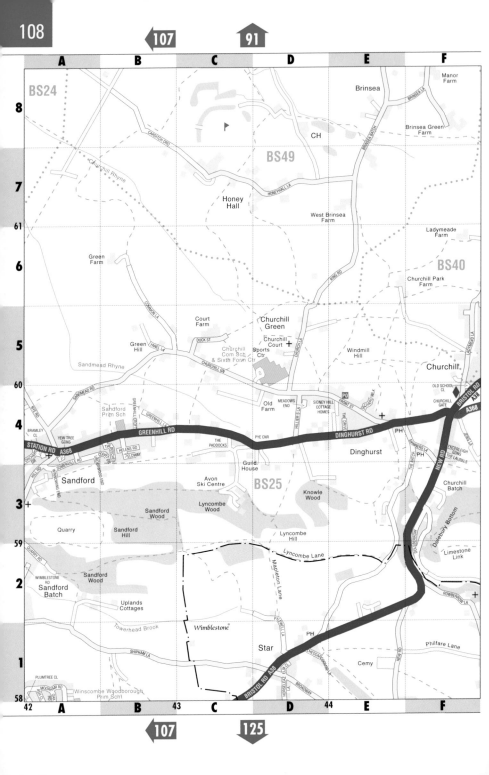

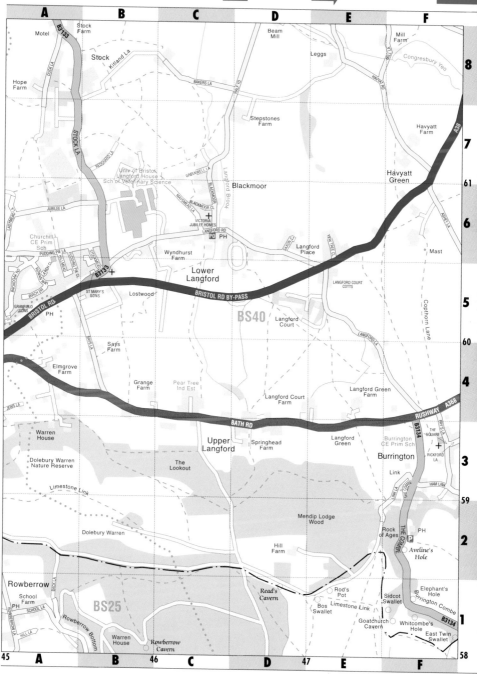

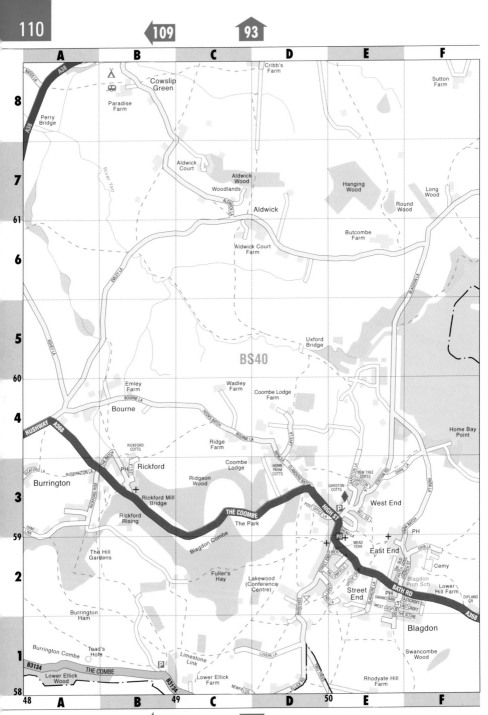

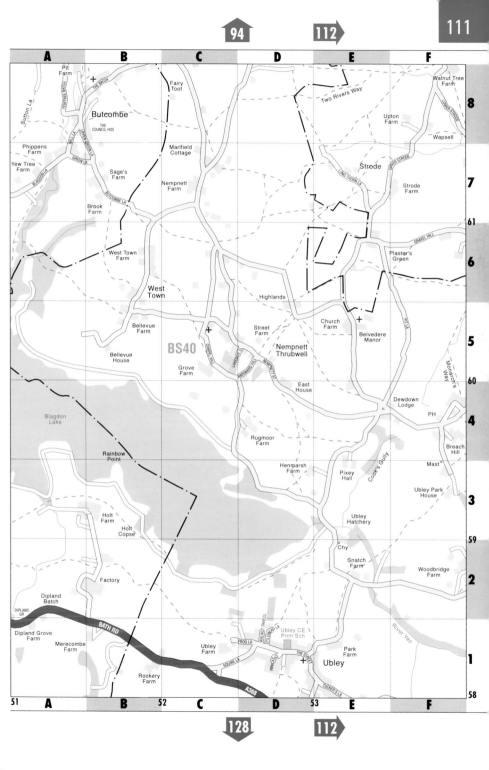

A   B   C   D   E   F

8

Pit
Farm
Butcombe
THE
COUNCIL HOS
Fairy
Toot
Walnut Tree
Farm
Two Rivers Way
Upton
Farm
Wapsell

7

Phippens
Farm
Yew Tree
Farm
Sage's
Farm
Marlfield
Cottage
Nempnett
Farm
Strode
Strode
Farm

61

Brook
Farm
West Town
Farm
Plaster's
Green
GRAVEL HILL

6

West
Town
Highlands
Church
Farm
Belvedere
Manor

5

Bellevue
Farm
Bellevue
House
BS40
Grove
Farm
Street
Farm
Nempnett
Thrubwell
East
House

60

Blagdon
Lake
Rainbow
Point
Dewdown
Lodge
PH
Monarch's Way

4

Rugmoor
Farm
Henmarsh
Farm
Pixey
Hall
Cook's Gully
Mast
Breach
Hill

3

Holt
Farm
Holt
Copse
Ubley
Hatchery
Ubley Park
House

59

Factory
Chy
Snatch
Farm
Woodbridge
Farm

2

Dipland
Batch
DIPLAND
GR
Dipland Grove
Farm
Merecombe
Farm
BATH RD
Rookery
Farm
A368
Ubley
Farm
FROG LA
SQUIRE LA
WALNUT TREE CL
STILEMEAD LA
INNOX CL
Ubley CE
Prim Sch
THE STREET
Park
Farm
Ubley
TUCKER'S LA
River Yeo

1

58

A   B   C   D   E   F

51   52   53

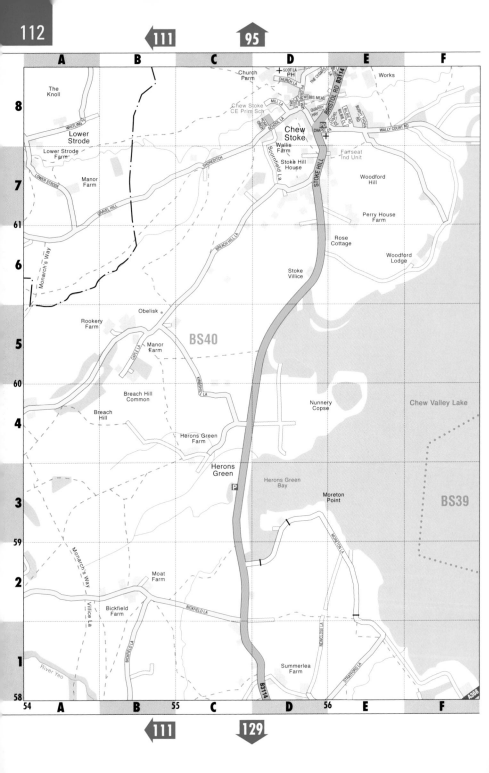

111
95

	A	B	C	D	E	F

8

The Knoll

Lower
Strode

Chew Stoke
CE Prim Sch

Church
Farm

SCOT LA
PH
CHURCH LA

THE COSMOS

BRISTOL RD B3114

Works

61

Lower Strode
Farm

WHITLING

LOWER STRODE

MILL LA

THE

SCHOOL LA

WEBBS MEAD

QUARRY
HAY

BIBBLE RD

BRISTOL RD

WALLY COURT RD

7

Manor
Farm

GRAVEL HILL

SHOREDITCH

Chew
Stoke

Wallis
Farm

Scornfield LA

Stoke Hill
House

STOKE HILL

CHAPEL LA
PO

Farrseat
Ind Unit

Woodford
Hill

Perry House
Farm

Rose
Cottage

Woodford
Lodge

6

Monarch's Way

BREACH HILL LA

Stoke
Villice

5

Rookery
Farm

Obelisk

Manor
Farm

CLAY LA

BS40

Chew Valley Lake

60

Breach
Hill

Breach Hill
Common

KINGS HILL LA

Nunnery
Copse

4

Herons Green
Farm

Herons
Green

Herons Green
Bay

Moreton
Point

BS39

3

P

59

Monarch's Way

Moat
Farm

2

Villice LA

Bickfield
Farm

BICKFIELD LA

BICKFIELD LA

MORETON LA

NEWCLOSE LA

STRATFORD LA

1

River Yeo

Summerlea
Farm

B3114

A368

58

54	A	B	55	C	D	56	E	F

111
129

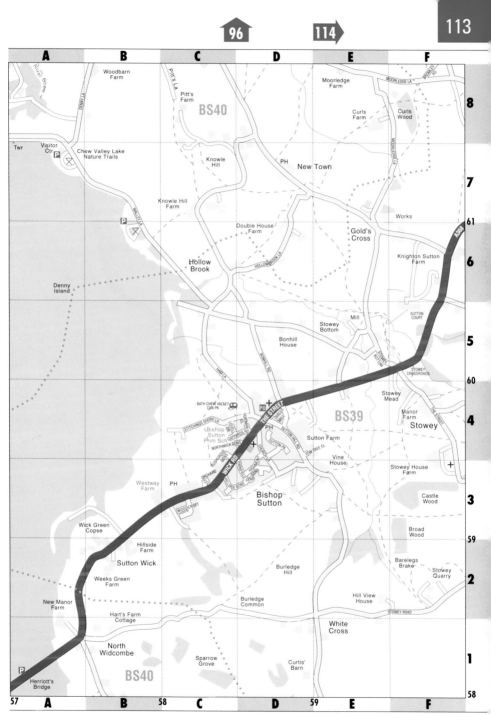

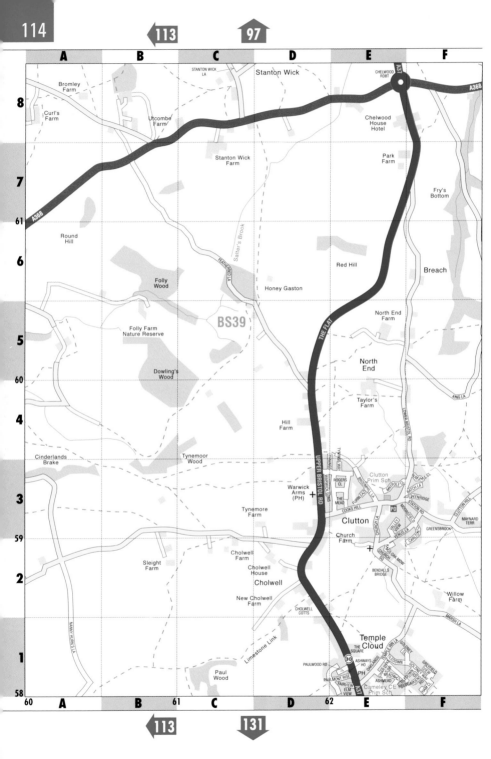

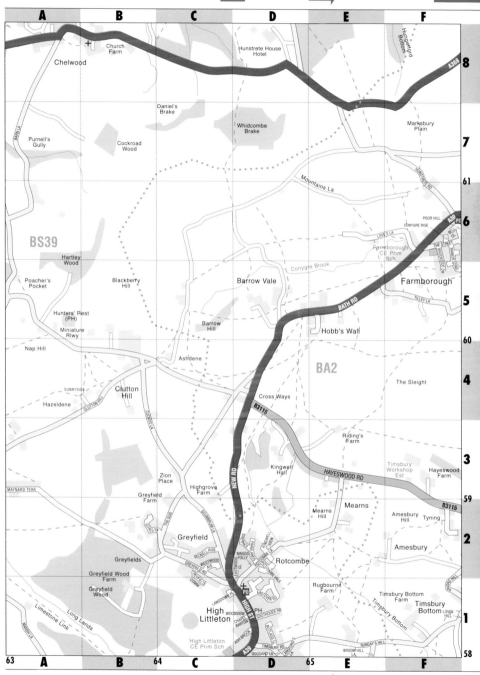

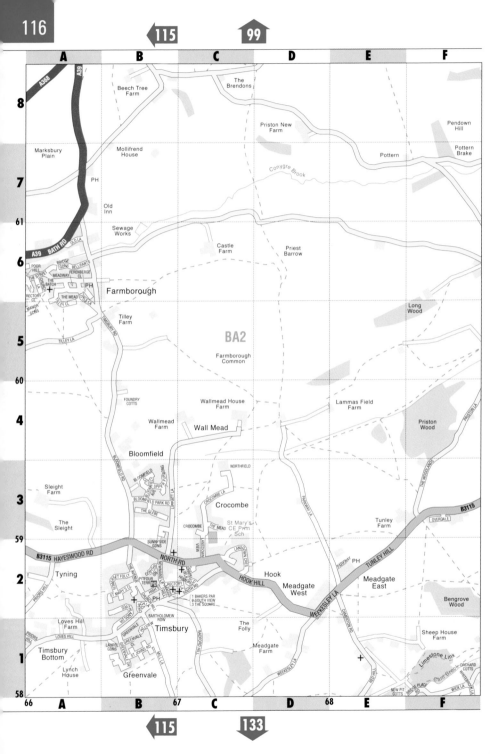

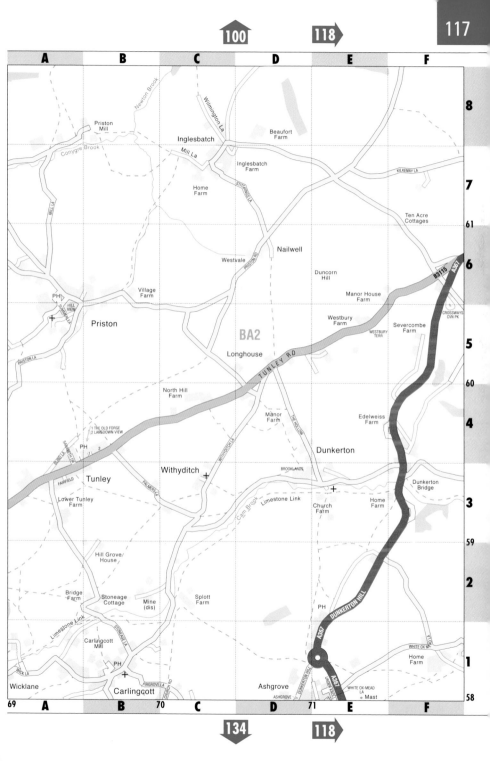

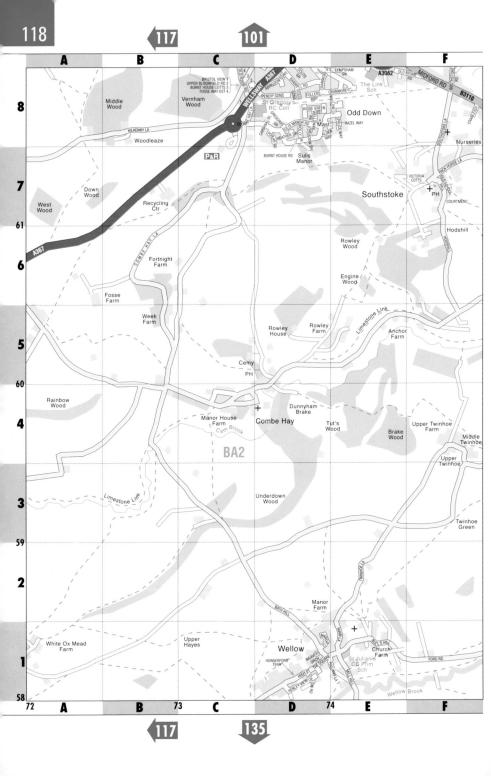

A B C D E F

8

7

61

6

5

60

4

3

59

2

1

58

A B C D E F

72 73 74

Middle Wood

Vernham Wood

BRISTOL VIEW 1
UPPER BLOOMFIELD RD 2
BURNT HOUSE COTTS 3
FOSSE WAY EST 4

Woodleaze

KILKENNY LA

WELLSWAY

A367

MENDIP GDNS

St Gregory's RC Coll

BATH RD

FULLERS WAY

CRANMORE 4

LYMPSHAM GN

The Link Sch

A3062

OLD FROME RD

MIDFORD RD

B3110

SOUTHSTOKE LA

CHALE EGS

Nurseries

BLACK HORSE LA

Odd Down

RIDGE GREEN CL

Mast

HAZEL WAY

Hodshill

Southstoke

VICTORIA COTTS

PH

COURTMEAD

HODSHILL

P&R

BURNT HOUSE RD

Sulis Manor

SULIS MANOR RD

HEATHER WAY

CARDINAL CL

CLOSE

Down Wood

West Wood

Recycling Ctr

COMBE HAY LA

Fortnight Farm

Fosse Farm

Week Farm

Rowley Wood

Engine Wood

Rowley House

Rowley Farm

Limestone Link

Anchor Farm

Cemy

PH

Rainbow Wood

Manor House Farm

Cam Brook

Combe Hay

Dunnyham Brake

Tut's Wood

Brake Wood

Upper Twinhoe Farm

Middle Twinhoe

Upper Twinhoe

BA2

Limestone Link

Underdown Wood

Twinhoe Green

White Ox Mead Farm

Upper Hayes

BATH HILL

Manor Farm

Wellow

HUNGERFORD TERR

WEAVERS ORCH

HENLEY VIEW

HIGH ST

THE SQUARE

FOX HILL

St Julian's CE Prim Sch

BULL'S HILL

Church Farm

FORD RD

Wellow Brook

WINSICK LA

TWINHOE LA

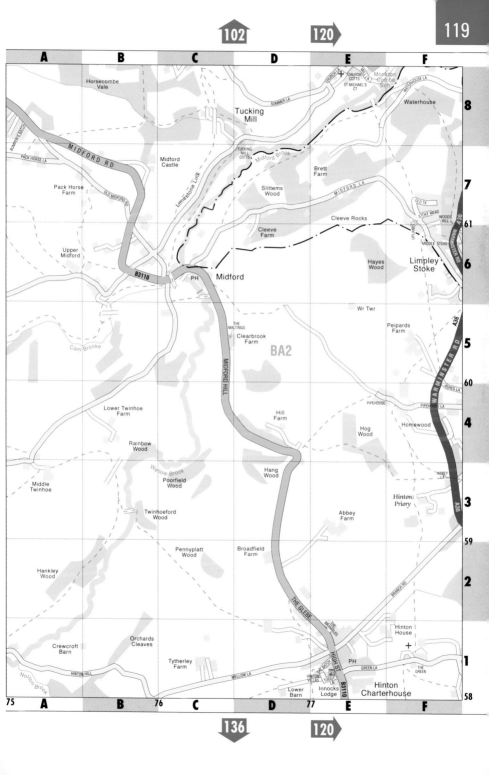

102
120

A   B   C   D   E   F

Horsecombe
Vale

CHURCH LA
CHURCH VILLA
ST MICHAEL'S CT
Monkton
Combe
Sch

8

SLAMMER LA

Tucking
Mill

Waterhouse

WATERHOUSE LA

MIDFORD RD

BUMPERS BATCH

PACK HORSE LA

Midford
Castle

Limestone Link

Tucking Mill Brook
TUCKING
MILL
COTTS

Midford Brook

Brett
Farm

7

MIDFORD LA

OLD TK

Pack Horse
Farm

OLD MIDFORD RD

Slittems
Wood

STOKE MEAD
WOODS
HILL

61

Cleeve
Farm

Cleeve Rocks

MIDDLE STOKE

UPR

A36

B3110

Upper
Midford

PH

Midford

Hayes
Wood

Limpley
Stoke

6

Cam Brooke

Wr Twr

Peipards
Farm

WARMINSTER RD

A36

THE
MALTINGS

Clearbrook
Farm

BA2

5

MIDFORD HILL

60

ASHES LA

Lower Twinhoe
Farm

Hill
Farm

PIPEHOUSE

PIPEHOUSE LA

Hog
Wood

Homewood

4

Rainbow
Wood

Wellow Brook

Poorfield
Wood

Hang
Wood

ABBEY
LA

A36

Middle
Twinhoe

Twinhoeford
Wood

Hinton
Priory

3

Abbey
Farm

59

Pennyplatt
Wood

Broadfield
Farm

Hankley
Wood

2

THE GLEBE

BRANSH RD

Hinton
House

Crewcroft
Barn

Orchards
Cleaves

HIGH ST

THE BRAMBLES

PH

Hinton
Charterhouse

1

Norton Brook

HINTON HILL

Tytherley
Farm

WELLOW LA

HINTON
VILLAS

THE BATCH

TURSY
LA

GREEN LA

THE
GREEN

B3110

Lower
Barn

Innocks
Lodge

58

75   A   B   76   C   D   77   E   F

136
120

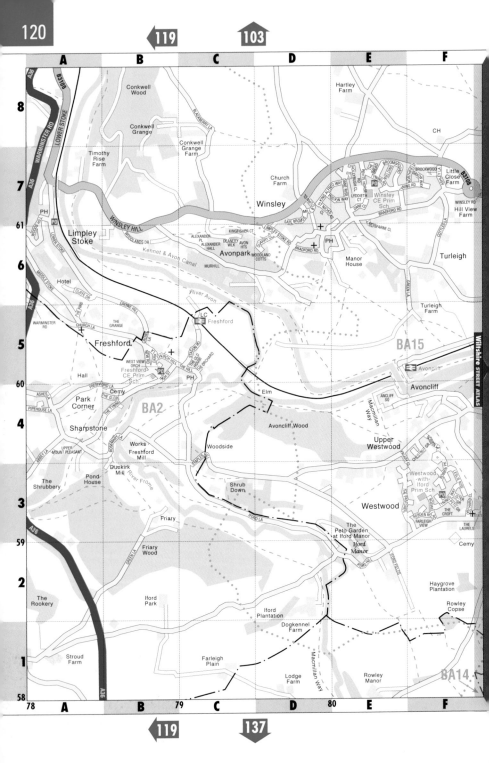

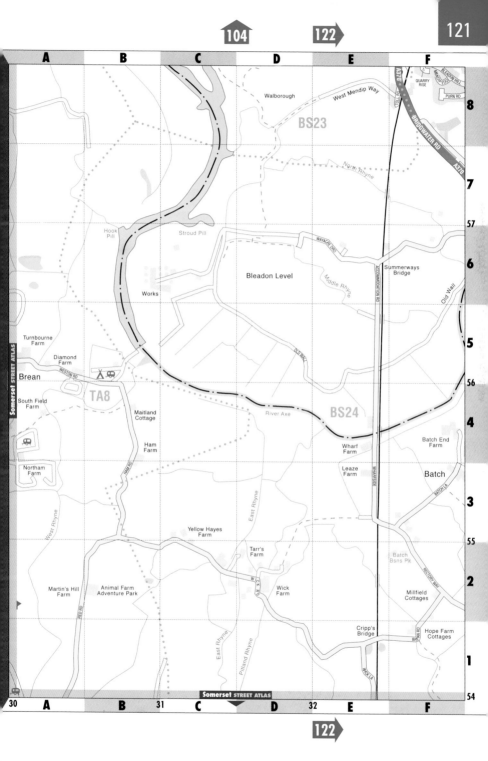

A **B** **C** **D** **E** **F**

8

Walborough

West Mendip Way

BS23

QUARRY RISE

BLEADON HILL
MENDIP CLOSE
PURN RD

A370

BRIDGWATER RD A370

North Rhyne

7

57

Hook Pill

Stroud Pill

WAYSIDE DRO

ACCOMMODATION RD

Summerways Bridge

6

Bleadon Level

Middle Rhyne

Old Wall

Works

5

Turnbourne Farm

Diamond Farm

WESTON RD

DLD WAY

56

Brean

TA8

South Field Farm

Maitland Cottage

River Axe

BS24

4

Wharf Farm

Batch End Farm

Northam Farm

Ham Farm

HAM RD

Leaze Farm

WHARFSIDE

Batch

BATCH LA

3

West Rhyne

East Rhyne

55

Yellow Hayes Farm

Batch Bsns Pk

RECTORY WAY

2

Martin's Hill Farm

Animal Farm Adventure Park

RED RD

Tarr's Farm

W.S.K. RD

Wick Farm

Millfield Cottages

1

East Rhyne

Pilland Rhyne

Cripp's Bridge

PURN RD

Hope Farm Cottages

WICK LA

54

30 **A** **B** 31 **C** **D** 32 **E** **F**

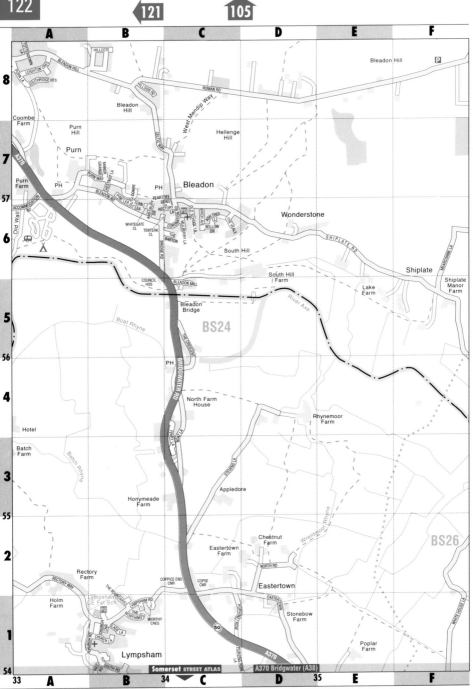

Somerset STREET ATLAS   ▽   A370 Bridgwater (A38)

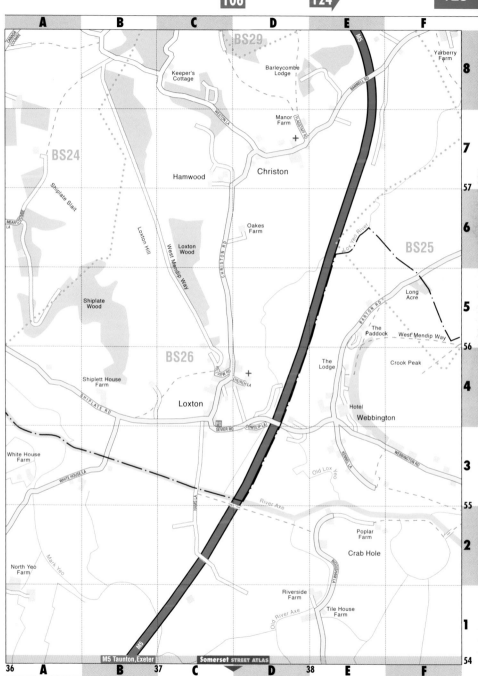

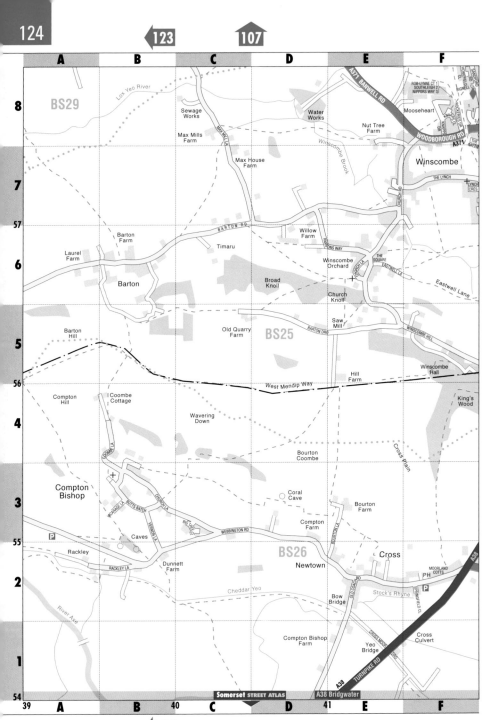

A B C D E F

8

BS29

Lox Yeo River

Sewage Works

Max Mills Farm

Water Works

Nut Tree Farm

Mooseheart

A371 BANWELL RD

WOODBOROUGH RD

A37V

ROB-LYNNE CT 1
SOUTHLEIGH 2
NIPPORS WAY 3

Max House Farm

Winscombe Brook

Winscombe

THE LYNCH

LYNCH CRES

7

57

BARTON RD

Barton Farm

Timaru

Willow Farm

Winscombe Orchard

THE SQUARE

EASTWELL LA

Eastwell Lane

6

Laurel Farm

Barton

Broad Knoll

Church Knoll

Eastwell Lane

5

Barton Hill

Old Quarry Farm

BS25

Saw Mill

BARTON DRO

Winscombe Hill

Winscombe Hall

56

West Mendip Way

Hill Farm

King's Wood

4

Compton Hill

Coombe Cottage

Wavering Down

Bourton Coombe

Cross Plain

3

Compton Bishop

Coral Cave

Bourton Farm

MCADAMS LA

BUTTS BATCH

CHURCH LA

BIG TREE

WEBBINGTON RD

Compton Farm

BOURTON LA

55

P

Rackley

Caves

VERNAL LA

Dunnett Farm

RACKLEY LA

BS26

Newtown

Cross

MOORLAND COTTS

PH

A38

2

River Axe

Cheddar Yeo

Bow Bridge

OLD CHAPEL RD

Stock's Rhyne

SPRINGFIELD CL

P

1

Compton Bishop Farm

Yeo Bridge

CROSS MOOR DRO

TURNPIKE RD

Cross Culvert

54

39 A B 40 C D 41 E F

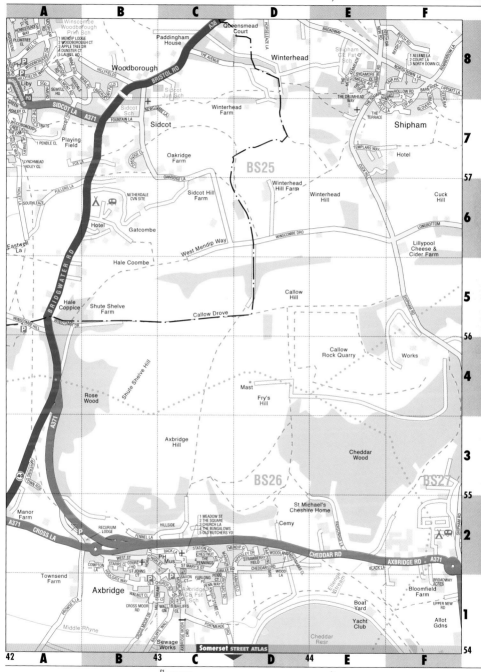

C1
1 OLD CHURCH RD
2 PEELERS CT

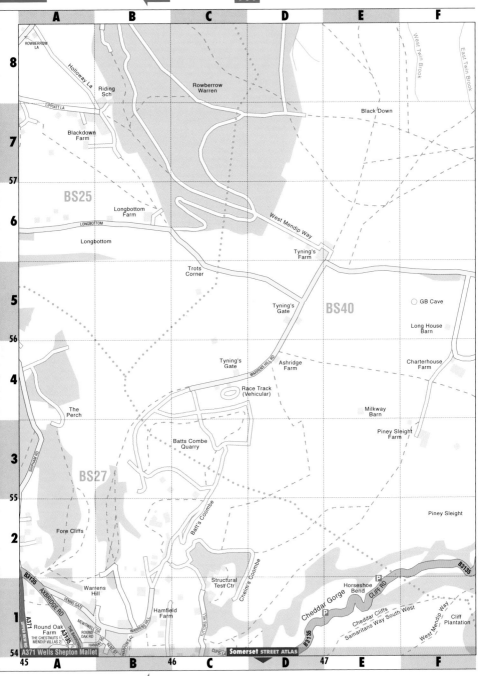

ROWBERROW LA

Holloway La

Riding Sch

Blackdown Farm

LIPPIATT LA

Rowberrow Warren

Black Down

West Twin Brook

East Twin Brook

BS25

57

Longbottom Farm

LONGBOTTOM

Longbottom

West Mendip Way

Tyning's Farm

Trots Corner

Tyning's Gate

BS40

GB Cave

Long House Barn

56

Tyning's Gate

WARRENS HILL RD

Ashridge Farm

Charterhouse Farm

The Perch

Race Track (Vehicular)

Milkway Barn

Piney Sleight Farm

BS27

Batts Combe Quarry

55

Fore Cliffs

Batt's Coombe

Piney Sleight

B3135

AXBRIDGE RD

YENNIS GATE

Warrens Hill

Chelm's Coombe

Structural Test Ctr

Cheddar Gorge

Horseshoe Bend

CLIFF RD

B3135

A371

Round Oak Farm

THE CHESTNUTS 1

MENDIP VILLAS 2

THE DRANGE

MEWSWELL DR

ROUND OAK RD

HANNAH

KENT RD

HARPERS LA

WARRENS HILL

Hamfield Farm

TITTONS

CUFIC LA

Cheddar Cliffs

Samaritans Way South West

West Mendip Way

Cliff Plantation

UPPER NEW RD

A3135

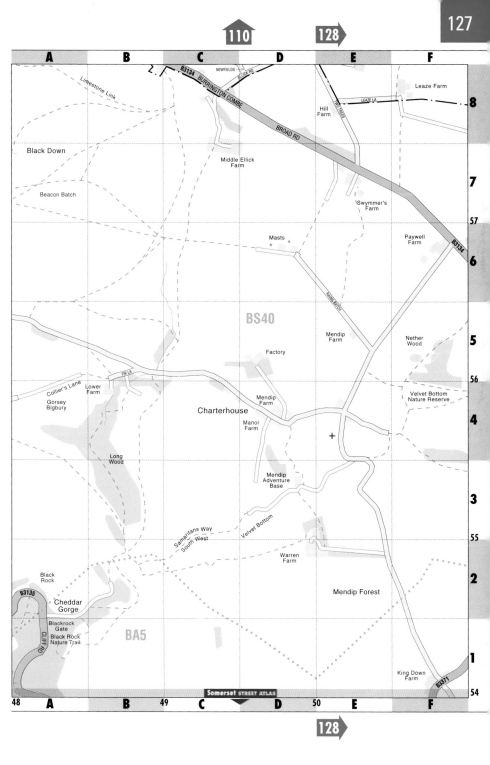

A   B   C   D   E   F

NEWFIELDS

ELLICK RD

B3134

BURRINGTON COMBE

Limestone Link

Leaze Farm

LEAZE LA

MILL TREES

Hill
Farm

8

BROAD RD

Black Down

Middle Ellick
Farm

7

Beacon Batch

Swymmer's
Farm

57

Masts

Paywell
Farm

B3134

6

BS40

RAINS BATCH

Mendip
Farm

Nether
Wood

5

Factory

56

Collier's Lane

FIR LA

Lower
Farm

Mendip
Farm

Velvet Bottom
Nature Reserve

Gorsey
Bigbury

Charterhouse

Manor
Farm

4

Long
Wood

Mendip
Adventure
Base

3

Samaritans Way
South West

Velvet Bottom

55

Warren
Farm

Black
Rock

Mendip Forest

2

B3135

Cheddar
Gorge

Blackrock
Gate
Black Rock
Nature Trail

BA5

CLIFF RD

King Down
Farm

1

B3371

48   A   B   49   C   Somerset STREET ATLAS   D   50   E   F   54

127
111

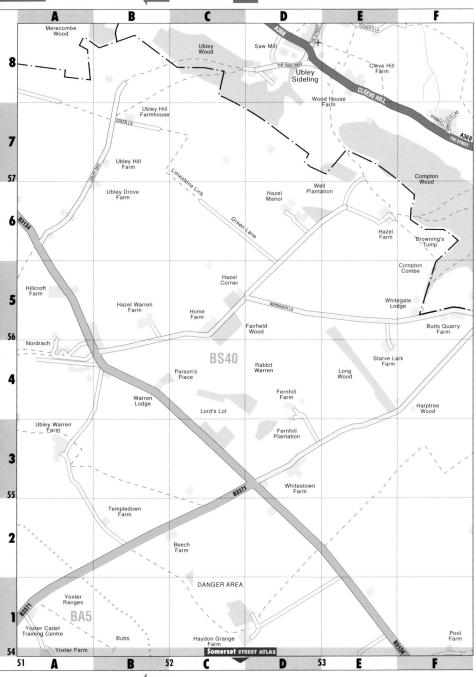

127

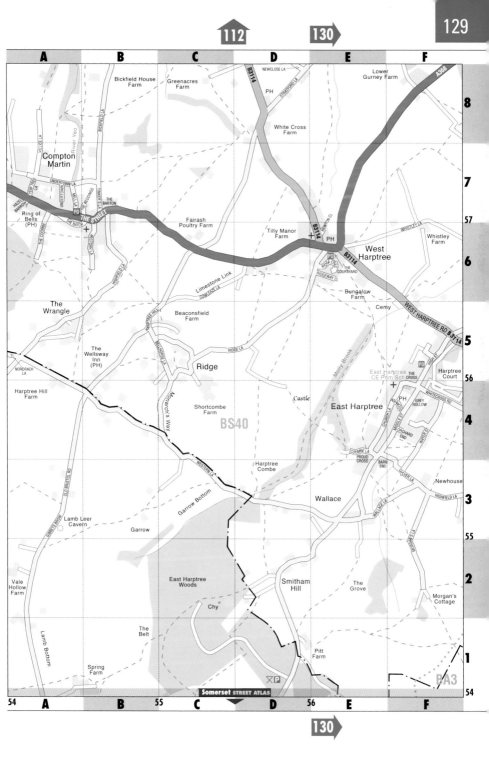

A   B   C   D   E   F

8

7

57

6

5

56

4

55

3

2

1

54

Compton Martin

VALE LA
FERN TREE LA
BICKFIELD LA
UNDERTOWN LA
MILL LA
THE REDDINGS
TINKER LA

Bickfield House Farm

Greenacres Farm

B3114

NEWCLOSE LA
STRATFORD LA

PH

Lower Gurney Farm

A368

White Cross Farm

River Yeo

HAZEL MANOR LA
Ring of Bells (PH)
THE COOMBE
THE BATCH
RECTORY LA
HIGHFIELD LA

UNDERTOWN LA
THE STREET
THE BARTON

Fairash Poultry Farm

Tilly Manor Farm

B3114

PH

NEWTON CL

WHISTLEY LA

Whistley Farm

West Harptree

VOLE CE
THE COURTYARD
RIDGEWAY CL

The Wrangle

HARPTREE HILL
BELMORE LA

Beaconsfield Farm

Limestone Link
COWLEAZE LA

RIDGE LA

Bungalow Farm

Cemy

WEST HARPTREE RD B3114

The Wellsway Inn (PH)

NORDRACH LA

Ridge

Molly Brook

PO
East Harptree CE Prim Sch
THE CROSS

RO
Harptree Court

56

Harptree Hill Farm

March's Way

Shortcombe Farm

Castle

BS40

PH
GREY HOLLOW

CHURCH LA
MIDDLE ST
WHITECROSS RD

East Harptree

OLD BRISTOL RD
GREEN'S BROW

Lamb Leer Cavern

Garrow

Garrow Bottom

WESTERN LA

Harptree Combe

COOMBE LA
PROUD CROSS

ORCHARD END
BARN END

SILVER LA
SILVER LA
HIGHFIELD LA

Wallace

Newhouse

Vale Hollow Farm

Lamb Bottom

East Harptree Woods

Smitham Hill

Chy

The Grove

Morgan's Cottage

The Belt

Pitt Farm

P

BA3

Spring Farm

54   A   B   55   C   D   56   E   F

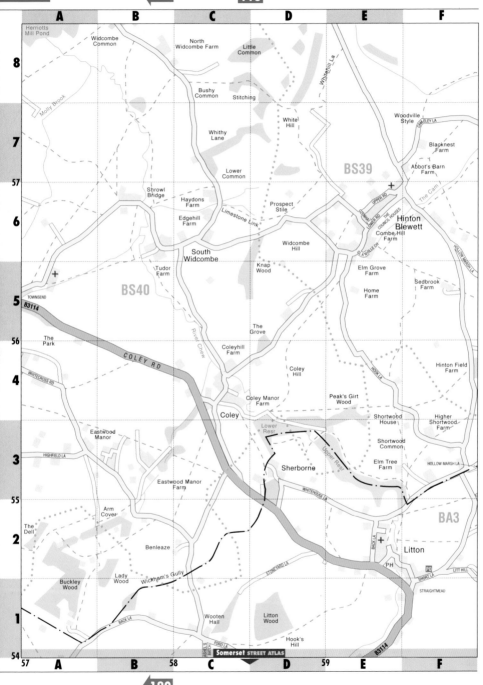

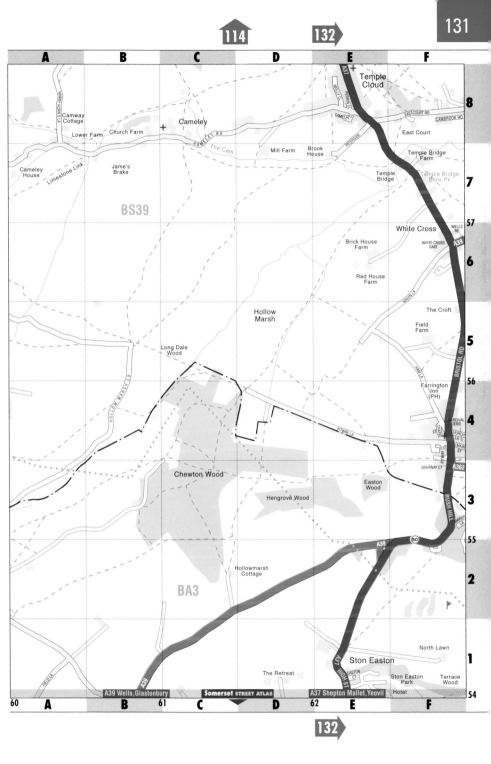

A　B　C　D　E　F

8

Camway
Cottage
Lower Farm
Church Farm
Cameley
Temple
Cloud
A37
EASTCOURT RD
CAMBROOK HO
East Court

Limestone Link
Cameley
House
Jame's
Brake
CAMELEY RD
The Cam
Mill Farm
Brook
House
PETERSH
Temple Bridge
Farm
East Court
Temple
Bridge
Temple Bridge
Bsns Pk

7

57

BS39
White Cross
WELLS RD
A39

Brick House
Farm
WHITE CROSS
GATE

6

Red House
Farm
GREEN LA

The Croft
Field
Farm

5

Hollow
Marsh
Long Dale
Wood
HOLLOW MARSH LA
HALL LA
BRISTOL RD
Farrington
Inn
(PH)

56

PERCIVAL
TERR
CHURCHILL
CHAPEL
A362

4

DITWAY LA
PLUM CT
MAIN
ST
GOURNAY CT

Chewton Wood
Easton
Wood
RUSH HILL

3

Hengrove Wood
MARSH
LA

55

A39
50

2

Hollowmarsh
Cottage

BA3

1

North Lawn
A37
HIGH ST
EASTON
CT
Ston Easton
Ston Easton
Park
Terrace
Wood

The Retreat
Hotel

FIELD LA

54

60　A　B　61　C　D　62　E　F

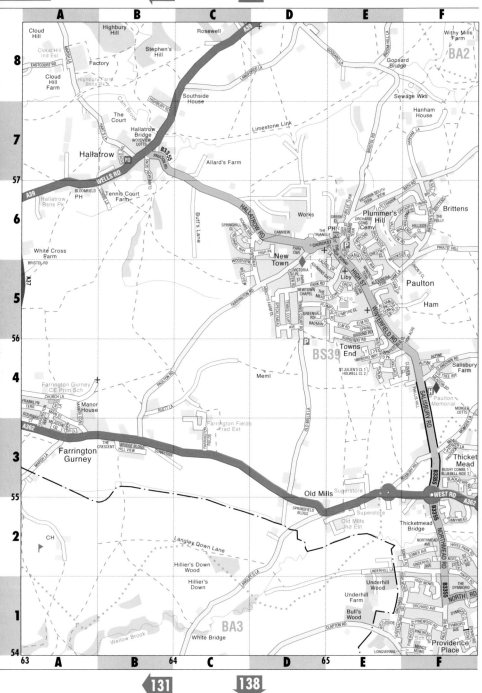

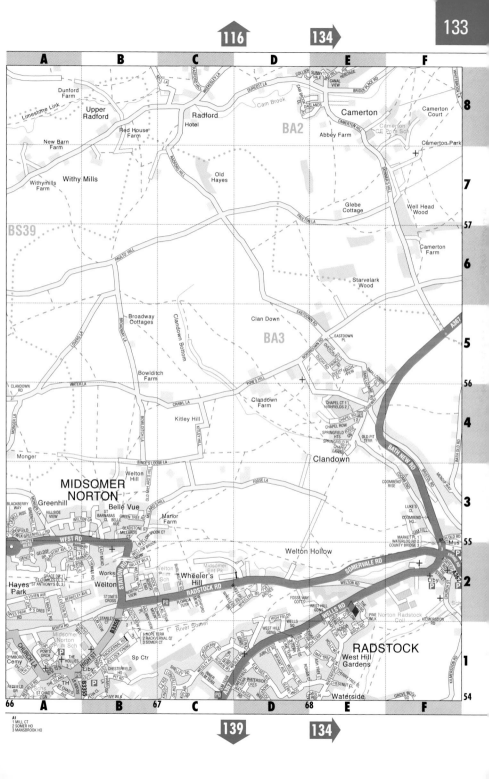

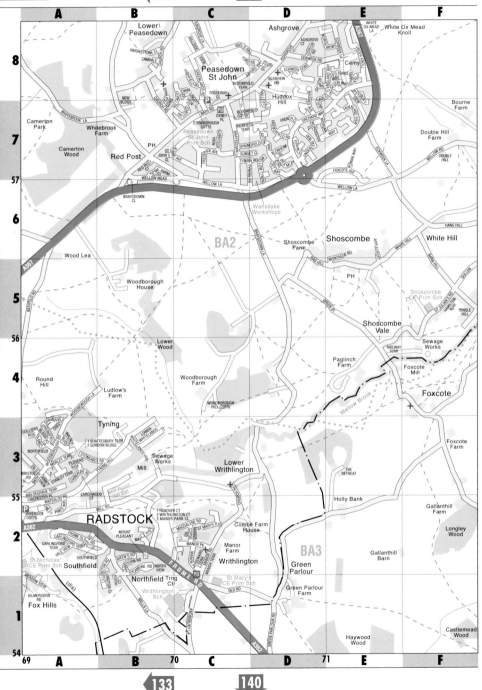

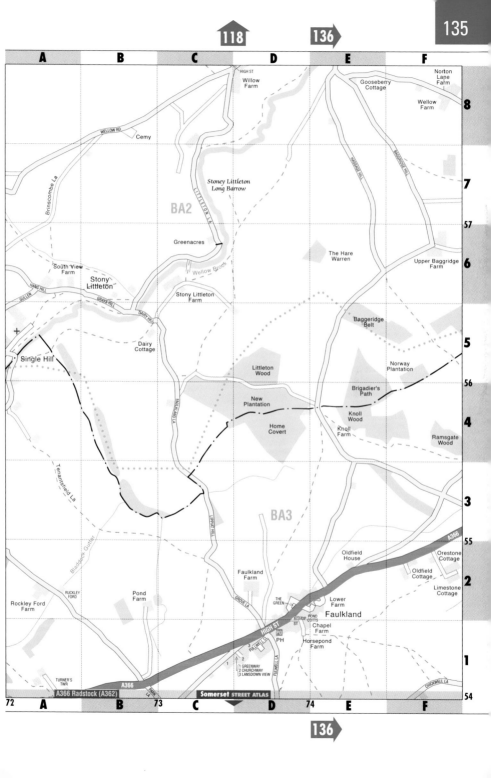

A | B | C | D | E | F

118   136

8
7
57
6
5
56
4
3
55
2
1
54

HIGH ST
Willow Farm

Norton Lane Farm
Gooseberry Cottage
Wellow Farm

WELLOW RD
Cemy

Stoney Littleton Long Barrow

BA2

LITTLETON LA

Greenacres

The Hare Warren

Upper Baggridge Farm

Brinscombe La

South View Farm

Wellow Brook

Stony Littleton

Stony Littleton Farm

HANG HILL
GULLEN
GRAYS HILL
DAIRY HILL

Baggeridge Belt

HASSAGE HILL
BAGGRIDGE HILL

Dairy Cottage

Littleton Wood

New Plantation

Norway Plantation

Single Hill

FAULKLAND LA

Home Covert

Brigadier's Path

Knoll Wood

Ramsgate Wood

Knoll Farm

Tenantsfield La

Blacjacks Gutter

LIPPIAT HILL

BA3

A366

Faulkland Farm

Oldfield House

Orestone Cottage

Oldfield Cottage

Limestone Cottage

Rockley Ford Farm

RUCKLEY FORD

Pond Farm

GROVE LA

THE GREEN

Lower Farm

Faulkland

Chapel Farm

Horsepond Farm

BISHOP ST
POND COTTS

HIGH ST
PO
PH

FAULWELLS

RUDWELL LA

1 GREENWAY
2 CHURCHWAY
3 LANSDOWN VIEW

TURNER'S TWR

A366

PARK LA

CHICKWELL LA

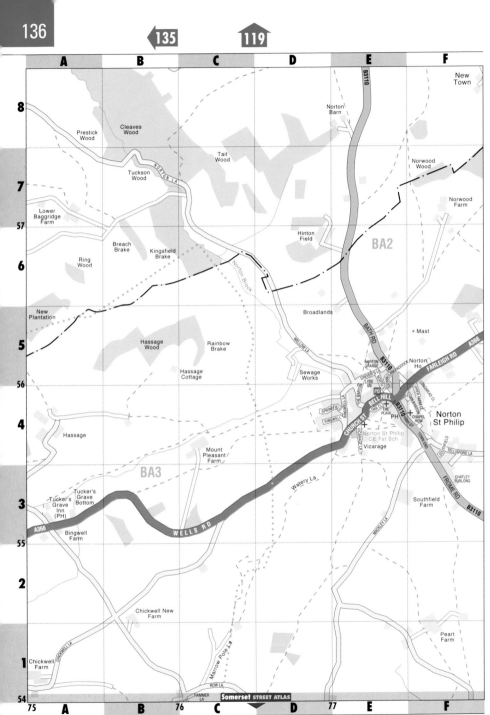

New Town

Norton Barn

Norwood Wood

Prestick Wood

Cleaves Wood

Tait Wood

Norwood Farm

Tuckson Wood

BA2

Lower Baggridge Farm

Breach Brake

Kingsfield Brake

Hinton Field

Ring Wood

Norton Brook

New Plantation

Broadlands

Mast

Hassage Wood

Rainbow Brake

BELLON LA

Norton Grange

Norton Ho

FARLEIGH RD

A366

Hassage Cottage

Sewage Works

CREVEL ST

LYDE GN

SOUTH PADDOCK

THE PLAIN

BELL HILL

PO

PH

CHAPEL ROW

Norton St Philip

BATH RD

B3110

B3110

Hassage

SPRINGFIELD

RINGWELL

CHURCH ST

VICARAGE LA

Norton St Philip CE Fst Sch

Vicarage

TOWN END

Chapel Row

Southfield Farm

FROME RD

CHATLEY FURLONG

BA3

Mount Pleasant Farm

Watery La

MACKLEY LA

Tucker's Grave Bottom

Tucker's Grave Inn (PH)

A366

WELLS RD

TELLSFORD LA

Bingwell Farm

Chickwell New Farm

Peart Farm

Chickwell Farm

CHICKWELL LA

MARROW POLE LA

ROW LA

HAMMER LA

Somerset STREET ATLAS

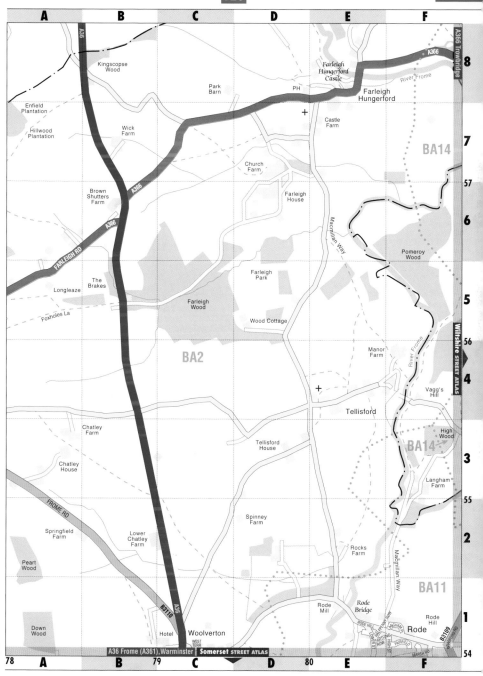

120

8

7

57

6

5

56

4

3

55

2

1

54

A366 Trowbridge

Wiltshire STREET ATLAS

A   B   C   D   E   F

78   79   80

Kingscope Wood

Enfield Plantation

Hillwood Plantation

Wick Farm

Park Barn

PH

Farleigh Hungerford Castle

Farleigh Hungerford

Castle Farm

BA14

A36

A366

Brown Shutters Farm

Church Farm

Farleigh House

Macmillan Way

Pomeroy Wood

River Frome

River Frome

FARLEIGH RD

The Brakes

Longleaze

Foxholes La

Farleigh Wood

Farleigh Park

Wood Cottage

Manor Farm

Vagg's Hill

BA2

High Wood

BA14

Tellisford

Chatley Farm

Tellisford House

Chatley House

Langham Farm

Macmillan Way

Spinney Farm

Springfield Farm

Lower Chatley Farm

Peart Wood

Rocks Farm

BA11

Down Wood

B3110

A36

Hotel

Woolverton

WEST TERR

Rode Mill

Rode Bridge

Rode Hill

Rode

B3109

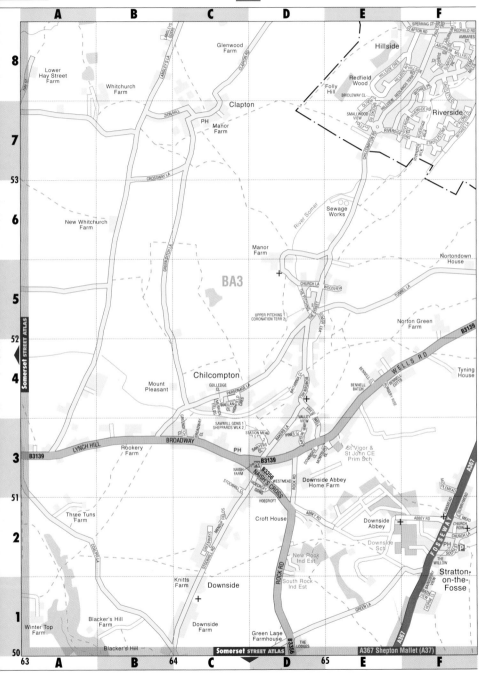

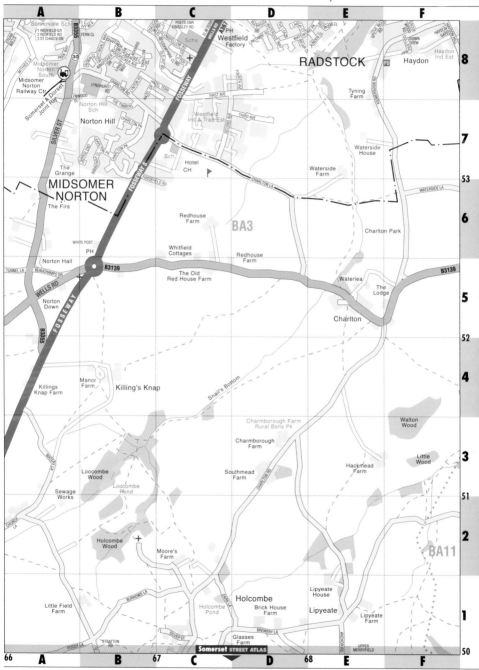

Somerset STREET ATLAS

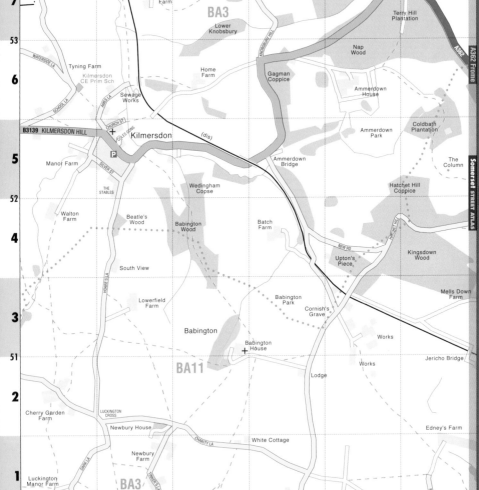

A B C D E F

Haydon
House

Huish
House

8

Upper Lentney
Farm

Peak's
Wood

Haywood
Wood

Haywood
Farm

A366 Trowbridge

A362

FROME RD

TERRY HILL

FROME RD

A366

AMMERDOWN
TERR

A366

Lentney
Farm

Upper Lentney Farm
Cottage

KNOBBURY LA

7

BA3

Upper
Knobsbury

B3139

Lower
Knobsbury

Terry Hill
Plantation

53

WATERSIDE LA

KNOBSBURY HILL

Nap
Wood

A362 Frome

Tyning Farm

Kilmersdon
CE Prim Sch

Home
Farm

Gagman
Coppice

Ammerdown
House

6

SCHOOL LA

AMES LA

Sewage
Works

Ammerdown
Park

Coldbath
Plantation

B3139 KILMERSDON HILL

CHURCH ST

COLES LANE

Kilmersdon

(dis)

The
Column

Somerset STREET ATLAS

5

Manor Farm

SILVER ST

P

Ammerdown
Bridge

Hatchet Hill
Coppice

52

THE
STABLES

Wedingham
Copse

52

HATCHET HILL

Walton
Farm

Beatle's
Wood

Babington
Wood

Batch
Farm

Kingsdown
Wood

4

HOME S LA

NEW RD

Upton's
Piece

South View

Mells Down
Farm

Lowerfield
Farm

Babington
Park

Cornish's
Grave

3

Babington

Works

Babington
House

Works

BA11

Jericho Bridge

51

Lodge

2

Cherry Garden
Farm

LUCKINGTON
CROSS

Newbury House

DARK LA

Edney's Farm

Newbury
Farm

CHARITY LA

White Cottage

1

AMBER LA

Luckington
Manor Farm

BA3

Newbury

Works

50

69 A B 70 C D 71 E F

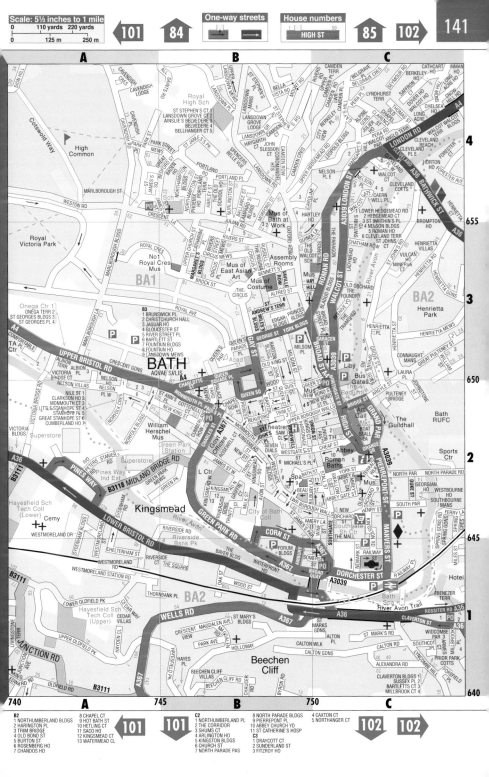

One-way streets

House numbers
HIGH ST

BATH

BA1

BA2

Royal Victoria Park

Royal High Sch

No1 Royal Cres Mus

Mus of East Asian Art

Mus of Costume

Assembly Rooms

THE CIRCUS

Mus of Bath at Work

LONDON RD

Henrietta Park

BA2

Kingsmead

Green Park Station

Superstore

Hayesfield Sch Tech Coll (Lower)

Hayesfield Sch Tech Coll (Upper)

City of Bath Coll

The Guildhall

Roman Baths

Abbey

Art Gall

Sports Ctr

Bath RUFC

Bath Spa

River Avon Trail

Beechen Cliff

WELLS RD

A367

A36

A4

A36

A3039

B2
1 NORTHUMBERLAND BLDGS
2 HARINGTON PL
3 TRIM BRIDGE
4 OLD BOND ST
5 BURTON ST
6 ROSENBERG HO
7 CHANDOS HO

8 CHAPEL CT
9 HOT BATH ST
10 HETLING CT
11 SACO HO
12 KINGSMEAD CT
13 WATERMEAD CL

C2
1 NORTHUMBERLAND PL
2 THE CORRIDOR
3 SHUMS CT
4 ARLINGTON HO
5 KINGSTON BLDGS
6 CHURCH ST
7 NORTH PARADE PAS

8 NORTH PARADE BLDGS
9 PIERREPONT PL
10 ABBEY CHURCH YD
11 ST CATHERINE'S HOSP
C3
1 DRAYCOTT CT
2 SUNDERLAND ST
3 FITZROY HO

4 CAXTON CT
5 NORTHANGER CT

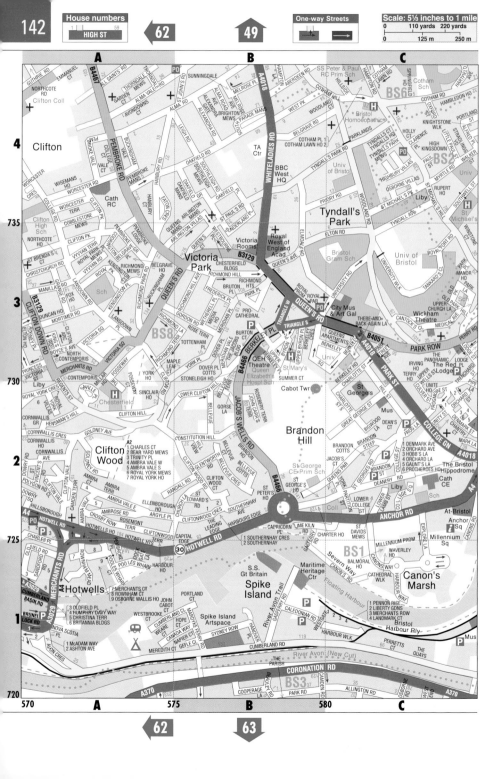

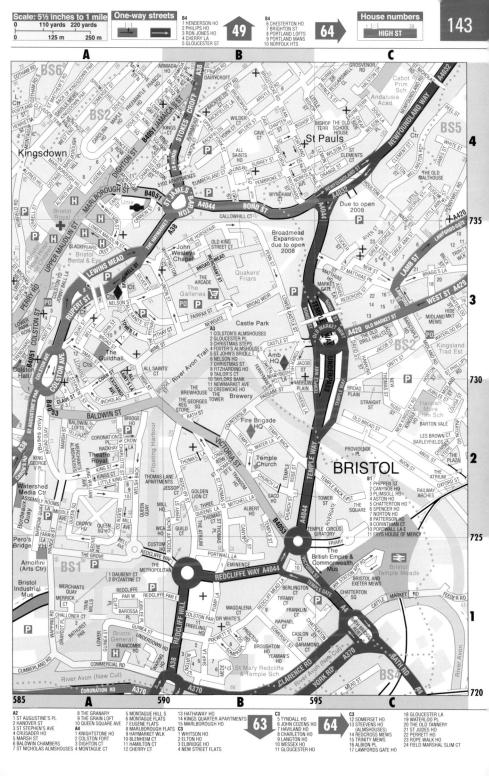

144

Index

Place name May be abbreviated on the map

Location number Present when a number indicates the place's position in a crowded area of mapping

Locality, town or village Shown when more than one place has the same name

Postcode district District for the indexed place

Page and grid square Page number and grid reference for the standard mapping

Church Rd 6 Beckenham BR2..........53 C6

Cities, towns and villages are listed in CAPITAL LETTERS   Public and commercial buildings are highlighted in magenta
Places of interest are highlighted in blue with a star ★

Abbreviations used in the index

Acad	Academy	Comm	Common	Gd	Ground	L	Leisure	Prom	Promenade
App	Approach	Cott	Cottage	Gdn	Garden	La	Lane	Rd	Road
Arc	Arcade	Cres	Crescent	Gn	Green	Liby	Library	Recn	Recreation
Ave	Avenue	Cswy	Causeway	Gr	Grove	Mdw	Meadow	Ret	Retail
Bglw	Bungalow	Ct	Court	H	Hall	Meml	Memorial	Sh	Shopping
Bldg	Building	Ctr	Centre	Ho	House	Mkt	Market	Sq	Square
Bsns, Bus	Business	Ctry	Country	Hospl	Hospital	Mus	Museum	St	Street
Bvd	Boulevard	Cty	County	HQ	Headquarters	Orch	Orchard	Sta	Station
Cath	Cathedral	Dr	Drive	Hts	Heights	Pal	Palace	Terr	Terrace
Cir	Circus	Dro	Drove	Ind	Industrial	Par	Parade	TH	Town Hall
Cl	Close	Ed	Education	Inst	Institute	Pas	Passage	Univ	University
Cnr	Corner	Emb	Embankment	Int	International	Pk	Park	Wk, Wlk	Walk
Coll	College	Est	Estate	Intc	Interchange	Pl	Place	Wr	Water
Com	Community	Ex	Exhibition	Junc	Junction	Prec	Precinct	Yd	Yard

Index of towns, villages, streets, hospitals, industrial estates, railway stations, schools, shopping centres, universities and places of interest

144   510–Alf

5102 Apartments
BS1.....................143 B4

A

Abbey Church Yd 10
BA1.....................141 C2
Abbey Cl BS31..........81 F6
Abbey Ct
Bath BA2...............102 B7
Bristol BS4..............64 F5
Abbeydale BS36........37 E6
Abbeyfield Ho BS37...28 C1
Abbey Gate St BA1...141 C2
Abbey Gdns BS22.....105 E8
Abbey Gn BA1..........141 C2
Abbey Gn 6 BS37.....39 D7
Abbey La
Hinton Charterhouse
BA2...................120 A4
Thornbury BS35........15 D6
Abbey Mews GL12.....11 F4
Abbey Pk BS31..........81 F6
Abbey Rd
Bristol BS9..............48 F7
Chilcompton BA3......138 D2
Stratton-on-t F BA3...138 F2
Abbey St
Bath BA1...............141 C2
Kingswood GL12........11 F5
Abbey View
Bath BA2...............102 B5
Radstock BA3..........134 A3
Abbey View Gdns
BA2...................102 B5
Abbeywood Dr BS9.....48 C5
Abbeywood Pk BS34....36 C2
Abbey Wood Ret Pk
BS34...................36 C2
Abbots Ave BS15.......65 C4
Abbotsbury Rd BS48...59 D1
Abbots Cl BS14.........80 A3
Abbot's Cl BS22........89 A3
Abbotsford Rd BS6.....49 B1
Abbots Horn BS48......59 D2
ABBOTSIDE...............9 F2
ABBOTS LEIGH.........62 A8
Abbots Leigh Rd BS8..62 C7
Abbots Rd BS15.........65 C2

Abbots Way BS9........49 E6
Abbotswood
Bristol BS15.............65 D7
Yate BS37................39 D7
Abbotswood Prim Sch
BS37...................39 D6
Abbott Rd BS35.........22 A5
Abbotts Farm Cl
BS39...................132 D5
Aberdeen Rd BS6.....142 B4
Abingdon Gdns BA2..118 D8
Abingdon Rd BS16.....51 A3
Ableton Ct BS35........22 A6
Ableton La
Hallen BS10............34 A8
Severn Beach BS35....22 A5
Ableton Wlk BS9.......48 C5
Abon Ho BS9.............48 C4
Abraham Cl BS5........64 B8
Abraham Fry Ho BS15..65 E7
ABSON...................53 D2
Abson Rd
Pucklechurch BS16....53 C3
Wick BS30................67 C8
Acacia Ave
Bristol BS16.............51 D4
Weston-S-M BS23....105 B8
Acacia Cl BS31..........81 C4
Acacia Ct BS31..........81 C4
Acacia Gr BA2..........101 C3
Acacia Mews 6 BS16..51 D4
Acacia Rd
Bristol BS16.............51 D4
Radstock BA3.........133 E1
Accommodation Rd
BS24...................121 E6
Acer Village BS14.......80 C7
Acid Rd BS11............33 C4
Aconite Cl BS22........89 B5
Acorn Gr BS13...........78 E6
Acraman's Rd 7 BS3...63 C4
Acresbush Cl BS13.....79 A5
Acton Rd BS16..........51 A3
ACTON TURVILLE......42 F6
Acton Turville Rd GL9..42 B4
Adams Cl BA2..........134 D8
Adams Ct 5 BS8........62 F6
Adams Hay 6 BS4......64 D1
Adams St BS36..........38 C7
Adastral Rd BS24.....106 D4
Adderly Gate BS16.....52 B7
Addicott Rd BS23.....104 E6

Addiscombe Rd
Bristol BS14.............80 B5
Weston-S-M BS23....104 E4
Addison Rd BS3.........63 E3
Adelaide Pl
Bristol, Fishponds
BS5...................50 F4
12 Bristol, Upper Easton
BS5...................64 B8
Adelaide Terr 1 BS16..51 A4
Adelante Cl BS34.......37 A4
Admiral Cl BS16.........50 E7
Admiral's Wlk BS20....45 B5
Adryan Ct 6 BS5.......64 C7
Aelfric Mdw BS20......45 F4
Agate St BS3.............63 B3
Aiken St BS5.............64 B6
Ainslie's Belvedere
BA1...................141 B4
Aintree Dr BS16........37 F1
Air Balloon Ct 1 BS5..65 A7
Air Balloon Hill Jun & Inf
Schs BS5...............65 A7
Air Balloon Rd BS5.....65 A7
Airport Rd BS14........80 A8
Airport Rdbt BS24....105 E7
Airport View Cvn Pk
BS24...................105 D7
Aisecome Way BS22..105 C6
Akeman Way BS11......47 C8
Alanscourt BS30........66 B5
Alard Rd BS4............79 F7
Albany BS23..............87 F1
Albany Ct 6 BA1......101 B6
Albany Gate BS34......36 E5
Albany Rd
Bath BA2................101 C6
Bristol BS6..............49 F1
Albany St BS15..........65 C8
Albany Way BS30.......66 C5
Albemarle Row 10
BS8...................62 F6
Albemarle Terr 7
BS8...................62 F6
Albert Ave
Peasedown St John
BA2...................134 C7
Weston-S-M BS23....104 E6
Albert Cres BS2.........64 B5
Albert Ct BS14..........104 E6
Albert Gr BS5............64 F8
Albert Gr S BS5.........64 F8
Albert Rd BS1..........143 B2

Alberton Rd BS16......50 F6
Albert Par BS5...........64 D8
Albert Park Pl BS6......49 F1
Albert Pk BS6............49 F1
Albert Pl
Bath BA2................102 C1
1 Bristol, Bedminster
BS3...................63 C3
Bristol, Eastfield BS9...49 A7
Portishead BS20........45 D4
Albert Quadrant BS23..104 E8
Albert Rd
Bristol, Hanham BS15..65 D5
Bristol, St Philip's Marsh
BS2...................64 A4
Bristol, Staple Hill BS16..51 E4
Clevedon BS21..........57 E3
Keynsham BS31.........81 E5
Portishead BS20........45 D5
Severn Beach BS35....22 A6
Weston-S-M BS23....104 E6
Albert St BS5.............64 C8
Albert Terr
Bath BA2................101 C6
Bristol BS16.............50 F4
Albion Bldgs BA1......101 D7
Albion Cl BS16...........51 F5
Albion Dr
Bath BA1................141 A3
16 Bristol BS2..........143 C3
Albion Rd BS5...........50 B1
Albion St BS5.............64 C8
Albion Terr
Bath BA1................141 A3
Bristol BS34.............24 B1
Alburys BS40.............92 D3
ALCOMBE...............86 F7
Alcove Rd BS16.........50 F3
Alden Ho BS36...........37 D4
Aldercombe Rd BS9....48 C8
Alder Ct BS14............80 B5
Alderdown Cl BS11....48 A8
Alder Dr BS5.............50 E1
Alderley Rd BA2........101 B4
Aldermoor Way BS30..65 E4
Alderney Ave BS4......64 F4
Aldes The BS16..........37 B1
Alder Terr BA3..........133 E2
ALDERTON..............31 F2
Alderton Rd
Bristol BS7..............49 E8
Burton SN14............43 D6
Alder Way BA2.........118 D8

ALDWICK...............110 D7
Aldwick Ave BS13......79 C3
Aldwick La BS40.......110 C7
Alec Ricketts Cl BA2..100 F5
Alexander Bldgs 12
BA1...................85 B1
Alexander Ct 4 BS3....63 A3
Alexander Hall BA2...120 C6
Alexander Ho 5
BS23...................104 F4
Alexander Hosea Prim Sch
GL12...................18 B5
Alexander Mews 5
BS23...................104 E7
Alexander Pl BA2.....120 C6
Alexander Way BS49...91 B7
Alexandra Apartments
BS6...................49 C3
Alexandra Cl BS16.....51 D4
Alexandra Ct
Bristol BS16.............50 F4
Clevedon BS21..........57 E4
Alexandra Gate BS8..142 B4
Alexandra Gdns BS16..51 D4
Alexandra Par BS23..104 E7
Alexandra Pk
Bristol, Cotham BS6....49 C2
Bristol, Ridgeway BS16..50 F4
Paulton BS39..........132 E5
Alexandra Pl
Bath BA2................102 C1
Bristol BS16.............51 D4
Alexandra Rd
Bath BA2................141 C1
Bristol BA2.............142 B4
Bristol, Eastfield BS10..49 C8
Bristol, Hanham BS15..65 D5
Bristol, Highridge BS13..78 F7
Clevedon BS21..........57 E4
Frampton Cotterell BS36..38 D7
Alexandra Terr BS39..132 E5
Alexandra Way BS35...8 B3
Alford Rd BS4............64 C2
Alfred Ct 4 BS23......104 E7
Alfred Hill BS2..........143 A4
Alfred Lovell Gdns 7
BS30...................66 A4
Alfred Par BS2..........143 A4
Alfred Pl BS2............142 C4
Alfred Rd
Bristol, Westbury Park
BS6...................49 A4

Alfred Rd continued
Bristol, Windmill Hill BS3 63 D3
Alfred St
Bath BA1 141 B3
Bristol, Moorfields BS5 64 D8
Bristol, Newton BS2 64 A6
Weston-S-M BS23 104 E8
Algars Dr BS37 26 E3
Algiers St BS3 63 D3
Alison Gdns BS48 76 A7
Allanmead Rd BS14 80 B8
Allans Way BS24 105 F7
Allengrove La SN14 31 C3
Allens La BS25 125 F8
Aller BS24 105 B2
Aller Par BS24 105 B2
Allerton Cres BS14 80 B4
Allerton Gdns BS14 80 B5
Allerton Rd BS14 80 B4
Allfoxton Rd BS7 50 A3
All Hallows Ct 11 BS5 64 B8
All Hallows Rd BS5 64 B8
Allington Dr BS30 65 F4
Allington Gdns BS48 75 C8
Allington Rd BS3 142 C1
Allison Ave BS4 64 E4
Allison Rd BS4 64 E3
All Saints Cl BS30 66 A3
All Saints' Ct BS1 143 A3
All Saints East Clevedon CE Prim Sch BS21 57 H4
All Saints Ho BS2 143 B4
All Saints La BS21 57 H4
All Saints' La BS1 143 A2
All Saints Pl BA2 102 E4
All Saints Rd BA1 141 B4
All Saints' Rd
Bristol BS8 142 A4
Weston-S-M BS23 87 E1
All Saints' St BS1 143 A3
Alma Cl BS15 65 E8
Alma Ct BS8 49 B1
Alma Rd
Bristol BS8 142 B4
Bristol, Kingswood BS15 51 E1
Alma Road Ave BS8 142 B4
Alma St
Bristol BS8 49 B1
Weston-S-M BS23 104 E7
Alma Vale Rd BS8 142 A4
Almeda Rd BS5 65 A6
Almond Cl BS22 89 A1
ALMONDSBURY 24 B5
Almondsbury Bsns Ctr BS32 24 D3
Almondsbury CE Prim Sch BS32 24 A4
Almondsbury Intc BS32 24 E4
Almond Way BS16 51 F5
Almorah Rd BS3 63 E3
Almshouses SN14 69 E8
Alonzo Pl BS21 57 F4
Alpha Ctr The BS37 27 C3
Alpha Rd BS3 63 D4
Alpine Cl BS39 132 F4
Alpine Gdns BA1 141 C4
Alpine Rd
Bristol BS5 50 C1
Paulton BS39 132 F4
Alsop Rd 4 BS15 51 D1
Alton Pl BA2 141 C1
Alton Rd BS7 49 F5
Altringham Rd BS5 64 D8
Alverstoke BS14 79 F7
ALVESTON 15 B4
ALVESTON DOWN 14 F5
Alveston Hill BS35 15 A6
Alveston Rd BS32 14 D3
Alveston Wlk BS9 48 B7
Alwins Ct 2 BS30 65 F4
Ambares Ct BA3 138 F8
Amberey Rd BS23 104 F5
Amberlands Cl BS48 76 A7
Amberley Cl
Bristol BS16 51 D7
Keynsham BS31 81 E4
Amberley Gdns 3 BS48 59 D1
Amberley House Sch BS8 49 A1
Amberley Rd
Bristol, Kingswood BS16 51 D7
Bristol, Patchway BS34 36 B8
Amberley Way GL12 18 B4
Amble Cl BS15 65 F7
Ambleside Ave BS10 35 B2
Ambleside Rd BA2 101 C2
Ambra Ct BS8 142 A2
Ambra Terr BS8 142 A2
Ambra Vale BS8 142 A2
Ambra Vale E BS8 142 A2
Ambra Vale S 5 BS8 142 A2
Ambra Vale W 4 BS8 142 A2
Ambrose Rd BS8 142 A2
Ambury BA1 141 B1
Amercombe Wlk BS14 80 D7
American Mus in Britain* BA2 103 A5
Amery La BA1 141 C2
AMESBURY 115 F2
Amesbury Dr BS24 122 B6
Ames La BA3 140 B6
Ammerdown Terr BA3 140 F7
Anchor Cl BS5 64 F6
Anchor Ho BS4 64 B2
Anchor Rd
Bath BA1 84 B1
Bristol BS1 142 C2
Bristol, Kingswood BS15 52 A2
Anchor Way BS20 47 D4
Ancliff Sq BA15 120 E4
Andalusia Acad BS2 143 C4
Andereach Cl BS14 80 B8
Andover Rd BS4 63 F2
Andrew Millman Ct BS37 27 F1
Andruss Dr BS41 78 D2
Angels Gd BS4 64 F6
Angers Rd BS4 64 A4
Anglesea Pl 15 BS8 49 A2
Anglo Terr BA1 141 C4
Animal Farm Adventure Pk* TA8 121 B2
Ankatel Cl BS23 105 A5
Annandale Ave BS22 88 E1
Annie Scott Cl 2 BS16 51 A4
Anson Cl BS31 82 D2
Anson Rd
Locking BS24 106 B6
Weston-S-M BS22 88 D4
Ansteys Cl BS15 65 B5
Anstey's Ct BS15 65 C5
Anstey's Rd BS15 65 C5
Anstey St BS5 50 B1
Anthea Rd BS5 50 E2
Antona Ct BS11 47 D7
Antona Dr BS11 47 D7
Antrim Rd BS9 49 B6
Anvil Rd BS49 74 F1
Anvil St BS2 143 C2
Apex Ct BS32 24 D3
Apperley Cl BS37 39 E8
Appleby Wlk BS4 79 D7
Applecroft BA2 134 E6
Appledore 4 BS22 88 F2
Appledore Cl BS14 80 B8
Apple Farm La BS24 89 C1
Applegate BS10 35 B3
Appleridge La GL13 3 C4
Appletree Ct BS22 89 B2
Apple Tree Dr BS25 125 A8
Appletree Mews BS22 89 B2
Applin Gn BS16 52 C6
Appsley Cl BS22 88 C1
Apseleys Mead BS32 24 C2
Apsley Cl BA1 101 B7
Apsley Garden Apartments BS6 49 E2
Apsley Mews BS8 49 A2
Apsley Rd
Bath BA1 101 A7
Bristol BS8 49 A1
Apsley St BS5 50 C3
Arbutus Dr BS9 48 C8
Arcade The BS1 143 B3
Arch Cl BS41 61 F1
Archer Ct
Bristol BS30 65 F3
Clevedon BS21 57 F4
Archer Wlk BS14 80 E6
Arches The
Bath BA2 101 A6
1 Bristol BS5 64 B7
Archfield Ct BS6 49 C1
Archfield Rd BS6 49 C1
Archgrove BS41 61 F1
Archway St BA2 102 B5
Ardagh Ct BS7 49 F7
Arden Cl
Bristol BS32 36 E6
Weston-S-M BS22 88 F3
Ardenton Wlk BS10 35 A3
Ardern Cl BS9 48 B8
Ardmore BS8 62 D7
Argus Ct BS3 63 C2
Argus Rd BS3 63 C3
Argyle Ave
Bristol BS5 50 C2
Weston-S-M BS23 104 F4
Argyle Dr BS37 27 E4
Argyle Pl BS8 142 A2
Argyle Rd
Bristol BS2 143 B4
Bristol, Chester Park BS16 51 B2
Clevedon BS21 57 F6
Argyle St
Bath BA2 141 C2
5 Bristol, Eastville BS5 50 C2
6 Bristol, Southville BS3 63 C4
Argyle Terr BA2 101 C6
Arkells Ct GL12 18 A6
Arley Cotts 5 BS6 49 D1
Arley Ct 4 BS6 49 D1
Arley Hill BS6 49 D1
Arley Pk BS6 49 D1
Arley Terr BS5 50 E1
Arlingham Way BS34 23 F1
Arlington Ho 4 BA1 141 C2
Arlington Mans BS8 142 B4
Arlington Rd
4 Bath BA2 101 D5
Bristol BS4 64 D5
Arlington Villas BS8 142 B3
Armada Ho BS2 143 A4
Armada Pl BS1 143 B4
Armes Ct BA2 141 C1
Armidale Ave 4 BS6 49 E1
Armidale Cotts 5 BS6 49 E1
Armoury Sq BS5 64 A8
Armstrong Cl BS35 15 D7
Armstrong Ct BS37 27 C3
Armstrong Dr BS30 66 B5
Armstrong Way BS37 27 B3
Arnall Dr BS10 34 F1
Arncliffe BS10 49 C8
Arneside Rd BS10 35 C1
Arnold Ct BS37 28 B1
Arnold Rd BS16 52 B3
Arnolds Field Trad Est GL12 18 A5
Arnold's Way BS49 74 A2
Arnolfini (Arts Ctr)* BS1 143 A1
Arnor Cl BS22 89 A4
Arno's St BS4 64 A3
ARNO'S VALE 64 B4
Arrowfield Cl BS14 80 A2
Artemesia Ave BS22 105 E8
Arthurs Cl BS16 52 C6
Arthur Skemp Cl BS5 64 B7
Arthur St
7 Bristol, Moorfields BS5 64 C8
Bristol, St Philip's Marsh BS2 64 A5
Arthurswood Rd BS13 79 A4
Arundel Cl BS13 79 B5
Arundel Ct BS7 49 D3
Arundell Ct BS23 104 E8
Arundell Rd BS23 87 E1
Arundel Rd
Bath BA1 85 A1
Bristol BS7 49 D3
Clevedon BS21 57 F3
Arundel Wlk BS31 81 D5
Ascension Ho BA2 101 D4
Ascot Cl BS16 37 F1
Ascot Rd BS10 35 E2
Ashbourne Cl 1 BS30 66 C6
Ash Brook BS39 115 D1
Ashbrooke House Sch BS23 104 D6
Ashburton Rd BS10 35 C1
Ashbury Dr BS22 88 B2
Ash Cl
Bristol, Hillfields BS16 51 C3
Bristol, Little Stoke BS34 36 D7
Weston-S-M BS22 89 D2
Winscombe BS25 108 A1
Yate BS37 27 D3
Ashcombe Cres BS30 66 D6
Ashcombe Ct 1 BS23 104 F7
Ashcombe Gdns BS23 105 A8
Ashcombe Park Rd BS23 88 A1
Ashcombe Pl 4 BS23 104 F7
Ashcombe Prim Sch BS23 105 A7
Ashcombe Rd BS23 104 F7
Ashcott BS14 79 F7
Ashcroft BS24 105 B2
Ashcroft Ave BS31 81 D5
Ashcroft Rd BS9 48 C7
Ash Ct BS14 80 A6
Ashdene Ave BS5 50 D3
Ashdene Rd BS23 105 A8
Ashdown Ct BS9 48 F8
Ashdown Rd BS20 45 A6
Asher La BS2 143 C3
Ashes La BA2 120 A4
Ashey La BS40 110 A5
Ashfield Pl BS6 49 F1
Ashfield Rd BS3 63 B3
Ashfield Terr 9 BS3 63 B3
Ashford Dr BS24 105 A1
Ashford Rd
Bath BA2 101 D4
Bristol BS34 36 A7
Redhill BS40 93 E4
Ashford Way BS15 66 A7
Ash Gr
Bath BA2 101 C4
Bristol BS16 51 D3
Clevedon BS21 57 G4
Weston-S-M BS23 104 E2
ASHGROVE 134 D8
Ashgrove
Peasedown St John BA2 134 D8
Thornbury BS35 8 C1
Ashgrove Ave
Abbots Leigh BS8 62 B7
Bristol BS7 49 F4
Ashgrove Cl BS7 49 F4
Ashgrove Ct BA2 134 D8
Ashgrove Rd
Bristol, Ashley Down BS7 49 F4
Bristol, Bedminster BS3 63 B3
Ash Hayes Dr BS48 59 E1
Ash Hayes Rd BS48 59 F1
Ash La BS32 23 D2
Ashland Rd BS13 79 A4
Ashleigh Cl
Paulton BS39 132 E6
Weston-S-M BS23 105 A8
Ashleigh Cres BS49 91 B8
Ashleigh Rd
Weston-S-M BS23 105 A8
Yatton BS49 91 B8
Ashley BS15 65 F8
Ashley Ave BA1 101 C7
Ashley Cl
Bristol BS7 49 F4
Winscombe BS25 125 A7
Ashley Court Rd 2 BS7 49 F2
Ashley Ct 1 BS2 49 F1
ASHLEY DOWN 49 E4
Ashley Down Jun & Inf Schs BS7 49 F5
Ashley Down Rd BS7 49 F4
Ashley Grove Rd
7 Bristol BS2 49 F2
1 Bristol BS2 50 A1
Ashley Hill BS6, BS7 49 F2
Ashley Ho BS34 23 F1
Ashley La BA15 120 F7
Ashley Par BS2 49 F2
Ashley Pk BS6 49 F3
Ashley Rd
Bathford BA1, SN13 86 D2
Bristol BS6 49 E1
Clevedon BS21 57 D1
Ashley St BS2 50 A1
Ashley Terr 1 BA1 101 C7
Ashley Trad Est 6 BS2 49 F2
Ashman Cl BS5 64 A8
Ashman Ct 1 BS16 50 E3
Ashmans Ct BA1 101 B6
Ashmans Gate BS39 132 E5
Ashmans Yd BA1 101 B6
Ashmead BS39 114 E1
Ashmead Bsns Pk BS31 82 B5
Ashmead Ho 12 BS5 64 C7
Ashmead Rd BS31 82 B5
Ashmead Road Ind Est BS31 82 B5
Ashmead Way 8 BS1 62 F5
Ash Rd
Banwell BS29 106 E4
Bristol BS7 49 E5
Ash Ridge Rd BS32 24 B3
Ashton BS16 37 C1
Ashton Ave BS1 142 A1
Ashton Cl BS21 57 D1
Ashton Court Est* BS41 62 C4
Ashton Cres BS48 59 D1
Ashton Dr BS3 62 F2
ASHTON GATE 62 F4
Ashton Gate Prim Sch BS3 63 A4
Ashton Gate Rd BS3 63 A4
Ashton Gate Stadium (Bristol City FC) BS3 62 F3
Ashton Gate Terr 4 BS3 63 A4
Ashton Gate Trad Est BS3 62 E3
Ashton Gate Underpass BS3 62 F3
Ashton Hill BA2 100 A7
Ashton Park Sch BS3 62 E3
Ashton Rd
Bristol, Ashton Gate BS3 62 F4
Bristol, Bower Ashton BS3 62 D3
ASHTON VALE 62 F2
Ashton Vale Prim Sch BS3 62 F2
Ashton Vale Rd BS3 62 E3
Ashton Vale Trad Est BS3 62 F1
Ashton Way BS31 81 E6
Ash Tree Cl BS24 122 C6
Ash Tree Ct BA3 133 E1
Ashvale Cl BS48 60 A2
Ashville Pk BS35 15 B7
Ashville Rd BS3 63 A4
Ashways Ho BS39 114 E1
Ashwell Cl BS14 80 E6
Ashwicke BS14 80 A6
Ashwicke Rd SN14 70 B3
Ash Wlk BS10 35 B3
Ashwood BS40 129 F4
Aspects L Pk BS15 65 E5
Aspen Cl SN14 70 F6
Aspen Park Rd BS22 105 E8
Assembly Rooms* BA1 141 B3
Assembly Rooms La BS1 143 A2
Aston Ho 4 BS1 143 B1
Astry Cl BS11 34 A1
At-bristol* BS1 142 C2
Atchley St 18 BS5 64 B7
Athena Ct 3 BS7 49 F4
Atherston BS30 66 D5
Athlone Wlk BS4 63 E1
Atholl Cl BS22 88 F3
Atkins Cl BS14 80 E6
Atlantic Rd
Bristol BS11 47 C8
Weston-S-M BS23 87 C1
Atlantic Rd S BS23 87 C1
Atlantic View Ct BS23 87 C1
Atlas Cl BS5 51 A2
Atlas Rd BS3 63 E3
Atlas St BS2 64 B5
Atlay Ct BS49 74 B1
Atrium The
Bristol BS1 143 B2
Bristol BS2 143 C2
Attewell Ct BA2 101 F4
Atwell Dr BS32 24 B1
Atwood Dr BS11 34 B2
Atyeo Cl BS3 62 E1
Aubrey Ho 10 BS3 63 B3
Aubrey Meads BS30 82 E8
Aubrey Rd BS3 63 B3
Auburn Ave BS30 66 B3
Auburn Rd BS6 49 B1
Auckland Cl BS23 104 F3
Auden Mead BS7 50 A8
Audley Ave BA1 101 D7
Audley Cl
Bath BA1 101 D7
Rangeworthy BS37 27 A8
Audley Gr BA1 101 C7
Audley Lo BA1 101 D7
Audley Park Rd BA1 101 C7
Audrey Wlk BS9 49 D7
Augusta Pl BA1 101 D7
Augustine's Cl BS20 44 E4
Augustus Ho BS15 65 B6
AUST 13 A6
Austen Dr BS22 89 B4
Austen Gr BS7 50 A8
Austen Ho BS7 50 A8
Austen Pl BS11 47 E7
Aust La BS9 49 A8
Aust Rd
Northwick BS35 12 D3
Olveston BS35 13 F5
Autumn Mews BS24 106 A8
Avalon Cl BS49 74 A1
Avalon Ho BS48 59 C1
Avalon La BS5 65 B6
Avalon Rd BS5 65 B6
Avebury Rd BS3 62 F2
Avening Cl BS48 76 A8
AVENING GREEN 10 D8
Avening Rd BS15 65 A8
Avenue Pl BA2 102 B1
Avenue The
Backwell BS48 76 A7
Bath, Bushey Norwood BA2 102 E5
Bath, Combe Down BA2 102 C1
Bristol, Ashley Down BS7 49 E3
Bristol, Clifton BS8 49 A1
Bristol, Crew's Hole BS5 64 F8
Bristol, Frenchay BS16 36 E1
Bristol, Little Stoke BS34 36 C6
Bristol, Patchway BS34 24 B2
Bristol, Sneyd Park BS9 48 E3
Clevedon BS21 57 G6
Keynsham BS31 81 E6
Timsbury BA2 116 B2
Weston-S-M BS22 89 C3
Winscombe BS25 125 C8
Yate BS37 27 D1
Yatton BS49 91 B8
Averay Rd BS16 50 C4
Averill Ct BS21 57 F4
Avonbank Ind Est BS11 47 B7
Avonbridge Trad Est BS11 47 C8
Avon Bsns Pk BS16 51 A3
Avon Cl
Bristol BS5 64 F6
Keynsham BS31 81 F6
Weston-S-M BS23 104 F2
AVONCLIFF 120 F4
Avoncliff Halt BA15 120 F5
Avon Cres
Bristol BS1 142 A1
Wickwar GL12 18 B6
Avon Ct
Batheaston BA1 86 A4
Bristol, Clifton BS8 49 A1
Bristol, Fishponds BS16 51 B5
Avondale Bldgs BA1 85 B2
Avondale Bsns Ctr BS15 51 C2
Avondale Ct
Bath BA1 101 B7
Bristol BS9 48 D3
Bristol, Oldland BS30 65 F3
Avondale Rd BA1 101 B6
Avondown Cl BS10 35 D2
Avondown Ct BS3 63 C2
Avondown Ho BA2 101 B5
Avondowns Ct BS8 142 A4
Avon Gorge Ind Est BS11 47 C7
Avon Gorge Nature Reserve* BS8 62 E7
Avon Gr BS9 48 D2
Avon Hts BA2 120 C6
Avon La BS31 82 F5
Avonlea
Bristol BS15 65 C5
Yate BS37 39 D8
Avonlea Ct BS30 66 A3
Avonleaze BS9 48 B5
Avonleigh Ct 4 BS3 63 B2
Avonleigh Rd BS3 63 B2
Avonmead BS2 143 B4
Avon Meads BS2 64 C5
Avon Mill La BS31 81 F6
AVONMOUTH 33 D2
Avonmouth CE Prim Sch BS11 47 C8
Avonmouth Rd
Avonmouth BS11 33 B1
Bristol BS11 47 C8
Avonmouth Sta BS11 33 B1
Avonmouth Way
Avonmouth BS11 33 D1
Bristol BS10 34 E3
Avonmouth Way W BS11 33 B1
AVONPARK 120 C6
Avon Pk
Bath BA1 101 A7
Bristol BS5 64 D7

Avon Prim Sch BS11 47 D8
Avon Rd
Bristol BS13 79 A6
Charfield GL12 11 A4
Keynsham BS31 81 F5
Pill BS20 47 C5
Avon Rise SN14 31 E4
Avon Riverside Est BS11 47 B7
Avon Riverside Sta* BS30 82 E6
Avonside Ind Est BS2 64 C6
Avonside Rd BS2 64 C6
Avonside Way BS4 64 F6
Avon Ski Ctr* BS25 108 C3
Avonsmere Residential Pk BS34 36 C3
Avon St
Bath BA1 141 B2
Bristol BS2 143 C2
Avon Trad Est BS2 64 A5
Avon Vale BS9 48 D4
Avonvale Pl BA1 85 F3
Avonvale Rd BS5 64 C7
Avon Valley Bsns Pk BS4 64 E6
Avon Valley Ctry Pk* BS31 82 D6
Avon Valley Farm Bsns Pk BS31 82 D5
Avon Valley Rly*
Bitton BS30 82 D7
Bristol BS30 66 C3
Avon View BS15 65 B3
Avon Way
Bristol BS9 48 C4
Bristol, Southmead BS10 49 D7
Portishead BS20 45 C5
Thornbury BS35 15 D7
Avonwood Cl BS11 47 E6
Awdelett Cl BS11 34 B1
AWKLEY 23 E8
Awkley La BS32 23 E8
Awkward Hill BS40 111 D5
AXBRIDGE 125 B1
Axbridge CE Fst Sch BS26 125 C1
Axbridge Cl BS48 75 E8
Axbridge Moor Dro BS26 125 C1
Axbridge Rd
Bath BA2 102 A2
Bristol BS4 63 F2
Cheddar BS27 125 F2
Axe Cl BS23 105 A5
Axe Ct 4 BS35 15 C8
Axford Way BA2 134 D8
Axis BS14 79 D5
Aycote Cl BS22 88 C2
Ayford La SN14 69 F4
Aylesbury Cres BS3 63 B1
Aylesbury Rd BS3 63 B1
Aylmer Cres BS14 80 B6
Aylminton Wlk BS11 34 B2
Ayr St BA2 101 D6
Azalea Rd BS22 89 A5
Azelin Ave BS13 79 B5
Aztec Ctr The BS32 24 A2
Aztec W BS32 24 A2

B

BABINGTON 140 C3
Backfield Farm BS37 26 F5
Backfields BS2 143 B4
Backfields Ct BS2 143 B4
Backfields La BS2 143 B4
Back La
Axbridge BS26 125 C2
Chewton Mendip BA3 130 B1
Keynsham BS31 81 E6
Kingston Seymour BS21 73 A5
Litton BA3 130 E2
Marshfield SN14 69 F8
Pill BS20 47 C5
Pucklechurch BS16 53 C4
Rowberrow BS25 109 A1
Wickwar GL12 18 A5
Back Of Kingsdown Par BS6 143 A4
Back Rd BS3 63 A4
Back St
Hawkesbury Upton GL9 20 A3
Weston-S-M BS23 104 E7
Back Stoke La BS9 48 F6
BACKWELL 76 B6
Backwell Bow BS48 60 C1
Backwell CE Jun Sch BS48 76 C5
Backwell Comm BS48 76 B8
BACKWELL COMMON 76 B8
BACKWELL GREEN 76 D8
Backwell Hill Rd BS48 76 E5
Backwell Sch BS48 76 B6
Backwell Wlk BS13 78 F8
Badenham Gr BS11 47 F8
Baden Hill Rd GL12 16 C6
Baden Ho BA1 141 B4
Baden Rd
Bristol, Kingswood BS15 66 A7
Bristol, Redfield BS5 64 C7
Bader Cl BS37 27 D3
Badger Cl BS30 65 F3
Badger Rise BS20 44 F3
Badgers Cl BS32 24 D3
Badger Sett BS5 65 B7
Badgers Holt BS14 80 C6
Badger's La BS32 23 C3
Badgers Rise BS10 35 E4
Badgers The BS22 89 D3
Badgers Way BS24 105 F8
Badgers Wlk BS4 64 D2
Badgeworth BS37 39 D6
Badman Cl BS39 132 D5
BADMINTON 30 F2
Badminton BS16 37 C1
Badminton Ct
17 Weston-S-M BS23 87 C1
Yate BS37 27 C2
Badminton Ctr The BS37 27 C2
Badminton Gdns BA1 101 C8
Badminton Rd
Bristol, Downend BS16 51 E7
Bristol, Montpelier BS2 49 F1
Chipping Sodbury BS37 41 B7
Frampton Cotterell BS36, BS37 38 C6
Badminton Road Trad Est BS37 27 B1
Badminton Sch BS9 49 A5
Badminton Wlk BS16 51 E7
Badock's Wood Prim Sch BS10 35 B1
Baggridge Hill BA2 135 F7
Baglyn Ave BS15 51 F3
Bagnell Cl BS14 80 E5
Bagnell Rd BS14 80 E5
BAGSTONE 17 A3
Bagstone Rd BS37, GL12 17 A2
Bagworth Dr BS30 65 F3
BAILBROOK 85 D3
Bailbrook Gr BA1 85 C3
Bailbrook La BA1 85 D3
Baildon Cres BS23 105 A4
Baildon Ct 2 BS23 104 F4
Baildon Rd BS23 105 A4
Bailey Cl BS22 105 E8
Bailey Ct BS20 45 F6
Bailey's Court Prim Sch BS32 36 F6
Baileys Court Rd BS32 36 F6
Baileys Ct BS32 36 F6
Baileys Mead Rd BS16 50 C5
Bailiffs Cl BS26 125 C1
Bailiffs' Wall BS26 125 B1
Bainsbury View BA3 138 F1
Baker Cl 7 BS21 57 D1
Baker's Bldgs BS40 92 D2
Bakersfield BS30 66 B3
Bakers Ground BS34 37 A5
Bakers La
Chilcompton BA3 138 D3
Lower Langford BS40 109 C8
Bakers Par BA2 116 B2
Bakers Pk BS13 79 B6
Baker St BS23 104 E8
Balaclava Ind Est BS16 50 F3
Balaclava Rd BS16 50 F3
Baldwin Chambers 6 BS1 143 A2
Baldwin Lofts BS1 143 A2
Baldwin St BS1 143 A2
Balfour Rd BS3 63 B3
Ballance St BA1 141 B4
Ballast La BS11 33 E2
Balls Barn La BS24 90 A2
Balmain St BS4 64 A4
Balmoral Cl BS34 36 D4
Balmoral Ct BS16 52 A5
Balmoral Ho BS1 142 C1
Balmoral Mans 3 BS7 49 F2
Balmoral Rd
Bristol, Longwell Green BS30 65 F2
Bristol, Montpelier BS7 49 F2
Keynsham BS31 81 E4
Balmoral Way BS22 88 D2
Baltic Pl BS20 47 D4
Balustrade 17 BA1 85 B1
Bamfield BS14 80 A6
Bampton 5 BS22 88 F2
Bampton Cl
Bristol, Emerson's Green BS16 52 C6
Bristol, Headley Park BS13 79 B7
Bampton Croft BS16 52 C6
Bampton Dr BS16 37 D1
Banfield Cl BS11 48 A8
Bangor Gr BS4 64 F5
Bangrove Wlk BS11 47 E8
Banister Gr BS4 79 D7
Bank Leaze Prim Sch BS11 34 B2
Bank Pl BS20 47 D4
Bank Rd
Avonmouth BS11 33 D7
Bristol BS15 65 D8
Pilning BS35 22 E6
Banks Cl BS21 73 D8
Bankside BS16 51 F4
Bankside Rd BS4 64 D3
Bannerdown Cl BA1 86 B4
Bannerdown Dr BA1 86 A4
Bannerdown Rd BA1 86 C5
Bannerleigh La BS8 62 E6
Bannerleigh Rd BS8 62 E6
Bannerman Rd BS5 64 B8
Bannerman Road Com Sch BS5 50 B1
Banner Rd BS6 49 E1
Bannetts Tree Cres BS35 15 A5
Bantock Cl BS4 79 D6
Bantry Rd BS4 79 E8
BANWELL 107 B3
Banwell Cl
Bristol BS13 79 A8
Keynsham BS31 82 A2
Banwell Prim Sch BS29 107 B3
Banwell Rd
Banwell BS26, BS29 123 E8
Bath BA2 118 D8
Bristol BS3 63 A3
Locking BS24 106 B3
Winscombe BS25, BS29 124 E8
Banyard Rd BS20 46 E5
BAPTIST MILLS 50 A2
Baptist St BS5 50 A1
Baranwheel Ct BS5 64 F6
Barberry Farm Rd BS49 74 B1
Barbour Gdns BS13 79 D3
Barbour Rd BS13 79 D3
Barcroft Cl BS15 65 C8
Barker Ct
5 Bristol BS5 64 C7
Long Ashton BS41 61 E1
Barkers Mead BS37 27 F4
Barker Wlk BS5 50 A1
Barkleys Hill BS16 50 C5
Barlands Ho BS10 34 F3
Barley Cl
Bristol BS16 52 A6
Frampton Cotterell BS36 38 C8
Barley Close Com Prim Sch BS16 52 A6
Barley Croft BS9 48 F5
Barley Cross BS22 89 A5
Barleyfields BS2 143 C2
Barley Wood Walled Gdn* BS40 92 F3
Barnabas Cl BS26 125 D2
Barnabas St 9 BS2 49 E1
Barnaby Cl BA3 133 B2
Barnack Trad Est BS3 63 C1
Barnard's Cl BS49 91 C7
Barnard Wlk BS31 81 D4
Barn Cl BS16 52 B6
Barn End
East Harptree BS40 129 E3
Marshfield SN14 70 A8
Barnes Ct BS34 36 E3
Barnes St BS5 64 D8
Barnfield Way BA1 86 B3
Barn Hill BA2 134 F5
Barnhill Cl BS37 28 A4
Barnhill Rd BS37 28 B1
Barn La BS39 115 A7
Barn Owl Way BS34 36 F5
Barn Pool BS25 125 F8
Barns Cl
Barrow Gurney BS48 77 E4
Nailsea BS48 59 E2
Barns Ground BS21 73 E8
Barnstaple Ct BS4 79 E8
Barnstaple Rd BS4 79 E8
Barnstaple Wlk BS4 79 F8
Barnwood Ct BS48 59 B1
Barnwood Rd BS37 39 C7
Baron Cl BS30 82 E8
Barons Cl BS3 62 F3
Barossa Pl BS1 143 A1
Barrack's La BS11 47 D8
Barratt St BS5 50 C1
Barrington Cl BS15 51 F2
Barrington Ct
Bristol BS4 64 A4
11 Bristol, Knowle BS2 63 F4
Bristol, New Cheltenham BS15 51 E1
BARROW COMMON 78 B4
Barrow Court La BS19 77 B5
Barrow Ct
Barrow Gurney BS48 77 A5
Tickenham BS21 58 F4
BARROW GURNEY 77 E5
Barrow Hill BS30 67 B5
Barrow Hill Cres BS11 47 C7
Barrow Hill Rd BS11 47 D6
Barrow La BS40 77 F1
Barrowmead Dr BS11 47 F7
Barrow Rd
Bath BA2 101 C1
Bristol BS2 64 A7
Hutton BS24 105 E2
Barrow St BS48 77 D5
Barrows The
Cheddar BS27 126 A1
Weston-S-M BS22 105 C7
BARROW VALE 115 D5
Barrs Court Ave BS30 66 A5
Barrs Court Prim Sch BS30 65 F5
Barrs Court Rd BS30 66 A5
Barrs La GL11 5 E4
Barry Cl
Bristol BS30 66 C1
Weston-S-M BS24 105 A1
Barry Rd BS30 66 C2
Barstaple Ho BS2 143 C3
Barter Cl BS15 65 D8
Bartholomew Row BA2 116 B2
Bartholomew Sq BS7 49 F7
Bartletts Ct BA2 141 C1
Bartlett's Rd BS3 63 C2
Bartlett St 6 BA1 141 B3
Bartletts Way BS24 106 A4
Bartley Ct BS5 64 D7
Bartley St BS3 63 D4
BARTON 124 B6
Barton Bldgs BA1 141 B3
Barton Cl
Alveston BS35 15 A5
1 Bristol BS4 64 F6
Winterbourne BS36 37 E5
Barton Ct BS5 64 C6
Barton Dro BS25 124 D5
Barton Gn BS5 64 B7
BARTON HILL 64 C6
Barton Hill Prim Sch BS5 64 B6
Barton Hill Rd BS5 64 B7
Barton Hill Trad Est 10 BS5 64 B6
Barton Ho BS5 64 C6
Bartonia Gr BS4 64 D1
Barton Manor BS2 64 A6
Barton Rd
Bristol BS2 143 C2
Winscombe BS26 124 C6
Barton St
Bath BA1 141 B2
Bristol BS1 143 A4
Barton The
Bleadon BS24 122 C6
Bristol BS15 65 C4
Compton Martin BS40 129 B7
Corston BA2 100 A7
Hawkesbury Upton GL9 19 F3
Norton St Philip BA2 136 E4
Barton Vale
6 Bristol BS2 64 A6
Bristol BS2 143 C2
Barwick Ho BS11 47 E7
Barwood Cl BS15 65 F8
BATCH 121 F3
Batch Bsns Pk BS24 121 F2
Batches The BS3 63 B2
Batchfield La BS16, BS37 53 D8
Batch La
Clutton BS39 114 F3
Lympsham BS24 121 F3
Batch The
Backwell BS48 76 D1
Batheaston BA1 85 F3
Burrington BS40 110 B3
Butcombe BS40 111 B8
Chew Magna BS40 96 B3
Churchill BS25 108 F4
Compton Martin BS40 129 A6
Farmborough BA2 116 A6
Hinton Charterhouse BA2 119 E1
Saltford BS31 82 F3
Yatton BS49 91 B7
Bates Cl BS5 64 A8
BATH 141 B3
Bath Abbey* BA1 141 C2
Bath Acad BA1 141 B3
BATHAMPTON 85 F1
Bathampton La BA2 85 E1
Bathampton Prim Sch BA2 85 F2
Bath Bldgs BS6 49 E1
Bath Bridge Rdbt BS1 143 C1
Bath Chew Valley Cvn Pk BS39 113 C4
BATHEASTON 85 F4
Batheaston CE Prim Sch BA1 85 F4
BATHFORD 86 C1
Bathford CE Prim Sch BA1 86 C2
Bathford Hill
Bathford BA1 86 B2
Compton Dando BS39 98 E5
Bathford Manor BA1 86 C2
Bath Foyer The BA2 101 A6
Bath Hill
Keynsham BS31 81 F5
Wellow BA2 118 D2
Bathings The 1 BS35 15 C8
Bath La GL9 19 E2
Bath New Rd BA3 133 F4
Bath Old Rd BA3 133 F4
Bath Postal Mus* BA1 141 C2
Bath Race Course* BA1 84 A6
Bath Rd
Bitton BS30 82 D8
Blagdon BS40 111 B1
Bristol, Brislington BS4 64 F1
Bristol BS2, BS4 143 C1
Bristol, Longwell Green BS30 65 F3
Bristol, North Common BS30 66 D6
Bristol, Totterdown BS4 64 B4
Bristol, Upper Knowle BS4 64 D2
Bristol, Willsbridge BS30 66 C1
Chipping Sodbury BS37, GL9 41 C4
Colerne SN14 70 E2
Farmborough BA2 115 E5
Kelston BA1, BS30 83 B6
Kingsdown SN13 86 F5
Norton St Philip BA2 136 E5
Bath Rd *continued*
Paulton BS39 132 F6
Peasedown St John BA2 134 C7
Saltford BS31 82 D3
Thornbury BS35 15 B8
Upper Langford BS40 109 D3
Wick BS30 67 E4
Bath Spa Sta BA1 141 C1
Bath Spa Univ BA1 84 E1
Bath Spa University Coll (Newton Pk Campus) BA2 100 B5
Bath St
Bath BA1 141 C2
Bristol, Ashton Gate BS3 63 A4
Bristol BS1 143 B2
Bristol, Staple Hill BS16 51 E4
Bathurst Par BS1 143 A1
Bathurst Rd BS22 105 C8
Bath View BA3 138 F1
Bathwell Rd BS4 64 A3
BATHWICK 102 B7
Bathwick Hill BA2 102 C6
Bathwick Rise BA2 102 B7
Bathwick St BA1, BA2 141 C4
Batley Ct BS30 66 D4
Batstone Cl BA1 85 B2
Battenburg Rd BS5 65 A8
Batten Ct BS37 28 C1
Batten's La BS5 65 A6
Battens Rd BS5 65 B7
Battersby Way BS10 34 E2
Battersea Rd BS5 64 C8
Battery La BS20 45 D7
Battery Rd BS20 45 D6
Battle La BS40 96 A3
Battson Rd BS14 80 E4
Baugh Gdns BS16 37 E1
Baugh Rd BS16 37 E1
Baxter Cl BS15 65 F8
Bayer Bldg The BA2 141 B1
Bay Gdns BS5 50 C2
Bayham Rd BS4 64 A3
Bayleys Dr BS15 65 C6
Baynham Ct 4 BS15 65 B5
Baynton Ho 2 BS5 64 B7
Baynton Mdw BS16 52 C6
Baynton Rd BS3 63 A4
Bay Rd BS21 57 F6
Bayswater Ave BS6 49 B3
Bayswater Rd BS7 49 F7
Bay Tree Cl BS34 35 F7
Baytree Ct BS22 88 D1
Baytree Rd BS22 88 C1
Bay Tree Rd
Bath BA1 85 B2
Clevedon BS21 57 G1
Baytree Sch BS24 106 A8
Baytree View BS22 88 D1
Bay Tree View BS22 88 D1
Bay Willow Dr BS6 49 B2
BEACH 67 C2
Beach Ave
Clevedon BS21 57 E2
Severn Beach BS35 22 A7
Beach Ct BS23 104 D6
Beach End Rd BS23 104 C2
Beachgrove Gdns BS16 51 C4
Beachgrove Rd BS16 51 B4
Beach Hill
Bristol BS30 66 F3
Portishead BS20 45 C6
Beach La BS30 67 C2
Beachlands Pk BS22 88 A6
Beachley Wlk BS11 47 D7
Beach Mews BS21 57 E4
Beach Rd
Severn Beach BS35 21 F7
Weston-S-M BS23 104 D6
Weston-S-M, Kewstoke BS22 88 A5
Beach Rd E BS20 45 D6
Beach Rd W BS20 45 C6
Beach The BS21 57 E4
BEACON HILL 84 F1
Beacon La BS16 37 C6
Beaconlea BS15 65 D6
Beacon Rd BA1 85 A1
Beacon Rise Prim Sch BS15 65 D6
Beaconsfield Cl 6 BS2 64 B6
Beaconsfield Rd
Bristol, Clifton BS8 49 A1
Bristol, Crew's Hole BS5 64 E7
Bristol, Kensington Park BS4 64 B3
Clevedon BS21 57 G3
Weston-S-M BS23 104 E7
Beaconsfield St 7 BS5 64 B6
Beafort Cl BS24 106 C3
Beale Cl BS14 80 E6
Beam St BS5 64 C7
Bean Acre The BS11 47 D8
Beanhill Cres BS35 15 A5
Beanwood Pk (Cvn Site) BS37 39 E3
Bearbridge Rd BS13 78 F4
BEAR FLAT 101 F4
Bear Yard Mews 2 BS8 142 A2
Beauchamp Rd BS7 49 D4
Beauchamps Dr BA3 139 A5
Beauford Sq BA1 141 B2
Beaufort BS16 37 C1

Beaufort Ave
  Midsomer Norton
   BA3 . . . . 133 A2
Yate BS37 . . . . 27 D2
Beaufort Bldgs [7] BS8 . . . 62 F7
Beaufort Cl BS5 . . . . 64 D7
Beaufort Cres BS34 . . . . . 36 E4
Beaufort Ct
  Bristol BS16 . . . . 52 A8
  Clevedon BS21 . . . . 57 E5
Beaufort E BA1 . . . . 85 C1
Beaufort Gdns [4] BS48 . . . 59 D1
Beaufort Ho [8] BS1 . . . . . 64 E7
Beaufort Hts BS5 . . . . 64 E7
Beaufort Mews
  [3] Bath BA1 . . . . 85 C1
  [11] Bristol BS8 . . . . 62 F7
Chipping Sodbury BS37 . . . 28 B1
Beaufort Pl
  Bath BA1 . . . . 85 C1
  Bristol, Frenchay BS16 . . . 37 B1
  Bristol, Upper Easton
   BS5 . . . . 64 A8
Beaufort Rd
  Bristol, Clifton BS8 . . . . . 49 A1
  Bristol, Horfield BS7 . . . . 49 F6
  Bristol, Kingswood BS15 . 51 C1
  Bristol, Pile Marsh BS5 . . 64 C7
  Bristol, Staple Hill BS16 . 51 E5
  Bristol, Vinney Green
   BS16 . . . . 52 A8
  Frampton Cotterell BS36 . 38 A8
  Weston-S-M BS23 . . . . . 104 F7
  Yate BS37 . . . . 27 D2
Beaufort St
  Bristol, Bedminster
   BS3 . . . . 63 C2
  Bristol, Upper Easton
   BS5 . . . . 64 A8
Beaufort Trad Pk BS16 . . . 53 B5
Beaufort View SN14 . . . . . 31 E4
Beaufort W [11] BA1 . . . . . 85 B1
Beaufort Way BS10 . . . . . 49 D8
Beauley Rd BS3 . . . . 63 B4
Beaumont BA1 . . . . 84 F1
Beaumont Cl
  Bristol BS30 . . . . 66 A3
  Weston-S-M BS23 . . . . . 104 F4
Beaumont St BS5 . . . . 64 A8
Beaumont Terr [6] BS5 . . . 64 A8
Beau St BA1 . . . . 141 B2
Beaver Cl BS36 . . . . 37 F7
Beavor Cl [5] BS16 . . . . . . 51 D3
Beck Cl BS16 . . . . 52 C7
Becket Ct BS16 . . . . 53 B5
Becket Dr BS22 . . . . 89 A3
Becket Prim Sch BS22 . . . 89 A2
Becket Rd BS22 . . . . 89 A4
Becket's La BS48 . . . . 75 E8
Beckford Ct BA2 . . . . 102 B7
Beckford Gdns
  BA2 . . . . 102 B8
  Bristol BS14 . . . . 80 A3
Beckford Rd BA2 . . . . 102 B7
Beckford's Twr & Mus*
  BA1 . . . . 84 D4
Beckhampton Rd
  BA2 . . . . 101 D5
Beck Ho BS34 . . . . 36 A8
Beckington Rd BS3 . . . . . 63 F2
Beckington Wlk BS3 . . . . 63 F2
Becks Bsns Pk BS23 . . . . 105 A7
Beckspool Rd BS16 . . . . . 37 C1
Bedford Cres BS7 . . . . . . 49 F5
Bedford Ct BA1 . . . . 102 B8
Bedford Rd BS23 . . . . . . 104 E4
Bedford St BA1 . . . . 102 B8
BEDMINSTER 63 C3
BEDMINSTER DOWN . . . 79 B8
Bedminster Down Rd BS3,
  BS13 . . . . 63 B1
Bedminster Down Sch
  BS13 . . . . 78 F7
Bedminster Par BS3 . . . . 63 D4
Bedminster Pl [9] BS3 . . . 63 D4
Bedminster Sta BS3 . . . . 63 C2
Bedminster Sta BS3 . . . . 63 C3
Bedwin Cl BS20 . . . . 44 F4
Beechacres BS35 . . . . 8 C1
Beech Ave BA2 . . . . 102 E5
Beech Cl
  Alveston BS35 . . . . 15 A5
  Bristol BS30 . . . . 66 A5
  Shipham BS25 . . . . 125 F8
Beechcroft BA1 . . . . 78 D2
Beech Croft BS14 . . . . . . 80 B5
Beechcroft Wlk BS7 . . . . 50 A8
Beech Ct BS14 . . . . 80 A5
Beech Dr
  Nailsea BS48 . . . . 60 A3
  Shipham BS25 . . . . 125 F8
BEECHEN CLIFF 141 B1
Beechen Cliff Rd BA2 . . . 141 B1
Beechen Cliff Sch
  BA2 . . . . 102 A4
Beechen Cliff Villas
  BA2 . . . . 141 B1
Beechen Dr BS16 . . . . 51 B3
Beeches Gr BS4 . . . . 64 D2
Beeches Ind Est BS37 . . . 27 B2
Beeches The
  Bath BA2 . . . . 101 D1
  Bristol, Bradley Stoke
   BS32 . . . . 36 D8
  Bristol BS9 . . . . 48 D3
  Bristol, Frenchay BS16 . . 37 B1

Beeches The *continued*
  Bristol, Oldland Common
   BS30 . . . . 66 C2
  Bristol, St Anne's BS4 . . . 64 E5
  Sandford BS25 . . . . 108 B4
Beechfield Cl BS41 . . . . . 62 C2
Beechfield Gr BS9 . . . . . . 48 C8
Beech Gr BA2 . . . . 101 D4
BEECH HILL 39 B7
Beech Ho
  Bristol BS16 . . . . 50 C5
  Clevedon BS21 . . . . 57 F4
Beech Leaze BS35 . . . . . . 15 A5
Beechmont Dr BS24 . . . . 105 A1
Beechmont Ct BS24 . . . . 104 F1
Beechmount Ct BS14 . . . . 80 B8
Beechmount Gr BS14 . . . . 80 B8
Beech Rd
  Bristol BS7 . . . . 49 E5
  Saltford BS31 . . . . 82 E3
  Shipham BS25 . . . . 125 F8
  Yatton BS49 . . . . 91 C8
Beech Terr BA3 . . . . 133 E1
Beechwood Ave
  Bristol BS15 . . . . 65 D5
  Locking BS24 . . . . 106 A5
Beechwood Cl BS14 . . . . 80 C8
Beechwood Dr BS20 . . . . 44 E5
Beechwood Ho BS16 . . . . 51 A4
Beechwood Rd
  Bath BA2 . . . . 102 B1
  Bristol BS16 . . . . 51 B4
  Easton-in-G BS20 . . . . . . 47 A4
  Nailsea BS48 . . . . 59 D2
  Portishead BS20 . . . . 44 E5
Beehive Trad Est BS5 . . . 64 E7
Beehive Yd BA1 . . . . 141 C3
Beek's La SN14, BA1 . . . . 69 D5
Bees Ho BS21 . . . . 57 E2
Beesmoor Rd BS36 . . . . . 38 B6
Begbrook Dr BS16 . . . . . . 50 F6
Begbrook La BS16 . . . . . . 50 F6
Begbrook Pk BS16 . . . . . . 51 A7
Begbrook Prim Sch
  BS16 . . . . 50 F6
Beggar Bush La BS8 . . . . 62 B6
Beggarswell Cl BS2 . . . . 143 C4
Belfast BS4 . . . . 79 E8
Belfields La BS16 . . . . . . 51 B3
Belfry BA1 . . . . 66 B6
Belfry Ave BS5 . . . . 65 A8
Belgrave Cres BA1 . . . . . 141 C4
Belgrave Hill [5] BS8 . . . . 49 A2
Belgrave Ho BS8 . . . . 142 A3
Belgrave Pl
  Bath BA1 . . . . 141 C4
  Bristol BS8 . . . . 142 A3
Belgrave Rd
  Bath BA1 . . . . 85 B1
  Bristol BS8 . . . . 142 B4
  Weston-S-M BS23 . . . . . 105 B8
Belgrave Terr [1] BA1 . . . 85 A1
Bellamy Ave BS13 . . . . . . 79 C4
Bellamy Cl BS15 . . . . 65 A5
Belland Dr BS14 . . . . 79 F4
Bell Ave BS1 . . . . 143 A1
Bella Vista Rd BA1 . . . . . 141 B4
Bell Barn Rd BS9 . . . . . . 48 D6
Bell Cl
  Bristol BS10 . . . . 49 E7
  Farmborough BA2 . . . . . 115 F6
Belle Ct [7] BS2 . . . . 63 F4
BELLE VUE 133 B3
Belle Vue Cl BS15 . . . . . . 65 E7
Belle Vue Cl BA2 . . . . . . 134 D7
Bellevue Cotts
  Bristol, Brandon Hill
   BS8 . . . . 142 A1
  [5] Bristol, Eastfield BS9 . . 49 F7
Bellevue Cres BS8 . . . . . 142 A2
Bellevue Ct
  Bristol, Brandon Hill
   BS8 . . . . 142 A2
  [6] Bristol, St George
   BS5 . . . . 65 A8
  Clevedon BS21 . . . . 57 F4
Bellevue Mans BS21 . . . . 57 F4
Bellevue Pk BS4 . . . . 64 D2
Bellevue Rd
  Bristol, Kingswood
   BS15 . . . . 65 F7
  [6] Bristol, Windmill Hill
   BS2 . . . . 63 F4
  Clevedon BS21 . . . . 57 F4
Belle Vue Rd BS5 . . . . . . 50 C1
Bellevue Terr
  Bristol, Bishopston BS4 . . 64 D2
  Bristol BS8 . . . . 142 B2
  [6] Bristol, Windmill Hill BS2 . . 63 F4
Bell Field The SN14 . . . . 31 E4
Bellhanger Ct BA1 . . . . . 141 B4
Bell Hill
  Bristol BS16 . . . . 50 C4
  Norton St Philip BA2 . . . 136 E4
Bell Hill Rd BS5 . . . . 64 F8
Bellhouse La BS40 . . . . . 129 C5
Bellhouse Wlk BS11 . . . . 34 B1
Bellifants BA2 . . . . 116 A6
Bell La BS1 . . . . 143 A3
Bell Language Sch The
  BA1 . . . . 101 C8
Bell Pit Brow BS48 . . . . . 60 B2
Bell Rd BS36 . . . . 38 C6

Bell Sq
  Blagdon BS40 . . . . 110 E3
  Marshfield SN14 . . . . 70 A8
Bellum SN14 . . . . 69 E8
BELLUTON 97 D6
Belluton La BS39 . . . . 97 D5
Belluton Rd BS4 . . . . 64 A3
Belluton Villas BS39 . . . . 97 D5
Bell Wlk BS40 . . . . 92 E2
Belmont Dr
  Bristol BS34 . . . . 36 E5
  Failand BS8 . . . . 61 B3
Belmont Hill BS48 . . . . . 61 B1
Belmont Pk BS7 . . . . 35 F1
Belmont Rd
  Bath BA2 . . . . 102 C1
  Bristol, Arno's Vale BS4 . . 64 C3
  Bristol, Montpelier BS6 . . 49 F2
  Winscombe BS25 . . . . . . 125 A8
Belmont St BS5 . . . . 50 B1
Belmont The BS21 . . . . . . 57 F3
Belmore Gdns BA2 . . . . . 101 B3
Beloe Rd BS7 . . . . 49 E5
Belroyal Ave BS4 . . . . . . 64 F3
Belsher Dr BS15 . . . . 66 A6
Belstone Wlk BS4 . . . . . . 79 C8
Belton Ct BA1 . . . . 84 B2
Belton Rd
  Bristol BS5 . . . . 64 B8
  Portishead BS20 . . . . 45 A6
Belvedere BA1 . . . . 141 B4
Belvedere Cres BS22 . . . . 88 C1
Belvedere Rd BS6 . . . . . . 49 B3
Belvoir Rd
  [6] Bath BA2 . . . . 101 D5
  Bristol BS6 . . . . 49 E2
Bence Ct [3] BS15 . . . . . . 65 B5
Bences Cl SN14 . . . . 69 F8
Benches La BS40 . . . . 94 D3
Bendalls Bridge BS39 . . . 114 E2
Benford Cl BS16 . . . . 51 D2
Bennell Batch BA3 . . . . . 138 E4
Bennell Cl BA3 . . . . 138 E4
Bennell Cotts BA3 . . . . . 138 E4
Bennett La BA1 . . . . 85 A1
Bennett Rd BS5 . . . . 64 E7
Bennett's Ct BS37 . . . . . . 28 A1
Bennett's Rd BA1 . . . . . . 85 C3
Bennett St BA1 . . . . 141 B3
Bennetts Way BS1, BS8 . . 62 F5
Bensaunt Gr BS10 . . . . . . 35 D4
Bentley Cl BS14 . . . . 79 F3
Bentley Rd BS22 . . . . 89 B3
Benville Ave BS9 . . . . 48 C8
Berchel Ho [4] BS3 . . . . . 63 D4
Berenda Dr BS30 . . . . 66 B3
Beresford Cl BS31 . . . . . . 82 E2
Beresford Gdns BA1 . . . . 84 A3
Berkeley Ave
  Bristol, Bishopston
   BS7 . . . . 49 D3
  Bristol BS8 . . . . 142 C3
  Midsomer Norton BA3 . . . 133 A2
Berkeley Cl
  Bristol BS16 . . . . 52 A8
  Charfield GL12 . . . . 11 A5
Berkeley Cres
  Bristol BS8 . . . . 142 B3
  Weston-S-M BS23 . . . . . 104 C2
Berkeley Ct
  Bath BA2 . . . . 102 C6
  Bristol, Bishopston BS7 . . 49 D3
Berkeley Ct Bsns Pk
  BS5 . . . . 64 B7
Berkeley Gdns BS31 . . . . 81 E4
Berkeley Gn BS16 . . . . . . 37 B1
Berkeley Gn Rd BS5 . . . . 50 D2
Berkeley Gr BS5 . . . . 50 C2
Berkeley Ho
  Bath BA1 . . . . 141 C4
  Bristol BS1 . . . . 142 C3
  [7] Bristol, Staple Hill
   BS16 . . . . 51 D5
Berkeley Pl
  Bath BA1 . . . . 141 C4
  Bristol, Brandon Hill
   BS8 . . . . 142 B3
  Bristol, Windmill Hill
   BS3 . . . . 63 D2
Berkeley Rd
  Bristol, Bishopston
   BS7 . . . . 49 D3
  Bristol, Kingswood BS15 . 65 D7
  Bristol, Mayfield Park
   BS16 . . . . 51 B2
  Bristol, Staple Hill BS16 . 51 D5
Berkeleys Mead BS34 . . . 37 A6
Berkeley Sq BS8 . . . . 142 C3
Berkeley St BS5 . . . . 50 C3
Berkeley Way BS16 . . . . . 52 B7
Berkshire Rd BS7 . . . . . . 49 D3
Berlington Ct BS1 . . . . . . 143 B1
Bernard Ireland Ho
  BA1 . . . . 84 B1
Berners Cl BS4 . . . . 79 D7
Berrow La BS23 . . . . 104 E5
Berrows Mead BS37 . . . . 27 A8
Berrow Wlk BS3 . . . . 63 E2
Berry Croft [5] BS3 . . . . . 63 D4
Berry Hill Cl BS10 . . . . . . 35 D1
Berry La BS7 . . . . 49 F6
BERWICK 34 D6
Berwick Cl BS10 . . . . 34 E8
Berwick Ct BS10 . . . . 34 E8
Berwick Dr BS10 . . . . 34 E5

Berwick La BS10 . . . . 34 D7
Berwick Rd BS5 . . . . 50 B2
Beryl Gr BS14 . . . . 80 C8
Beryl Rd BS3 . . . . 63 B3
Besom La BS37 . . . . 39 D5
Bethel Rd BS5 . . . . 64 F8
Betjeman Ct [4] BS30 . . . 66 A5
Betts Gn BS16 . . . . 52 C7
Bevan Ct BS34 . . . . 35 F2
Beverley Ave BS16 . . . . . 37 F1
Beverley Cl BS5 . . . . 65 B6
Beverley Ct BS7 . . . . 49 F8
Beverley Gdns BS9 . . . . . 48 D7
Beverley Rd BS7 . . . . 49 F8
Beverstone BS15 . . . . 65 C8
Beverston Gdns BS11 . . . 34 B2
BEVINGTON 2 F6
Bevington Cl BS34 . . . . . . 23 E1
Bevington La GL13 . . . . . . 2 F7
Bevington Wlk BS34 . . . . 23 E1
Bewdley Rd BA2 . . . . 102 B4
Bexley Rd BS16 . . . . 51 E8
BIBSTONE 10 C3
Bibstone BS15 . . . . 66 A8
Bibury Ave BS34 . . . . 36 B8
Bibury Cl
  Bristol BS9 . . . . 49 D7
  Nailsea BS48 . . . . 60 A1
Bibury Cres
  Bristol, Hanham BS15 . . . 65 C5
  Bristol, Henleaze BS9 . . . 49 D7
Bibury Ho BA1 . . . . 84 B2
Bickerton Cl BS10 . . . . . . 34 F3
Bickfield La BS40 . . . . . . 129 B8
Bickford Cl BS30 . . . . 66 A6
Bickley Cl BS15 . . . . 65 C2
Biddestone Rd BS7 . . . . . 35 E1
Biddisham Cl [6] BS48 . . . 59 E1
Biddle St BS49 . . . . 91 B7
Bideford Cres BS4 . . . . . . 79 F8
Bideford Rd BS22 . . . . . . 88 F2
Bidwell Cl BS10 . . . . 35 B3
Bifield Cl BS14 . . . . 80 F5
Bifield Gdns BS14 . . . . . . 80 E5
Bifield Rd BS14 . . . . 80 F5
Bignell Cl BS25 . . . . 124 F8
Big Tree Cl BS26 . . . . 124 C3
Bigwood La BS1 . . . . 142 C2
Bilberry Cl BS9 . . . . 48 C8
Bilbie Cl
  Bristol BS10 . . . . 49 E7
  Chew Stoke BS40 . . . . . 112 E8
Bilbie Rd
  Chew Stoke BS40 . . . . . 112 E8
  Weston-S-M BS22 . . . . . 89 B3
Bilbury La BA1 . . . . 141 B2
Billand Cl BS13 . . . . 78 E3
Billingham La BS35 . . . . . 12 C2
Bimbes La BA2 . . . . 99 E3
Bince's Lodge La BA3 . . . 133 B3
Bindon Dr BS10 . . . . 35 D4
Binhay Rd BS49 . . . . 91 C7
Binley Gr BS14 . . . . 80 D5
Binmead Gdns BS13 . . . . 79 B4
Birbeck Rd BS9 . . . . 48 E5
Birchall Rd BS6 . . . . 49 C4
Birch Ave
  Bleadon BS24 . . . . 122 C6
  Clevedon BS21 . . . . 57 G4
Birch Cl
  Bristol BS34 . . . . 35 E7
  Locking BS24 . . . . 106 B4
Birch Croft BS14 . . . . 80 A3
Birch Ct
  Keynsham BS31 . . . . 81 C4
  Weston-S-M BS22 . . . . . 89 C2
  Yate BS37 . . . . 27 D2
Birchdale Rd BS14 . . . . . . 80 A8
Birchdene BS48 . . . . 60 A2
Birch Dr
  Alveston BS35 . . . . 14 F4
  Churchill BS40 . . . . 109 A5
  Pucklechurch BS16 . . . . . 53 B5
Birches The BS48 . . . . . . 60 A2
Birch Gr BS20 . . . . 45 C4
Birch Ho BS16 . . . . 51 B5
Birchills Trad Est BS4 . . . 64 F1
Birch Rd
  Bristol, Kingswood
   BS15 . . . . 51 F1
  Bristol, Southville BS3 . . 63 B4
  Radstock BA3 . . . . 133 E1
  Yate BS37 . . . . 27 D2
Birchwood Ave BS23 . . . . 105 A7
Birchwood Ct BS4 . . . . . . 64 F6
Birchwood Dr BS8 . . . . . . 61 B3
Birchwood La BS39 . . . . . 97 F2
Birchwood Rd BS4 . . . . . . 64 F4
Birdale Cl BS10 . . . . 34 E3
Birdcombe Cl BS48 . . . . . 59 E3
Birdlip Cl BS48 . . . . 60 A1
Birds Bush La GL12 . . . . . 18 A1
Birdwell La BS41 . . . . 61 F1
Birdwell Prim Sch
  BS41 . . . . 78 A8
Birdwell Rd BS41 . . . . . . 61 F1
Birdwood BS15 . . . . 65 C4
Birgage Rd GL9 . . . . 19 F2
Birkdale
  Bristol BS30 . . . . 66 B6
  Yate BS37 . . . . 39 E8
Birkett Rd BS23 . . . . 87 B1
Birkin St [6] BS2 . . . . 64 A6
Birnbeck Ct BS23 . . . . . . 104 D7
Birnbeck Rd BS23 . . . . . . 87 C1
Biscay Dr BS20 . . . . 45 F6
Bisdee Rd BS24 . . . . 105 E7
Bishop Ave BS22 . . . . 89 A3

Bishop La BS7 . . . . 49 E4
Bishop Manor Rd BS10 . . 49 D7
Bishop Rd
  Bristol, Bishopston
   BS7 . . . . 49 D4
  Bristol, Emerson's Green
   BS16 . . . . 52 C6
Bishop Road Prim Sch
  BS7 . . . . 49 D4
Bishops Cl BS9 . . . . 48 E3
Bishops Cove BS13 . . . . . 78 F5
Bishops Ct BS9 . . . . 48 C3
Bishops Knoll BS9 . . . . . . 48 C3
Bishops Mead BS49 . . . . . 92 A8
Bishops Rd BS49 . . . . 92 A8
Bishop St
  Bristol BS2 . . . . 143 B4
  Faulkland BA3 . . . . 135 C2
BISHOPSTON 49 C3
BISHOP SUTTON 113 D3
Bishop Sutton Prim Sch
  BS39 . . . . 113 D4
Bishop's Wood BS32 . . . . 24 C6
BISHOPSWORTH 79 A5
Bishopsworth CE Jun Sch
  BS13 . . . . 78 F6
Bishopsworth Rd BS13 . . 79 A7
Bishop Terr BS2 . . . . 143 C4
Bishopthorpe Rd BS10 . . 49 E7
Bishport Ave BS13 . . . . . . 79 C3
Bishport Cl BS13 . . . . 79 B4
Bishport Gn BS13 . . . . . . 79 C3
Bisley BS37 . . . . 39 C7
Bissex Mead BS16 . . . . . . 52 B5
Bittern Cl BS22 . . . . 88 F1
Bitterwell Cl BS36 . . . . . . 38 D3
Bittlemead BS13 . . . . 79 F4
BITTON 82 E7
Bitton Sta * BS30 . . . . . . 66 B1
Blackacre BS14 . . . . 80 C4
Blackberry Ave [5]
  BS16 . . . . 50 E5
Blackberry Dr
  Frampton Cotterell
   BS36 . . . . 38 C4
  Weston-S-M BS22 . . . . . 89 A2
Blackberry Hill BS16 . . . . 50 E5
Blackberry Hill Hospl
  BS16 . . . . 50 F5
Blackberry La
  Portishead BS20 . . . . 44 F2
  Winsley BA2 . . . . 120 C8
Blackberry Way BA3 . . . . 132 F3
Blackbird Cl BA3 . . . . 139 B8
Blackcurrant Dr BS41 . . . 77 F8
Blackdown Cl BS14 . . . . . 80 B5
Blackdown Ct BS14 . . . . . 80 B5
Blackfriars BS1 . . . . 143 A3
Blackfriars Rd BS48 . . . . 59 B1
BLACKHORSE 52 A7
Blackhorse Cl BS16 . . . . . 52 A8
Blackhorse Ct BS15 . . . . . 65 C8
Blackhorse Hill BS35,
  BS10 . . . . 35 B8
Blackhorse La BS16 . . . . . 52 A8
Blackhorse Pl BS16 . . . . . 52 A6
Blackhorse Prim Sch
  BS16 . . . . 52 A8
Blackhorse Rd
  Bristol, Kingswood
   BS15 . . . . 65 C8
  Bristol, Mangotsfield
   BS16 . . . . 52 A7
Black La BS26 . . . . 125 E2
BLACKMOOR 95 C3
Blackmoor BS21 . . . . 57 E1
BLACKMOOR 109 D6
Blackmoor
  Lower Langford BS40 . . . 109 C6
  [3] Weston-S-M BS22 . . . 88 F2
Blackmoor Cl BS40 . . . . . 109 C6
Blackmoor Rd BS8 . . . . . 47 E2
Blackmoors La BS3 . . . . . 62 E4
Blackmore Dr BA2 . . . . . 101 C5
Black Nore Point BS20 . . 44 F1
BLACKROCK 97 E8
Blackrock La BS39 . . . . . 97 E7
Black Rock Nature Trail*
  BA5 . . . . 127 A1
Blackrock Villas BS20 . . . 45 B1
Blacksmith La BA1 . . . . . 85 B6
Blacksmith's La BA1 . . . . 83 B3
Blackswarth Ho [4]
  BS5 . . . . 64 D7
Blackswarth Rd BS5 . . . . 64 D7
Blackthorn Cl BS13 . . . . . 79 D5
Blackthorn Dr
  Portishead BS20 . . . . 45 E5
Blackthorn Gdns BS22 . . 89 A1
Blackthorn Rd BS13 . . . . 79 D5
Blackthorn Sq BS21 . . . . 57 F1
Blackthorn Terr BS22 . . . 89 A1
Blackthorn Way BS48 . . . 60 A2
Blackthorn Wlk BS15 . . . 51 E2
Bladen Cl [4] BS20 . . . . . . 45 E4
Bladud Bldgs BA1 . . . . . . 141 C3
BLAGDON 110 E1
Blagdon Cl
  Bristol BS3 . . . . 63 E2
  Weston-S-M BS24 . . . . . 104 F1
Blagdon La BS40 . . . . 110 F6
Blagdon Pk BA2 . . . . 101 A4
Blagdon Prim Sch
  BS40 . . . . 110 E2

Blagrove Cl BS13..........79 C3
Blagrove Cres BS13.......79 C3
Blaisdon
　Weston-S-M BS22.......105 D7
　Yate BS37................39 E7
Blaisdon CI BS10..........35 A1
Blaise Castle Mus *
　BS10....................34 E2
Blaisedell View BS10.......34 D3
Blaise Hamlet BS11........34 D2
Blaise Prim Sch BS10......34 F2
Blaise Wlk BS9............48 C6
Blakeney Gr BS34..........75 C8
Blakeney Mills BS37........27 E1
Blakeney Rd
　Bristol BS34..............23 E1
　Bristol, Horfield BS7......50 A7
Blake Rd BS7..............50 B6
Blakes Rd BS5..............8 B1
Blanchards BS37...........40 D8
Blanchards Cotts BS37.....40 D8
Blandford Cl
　2 Bristol BS9...........49 B6
　Nailsea BS48.............59 E1
Blandmour Way BS10.......35 D2
Blands Row BS35...........12 B1
BLEADON..................122 C7
Bleadon Hill BS23,
　BS24....................122 A8
Bleadon Mill BS24.........122 C5
Bleadon Rd BS24..........122 B7
Blenheim Cl
　Peasedown St John
　BA2.....................134 D7
　Weston-S-M BS22.........89 A2
Blenheim Ct
　10 Bristol, Kingsdown
　BS1.....................143 A4
　Bristol, Patchway BS32...24 D3
Blenheim Dr
　Bristol BS34..............36 B4
　Yate BS37................27 D3
Blenheim Gdns BA1........85 A2
Blenheim Rd BS6...........49 B3
Blenheim St BS5...........50 A1
Blenheim Way BS20.........45 E5
Blenman Cl BS16...........51 A7
Blethwin Cl BS10...........34 F1
Blind La
　Bath BA1.................84 C2
　Chew Stoke BS40.........112 E8
　Congresbury BS49.........91 F6
　Tunley BA2...............117 A4
Blind La BS37.............101 E3
Bloomfield BS39...........132 A6
BLOOMFIELD...............116 B4
Bloomfield BS24...........105 A2
Bloomfield Ave
　Bath BA2.................101 E4
　Timsbury BA2............116 B3
Bloomfield Cl BA2.........116 B3
Bloomfield Cotts BA2......134 C7
Bloomfield Cres BA2.......101 D2
Bloomfield Dr BA2.........101 D2
Bloomfield Gr BA2.........101 E3
Bloomfield La BS39........132 E5
Bloomfield Park Rd
　BA2.....................116 B3
Bloomfield Pk BA2.........101 E3
Bloomfield Rd
　Bath BA2.................101 E4
　Bristol BS4...............64 D4
　Timsbury BA2............116 B3
Bloomfield Rise BA2.......101 D2
Bloomfield Rise N
　BA2.....................101 D2
Bloomfield Road Link
　BS4.....................64 C4
Bloomfield Terr BA2.......134 C7
Bloy St BS5...............50 C1
Bluebell Cl
　Bristol BS9..............48 B6
　Thornbury BS35...........8 D2
Bluebell Rd BS22..........89 A6
Bluebell Rise BA3.........132 F3
Bluebells The BS32........36 E7
Blueberry Way BS22........88 F1
Blue Falcon Rd BS15.......51 E1
Blue Water Dr BS4........106 D3
Blythe Gdns BS22..........89 A3
Boat La BS24..............122 C3
Boat Stall La BA2.........141 C2
Bobbin La BA15...........120 F4
Bobbin Pk BA15...........120 F3
Bockenem Cl BS35.........15 D7
Bodey Cl BS30.............66 A5
Bodley Way BS24..........105 E2
Bodmin Wlk BS4...........79 F8
Bodyce Rd **4** BS35.......15 A5
Boiling Wells La BS2.......50 A3
Bolton Rd BS7.............49 E3
Bond's La SN14............69 E8
Bond St BS1..............143 B4
Bonhill Rd BS39..........113 D5
Bonnington Wlk BS7........50 B7
Bonville Bsns Ctr BS4......64 F2
Bonville Rd BS4...........64 F2
Boon Villas BS11...........47 E7
Booth Rd BS3..............63 C4
Boot La BS3...............63 D4
Bordesley Rd BS14.........80 A3
Boreal Way **4** BS24......105 F7
Borgie Pl BS22.............88 F3
Borleyton Wlk BS13........78 F4

Britannia Rd *continued*
Bristol, Lower Easton BS5 . . . 50 C1
Bristol, Patchway BS34 . . . 35 E7
Britannia Way BS21 . . . 57 E1
British Empire & Commonwealth Mus The* BS1 . . . 143 C1
British Rd BS3 . . . 63 C3
British The BS37 . . . 27 B4
Brittan Pl BS20 . . . 46 E3
Britten Ct 10 BS30 . . . 65 F4
BRITTENS . . . 132 F6
Brittens BS39 . . . 132 F6
Britten's Cl BS39 . . . 132 F6
Britten's Hill BS39 . . . 132 F6
Britton Bottom GL9 . . . 20 B1
Britton Gdns BS15 . . . 51 C1
Britton Ho BS15 . . . 66 B8
Brittons Pass SN14 . . . 69 F8
Brixham Rd BS3 . . . 63 C1
Brixton Rd BS5 . . . 64 B8
Brixton Road Mews 22 BS5 . . . 64 B8
Broadbury Rd BS4 . . . 79 E8
Broadcroft BS40 . . . 95 F3
Broad Croft BS32 . . . 24 C2
Broadcroft Ave BS49 . . . 74 F1
Broadcroft Cl BS49 . . . 74 F1
Broadfield Ave BS15 . . . 51 C1
Broadfield Ct BS15 . . . 65 C8
Broadfield Rd
Bristol BS4 . . . 64 B1
Bristol BS4 . . . 80 A8
Broad La
Henfield BS36 . . . 38 D5
Westerleigh BS37 . . . 39 A4
Yate BS37 . . . 27 C4
Broadlands BS21 . . . 57 H3
Broadlands Ave BS31 . . . 81 D6
Broadlands Dr BS11 . . . 34 A1
Broadlands Sch BS31 . . . 81 D6
Broadleas BS13 . . . 79 C7
Broadleaze BS11 . . . 47 E7
Broadleaze Way BS25 . . . 107 F2
Broadleys Ave BS9 . . . 49 C7
Broadmead
Bristol BS1 . . . 143 B3
Keynsham BS31 . . . 82 B5
Broadmead La BS31 . . . 82 A6
Broad Mead La BS40 . . . 95 A3
Broadmead Lane Ind Est BS31 . . . 82 B7
Broadmoor La BA1 . . . 84 A3
Broadmoor Pk BA1 . . . 84 B2
Broadmoor Vale BA1 . . . 84 A3
Broadoak Hill BS41 . . . 78 F2
Broadoak Mathematics & Computing Coll BS23 . . . 104 E3
Broadoak Rd
Churchill BS40 . . . 109 A5
Weston-S-M BS23 . . . 104 D3
Broad Oak Rd BS13 . . . 78 F4
Broad Oaks BS8 . . . 62 E6
Broadoak Wlk BS16 . . . 51 B4
Broad Plain BS2 . . . 143 C2
Broad Quay
Bath BA1 . . . 141 C1
Bristol BS1 . . . 143 A2
Broad Rd
Blagdon BS40 . . . 127 D8
Bristol BS15 . . . 51 C1
Broad St
Bath BA1 . . . 141 C3
Bristol BS1 . . . 143 A3
Bristol, Staple Hill BS16 . . . 51 F4
Chipping Sodbury BS37 . . . 28 B1
Congresbury BS49 . . . 91 D4
Wrington BS40 . . . 92 D2
Broadstone La BS21 . . . 72 F3
Broadstones BA15 . . . 103 E7
Broadstone Wlk BS13 . . . 79 D5
Broad Street Pl BA1 . . . 141 C3
Broadwalk Sh Ctr BS4 . . . 64 B2
Broadway
Bath BA2 . . . 102 B6
Chilcompton BA3 . . . 138 C3
Locking BS24 . . . 106 D4
Saltford BS31 . . . 82 D3
Shipham BS25 . . . 125 E8
Weston-S-M BS24 . . . 105 A2
Yate BS37 . . . 27 F2
Broadway Acres BS27 . . . 125 F1
Broadway Ave BS9 . . . 49 D6
Broadway Cl BA3 . . . 138 C3
Broadway Inf Sch BS37 . . . 27 F2
Broadway La BA3 . . . 133 B5
Broadway Rd
Bristol, Bishopston BS7 . . . 49 D3
Bristol, Bishopsworth BS13 . . . 78 F5
Broadways Dr BS16 . . . 50 F7
Broadway The GL11 . . . 5 F8
Broad Weir BS1 . . . 143 B3
Broad Wlk BS4 . . . 64 A2
Brock End BS20 . . . 44 F3
Brockeridge Inf Sch BS36 . . . 38 C7
Brockhurst Gdns BS15 . . . 65 A8
Brockhurst Rd BS15 . . . 65 A8
BROCKLEY . . . 75 C2
Brockley Cl
Bristol BS34 . . . 36 C7
Nailsea BS48 . . . 59 D1
Weston-S-M BS24 . . . 104 F1
Brockley Combe Rd BS48 . . . 76 B1
Brockley Cres BS24 . . . 104 F1
Brockley La BS48 . . . 75 D4
Brockley Mini Farm (Open Farm)* BS48 . . . 92 F7
Brockley Rd BS31 . . . 82 D3
Brockley Way BS49 . . . 75 B3
Brockley Wlk BS13 . . . 79 A8
Brockridge La BS36 . . . 38 C7
Brocks 4 BS4 . . . 64 D1
Brocks La BS41 . . . 61 F1
Brocks Rd BS13 . . . 79 C3
Brock St BA1 . . . 141 B3
Brockway BS48 . . . 59 F2
Brockwood BA15 . . . 120 F7
Brockworth BS37 . . . 39 C6
Brockworth Cres BS16 . . . 50 F6
Bromfield Wlk BS16 . . . 52 B7
Bromley Dr BS16 . . . 51 D8
Bromley Farm BS16 . . . 37 D1
BROMLEY HEATH . . . 37 D1
Bromley Heath Ave BS16 . . . 51 D8
Bromley Heath Jun & Inf Schs BS16 . . . 51 E8
Bromley Heath Rd BS16 . . . 51 D8
Bromley Heath Rdbt BS16 . . . 37 D1
Bromley Rd
Bristol BS7 . . . 49 F5
Stanton Drew BS39 . . . 96 F1
Brompton Cl BS15 . . . 66 A8
Brompton Ho BA2 . . . 141 C4
Brompton Rd BS24 . . . 105 A2
Broncksea Rd BS7 . . . 35 F1
Bronte Cl BS23 . . . 105 B4
Bronte Wlk BS7 . . . 50 A8
Brook Cl BS41 . . . 62 B1
Brookcote Dr BS34 . . . 36 D6
Brook Cotts BA2 . . . 100 B7
Brook Ct BS13 . . . 79 A6
Brookdale Rd BS13 . . . 79 B6
Brook End SN14 . . . 31 F5
Brookfield Ave BS7 . . . 49 D3
Brookfield Cl BS37 . . . 28 C2
Brookfield La 2 BS6 . . . 49 D2
Brookfield Pk BA1 . . . 84 B2
Brookfield Rd
3 Bristol, Montpelier BS6 . . . 49 D2
Bristol, Patchway BS34 . . . 36 B8
Brookfield Wlk
Bristol BS30 . . . 66 C3
Clevedon BS21 . . . 57 H3
Brook Gate BS3 . . . 62 E1
Brook Hill BS6 . . . 49 F1
Brook Ho
Bristol BS34 . . . 36 C8
3 Thornbury BS35 . . . 15 C8
Brook La
Bristol, Montpelier BS6 . . . 49 F1
Bristol, Stapleton BS16 . . . 50 E6
Brookland Rd
Bristol BS6 . . . 49 D5
Weston-S-M BS22 . . . 105 B7
Brooklands BA2 . . . 117 D3
Brooklea BS30 . . . 66 B3
Brookleaze BS9 . . . 48 C5
Brookleaze Bldgs BA1 . . . 85 B2
Brook Lintons BS4 . . . 64 D3
Brooklyn BS40 . . . 92 D2
Brooklyn Rd
Bath BA1 . . . 85 C2
Bristol BS13 . . . 79 B8
Brookmead BS35 . . . 15 D7
Brook Office Pk BS16 . . . 38 B2
Brook Rd
Bath BA2 . . . 101 D6
Bristol, Hillfields BS16 . . . 51 B4
Bristol, Mangotsfield BS16 . . . 51 F6
Bristol, Montpelier BS6 . . . 49 F1
Bristol, Southville BS3 . . . 63 D4
Bristol, Speedwell BS5 . . . 50 F1
Bristol, Warmley BS15 . . . 66 B8
Brookridge Ct 6 BS16 . . . 51 D4
Brookridge Ho BS10 . . . 34 F3
Brookside
Paulton BS39 . . . 132 E6
Pill BS20 . . . 47 D3
Winford BS40 . . . 94 F7
Brookside Cl
Batheaston BA1 . . . 85 F5
Paulton BS39 . . . 132 E6
Brookside Dr
Farmborough BA2 . . . 115 F6
Frampton Cotterell BS36 . . . 38 B8
Brookside Ho BA1 . . . 84 B1
Brookside Rd BS4 . . . 64 E2
Brook St BS5 . . . 64 C7
Brookthorpe BS37 . . . 39 D8
Brookthorpe Ave BS11 . . . 34 A1
Brookthorpe Ct BS37 . . . 39 D8
Brookview Wlk BS13 . . . 79 B7
Brook Way BS32 . . . 36 D8
Broom Farm Cl BS48 . . . 75 E8
Broomground BA15 . . . 120 E7
BROOMHILL . . . 50 E6
BROOM HILL . . . 64 F3
Broom Hill BS16 . . . 50 E5
Broomhill Inf Sch BS4 . . . 64 F3
Broomhill Jun Sch BS4 . . . 64 F3
Broomhill La BS39 . . . 114 E3
Broom Hill La BS39 . . . 132 E8
Broomhill Rd BS4 . . . 65 A2
Brooms The BS16 . . . 38 A1
Brotherswood Ct BS32 . . . 24 D4
Brougham Hayes BA2 . . . 101 D6
Brougham Pl 2 BA1 . . . 85 C2
Broughton Ho BS1 . . . 143 B1
Brow Hill BA2 . . . 85 F4
Browne Ct 4 BS8 . . . 62 F6
Browning Ct BS7 . . . 50 B8
Brownlow Rd BS23 . . . 104 E4
Browns Ct BS23 . . . 104 E6
Brown's Folly Nature Reserve BA15 . . . 86 D1
Brow The
Bath BA2 . . . 101 B5
Bath, Combe Down BA2 . . . 102 C1
Broxholme Wlk BS11 . . . 47 F8
Bruce Ave BS5 . . . 50 C1
Bruce Rd BS5 . . . 50 C1
Brue Cl BS23 . . . 105 A5
Brummel Way BS39 . . . 132 C6
Brunel Cl
Bristol BS30 . . . 66 C7
Weston-S-M BS24 . . . 104 F1
Brunel Ct
Portishead BS20 . . . 45 D6
Yate BS37 . . . 27 C2
Brunel Ho BA2 . . . 101 A6
Brunel Lock Rd BS1 . . . 62 F5
Brunel Rd
Bristol BS13 . . . 79 A8
Nailsea BS48 . . . 59 B1
Brunel Way
Bristol BS1, BS3 . . . 62 F4
Thornbury BS35 . . . 15 B7
Brunswick Pl
1 Bath BA1 . . . 141 B3
10 Bristol BS1 . . . 62 F5
Brunswick Sq BS2 . . . 143 B4
Brunswick St
1 Bath BA1 . . . 85 B1
Bristol BS2 . . . 143 B4
Bristol, Redfield BS5 . . . 64 C7
Bruton BS24 . . . 105 A2
Bruton Ave
Bath BA2 . . . 101 F4
Portishead BS20 . . . 45 A5
Bruton Avenue Garages BA2 . . . 101 F4
Bruton Cl
Bristol BS5 . . . 64 F8
Nailsea BS48 . . . 75 E8
Bruton La GL12 . . . 11 F5
Bruton Pl BS8 . . . 142 B3
Bryansons Cl BS16 . . . 50 D6
Bryant Ave BA3 . . . 133 D1
Bryant Gdns BS21 . . . 57 E1
Bryants Cl BS16 . . . 37 C1
Bryant's Hill BS5 . . . 65 B6
Brynland Ave BS7 . . . 49 E4
Brynland Ct BS7 . . . 49 E5
Buckingham Ct BS32 . . . 24 D3
Buckingham Dr BS34 . . . 36 D5
Buckingham Gdns BS16 . . . 51 E6
Buckingham Ho BS34 . . . 35 F2
Buckingham Lo 1 BS31 . . . 81 F6
Buckingham Par 11 BS35 . . . 8 B1
Buckingham Pl
Bristol BS8 . . . 142 A3
Bristol, Mangotsfield BS16 . . . 51 E6
Buckingham Rd
Bristol BS4 . . . 64 D5
Weston-S-M BS24 . . . 105 B2
Buckingham St BS3 . . . 63 C2
Buckingham Vale BS8 . . . 142 A4
Buckland Gn BS22 . . . 89 A5
Bucklands Batch BS48 . . . 75 F8
Bucklands Dr BS48 . . . 76 A8
Bucklands End BS48 . . . 75 F8
Bucklands Gr BS48 . . . 75 F8
Bucklands La BS48 . . . 75 F8
Bucklands View BS48 . . . 76 A8
Bucklewell Cl BS11 . . . 47 F6
BUCKOVER . . . 9 B1
Bude Ave BS5 . . . 65 A8
Bude Cl BS48 . . . 60 B1
Bude Rd BS34 . . . 36 B4
Building of Bath Mus* BA1 . . . 141 C3
Bullens Cl BS32 . . . 24 D2
Buller Rd BS4 . . . 64 C2
Bull La
Bristol BS5 . . . 64 F6
Pill BS20 . . . 47 C4
Bullocks La BS21 . . . 73 C4
Bull's Hill BA2 . . . 118 E1
Bully La BS37 . . . 17 D1
Bumper's Batch BA2 . . . 119 A8
Bungalows The BS26 . . . 125 C2
Bungay's Hill BA2, BS39 . . . 115 E1
Bunting Ct BS22 . . . 88 E1
Burbank Cl BS30 . . . 66 A3
Burchells Ave BS15 . . . 51 B1
BURCHELLS GREEN . . . 51 B1
Burchells Green Cl BS15 . . . 51 B1
Burchells Green Rd BS15 . . . 51 B1
Burchill Cl BS39 . . . 114 F3
Burcombe Cl BS36 . . . 38 D6
Burcott Rd BS11 . . . 33 D5
Burden Cl BS32 . . . 36 F6
Burfoote Gdns BS14 . . . 80 E4
Burfoot Rd BS14 . . . 80 E4
Burford Ave BS34 . . . 36 C8
Burford Cl
Bath BA2 . . . 101 B3
Portishead BS20 . . . 45 E4
Burford Gr BS11 . . . 47 F5
Burgage Cl BS37 . . . 40 B8
Burgess Green Cl BS4 . . . 64 E7
Burghill Rd BS10 . . . 35 A1
Burghley Ct BS36 . . . 37 E5
Burghley Rd BS6 . . . 49 E2
Burgis Rd BS14 . . . 80 D6
Burleigh Gdns BA1 . . . 101 A8
Burleigh Way GL12 . . . 18 B5
Burley Ave BS16 . . . 51 F5
Burley Crest BS16 . . . 51 F5
Burley Gr BS16 . . . 51 F5
Burlington Ct
9 Bristol BS6 . . . 49 B2
Portishead BS20 . . . 45 E6
Burlington Rd
Bristol BS6 . . . 49 B2
Midsomer Norton BA3 . . . 133 C2
Portishead BS20 . . . 45 E7
Burlington St
Bath BA1 . . . 141 B4
15 Weston-S-M BS23 . . . 104 E8
Burltons The GL12 . . . 10 B2
Burnbush Cl BS14 . . . 80 E6
Burnbush Prim Sch BS14 . . . 80 D5
Burnell Dr BS2 . . . 143 C4
Burneside Cl BS10 . . . 35 C2
BURNETT . . . 99 B7
Burnett Bsns Pk BS31 . . . 82 B1
Burnett Hill BS31 . . . 99 B8
Burnett Ind Est BS40 . . . 92 E1
Burney Way BS30 . . . 66 A3
Burnham Cl
Bristol BS15 . . . 51 F1
Weston-S-M BS24 . . . 104 F1
Burnham Dr
Bristol BS15 . . . 51 F1
Weston-S-M BS24 . . . 104 F1
Burnham Rd
Bath BA2 . . . 101 C6
Bristol BS11 . . . 47 D6
Burnt House Cotts BA2 . . . 118 C8
Burnt House Rd BA2 . . . 118 D8
BURRINGTON . . . 109 F3
Burrington Ave BS24 . . . 104 F1
Burrington CE Prim Sch BS40 . . . 109 F3
Burrington Cl
Nailsea BS48 . . . 59 E1
Weston-S-M BS24 . . . 104 F1
Burrington Combe BS40 . . . 127 C8
Burrington Coombe* BS40 . . . 110 A1
Burrington La BS40 . . . 110 A3
Burrington Wlk BS13 . . . 79 A8
Burrough Way BS36 . . . 37 E6
Burrows La BA3 . . . 139 B1
Burrows The BS22 . . . 89 D3
BURTON . . . 43 B3
Burton Cl BS1 . . . 143 B1
Burton Ct
Bristol BS8 . . . 142 B3
2 Bristol, Upper Eastville BS16 . . . 50 E3
Burton Farm Cl SN14 . . . 43 B3
Burton Rd GL9 . . . 42 F6
Burton St 5 BA1 . . . 141 B2
Burwalls Rd BS8 . . . 62 E6
Burycourt Cl BS11 . . . 34 A1
Bury Hill BS36 . . . 37 F3
Bury Hill La BS37 . . . 28 A8
Bury Hill View BS16 . . . 37 E1
Bury La BS30 . . . 67 F7
Bury The BS24 . . . 106 A3
Bury View BA2 . . . 99 C5
Bushacre Bsns Pk BS22 . . . 105 C8
Bush Ave BS34 . . . 36 D5
Bush Ct
Alveston BS32 . . . 14 F5
10 Bristol BS2 . . . 63 F4
Bushes La BS37 . . . 29 A6
BUSHEY NORWOOD . . . 102 F6
Bush Ind Est BS5 . . . 64 D8
Bushy Combe BA3 . . . 132 F3
Bushy Ho BS2 . . . 63 F3
Bushy Pk BS2 . . . 63 F3
Bushy Thorn Rd BS40 . . . 112 E8
Business Pk The BS13 . . . 79 E3
BUTCOMBE . . . 111 B8
Butcombe BS24 . . . 105 A2
Butcombe La BS40 . . . 111 B7
Butcombe Wlk BS14 . . . 80 B5
Butham La
Chew Magna BS40 . . . 96 B3
Chew Magna BS40 . . . 96 B4
Buthay La GL12 . . . 18 A5
Buthay The GL12 . . . 18 A5
Butlass Cl BS39 . . . 115 D1
Butler Ho BS5 . . . 64 F8
Butlers Cl BS5 . . . 64 F7
Butlers Wlk 3 BS5 . . . 64 F6
Buttercliffe Rise BS41 . . . 62 C3
Butterfield Cl
Bristol BS10 . . . 49 E7
Frampton Cotterell BS36 . . . 38 B6
Butterfield Pk BS21 . . . 57 E1
Butterfield Rd BS10 . . . 49 E7
Buttermere Rd BS23 . . . 105 A5
Butterworth Ct BS4 . . . 79 D7
Butt La BS35 . . . 8 C3
Button Cl BS14 . . . 80 A6
Butts Batch BS26 . . . 124 B3
BUTT'S BATCH . . . 92 D1
Butt's Batch BS40 . . . 92 D1
Butt's La SN14 . . . 55 B4
Butts Orch BS40 . . . 92 D1
Buxton Wlk BS7 . . . 50 A8
BW Ests BS24 . . . 105 A3
Bye Mead BS16 . . . 52 B8
Byfield BA2 . . . 102 B1
Byfield Pl BA2 . . . 102 B1
Byfields BS21 . . . 73 C8
Byron Cl BS24 . . . 106 A4
Byron Ct BS23 . . . 104 F8
Byron Pl
Bristol BS8 . . . 142 B3
Bristol, Staple Hill BS16 . . . 51 E4
Byron Rd
Bath BA2 . . . 101 F4
Locking BS24 . . . 106 A4
Weston-S-M BS23 . . . 105 A4
Byron St
Bristol, Moorfields BS5 . . . 64 C7
5 Bristol, St Pauls BS2 . . . 50 A1
Byways Cvn Pk BS21 . . . 57 E1
Byzantine Ct BS1 . . . 143 A1

C

Cabot Cl
Bristol BS15 . . . 65 C7
Saltford BS31 . . . 82 D2
Yate BS37 . . . 27 F1
Cabot Ct BS7 . . . 35 F1
Cabot Gn BS5 . . . 64 B7
Cabot Ho 6 BS35 . . . 15 C8
Cabot Pk BS11 . . . 33 D6
Cabot Prim Sch BS2 . . . 143 C4
Cabot Rise BS20 . . . 45 A5
Cabot Twr* BS8 . . . 142 B2
Cabot Way
Bristol BS8 . . . 62 F5
Pill BS20 . . . 47 D3
Weston-S-M BS22 . . . 89 A3
Cabstand BS20 . . . 45 D6
Cadbury Camp La BS20 . . . 59 D6
Cadbury Camp La W BS21 . . . 58 C5
Cadbury Farm Rd BS49 . . . 91 C7
Cadbury Gdns BS30 . . . 66 B6
Cadbury Halt BS20 . . . 44 F1
CADBURY HEATH . . . 66 B5
Cadbury Heath Prim Sch BS30 . . . 66 B6
Cadbury Heath Rd BS30 . . . 66 B5
Cadbury Ho 5 BS20 . . . 45 E4
Cadbury La BS20 . . . 44 F1
Cadbury Rd
Keynsham BS31 . . . 82 A2
Portishead BS20 . . . 45 E4
Cadbury Sq BS49 . . . 91 E3
Cadby Ho BA2 . . . 101 A6
Caddick Cl BS15 . . . 51 F2
Cade Cl
Bristol, Kingswood BS15 . . . 65 F6
Bristol, Stoke Gifford BS34 . . . 36 E5
Cadmium Rd BS11 . . . 33 C4
Cadogan Gr BS48 . . . 76 B6
Cadogan Rd BS14 . . . 80 A8
Caen Rd BS3 . . . 63 D3
Caernarvon Rd BS31 . . . 81 C4
Caern Well Pl BA1 . . . 141 C4
Caine Rd BS7 . . . 49 F7
Cains Cl BS15 . . . 65 E6
Cairn Cl BS48 . . . 60 A1
Cairn Gdns BS36 . . . 37 E4
Cairns' Cres 12 BS2 . . . 49 F1
Cairns Ct BS6 . . . 49 C4
Cairns Rd BS6 . . . 49 C4
Cairo Ct 18 BS23 . . . 87 C1
Caitlin Ct BS14 . . . 80 D6
Cala Trad Est BS3 . . . 62 F3
Calcott Rd BS4 . . . 64 A3
Caldbeck Cl BS10 . . . 35 D2
Calder Cl BS31 . . . 82 A4
Caldicot Cl
Bristol, Lawrence Weston BS11 . . . 34 C2
Bristol, Willsbridge BS30 . . . 66 B2
Caledonia Mews BS8 . . . 62 F6
Caledonian Rd
Bath BA2 . . . 101 D6
Bristol BS1 . . . 142 B1
Caledonia Pl BS8 . . . 62 F7
California Rd BS30 . . . 66 B3
Callicroft Prim Sch BS10 . . . 35 F8
Callicroft Rd BS34 . . . 36 A7
Callington Rd BS4 . . . 64 D1
Callowhill Ct BS1 . . . 143 B3
Calluna Cl BS22 . . . 89 A5
Calton Gdns BA2 . . . 141 C1
Calton Rd BA2 . . . 141 C1
Calton Wlk BA2 . . . 141 B1
Camberley Dr BS36 . . . 37 F8
Camberley Rd BS4 . . . 79 D8
Camberley Wlk BS22 . . . 105 E8

Camborne Rd BS7 50 A7
Cambrian Dr BS37 27 E3
CAMBRIDGE BATCH 77 C8
Cambridge Cres BS9 49 A7
Cambridge Ct BS40 92 D2
Cambridge Gr BS21 57 F5
Cambridge Pk BS6 49 B3
Cambridge Pl
Bath BA2 102 B5
Weston-S-M BS23 104 D8
Cambridge Rd
Bristol BS7 49 E4
Clevedon BS21 57 F5
Cambridge St
[8] Bristol, Redfield BS5 64 C7
Bristol, Windmill Hill BS3 63 F4
Cambridge Terr BA2 102 B5
Cam Brook Cl BA2 133 D8
Cambrook Ho BS39 131 F8
Camden Cres BA1 141 B4
Camden Ct BA1 141 B4
Camden Rd
Bath BA1 85 A1
Bristol BS3 142 B1
Camden Row BA1 141 B4
Camden Terr
Bath BA1 141 C4
Bristol BS8 142 A2
Weston-S-M BS23 104 E7
CAMELEY 131 C8
Cameley CE Prim Sch BS39 114 E1
Cameley Cl BS39 131 E8
Cameley Gn BA2 100 F6
Cameley La BS39 130 F7
Cameley Rd BS39 131 C8
Camelford Rd BS5 50 D1
Cameron Wlk BS7 50 C6
Cameroons Cl BS31 81 E4
CAMERTON 133 E8
Camerton CE Prim Sch BA2 133 E8
Camerton Cl BS31 82 E3
Camerton Hill BA2 133 E8
Camerton Rd
Bristol BS5 50 D1
Timsbury BA2 116 E1
Camomile Wlk BS20 45 F5
Campbell Ct BS11 33 F1
Campbell Farm BS11 33 F1
Campbell Farm Dr BS11 33 F1
Campbell St BS2 49 E1
Campian Wlk BS4 79 D6
Campion Cl
Thornbury BS35 8 D2
[4] Weston-S-M BS22 105 D7
Campion Dr BS32 24 D2
Camp La SN14 55 C4
Camplins BS21 57 E1
Camp Rd
Bristol BS8 62 F7
Oldbury-on-S BS35 7 B6
Weston-S-M BS23 87 C1
Camp Rd N BS23 87 B1
Camp View
Nailsea BS48 59 D2
Winterbourne BS36 37 E4
Camvale BA2 134 B8
Camview BS39 132 D6
Camwal Ind Est BS2 64 A5
Camwal Rd BS2 64 A5
Canada Coombe BS24 106 A1
Canada Way BS1 142 B1
Canal Terr BA2 85 F1
Canal View BA2 133 E8
Canberra Cres BS24 106 B6
Canberra Gr BS34 36 B4
Canberra Rd BS23 104 F3
Candy Ct BS4 64 D5
Canford La BS9 48 E8
Canford Rd BS9 48 F8
Cannans Cl BS36 37 E7
Cann La BS30 66 E6
Cannons Gate BS21 73 C8
CANNON'S MARSH 142 C1
Cannon St
Bristol BS1 143 A4
Bristol, Southville BS3 63 C4
Canons Cl BA2 101 B2
Canons Rd BS1 142 C2
Canon's Rd BS1 142 C1
Canon St BS5 64 C8
Canons Way BS1 142 C1
Canons Wlk BS22 88 D2
Canon's Wlk BS15 51 F2
Canowie Rd BS6 49 B3
Cantell Gr BS14 80 F5
Canterbury Cl
Weston-S-M BS22 89 B3
Yate BS37 27 E3
Canterbury Ct BS16 50 E6
Canterbury Rd BA2 101 D5
Canterbury St [5] BS5 64 B6
Canters Leaze GL12 18 B4
Cantock's Cl BS8 142 C3
Canvey Cl BS10 49 E7
Canynge Ho [2] BS1 143 B1
Canynge Rd BS8 62 F8
Canynge Sq BS8 62 F8
Canynge St BS1 143 B2
Capel Cl BS15 66 B8
Capell Cl BS22 105 B8
Capel Rd BS11 34 B1
Capenor Cl BS20 45 C4
Capgrave Cl BS4 65 A3
Capgrave Cres BS4 65 A3
Capital Edge BS8 142 B1
Caple La BS40 112 B5
Cappards Rd BS39 113 D4
Capricorn Pl BS8 142 B2
Capri Villas BS23 87 C2
Caraway Gdns BS5 50 C2
Carberry View BS24 106 A8
Cardigan Cres BS22 105 C8
Cardigan Mews BS9 49 B5
Cardigan Rd BS9 49 B6
Cardill Cl BS13 79 A8
Cardinal Cl BA2 118 D8
Carditch Dro BS49 108 B8
Carey Developments [1] BS21 57 E1
Carey's Cl BS21 57 H4
Careys Way BS24 105 E7
Carfax Ct BS6 49 A3
Carice Gdns BS21 73 D8
Carisbrooke Lo BS6 49 A3
Carisbrooke Rd BS4 79 D7
CARLINGCOTT 117 B1
Carlingford Terr BA3 134 A2
Carlingford Terrace Rd BA3 134 A2
Carlow Rd BS4 79 E8
Carlton Cl BS39 114 F3
Carlton Ct
[1] Bristol, Ashley Down BS7 49 F4
[3] Bristol, Eastfield BS9 49 A7
Carlton Ho [2] BS9 49 A7
Carlton Mans BS23 104 D7
Carlton Pk BS5 64 C8
Carlton St BS23 104 D7
Carlyle Rd BS5 50 C1
Carmarthen Cl BS37 27 F4
Carmarthen Gr BS30 66 B1
Carmarthen Rd BS9 49 A5
Carnarvon Rd BS6 49 D2
Carolina Ho BS2 143 A4
Caroline Bldgs BA2 102 B5
Caroline Cl
Chipping Sodbury BS37 28 B2
Keynsham BS31 81 C4
Caroline Pl BA1 141 B4
Carousel La BS24 105 E7
Carpenter Cl BS23 105 A7
Carpenters La BS31 81 E5
Carpenter's Shop La BS16 51 E6
Carre Gdns BS22 88 F4
Carr Ho
Bath BA2 101 A6
[3] Bristol BS2 49 F1
Carriage Dr BS10 35 B2
Carrick Ho [8] BS8 62 F6
Carrington Rd BS3 63 A3
Carroll Ct BS16 36 E1
Carrs Cl BA2 101 A6
Carsons Rd BS16 52 B2
Carter Rd BS39 132 D5
Carters Bldgs [12] BS8 62 F7
Carters Way BA3 138 D3
Carter Wlk BS32 36 D8
Cartledge Rd [6] BS5 50 C1
Cary Ct [2] BS2 49 F1
Cashmore Ho [9] BS5 64 B7
Caslon Ct BS1 143 B1
Cassell Rd BS16 51 C5
Cassey Bottom La BS5 65 A7
Casson Dr BS16 50 E8
Castle Batch Com Prim Sch BS22 89 A5
Castle Cl
Bristol BS10 34 E2
Flax Bourton BS48 76 F7
Castle Coombe BS35 8 C1
Castle Cotts SN14 55 E2
Castle Ct
Bristol, Arno's Vale BS4 64 C4
Bristol BS34 37 A4
Thornbury BS35 8 B1
Castle Farm La BS41 78 B2
Castle Farm Rd BS15 65 C2
Castlegate Ho BS4 64 E3
Castle Gdns BA2 101 E3
Castle Hill BS29 107 C2
Castle La SN14 55 E2
Castlemead Sh Ctr BS22 89 A5
Castle Prim Sch BS31 81 D4
Castle Rd
Bristol, Kingswood BS15 51 D2
Bristol, Oldland Common BS30 66 D3
Clevedon BS21 57 G6
Pucklechurch BS16 53 C6
Weston-S-M BS22 88 E3
Castle Sch Sixth Form Ctr The BS35 8 B1
Castle Sch The BS35 8 B2
Castle St
Bristol BS1 143 B3
Thornbury BS35 8 B1
Castle View [2] BS24 105 F8
Castle View Rd BS21 57 F5
Castlewood Cl BS21 57 F4
Caswell Hill BS20 46 B1
Caswell La BS20 46 B2
CATBRAIN 35 B6
Catbrain Hill BS10 35 B6
Catbrain La BS10 35 B6
Catchpot La BS37 41 A6
Catemead BS21 73 C8
Cater Rd BS13 79 B6
Catharine Pl BA1 141 B3
Cathcart Ho [6] BA1 85 A1
Cathedral Church of The Holy & Undivided Trinity* BS1 142 C2
Cathedral Wlk BS1 142 C1
Catherine Ct [14] BS6 49 E1
Catherine Hill BS35 13 F2
Catherine Mead St BS3 63 D4
Catherine St BS11 47 C8
Catherine Way BA1 86 A5
Catley Gr BS41 62 B2
Cato St BS5 50 B2
Cattistock Dr BS5 65 A6
Cattle Market Rd BS1 143 C1
Cattybrook Rd BS16 52 D5
Cattybrook Rd N BS16 52 D6
Cattybrook St
[7] Bristol BS5 64 B7
[23] Bristol BS5 64 B8
Caulfield Rd BS22 89 B4
Causeway BS48 59 B3
Causeway The
Congresbury BS49 91 D4
Frampton Cotterell BS36 38 D7
Yatton BS49 91 C7
Causeway View BS48 59 C2
Causley Dr BS30 66 A5
Cautletts Cl BA3 138 F8
Cavan Wlk BS4 63 D1
Cave Cl BS16 51 D6
Cave Ct BS2 143 B4
Cave Dr BS16 51 D6
Cave Gr BS16 52 B7
Cavell Ct BS21 57 E1
Cavendish Cl
Saltford BS31 82 D2
Tormarton GL9 41 E2
Cavendish Cres BA1 141 A4
Cavendish Gdns BS9 48 C4
Cavendish Lo BA1 141 A4
Cavendish Pl BA1 141 A4
Cavendish Rd
Bath BA1 141 A4
Bristol, Henleaze BS9 49 A5
Bristol, Patchway BS34 35 F8
Caveners Ct BS22 88 B1
Caversham Dr BS48 60 A2
Caves Cotts BS16 51 E7
Cave St BS2 143 B4
Caxton Ct [4] BA2 141 C3
Cecil Ave BS5 50 F1
Cecil Rd
Bristol, Clifton BS8 62 F8
Bristol, Kingswood BS15 65 D8
Weston-S-M BS23 87 E1
Cedar Ave BS22 88 C1
Cedar Cl
Bristol, Oldland BS30 66 B4
Bristol, Patchway BS34 35 F7
Long Ashton BS41 61 F1
Cedar Ct
Bristol BS9 48 C4
Bristol, Combe Dingle BS9 48 D7
Bristol, Mangotsfield BS16 51 E6
Bristol, Westbury on T BS9 48 F8
Cedar Dr BS31 81 D4
Cedar Gr
Bath BA2 101 D3
Bristol BS9 48 D5
Cedar Hall BS16 51 C8
Cedarhurst Rd BS20 44 E4
Cedarn Ct BS22 88 B4
Cedar Pk BS9 48 D5
Cedar Row BS11 47 F6
Cedars The
Bristol BS9 48 D3
Chew Stoke BS40 112 D8
Cedars Way BS36 37 D5
Cedar Terr BA3 133 D1
Cedar Villas BA2 141 A1
Cedar Way
Bath BA2 141 A1
Nailsea BS48 60 A2
Portishead BS20 45 C4
Pucklechurch BS16 53 C5
Cedern Ave BS24 106 C3
Cedric Cl BA1 101 C7
Cedric Rd BA1 101 C8
Celandine Cl BS35 8 D2
Celestine Rd BS37 27 C3
Celia Terr BS4 64 F6
Celtic Way BS24 122 B7
Cemetery Rd BS4 64 A3
Cennick Ave BS15 51 E1
Centaurus Rd BS34 35 D7
Central Ave
Bristol BS15 65 C5
Severn Beach BS10 22 A3
Central Pk BS14 80 B7
Central Trad Est BS4 64 B4
Central Way
Bristol BS10 49 E8
Clevedon BS21 57 G1
Centre Dr BS29 106 E4
Centre Quay BS20 45 E7
Centre The
Keynsham BS31 81 F5
[10] Weston-S-M BS23 104 E7
Ceres Cl BS30 65 F2
Cerimon Gate BS34 36 E5
Cerney Gdns BS48 60 A2
Cerney La BS11 47 E5
Cesson Cl BS37 40 C8
Chadleigh Gr BS4 79 D7
Chaffinch Dr BA3 139 B8
Chaffins The BS21 57 G2
Chaingate La BS37 27 A6
Chakeshill Cl BS10 35 C3
Chakeshill Dr BS10 35 C4
Chalcombe Cl BS34 36 C8
Chalcroft Ho [2] BS3 63 A4
Chalcroft Wlk BS13 78 E4
Chalet The BS10 34 F3
Chalfield Cl BS31 82 A2
Chalfont Rd BS22 105 C8
Chalford Cl BS37 39 D8
Chalk Farm Cl BS39 97 A7
Chalks Rd BS5 64 D8
Chalks The BS40 96 B3
Challender Ave BS10 34 F2
Challoner Ct BS1 143 A1
Challow Dr BS22 88 B2
Champion Rd BS15 52 A2
Champneys Ave BS10 34 F3
Champs Sur Marne BS32 36 E8
Chancel Cl
Bristol BS9 48 D3
Nailsea BS48 59 D1
Chancellor's Pound BS40 93 D3
Chancery St BS5 64 B7
Chandag Inf Sch BS31 82 A4
Chandag Jun Sch BS31 82 A4
Chandag Rd BS31 82 A4
Chandler Cl BA1 84 B1
Chandos BS6 49 C2
Chandos Ct BS23 104 D6
Chandos Ho [7] BA1 141 B2
Chandos Rd
Bristol BS6 49 C1
Keynsham BS31 81 E7
Chandos Trad Est BS2 64 A5
Channel Ct BS22 88 B3
Channel Hts BS24 104 F1
Channell's Hill BS9 49 A8
Channel Rd BS21 57 G5
Channel View Cres BS20 45 B5
Channel View Rd BS20 45 B5
Channon's Hill BS16 50 F4
Chantry Cl BS48 59 C1
Chantry Ct BS1 142 C2
Chantry Dr BS22 89 A4
Chantry Gr BS11 34 C2
Chantry La BS16 37 F1
Chantry Mead Rd BA2 101 E3
Chantry Rd
Bristol BS8 49 B1
Thornbury BS35 8 B2
Chapei Way BS10 49 D8
Chapel Barton
[7] Bristol BS3 63 B2
High Littleton BS39 115 D1
Nailsea BS48 59 C2
Chapel Cl
Bristol BS15 66 B8
Chew Stoke BS40 112 E8
Farrington Gurney BS39 131 F4
Nailsea BS48 59 E2
Winford BS40 95 A6
Chapel Ct
[8] Bath BA1 141 B2
Bristol, Brentry BS10 35 D3
Bristol, St Philip's Marsh BS2 64 A5
Clandown BA3 133 E4
Clevedon BS21 57 F3
Chapel Field BA2 134 E8
Chapel Gdns BS10 35 A1
Chapel Green La BS6 49 B2
Chapel Hill
Backwell BS48 76 D7
Clevedon BS21 57 F3
Newport GL13 4 B7
Ubley BS40 111 C5
Wrington BS40 92 D3
Chapel La
Acton Turville GL9 43 A6
Bristol, Clay Hill BS5 50 E2
Bristol, Fishponds BS16 51 A4
Bristol, Frenchay BS16 51 C7
Bristol, Lawrence Weston BS11 34 C2
Bristol, Warmley BS15 66 B8
Chew Stoke BS40 112 D8
Chipping Sodbury BS37 41 A7
Claverham BS49 91 F8
Cleeve BS49 92 B7
Hillesley GL12 19 E8
Hinton SN14 54 C5
Thornbury BS35 9 A1
Winford BS40 95 A6
Chapel Lawns BA3 133 E4
Chapel Orch BS37 27 C2
Chapel Pill La BS20 47 E4
Chapel Rd
Bristol, Bishopsworth BS13 79 A6
Bristol, Hanham BS15 65 C5
[2] Bristol, Lower Easton BS5 50 B1
Clandown BA3 133 E4
Oldbury-on-S BS35 7 C5
Chapel Row
Bath BA1 141 B2
Bathford BA1 86 C2
Clandown BA3 133 E4
Luckington SN14 31 E4
Norton St Philip BA2 136 F4
Pill BS20 47 C4
Chapel St
Bristol BS2 64 A5
Thornbury BS35 15 B8
Chapel Way BS4 64 E6
Chapel Wlk BA2 116 C2
Chaplains Wood BS20 44 E5
Chaplin Rd BS5 50 B1
Chapter St BS2 143 B4
Chapter Wlk BS6 49 B3
Charbon Gate BS34 36 F5
Charborough Ct
Bristol BS34 35 F2
Bristol BS34 36 A2
Charborough Rd BS34 35 F2
Charborough Road Prim Sch BS34 35 F2
Charbury Wlk BS11 47 E5
Chard Cl BS48 75 F8
Chard Ct BS14 80 B6
Chard Rd BS21 57 G1
Chardstock Ave BS9 48 D8
Char Dyke Dr BS39 114 E1
CHARFIELD 11 B4
Charfield [4] BS15 66 A8
CHARFIELD GREEN 11 B5
CHARFIELD HILL 10 F5
Charfield Prim Sch GL12 10 F5
Charfield Rd
Bristol BS10 35 D1
Kingswood GL12 11 E5
Chargrove
[2] Bristol BS30 66 C6
Yate BS37 39 D7
Charis Ave BS10 49 C7
Charity La BA11 140 C1
CHARLCOMBE 84 E3
Charlcombe La BA1 84 F3
Charlcombe Pk BS20 44 D3
Charlcombe Rise BA1 84 F2
Charlcombe View Rd BA1 85 A2
Charlcombe Way BA1 84 F2
Charlcome Rise BS20 44 D3
Charlecombe Ct BS9 48 F6
Charlecombe Rd BS9 48 F6
Charlecote BA1 84 F1
Charles Ave BS34 36 E4
Charles Cl BS35 8 C3
Charles Ct [1] BS8 142 A2
Charles England Ho BS34 35 F7
Charles Pl BS8 142 A2
Charles Rd BS34 36 B3
Charles St
Bath BA1 141 B2
Bristol BS1 143 A4
Charles Wesley Ct BS5 65 A6
Charleton Ho [8] BS2 143 C3
Charlock Cl [3] BS22 105 D7
Charlock Rd BS22 105 D7
Charlotte St S BS1 142 C2
Charlotte St
Bath BA1 141 B2
Bristol, Brandon Hill BS1 142 C3
CHARLTON 139 E5
Charlton Ave
Bristol BS34 35 F2
Weston-S-M BS23 104 D4
Charlton Ct BS34 23 F1
Charlton Dr BS48 60 C7
Charlton Gdns BS10 35 D4
Charlton La
Bristol BS10 35 A3
Radstock BA3 139 D6
Charlton Leaze BS10 35 A6
Charlton Mead Ct BS10 35 D4
Charlton Mead Dr BS10 35 D3
Charlton Pk
Keynsham BS31 81 D5
Midsomer Norton BA3 139 B7
Charlton Pl BS10 35 D4
Charlton Rd
Bristol, Brentry BS10 35 C3
Bristol, Kingswood BS15 51 B1
Holcombe BA3 139 D3
Keynsham BS31, BS14 81 C3
Midsomer Norton BA3 139 B8
Weston-S-M BS23 104 D4
Charlton St [17] BS5 64 B7
Charlton View BS20 45 C5
Charmborough Farm Rural Bsns Pk BA3 139 D3
Charminster Rd BS16 51 B3
Charmouth Ct BS3 63 D1
Charmouth Rd BA1 101 B7
Charnell Rd BS16 51 E4
Charnhill Brow BS16 52 A4
Charnhill Cres BS16 51 F4
Charnhill Dr BS16 51 F4
Charnhill Ridge BS16 52 A4
Charnhill Vale BS16 51 F4
Charnwood BS16 52 A4
Charnwood Rd BS14 80 B4
Charter Ho BS1 142 B2
CHARTERHOUSE 127 C4
Charterhouse Cl BS48 59 F1
Charterhouse Rd BS5 64 D8

Charter Rd BS22.....105 B8
Charter Wlk BS14.....80 A6
Chartley BS9.....48 D2
Chasefield La **1** BS16...51 B4
Chase La GL12.....18 C6
Chase Rd BS15.....51 D2
Chase The BS16.....51 C3
Chatcombe BS37.....39 E7
Chatford Ho BS8.....62 F8
Chatham Pk BA2.....102 C6
Chatham Row BA1.....141 C3
Chatley Furlong BA2..136 F3
Chatsworth Rd
  Bristol, Arno's Vale
  BS4.....64 C4
  Bristol, Hillfields BS16...51 B3
Chattenden Ho BS9.....48 F3
Chatterton Gn BS14.....79 F3
Chatterton Ho **5** BS1..143 B1
Chatterton Rd BS37.....27 D1
Chatterton Sq BS1.....143 C1
Chatterton St BS1.....143 C1
Chaucer Rd
  Bath BA2.....101 F4
  Midsomer Norton BA3..139 B8
  Weston-S-M BS23.....105 A8
Chaundey Gr BS13.....79 B5
Chavenage BS15.....52 A1
Cheapside BS2.....143 C4
Cheapside St **8** BS3...63 F4
Cheap St BA1.....141 C2
Cheddar Cl BS48.....75 F8
Cheddarcoombe La
  BS25.....108 D1
Cheddar Gorge*
  BS27.....126 E1
Cheddar Gr BS13.....79 A8
Cheddar Grove Prim Sch
  BS13.....79 A8
Cheddar Rd BS26.....125 E2
Chedworth
  Bristol BS15.....51 F3
  Yate BS37.....39 B7
Chedworth Cl BA2.....102 F3
Chedworth Rd BS7.....50 A6
Cheese La BS2.....143 B2
Chelford Gr BS34.....36 B8
Chelmer Gr BS31.....81 F4
Chelmsford Wlk BS4...64 F5
Chelscombe BA1.....84 B1
Chelsea Cl BS31.....82 A5
Chelsea Ho BA1.....141 C4
Chelsea Pk BS5.....64 C8
Chelsea Rd
  Bath BA1.....101 C7
  Bristol BS5.....76 B1
Chelsfield BS48.....76 A7
Chelston Rd BS4.....79 D7
Chelswood Ave BS22...105 D8
Chelswood Gdns
  BS22.....105 D8
Cheltenham Cres **2**
  BS6.....49 D1
Cheltenham La BS6.....49 D2
Cheltenham Rd BS6.....49 E1
Cheltenham St BA2....141 A1
CHELVEY.....75 D5
Chelvey Batch BS48.....75 F3
Chelvey La BS48.....75 E4
Chelvey Rd BS48.....75 A4
Chelvey Rise BS48.....60 A1
Chelvy Cl BS13.....79 D3
CHELWOOD.....115 A8
Chelwood BS23.....104 F8
Chelwood Dr BA2.....101 D1
Chelwood Rd
  Bristol BS11.....47 D7
  Saltford BS31.....82 E4
Chelwood Rdbt BS39...114 C8
Chepstow Pk BS16.....37 F1
Chepstow Rd BS4.....79 D8
Chepstow Wlk BS31.....81 D5
Chequers Cl BS30.....66 C3
Chequers Ct BS34.....37 A6
Cherington
  Bristol BS15.....65 B5
  Yate BS37.....39 D6
Cherington Rd
  Bristol BS10.....49 D7
  Nailsea BS48.....60 A2
Cheriton Pl
  Bristol, Eastfield BS9...49 B7
  Bristol, Warmley BS30...66 C5
Cherry Ave BS21.....57 G2
Cherry Ct **12** BS1.....143 A4
Cherry Garden La
  BS30.....66 B2
Cherry Garden Prim Sch
  BS30.....66 C1
Cherry Garden Rd
  BS30.....66 C1
Cherry Gdns BS30.....66 C1
Cherry Gr
  Bristol BS16.....52 A6
  Yatton BS49.....91 B8
Cherry Hay BS21.....57 F1
Cherry La **4** BS1.....143 B4
Cherry Orchard La
  4 Bristol BS5.....64 F8
  Luckington SN14.....31 C5
Cherry Rd
  Chipping Sodbury BS37...28 A1
  Long Ashton BS41.....61 F1
  Nailsea BS48.....59 D1
Cherry Tree Cl
  Bristol BS16.....51 C2

Cherry Tree Cl continued
  Keynsham BS31.....81 C4
  Radstock BA3.....133 E1
Cherrytree Cres BS16...51 C2
Cherrytree Ct BS16.....53 C5
Cherry Tree Ct BS21...73 C2
Cherrytree Rd BS16.....51 C2
Cherry Wood BS30.....66 B2
Cherrywood Rd BS22...88 F2
Cherrywood Rise BS22..88 F2
Chertsey Rd BS6.....49 B1
Cherwell Cl BS35.....15 C7
Cherwell Rd BS31.....82 A4
Chescombe Rd BS49.....91 B7
Chesham Rd N BS22...105 B8
Chesham Rd S BS22...105 B8
Chesham Way BS15.....51 D1
Cheshire Cl BS37.....27 E3
Chesle Cl BS20.....44 E3
Cheslefield BS20.....44 E3
Chesle Way BS20.....44 E3
Chesley Hill BS30.....66 F7
Chessel Cl BS32.....24 C2
Chessel Ct **8** BS3.....63 B2
Chessel Mews BS3.....63 C3
Chessel St BS3.....63 B3
Chessington Ave BS14...80 B5
Chester Cl BS24.....106 A8
Chester Ct **4** BS5.....64 C7
Chesterfield Ave BS6...49 E2
Chesterfield Bldgs
  BS8.....142 B3
Chesterfield Cl BS29...106 F3
Chesterfield Ho
  Bristol BS10.....34 F1
  Midsomer Norton BA3..133 B1
Chesterfield Hospl
  BS8.....142 A2
Chesterfield Rd
  Bristol, Mangotsfield
  BS16.....51 E5
  Bristol, Montpelier BS6...49 E1
Chestermaster Cl BS32..24 A5
CHESTER PARK.....51 B2
Chester Park Jun & Inf
  Schs BS16.....51 B2
Chester Park Rd BS16...51 B2
Chester Pk BS5.....50 E1
Chester Rd BS5.....50 E1
Chesters BS30.....66 A4
Chester St BS5.....50 B2
Chesterton Dr BS48.....60 A7
Chesterton Ho **6**
  BS2.....143 B4
Chestertons The BA2...102 F8
Chestnut Ave
  Axbridge BS26.....125 C2
  Weston-S-M BS22.....89 A1
Chestnut Barn Ind Est
  BS24.....90 D3
Chestnut Chase BS48...60 A3
Chestnut Cl
  Acton Turville GL9.....43 A6
  Banwell BS29.....107 A3
  Bristol BS14.....80 E5
  Congresbury BS49.....91 D4
  Paulton BS39.....132 E6
  Radstock BA3.....133 E1
Chestnut Ct
  Bristol BS13.....79 A7
  Bristol, Hillhouse BS16...52 A5
Chestnut Dr
  Bristol BS13.....79 A7
  Claverham BS49.....74 F1
  Thornbury BS35.....8 C1
Chestnut Gr
  Bath BA2.....101 C4
  Clevedon BS21.....57 G4
  Westwood BA15.....120 F4
Chestnut Ho BS13.....79 D3
Chestnut La BS24.....122 B7
Chestnut Park Est
  GL12.....11 F4
Chestnut Rd
  Bristol, Lower Soundwell
  BS15.....51 F3
  Bristol, Mangotsfield
  BS16.....51 D6
  Long Ashton BS41.....62 B2
  Radstock BA3.....133 E1
Chestnut Springs BS37..27 B4
Chestnuts The
  Cheddar BS27.....126 A1
  Winscombe BS25.....125 A1
Chestnut Way BS15.....51 F3
Chestnut Wlk
  Bristol BS13.....79 A6
  Saltford BS31.....82 E3
Chetwode Cl BS10.....35 D3
Chetwood Ho BS5.....64 C6
Chevening Cl BS34.....36 D6
Chever's La BA2.....136 E5
Cheviot Dr BS35.....15 E8
Cheviot Way BS30.....66 C5
Chew Cotts BS31.....81 F5
Chew Court Farm
  BS40.....96 B3
Chew Hill BS40.....96 A4
Chew La BS40.....95 F1
CHEW MAGNA.....96 B3
Chew Magna Prim Sch
  BS40.....96 B3
Chew Rd BS40.....95 C5
Chew St BS40.....96 A3
CHEW STOKE.....112 D8
Chew Stoke CE Prim Sch
  BS40.....112 D8
Chewton Cl BS16.....51 B3

CHEWTON KEYNSHAM....81 B2
Chewton Rd BS31.....81 B2
Chew Valley Lake Nature
  Trails* BS39.....113 B7
Chew Valley Lake Visitor
  Ctr* BS39.....113 A7
Chew Valley Sch BS40...95 F1
Cheyne Rd BS9.....48 D6
Chichester Ho BS4.....64 F6
Chichester Pl BA3.....134 A2
Chichester Way
  Weston-S-M BS24.....106 A8
  Yate BS37.....27 D3
Chickwell La BA3.....136 A1
CHILCOMPTON.....138 C4
Chilcompton Rd BA3...138 C7
Chillwood Cl BS41.....62 A1
Chillyhill La BS40.....95 F2
Chiltern Cl
  Bristol BS14.....80 B4
  Bristol, Warmley BS30...66 C5
Chiltern Pk BS35.....15 E8
Chilton Cl **7** BA1.....85 B1
Chilton Rd
  Bath BA1.....85 B1
  Bristol BS4.....80 A8
Chilwood Cl BS37.....26 E3
Chimes The BS48.....75 C8
Chimney Stps BS2.....143 C2
Chine The BS16.....50 D5
Chine View BS16.....51 F8
Chiphouse Rd BS15.....51 F3
Chippenham Rd SN14...70 A8
Chipperfield Dr BS15...51 F1
Chipping Cross BS21...73 C8
Chipping Edge Est
  BS37.....28 C1
Chipping Sodbury Sch
  BS37.....28 D1
CHIPPING SODBURY....28 B1
Chippings The BS16.....50 D5
Chipping The GL12.....11 F4
Chisbury St BS5.....50 C3
Chittening Ind Est
  BS11.....33 D7
Chittening Rd BS11.....33 E7
Chock La BS9.....49 A7
CHOLWELL.....114 D2
Cholwell Cotts BS39...114 D2
Christchurch Ave BS16...51 D5
Christ Church CE Inf Sch
  BS16.....51 D5
Christ Church CE Jun Sch
  BS16.....51 D5
Christ Church CE Prim
  Sch
  Bristol BS8.....142 A3
  Weston-S-M BS23.....104 E8
Christ Church Cl **1**
  BS48.....59 E2
Christchurch Hall **2**
  BA1.....141 B3
Christ Church Hanham CE
  Prim Sch BS15.....65 B4
Christchurch La BS16...51 D5
Christ Church Path S **2**
  BS23.....104 E8
Christchurch Rd BS8...142 A3
Christian Cl BS22.....89 A3
Christina Terr BS8.....142 A1
Christmas St **7** BS1...143 A3
Christmas Stps **3**
  BS1.....143 A3
Christmas Tree BS34...35 D6
CHRISTON.....123 D7
Christon Rd
  Banwell BS29.....107 A1
  Loxton BS26.....123 C6
Christon Terr BS23.....104 F2
Christ the King RC Prim
  Sch BS35.....8 D1
Chubb Cl BS30.....65 F5
Church Ave
  Bristol BS9.....48 E4
  3 Bristol, Upper Easton
  BS5.....50 B1
  Bristol, Warmley BS30...66 D7
  Falfield GL12.....9 E7
Church Cl
  Bathampton BA2.....85 F2
  Bathford BA1.....86 B2
  Bristol BS10.....34 E2
  Clevedon BS21.....57 C2
  Frampton Cotterell BS36..38 B8
  Portishead BS20.....45 D5
  Yatton BS49.....91 C7
Church Cnr BS24.....122 B1
Church Cotts
  Monkton Combe BA2...119 E8
  Newton St Loe BA2.....100 B8
Church Ct
  8 Bristol BS16.....51 D3
  Midsomer Norton BA3..133 A1
  Redhill BS40.....93 D3
Churchdown Wlk BS11...47 E5
Church Dr
  Bristol BS5.....64 F8
  Congresbury BS49.....91 D4
CHURCHEND.....10 F3
Churchend La GL12.....10 F3
Church Farm Bsns Pk
  BA2.....100 A7
Churchfarm Cl BS37.....27 F3
Church Farm Cl BA2.....99 B1
Church Farm Rd BS16...52 C6
Church Hayes Cl BS48...75 E8
Church Hayes Dr BS48...75 E8

Church Hill
  Bristol BS4.....64 E2
  Burton SN14.....43 B3
  Freshford BA2.....120 B5
  Oldbury-on-S BS35.....7 B5
  Olveston BS35.....13 F3
  Radstock BA3.....134 C3
  Timsbury BA2.....116 B2
Church Hill Ho BS4.....64 E2
Church Ho BS7.....49 F8
CHURCHILL.....108 F5
Churchill Ave BS21.....57 E2
Churchill Bsns Pk
  BS23.....105 A7
Churchill CE Prim Sch
  BS40.....109 A5
Churchill Cl
  Bristol BS50.....66 A5
  5 Clevedon BS21.....57 E2
Churchill Com Sch & Sixth
  Form Ctr BS25.....108 D5
Churchill Dr BS9.....48 D7
Churchill Gate BS25...108 F4
Churchill Gn BS25.....108 C5
CHURCHILL GREEN....108 C5
Churchill Rd
  Bristol BS4.....64 C4
  Weston-S-M BS23.....105 A7
Churchill Sch & Sixth
  Form Ctr BS25.....108 D5
Church La
  Axbridge BS26.....125 C2
  Backwell BS48.....76 C5
  Badminton GL9.....30 E5
  Bath BA2.....102 C4
  Bathampton BA2.....85 E7
  Bishop Sutton BS39.....113 D4
  Bitton BS30.....82 E7
  Bristol, Bromley Heath
  BS16.....37 F1
  Bristol, Clifton Wood
  BS8.....142 B2
  Bristol, Dundry Hill BS14..80 B3
  Bristol, Henbury BS10...34 E2
  Bristol, Southville BS3...63 D3
  Chew Stoke BS40.....112 D8
  Chipping Sodbury BS37..41 B8
  Churchill BS25.....108 C5
  Clutton BS39.....114 C3
  Compton Bishop BS26...124 C3
  Compton Dando BS39...98 D6
  Cromhall GL12.....10 A1
  East Harptree BS40.....129 E4
  Farmborough BA2.....116 A6
  Farrington Gurney
  BS39.....132 A4
  Flax Bourton BS48.....76 D6
  Frampton Cotterell BS36..38 C6
  Hambrook BS16.....37 E2
  Hutton BS24.....105 E2
  Limpley Stoke BA2.....120 A5
  Long Ashton BS41.....62 C3
  Loxton BS26.....123 D4
  Lympsham BS24.....122 B1
  Marshfield SN14.....70 A8
  Midsomer Norton BA3..133 A1
  Monkton Combe BA2...119 E8
  Nailsea BS48.....59 C1
  Paulton BS39.....132 E6
  Portbury BS20.....46 E3
  Rangeworthy BS37.....16 F1
  Stratton-on-t-F BA3.....138 F2
  Ticknenham BS21.....59 C4
  Timsbury BA2.....116 B2
  Wickwar GL12.....18 A6
  Winscombe BS25.....124 E6
  Winterbourne BS36.....37 C6
  Yatton BS49.....91 C7
Churchlands Rd **8**
  BS3.....63 B2
Churchland Way
  BS22.....106 B8
Church Lane End BS48...76 F8
Church Mdws BS14.....80 C5
Church Par BS4.....64 E2
Church Path Rd BS20...47 C4
Church Pl BS20.....47 C4
Church Rd
  Abbots Leigh BS8.....62 A8
  Almondsbury BS32.....24 A5
  Alveston BS35.....15 A5
  Bath, Combe Down
  BA2.....102 C1
  Bath, Weston Park BA1...84 C1
  Bitton BS30.....82 E7
  Bristol, Bedminster BS3...63 C3
  Bristol, Bishopsworth
  BS13.....79 A6
  Bristol BS9.....48 D3
  Bristol, Filton BS34.....36 A3
  Bristol, Frenchay BS16...51 C7
  Bristol, Hanham BS15...65 B5
  Bristol, Horfield BS7.....49 E5
  Bristol, Kingswood BS15..65 E8
  Bristol, Moorfields BS5...64 D8
  Bristol, Stoke Gifford
  BS34.....36 E4
  Bristol, Upper Soundwell
  BS16.....51 E3
  Bristol, Westbury on Trym
  BS9.....49 A7
  Doynton BS30.....54 A1
  Dundry BS41.....78 D2
  Easter Compton BS35....23 A1
  Easton-in-G BS20.....47 A4

Church Rd continued
  Frampton Cotterell BS36..38 C8
  Leigh Woods BS8.....62 D6
  Luckington SN14.....31 F4
  Lympsham BS24.....122 B1
  Oldbury-on-S BS35.....7 B5
  Peasedown St John
  BA2.....134 B8
  Pensford BS39.....97 A7
  Pilning BS35.....22 B7
  Redhill BS40.....93 D3
  Severn Beach BS35.....22 A6
  Thornbury BS35.....8 B2
  Tormarton GL9.....41 D2
  Weston-S-M BS22.....88 E2
  Whitchurch BS14.....80 C4
  Wick BS30.....67 B6
  Winford BS40.....95 A7
  Winscombe BS25.....124 E7
  Winterbourne BS36.....37 E4
  Yate BS37.....27 E3
  Yate BS37.....27 F2
  Yatton BS49.....91 C7
Church Rd N BS20.....45 D5
Church Rd S BS20.....45 D4
Church Rise BS40.....95 A7
Church Row BA3.....138 F2
Churchside BS16.....51 B7
Church Sq
  Clutton BS39.....114 C2
  Midsomer Norton BA3...133 A1
Church St
  Banwell BS29.....107 B3
  6 Bath BA1.....141 C2
  Bathford BA1.....86 B2
  Bath, Weston Park BA1...84 B1
  Bath, Widcombe BA2....102 B4
  Blagdon BS40.....110 F2
  Bristol BS1.....143 B2
  Bristol, Lower Easton
  BS5.....50 B1
  Bristol, Russell Town
  BS5.....64 B6
  Kilmersdon BA3.....140 B5
  Norton St Philip BA2....136 E4
  Paulton BS39.....132 D6
  Pensford BS39.....97 D4
  Radstock BA3.....133 F2
  Woolley BA1.....84 F6
CHURCH TOWN.....76 C5
Church Town BS48.....76 C5
Church View
  Almondsbury BS32.....23 F4
  6 Bristol BS15.....65 E8
  Bristol, Filton BS34.....36 A3
  Hillesley GL12.....19 D8
  Newport GL13.....4 C8
  Pucklechurch BS16.....53 B6
  Wrxall BS48.....8 E7
  Wrxall BS48.....60 B2
Churchward Cl BS15.....65 B5
Churchward Rd
  Weston-S-M BS22.....89 B3
  Yate BS37.....27 B3
Churchway BA3.....135 D1
Churchways BS14.....80 C4
Churchways Ave BS7....49 E6
Churchways Cres BS7...49 E6
Church Wlk
  Pill BS20.....47 C4
  Wrington BS40.....92 D2
Churston Cl BS14.....80 A3
Cicil Rd **1** BS15.....65 D8
Circle The BS40.....101 B3
Circuit 32 BS5.....64 B8
Circular Rd BS9.....48 E2
Circus Mews BA1.....141 B3
Circus Pl BA1.....141 B3
Circus The BA1.....141 B3
City Academy Bristol The
  BS5.....64 C8
City Bsns Pk BS5.....64 A8
City Mus & Art Gal*
  BS8.....142 C3
City of Bath Coll BA1...141 B2
City of Bristol Coll
  BS1.....142 C2
City of Bristol Coll, Ashley
  Down Ctr BS7.....49 F4
City of Bristol Coll,
  Bedminster Ctr BS3.....63 C2
City of Bristol Coll,
  Brunel Ctr BS16.....52 A8
City of Bristol College
  Lawrence Weston Ctr
  BS11.....34 B1
City of Bristol Coll (Folly
  La Ctr) BS2.....64 A6
City of Bristol Coll
  (Hartcliffe Ctr) BS13...79 D4
  (Kingswood Ctr)
  BS15.....65 E8
City of Bristol Coll,
  Parkway Transport Tech
  Ctr BS34.....36 D3
City of Bristol Coll,
  Soundwell Ctr BS16...51 E2
City Rd BS2.....143 B4
City View
  Bath BA1.....141 C4
  Bristol BS4.....64 A3
Clamp The BS30.....66 C3
Clanage Rd BS3.....62 E4
Clanders Batch BS40...110 D3

CLANDOWN 133 E4
Clandown Rd BS39 ....132 F4
Clan Ho BA2 ....102 C7
CLAPTON 138 C7
Clapton Dro BS20......45 D1
CLAPTON IN GORDANO
...................45 E1
Clapton La BS20.......45 E2
Clapton Rd BA3 ....132 D1
Clapton Wlk BS9 ....48 C5
Clara Cross La BA2 ....101 E1
Clare Ave BS7 ....49 C3
Clare Gdns BA2........101 D1
Claremont Ave BS7 .....49 D3
Claremont Bldgs BA1....85 A1
Claremont Cres BS23 ...87 B1
Claremont Ct BS9 ......49 C5
Claremont Gdns
  Clevedon BS21.......57 G1
  Hallatrow BS39.......132 B7
  ◆ Nailsea BS48.......59 D1
Claremont Hall BS21....57 G4
Claremont Pl ⓬ BA1....85 A1
Claremont Rd
  Bath BA1............85 B1
  Bristol BS7..........49 D3
Claremont Specl Sch
  BS9................49 C5
Claremont St BS5.......50 A1
Claremont Terr ⓾ BS5...64 D7
Claremont Wlk BA1.....85 A1
Clarence Ave BS24.....105 C6
Clarence Ave BS16.....51 E5
Clarence Ct ❸ BS15....51 B1
Clarence Gdns BS16....51 E5
Clarence Grove Rd
  BS23...............104 E5
Clarence Ho ❷ BS15....51 B1
Clarence Pl
  Bath BA1...........101 B6
  Bristol BS2.........142 C4
Clarence Rd
  Bristol BS1.........143 B1
  Bristol, Kingswood BS15..51 B1
  Bristol, Newton BS2....64 A7
  Bristol, Staple Hill BS16..51 E5
Clarence Rd E BS23.....104 E5
Clarence Rd N BS23....104 D5
Clarence Rd S BS23....104 D5
Clarence St BA1.......141 C4
Clarence Terr BA2.....102 D5
Clarendon Mews BS16..51 B8
Clarendon Rd
  Bath BA2...........102 B5
  Bristol BS6..........49 C2
  Weston-S-M BS23....104 F8
Clarendon Villas BA2..102 B5
Clare Rd
  Bristol, Cotham BS6...49 D1
  Bristol, Kingswood BS15..51 C2
  Bristol, Lower Easton
  ....50 A2
Clare St
  Bristol BS1.........143 A2
  Bristol, Moorfields BS5..64 C8
Clare Wlk BS35.........8 B2
Clark Cl BS48..........60 B2
Clark Dr BS16..........50 F7
Clarken Cl BS48........59 E1
Clarken Coombe BS41...62 B3
Clarke St BS3..........63 D4
Clarkson Ave BS22.....88 C1
Clarkson Ho BA1.......141 A2
Clark St BS5...........64 A8
Clarks Way BA2........101 C2
Clatworthy Dr BS14.....80 A7
Claude Ave BA2........101 C5
Claude Terr BA2.......101 C5
Clavell Rd BS10........34 F2
CLAVERHAM 74 E1
Claverham Cl BS49......91 D7
Claverham Dro BS49....74 D5
Claverham Pk BS49......91 F8
Claverham Rd
  Bristol BS16.........51 A5
  Yatton BS49..........91 E8
CLAVERTON 103 B5
Claverton Bldgs BA1...141 C1
Claverton Ct BA2......102 E4
CLAVERTON DOWN ..102 F3
Claverton Down Rd
  BA2................102 F3
Claverton Dr BA2......102 F3
Claverton Hill BA2.....103 A4
Claverton Lo BA2......102 C5
Claverton Pumping Sta*
  BA2................103 C3
Claverton Rd BS31......82 E2
Claverton Rd W BS31...82 D3
Claverton St BA2......141 C1
Clay Bottom BS5........50 E2
Claydon Gn BS14........79 F3
Clayfield BS37.........27 E5
Clayfield Rd BS4.......64 E3
CLAY HILL 50 E2
Clay Hill BS5...........50 E2
Clay La
  Bitton BS30.........82 D8
  Bristol, Little Stoke BS34..36 C7
  Bristol, Willsbridge
  BS30................66 D1
  Thornbury BS35.......8 E1
Claymore Cres ❶ BS15..51 B1
Claypiece Rd BS13......79 A4

Clay Pitch BS37........29 E3
Claypit Hill BS37......40 B7
Clay Pit Rd BS6........49 A3
Claypool Rd BS15......65 E7
CLAYS END 100 D6
Clayton Cl BS20........45 E4
Clayton St
  Avonmouth BS11.....33 A1
  ㉑ Bristol BS5.......64 B8
Cleave St BS2..........50 A2
CLEEVE 92 B8
Cleeve Ave BS16........51 D7
Cleeve Ct BS16.........51 D7
Cleevedale Rd BA2.....102 A1
Cleeve Dr BS49.........92 B8
Cleeve Gdns BS16......51 D7
Cleeve Gn BA2.........101 A6
Cleeve Gr BS31.........81 D5
Cleeve Hill
  Bristol BS16.........51 D7
  Ubley BS40.........128 E8
Cleeve Hill Extension
  BS16...............51 E6
Cleeve Hill Rd BS40....92 C7
Cleeve La BS30.........53 D1
Cleeve Lawns BS16.....51 D7
Cleeve Lodge Cl BS16..51 E6
Cleeve Lodge Rd BS16..51 E6
Cleeve Park Rd BS16...51 E7
Cleeve Pl BS48.........60 A1
Cleeve Rd
  Bristol BS4..........64 B3
  Bristol, Frenchay BS16..51 C8
  Bristol, Mangotsfield
  BS16...............51 D7
  Yate BS37............27 E1
Cleeves Ct BS30........65 F2
Cleeve Wood Pk BS16...51 C8
Cleeve Wood Rd BS16...51 D7
Clement St BS2........143 C4
Clermont Cl BS34.......35 F8
Cleve Ct
  ❸ Bristol, Clifton Wood
  BS8................62 F6
  Bristol, Filton BS34...36 B4
Clevedale BS16.........51 D7
Clevedale Ct BS16......51 D7
CLEVEDON 57 D3
Clevedon Com Sch
  BS21...............57 H5
Clevedon Craft Ctr*
  BS21...............58 A1
Clevedon Ct* BS21.....58 A4
Clevedon Hospl BS21...57 G3
Clevedon La BS21......59 C7
Clevedon Min Rly*
  BS21...............57 D3
Clevedon Pier* BS21...57 E4
Clevedon Rd
  Bristol BS7.........49 D4
  Flax Bourton BS48....60 F2
  Midsomer Norton BA3..133 A2
  Nailsea BS48........60 B4
  Portishead BS20......45 D3
  Tickenham BS21......59 B4
  Weston-S-M BS23....104 E6
  Wraxall BS48........60 D6
Clevedon Terr BS6.....143 A4
Clevedon Wlk ❷ BS48..59 E2
Cleve House Sch BS4...64 B3
Cleveland Cl BS35......15 E8
Cleveland Cotts BA1...141 C4
Cleveland Ct BA2......102 C6
Cleveland Pl BA1......141 C4
Cleveland Pl E BA1....141 C4
Cleveland Pl W BA1....141 C4
Cleveland Reach BA1..141 C4
Cleveland Row BA1....102 B8
Cleveland Terr BA1....141 C4
Cleveland Wlk BA2....102 C6
Cleve Rd BS34..........36 A4
Clevewood Ho BS16....51 C7
Clevewyn Rise BS14....79 F3
Cliff Court Dr BS16....51 B7
Cliffe Dr BA2.........120 A6
Clift House Rd BS3.....63 A4
Clift House Spur BS3...62 F4
CLIFTON 142 A4
Clifton Arc BS8.......142 A3
Clifton Ave BS23.....104 E5
Clifton Cl ❶ BS8.......62 F7
Clifton Coll (Jun Sch)
  BS8................142 A4
Clifton Coll Prep Sch
  BS8................48 F1
Clifton Ct ⓾ BS21......57 E2
Clifton Down BS8.......62 F7
Clifton Down Rd BS8...62 F6
Clifton Down Sh Ctr ⓬
  BS8................49 B1
Clifton Down Sta BS8..49 B1
Clifton High Gr BS9....48 E5
Clifton High Sch BS8..142 A4
Clifton Hill BS8......142 A2
Clifton Metro ⓾ BS16..49 B1
Clifton Park Rd BS8...62 F8
Clifton Pk BS8.......142 A3
Clifton Pl BS5.........64 A8
Clifton Rd
  Bristol BS8.........142 A2
  Weston-S-M BS23....104 E5

Clifton St
  Bristol, Bedminster
  BS3................63 C3
  Bristol, Upper Easton
  BS5................64 A8
  Portishead BS20......45 C2
Clifton Suspension
  Bridge* BS8........62 E7
Clifton Vale BS8......142 A2
Clifton Vale Cl BS8...142 A2
Clifton View
  Bristol, Bedminster Down
  BS13...............63 A1
  ❶ Bristol, Windmill Hill
CLIFTON WOOD 142 A2
Cliftonwood Cres
  BS8................142 B2
Clifton Wood Ct BS8..142 B2
Clifton Wood Rd BS8..142 B2
Cliftonwood Terr BS8..142 A2
Clift Pl BS1..........143 A1
Clift Rd BS3...........63 A4
Clinton Rd BS3.........63 C2
Clive Rd BS14..........80 C8
Clockhouse Mews
  BS20...............45 D6
Cloisters Ct BS8.......62 F8
Cloisters Rd BS36......37 F6
Cloisters The BS36.....49 C3
Clonmel Rd BS4.........63 D1
Closemead BS21........57 F1
Close The
  Bristol BS16.........36 F1
  Bristol, Henbury BS10..35 A5
  Bristol, Little Stoke BS34..36 C6
  Bristol, Patchway BS32..24 C1
  Bristol, Upper Soundwell
  BS16...............51 E6
  Frampton Cotterell BS36..38 C6
  Portishead BS20......44 F1
  Thornbury BS35........15 B8
Clothier Rd BS4........64 F2
Cloud Hill Ind Est
  BS39...............132 A8
Clouds Hill Ave BS5....64 D8
Clouds Hill Rd BS5.....64 F8
Clovelly Cl BS5........64 F8
Clovelly Rd
  Bristol BS5..........64 F8
  Weston-S-M BS22.....89 A2
Clover Cl
  Clevedon BS21........57 H3
  Paulton BS39........132 E4
Clover Ct ❷ BS22.....105 D7
Cloverdale Dr BS30.....66 A3
Clover Ground BS9.....49 B7
Cloverlea Bsns Ctr
  BS36...............38 C3
Cloverlea Rd BS30......66 C5
Clover Leaze BS32......36 D6
Clover Rd BS22.........89 A6
CLUTTON 114 E3
CLUTTON HILL 115 B4
Clutton Hill BS39.....115 B4
Clutton Prim Sch
  BS39...............114 E3
Clyde Ave BS31.........81 F4
Clyde Ct ❷ BS3........63 C3
Clyde Gdns
  Bath BA2...........101 B6
  Bristol BS5..........65 B6
Clyde Gr BS34..........35 F2
Clyde Ho ⓭ BS35.......15 C8
Clyde La BS6...........49 C2
Clyde Mews ❸ BS6......49 C2
Clyde Rd
  Bristol, Redland BS6...49 B2
  Bristol, Totterdown BS4..64 A3
  Frampton Cotterell BS36..38 B8
Clydesdale Cl BS14.....80 A6
Clyde Terr
  Bristol, Bedminster
  BS3................63 C3
  Bristol, Totterdown BS4..64 A3
Clynder Gr BS21........57 G6
Clyntonville BS22......88 A4
Coach House La BS5.....64 B8
Coach House Mews
  BS3................87 D1
Coalbridge Cl BS22.....88 F2
Coaley Rd BS11.........47 D5
COALPIT HEATH 38 D6
Coalpit La BA3.......138 A2
Coalpit Rd BA1.........86 A4
Coalsack La BS36.......38 B3
Coalville Rd BS36......38 D7
Coape Rd BS14.........80 F5
Coast Cvn Pk BS21.....44 B1
Coates Est BS48........59 F3
Coates Rd BS48.........60 A2
Coates Wlk BS4........79 D6
Cobblestone Mews
  BS8................142 A4
Cobden Ctr The BS16...38 B2
Cobden St BS5..........64 C7
Coberley BS15..........65 C6
Cobhorn Dr BS13........78 F4
Cobley Croft BS21......73 C8
Cobourg Rd BS6........49 F2
Cobthorn Way BS49.....91 E5
Coburg Villas ⓾ BA1...85 A1
Cockers Hill BS39......98 C5
Cock La SN14...........54 D5
Cock Rd BS15...........65 F6
Cock & Yew Tree Hill
  BS40...............95 A2

CODRINGTON 40 C2
Codrington Pl BS8....142 A3
Codrington Rd BS7.....49 D3
Cody Ct ❷ BS15........65 B5
Cogan Rd BS16.........51 E3
Cogsall Rd BS14........80 F6
Coity Pl BS21..........57 E4
Coker Rd BS22..........89 B2
Colbourne Rd BA2.....101 D1
Colburn Ct BS7........49 F7
Colchester Cres BS4....79 D7
COLD ASHTON 68 F6
Coldharbour La
  Bristol BS16.........50 E8
  Weston-S-M BS23.....104 D3
Coldharbour Rd BS6....49 B4
Coldpark Gdns BS13....78 E5
Coldpark Rd BS13......78 E5
Coldrick Cl BS14.......79 F3
Colebrook Rd BS15......65 C8
Coleford Rd BS10.......35 D1
Colehouse La BS21......73 D8
Coleman BS13..........79 B5
Cole Rd BS2............64 B6
Coleridge Ct ⓾ BS3....63 C3
Coleridge Ho BS34.....24 A1
Coleridge Rd
  Bristol BS5..........50 C3
  Clevedon BS21........57 E3
  Weston-S-M BS23....105 A4
Coleridge Vale Rd E ❶
  BS21...............57 F2
Coleridge Vale Rd N
  BS21...............57 E2
Coleridge Vale Rd S
  BS21...............57 F2
Coleridge Vale Rd W ❷
  BS21...............57 E2
COLERNE 70 E6
Colesborne Cl BS37.....39 E8
Coles Gdns BA3.......140 B5
Coleshill Dr BS13......79 B5
COLEY 130 C4
Coley Rd BS40.........130 B4
Colin Cl BS35..........8 C1
Collard Ho ❷ BS16.....50 F4
College Ave BS16.......51 A5
College Ct
  Bristol BS8.........142 A4
  Bristol, Fishponds BS16..51 A5
College Fields BS8.....62 F8
College Gn BS1.......142 C2
College Mews BS9......49 A7
College Park Dr BS10...34 F1
College Rd
  Bath BA1............84 E1
  Bristol, Clifton BS8...62 F8
  Bristol, Fishponds BS16..51 A5
  Bristol, Westbury on Trym
  BS9................49 A7
College Sq BS1.......142 C2
College St BS1........142 C2
College View ⓲ BA1....85 A1
Colliers Break BS16....52 B5
Colliers Gdns BS16.....51 B5
Colliers La BA1........84 F4
Colliers Rise BA3.....134 A3
Colliers Way BA3.....139 F8
Colliers Wlk ❹ BS48...59 E2
Collingwood Ave BS15..51 E1
Collingwood Cl
  Saltford BS31........82 E2
  Weston-S-M BS22.....88 B4
Collingwood Rd ❹
  BS6................49 B1
Collin Rd BS4..........64 D4
Collins Ave BS34.......36 C6
Collins Dr BS35........22 C3
Collinson Rd BS13......79 B5
Collins St BS11........47 B8
Colliter Cres BS3......63 B2
Collum La BS22.........88 E6
Colne Gn BS31.........82 A4
Colin Sq BS35..........15 C8
Colombo Cres BS23....104 E3
Colston Ave BS1......143 A3
Colston Cl
  Bristol BS16.........51 D3
  Winterbourne BS36....37 E4
Colston Ct BS7.........49 D3
Colston Dale BS16.....50 E4
Colstone Ct ❸ BS16....50 E3
Colston Hill BS16......50 D4
Colston Mews BS6......49 E1
Colston Par BS1......143 B1
Colston Pl BS5.........50 C1
Colston's Almshouses ❶
  BS1................143 A3
Colstons Girls' Sch
  BS6................49 E1
Colston's Lower Sch
  BS16...............50 D5
Colston's Prim Sch
  BS6................49 D1
Colston's Sch BS16....50 C4
Colston St
  Bristol BS1.........143 A3
  Bristol, Upper Soundwell
  BS16...............51 D3
Colston Yd BS1.......143 A3

Colthurst Dr BS15......65 E5
Colthurst Mews BS2....64 B4
Colts Gn BS37..........40 E8
Colts Green Rd BA2....40 E8
Columbus Ho BA2......102 D8
Colwyn Rd ❷ BS5......50 C1
Colyton ⓫ BS22........89 A2
Colyton Ct BS3.........63 D1
Combe Ave BS20........45 C6
COMBE DOWN 102 B1
Combe Down CE Prim Sch
  BA2................102 B1
Combe Fields BS20.....45 C6
Combe Gr BA1........101 B8
COMBE HAY 118 D4
Combe Hay La BA2.....118 B6
Combe La BS39.........132 B6
Combe Pk BA1.........101 C8
Combe Rd
  Bath BA2...........102 B1
  Portishead BS20......45 D5
Combermere BS35......15 D8
Combe Road Cl BA2...102 B1
Combeside BA2........102 A3
Combe Side BS48.......76 A7
Combe The BS40.......109 F2
Combfactory La ⓭
  BS5................64 B8
Comb Paddock BS9.....49 B7
Comfortable Pl BA1...141 A3
Commercial Rd BS1...143 A1
Commercial Way BS22..89 B2
Common (East) The
  BS32...............24 C1
Commonfield Rd BS11..34 B1
Common La
  Churchill BS25......108 B5
  Easton-in-G BS20.....47 B2
Commonmead La BS37...40 F8
Common Mead La
  BS16...............37 A1
Common Rd
  Bristol BS15.........65 B3
  Winterbourne BS36....37 F7
Common The
  Bristol, Frenchay BS16..51 B7
  Bristol, Patchway BS32..24 C1
  Olveston BS35........13 F3
Como Cl BS20...........45 C6
COMPTON BISHOP ..124 A3
COMPTON COMMON ..98 C5
COMPTON DANDO 98 D6
Compton Dr
  Bristol BS9..........48 C7
  Weston-S-M BS24.....105 E7
Compton Gn BS31.......81 E4
COMPTON GREENFIELD
  ....34 F8
Compton La BS26......125 B3
Compton Lo ❸ BS6......49 B1
COMPTON MARTIN ..129 A7
Compton St BS5.........64 C7
Comrade Ave BS25.....125 E8
Comyn Wlk BS16........51 A5
Concorde Dr
  Bristol BS10.........35 B1
  Clevedon BS21........57 D1
Concorde Ho BS34......35 F2
Concorde Rd BS34.....35 F2
Condor Cl BS22.......105 D8
Condor Ho BS7.........50 C7
Condover Rd BS4.......65 A3
Conduit Pl ❷ BS2......50 A1
Conduit Rd BS2........50 A1
Cone The BS10, BS34...35 C6
Coneygree BS13........78 F6
Conference Ave BS20...45 F5
Conference Cl BS20....45 F4
Congleton Rd BS5......64 D8
CONGRESBURY 91 E4
CONHAM 65 A5
Conham Hill BS15......65 A5
Conham Rd BS15.......65 A5
  BS15...............64 F5
Conifer Cl
  Bristol BS16.........51 D6
  Frampton Cotterell BS36..26 A1
Conifer Way BS24.....105 E5
Coniston Ave BS9......48 E6
Coniston Cl BS30......66 D6
Coniston Cres BS23...104 E4
Coniston Prim Sch
  BS34...............23 F1
Coniston Rd BS34......23 F1
CONKWELL 103 C1
Connaught Mans BA1..141 C3
Connaught Pl BS23....104 D8
Connaught Prim Sch
  BS4................79 E8
Connaught Rd BS4......79 E8
Connection Rd BA2....101 A6
Constable Cl BS31.....81 F6
Constable Dr BS22.....89 A4
Constable Rd BS7......50 B6
Constantine Ave BS34..36 E5
Constitution Hill BS8..142 B2
Contemporis BS8......142 A3
Convent Cl BS10........34 D3
Convocation Ave BA2..102 E5
Conway Gn BS31.......82 A4
Conway Rd BS4.........64 C4
Conygar Cl BS21.......57 H5
Conygre Gn BA2.......116 B2
Conygre Gr BS34.......36 B3
Conygre Rd BS34.......36 B3
Conygre Rise BA2.....115 F6
  BS34...............66 B3
Cook Cl BS30...........66 C5

Cooke's Dr BS35 . . . . .23 A1
Cooks Bridle Path
BS48 . . . . .93 D8
Cooks Cl BS32 . . . . .24 D3
Cook's Folly Rd BS9 . . . . . . .48 C3
Cooks Gdns BS48 . . . . .60 A2
Cooks La BS36 . . . . .38 D3
Cook's La
 Banwell BS29 . . . . .107 A4
 Clevedon BS21 . . . . .58 B2
Cooksley Rd BS5 . . . . .64 C8
Cook St BS11 . . . . .47 C8
Cookworthy Cl ➋ BS5 . . . . .64 B6
Coombe Ave BS35 . . . . .8 B2
Coombe Bank Mews
BS23 . . . . .87 D1
Coombe Bridge Ave
BS9 .48 D6
Coombe Brook La BS5 . . . . .50 E2
Coombe Cl BS10 . . . . .34 D3
Coombe Dale
 Backwell BS48 . . . . .94 A8
 Bristol BS9 . . . . .48 C6
COOMBE DINGLE 48 C8
Coombe Gdns BS9 . . . . .48 C6
Coombe Ho ➍ BS15 . . . . . . .65 E8
Coombe La
 Bristol BS9 . . . . .48 B2
 Compton Bishop BS26 . . .124 B4
 East Harptree BS40 . . . . . .129 E4
 Easton-in-G BS8 . . . . .47 A2
Coomb End BA3 . . . . .133 F3
Coombend Ho BA3 . . . . . . .133 F3
Coombend Rise BA3 . . . . . .133 F3
Coombe Rd
 Bristol BS5 . . . . .50 C2
 Nailsea BS48 . . . . .59 E1
 Weston-S-M BS23 . . . . . . .87 E1
Coombes Way BS30 . . . . . . .66 C6
Coombe The
 Blagdon BS40 . . . . .110 C3
 Compton Martin BS40 . . .129 A6
Coombe Way BS10 . . . . .34 F1
Coomb Rocke BS9 . . . . .48 D6
COOMB'S END 41 A6
Cooperage La BS3 . . . . .142 B1
Cooperage Rd BS5 . . . . .64 D7
Co-operation Rd BS5 . . . . .50 C1
Cooper Rd
 Bristol BS9 . . . . .48 F7
 Thornbury BS35 . . . . .15 B7
Coopers Dr BS37 . . . . .27 F5
Coots The BS14 . . . . .80 E6
Copeland Dr BS14 . . . . .80 B5
Cope Pk BS32 . . . . .24 C5
Copford La BS41 . . . . .62 B1
Copley Ct BS15 . . . . .65 E5
Copley Gdns
 Bristol BS7 . . . . .50 B6
 Weston-S-M BS22 . . . . . . .88 F2
Coppack Ho ➏ BS21 . . . . . .57 E2
Copperfield Dr BS22 . . . . . .88 F4
Coppice End Cnr
BS24 . . . . .122 C2
Coppice Mews BS21 . . . . . . .57 E4
Coppice The
 Bristol, Bradley Stoke
 BS32 . . . . .36 E7
 Bristol, Highridge BS13 . . .78 E4
Copse Cl BS24 . . . . .105 A1
Copse Cnr BS24 . . . . .122 C2
Copse End BS25 . . . . .107 F2
Copseland BA2 . . . . .102 D5
Copse Rd
 Bristol BS4 . . . . .64 B3
 Clevedon BS21 . . . . .57 E4
 Keynsham BS31 . . . . .82 C4
Copse The BS22 . . . . .89 D2
Copthorne Cl BS14 . . . . . . .80 B5
Coralberry Dr BS22 . . . . . . .88 F1
Corbet Cl BS11 . . . . .34 C2
Corbett Cl BS37 . . . . .27 F4
Corbett Ho ➍ BS5 . . . . .64 C7
Cordwell Wlk BS10 . . . . . . .49 D7
Corey Cl ➍ BS2 . . . . .49 F1
Corfe Cl BS48 . . . . .59 D1
Corfe Cres BS31 . . . . .81 E4
Corfe Pl BS30 . . . . .66 B1
Corfe Rd BS4 . . . . .79 D7
Coriander Dr BS34 . . . . .37 A7
Coriander Wlk BS5 . . . . . . .50 C2
Corinthian Ct ➒ BS1 . . . . .143 B1
Corinum Cl BS16 . . . . .52 C6
Corker's Hill ➌ BS5 . . . . . .64 F6
Cork Pl BA1 . . . . .101 D7
Cork St BA1 . . . . .101 D7
Cork Terr BA1 . . . . .101 D7
Cormorant Cl BS22 . . . . . . .88 F1
Corner Croft BS21 . . . . .57 F1
Cornfield Cl BS32 . . . . .24 C1
Cornfields The BS22 . . . . . . .88 F5
Cornhill Dr BS14 . . . . .80 A7
Cornish Gr BS14 . . . . .80 E6
Cornish Rd BS14 . . . . .80 E6
Cornish Wlk BS14 . . . . .80 E6
Cornleaze BS13 . . . . .79 A5
Corn St
 Bath BA1 . . . . .141 B2
 Bristol BS1 . . . . .143 A3
Cornwall Cres BS37 . . . . . . .27 F3
Cornwallis Ave
 Bristol BS8 . . . . .142 A2
 Weston-S-M BS22 . . . . . . .88 F4
Cornwallis Cres BS8 . . . . . .142 A2
Cornwallis Gr BS8 . . . . . . .142 A2
Cornwallis Ho BS8 . . . . . . .142 A2
Cornwall Rd BS7 . . . . .49 D4

Coromandel Hts BA1 . . . . .141 B4
Coronation Ave
 Bath BA2 . . . . .101 C4
 Bristol BS16 . . . . .51 A4
 Keynsham BS31 . . . . .81 D4
Coronation Cl BS30 . . . . . . .66 A5
Coronation Est BS23 . . . . .104 F3
Coronation Pl BS1 . . . . . . .143 A2
Coronation Rd
 Banwell BS29 . . . . .107 A3
 Bath BA1 . . . . .101 D7
 Bleadon BS24 . . . . .122 C6
 Bristol BS3 . . . . .142 B1
 Bristol, Cadbury Heath
 BS30 . . . . .66 B5
 Bristol, Mangotsfield
 BS16 . . . . .51 E5
 Bristol, Warmley BS15 . . . .66 A7
 Weston-S-M BS22 . . . . . . .88 C2
Coronation Terr BA3 . . . . .138 D5
Corondale Rd BS22 . . . . . .105 D8
Corpus Christi RC Prim
 Sch BS23 . . . . .104 D6
Corridor The ➋ BA1 . . . . .141 C2
Corsley Wlk BS4 . . . . .79 F8
CORSTON 100 B7
Corston BS24 . . . . .105 A2
Corston Dr BA2 . . . . .100 B6
Corston La BA2 . . . . .100 A8
Corston View BA2 . . . . . . .101 C2
Corston Wlk BS11 . . . . .47 D7
Cossham Cl BS35 . . . . .8 C2
Cossham Meml Hospl
 BS16 . . . . .51 C2
Cossham Rd BS5 . . . . .64 D7
Cossham St BS16 . . . . .52 B5
Cossham Wlk BS5 . . . . .51 A1
Cossington Rd BS4 . . . . . . .79 F8
Cossins Rd BS6 . . . . .49 B3
Costers Cl BS35 . . . . .15 A5
Costiland Dr BS13 . . . . .78 F6
Cote Bank Ho BS9 . . . . .49 B7
Cote Dr BS9 . . . . .49 A4
Cote House La BS9 . . . . . . .49 A5
Cote La BS9 . . . . .49 A5
Cote Lea Pk BS9 . . . . .49 B7
Cote Paddock BS9 . . . . .48 F4
Cote Pk BS9 . . . . .48 E6
Cote Rd BS9 . . . . .49 A4
COTHAM 49 C1
Cotham Brow BS6 . . . . .49 D1
Cotham Gdns ➊➎ BS6 . . . .49 B1
Cotham Gr BS6 . . . . .49 D1
Cotham Gram Sch
 (Charnwood Annex)
 BS6 . . . . .49 C1
Cotham Hill BS6 . . . . .142 C4
Cotham Lawn Ho BS6 . . . .142 C4
Cotham Lawn Rd
 BS6 . . . . .49 C1
 Bristol BS6 . . . . .142 C4
Cotham Pk BS6 . . . . .49 C1
Cotham Pk N BS6 . . . . .49 C1
Cotham Pl BS6 . . . . .142 C4
Cotham Rd BS6 . . . . .142 C4
Cotham Rd S BS6 . . . . . . .143 A4
Cotham Sch BS6 . . . . .142 C4
Cotham Side BS6 . . . . .49 D1
Cotham Vale BS6 . . . . .49 C1
Cotman Wlk
 Bristol BS7 . . . . .50 B6
 Weston-S-M BS22 . . . . . . .88 F2
Cotrith Gr BS10 . . . . .34 E3
Cotswold Cl ➌ BS20 . . . . . .45 E4
Cotswold Ct
 Bristol BS16 . . . . .36 E1
 Chipping Sodbury BS37 . . .28 B1
Cotswold Ed Ctr The
 BS34 . . . . .35 F2
Cotswold Rd
 Bath BA2 . . . . .101 C4
 Bristol BS3 . . . . .63 D3
 Chipping Sodbury BS37 . . .40 B8
Cotswold View
 Bath BA2 . . . . .101 B5
 Bristol, Filton BS34 . . . . . .36 A3
 Bristol, Kingswood BS15 . .51 D2
 Charfield GL12 . . . . .11 B5
 Wickwar GL12 . . . . .18 B6
Cotswold Way SN14 . . . . . .69 A6
Cottage Gdns BS5 . . . . .65 A7
Cottage Pl
 ➌ Bath BA1 . . . . .85 C2
 Bristol BS2 . . . . .143 A4
Cottages The BS40 . . . . .92 D2
Cotterell Ct BA1 . . . . .141 B2
Cottington Ct BS15 . . . . . . .65 E5
Cottisford Rd BS5 . . . . .50 B4
Cottle Gdns BS14 . . . . .80 F6
Cottle Rd BS14 . . . . .80 F6
Cottles La BA15 . . . . .120 F6
Cotton Mead BA2 . . . . . . .100 B7
Cotton Mill La BS5 . . . . . . .64 B6
Cottonwood Dr BS30 . . . . . .66 A3
Cottrell Ave BS15 . . . . .51 C2
Cottrell Rd BS5 . . . . .50 C3
Coulson Dr BS22 . . . . .89 B3
Coulson Ho ➋ BS7 . . . . . . .49 F4
Coulson's Cl BS14 . . . . .80 A3
Coulson's Rd BS14 . . . . . . .80 A3
Coulson Wlk BS15 . . . . .51 C2
Council Hos
 Bleadon BS24 . . . . .122 B5
 Kingston Seymour BS21 . .73 C3
 Wick St L BS22 . . . . .89 B8
Council Hos The
 BS40 . . . . .111 B8

Council Houses BS24 . . . . .90 C3
Council Houses The
 BS39 . . . . .130 E6
Counterpool Rd BS15 . . . . .65 C7
Countership BS1 . . . . .143 B2
Countership Gdns BS14 . . .80 C6
Countess Wlk BS16 . . . . . . .50 D6
County Bridge BA3 . . . . . .133 F2
County St BS4 . . . . .64 A4
County Way BS34 . . . . .37 A4
Court Ave
 Bristol BS34 . . . . .36 F5
 Yatton BS49 . . . . .91 C7
Court Cl
 Backwell BS48 . . . . .76 C5
 Bristol BS7 . . . . .49 E7
 Portishead BS20 . . . . .45 D4
Court Cotts BS37 . . . . .29 D6
Court-de-Wyck CE Prim
 Sch BS49 . . . . .74 F1
Court Dr BS25 . . . . .108 B4
Courtenay Cres BS4 . . . . . . .79 D7
Courtenay Rd BS31 . . . . . . .82 B2
Courtenay Wlk BS22 . . . . . .89 A3
Court Farm Pk* . . . .
Court Farm Rd
 Bristol BS14 . . . . .79 F3
 Bristol, Longwell Green
 BS30 . . . . .65 E2
Courtfield Gr BS16 . . . . .51 A4
Court Gdns
 Batheaston BA1 . . . . .86 A4
 Yate BS37 . . . . .39 E8
Court Hay BS20 . . . . .47 A4
Court Hill BS39 . . . . .98 D5
Court Ho BS26 . . . . .125 B2
Court La
 Bathford BA1 . . . . .86 B2
 Clevedon BS21 . . . . .58 A3
 Shipham BS25 . . . . .125 F8
 Wick BS30 . . . . .67 B6
Courtlands
 Bristol BS32 . . . . .24 C1
 Keynsham BS31 . . . . .81 E5
Courtlands La BS3 . . . . .62 E4
Court Mdw GL13 . . . . .3 E3
Courtmead BA2 . . . . .118 F7
Court Mead GL13 . . . . .3 E3
Courtney Prim Sch
 BS15 . . . . .65 F7
Courtney Rd BS15 . . . . .65 E7
Courtney Way BS15 . . . . . . .66 A7
Court Pl BS22 . . . . .88 F2
Court Rd
 Bristol, Horfield BS7 . . . . .49 F6
 Bristol, Kingswood BS15 . .65 D7
 Bristol, Oldland Common
 BS30 . . . . .66 C3
 Frampton Cotterell BS36 . .37 F8
 Weston-S-M BS22 . . . . . . .88 A5
Courtside Mews BS6 . . . . . .49 C1
Court View BS30 . . . . .67 C6
Court View Cl BS32 . . . . . . .24 A5
Courtyard The BS40 . . . . . .129 E6
Courville Cl BS35 . . . . .15 A4
Cousins Cl BS10 . . . . .34 D3
Cousins La BS5 . . . . .64 F8
Cousins Mews BS4 . . . . .64 F6
Cousins Way BS16 . . . . .52 B8
Couzens Cl BS37 . . . . .28 B2
Couzens Pl BS34 . . . . .36 F5
Coventry Wlk BS4 . . . . .64 F6
Cowdray Rd BS4 . . . . .79 D7
COWHILL 7 B3
Cowhorn Hill BS30 . . . . . . .66 C4
Cowleaze La BS40 . . . . . . .129 C6
Cowler Wlk BS13 . . . . .78 F4
Cowling Dr BS14 . . . . .80 C5
Cowling Rd BS14 . . . . .80 D5
Cowper Rd BS6 . . . . .49 C1
Cowper St BS5 . . . . .64 C7
Cowship La GL12 . . . . .17 D6
COWSLIP GREEN 110 B8
Cowslip La BS26 . . . . .123 D3
Cox Ct BS30 . . . . .65 F4
Coxgrove Hill BS16 . . . . . . .52 F6
Coxley Dr BA1 . . . . .85 B2
Cox's Gn BS40 . . . . .92 E1
COX'S GREEN 92 E1
Coxway BS21 . . . . .57 H2
Coxwynne Cl BA3 . . . . . . .139 C8
CRAB HOLE 123 E2
Crabtree Cl BS41 . . . . .78 D1
Crabtree La BS41 . . . . .78 D2
Crabtree Wlk BS5 . . . . .50 D2
Cradock Cl BS30 . . . . .66 B4
Craftes Ct BS5 . . . . .50 E1
Cranberry Wlk BS9 . . . . . . .48 C8
Cranbourne Chase
 BS23 . . . . .88 A1
Cranbourne Rd BS34 . . . . . .35 F7
Cranbrook Rd BS6 . . . . .49 B3
Crandale Rd ➍ BA2 . . . . .101 D5
Crandell Cl BS10 . . . . .34 F4
Crane Cl BS15 . . . . .66 B8
Cranford Cl BS22 . . . . .88 D1
Cranford Ct ➊ BS9 . . . . . . .49 B6
Cranham BS37 . . . . .39 C7
Cranham Cl BS15 . . . . .51 F2
Cranham Dr BS34 . . . . .24 C1
Cranham Rd BS10 . . . . .49 C8
Cranhill Rd BA1 . . . . .101 D8
Cranleigh BA2 . . . . .118 F8
Cranleigh Court Inf Sch
 BS37 . . . . .27 D3
Cranleigh Court Rd
 BS37 . . . . .27 D2

Cranleigh Gdns BS9 . . . . . .48 E4
Cranleigh Rd BS14 . . . . . . .80 B5
Cranmoor Gn BS35 . . . . . . .22 D6
Cranmore BS24 . . . . .105 A2
Cranmore Ave BS31 . . . . . . .81 E6
Cranmore Cres BS10 . . . . . .35 D1
Cranmore Pl BA2 . . . . .118 C8
Cranside Ave BS6 . . . . .49 C4
Cransley Cres BS9 . . . . .49 C7
Crantock Ave BS13 . . . . .79 B8
Crantock Dr BS32 . . . . .24 B5
Crantock Rd BS37 . . . . .27 D1
Cranwell Gr BS14 . . . . .80 A5
Cranwell Rd BS24 . . . . . . .106 C5
Cranwells Pk BA1 . . . . .101 D8
Crates Cl BS15 . . . . .65 D8
Craven Cl BS30 . . . . .65 F5
Craven Way BS30 . . . . .65 F5
Crawford Cl ➊ BS21 . . . . . .57 D1
Crawl La BA3 . . . . .133 C4
Craydon Gr BS14 . . . . .80 D4
Craydon Rd BS14 . . . . .80 D4
Craydon Wlk BS14 . . . . .80 D5
Create Ctr* BS1 . . . . .62 F5
Crediton ➋ BS22 . . . . .89 A2
Crediton Cres BS4 . . . . .63 F1
Crescent Gdns BA1 . . . . . .141 A3
Crescent La BA1 . . . . .141 B3
Crescent Place Mews
 BA2 . . . . .101 C1
Crescent Rd BS16 . . . . .51 C6
Crescent The
 Backwell BS48 . . . . .76 A6
 Bristol BS16 . . . . .36 F1
 Bristol, Frenchay BS16 . . . .36 F7
 Bristol, Henleaze BS9 . . . . .49 C6
 Bristol, Sea Mills BS9 . . . . .48 C6
 Bristol, Upper Soundwell
 BS16 . . . . .51 D3
 Farrington Gurney
 BS39 . . . . .132 B3
 Lympsham BS24 . . . . . . .122 C5
 Olveston BS35 . . . . .14 D4
 Stanton Drew BS39 . . . . . .96 F1
 Weston-S-M BS22 . . . . . . .88 B1
 Wick BS30 . . . . .67 C7
Crescent View BA2 . . . . . . .141 B1
Crescent View Ct BS22 . . . .88 B1
Crest The
 Bristol BS4 . . . . .64 C2
 West Kington SN14 . . . . . .56 F3
Creswicke Ave BS15 . . . . . . .65 C5
Creswicke Ho ➊➐ BS1 . . .143 A3
Creswicke Rd BS4 . . . . .79 E7
Crewkerne Cl BS48 . . . . . . .60 B1
CREW'S HOLE 64 E7
Crew's Hole Rd BS5 . . . . . . .64 C7
CRIBBS CAUSEWAY 35 C6
Cribbs Causeway Ctr
 BS34 . . . . .35 A6
Cribbs Causeway Ret Pk
 BS10 . . . . .35 A6
Cribbs Cswy BS10 . . . . .35 A6
Cribb's La BS40 . . . . .93 D1
Crickback La BS40 . . . . .96 A3
Cricket Field Gn BS48 . . . . .59 D2
Cricket La BS10 . . . . .49 A8
Cricklade Ct BS48 . . . . .60 A1
Cricklade Rd BS7 . . . . .49 F4
Cripps Rd BS3 . . . . .63 C3
Crispin La ➍ BS35 . . . . .8 B1
Crispin Way BS15 . . . . .51 F2
Crockerne CE Prim Sch
 BS20 . . . . .47 D4
Crockerne Dr BS20 . . . . . . .47 D3
Crockerne Ho BS20 . . . . . . .47 D4
CROCOMBE 116 C3
Crocombe BA2 . . . . .116 C3
Crocombe La BA2 . . . . . . .116 C3
Croft Ave BS16 . . . . .50 C4
Croft Cl BS30 . . . . .82 D8
Crofters Wlk BS32 . . . . .36 D8
Crofton Ave BS7 . . . . .49 F6
Crofton Cres BS7 . . . . .49 F6
Crofton Fields BS36 . . . . . . .37 E6
Crofton Mews BS15 . . . . . . .65 E7
Croft Rd BA1 . . . . .85 B1
Crofts End Ind Est BS5 . . . .50 E1
Crofts End Rd BS5 . . . . .50 E1
Croft The
 Backwell BS48 . . . . .76 A7
 Bristol, Mangotsfield
 BS16 . . . . .51 F5
 Bristol, Oldland Common
 BS30 . . . . .66 C3
 Clevedon BS21 . . . . .57 H4
 Hutton BS24 . . . . .105 A3
 Monkton Combe BA2 . . .102 E1
 Westwood BA15 . . . . .120 F3
Croft View BS9 . . . . .49 A6
Crokeswood Wlk BS11 . . . .34 A1
Crome Rd BS7 . . . . .50 B7
Cromer Rd
 Bristol BS5 . . . . .50 C2
 Weston-S-M BS23 . . . . . .104 E5
CROMHALL 10 A1
Cromhall La GL12 . . . . .9 D1
Cromwell Ct BS15 . . . . .65 E5
Cromwell Dr BS22 . . . . .89 A4
Cromwell Rd
 Bristol, Montpelier BS6 . . .49 E2
 Bristol, St George BS5 . . . .65 A8
Cromwells Hide BS16 . . . . .50 E5
Cromwell St BS3 . . . . .63 C3

Cromwell View BS6 . . . . . . .49 E2
Crookes La BS22 . . . . .88 A4
Croomes Hill BS16 . . . . . . .51 D6
Cropthorne Rd BS7 . . . . . . .36 A1
Cropthorne Road S
 BS7 . . . . .50 A8
Crosby Hall BS23 . . . . .104 D8
Crosby Row BS8 . . . . .142 A2
CROSS 124 E2
Crosscombe Dr BS13 . . . . . .79 C3
Cross Combe Wlk
 BS13 . . . . .79 B3
Cross Cotts GL13 . . . . .2 C3
Cross Elms La BS9 . . . . .48 E5
Crossfield Rd BS16 . . . . .51 E3
Cross Hands Rd BS35 . . . . .22 D7
Cross La BS26 . . . . .125 A2
Cross Lanes BS20 . . . . .47 C4
Crossleaze Rd BS15 . . . . . . .65 C3
Crossley Cl BS36 . . . . .37 F7
Crossley Farm Bsns Ctr
 BS36 . . . . .37 E7
Crossman Ave BS36 . . . . . . .37 E5
Crossman Wlk BS21 . . . . . . .57 H2
Cross Moor Dr BS26 . . . . .124 C1
Cross Moor Dro BS26 . . . .124 E1
Cross Moor Rd BS26 . . . . .125 B1
Crosspost La BA2 . . . . .99 B4
Cross St
 Bristol BS15 . . . . .51 D1
 Keynsham BS31 . . . . .81 F5
 ➌ Weston-S-M BS23 . . . .104 E7
Cross The BS40 . . . . .129 F4
Cross Tree Gr BS32 . . . . . . .36 D8
Crossway La BA3 . . . . .138 B7
Crossways Ct 8 E2
CROSSWAYS 8 F2
Crossways ➊ 4 F8
Crossways Cvn Pk
 BA2 . . . . .117 F5
Crossways Jun & Inf Schs
 BS35 . . . . .8 D1
Crossways La BS35 . . . . .8 E2
Crossways Rd
 Bristol BS4 . . . . .64 A1
 Thornbury BS35 . . . . .8 D1
Crow La
 Bristol BS1 . . . . .143 A2
 Bristol, Henbury BS10 . . . .34 F2
Crowley Way BS11 . . . . .33 B1
Crow Mdw GL12 . . . . .11 F4
Crowndale Rd BS4 . . . . .64 A3
Crown Gdns BS30 . . . . .66 B7
Crown Glass Pl ➎
 BS48 . . . . .59 E2
Crown Hill
 Bath BA1 . . . . .84 C1
 Bristol BS5 . . . . .64 F8
 Winford BS40 . . . . .95 A5
Crown Hill Wlk BS5 . . . . . . .50 E1
Crown Ho
 Bristol BS1 . . . . .143 A2
 Nailsea BS48 . . . . .59 C1
Crown Ind Est BS30 . . . . . . .66 C7
Crown La BS16 . . . . .51 D3
Crownleaze BS16 . . . . .51 D3
Crown Rd
 Bath BA1 . . . . .84 B1
 Bristol, Upper Soundwell
 BS15 . . . . .51 D2
 Bristol, Warmley BS30 . . . .66 C7
Crow Way BS30 . . . . .66 C7
Crows Gr BS32 . . . . .24 D3
Crowther Rd BS7 . . . . .50 A4
Crowther Rd BS7 . . . . .50 A4
Crowthers Ave BS37 . . . . . .27 E3
Crowther St BS3 . . . . .63 B3
Croydon Ho ➊ BS5 . . . . . . .64 B8
Croydon St BS5 . . . . .64 B8
Crunnis The BS32 . . . . .36 E6
Crusader Ho ➍ BS1 . . . . . .143 A2
Crusty La BS20 . . . . .47 C5
Crystal Way BS32 . . . . .36 E8
Cuck Hill BS25 . . . . .125 E2
Cuckoo La
 High Littleton BS39 . . . . .115 B3
 Winterbourne BS36 . . . . . .37 F3
 Wraxall BS48 . . . . .60 A6
Cuffington Ave BS4 . . . . . . .64 D4
Culleysgate La BS30 . . . . . .67 F6
Culverhay BS39 . . . . .98 D6
Culverhay Sch BA2 . . . . . .101 B2
Culverhill Rd BS37 . . . . .28 A1
Culverhill Sch BS37 . . . . . . .39 D7
Culver La BS40 . . . . .129 F3
Culvers Cl BS31 . . . . .81 E6
Culvers Rd BS31 . . . . .81 E6
Culver St BS1 . . . . .142 C2
Culvert The BS32 . . . . .27 B1
Culverwell Rd BS13 . . . . . . .79 A4
Cumberland Basin Rd
 BS8 . . . . .62 F5
Cumberland Cl BS1 . . . . . .142 A1
Cumberland Gr ➎ BS6 . . . .49 F2
Cumberland Ho BA1 . . . . .141 A2
Cumberland Pl ➏ BS8 . . . .62 F6
Cumberland Rd BS1 . . . . . .142 B1
Cumberland Row
 BA1 . . . . .141 B2
Cumberland St BS2 . . . . . .143 B4
Cumbria Cl BS35 . . . . .8 E1

Cunningham Gdns BS16 .... 51 B5
Cunnington Cl BS30 .... 66 B1
Curland Gr BS14 .... 80 B5
Curlew Cl BS16 .... 50 F6
Curlew Gdns BS22 ...... 88 F1
Curlew Pl BS20 .... 45 C6
Currells La BS40 .... 77 B1
Curtis La BS34 .... 37 A4
Custom Cl BS14 .... 80 A7
Custom Ho BS1 .... 143 A1
Cutler Rd BS13 .... 78 F6
Cutters Row BS3 .... 63 E4
Cuttsheath Rd GL12 ... 16 C8
Cutts Heath Rd BS25 ... 9 A1
Cygnet Cres BS22 ..... 88 F1
Cylde Pk BS6 .... 49 B2
Cynder Way BS16 ...... 38 A1
Cynthia Rd BA2 ...... 101 D5
Cypress Ct BS9 .... 48 D3
Cypress Gdns BS8 ..... 62 E6
Cypress Gr BS9 .... 49 C6
Cypress Terr BA3 .... 133 D1
Cypress Wlk SN14 ..... 70 F6
Cyrus Ct BS16 .... 52 B7

D

Dafford's Bldgs BA1 ... 85 C2
Dafford St BA1 .... 85 C2
Daglands The BA2 ... 133 E8
Dahlia Gdns BA2 ..... 102 B7
Daines Ct ⑲ BS16 .... 50 E3
Dairy Cl BS49 .... 74 A2
Dairycroft BS2 ...... 143 B4
Dairy Hill BA2 ...... 135 B5
Daisy Bank BA2 ..... 102 B4
Daisy Green La GL12 ... 5 D2
Daisy Rd BS5 .... 50 C2
Dakin Cl BS4 .... 60 A4
Dakota Dr BS14 ...... 80 A4
Dalby Ave BS3 .... 63 D4
Daldry Gdns BS35 .... 14 A3
Dale St BS5 .... 64 F8
Daley Cl BS22 .... 89 B3
Dalkeith Ave BS15 .... 51 C1
Dalrymple Rd ⑩ BS2 .. 49 E1
Dalston Rd BS3 .... 63 B4
Dalton Sq BS2 ...... 143 B4
Dalwood ⑲ BS22 ..... 89 A2
Dame Court Cl BS22 .. 88 F4
Damery La
  Stone GL13 .... 3 F3
  Woodford GL13 .... 4 A4
Dampier Rd BS3 .... 63 A3
Damson Rd BS22 .... 105 E7
Danbury Cres BS10 ... 35 C1
Danbury Wlk BS10 .... 35 C1
Danby Ho BS7 .... 50 A5
Dancey Mead BS13 ... 78 F6
Dandy's Mdw BS20 ... 45 E4
Daneacre Rd BA3 ... 134 A3
Dane Cl BA15 .... 120 F2
Dane Rise BA15 ..... 120 E7
Dangerfield Ave BS13 . 78 F6
Daniel Cl BS21 .... 57 H3
Daniel Mews BA2 .... 102 B7
Daniel St BA2 .... 102 B7
Dapps Hill BS31 ...... 81 F5
Dapwell La BS14, BS31 . 81 A1
Dark La
  Backwell BS48 .... 76 B5
  Banwell BS29 .... 107 C2
  Bathampton BA2 ..... 85 F1
  Blagdon BS40 .... 110 E3
  Chew Magna BS40 .... 95 F3
  Freshford BA2 ...... 120 B5
  Holcombe BA3 ...... 139 C1
  Kilmersdon BA11 ... 140 A1
Darley Cl BS10 .... 34 D3
Darlington Mews BA2 . 102 B7
Darlington Pl BA2 ... 102 B6
Darlington Rd BA2 ... 102 B7
Darmead BS34 .... 89 B1
Darnley Ave BS7 ..... 49 F6
Dart Cl BS35 .... 15 B8
Dartmoor St BS3 ..... 63 B3
Dartmouth Ave BA2 . 101 C5
Dartmouth Cl BS22 .. 89 A2
Dartmouth Wlk BS31 . 81 D4
Dart Rd BS21 .... 57 H3
Daubeny Cl BS16 ..... 51 B5
Daubeny Ct BS1 .... 143 A1
Davenport Cl BS30 ... 66 A2
Daventry Rd BS4 ..... 63 F1
Davey St BS2 .... 49 F1
Davey Terr ⑧ BS2 ... 49 F1
Davids Cl BS35 .... 15 A4
David's La BS35 ...... 15 A4
David's Rd
  Bristol BS14 .... 80 C6
  Thornbury BS35 ...... 8 C1
David St BS2 .... 143 C3
David Thomas Ho BS6 . 49 E2
Davies Dr BS4 .... 64 F5
Davin Cres BS20 ..... 47 C3
Davis Cl BS30 .... 65 F5
Davis Ct BS35 .... 8 F1
Davis La BS21 .... 73 F8
Davis St BS11 .... 47 B8
Davron Ct BS3 .... 63 E4
Dawes Ct BS21 .... 57 F1

Dawes Ct ❷ BS8 .... 62 F6
Dawley Cl BS36 .... 37 E7
Dawlish Rd BS3 .... 63 D2
Dawn Rise BS15 ...... 52 A1
Daws Ct BS16 .... 51 B4
Day Cres BA2 .... 100 F6
Day House La GL12 ... 19 C8
Day's Rd BS2 .... 64 A6
Days Road Commercial
  Ctr BS2 .... 64 A7
Deacon Cl BS15 ...... 37 E5
Deacons Cl BS22 ..... 88 E2
Deacons Ct BS22 ..... 88 C1
Deadmill La BA1 ..... 85 C3
Dean Ave BS35 .... 8 C2
Dean Cl
  Bristol BS15 .... 51 E3
  Weston-S-M BS22 ... 89 B3
Dean Cres
  ❶ Bristol BS3 ...... 63 C4
  Bristol BS3 .... 63 D4
Dean Ct BS37 .... 27 C3
Deanery Cl BS15 ..... 66 B8
Deanery Rd
  Bristol BS1 .... 142 C2
  Bristol, Warmley BS15 . 66 B8
Deanery Rd Rdbt BS15 . 66 B8
Deanery Wlk BA2 .... 120 A6
Deanhill La BA1 ...... 84 A2
Dean La BS3 .... 63 C4
Deanna Ct BS16 ...... 51 E6
Dean Rd
  Avonmouth BS11 .... 33 C5
  Yate BS37 .... 27 C3
Dean's Ct BS1 ...... 142 C2
Dean's Dr BS5 .... 51 A2
Deans Mead BS11 .... 48 A8
Dean St
  Bristol BS2 .... 143 B4
  Bristol, Southville BS3 63 C4
Deans The BS20 ...... 45 B4
Debecca's La BS20 ... 47 B4
De Clifford Rd BS11 .. 34 C2
Deep Coombe Rd BS3 . 63 A2
Deep Pit Rd BS5 ...... 50 F2
Deep St BS1 .... 143 A3
Deerhurst
  Bristol BS15 .... 51 E3
  Yate BS37 .... 39 C8
Deering Cl BS11 ...... 34 B1
Deerleap BS25 ...... 125 F8
Deer Mead BS21 ..... 57 D1
Deerswood BS15 ..... 52 A2
Delabere Ave BS16 ... 51 B5
Delapre Rd BS23 .... 104 D3
De La Warre Ct ❶ BS4 . 64 A1
Delius Gr BS4 .... 79 D7
Dell The
  Bristol, Bradley Stoke
    BS32 .... 36 E7
  Bristol, Oldland Common
    BS30 .... 66 C5
  Bristol, Westbury on T
    BS9 .... 48 F5
  Nailsea BS48 .... 59 D2
  Weston-S-M BS22 ... 88 E4
Delvin Rd BS10 ...... 49 C8
De Montalt Pl BA2 ... 102 B1
Denbigh St BS2 ...... 49 F1
Dene Cl BS31 .... 81 F3
Dene Rd BS14 .... 80 C4
Denleigh Cl BS14 .... 80 A4
Denmark Ave BS1 ... 142 C2
Denmark Pl BS7 ..... 49 E3
Denmark Rd BA2 ... 101 D6
Denmark St BS1 .... 142 C2
Denning Ct BS22 .... 89 B4
Dennisworth BS16 ... 53 B5
Dennor Pk BS14 ..... 80 B7
Denny Cl BS20 ...... 45 A5
Denny Isle Dr BS35 .. 22 A6
Denny La BS40 ...... 96 B1
Denny View BS20 .... 45 A5
Dennyview Rd BS8 ... 61 F8
Denston Dr BS20 .... 45 E4
Denston Wlk BS13 ... 79 A7
Denton Patch BS16 .. 52 B7
Dentwood Gr BS9 ... 48 B8
Denys Ct BS35 ...... 14 A3
Derby Rd BS7 .... 49 F4
Derby St BS5 .... 64 D7
Derham Cl BS49 ..... 91 B8
Derham Ct BS49 ..... 91 B8
Derham Pk BS49 ..... 91 B8
Derham Rd BS13 .... 79 A5
Derricke Rd BS14 ... 80 F6
Derrick Rd BS15 .... 65 D8
Derry Rd BS3 .... 63 B2
Derwent Cl BS34 .... 36 A8
Derwent Ct BS35 .... 15 D8
Derwent Gr BS31 .... 82 A5
Derwent Rd
  Bristol BS5 .... 50 F1
  Weston-S-M BS23 .. 105 A5
Devaney Cl BS4 ..... 64 F6
Deveron Gr BS31 .... 82 A4
De Verose Ct BS15 .. 65 E8
Devil's La GL12 ..... 11 A2
Devon Gr BS5 .... 64 C8
Devon Rd BS5 .... 50 C1
Devonshire Bldgs
  Bath BA2 .... 101 F4
  Bristol BS3 .... 63 E4
Devonshire Ct BS23 . 104 E4
Devonshire Dr BS20 . 44 F5

Devonshire Mews
  BA2 .... 101 F3
Devonshire Pl BA2 .. 101 F4
Devonshire Rd
  Bathampton BA2 .... 85 E1
  Bristol BS6 .... 49 B4
  Weston-S-M BS23 .. 104 E4
Devonshire Villas
  BA2 .... 101 F3
Dewfalls Dr BS32 ... 24 D1
Dial Hill Rd BS21 ... 57 F4
Dial La
  Bristol BS16 .... 51 D6
  Felton BS40 .... 77 D1
Diamond Batch BS24 . 89 B1
Diamond Rd BS5 .... 64 F7
Diamond St BS3 .... 63 C3
Diamonite Ind Pk
  BS16 .... 51 A3
Diana Gdns BS32 ... 36 E8
Dibden Cl BS16 .... 52 A8
Dibden La BS16 .... 52 B7
Dibden Rd BS16 .... 52 A7
Dickens Cl BS7 ..... 50 A8
Dickenson Rd BS23 . 104 E6
Dickenson's Gr BS49 . 91 E3
Dickinsons Fields BS3 . 63 D2
Didsbury Cl BS10 ... 34 F1
Dighton Ct ❸ BS2 .. 143 A4
Dighton Gate BS34 . 36 E5
Dighton St BS2 .... 143 A4
Dillon Ct ⑱ BS5 ... 64 D7
Dinder Cl BS48 ..... 75 E8
DINGHURST 108 E4
Dinghurst Rd BS25 . 108 E4
Dingle Cl BS9 ...... 48 C4
Dingle Ct BS13 ..... 78 F7
Dingle Rd BS9 ...... 48 D7
Dingle The
  Bristol BS9 .... 48 D7
  Winterbourne BS36 . 37 F3
Dingle View BS9 ... 48 C7
Dinglewood Cl BS9 . 48 D7
DINGS THE 64 A6
Dings Wlk ❹ BS2 .. 64 A6
Dipland Gr BS40 .. 110 F2
Dirac Rd BS7 ...... 49 F4
District Ctr BS32 . 36 D8
Dixon Gdns BA1 ... 84 F1
Dixon Rd BS4 ..... 64 F2
Dock Gate La BS8 . 142 A1
DODINGTON 40 F5
Dodington Ash BS37 . 41 B2
Dodington La BS37 . 40 D5
Dodington Rd BS37 . 40 B7
Dodisham Wlk BS16 . 51 B6
Doleberrow BS25 .. 108 F3
Dolebury Warren Nature
  Reserve* BS25 ... 109 A3
DOLEMEADS 102 B5
Dolemoor La
  Congresbury BS49 . 91 C3
  Puxton BS49 ...... 91 A4
Dolman Cl BS10 ... 34 F3
Dolman Cl BS10 ... 34 F3
Dolman Cl BS37 ... 27 D1
Dolphin Sq BS23 . 104 D7
Dominion Rd
  Bath BA2 .... 101 A6
  Bristol BS16 ..... 50 F3
Donald Rd BS13 ... 78 F7
Donal Early Way BS7 . 49 E8
Doncaster Rd BS10 . 49 C8
Doncombe Hill SN14 . 70 F7
Doncombe La SN14 . 70 F7
Donegal Rd BS4 ... 63 D1
Dongola Ave BS7 .. 49 E4
Dongola Rd BS7 ... 49 E4
Don John's Cross BS4 . 64 E8
Donnington Wlk BS31 . 81 D4
Doone Rd BS7 ...... 49 F8
Dorcas Ave BS34 .. 36 F5
Dorchester Cl ❻ BS48 . 59 D1
Dorchester Rd BS7 . 50 A7
Dorchester St BA1 . 141 C1
Dorester Cl BS10 .. 35 C4
Dorian Cl BS7 ..... 49 F7
Dorian Rd BS7 .... 49 F7
Dorian Way BS7 .. 49 E8
Dormeads View ❻
  BS24 .... 105 F7
Dormer Cl BS36 ... 38 C6
Dormer Rd BS5 .... 50 B3
Dorset Cl BA2 .... 101 D6
Dorset Gr BS2 .... 50 A2
Dorset Ho BA2 ... 101 D3
Dorset Rd
  Bristol, Kingswood
    BS15 .... 51 D1
  Bristol, Westbury on Trym
    BS9 .... 49 B6
Dorset St
  Bath BA2 .... 101 D6
  Bristol BS3 ...... 63 B3
Dorset Way BS37 . 28 A3
Double Hill BA2 .. 134 F7
Doudney Ct BS3 .. 63 E4
Douglas Ct ❸ BS23 . 104 F5
Douglas Rd
  Bristol, Horfield BS7 . 49 F7
  Bristol, Kingswood BS15 . 65 D7
  Weston-S-M BS23 . 104 F5
Douglas Road Ind Pk
  BS15 .... 65 D7
Doulton Way BS14 . 80 B5
Dovecote BS37 .... 39 E7
Dovedale BS35 .... 15 D8

Dove La
  Bristol BS2 ...... 143 C4
  Bristol, Russell Town
    BS5 .... 64 C7
Dovercourt Rd BS7 . 50 A6
Dover Ho BA1 .... 141 C4
Dover Pl
  ❺ Bath BA1 ..... 85 A1
  Bristol BS8 ..... 142 B3
Dove Place Cotts
  BS8 .... 142 B3
Dovers La BA1 .... 86 C2
Dovers Pk BA1 .... 86 C2
Dove St S BS2 ... 143 A4
Dove St BS2 ..... 143 A4
Doveswell Gr BS13 . 79 A4
Dovetail Dr BS23 . 105 A7
Dovey Ct BS30 ... 66 C6
Dowdeswell Cl BS10 . 34 F3
Dowding Cl BS37 . 28 C2
Dowding Rd BA1 . 85 B1
Dower Ho The BS16 . 50 E7
Dowland ⑱ BS22 . 89 A2
Dowland Gr BS4 .. 79 D6
Dowling Rd BS13 . 79 D3
Down Ave BA2 ... 102 A1
Down Cl BS20 ... 44 F4
DOWNEND 51 E8
Downend Comp Sch
  BS16 .... 51 F7
Downend Park Rd
  BS16 .... 51 D5
Downend Pk BS7 . 49 F5
Downend Rd
  Bristol, Fishponds
    BS16 .... 51 C5
  Bristol, Horfield BS7 . 49 F5
  Bristol, Kingswood BS15 . 51 D1
  Bristol, Mangotsfield BS16 . 37 E1
Downfield
  Keynsham BS31 .. 81 D5
Downfield Cl ⑲ BS35 . 15 A5
Downfield Dr BS36 . 38 B8
Downfield Lo BS8 . 49 A1
Downfield Rd BS8 . 49 A1
Down La BA2 ..... 85 F1
Downland Cl ❺ BS48 . 59 D1
Downleaze
  Bristol, Downend BS16 . 51 D8
  Portishead BS20 .. 45 A5
  Stoke Bishop BS9 . 48 C7
Down Leaze ❷ BS35 . 15 A5
Downleaze Dr BS37 . 40 B8
Downleaze Rd BS9 . 48 F3
Downman Rd BS7 . 50 A5
Down Rd
  Alveston BS35 ... 15 A5
  Marshfield SN14 . 56 C2
  Portishead BS20 . 44 F4
  Winterbourne BS36 . 37 F4
Downs Cl
  ❸ Alveston BS35 . 15 A5
  Weston-S-M BS22 . 88 F1
Downs Cote Ave BS9 . 48 F6
Downs Cote Dr BS9 . 48 F6
Downs Cote Gdns BS9 . 49 A6
Downs Cote Pk BS9 . 49 A6
Downs Cote View BS9 . 49 A6
Downs Ct BS9 .... 49 B6
DOWNSIDE 138 C1
  Chilcompton 138 C1
  Nailsea 76 D1
Downside BS20 ... 45 C5
Downside Abbey*
  BA3 .... 138 E2
Downside Cl
  Bathampton BA2 . 85 F1
  Bristol BS30 .... 65 F5
  Chilcompton BA3 . 138 D3
Downside Rd
  Backwell BS48 .. 93 E8
  Bristol BS8 ..... 49 A1
  Weston-S-M BS23 . 104 F4
Downs Pk E BS6 .. 49 A4
Downs Pk W BS6 . 49 A4
Downs Rd
  Bristol BS9 ..... 49 A6
  Dundry BS41 .... 78 D2
Downs Sch The BS48 . 60 C8
Downs The
  Portishead BS20 . 45 B4
  Wickwar GL12 ... 17 F7
Downsview BS8 .. 49 A1
Downsway BS39 . 132 D6
Down The
  Alveston BS35 .. 14 F5
  Tockington BS32 . 14 D3
Downton Rd BS4 . 63 D1
Down View
  Bristol BS7 ..... 49 F3
  Radstock BA3 ... 139 F8
Dowry Pl BS8 .... 62 F5
Dowry Rd BS8 ... 142 A2
Dowry Sq BS8 ... 142 A2
DOYNTON 54 A1
Doynton La SN14, BS30 . 54 B3
Doynton Mill BS30 . 53 F1
Dragon Cr BS5 ... 50 E1
Dragonfly Cl BS15 . 65 D7
Dragon Rd BS36 . 37 D5
Dragons Hill Cl BS31 . 81 F5
Dragons Hill Ct BS31 . 81 F5
Dragons Hill Gdns
  BS31 .... 81 F5
Dragonswell Rd BS10 . 35 A2
Dragon Wlk BS5 . 51 F1

Drake Ave BA2 .... 101 F2
Drake Cl
  Saltford BS31 .... 82 D2
  Weston-S-M BS22 . 88 F4
Drake Rd BS3 ..... 63 A3
Drakes Way BS20 . 45 B5
Dram La BS5 ..... 65 A6
Dransfield Way BA2 . 101 C4
Draper Ct ❸ BS5 . 64 C7
Draycot Pl BS1 .. 143 A1
Draycott Cl ⑴ BA2 . 141 C3
Draycott Rd BS7 . 49 F5
Draydon Rd BS4 . 79 D8
Drayton BS24 ... 105 A2
Drayton Cl BS14 . 80 B8
Drayton Rd BS9 . 48 C8
Drifton Hill SN14 . 56 F7
Dring The BA3 .. 133 E2
Drive The
  Bristol BS14 .... 80 C6
  Bristol, Henleaze BS9 . 49 B5
  Churchill BS25 .. 108 E4
  Keynsham BS31 . 81 E6
  Shipham BS25 .. 125 E8
  Stanton Drew BS39 . 96 F1
  Weston-S-M BS23 . 104 F8
Drove Ct BS48 ... 59 E3
Drove Rd
  Congresbury BS49 . 91 D3
  Weston-S-M BS23 . 104 F5
Drove The BS20 . 46 D6
Drove Way BS24, BS25 . 107 E7
Druetts Cl BS10 .. 49 E6
Druid Cl BS9 ..... 48 E5
Druid Hill BS9 ... 48 E5
Druids Garth BA2 . 85 D1
Druid Stoke Ave BS9 . 48 C6
Druid Woods BS9 . 48 B5
Drumhead Way The
  BS25 .... 125 E8
Drummond Ct BS30 . 65 F4
Drummond Rd
  Bristol, Fishponds
    BS16 .... 50 F3
  Bristol, St Pauls BS2 . 49 E1
Dr White's Cl BS1 . 143 B1
DRY HILL 45 C6
Dryleaze
  Keynsham BS31 . 81 E7
  Yate BS37 ...... 27 E5
Dryleaze Rd BS16 . 50 F6
Drysdale Cl BS22 . 88 D1
Dubbers La BS5 . 50 E2
Dublin Cres BS9 . 49 B6
Duchess Rd BS8 . 49 A1
Duchess Way BS16 . 50 D6
Duchy Cl BA3 ... 133 E5
Duchy Rd BA3 .. 133 E5
Ducie Cl GL12 ... 10 B2
Ducie Ct BS16 ... 51 A4
Ducie Rd
  Bristol, Russell Town
    BS5 .... 64 B7
  Bristol, Staple Hill BS16 . 51 E5
Ducie Rd Bsns Pk ❻
  BS5 .... 64 B7
DUCKHOLE 8 C5
Duck La
  Churchill BS40 . 109 A4
  Kenn BS21 ..... 74 A6
Duckmoor Rd BS3 . 63 A3
Duckmoor Road Ind Est
  BS3 .... 63 A4
Ducks La BS22 .. 89 A8
Duck St
  Churchill BS40 . 108 C5
  Tytherington BS35 . 16 C5
Dudley Cl BS31 .. 81 E4
Dudley Ct ❸ BS30 . 65 F4
Dudley Gr BS7 ... 50 A8
Dugar Wlk BS6 .. 49 C3
Duke St BA2 .... 141 C2
Dulverton Rd BS7 . 49 D4
Dumaine Ave BS34 . 36 E5
Dumfries Pl BS23 . 104 E5
Dumpers La BS40 . 96 B2
Duncan Gdns BA1 . 84 A3
Duncan Ho BS6 . 142 A3
Duncombe La BS15 . 51 B2
Duncombe Rd BS15 . 51 B1
Dundas Cl BS10 . 35 A2
Dundonald Rd BS6 . 49 A3
Dundridge Gdns BS5 . 65 A6
Dundridge La BS5 . 65 A6
DUNDRY 78 D2
Dundry CE Prim Sch
  BS41 .... 78 D2
Dundry La BS13, BS15 . 65 D2
DUNDRY HILL 80 B3
Dundry La
  Bristol BS48 ... 78 C3
  Winford BS40 .. 95 A7
Dundry View BS4 . 64 A1
Dunedin Way BS22 . 89 C4
Dunford Rd BS3 . 63 D3
Dungarvon Rd BS24 . 105 F7
Dunkeld Ave BS34 . 36 F5
Dunkerry Rd BS3 . 63 E3
DUNKERTON 117 E4
Dunkery Cl BS48 . 59 E1
Dunkery Rd BS23 . 87 F1
DUNKIRK 50 F3
Dunkirk Rd BS16 . 50 F3
Dunlin Dr BS20 . 45 F6
Dunmail Rd BS10 . 35 C2

Dunmore St 3 BS2 ... 63 F4
Dunmurry BS9 ... 48 D3
Dunsdown La SN14 ... 55 B5
Dunsford Pl BA2 ... 102 B6
Dunster Cres BS24 ... 105 A2
Dunster Ct BS25 ... 125 A8
Dunster Gdns
Bristol BS30 ... 66 B2
5 Nailsea BS48 ... 59 E1
Dunster Ho BA2 ... 102 A2
Dunster Rd
Bristol BS4 ... 79 F8
Keynsham BS31 ... 81 E4
Dunsters Rd BS49 ... 74 F1
Durban Rd BS34 ... 35 F8
Durban Way BS49 ... 74 B1
Durbin Park Rd BS21 ... 57 F5
Durbin Wlk BS5 ... 64 A8
Durcott La BA2 ... 133 D8
Durdham Ct BS6 ... 49 A3
Durdham Pk BS6 ... 49 A3
Durham Gr BS31 ... 81 D4
Durham Rd
11 Bristol BS2 ... 50 A2
Charfield GL12 ... 11 A5
Durleigh Cl BS13 ... 79 A7
Durley Hill BS31 ... 81 C7
Durley La BS31 ... 81 D7
Durley Pk BA2 ... 101 E4
Durnford Ave BS3 ... 63 A4
Durnford St BS3 ... 63 A4
Durnhill BS40 ... 128 F7
Dursley Cl BS37 ... 27 E1
Dursley Rd BS11 ... 47 E5
Durston BS24 ... 105 A2
Durville Rd BS13 ... 79 B6
Durweston Wlk BS14 ... 80 C8
Dutton Cl BS14 ... 80 D6
Dutton Rd BS14 ... 80 D6
Dutton Wlk BS14 ... 80 D6
Dye House Rd GL12 ... 11 F5
Dyers Cl BS13 ... 79 D4
DYER'S COMMON ... 22 C3
Dyer's La BS37 ... 27 A4
Dylan Thomas Ct 4
BS30 ... 66 A5
Dymboro Ave BA3 ... 132 F1
Dymboro Cl BA3 ... 132 F1
Dymboro Gdns BA3 ... 132 F1
Dymboro The BA3 ... 132 F1
DYRHAM ... 54 D4
Dyrham BS16 ... 37 C1
Dyrham Cl
Bristol, Henleaze BS9 ... 49 D6
Bristol, Kingswood BS15 ... 65 F8
Pucklechurch BS16 ... 53 C4
Thornbury BS35 ... 8 C3
Dyrham Par BS34 ... 36 C8
Dyrham Park* SN14 ... 54 F5
Dyrham Rd BS15 ... 65 F8
Dyrham View BS16 ... 53 C4
Dyson Cl BS49 ... 91 B8

E

Eagle Cl BS22 ... 105 D8
Eagle Cres BS16 ... 53 C5
Eagle Dr BS34 ... 35 E8
Eagle Pk BA1 ... 85 F5
Eagle Rd
Batheaston BA1 ... 85 F5
Bristol BS4 ... 64 D2
Eagles The BS49 ... 91 B8
Eagles Wood BS32 ... 24 D3
Eagles Wood Bsns Pk
BS32 ... 24 C3
Earlesfield BS48 ... 59 C1
Earlham Gr BS23 ... 105 A7
Earl Russell Way BS5 ... 64 B7
Earlsmead BS16 ... 50 E4
Earl St BS1 ... 143 A4
Earlstone Cl BS30 ... 66 A4
Earlstone Cres BS30 ... 66 A4
EARTHCOTT GREEN ... 25 E7
Earthcott Rd BS35 ... 15 F1
Easedale Cl BS10 ... 35 D2
Eastbourne Ave 15
BA1 ... 85 B1
Eastbourne Rd 9 BS5 ... 64 B8
Eastbury Cl BS35 ... 8 C1
Eastbury Rd
Bristol BS16 ... 51 A4
Thornbury BS35 ... 8 C1
East Cl BA2 ... 101 A5
EAST CLEVEDON ... 57 H3
East Clevedon Triangle
BS21 ... 57 H3
Eastcliff BS20 ... 45 E7
Eastcombe Gdns BS23 ... 87 F1
Eastcombe Rd BS23 ... 87 F1
Eastcote Pk BS14 ... 80 B5
Eastcourt Rd BS39 ... 131 F8
Eastcroft BS40 ... 110 E2
East Croft BS9 ... 49 C7
Eastcroft Cl BS40 ... 110 E2
East Ct BS3 ... 62 F3
Eastdown Pl BA3 ... 133 E5
Eastdown Rd BA3 ... 133 D5
EAST DUNDRY ... 79 A1
East Dundry La BS41 ... 79 A1
East Dundry Rd BS13,
BS14 ... 79 F2
EAST END
Blagdon ... 110 E2
Marshfield ... 70 A8
Nailsea ... 60 A1
EASTER COMPTON ... 23 A2
Easter Ct BS37 ... 27 B1
Eastermead La BS29 ... 107 C3
Eastern Ho BS23 ... 87 E1
EASTERTOWN ... 122 D2
Eastertown BS24 ... 122 D1
EASTFIELD ... 49 B7
Eastfield BS9 ... 49 B7
Eastfield Ave BA1 ... 84 B2
Eastfield Dr BS37 ... 27 E4
Eastfield Gdns BS23 ... 87 F1
Eastfield Pk BS23 ... 87 F1
Eastfield Rd
Bristol, Eastfield BS9 ... 49 B7
Bristol, Montpelier BS6 ... 49 D2
Bristol, Westbury on Trym
BS9 ... 49 A7
Hutton BS24 ... 105 E2
Eastfield Terr BS9 ... 49 B6
Eastgate Office Ctr
BS5 ... 50 B3
Eastgate Ret Pk BS5 ... 50 B3
East Gr BS6 ... 49 F1
EAST HARPTREE ... 129 E4
East Harptree CE Prim Sch
BS40 ... 129 F4
EAST HEWISH ... 90 B6
East Hill BS9 ... 49 B7
Eastlake Cl BS7 ... 50 B7
Eastland Ave BS35 ... 8 C2
Eastland Rd BS35 ... 8 C2
Eastlea BS21 ... 57 D1
East Lea Rd BA1 ... 101 A8
Eastleigh Cl BS16 ... 51 E4
Eastleigh Rd
Bristol, Brentry BS10 ... 35 D1
Bristol, Staple Hill BS16 ... 51 E3
Eastley Cl GL12 ... 9 E7
Eastlyn Rd BS13 ... 79 B8
East Mead BA3 ... 133 B2
Eastmead Ct BS9 ... 48 E4
Eastmead La BS9 ... 48 E4
Eastnor Rd BS14 ... 80 A3
Easton Bsns Ctr BS5 ... 64 B8
Easton CE Prim Sch
BS5 ... 64 A8
Easton Ct BA3 ... 131 E1
Easton Gdns BA1 ... 85 F5
Easton Hill Rd BS35 ... 8 D1
Easton Ho 9 BA1 ... 85 C1
EASTON-IN-GORDANO
... 47 A4
Easton Rd
Bristol, Newton BS5 ... 64 A7
Bristol, Upper Easton
BS5 ... 64 B8
Pill BS20 ... 47 C4
Easton Way BS5 ... 64 A8
Eastover Cl BS9 ... 49 A8
Eastover Gr BA2 ... 101 C1
Eastover Rd BS39 ... 115 D1
East Par BS9 ... 48 C6
East Park Dr BS5 ... 50 C2
Eastpark Trad Est BS5 ... 50 D1
East Pk BS5 ... 50 C2
East Priory Cl BS9 ... 49 A7
East Ridge Dr BS13 ... 78 F5
EAST ROLSTONE ... 90 B1
East Shrubbery 3 BS6 ... 49 B2
East St
Avonmouth BS11 ... 33 A1
Banwell BS29 ... 107 C3
Bristol, Southville BS3 ... 63 D4
EAST TWERTON ... 101 D6
East View BS16 ... 51 F6
EASTVILLE ... 50 C3
Eastville BA1 ... 85 B1
Eastway BS48 ... 59 E3
East Way BA2 ... 101 A5
Eastway Cl BS48 ... 59 D2
Eastway Sq BS48 ... 59 E3
Eastwell La BS25 ... 124 E6
East Wlk BS37 ... 27 E1
Eastwood BA2 ... 102 F6
Eastwood Cl BS39 ... 115 C1
Eastwood Cres BS4 ... 64 F3
East Wood Pl BS20 ... 45 E7
Eastwood Rd BS4 ... 64 F4
Eastwoods BA1 ... 86 B3
Eaton Cl
Bristol BS14 ... 80 E5
Bristol, Fishponds BS16 ... 51 B4
Eaton Cres BS8 ... 142 A4
Eaton St 14 BS3 ... 63 C3
Ebden Lo 15 BS22 ... 89 A2
EBDON ... 89 B6
Ebdon La BS22 ... 89 C5
Ebdon Rd BS22 ... 88 F4
Ebenezer La BS9 ... 48 E5
Ebenezer St BS5 ... 64 D7
Ebenezer Terr BA2 ... 141 C1
Eccleston Ho 1 BS5 ... 64 B6
Eckweek Gdns BA2 ... 134 D8
Eckweek La BA2 ... 134 E8
Eckweek Rd BA2 ... 134 D8
Eclipse Ct 1 BS16 ... 51 C4
Eclipse Office Pk 2
BS16 ... 51 C4
Eddington Ct BS23 ... 104 D7
Eden Croft BS22 ... 105 E8
Eden Gr BS7 ... 36 A1
Eden Office Pk BS20 ... 47 E4
Eden Park Cl BA1 ... 86 A4
Eden Park Dr BA1 ... 86 A4
Eden Terr BA1 ... 85 B2
Eden Villas 4 BA1 ... 85 C2
Edgar Bldgs BA1 ... 141 B3
Edgarley Ct BS21 ... 57 E5
Edgecombe Ave BS22 ... 88 D2
Edgecombe Cl BS15 ... 51 F1
Edgecombe Mews BA1 ... 84 B1
Edgecorner La SN14 ... 43 A3
Edgecumbe Rd BS6 ... 49 D2
Edgefield Cl BS14 ... 79 F3
Edgefield Rd BS14 ... 79 F3
Edgehill Rd BS21 ... 57 F6
Edgeware Rd
Bristol, Southville BS3 ... 63 C4
Bristol, Staple Hill BS16 ... 51 D4
Edgewood Cl
Bristol BS14 ... 80 B8
Bristol, Longwell Green
BS30 ... 66 A3
Edgeworth BS37 ... 39 C6
Edgeworth Rd BA2 ... 101 C2
Edinburgh Pl 1 BS23 ... 104 E8
Edinburgh Rd BS31 ... 81 E4
Edington Gr BS10 ... 35 A2
Edmund Cl BS16 ... 51 D6
Edmund Ct BS16 ... 53 B6
Edna Ave BS4 ... 64 E3
Edward Bird Ho BS7 ... 50 B6
Edward Ct BS31 ... 81 F4
Edward Rd
Bristol, Kingswood
BS15 ... 65 E8
Bristol, Totterdown BS4 ... 64 B4
Clevedon BS21 ... 57 G5
Edward Rd S BS21 ... 57 G5
Edward Rd W BS21 ... 57 G6
Edwards Ct 17 BS5 ... 64 D7
Edward St
Bath, Bathwick BA2 ... 102 B7
Bath, Lower Weston
BA1 ... 101 C7
Bristol, Eastville BS5 ... 50 D2
Bristol, Moorfields BS5 ... 64 C7
Edwin Short Cl BS30 ... 82 E8
Effingham Rd BS6 ... 49 E2
Egerton Brow BS7 ... 49 D4
Egerton Ct BS7 ... 49 E4
Egerton Rd
Bath BA2 ... 101 E4
Bristol BS7 ... 49 D4
Eggshill La BS37 ... 27 D1
Eglin Croft BS13 ... 79 B4
Eighth Ave
Bristol BS14 ... 80 A7
Bristol, Filton BS7 ... 36 B1
Eirene Terr BS20 ... 47 D4
ELBERTON ... 14 A6
Elberton BS15 ... 66 A8
Elberton Rd
Bristol BS9 ... 48 B7
Elberton BS35 ... 13 F5
Elborough Ave BS49 ... 91 B8
Elborough Gdns BS24 ... 106 C3
Elbridge Ho 3 BS2 ... 143 C3
Elbury Ave BS15 ... 51 C2
Elbury View GL12 ... 11 B5
Elderberry Wlk
Bristol BS10 ... 35 C3
Weston-S-M BS22 ... 88 F1
Elderwood Dr BS30 ... 66 A3
Elderwood Rd BS14 ... 80 B7
Eldon Pl BA1 ... 85 B2
Eldon Terr BS3 ... 63 D3
Eldonwall Trad Est
BS4 ... 64 C5
Eldon Way BS4 ... 64 C5
Eldred Cl BS9 ... 48 D5
Eleanor Cl BA2 ... 101 A5
Eleanor Cotts BA2 ... 101 A6
Eleventh Ave BS7 ... 36 B1
Elfin Rd BS16 ... 51 A5
Elgar Cl
Bristol BS4 ... 79 D6
Clevedon BS21 ... 57 G1
Elgin Ave BS7 ... 35 F1
Elgin Pk BS6 ... 49 B2
Elgin Rd BS16 ... 51 B2
Eliot Cl
Bristol BS7 ... 36 A1
Weston-S-M BS23 ... 105 A3
Elizabeth Cl
Hutton BS24 ... 105 D3
Thornbury BS35 ... 15 D8
Elizabeth Cres BS34 ... 36 E4
Elizabeths Mews 12
BS4 ... 64 F6
Elizabeth Way BS16 ... 52 B3
Elkstone Wlk BS30 ... 66 C2
Ella Cl BS16 ... 51 C6
Ellacombe Rd BS30 ... 65 F2
Ellan Hay Rd BS34 ... 37 A6
Ellbridge Cl BS9 ... 48 D5
Ellenborough Cres
BS23 ... 104 E6
Ellenborough Ct
BS23 ... 104 E6
Ellenborough Ho BS8 ... 142 A2
Ellenborough Park Rd
BS23 ... 104 E6
Ellenborough Pk N
BS23 ... 104 D6
Ellenborough Pk S
BS23 ... 104 D6
Ellen Ho BA2 ... 101 A5
Ellerncroft Rd GL12 ... 11 F8
Ellesmere BS35 ... 15 C8
Ellesmere Rd
1 Bristol BS4 ... 64 D1
Weston-S-M BS23 ... 104 D2
Ellfield Cl BS13 ... 78 F6
Ellick Rd BS40 ... 110 D1
Ellicks Cl BS32 ... 24 E2
Ellicott Rd BS7 ... 49 F5
Ellinghurst Cl BS10 ... 35 A2
Elliott Ave BS16 ... 37 C1
Elliott Ho BS7 ... 50 A3
Ellis Ave BS13 ... 79 A8
Ellis Pk BS22 ... 89 C4
Elliston Dr BA2 ... 101 B4
Elliston La BS6 ... 49 C2
Elliston Rd BS6 ... 49 C2
Ellsbridge Cl BS31 ... 82 B5
Ellsbridge Ho Norton
Radstock Coll BS31 ... 82 B5
Ellsworth Rd BS10 ... 34 F2
Ellyott Ct 5 BS16 ... 50 E3
Elmbrook BA1 ... 101 D8
Elm Cl
Banwell BS29 ... 106 E4
Bristol BS34 ... 36 D7
Bristol, Lawrence Weston
BS11 ... 33 F1
Chipping Sodbury BS37 ... 28 A1
Nailsea BS48 ... 59 C1
Star BS25 ... 108 D1
Yatton BS49 ... 91 B7
Elmcroft Cres BS7 ... 50 A4
Elm Ct
Bristol BS14 ... 80 A6
Bristol, Redland BS6 ... 49 B2
Keynsham BS31 ... 81 C4
Elmdale Cres BS35 ... 8 C1
Elmdale Gdns 4 BS16 ... 51 A4
Elmdale Rd
Bristol, Bedminster
BS3 ... 63 B2
Bristol BS8 ... 142 B3
Elm Farm BS48 ... 60 A2
Elmfield BS15 ... 65 E6
Elmfield Cl BS15 ... 65 E6
Elmfield Rd BS9 ... 49 A8
Elmfield Sch for Deaf
Children BS10 ... 49 B8
Elm Gr
Bath, Larkhill BA1 ... 85 C2
Bath, The Oval BA2 ... 101 C4
Locking BS24 ... 105 F4
Elmgrove Ave 10 BS5 ... 64 B8
Elmgrove Dr BS37 ... 27 F2
Elmgrove Pk 1 BS6 ... 49 D1
Elmgrove Rd
Bristol, Fishponds
BS16 ... 50 E3
Bristol, Redland BS6 ... 49 D1
Elmham Way BS24 ... 89 B1
Elm Hayes BS13 ... 78 F6
Elmhirst Gdns BS37 ... 28 A2
Elmhurst Ave BS5 ... 50 D3
Elmhurst Est BA1 ... 86 A4
Elmhurst Gdns BS41 ... 77 F8
Elmhurst Rd BS24 ... 105 E2
Elmhyrst Rd BS23 ... 104 F8
Elming Down Cl BS32 ... 36 D6
Elm La BS6 ... 49 B2
Elmlea Ave BS9 ... 48 F5
Elmlea Jun & Inf Schs
BS9 ... 48 F5
Elmleigh Ave BS16 ... 52 B5
Elmleigh Cl BS16 ... 52 B5
Elmleigh Rd BS16 ... 52 B5
Elm Lodge Rd BS48 ... 60 B2
Elmore
Bristol BS15 ... 51 F2
Yate BS37 ... 39 D8
Elmore Rd
Bristol BS34 ... 23 F1
Bristol, Horfield BS7 ... 50 A6
Elm Park Prim Sch
BS36 ... 37 E6
Elm Pk BS34 ... 36 A2
Elm Pl BA2 ... 101 F4
Elm Rd
Bristol, Horfield BS7 ... 49 E5
Bristol, Kingswood BS15 ... 65 E6
Paulton BS39 ... 132 E5
Elms Gr BS34 ... 24 B1
Elmsleigh Rd BS23 ... 104 E4
Elmsley La BS22 ... 88 C5
Elms The
Banwell BS29 ... 107 A4
Bath, Lambridge BA1 ... 85 C2
Bath, Weston Park BA1 ... 84 C1
Bristol, Frenchay BS16 ... 37 C1
Bristol, Henbury BS10 ... 34 F2
Tockington BS32 ... 14 B2
Elmswood BS23 ... 104 F8
Elm Terr BA3 ... 139 C8
Elmtree Ave BS16 ... 52 A7
Elm Tree Ave
Nailsea BS21 ... 59 A4
Radstock BA3 ... 133 D1
Elmtree Cl BS15 ... 51 D1
Elmtree Dr BS13 ... 78 F5
Elm Tree Pk BS20 ... 46 D3
Elm Tree Rd
Clevedon BS21 ... 57 F2
Locking BS24 ... 106 A4
Elmtree Way BS15 ... 51 D1
Elmvale Dr BS24 ... 105 F3
Elm View
Midsomer Norton
BA3 ... 133 B1
Temple Cloud BS39 ... 114 E1
Elm Wlk
Portishead BS20 ... 45 C4
Yatton BS49 ... 91 B7
Elm Wood BS37 ... 39 E8
Elsbert Dr BS13 ... 78 E6
Elstree Rd BS5 ... 50 E1
Elton Ho
Bristol, Clifton BS8 ... 142 A3
Elton Ho *continued*
2 Bristol, Newton BS2 ... 143 C3
Elton La BS7 ... 49 D2
Elton Mans 5 BS7 ... 49 D2
Elton Rd
Bristol, Bishopston
BS7 ... 49 D2
Bristol BS8 ... 142 C3
Bristol, Kingswood BS15 ... 51 C1
Clevedon BS21 ... 57 E3
Weston-S-M BS22 ... 89 A4
Elton St BS2 ... 143 C4
Elvard Cl BS13 ... 79 A4
Elvard Rd BS13 ... 79 A4
Elvaston Rd BS3 ... 63 E3
Elwell La BS40, BS41 ... 78 A1
Ely Gr BS9 ... 48 B7
Embassy Rd BS5 ... 50 E1
Embassy Wlk BS5 ... 50 E1
Embercourt Dr BS48 ... 76 A6
Embleton Rd BS10 ... 35 C2
EMERSON'S GREEN ... 52 C6
Emersons Green La
BS16 ... 52 B6
Emersons Green Prim Sch
BS16 ... 52 B7
Emerson Sq BS7 ... 50 A8
Emerson Way BS16 ... 52 C7
Emery Gate BS29 ... 107 B3
Emery Rd BS4 ... 64 F1
Emet Gr BS16 ... 52 B6
Emet La BS16 ... 52 B6
Eminence BS1 ... 143 B1
Emley La BS40 ... 110 B6
Emlyn Cl 6 BS22 ... 89 B4
Emlyn Rd BS5 ... 50 C2
Emma-Chris Way
BS34 ... 36 C2
Emmanuel Ct BS8 ... 142 A4
Emmett Wood BS14 ... 80 B3
Empire Cres BS15 ... 65 E4
Empress Menen Gdns
BA1 ... 101 A8
Emra Cl BS5 ... 50 F1
Emra Ho 10 BS5 ... 64 A8
Enderleigh Gdns
BS25 ... 108 F4
Enfield Rd BS16 ... 51 A3
ENGINE COMMON ... 27 B5
Engine Common La
BS37 ... 27 C5
Engine La BS48 ... 75 B8
England's Cres BS36 ... 37 E7
ENGLISHCOMBE ... 100 F2
Englishcombe La
BA2 ... 101 D3
Englishcombe Rd
BS13 ... 79 C3
Englishcombe Rise
BA2 ... 101 A3
Englishcombe Tithe
Barn* BA2 ... 100 F2
Englishcombe Way
BA2 ... 101 E3
Enmore BS24 ... 105 A2
Ennerdale Cl BS23 ... 105 A5
Ennerdale Rd BS10 ... 35 D2
Enterprise Ctr The
BS24 ... 105 A3
Enterprise Trade Ctr
BS4 ... 79 E7
Entry Hill BA2 ... 101 F2
Entry Hill Dr BA2 ... 101 F3
Entry Hill Gdns BA2 ... 101 F3
Entry Hill Pk BA2 ... 101 F2
Entry Rise BA2 ... 101 F1
Epney Cl BS34 ... 23 F1
Epsom Cl BS16 ... 37 F1
Epworth Rd BS10 ... 35 A3
Equinox BS32 ... 24 C3
Erin Wlk BS4 ... 79 D8
Ermine Way BS11 ... 47 C7
Ermleet Rd 1 BS6 ... 49 C2
Ernest Barker Cl 15
BS5 ... 64 B7
Ernestville Rd BS16 ... 50 F3
Ervine Terr BS2 ... 143 C4
Esgar Rise BS22 ... 88 E3
Eskdale BS35 ... 15 D7
Eskdale Cl BS22 ... 105 D8
Esmond Gr BS21 ... 57 F4
Esplanade Rd BS20 ... 45 C7
Essery Rd BS5 ... 50 C2
Esson Rd BS15 ... 51 B1
Estcourt Gdns BS16 ... 50 D5
Estoril BS37 ... 27 F1
Estuary Ho BS20 ... 45 E7
Estune Wlk BS41 ... 62 A2
Etloe Rd BS6 ... 49 A4
Etonhurst BS23 ... 104 D6
Eton La BS29 ... 106 E7
Eton Rd BS4 ... 64 D3
Ettlingen Way BS21 ... 57 H2
Ettricke Dr BS16 ... 51 B5
Eugene Flats 7 BS2 ... 143 A4
Eugene St
Bristol, Kingsdown
BS2 ... 143 A4
Bristol, St Pauls BS2,
BS5 ... 143 C4
Evans Cl BS4 ... 64 F5
Evans Rd BS6 ... 49 B2
Eveleigh Ave BA1 ... 85 D3
Evelyn Rd
Bath BA1 ... 101 B8

Evelyn Rd continued
Bristol BS10 . . . . .49 C7
Evelyn Terr 🔟 BA1 . . . . . . .85 A1
Evenlode Gdns BS11 . . . . . .47 F5
Evenlode Way BS31 . . . . . . .82 A3
Evercreech Rd BS14 . . . . . .80 B4
Eve Rd BS5 . . . . .50 B1
Everest Ave BS16 . . . . .50 E4
Everest Rd BS16 . . . . .50 E4
Evergreen Cl BS25 . . . . . . .107 F1
Ewart Rd BS22 . . . . .105 C8
Ewell Rd BS14 . . . . .80 B6
Exbourne 🔟 BS22 . . . . .89 A2
Excelsior St BA2 . . . . .102 B5
Excelsior Terr BA3 . . . . . . .133 B1
Exchange Ave BS1 . . . . . . .143 A2
Exchange Ct 🔟 BS15 . . . . . .65 D8
Exeter Bldgs BS6 . . . . .49 B2
Exeter Rd
Bristol BS3 . . . . .63 B4
Portishead BS20 . . . . .45 E4
Weston-S-M BS23 . . . . . . .104 E5
Exford Cl BS23 . . . . .104 F2
Exley Cl BS30 . . . . .66 D5
Exmoor Rd BA2 . . . . .101 C2
Exmoor St BS3 . . . . .63 B3
Exmouth Rd BS4 . . . . .63 F1
Explore La BS1 . . . . .142 C2
Exton BS24 . . . . .105 A2
Exton Cl BS14 . . . . .80 B5
Eyer's La BS2 . . . . .143 C3
Eyers Rd BS24 . . . . .105 F7

F

Faber Gr BS13 . . . . .79 C4
Fabian Dr BS34 . . . . .36 E5
Factory Rd BS36 . . . . .37 F7
FAILAND 61 C3
Failand Cres BS9 . . . . .48 C5
Failand La
Easton-in-G BS8 . . . . .47 A1
Portbury BS20 . . . . .46 F2
Failand Wlk BS9 . . . . .48 C6
Fairacre Cl
Bristol BS7 . . . . .50 B5
Locking BS24 . . . . .106 D4
Fairacres Cl BS31 . . . . .81 F5
Fair Cl BA2 . . . . .136 E4
Fairfax St BS1 . . . . .143 B3
Fairfield
Rode BA11 . . . . .137 F1
Tunley BA2 . . . . .117 A3
Fairfield Ave BA1 . . . . .85 A2
Fairfield Cl
Backwell BS48 . . . . .76 D7
Marshfield SN14 . . . . .69 F8
Weston-S-M BS22 . . . . .88 B1
Fairfield High Sch
Bristol BS5, BS7 . . . . .50 A3
Bristol BS6 . . . . .49 F2
Fairfield Mead BS48 . . . . . .76 D7
FAIRFIELD PARK 85 A2
Fairfield Park Rd BA1 . . . . .85 A2
Fairfield Pl BS3 . . . . .63 B4
Fairfield Pneu Sch
BS48 . . . . .76 C6
Fairfield Rd
Bath BA1 . . . . .85 B1
Bristol, Montpelier BS6 . . . .49 F2
Bristol, Southville BS3 . . . . .63 B4
Fairfield Terr
Bath BA1 . . . . .85 A1
Peasedown St John
BA2 . . . . .134 C7
Fairfield View BA1 . . . . .85 A2
Fairfield Way BS48 . . . . .76 D7
Fairfoot Rd BS4 . . . . .64 A3
Fairford Cl BS15 . . . . .51 F2
Fairford Cres BS34 . . . . . . .36 C8
Fairford Rd BS11 . . . . .47 D7
Fair Furlong BS13 . . . . .79 A4
Fair Furlong Prim Sch
BS13 . . . . .79 B4
Fairhaven BS37 . . . . .27 E1
Fairhaven Rd BS6 . . . . .49 C4
Fair Hill BS25 . . . . .125 F8
Fairlawn BS16 . . . . .51 D4
Fair Lawn BS30 . . . . .66 B4
Fairlawn Ave BS34 . . . . . . .36 A3
Fairlawn Rd BS6 . . . . .49 F2
Fairlyn Dr BS15 . . . . .51 F3
Fairoaks BS30 . . . . .66 A3
Fairseat Ind Unit
BS40 . . . . .112 E7
Fairview BS22 . . . . .88 F4
Fairview Ct BS15 . . . . .65 D6
Fair View Dr BS6 . . . . .49 C2
Fairview Ho BS9 . . . . .48 F8
Fairview Rd BS15 . . . . .65 F8
Fairway BS4 . . . . .64 D1
Fairway Cl
Bristol BS30 . . . . .66 B4
Weston-S-M BS22 . . . . .88 B2
Fairway Ind Ctr BS34 . . . . .35 F3
Fairways BS31 . . . . .82 E2
Fairy Hill BS39 . . . . .98 D6
Falcon Cl
Bristol, Patchway BS34 . . . .35 E8
Bristol, Westbury on T
BS9 . . . . .48 F8
Portishead BS20 . . . . .45 D4
Falcon Cres BS22 . . . . .105 D8
Falcon Ct BS9 . . . . .49 A7

Falcondale Rd BS9 . . . . . . .48 F7
Falcondale Wlk BS9 . . . . . .49 A8
Falcon Dr BS34 . . . . .35 E8
Falconer Rd BA1 . . . . .84 A3
Falcons Gate BS37 . . . . . . .27 C3
Falcon Way BS35 . . . . .8 D2
Falcon Wlk BS34 . . . . .23 E1
FALFIELD 9 E7
Falfield Rd BS4 . . . . .64 C3
Falfield Wlk BS10 . . . . .49 C8
Falkland Rd 🔟 BS6 . . . . . . .49 F2
Fallodon Ct BS9 . . . . .48 B5
Fallodon Way BS9 . . . . .49 B5
Fallowfield
Blagdon BS40 . . . . .110 E2
Bristol BS30 . . . . .66 D5
Weston-S-M BS22 . . . . .88 F3
Falmouth Cl BS48 . . . . .60 A1
Falmouth Rd BS7 . . . . .49 E4
Fane Cl BS10 . . . . .35 A3
Fanshawe Rd BS14 . . . . . . .80 A7
Faraday Rd 🔟 BS8 . . . . . . .62 F5
Farendell Rd BS16 . . . . .38 B1
Far Handstones BS30 . . . . .66 A4
Farington Rd BS10 . . . . .49 D7
Farlands BS16 . . . . .53 B6
FARLEIGH 76 D7
Farleigh Ct BS48 . . . . .77 B8
FARLEIGH HUNGERFORD
. . . . .137 E8
**Farleigh Hungerford
Castle*** BA2 . . . . .137 E8
Farleigh La GL12 . . . . .10 C2
Farleigh Rd
Backwell BS48 . . . . .76 C6
Clevedon BS21 . . . . .57 D1
Keynsham BS31 . . . . .81 D4
Norton St Philip BA2 . . . . .136 F5
Farleigh Rise BA15 . . . . . . .86 E1
Farleigh View BA15 . . . . . .120 F3
FARLEIGH WICK 103 E4
Farleigh Wlk BS13 . . . . .79 A8
Farler's End BS48 . . . . .75 F8
FARLEY 44 B1
Farley Cl BS34 . . . . .36 C7
FARMBOROUGH 116 B6
Farmborough CE Prim Sch
BA2 . . . . .115 F6
Farm Cl
Bristol BS7 . . . . .50 B6
Weston-S-M BS22 . . . . .89 C4
Farmcote GL12 . . . . .19 D8
Farm Ct BS16 . . . . .51 E7
Farmer Rd BS13 . . . . .78 E4
Farmhouse Cl 🔟 BS48 . . . .59 E2
Farmhouse Ct 🔟 BS48 . . . .59 E1
Farm La
Easter Compton BS35 . . . . .22 E2
Yellow BA2 . . . . .118 E1
Farm Lees GL12 . . . . .11 A6
Farm Rd
Bristol BS16 . . . . .51 E7
Hutton BS24 . . . . .105 E2
Weston-S-M BS22 . . . . .88 B1
Farmwell Cl BS13 . . . . .79 B5
Farnaby Cl BS4 . . . . .79 C7
Farnborough Rd
BS24 . . . . .106 C4
Farndale BS5 . . . . .65 A6
Farndale Rd BS22 . . . . .105 D8
Farne Cl BS9 . . . . .49 B5
Farrant Cl BS4 . . . . .79 D6
Farringford Ho BS5 . . . . . . .50 D2
Farrington Fields
BS39 . . . . .132 C3
Farrington Fields Trad Est
BS39 . . . . .132 C3
FARRINGTON GURNEY
. . . . .132 A3
**Farrington Gurney CE
Prim Sch** BS39 . . . . .132 A4
Farrington Rd BS39 . . . . . .132 C5
Farrington Way BS39 . . . . .132 A3
Farrs La BA2 . . . . .102 B2
Farr's La BS1 . . . . .143 A2
Farr St BS11 . . . . .47 B8
Farthing Combe
BS26 . . . . .125 D2
Farthing Row BA11 . . . . . .137 E1
FAULKLAND 135 E2
Faulkland La BA2,
BA3 . . . . .135 C4
Faulkland Rd BA2 . . . . .101 D5
Faulkland View BA2 . . . . . .134 E7
Faversham Dr BS24 . . . . . .105 A1
Fawkes Cl BS15 . . . . .66 B8
Featherbed La
Chew Stoke BS40 . . . . .95 A3
Clutton BS39 . . . . .114 C6
Oldbury-on-S BS35 . . . . .7 B6
Featherstone Rd 🔟
BS16 . . . . .50 F4
Fedden Village BS21 . . . . . .44 F5
Feeder Rd BS2 . . . . .64 A5
Felix Rd BS5 . . . . .64 B8
Felstead Rd BS10 . . . . .35 E1
Feltham Ct BS34 . . . . .35 F2
Feltham Rd BS16 . . . . .53 C6
FELTON 94 D8
Felton Gr BS13 . . . . .79 A8
Felton La BS40 . . . . .94 E7
Felton St BS40 . . . . .94 C7
Fenbrook Cl BS16 . . . . .37 B1
Feniton 🔟 BS22 . . . . .89 A2
Fennel Dr BS34 . . . . .37 A7
Fennel La BS26 . . . . .125 B2
Fennell Gr BS10 . . . . .35 A3
Fenners BS22 . . . . .89 B4

Fenns La BS41 . . . . .61 E1
Fenshurst Gdns BS41 . . . . .77 F8
Fenswood Cl BS41 . . . . .61 F1
Fenswood Ct BS41 . . . . .61 E1
Fenswood Mead BS41 . . . . .61 E1
Fenswood Rd BS41 . . . . . . .61 E1
Fenton Cl BS31 . . . . .82 D3
Fenton Ct BS7 . . . . .49 D4
Fenton Rd BS7 . . . . .49 D4
Ferenberge Cl BA2 . . . . . . .116 A6
Fermaine Ave BS4 . . . . .64 F3
Fernbank Ct 🔟 BS6 . . . . . .49 C2
Fernbank Rd BS6 . . . . .49 C2
Fernbrook Cl BS16 . . . . .37 B1
Fern Cl
Bristol BS10 . . . . .35 B3
Midsomer Norton BA3 . . . .133 B1
Ferncliffe BS8 . . . . .62 E7
Ferndale Ave BS30 . . . . . . .66 A3
Ferndale Cl BS32 . . . . .24 D7
Ferndale Rd
Bath BA1 . . . . .85 C3
Bristol BS34 . . . . .36 A2
Portishead BS20 . . . . .46 E5
Portbury BS20 . . . . .46 E5
Radstock BA3 . . . . .139 C8
Ferndene BS32 . . . . .24 C2
Ferndown BS37 . . . . .27 E1
Ferndown Cl BS11 . . . . .48 A7
Ferndown Grange BS9 . . . . .49 B6
Fern Gr
Bristol BS32 . . . . .36 D8
Nailsea BS48 . . . . .75 C8
Fernhill BS32 . . . . .24 C7
Fernhill Ct
Bristol BS11 . . . . .34 B1
Tockington BS32 . . . . .24 C7
Fernhurst Rd BS5 . . . . .50 F1
Fern La BS24 . . . . .122 B6
Fernlea Gdns BS20 . . . . . . .47 B4
Fernlea Rd BS22 . . . . .105 C7
Fernleaze BS36 . . . . .38 C6
Fernleigh Ct 🔟 BS6 . . . . . .49 B2
Fern Lo BS23 . . . . .104 D6
Fern Rd BS16 . . . . .51 D5
Fernside BS48 . . . . .76 A7
Fern St BS2 . . . . .49 F1
Fernsteed Rd BS13 . . . . . . .78 F6
Fernville Est BS21 . . . . .57 E2
Ferry Ct BA2 . . . . .102 B6
Ferry La
Bath BA2 . . . . .102 B6
Lympsham BS24 . . . . .122 C3
Ferryman's Ct BS2 . . . . . . .143 B2
Ferry Rd BS15 . . . . .65 D1
Ferry St BS1 . . . . .143 B2
Ferry Steps Ind Est
BS2 . . . . .64 A4
Fersfield BA2 . . . . .102 B3
Fiddes Rd BS6 . . . . .49 C4
Fiddlers Wood La
BS32 . . . . .36 E8
Fielders The BS22 . . . . .89 B4
Fieldfare Ave BS20 . . . . . . .46 A6
Field Farm Cl BS34 . . . . . . .36 F4
Fieldgardens Rd
BS39 . . . . .114 F1
Fielding Ho BA2 . . . . .101 A6
Fielding's Rd BA2 . . . . .101 C6
Fieldins BA15 . . . . .120 E7
Field La
Bristol BS30 . . . . .65 F3
Dyrham SN14 . . . . .54 F6
Littleton-u-S BS35 . . . . .14 A8
Tytherington BS35 . . . . .9 C2
Field Marshal Slim Ct 🔟
. . . . .64 A4
Florida Terr BA3 . . . . .133 C2
Flowerdown Bridge
BS22 . . . . .105 D2

Finch Cl
Thornbury BS35 . . . . .8 C2
Weston-S-M BS22 . . . . .105 E8
Finches The BS20 . . . . .45 F6
Finch Rd BS37 . . . . .40 A8
Finisterre Par BS20 . . . . . . .45 F6
Finmere Gdns BS22 . . . . . . .89 A4
Fircliff Pk BS20 . . . . .45 D7
Fireclay Rd BS5 . . . . .64 D6
Fire Engine La BS36 . . . . . .38 D7
Fire Station La BS11 . . . . . .33 B2
Firework Cl BS15 . . . . .66 B8
Firfield St BS4 . . . . .64 A4
Firgrove Cres BS37 . . . . . . .28 A2
Firgrove La BA2 . . . . .117 B1
Fir La BS40 . . . . .127 B5
Fir Leaze BS48 . . . . .59 B1
Fir Rd SN14 . . . . .70 F6
Firs Ct BS31 . . . . .81 C4
First Ave
Bath BA2 . . . . .101 E4
Bristol BS14 . . . . .80 A7
Bristol, St Anne's BS4 . . . . .64 E5
Portbury BS20 . . . . .46 E5
Radstock BA3 . . . . .139 C8
First Way BS11 . . . . .33 C1
Fir Tree Ave
Paulton BS39 . . . . .132 F4
Weston-S-M BS24 . . . . . . .105 E4
Fir Tree Cl BS34 . . . . .36 A8
Fir Tree La BS5 . . . . .65 A7
Fisher Ave BS15 . . . . .52 A1
Fisher Rd BS15 . . . . .52 A1
Fishers Mead BS41 . . . . . . .61 E1
FISHPONDS 51 A5
Fishponds Rd BS5 . . . . .50 D3
Fishponds Trad Est
BS5 . . . . .50 E2
Fishpool Hill BS10 . . . . .35 B4
Fitchett Wlk BS10 . . . . .34 F3
Fitzgerald Rd BS3 . . . . .63 F3
Fitzharding Ho 🔟
BS1 . . . . .142 C1
Fitzharding Rd BS20 . . . . . .47 E3
Fitzroy Circ BS20 . . . . .45 F6
Fitzroy Ho 🔟 BA2 . . . . . . .141 C3
Fitzroy Rd BS16 . . . . .51 B2
Fitzroy St BS4 . . . . .64 A4
Fitzroy Terr 🔟 BS6 . . . . . . .49 B2
Five Acre Dr BS16 . . . . .51 B7
Five Arches Cl BA3 . . . . . . .133 D2
Five C Doors Ctr BS21 . . . .57 D1
Flagstaff Rd BS26 . . . . .123 D7
Flamingo Cres BS22 . . . . . .105 E8
Flat The BS39 . . . . .114 D5
Flatwoods Cres BA2 . . . . . .102 F3
Flatwoods Rd BA2 . . . . .102 F3
FLAX BOURTON 76 F7
Flax Bourton CE Prim Sch
BS48 . . . . .76 F6
Flax Bourton Rd BS8 . . . . . .61 B3
Flaxman Cl BS7 . . . . .50 B6
FLAXPITS 38 A1
Flaxpits La BS36 . . . . .37 E5
Florence Brown Com Sch
BS4 .64 E1
Florence Gr BS22 . . . . .105 D8
Florence Pk
Almondsbury BS32 . . . . . . .24 C5
Bristol BS6 . . . . .49 B4
Florence Rd BS16 . . . . .51 E3

Forde Cl BS30 . . . . .65 F5
Fordell Pl BS4 . . . . .64 A3
Ford La BS16 . . . . .52 B6
Ford Rd
Peasedown St John
BA2 . . . . .134 D8
Wellow BA2 . . . . .118 F1
Ford St BS5 . . . . .64 C6
Fordfield Pl BA2 . . . . .141 C1
Forefield Rise BA2 . . . . . . .102 B4
Forefield Terr BA2 . . . . . . .102 A4
Forelands BS23 . . . . .87 B1
Forest Ave BS16 . . . . .51 B3
Forest Dr
Bristol BS10 . . . . .35 C3
Weston-S-M BS23 . . . . .88 A1
Forest Edge BS15 . . . . .65 C4
Forester Ave BA2 . . . . .102 B8
Forester Ct BA2 . . . . .141 C4
Forester La BA2 . . . . .102 B8
Forester Rd
Bath BA2 . . . . .102 B8
Portishead BS20 . . . . .45 D4
Forest Hills BS32 . . . . .24 B5
Forest Rd
Bristol, Fishponds
BS16 . . . . .51 B4
Bristol, Kingswood BS15 . . .65 D7
Forest Wlk
Bristol, Fishponds
BS16 . . . . .51 B2
Bristol, Kingswood BS15 . . .65 C7
Forge Rd BS20 . . . . .46 E3
Fortescue Rd BA3 . . . . .133 F2
Fortfield Rd BS14 . . . . .80 B5
Forth Ave BS20 . . . . .45 F6
FORTHAY 5 E5
Forty Acres La BS35 . . . . . .15 B3
Forum Bldgs BA1 . . . . .141 C1
Foss Cl 🔟 BS5 . . . . .64 F8
Fosse Barton BS48 . . . . . . .59 C2
Fosse Cl BS48 . . . . .59 C2
Fossedale Ave BS14 . . . . . .80 C6
Fossefield Rd BA3 . . . . .139 B6
Fosse Gdns BA2 . . . . .118 D8
Fosse Gn BA3 . . . . .133 E4
Fosse La
Batheaston BA1 . . . . .86 A4
Clandown BA3 . . . . .133 D3
Nailsea BS48 . . . . .59 D2
Fosseway
Clandown BA3 . . . . .133 E4
Clevedon BS21 . . . . .57 E2
Midsomer Norton BA3 . . . .139 A5
Radstock BA3 . . . . .139 C8
Fosse Way BS48 . . . . .59 C2
Fosseway Cl BA2 . . . . .134 C7
Fosse Way Cotts BA3 . . . . .139 C8
Fosseway Ct BS8 . . . . .142 A2
Fosse Way Est BA2 . . . . . .101 D1
Fosseway Gdns BA3 . . . . . .133 D1
Fosseway S BS37 . . . . .139 D7
Fosseway The BS8 . . . . . . .142 A3
Foster's Almshouses 🔟
BS1 . . . . .143 A3
Foster St BS5 . . . . .50 B2
Foundry Cotts BA2 . . . . . . .116 A4
Foundry La BS5 . . . . .50 F2
Foundry The BA1 . . . . .141 C3
Foundry Yd BS5 . . . . .50 F2
Fountain Bldgs 🔟
BA1 . . . . .141 B3
Fountain Ct
Bristol BS32 . . . . .24 C3
🔟 Yate BS37 . . . . .39 D7
Fountaine Ct 🔟 BS5 . . . . . .50 C2
Fountain Ho 🔟 BA1 . . . . . .141 B3
Fountain La BS25 . . . . .125 B7
Fountains Dr BS30 . . . . .65 F6
Four Acre Ave BS16 . . . . . .51 E8
Four Acre Cres BS16 . . . . . .37 E1
Four Acre Rd BS16 . . . . . . .51 E8
Four Acres BS13 . . . . .78 E4
Four Acres Cl
Bristol BS13 . . . . .78 F4
Nailsea BS48 . . . . .59 D1
Four Acres Prim Sch
BS13 . . . . .78 E4
Four Seasons Sq BS37 . . . .27 E1
Fourth Ave
Bristol BS14 . . . . .80 B7
Bristol, Filton BS7 . . . . .36 A1
Radstock BA3 . . . . .139 D8
Fourth Way BS11 . . . . . . .33 E1
Fowey Cl BS48 . . . . .76 A8
Fowey Rd BS22 . . . . .89 A4
Fox Ave BS37 . . . . .27 D2
Foxborough Gdns
BS32 . . . . .24 D2
Fox Cl
Bristol BS4 . . . . .64 F5
Hawkesbury Upton GL9 . . . .19 F3
Foxcombe Rd
Bath BA1 . . . . .101 B7
Bristol BS14 . . . . .80 B4
FOXCOTE 134 F4
Foxcote BS15 . . . . .65 F7
Foxcote Ave BA2 . . . . .134 F7
Foxcote Rd BS3 . . . . .63 A3
Foxcroft Cl BS32 . . . . .36 F6
Foxcroft Rd BS5 . . . . .64 D8
Fox Ct BS30 . . . . .65 F3
Fox Den Rd BS36 . . . . .36 D3
Foxe Rd BS36 . . . . .38 B8
Foxfield Ave BS32 . . . . .24 D3

Foxglove Cl
  Bristol BS16. . . . . .50 E5
  Thornbury BS35. . . . . .8 C2
  Weston-S-M BS22 . . . . .89 A5
FOX HILL 102 A2
Fox Hill Rd BA2 . . . . .102 A2
Foxhill Ho BA2 . . . . .102 A1
FOX HILLS 134 A1
Fox Ho
  Bristol, Broom Hill BS4 . . .64 E3
  Bristol, Victoria Park
  BS3. . . . . .142 A3
Foxholes La BA2 . . . . .14 C4
Fox & Hounds La BS31. . . .81 F5
Fox La BS25 . . . . .125 A7
Fox Rd BS5. . . . . .50 B1
Foye Ho BS40 . . . . .62 E6
Fraley Rd BS9 . . . . .49 C7
FRAMPTON COTTERELL
  . . . . .38 B7
Frampton Cotterell CE
  Prim Sch BS36 . . . . .38 A8
Frampton Cres BS16. . . . . .51 C4
Frampton Ct
  8 Bristol, Longwell Green
  BS30. . . . . .65 F4
  16 Bristol, Pile Marsh
  BS5. . . . . .64 D7
FRAMPTON END 38 D8
Frampton End Rd
  BS37. . . . . .26 D2
France La GL9 . . . . .20 B2
Frances Greeves Ct
  BS10. . . . . .34 F1
Frances Mews 12 BS3. . . . .63 C4
Francis Ct BS5 . . . . .64 E8
Francis Fox Rd 7
  BS23. . . . . .104 E7
Francis Ho BS2 . . . . .143 A4
Francis Pl BS30. . . . . .65 F4
Francis Rd
  Bristol, Bedminster
  BS3. . . . . .63 C2
  Bristol, Westbury on Trym
  BS10. . . . . .49 C8
Francis Way BS30 . . . . .66 D6
Francombe Gr BS10 . . . . . .49 E6
Francombe Ho BS1 . . . . . .143 A1
Frankcom Ho BA2. . . . . . . .102 B7
Frankfort Mans 7
  BS23. . . . . .87 C1
Frankland Cl BA1 . . . . .85 B1
Frankley Bldgs BA1. . . . . . .85 B1
Frankley Terr 6 BA1. . . . . .85 B1
Franklin Ct BS1 . . . . .143 B1
Franklin's Way BS49 . . . . . .74 F1
Franklyn Ct 6 BS16 . . . . . .50 E3
Franklyn La 10 BS2 . . . . . . .49 F1
Franklyn St BS2 . . . . .49 F1
Franklyn Terr BS39. . . . . . .132 A4
Fraser Cl BS22 . . . . .88 F4
Fraser St BS3 . . . . .63 D3
Frayne Rd BS3 . . . . .63 A4
Frederick Ave BA2 . . . . . . .134 C7
Frederick Pl BS8 . . . . .142 B3
Fredrick St BS4 . . . . .64 A4
Freeland Bldgs 1 BS5. . . .50 C4
Freeland Pl BS8 . . . . .62 F6
Freelands BS21. . . . . .73 C8
Freeling Ho BS1. . . . . .143 B1
Freemans La BS48 . . . . .77 B2
Freemantle Gdns BS5. . . . .50 C3
Freemantle Ho BS2 . . . . .143 A4
Freemantle La BS5 . . . . . . .50 C3
Freestone Rd BS2 . . . . .64 A6
Freeview Rd BA2 . . . . .101 A5
Freezinghill La BS30 . . . . . .68 B4
Fremantle La 9 BS6. . . . . .49 D1
Fremantle Rd BS6 . . . . .49 D1
Fremantle Sq BS6 . . . . .49 D1
FRENCHAY 51 B8
Frenchay CE Prim Sch
  BS16. . . . . .51 B7
Frenchay Cl BS16. . . . . .51 B7
Frenchay Hill BS16 . . . . . . .51 C7
Frenchay Hospl BS16 . . . . .51 B7
Frenchay Park Rd
  BS16. . . . . .50 F6
Frenchay Rd
  Bristol BS16. . . . . .51 B7
  Weston-S-M BS23 . . . . . .104 E4
Frenchay Village Mus *
  BS16. . . . . .51 A8
French Cl
  Nailsea BS48 . . . . .59 F3
  Peasedown St John
  BA2. . . . . .134 D7
Frenchfield Rd BA2 . . . . . .134 D7
FRESHFORD 120 B5
Freshford CE Prim Sch
  BA2 . . . . .120 B5
Freshford La BA2 . . . . .120 A4
Freshford Sta BA2 . . . . . . .120 C5
Freshland Way BS15 . . . . . .65 B8
Freshmoor 8 BS21 . . . . . . .57 H3
Friar Ave BS22 . . . . .88 E3
Friars Ho 4 BS37 . . . . .39 D7
Friary St BS1 . . . . .143 C1
Friary Cl
  Clevedon BS21. . . . . .57 E5
  Westwood BA15. . . . . . . .120 A3
Friary Grange Pk BS36. . . .37 E6
Friary Rd
  Bristol BS7. . . . . .49 D4
  Portishead BS20 . . . . .45 A4
Friendly Row BS20. . . . . . . .47 C5
Friendship Gr 2 BS48 . . . .59 F2

Friendship Rd
  Bristol BS4. . . . . .64 A2
  Nailsea BS48 . . . . .59 F3
Friezewood Rd BS3. . . . . . .63 A4
Fripp Cl BS5 . . . . .64 B6
Frith La GL12 . . . . .17 F3
Frobisher Ave BS20. . . . . . .45 B5
Frobisher Cl
  Portishead BS20 . . . . .45 A5
  Weston-S-M BS22 . . . . . . .88 E4
Frobisher Rd BS3. . . . . .63 A3
Frog La
  Bristol BS1. . . . . .142 C2
  Felton BS40 . . . . .94 C8
  Frampton Cotterell BS36. . .38 E7
  North Nibley GL11 . . . . . . .5 C5
  Ubley BS40 . . . . .111 D1
  Winford BS40 . . . . .94 F5
Frogmore St BS1 . . . . .142 C2
Frome Bank Gdns
  BS36. . . . . .37 E3
Frombank Jun Sch
  BS37. . . . . .27 D3
Frome Ct BS35. . . . . .15 C8
Frome Glen BS36 . . . . .37 E4
Frome Old Rd BA3 . . . . . .134 A2
Frome Pl 1 BS16. . . . . .50 E5
Frome Rd
  Bristol BS16. . . . . .101 D1
  Chipping Sodbury BS37 . . .28 C1
  Norton St Philip BA2. . . .136 F3
  Radstock BA3 . . . . .134 B2
  Radstock BA3 . . . . .140 E8
Fromeside Pk BS16. . . . . . .51 B8
Frome Terr BS16. . . . . .51 E5
Frome Valley Rd BS16. . . . .50 F6
Frome View BS36 . . . . .38 B7
Frome Villas BS16 . . . . .51 C7
Frome Way BS36 . . . . .38 A7
Front St BS25 . . . . .108 E4
Froomshaw Rd BS16. . . . . .51 A7
FROST HILL 91 C6
Frost Hill BS49 . . . . .91 D7
Frost & Reed Ho 3
  BS5. . . . . .64 F8
Fry Ct 2 BS3. . . . . .63 C4
Fry's Cl BS16 . . . . .50 D4
Frys Hill BS15 . . . . .51 E2
Fry's Hill BS4 . . . . .64 D2
Fry's House of Mercy 11
  BS3. . . . . .143 B1
Fry's La BS40. . . . . .109 F3
Frys Leaze BA1 . . . . .85 B2
Fry's Well BA3. . . . . .138 D3
Fryth Ho BS48 . . . . .60 D3
Fryth Way BS48 . . . . .59 C2
Fuddlebrook Cotts
  SN14 . . . . .69 F6
Fulford Rd BS13. . . . . .79 C5
Fulford Wlk BS13 . . . . .79 B5
Fullens Cl BS22 . . . . .105 D7
Fuller Rd BA1 . . . . .85 C2
Fullers La BS25 . . . . .125 A6
Fullers Way BA2. . . . . .118 D8
Fullwell Cl BA1 . . . . .135 D1
Fulmar Cl BS35. . . . . .8 D2
Fulmar Rd BS22 . . . . .88 F1
Fulwell La BA3 . . . . .135 D1
Furber Ct BS5. . . . . .65 B6
Furber Rd BS5 . . . . .65 B6
Furber Ridge BS5 . . . . .65 B6
Furber Vale BS5 . . . . .65 B6
Furland Rd BS22 . . . . .88 E2
Furlong Cl BA3 . . . . .138 F7
Furlong Pl BS26 . . . . .125 C1
Furlong The BS6. . . . . .49 D6
Furnleaze BS39. . . . . .114 E3
Furnwood BS5. . . . . .65 A6
Furze Cl BS22 . . . . .88 B2
Furze Rd
  Bristol BS16. . . . . .51 C3
  Weston-S-M BS22 . . . . . . .88 A3
Furzewood Rd BS15 . . . . . .65 F8
Fussell Ct BS15. . . . . .65 F8
Fylton Croft BS14. . . . . .80 B3

G

Gable Cl BS35 . . . . .23 A2
Gable Rd 8 BS5. . . . . .50 A1
Gables Cl BS29 . . . . .107 B3
Gadshill Dr BS34 . . . . .36 E5
Gadshill Rd BS5 . . . . .50 C2
Gages Cl BS15. . . . . .65 F7
Gages Rd BS15 . . . . .65 F7
Gainsborough Ct BA1. . . . .84 B1
Gainsborough Dr BS22. . . .88 F3
Gainsborough Gdns
  BA1 . . . . .101 C8
Gainsborough Mews
  BS10. . . . . .35 B2
Gainsborough Rd BS31. . . .81 F5
Gainsborough Sq BS7. . . . .50 B7
Galingale Way BS20 . . . . . .45 F5
Gallagher Ret Pk
  Bristol BS30. . . . . .65 E4
  Weston-S-M BS23 . . . . . .105 A5
Galleries The BS1. . . . . . . .143 B3
Gallivan Cl BS34. . . . . .36 B8
Galway Rd BS4 . . . . .63 E1
Gambril La GL12 . . . . .9 F5
Gander Cl BS13. . . . . .79 B5
Gannet Rd BS22 . . . . .88 F1
Garamond Ct BS1 . . . . . . .143 B1
Garden Cl
  Bristol BS9. . . . . .48 C5
  Weston-S-M BS22 . . . . . . .88 E2

Garden Ct BS8 . . . . .142 A4
Gardeners Wlk BS41 . . . . . .62 B1
Gardens Rd BS21 . . . . .57 E4
Gardens The
  Bristol, Frenchay BS16 . . . .36 F1
  Bristol, Upper Soundwell
  BS16. . . . . .51 D3
Gardner Ave BS13 . . . . .78 F7
Gardner Rd BS20 . . . . .45 D6
Garfield Ct BS5. . . . . .64 F8
Garfield Rd BS5 . . . . .65 A8
Garland Ho 7 BS21. . . . . . .57 E2
Garner Ct 4 BS22 . . . . .89 B4
Garnet St BS3 . . . . .63 B3
Garnett Pl BS16 . . . . .51 F7
Garonor Way BS20. . . . . . . .46 F5
Garre Ho BS2 . . . . .100 F5
Garrett Dr BS32 . . . . .36 D7
Garrick Rd BA2. . . . . .100 F5
Garsdale Rd BS22 . . . . . . .105 D8
Garston Cotts BS40. . . . . .110 E3
Garston La BS40. . . . . .110 E3
Garstons
  Bathford BA1. . . . . .86 D2
  6 Clevedon BS21. . . . . . . .57 D1
  Wrington BS40 . . . . .92 E1
Garstons Cl
  Backwell BS48. . . . . .75 F6
  Wrington BS40 . . . . .92 D1
Garstons Orch BS40 . . . . . .92 D1
Garstons The BS20 . . . . . . .45 D4
Garth Rd BS13. . . . . .79 A8
Garton Ho 3 BS16. . . . . . . .51 D5
Gaston Ave BS31. . . . . .81 F6
Gastons The BS11. . . . . .48 A8
Gatcombe Dr BS34 . . . . . . .36 E4
Gatcombe Farm Ind Est
  BS40. . . . . .92 D3
Gatcombe Rd BS13 . . . . . . .79 B5
Gatehouse Ave BS13 . . . . . .79 A5
Gatehouse Cl BS13 . . . . . . .79 B5
Gatehouse Ctr The
  BS13. . . . . .79 B5
Gatehouse Way BS13 . . . . .79 A5
Gatesby Mead BS34. . . . . .36 E5
Gateway Terr BS20 . . . . . . .45 E6
Gathorne Cres BS37 . . . . . .27 D2
Gathorne Rd BS3 . . . . .63 B4
Gatton Rd BS2. . . . . .50 A1
Gaunts Cl BS20 . . . . .44 F4
GAUNT'S EARTHCOTT
  . . . . .25 B5
Gaunts Earthcott La
  BS32. . . . . .25 A4
Gaunt's La BS1 . . . . .142 C2
Gaunt's Rd BS37 . . . . .40 B8
Gay Ct BA1. . . . . .85 E3
Gay Elms Prim Sch
  BS13. . . . . .79 A4
Gay Elms Rd BS13 . . . . .79 A4
Gayner Rd BS7 . . . . .36 A1
Gay's Hill BA1 . . . . .141 C4
Gays Rd BS15 . . . . .65 B4
Gay St BA1 . . . . .141 B3
Gaywood Ho 7 BS3 . . . . . .63 B3
Gazelle Rd BS24 . . . . .105 B3
Gazzard Cl BS36 . . . . .37 C7
Gazzard Rd BS36. . . . . .37 C7
GEE MOOR 65 F6
Gee Moors BS15 . . . . .65 F7
Gefle Cl BS1 . . . . .142 B1
Geldof Dr BA3. . . . . .133 A2
Geoffrey Cl BS13 . . . . .78 E6
George Cl BS48 . . . . .76 D7
George Cl 12 BS6. . . . . .49 B1
George & Dragon La 11
  BS5. . . . . .64 A6
George Jones Rd BS2 . . . . .64 A6
George La SN14 . . . . .55 E1
Georges Bldgs BA1 . . . . . . .85 C3
Georges Ho BA2. . . . . .102 B6
George's Pl BA2 . . . . .102 B6
George's Rd BA1. . . . . .85 A1
George Sq BS1 . . . . .143 B2
George St
  Bath BA1 . . . . .141 B3
  Bath, Bathwick BA2. . . . .102 B6
  Bristol BS5. . . . . .64 C8
  Portishead BS20 . . . . .45 C2
  Weston-S-M BS23 . . . . . .104 E7
Georgian Ho BA2 . . . . . . .141 C2
Georgian House (Mus)*
  BS1. . . . . .142 C2
Georgian Mansions
  BS1. . . . . .142 C2
Gerald Rd BS3 . . . . .63 A3
Gerard Rd BS23 . . . . .104 F8
Gerrard Bldgs BA2 . . . . . .102 B7
Gerrard Cl BS4 . . . . .79 D7
Gerrish Ave
  Bristol, Moorfields BS5 . . .64 C8
  Bristol, Staple Hill BS16. . .51 D3
Gibbet La BS14. . . . . .80 D1
Gibbets Brow BS40 . . . . . .129 A3
Gibbs Ct 15 BS3 . . . . .64 D7
Gibbsfold Rd BS13. . . . . . . .79 C4
Gibson Rd BS6 . . . . .49 D1
Giffard Ho BS34 . . . . .36 D6
Gifford Cl BS37 . . . . .27 A8
Gifford Cres BS34. . . . . .36 C6
Gifford Ct BS34 . . . . .24 A1
Gifford Ho BS1 . . . . .143 A4
Gifford Rd BS10 . . . . .34 F4
Giffords Pl BS13. . . . . .79 A7

Gilbeck Rd BS48. . . . . .59 C2
Gilbert Rd
  Bristol, Kingswood
  BS15. . . . . .51 D1
  Bristol, Moorfields BS5 . . .64 C8
Gilberyn Dr BS22 . . . . .89 A3
Gilda Cl BS14. . . . . .80 C5
Gilda Cres BS14 . . . . .80 B6
Gilda Par BS14 . . . . .80 C5
Gilda Sq W BS14 . . . . .80 B5
Gillard Cl 2 BS15 . . . . .65 B8
Gillard Rd BS15. . . . . .65 B8
Gill Ave BS16 . . . . .51 B6
Gillebank Cl BS14 . . . . .80 D5
Gilham Ho BA2 7. . . . . . . .49 D2
Gillingham Hill 7
  BS15. . . . . .65 B5
Gillingham Terr 3
  BA1 .85 B1
Gillingstool BS35 . . . . .15 C8
Gillingstool Prim Sch
  BS35. . . . . .15 B8
Gill Mews BS22. . . . . .89 B4
Gillmore Cl BS22 . . . . .88 D1
Gillmore Rd BS22. . . . . .88 D1
Gillray Cl BS7 . . . . .50 B6
Gillson Cl BS24 . . . . .105 D2
Gilpin Cl BS15 . . . . .51 F1
Gilroy Cl BS30 . . . . .66 B3
Gilslake Ave BS10 . . . . .35 B3
Gilton Ho BS4 . . . . .64 E2
Gimblet Rd BS22 . . . . .89 B4
Gingell's Gn 4 BS5. . . . . . .65 A8
Gipsy Patch La BS34. . . . . .36 C6
Glades The BS5. . . . . .50 E2
Gladstone Ct
  Bath BA2 . . . . .102 C2
  Bristol BS16. . . . . .51 E4
Gladstone La BS36. . . . . . . .38 C7
Gladstone Pl BA2 . . . . . . .102 C2
Gladstone Rd
  Bath BA2 . . . . .102 C2
  Bristol BS16. . . . . .80 B6
  2 Bristol, Kingswood
  BS15. . . . . .51 D1
Gladstone St
  Bristol, Bedminster
  BS3. . . . . .63 B3
  Bristol, Kingswood BS16. . .51 D3
  13 Bristol, Pile Marsh
  BS5. . . . . .64 D7
  Midsomer Norton BA3. . .133 B3
Glaisdale Rd BS16 . . . . .51 A5
Glamis Ct BS24. . . . . .105 E7
Glanville Dr BS39 . . . . .130 E6
Glanville Gdns BS15 . . . . . .65 E7
Glass House La BS2 . . . . . .64 B5
Glastonbury Cl
  Bristol BS30. . . . . .65 F5
  Nailsea BS48 . . . . .60 B1
Glastonbury Way BS22. . . .89 A2
Glebe Ave BS20 . . . . .45 E4
Glebe Cl BS41 . . . . .62 C2
Glebe Field BS32 . . . . .24 A5
Glebe Ho
  Bath BA2 . . . . .102 B5
  Portishead BS20 . . . . .45 E4
  Weston-S-M BS22 . . . . . . .88 F3
Glebe Inf Sch The
  BS49. . . . . .91 C4
Glebelands BA3 . . . . .133 D1
Glebelands Rd BS34 . . . . . .36 A3
Glebe Rd
  Bath BA2 . . . . .101 B4
  Bristol BS5. . . . . .64 E8
  Clevedon BS21. . . . . .57 E2
  Long Ashton BS41 . . . . . . .62 C2
  Portishead BS20 . . . . .45 E4
  Weston-S-M BS23 . . . . . .104 E8
Glebes The BS5. . . . . .64 E8
Glebe The
  Freshford BA2 . . . . .120 B4
  Hinton Charterhouse
  BA2. . . . . .119 D2
  Pilning BS35 . . . . .22 C3
  Timsbury BA2 . . . . .116 B3
  Wrington BS40 . . . . .92 D2
Glebe Wlk BS31 . . . . .81 C4
Gledemoor Dr BS36. . . . . . .38 D7
Glena Ave BS4 . . . . .64 B2
Glenarm Rd BS4 . . . . .64 E2
Glenarm Wlk BS4. . . . . .64 E2
Glen Ave BS8. . . . . .61 D7
Glenavon Cl BS9 . . . . .48 C4
Glenavon Pk BS9 . . . . .48 C4
Glen Brook BS9 . . . . .48 D4
Glenburn Rd BS15. . . . . . . .51 D1
Glencairn Ct BA2 . . . . .102 B6
Glencoe Bsns Pk
  BS23. . . . . .105 A3
Glencoyne Ct 1 BS10. . . . .35 C2
Glencoyne Sq BS10 . . . . . . .35 C2
Glencroft Way BS22. . . . . . .88 E3
Glendale
  17 Bristol BS8. . . . . .62 F6
  Bristol, Downend BS16 . . .51 C6
  Bristol, Hillfields BS16. . . .51 C4
Glendare St BS5. . . . . .64 C6
Glendevon Rd BS14. . . . . . .80 A3
Glendower Ho BS8 . . . . . . .62 F7
Glen Dr BS9 . . . . .48 D5
Gleneagles BS37. . . . . .27 E1
Gleneagles Cl
  Nailsea BS48 . . . . .60 A1
  Weston-S-M BS22 . . . . . . .88 E3
Gleneagles Dr BS10. . . . . . .34 D3
Gleneagles Rd BS30 . . . . . .66 B6

Gilbeck Rd BS48. . . . . .59 C2

Fox–Goo   157

Glenfall BS37. . . . . .39 D7
Glenfrome Prim Sch
  BS5. . . . . .50 B4
Glenfrome Rd BS2 . . . . .50 B3
Glen Hospl The BS6. . . . . . .49 A2
Glen La BS4 . . . . .64 D2
Glen Park Gdns BS5 . . . . . .65 A8
Glen Pk
  Bristol, Eastville BS5 . . . . .50 C2
  Bristol, St George BS5. . . .65 A8
Glenroy Ave BS15. . . . . .51 E1
Glenside Cl BS16 . . . . .51 C7
Glenside Hospl Mus*
  . . . . .50 E5
Glenside Pk 3 BS16. . . . . . .50 E5
Glen The
  Bristol, Hanham BS15 . . . .65 B4
  Bristol, Redland BS6 . . . . .49 B3
  Saltford BS31 . . . . .82 F1
  Weston-S-M BS22 . . . . . . .88 B2
  Yate BS37 . . . . .27 C1
Glentworth Ct 10 BS23 . . . .87 C1
Glentworth Rd
  Bristol BS8. . . . . .142 B4
  Bristol, Redland BS6 . . . . .49 C2
Glenview Ho BA2 . . . . .134 D8
Glenview Rd BS4 . . . . .64 D2
Glenwood BS16. . . . . .51 C1
Glenwood Dr BS30. . . . . . . .66 B4
Glenwood Mans BS23 . . . . .87 D1
Glenwood Rd BS10 . . . . . . .49 C7
Glenwood Rise BS20 . . . . . .44 F5
Glen Yeo Terr BS49. . . . . . . .91 C4
Glevum Cl BS16 . . . . .52 C7
Gloster Ave BS5 . . . . .50 D3
Gloucester Cl BS34 . . . . . . .36 D5
Gloucester Ho 11
  BS2. . . . . .143 C3
Gloucester Pl 2 BS2 . . . . .143 A3
Gloucester Rd
  Almondsbury BS32,
  BS35. . . . . .24 C6
  Avonmouth BS11. . . . . . . .33 A1
  Bath BA1 . . . . .85 C3
  Bristol, Bishopston BS7 . . .49 F4
  Bristol, Patchway BS34 . . .36 B7
  Bristol, Staple Hill BS16 . . .51 E3
  Stone GL13 . . . . .3 F3
  Thornbury BS35. . . . . .8 C1
  Upper Swainswick BA1. . . .85 A7
Gloucester Rd N BS7,
  BS34. . . . . .36 A4
Gloucester Row
  8 Bristol BS8. . . . . .62 F7
  Kingswood GL12 . . . . .11 F8
Gloucestershire County
  Cricket Club* BS7 . . . . . . .49 F4
Gloucester St
  4 Bath BA1 . . . . .141 B3
  5 Bristol BS2. . . . . .143 B4
  Bristol, Clifton BS8. . . . . . .62 F7
  Bristol, Eastville BS5 . . . . .50 D3
  Weston-S-M BS23 . . . . . .104 D7
Gloucester Terr 12 BS35. . . .8 B1
Glovers Field BS25 . . . . . . .125 F7
Glyn Vale BS3 . . . . .63 E1
Goddard Dr BS22 . . . . .89 B4
Goddard Way BS10. . . . . . . .35 A1
Godfrey Ct 3 BS30 . . . . . . .65 F4
Godwin Dr BS48. . . . . .59 C3
Goffenton Dr BS16. . . . . . . .51 B6
Goldcrest Rd BS37 . . . . .39 F7
Goldcrest Way BS20 . . . . . .45 F6
GOLDEN HILL 49 D5
Golden Hill BS6. . . . . .49 C5
Golden La GL12. . . . . .11 F4
Golden Lion Ct BS1. . . . . .143 B2
Golden Valley La
  BS30. . . . . .82 E8
  Upton Cheyney BS30. . . . .66 F2
Golden Valley Prim Sch
  BS48. . . . . .59 C2
Goldfinch Way BS16 . . . . . .53 C4
Goldney Ave
  Bristol BS8. . . . . .142 A2
  Bristol, Warmley BS30. . . .66 C7
Goldney Cl BS39 . . . . .114 F1
Goldney Ct 7 BS30 . . . . . . .50 E3
Goldney Rd BS8 . . . . .142 A2
Goldney Way BS30. . . . . . .114 F1
GOLD'S CROSS 113 C6
Gold Club La BS31 . . . . . . .82 E2
Golf Course La BS34 . . . . . .35 F3
Golf Course Rd BA2 . . . . .102 D6
Golledge Cl BA3 . . . . .138 C4
Gooch Cl BS30 . . . . .66 D6
Gooch Way BS22. . . . . .89 B3
Goodeve Pk BS9. . . . . .48 D3
Goodeve Rd BS9 . . . . .48 D3
Goodhind St BS5. . . . . .64 A8
Goodneston Rd BS16 . . . . .51 A3
Goodrich Cl BS37 . . . . .27 B1
Goodring Hill BS11 . . . . . . .34 A1
Good Shepherd Cl BS7 . . . .49 C4
Goodwin Dr BS14. . . . . .79 F4
Goodwood Gdns BS16 . . . .37 F1
Goold Cl BA2 . . . . .100 A8
Goolden St BS4 . . . . .64 A3
Goosard La BS39 . . . . .132 E8
Goose Acre BS32 . . . . .36 F6
Goose Gn
  Bristol BS30. . . . . .52 C1
  Frampton Cotterell BS36. . .38 C8

Goose Gn *continued*
Yate BS37 .... 27 E3
GOOSE GREEN
Bristol 52 C1
Yate 27 E3
Goose Green Way BS37 .... 27 E4
Gooseham Mead BS49 .... 91 D4
Gooseland Cl BS14 .... 79 F3
Goosey La BS22 .... 89 C2
Gordano Ct BS20 .... 45 E5
Gordano Gate Bsns Pk BS20 .... 45 E5
Gordano Gdns BS20 .... 47 B4
Gordano Rd BS20 .... 46 D7
Gordano Sch BS20 .... 45 D3
Gor Dano View BS20 .... 45 C5
Gordano Way BS20 .... 46 F5
Gordon Ave BS5 .... 50 E1
Gordon Bldgs BA3 .... 134 A3
Gordon Cl BS5 .... 50 E1
Gordon Rd
Bath BA2 .... 102 B5
Bristol BS8 .... 142 B3
14 Bristol, St Pauls BS2 .... 49 F1
Bristol, Whitehall BS5 .... 50 D1
Peasedown St John BA2 .... 134 D8
Weston-S-M BS23 .... 104 F7
Gore Rd BS3 .... 63 A3
Gore's Marsh Rd BS3 .... 63 A2
Gores Pk BS39 .... 115 B2
Gorham Cl BS11 .... 34 C2
Gorlands Rd BS37 .... 28 C1
Gorlangton Cl BS14 .... 80 A7
Gorse Cover Rd BS35 .... 22 A7
Gorse Hill BS16 .... 51 C3
Gorse La
Bristol BS8 .... 142 B2
Cold Ashton BS30, SN14 .... 68 D7
Gosford Mans 6 BS23 .... 87 C1
Gosforth Cl BS10 .... 35 B1
Gosforth Rd BS10 .... 35 B1
Goslet Rd BS14 .... 80 E5
Goss Barton BS48 .... 59 D1
Goss Cl BS48 .... 59 C1
Goss La BS48 .... 59 C1
Goss View BS48 .... 59 C1
Gotley Rd BS4 .... 64 D2
Gott Dr BS4 .... 64 D5
Goulston Rd BS13 .... 79 A5
Goulston Wlk BS13 .... 79 A5
Goulter St BS5 .... 64 B6
Gournay Ct BS39 .... 132 A3
Gourney Cl BS11 .... 34 B2
Governors Ho 2 BA2 .... 101 D6
Gover Rd BS15 .... 65 C3
Govier Way BS35 .... 22 C4
Grace Cl
Chipping Sodbury BS37 .... 28 C1
Yatton BS49 .... 91 B8
Grace Ct BS16 .... 51 D6
Grace Dr
Bristol BS15 .... 66 A8
Midsomer Norton BA3 .... 133 A2
Gracefield Sch BS16 .... 51 C5
Grace Park Rd BS4 .... 64 D1
Grace Rd
Bristol BS16 .... 51 C5
Weston-S-M BS22 .... 89 B4
Gradwell Cl BS22 .... 89 B3
Graeme Cl BS16 .... 51 A4
Graham Rd
3 Bristol, Bedminster BS3 .... 63 C3
Bristol, Downend BS16 .... 51 F6
21 Bristol, Upper Easton BS5 .... 50 B1
Weston-S-M BS23 .... 104 E7
Grainger Ct BS11 .... 47 E7
Grain Loft The 9 BS1 .... 143 A2
Graitney Cl BS49 .... 92 A8
Grampian Cl BS30 .... 66 C4
Granary The 8 BS1 .... 143 A2
Granby Ct 18 BS8 .... 62 F6
Granby Hill BS8 .... 62 F6
Grandmother's Rock La BS30 .... 67 D2
Grand Par BA2 .... 141 C2
Grand Pier* BS23 .... 104 D7
Granfield Gdns BS40 .... 109 A5
Grange Ave
Bristol, Hanham BS15 .... 65 D5
Bristol, Little Stoke BS34 .... 36 C6
Grange Bsns Pk The BS24 .... 90 A5
Grange Cl
Bristol, Patchway BS32 .... 24 C2
Bristol, Stoke Gifford BS34 .... 37 A4
Weston-S-M BS23 .... 104 E1
Grange Cl N BS9 .... 49 B6
Grange Court Rd BS9 .... 49 A6
Grange Ct
Bristol BS15 .... 65 D5
Bristol, Henleaze BS9 .... 49 B6
Bristol, Westbury on Trym BS9 .... 49 A8
Grange Dr BS16 .... 51 C6
Grange End BA3 .... 139 B7
Grange Farm Rd BS49 .... 74 A1
Grange Pk
Bristol, Frenchay BS16 .... 51 C8

Grange Pk *continued*
Bristol, Westbury on Trym BS9 .... 49 B6
Grange Rd
Bristol, Bishopsworth BS13 .... 79 A5
Bristol BS8 .... 142 A3
Saltford BS31 .... 82 C3
Weston-S-M BS23 .... 104 E1
Grange Sch & Sports Coll The BS30 .... 66 B7
Grange The
Bath BA1 .... 84 C1
Bristol, Coombe Dingle BS9 .... 48 D7
Bristol, Sneyd Park BS9 .... 48 F3
Flax Bourton BS48 .... 76 F7
Limpley Stoke BA2 .... 120 B5
Grangeville Cl BS30 .... 66 B3
Grangewood Cl 4 BS16 .... 51 C6
Granny's La BS15 .... 65 E6
Grantham Ct 1 BS15 .... 65 C8
Grantham Ho BS15 .... 51 C1
Grantham La BS15 .... 65 C8
Grantham Rd BS15 .... 51 C1
Grantson Cl BS4 .... 64 E2
Granville Cl BS15 .... 65 B3
Granville Rd BA1 .... 84 E4
Granville St BS5 .... 64 C6
Grasmere Cl BS10 .... 49 A8
Grasmere Dr BS23 .... 104 F4
Grassington Dr BS37 .... 40 A8
Grass Meers Dr BS14 .... 80 A4
Grassmere Gdns BS30 .... 66 D6
Grassmere Rd BS49 .... 91 B8
Gratitude Rd BS5 .... 50 C1
Gravel Hill BS40 .... 112 B7
Gravel Hill Rd N BS37 .... 28 A5
Graveney Cl BS4 .... 64 D1
Gray Cl BS10 .... 34 E2
Grayle Rd BS10 .... 35 A2
Grayling Ho BS9 .... 48 F7
Grays Hill BA2 .... 135 B5
Great Ann St BS2 .... 143 C3
Great Bedford St BA1 .... 141 B4
Great Britain SS* BS1 .... 142 B1
Great Brockeridge BS9 .... 48 F6
Great Dowles BS30 .... 66 A4
Great George St
Bristol, Brandon Hill BS1 .... 142 C2
Bristol, St Pauls BS2 .... 143 C3
Great Hayles Rd BS14 .... 80 A6
Great Leaze BS30 .... 66 A4
Great Mdw BS34 .... 37 A6
Great Meadow Rd BS32 .... 36 F6
Great Park Rd BS32 .... 24 C3
Great Pulteney St BA2 .... 141 C3
Great Stanhope St BA1 .... 141 A2
GREAT STOKE 36 F5
Great Stoke BS34 .... 37 A5
Great Stoke Way
Bristol, Great Stoke BS34 .... 37 A5
Bristol, Harry Stoke BS34 .... 36 D3
Greatstone La BS40 .... 94 F5
Great Western Bsns Pk BS37 .... 27 B3
Great Western Ct BS34 .... 36 F4
Great Western La BS5 .... 64 C6
Great Western Rd BS21 .... 57 F2
Great Wood Cl BS13 .... 79 C4
Greenacre BS22 .... 88 B2
Green Acre Rd BS14 .... 80 A3
Greenacres
Bath BA1 .... 84 B3
Bristol BS9 .... 48 E7
Midsomer Norton BA3 .... 132 E1
Greenacres Park Homes BS36 .... 38 E5
Greenbank Ave E BS5 .... 50 C1
Greenbank Ave W BS5 .... 50 C1
Greenbank Gdns BA1 .... 84 B1
Greenbank Rd
Bristol, Hanham BS15 .... 65 D5
Bristol, Lower Easton BS5 .... 50 D2
Bristol, Southville BS3 .... 63 A4
Greenbank View
Bristol, Kingswood BS15 .... 65 E7
Bristol, Lower Easton BS5 .... 50 D2
Green Cl
Bristol BS7 .... 50 A8
Paulton BS39 .... 132 E6
Green Cotts BA2 .... 102 C2
Green Croft BS5 .... 51 A1
Green Ct BS35 .... 14 A2
Greendale Rd
Bristol, Lower Knowle BS3 .... 63 E2
Bristol, Redland BS6 .... 49 B3
Green Dell Cl BS10 .... 34 D3
Greenditch Ave BS13 .... 79 C5
Greenditch Cl BA3 .... 138 C3
Green Ditch La BA3 .... 138 B6
Greenditch St BS35 .... 13 D1
Greendown BS5 .... 65 A7
Greendown Pl BA2 .... 102 A1

Green Dragon Rd BS36 .... 37 D5
Greenfield Ave BS10 .... 49 D8
Greenfield Cres BS48 .... 59 E3
Greenfield Ct BS10 .... 35 D1
Greenfield Pk BS20 .... 45 C3
Greenfield Pl BS23 .... 104 C8
Greenfield Prim Sch BS4 .... 79 C7
Greenfield Rd BS10 .... 35 D1
Greenfields Ave BS29 .... 107 A3
Greenfield Wlk BA3 .... 133 A3
Greenfinch Lo BS16 .... 50 E6
Greengage Cl 6 BS22 .... 105 E8
Greenhaven 5 BS5 .... 50 C1
Greenhayes BS37 .... 40 C8
GREENHILL 133 A3
Greenhill BS35 .... 15 A4
Green Hill BS35 .... 15 A4
Greenhill Cl
Nailsea BS48 .... 59 D2
Weston-S-M BS22 .... 89 A3
Greenhill Croft BS25 .... 108 B4
Greenhill Down BS35 .... 15 A5
Greenhill Gdns BS35 .... 15 A4
Greenhill Gr BS3 .... 63 A2
Greenhill La
Alveston BS35 .... 14 F4
Bristol BS11 .... 34 C1
Sandford BS25 .... 108 B4
Greenhill Par 5 BS35 .... 15 A5
Greenhill Pl BA3 .... 133 A3
Greenhill Rd
Alveston BS35 .... 15 A5
Midsomer Norton BA3 .... 133 A3
Sandford BS25 .... 108 B4
Green La
Avonmouth BS11 .... 33 B1
Bristol BS11 .... 47 B8
Butcombe BS40 .... 111 A7
Easter Compton BS35 .... 22 C1
Failand BS8 .... 61 C4
Farrington Gurney BS39 .... 131 F6
Felton BS40 .... 94 C3
Freshford BA2 .... 120 B2
Hinton Charterhouse BA2 .... 119 E1
Marshfield SN14 .... 69 E8
Priddy BS40 .... 128 B7
Rangeworthy BS37, GL12 .... 17 B2
Severn Beach BS35 .... 22 B8
Stratton-on-t-F BA3 .... 138 E1
Tytherington GL12 .... 16 B8
Winsley BA15 .... 120 F6
Winterbourne BS36 .... 37 C7
Greenland Rd BS22 .... 88 D1
Greenlands Rd BA2 .... 134 C8
Greenlands Way BS10 .... 34 F4
Greenleaze BS4 .... 64 B1
Greenleaze Ave BS16 .... 37 D1
Greenleaze Cl BS16 .... 37 D1
Greenmore Rd BS4 .... 64 B2
Greenore BS15 .... 65 C7
Green Park Mews BA1 .... 141 A2
Greenpark Rd BS10 .... 35 E1
Green Park Rd BA1 .... 141 B2
Green Park Sta BA1 .... 141 B2
GREEN PARLOUR 134 D2
Green Parlour Rd BA3 .... 134 D1
Green Pastures Rd BS48 .... 60 B2
Green Pk BA1 .... 141 B2
Greenridge BS39 .... 114 F3
Greenridge Cl BS13 .... 78 E4
Greensbrook BS39 .... 114 F3
Green's Hill BS16 .... 50 E3
Green Side BS16 .... 52 A6
Greenside Cl BS10 .... 34 D3
Greenslade Gdns BS48 .... 59 D3
Greensplott Rd BS11 .... 33 E7
Green St
Bath BA1 .... 141 C2
Bristol BS3 .... 63 F4
Shoscombe BA2 .... 134 E5
Green The
Backwell BS48 .... 76 A5
Bath BA2 .... 101 D1
Bristol, New Cheltenham BS15 .... 51 E2
Bristol, Stoke Gifford BS34 .... 36 E4
Chipping Sodbury BS37 .... 41 A8
Cromhall GL12 .... 17 B8
Faulkland BA3 .... 135 D2
Hinton Charterhouse BA2 .... 119 F1
Iron Acton BS37 .... 26 D4
Locking BS24 .... 106 A4
Luckington SN14 .... 31 E4
Olveston BS35 .... 14 A2
Pill BS20 .... 47 D4
Winscombe BS25 .... 125 A7
Green Tree Rd BA3 .... 133 B3
GREENVALE 116 B1
Greenvale BA2 .... 116 B1
Greenvale Cl BA2 .... 116 B1
Greenvale Dr BA2 .... 116 B1
Greenvale Rd BS39 .... 132 D5
Greenview BS30 .... 66 A2
Greenway BA3 .... 135 C1
Greenway Bush La BS3 .... 63 B4
Greenway Ct BA2 .... 101 F4
Greenway Dr BS10 .... 49 D8
Greenway Farm BS30 .... 67 E5

Greenway Ho 10 BS6 .... 49 B2
Greenway La
Bath BA2 .... 102 A4
Cold Ashton SN14 .... 68 D5
Greenway Pk
Bristol BS10 .... 49 D8
3 Clevedon BS21 .... 57 H3
Greenway Rd BS6 .... 49 B2
Greenways
Bristol BS15 .... 52 A1
Chilcompton BA3 .... 138 C2
Greenways Rd BS37 .... 27 E3
Greenway The BS16 .... 51 C3
Greenwell La BS40 .... 109 C7
Greenwich Apartments BS6 .... 49 C3
Green Wlk BS4 .... 64 A1
Greenwood Cl BS7 .... 49 E7
Greenwood Dr BS35 .... 14 F4
Greenwood Rd
Bristol BS4 .... 64 A1
Weston-S-M BS22 .... 88 E2
Gregory Ct BS30 .... 66 A6
Gregory Mead BS49 .... 74 A1
Gregorys Gr BA2 .... 118 D8
Gregorys Tyning BS39 .... 132 F6
Greinton BS24 .... 105 A2
Grenville Ave BS24 .... 106 A4
Grenville Chapel 5 BS8 .... 62 F5
Grenville Cl BS5 .... 64 F8
Grenville Pl 7 BS1 .... 62 F5
Grenville Rd BS6 .... 49 E3
Greve Ct 5 BS30 .... 65 F4
Greville Rd BS3 .... 63 B4
Greville St BS3 .... 63 C4
GREYFIELD 115 C2
Greyfield Comm BS39 .... 115 C2
Greyfield Rd BS39 .... 115 C2
Greyfield View BS39 .... 114 F1
Grey Gables BS35 .... 14 A3
Grey Hollow BS40 .... 129 F4
Greylands Rd BS13 .... 78 F7
Greystoke Ave BS10 .... 35 C1
Greystoke Bsns Ctr BS20 .... 45 D4
Greystoke Gdns BS10 .... 49 A8
Greystones BS16 .... 37 E1
Grib La BS40 .... 110 F2
Griffen Rd BS24 .... 105 E7
Griffin Cl BS22 .... 89 B2
Griffin Ct BA1 .... 141 B2
Griffin Ho BS21 .... 73 D8
Griffin Rd BS21 .... 57 G3
Griggfield Wlk BS14 .... 80 A7
Grimsbury Rd BS15 .... 66 A7
Grindell Rd BS5 .... 64 D7
Grinfield Ave BS13 .... 79 C4
Grinfield Ct BS13 .... 79 C4
Grittleton Rd BS7 .... 49 E8
GROSVENOR 85 C1
Grosvenor Bridge Rd BA1 .... 85 C1
Grosvenor Ct 2 BS6 .... 49 B1
Grosvenor Pk BA1 .... 85 C1
Grosvenor Pl BA1 .... 85 C1
Grosvenor Rd
Bristol BS2 .... 49 F1
Bristol BS2 .... 143 C4
Grosvenor Terr BA1 .... 85 C2
Grosvenor Villas 9 BA1 .... 85 B1
Grove Ave
Bristol BS1 .... 143 A1
Bristol, Coombe Dingle BS9 .... 48 C7
3 Bristol, Fishponds BS16 .... 50 F4
Grove Bank BS16 .... 37 C1
Grove Ct BS9 .... 48 E5
Grove Dr BS22 .... 88 C1
Grove Hall BS4 .... 64 D2
Grove Ho BA2 .... 102 B6
Grove Ind Est The BS34 .... 36 B8
Grove Jun Sch BS48 .... 75 D8
Grove La
Faulkland BA3 .... 135 D2
Hinton SN14 .... 54 C6
Weston-S-M BS23 .... 104 D8
Grove Leaze BS11 .... 47 D6
Grove Mews The BS36 .... 37 E7
Grove Orch BS40 .... 110 E2
Grove Park Ave BS4 .... 64 D2
Grove Park Ct BS23 .... 87 D1
Grove Park Rd
Bristol BS4 .... 64 D2
Weston-S-M BS23 .... 87 D1
Grove Park Terr BS16 .... 50 F4
Grove Pk
Bristol, Brislington BS4 .... 64 D2
Bristol, Redland BS6 .... 49 C2
Grove Rd
Banwell BS29 .... 106 E4
Bristol, Coombe Dingle BS9 .... 48 D8
Bristol, Fishponds BS16 .... 50 F4
Bristol, Redland BS6 .... 49 A2
Weston-S-M BS23 .... 104 D8
Weston-S-M, Milton BS22 .... 88 C1
Grovesend Rd BS35 .... 15 D8
Grove St BA2 .... 141 C3
Groves The BS13 .... 79 D4
Grove The
Bath BA1 .... 84 C1

Grove The *continued*
Bristol BS1 .... 143 A1
Bristol, Oldland BS30 .... 66 A4
Bristol, Patchway BS34 .... 36 B7
Hallatrow BS39 .... 132 B7
Rangeworthy BS37 .... 27 A8
Winscombe BS25 .... 107 F1
Wraxall BS48 .... 60 C3
Grove View BS16 .... 50 E6
Grove Wood Rd BA3 .... 133 F1
Guardian Ct 8 BS8 .... 62 F7
Guernsey Ave BS4 .... 64 F4
Guest Ave BS16 .... 52 B7
Gug The BS39 .... 115 C2
Guild Ct BS1 .... 143 B2
Guildford Rd BS4 .... 64 E6
Guildhall The*
Bath BA1 .... 141 C2
Bristol BS1 .... 143 A3
Guinea La
Bath BA1 .... 141 C3
Bristol BS16 .... 51 A4
Bristol, Fishponds BS16 .... 51 A5
Guinea St BS1 .... 143 A1
Gullen BA2 .... 135 A6
Gulliford's Bank BS21 .... 57 H2
Gullimores Gdns BS13 .... 79 B4
Gullivers Pl BS37 .... 40 A8
Gullock Tyning BA3 .... 133 B1
Gullons Cl BS13 .... 79 A6
Gullon Wlk BS13 .... 78 F5
Gullybrook La 3 BS5 .... 64 B6
Gully La BS35 .... 8 E7
Gully The BS36 .... 37 F7
Gunning Cl BS15 .... 65 D6
Gunter's Hill BS5 .... 65 A6
Guthrie Rd BS8 .... 142 A4
Gwilliam St BS3 .... 63 D3
Gwyn St BS2 .... 49 E1
Gypsy La
Keynsham BS31 .... 99 B8
Marshfield SN14 .... 69 F7

H

Haberfield Hill BS8 .... 47 E2
Haberfield Ho 1 BS8 .... 62 F6
Hacket Hill BS35 .... 15 F8
Hacket La BS35 .... 15 F8
Haddrell Ct BS35 .... 14 F5
Hadley Ct BS30 .... 66 B6
Hadley Rd BA2 .... 102 B2
Hadrian Cl BS9 .... 48 C4
Hadrians Wlk BS16 .... 52 C6
Haig Cl BS9 .... 48 B7
Halbrow Cres BS16 .... 51 C5
Haldon Cl BS3 .... 63 D1
Hale Cl BS15 .... 65 D4
Hales Horn Cl BS32 .... 36 D6
Half Acre Cl BS14 .... 80 A3
Halfacre La BS14 .... 80 B4
Halfpenny Row BA11 .... 137 E1
Half Yd BS40 .... 109 D8
Halifax Rd BS37 .... 27 D4
Hallam Ct BS21 .... 57 E4
Hallam Rd BS21 .... 57 E4
Hallards Cl BS11 .... 47 F8
HALLATROW 132 B7
Hallatrow Bsns Pk BS39 .... 132 A6
Hallatrow Rd BS39 .... 132 C6
HALLEN 34 C5
Hallen Cl
Bristol, Emerson's Green BS16 .... 52 C6
Bristol, Henbury BS10 .... 34 D3
HALL END 17 D2
Hall End La BS37 .... 17 D2
Hallen Dr BS9 .... 48 C7
Hallen Ind Est BS10 .... 34 A7
Hallen Rd BS10 .... 34 D4
Halletts Way BS20 .... 45 D5
Halliwell Rd BS20 .... 44 D4
Hall La
Cold Ashton BA1 .... 68 B3
Horton BS37 .... 29 E5
Halls Gdns BS34 .... 37 A4
Halls Rd BS15 .... 65 D8
Hall St BS3 .... 63 C2
Hall The BS20 .... 44 F5
Halsbury Rd BS6 .... 49 B4
Halstock Ave BS16 .... 50 F3
Halston Dr BS2 .... 143 C4
Halswell Gdns BS13 .... 79 B4
Halswell Rd BS21 .... 57 F1
Halt End BS14 .... 80 C3
Halwyn Cl BS9 .... 48 D5
HAM 132 F5
Hamble Cl BS35 .... 15 C8
Hambledon Ho BS6 .... 142 C4
Hambledon Rd BS22 .... 89 C4
HAMBROOK 37 C3
Hambrook La BS34 .... 37 A3
Hambrook Prim Sch BS16 .... 37 D3
Ham Cl BS39 .... 114 F1
Ham Farm La BS16 .... 52 B6
Ham Gn BS20 .... 47 D3
Ham Gr BS39 .... 132 E5
HAM GREEN 47 E4
Ham Hill BA3 .... 133 F3
Hamilton Ct 11 BS1 .... 143 A4
Hamilton Ho BA1 .... 84 E3
Hamilton Rd
Bath BA1 .... 84 E2
Bristol, Southville BS3 .... 63 B4

Hamilton Rd *continued*
Bristol, Upper Easton BS5 64 B8
8 Weston-S-M BS23 87 C1
Hamilton Terr BA2 134 F5
Ham La
Bishop Sutton BS39 113 C5
Bristol BS16 50 E6
Doynton BS30 53 E1
Dundry BS41 78 D3
Farrington Gurney BS39 131 F5
Kingston Seymour BS21 73 B2
Oldbury-on-S BS35 7 C7
Paulton BS39 132 E5
Wraxall BS48 60 B4
Yatton BS49 74 A3
Hamlet The BS48 60 A3
Ham Link BS40 109 F3
Hammersmith Rd BS5 64 D8
Hammond Cl BS4 64 E1
Hammond Gdns BS9 48 E7
Hampden Cl BS37 27 D4
Hampden Rd
Bristol BS4 64 B3
Weston-S-M BS22 88 E2
Hampshire Way BS37 27 F4
Hampstead Rd BS4 64 C3
Hampton Cl BS30 66 A5
Hampton Cnr BS11 47 E6
Hampton Ct BS6 49 B1
Hampton Hall BA2 102 D8
Hampton Ho 10 BA1 85 C1
Hampton La
17 Bristol BS6 49 B1
Bristol BS6 142 B4
Hampton Pk BS6 49 B1
Hampton Rd BS6 49 B1
Hampton Row BA2 102 B8
Hampton St BS15 51 D1
Hampton View BA1 85 B1
Ham Rd BS24, TA8 121 B3
Hams La BS26 123 C3
Hams Rd BS31 81 F7
HAMWOOD 123 C7
Ham Wood Cl BS24 105 B2
Hanbury Cl BS15 65 D5
Hanbury Ct BS8 142 A4
Hanbury Rd BS8 142 A4
Handel Ave 2 BS5 64 D7
Handel Cossham Ct 3 BS15 51 C1
Handel Rd BS31 81 E5
Handford Way BS30 66 B3
Hanford Ct BS14 80 D7
Hang Hill BA2 135 A6
HANHAM 65 C4
Hanham Abbots Jun Sch BS15 65 C4
Hanham Bsns Pk BS15 65 B5
HANHAM GREEN 65 C3
Hanham High Sch BS15 65 C4
Hanham La BS39 132 F7
Hanham Lo BS15 65 D7
Hanham Mills BS15 65 D1
Hanham Rd BS15 65 D7
Hanham Way BS48 59 B2
Hanna Cl BA2 101 B6
Hannah More Cl BS40 92 E2
Hannah More Inf Sch BS48 75 D8
Hannah More Prim Sch BS2 143 C2
Hannah More Rd BS48 75 C8
Hannay Rd BS27 126 B1
Hanny's La BS40 96 C3
Hanover Cl BS22 89 A4
Hanover Ct
Bath BA1 85 B2
Bristol, Filton BS34 36 A3
Radstock BA3 134 C2
Hanover Ho
Bristol BS2 64 A7
Portishead BS20 45 B5
Hanover Pl
Bath BA1 102 B8
Bristol BS1 142 B1
Hanover St
2 Bath BA1 85 B1
2 Bristol BS1 143 A2
Bristol, Russell Town BS5 64 C7
Hanover Terr 5 BA1 85 B1
Hansford Cl BA2 101 E1
Hansford Mews BA2 101 F1
Hansford Sq BA2 101 E1
Hanson's Way 4 BS21 57 E2
Hans Price Cl 18 BS23 104 E8
Hans Price Ho 13 BS23 104 E8
Hantone Hill BA2 102 F8
Happerton La BS20 47 D2
Hapsburg Cl BS22 89 A4
Harbour Cres BS20 45 E5
Harbour Ho BS8 142 A1
Harbour Rd BS20 45 D6
Harbour Road Trad Est BS20 45 F6
Harbours Edge BS8 142 B2
Harbour Wall BS9 48 B4
Harbour Way BS1 142 C1
Harbour Wlk BS1 142 C1
Harbury Rd BS9 49 C7
Harbutts BA2 85 F1
Harcombe Hill BS36 37 E4
Harcombe Rd BS36 37 D5
Harcourt Ave BS5 65 A6
Harcourt Cl BS31 82 E2
Harcourt Gdns BA1 84 B2
Harcourt Hill BS6 49 C3
Harcourt Rd BS6 49 B3
Hardenhuish Rd BS4 64 D5
Harden Rd BS14 80 E5
Harding Pl BS31 82 B5
Hardings Row BS2 64 B4
Hardington Dr BS31 82 A2
Hardwick Cl
Bristol, Broom Hill BS4 64 E3
Bristol, North Common BS30 66 D5
Hardwicke BS37 39 C7
Hardwick Rd BS20 47 C5
Hardy Ave BS3 63 A4
Hardy Ct BS30 65 F5
Hardy La BS32 14 A1
Hardy Rd BS3 63 B2
Hareclive Prim Sch BS13 79 C4
Hareclive Rd BS13 79 C4
Harefield Cl BS15 65 C2
Harescombe BS37 39 E7
Harewood Ho BS6 49 A3
Harewood Rd BS5 51 A1
Harford Cl BS9 48 C7
Harford Dr BS16 37 C1
Harford Sq BS40 96 B3
Harington Pl 2 BA1 141 B2
Harlech Way BS30 66 B2
Harleston St 1 BS5 64 A8
Harley Ct 3 BS8 62 F7
Harley La BS21 58 C6
Harley Mews 2 BS8 62 F7
Harley Pl 4 BS8 62 F7
Harley St BA1 141 B4
Harmer Cl BS10 34 F3
Harmony Dr BS20 44 F4
Harnhill Cl BS13 79 B4
Harolds Way BS15 65 C6
Harptree BS24 105 A2
Harptree Cl BS48 75 D8
Harptree Ct 5 BS30 66 A4
Harptree Gr BS3 63 B2
Harptree Hill BS40 129 B5
Harrier Path 3 BS22 105 E8
Harriets Yd BS31 81 F5
Harrington Ave BS14 80 E6
Harrington Cl BS30 82 E8
Harrington Gr BS14 80 E6
Harrington Rd BS14 80 E6
Harrington Wlk BS14 80 E6
Harris Barton BS36 38 B7
Harris Ct BS30 65 F4
Harris Gr BS13 79 B3
Harris La BS8 61 F8
Harrison Cl BS16 52 B6
Harrowdene Rd BS4 64 B3
Harrow Rd BS4 64 D3
HARRY STOKE 36 E2
Harry Stoke Rd BS34 36 E2
Hart Cl BS20 47 E4
HARTCLIFFE 79 C4
Hartcliffe Engineering Com Coll BS13 79 E4
Hartcliffe Rd BS4 79 E8
Hartcliffe Way BS3, BS4, BS13 79 C7
Hartcliffe Wlk BS4 79 F8
Hartfield Ave BS6 142 C4
Hartgill Cl BS13 79 B3
Hartington Pk BS6 49 C2
Hartland 14 BS22 89 A2
Hartland Ho BS5 64 C6
Hartley Cl BS37 28 C1
Hartley Ho BA1 141 B3
Harts Croft BS37 27 F4
Hart's La BS39 132 B7
Harts Paddock BA3 132 F3
Harvest Cl BS32 24 D1
Harvest La BS22 106 B8
Harvest Way BS22 89 A5
Harvey Cl BS22 89 A4
Harvey's La 6 BS5 64 F8
Harwood Gn BS22 88 E4
Harwood Ho 14 BS5 64 B7
Harwood Sq BS7 49 E5
Haselbury Gr BS31 82 E2
Haskins Ct 4 BS30 66 A4
Haslands BS48 75 D8
Haslemere Ind Est BS11 33 C2
Hassage Hill BA2 135 E7
Hassell Dr BS2 64 A7
Hastings Cl BS3 63 C1
Hastings Rd BS3 63 C1
Hatchet Hill BA3, BA11 140 E4
Hatchet La BS34 36 E4
Hatchet Rd BS34 36 E5
Hatchmere BS35 15 D8
Hatfield Bldgs BA2 102 B5
Hatfield Rd
Bath BA2 101 F3
Weston-S-M BS23 105 A8
Hathaway Ho 13 BS2 143 A4
Hatherley BS37 39 E7
Hatherley Rd BS7 49 E4
Hathway Wlk BS5 64 A8
Hatters' La BS37 28 C1
Havage Dro BS24 107 D8
Haven The BS15 51 E1
Haversham Cl BS22 88 D1
Haverstock Rd BS4 64 A3
Haviland Gr BA1 84 B3
Haviland Ho 7 BS2 143 C3
Haviland Pk BA1 84 B2
Havory BA1 85 C1
Havyat Rd BS40 109 E8
Havyat Road Trad Est BS40 92 E1
HAVYATT GREEN 109 F7
Hawarden Terr BA1 85 B1
Hawburn Cl BS4 64 D2
Haweswater BS10 35 B2
Haweswater Cl BS30 66 D6
Hawke Rd BS22 88 E4
HAWKESBURY 19 D2
Hawkesbury CE Prim Sch GL9 19 F3
Hawkesbury Grange GL9 20 A2
Hawkesbury Rd
Bristol BS16 50 E3
Hillesley GL12 19 D6
HAWKESBURY UPTON 20 A3
Hawkesley Dr BS34 36 D6
Hawkesworth Rd BS37 27 C3
Hawkfield Bsns Pk BS14 79 D5
Hawkfield Cl BS14 79 D5
Hawkfield Rd BS13 79 D5
Hawkfield Way BS14 79 D5
Hawkins Cl BS30 66 C5
Hawkins Cres BS32 36 E8
Hawkins St BS2 143 C3
Hawkley Dr BS32 24 D3
Hawkridge Dr BS16 53 C5
Hawksmoor Cl BS14 80 A6
Hawksmoor La BS16 50 E8
Hawksworth Dr
Bristol BS15 65 B5
Weston-S-M BS22 89 C4
Haw La BS35 14 B3
Hawthorn Ave BS15 65 B5
Hawthorn Cl
Bristol BS34 35 E7
Charfield GL12 11 A4
Portishead BS20 44 F5
Hawthorn Coombe BS22 88 E3
Hawthorn Cres
Thornbury BS35 8 C2
Yatton BS49 74 A2
Hawthorne Cl BS16 53 C5
Hawthorne Gdns BS16 51 F4
Hawthorne Rise BS10 35 C3
Hawthorne St BS4 64 A3
Hawthornes The BS16 51 F4
Hawthorn Gdns BS22 88 D2
Hawthorn Gr BA2 102 A1
Hawthorn Hill BS22 88 E2
Hawthorn Hts BS22 88 D3
Hawthorn Pk BS22 88 E3
Hawthorn Rd BA3 134 B2
Hawthorns La BS31 81 E5
Hawthorns The BS21 57 E3
Hawthorn Way
Bristol BS34 36 E5
Nailsea BS48 60 A2
Hayboro Way BS39 132 E4
Haycombe BS14 79 F6
Haycombe Dr BA2 101 A4
Haycombe La BA2 101 A3
Haycroft La GL13 4 C6
Haycroft Rd BS34 36 A3
Hayden Cl BA2 141 A1
Haydock Cl BS16 37 F1
HAYDON 139 F8
Haydon Ct 12 BS8 49 A2
Haydon Gate BA3 139 F8
Haydon Gdns BS7 50 B5
Haydon Hill BA3 140 A8
Haydon Ind Est BA3 139 F8
Hayeley Dr BS32 36 E6
Hayes Cl BS2 64 A7
Hayes Ct BS34 36 A7
Hayesfield Pk BA2 141 B1
Hayesfield School Tech Coll (Upper) BA2 141 A1
Hayesfield Sch Tech Coll (Lower) BA2 101 D6
Haye's La GL9 30 F2
HAYES PARK 133 A2
Hayes Park Rd BA3 132 F2
Hayes Pl BA2 141 B1
Hayes Rd BA3 132 F1
Hayeswood Farm BA15 103 F5
Hayeswood Rd BA2 115 E3
Hayfield SN14 70 A8
Haygarth Ct BA1 141 B4
Hay Hill BA1 141 B3
Hay La BS40 94 D6
Hay Leaze BS37 27 D4
Hayleigh Ho BS13 79 C4
Haymarket The BS1 143 A3
Haymarket Wlk 9 BS1 143 A4
Haynes Ho 3 BS16 51 D4
Haynes La BS16 51 D5
Hay St
Farrington Gurney BA3 138 A8
Marshfield SN14 70 A8
Hayter Ct BS10 35 D3
Haythorn Ct BS16 51 F5
Haythorne Ct 8 BS16 50 E3
Haytor Pk BS9 48 D6
Hayward Cl BS21 57 E1
Hayward Ind Est 1 BS16 51 D3
Hayward Rd
Bristol, Russell Town BS5 64 C7
Bristol, Staple Hill BS16 51 D3
Haywood Cl BS24 105 A1
Haywood Gdns BS24 105 B1
Hazel Ave BS6 49 B2
Hazel Barrow BS40 129 A7
Hazelbury Dr BS30 66 C6
Hazelbury Rd
Bristol BS14 80 C7
Nailsea BS48 59 D1
Hazel Cote Rd BS14 80 B4
Hazel Cres BS35 8 D1
Hazeldene Rd
Bristol BS34 36 A7
Weston-S-M BS23 105 A8
Hazel Gdns BS35 15 A4
Hazel Gr
Bath BA2 101 D4
Bristol BS7 50 A8
Midsomer Norton BA3 139 B8
Hazelgrove BS36 37 E5
Hazel La BS32, BS35 14 E3
Hazell Cl BS21 57 G1
Hazel Terr BA3 139 C8
Hazelton Rd BS7 49 D3
Hazel Way BA2 118 D8
Hazelwood Ct BS9 48 D3
Hazelwood Rd BS9 48 D3
Hazleton Gdns BA2 102 F3
Head Croft BS48 77 B8
Headford Ave BS5 65 B7
Headford Rd BS4 63 D1
Headington Cl BS15 65 D4
Headley Ct BS13 79 B6
Headley La BS13 79 B7
HEADLEY PARK 79 B6
Headley Park Ave BS13 79 B7
Headley Park Prim Sch BS13 79 B6
Headley Park Rd BS13 79 A7
Headley Rd BS13 79 A6
Headley Wlk BS13 79 B7
Healey Dr SN14 54 C6
Heart Meers BS14 80 B5
Heath Cl BS36 37 E6
Heathcote Dr BS36 38 D7
Heathcote La BS36 38 D7
Heathcote Rd
Bristol, Chester Park BS16 51 B2
Bristol, Staple Hill BS16 51 E5
Heathcote Wlk BS16 51 C2
Heath Ct BS16 51 D7
HEATH END 17 B8
Heather Ave BS36 38 B6
Heather Cl BS15 65 B8
Heatherdene BS14 79 F7
Heather Dr BA2 118 D8
Heathfield Cl
Bath BA1 84 A3
Keynsham BS31 81 C5
Heathfield Cres BS14 80 B4
Heathfield Rd BS48 59 E3
Heathfields BS16 51 D8
Heathfield Way BS48 59 E2
Heathgate BS49 91 B8
Heathgates BS23 104 D4
Heath Gdns
Bristol BS16 51 D8
Frampton Cotterell BS36 38 C5
Heath House La BS7, BS16 50 C5
Heath House Priory Hospl BS16 50 B4
Heath Rd
Bristol, Downend BS16 51 D8
Bristol, Eastville BS5 50 B3
Bristol, Hanham BS15 65 B4
Nailsea BS48 59 F3
Heath Ridge BS41 62 A2
Heath Rise BS30 66 B5
Heath St BS5 50 C3
Heath The BS9 48 E3
Heath Wlk BS16 51 D7
Hebden Rd BA15 120 F3
Heber St BS5 64 C7
Hebron Ct BS3 63 C3
Hebron Rd BS3 63 C3
Hedgemead Cl BS16 50 D5
Hedgemead Ct BA1 141 C4
Hedgemead View BS16 50 E5
Hedgerows 2 BS32 24 D1
Hedgers Cl BS3 63 A2
Hedges Cl 3 BS21 57 D1
Hedges The BS22 89 C3
Hedwick Ave BS5 64 E7
Hedwick St BS5 64 E7
Heggard Cl BS13 79 A5
Helens Rd BS25 108 B4
Heligan Wlk BS24 105 E7
Hellier Wlk BS13 79 C3
Helston Rd BS48 60 A1
Hemmings Par 4 BS5 64 B7
Hemming Way BS24 105 E3
Hemplow Cl BS14 80 D7
Hempton La BS32 24 B2
Henacre Rd BS11 47 F8
HENBURY 34 E2
Henbury Court Prim Sch BS10 34 F3
Henbury Ct BS10 34 E3
Henbury Gdns BS10 34 E2
Henbury Hill
Bristol BS9 34 F1
Bristol BS9 48 F8
Henbury Ho BA2 102 E4
Henbury Rd
Bristol BS9 48 F8
Bristol, Hanham BS15 65 B5
Bristol, Henbury BS10 34 F2
Bristol, Westbury on Trym BS9 49 A8
Henbury Sch BS10 34 E3
Hencliffe Rd BS14 80 D7
Hencliffe Way BS15 65 B3
Henderson Ho 1 BS2 143 B4
Henderson Rd BS15 65 B5
Hendre Rd BS3 63 A2
Heneage La GL12 9 F8
HENFIELD 38 D3
Henfield Bsns Pk BS36 38 D2
Henfield Cres BS30 66 B3
Henfield Rd BS36 38 C4
Hengaston St BS3 63 B2
HENGROVE 80 B6
Hengrove Ave BS14 80 B8
Hengrove Com Arts Coll BS14 80 B7
Hengrove La BS14 80 B8
Hengrove Rd BS4 64 A2
Hengrove Way BS14 79 E6
Hen La BS40 94 E3
HENLEAZE 49 C6
Henleaze Ave BS9 49 A5
Henleaze Gdns BS9 49 A5
Henleaze Jun & Inf Schs BS9 49 C5
Henleaze Park Dr BS9 49 C6
Henleaze Pk BS9 49 C5
Henleaze Rd BS9 49 B6
Henleaze Terr BS9 49 B7
Henley Gr BS9 49 B5
Henley Grove Ct BS9 49 B5
Henley La BS49 91 D7
Henley Lo BS49 91 D7
Henley Pk BS49 91 C7
Henley View BA2 118 D1
Hennessy Cl BS14 79 F3
Henrietta Ct BA2 141 C4
Henrietta Gdns BA2 141 C3
Henrietta Mews BA2 141 C3
Henrietta Pl BA2 141 C3
Henrietta Rd BA2 141 C3
Henrietta St
Bath BA2 141 C3
Bristol BS2 143 A4
5 Bristol, Lower Easton BS5 50 B1
Henrietta Villas BA2 141 C3
Henry Butt Ho 11 BS23 104 E8
Henry St
Bath BA1 141 C2
Bristol BS3 63 F4
Henry Williamson Ct 1 BS30 66 A5
Henshaw Cl BS15 51 C2
Henshaw Rd BS15 51 C2
Henshaw Wlk BS15 51 C2
Hensley Gdns BA2 101 E4
Hensley Rd BA2 101 E3
Hensman's Hill BS8 142 A2
Hepburn Rd BS2 143 B4
Herald Cl BS9 48 D5
Herapath St BS5 64 C6
Herbert Cres BS5 50 D3
Herbert Rd
Bath BA2 101 D5
Clevedon BS21 57 F4
Herbert St
Bristol, Moorfields BS5 64 C8
Bristol, Southville BS3 63 D4
Hercules Cl BS34 36 D6
Hereford Rd BS2 50 A2
Hereford St BS3 63 D3
Heritage Cl BA2 134 D8
Heritage The BA2 133 E8
Herkomer Cl BS7 50 B7
Herluin Way BS22, BS23 105 B6
Hermes Cl BS31 82 D2
Hermitage Cl BS11 47 E7
Hermitage Rd
Bath BA1 84 E1
Bristol BS16 51 E5
Hern La BS48 77 E5
Heron Cl BS22 105 E8
Heron Ct BS21 57 E2
Heron Gdns BS20 45 E4
Heron Rd BS5 50 B1
HERONS GREEN 112 C3
Herons Moor Com Prim Sch BS24 106 A8
Heron Way BS37 40 A8
Heron Wlk BS21 44 B1
Herridge Cl BS13 79 B4
Herridge Rd BS13 79 B4
Hersey Gdns BS13 78 E3
Hesding Cl BS15 65 C3
Hestercombe Cl BS24 105 E7
Hestercombe Rd BS13 79 B6
Hester Wood BS37 27 F4
Hetling Ct 10 BA1 141 B2
HEWISH 90 C5
Hewish Ct BS23 104 E8
Hewland Ct BS11 34 C2
Hexagon The BA2 101 E1
Heyford Ave BS5 50 B4
Heyron Wlk BS13 79 B4
Heywood Rd BS20 47 C4

Heywood Terr BS20 . . . . . .47 C4
Hibbs Cl SN14 . . . . .69 F8
Hicking Ct **8** BS15 . . . . . .51 D1
Hicks Ave BS16 . . . . .52 B8
HICKS COMMON 37 F5
Hicks Common Rd
BS36 . . . . .37 E5
Hicks Ct
Bristol, Crofts End BS5 . . . . .64 F8
Bristol, Stone Hill BS30 . . . .65 F4
HICKS GATE 81 B8
Hidcote Mews BS24 . . . . . .105 E7
Hide Mkt BS2 . . . . .143 C3
High Acre BS39 . . . . .132 F4
Higham St **4** BS2 . . . . .63 F4
High Bannerdown BA1 . . . . .86 B4
Highbury Cotts **7** BA1 . . . .85 A1
Highbury Ct **16** BS23 . . . . . .87 C1
Highbury Farm Bsns Pk
BS39 . . . . .132 A8
Highbury Par BS23 . . . . .87 C1
Highbury Pl BA1 . . . . .85 A1
Highbury Rd
Bristol, Bedminster
BS3 . . . . .63 C2
Bristol, Horfield BS7 . . . . . . .49 F7
Hallatrow BS39 . . . . .132 B7
Weston-S-M BS23 . . . . .87 C1
Highbury Terr **9** BA1 . . . . .85 A1
Highbury Villas
8 Bath BA1 . . . . .85 A1
Bristol BS2 . . . . .142 C4
High Cnr BS10 . . . . .34 F1
Highcroft
8 Bristol BS30 . . . . .66 C6
Weston-S-M BS23 . . . . .87 F1
Highcroft Jun Sch
BS36 . . . . .38 C8
Highdale Ave BS21 . . . . .57 G3
Highdale Cl BS14 . . . . .80 B4
Highdale Ct BS21 . . . . .57 F3
Highdale Rd BS21 . . . . .57 G3
High Down Jun & Inf Schs
BS20 . . . . .45 A4
High Elm BS15 . . . . .65 E6
Highett Dr BS5 . . . . .50 A1
Highfield Ave BS15 . . . . . . .65 D5
Highfield Cl BA2 . . . . .101 B5
Highfield Cres BA3 . . . . . .138 C4
Highfield Dr BS20 . . . . .44 E3
Highfield Gdns BS30 . . . . . .66 C2
Highfield Gr BS7 . . . . .49 D5
Highfield La
Compton Martin BS40 . . . .129 B6
East Harptree BS40 . . . . . .130 A3
Horton BS37, GL9 . . . . .29 E7
Highfield Rd
Chipping Sodbury BS37 . . . .28 A1
Keynsham BS31 . . . . .81 D4
Peasedown St John
BA2 . . . . .134 C8
Weston-S-M BS24 . . . . . . .105 A1
Highfields
Clandown BA3 . . . . .133 E4
Hawkesbury Upton GL9 . . . .19 F2
Stanton Drew BS39 . . . . . . .96 F3
High Fields BA3 . . . . .133 D2
Highfields Cl BS34 . . . . .36 F3
High Gr BS9 . . . . .48 B7
Highgrove St **4** BS4 . . . . . .64 A4
Highgrove Wlk BS24 . . . . .106 A8
High Kingsdown BS2 . . . . .142 C4
High La BS36 . . . . .37 C8
Highland Cl BS22 . . . . .88 B2
Highland Cres **3** BS8 . . . . .49 A2
Highland Pl **12** BS8 . . . . . . .49 A2
Highland Rd BA2 . . . . .101 B5
Highlands Dr GL11 . . . . .5 E4
Highlands La BS24 . . . . . . .106 A8
Highland Sq **4** BS8 . . . . . . .49 A2
Highlands Rd
Long Ashton BS41 . . . . .62 A2
Portishead BS20 . . . . .45 B5
Highland Terr **3** BA2 . . . .101 D6
Highleaze Rd BS30 . . . . .66 C4
HIGH LITTLETON 115 C1
High Littleton CE Prim
Sch BS39 . . . . .115 C1
High Mdws BA3 . . . . .132 F1
Highmead Gdns
Bishop Sutton BS39 . . . . . .113 D3
Bristol BS13 . . . . .78 E4
Highmore Ct BS7 . . . . .50 B7
Highmore Gdns BS7 . . . . . .50 C7
Highnam Ct BS34 . . . . .24 D1
High Pk
Bristol BS14 . . . . .64 B1
Paulton BS39 . . . . .132 D6
High Point Ho **8** BS15 . . . . .51 C1
HIGHRIDGE
Bristol 78 F7
Dundry 78 D3
Highridge Cres BS13 . . . . . .78 F5
Highridge Gn BS13 . . . . .78 E6
Highridge Inf Sch
BS13 . . . . .78 F6
Highridge Pk BS13 . . . . .78 F6
Highridge Rd
Bristol, Bedminster
BS3 . . . . .63 B2
Bristol, Withywood BS13,
BS41 . . . . .78 E4
Highridge Wlk BS13 . . . . . .78 E7
High St
Axbridge BS26 . . . . .125 B2

High St continued
Badminton GL9 . . . . .30 E2
Banwell BS29 . . . . .107 A2
Bathampton BA2 . . . . .85 F1
Bath BA1 . . . . .141 C2
Batheaston BA1 . . . . .85 F3
Bathford BA1 . . . . .86 D2
Bath, Twerton BA2 . . . . . .101 B6
Bath, Weston BA1 . . . . .84 B1
Bitton BS30 . . . . .82 E8
Blagdon BS40 . . . . .110 E3
Bristol BS1 . . . . .143 A2
Bristol, Clifton BS8 . . . . . . .49 A2
Bristol, Jefferies Hill
BS15 . . . . .65 C5
Bristol, Kingswood BS15 . . .65 E8
Bristol, Lower Easton
BS5 . . . . .50 B1
Bristol, Oldland Common
BS30 . . . . .66 D4
Bristol, Shirehampton
BS11 . . . . .47 E6
Bristol, Staple Hill BS16 . . .51 D4
Bristol, Warmley BS15 . . . . .66 B8
Bristol, Westbury on Trym
BS9 . . . . .49 A7
Chew Magna BS40 . . . . .96 A3
Chipping Sodbury BS37 . . . .28 B1
Claverham BS49 . . . . .74 F1
Congresbury BS49 . . . . .91 D4
Doynton BS30 . . . . .53 F1
East Harptree BS40 . . . . . .129 F5
Faulkland BA2 . . . . .135 D1
Freshford BA2 . . . . .120 B5
Hawkesbury Upton GL9 . . . .19 F3
High Littleton BS39 . . . . . .115 D1
Hillesley GL12 . . . . .19 D8
Hinton Charterhouse
BA2 . . . . .119 E1
Iron Acton BS37 . . . . .26 D4
Keynsham BS31 . . . . .81 E6
Kingswood GL12 . . . . .11 F4
Marshfield SN14 . . . . .69 F8
Midsomer Norton BA3 . . . .133 B1
Nailsea BS48 . . . . .59 F3
Norton St Philip BA2 . . . . .136 E4
Paulton BS39 . . . . .132 E5
Paulton, Plummer's Hill
BS39 . . . . .132 E6
Pensford BS39 . . . . .97 E4
Portbury BS20 . . . . .46 E3
Portishead BS20 . . . . .45 D5
Saltford BS31 . . . . .82 F3
Thornbury BS35 . . . . .15 B8
Timsbury BA2 . . . . .116 B2
Tormarton GL9 . . . . .41 D2
Wellow BA2 . . . . .118 D1
Weston-S-M BS23 . . . . . .104 D8
Weston-S-M, Worle
BS22 . . . . .88 E2
Wick BS30 . . . . .67 D6
Wickwar GL12 . . . . .18 A5
Winford BS40 . . . . .95 A7
Winterbourne BS36 . . . . . . .37 D6
Woolley BA1 . . . . .84 F6
Wrington BS40 . . . . .92 D2
Yatton BS49 . . . . .91 C8
High View BS20 . . . . .45 A4
Highview Rd BS15 . . . . .51 F1
Highwall La BS14, BS31 . . . .80 F1
Highway BS37 . . . . .27 F2
Highwood Bsns Pk
BS34 . . . . .35 C7
Highwood La BS10,
BS34 . . . . .35 D7
Highwood Pk Cvn Site
BS34 . . . . .35 E6
Highwood Rd BS34 . . . . .35 E6
Highworth Cres BS37 . . . . . .39 D8
Highworth Rd BS4 . . . . .64 D6
Hildesheim Bridge
BS23 . . . . .104 F7
Hildesheim Cl BS23 . . . . . .104 F6
Hildesheim Ct **9**
BS23 . . . . .104 E7
Hilhouse BS9 . . . . .48 C6
HILL .2 D3
Hill Ave
Bath BA2 . . . . .101 F1
Bristol BS3 . . . . .63 E3
Hillbrook Rd **5** BS35 . . . . .15 D8
Hill Burn BS9 . . . . .49 C6
Hillburn Rd BS5 . . . . .65 A8
Hill Cote BS16 . . . . .52 B8
Hillcote BS24 . . . . .122 B8
Hillcrest
Peasedown St John
BA2 . . . . .134 C7
Pensford BS39 . . . . .97 E3
Thornbury BS35 . . . . .8 B1
Hill Crest BS4 . . . . .64 B1
Hillcrest Cl BS48 . . . . .59 E1
Hillcrest Dr BA2 . . . . .101 C4
Hillcrest Prim Sch BS4 . . . . .64 A3
Hillcrest Rd
Nailsea BS48 . . . . .59 E1
Portishead BS20 . . . . .44 E4
Hillcroft Cl
Bristol BS15 . . . . .65 E4
Weston-S-M BS22 . . . . .88 A2
Hill Ct BS39 . . . . .132 E6
Hilldale Rd BS48 . . . . .76 B5
Hill Dr BS8 . . . . .61 C3
Hillend BS22 . . . . .88 E3
Hill End Dr BS10 . . . . .34 D3
HILLESLEY 19 E8
Hillesley CE Prim Sch
GL12 . . . . .19 E8

Hillesley Rd GL12 . . . . .11 F4
HILLFIELDS 51 B3
Hillfields Ave BS16 . . . . . . .51 C3
Hillfields Prim Sch
BS16 . . . . .51 C2
Hill Gay Cl BS20 . . . . .44 F4
Hill Gr BS9 . . . . .49 C6
Hillgrove St BS2 . . . . .143 B4
Hillgrove Terr BS23 . . . . . .104 D1
HILLHOUSE 52 A5
Hill House Rd BS16 . . . . . . .51 F5
Hillier's La BS25 . . . . .108 D4
Hill La
Chipping Sodbury BS37 . . . .41 B7
Clevedon BS21 . . . . .58 C4
Portishead BS20 . . . . .44 F1
Rowberrow BS25 . . . . .109 A1
Thornbury BS35, GL13 . . . . .2 C1
Hill Lawn BS4 . . . . .64 D3
Hillmead BS40 . . . . .109 A1
Hillmer Rise BS29 . . . . . . .106 F3
Hill Moor BS21 . . . . .57 G2
Hillpath BS29 . . . . .107 B2
Hill Pk BS49 . . . . .91 E5
Hill Rd
Clevedon BS21 . . . . .57 F4
Dundry BS41 . . . . .78 D2
Sandford BS25 . . . . .108 A3
Weston-S-M BS23 . . . . . . .104 F8
Weston-S-M, Worle
BS22 . . . . .88 E2
Hill Rd E BS22 . . . . .88 E2
Hill's Barton BS13 . . . . .63 A1
Hillsborough BS8 . . . . .142 A2
Hillsborough Ho
BS23 . . . . .105 A4
Hillsborough Rd BS4 . . . . . .64 C4
Hills Cl BS31 . . . . .82 A5
Hillsdon Rd BS9 . . . . .48 F8
HILLSIDE 138 E8
Hillside
Axbridge BS26 . . . . .125 C2
Bristol BS6 . . . . .142 C4
Bristol, Mangotsfield
BS16 . . . . .52 A5
Burton SN14 . . . . .43 A4
Portbury BS20 . . . . .46 D3
Hillside Ave
Bristol BS15 . . . . .65 C8
Midsomer Norton BA3 . . . .138 F8
Hillside Cl
Frampton Cotterell
BS36 . . . . .38 C7
Paulton BS39 . . . . .132 F6
Hillside Cres BA3 . . . . .138 E8
Hillside Ct BS5 . . . . .65 B7
Hillside Fst Sch BS22 . . . . .88 E2
Hillside Gdns
Bishop Sutton BS39 . . . . . .113 C3
Weston-S-M BS22 . . . . .88 B1
Hillside Ho **6** BS6 . . . . . . .49 D1
Hillside La BS36 . . . . .38 C7
Hillside Rd
Backwell BS48 . . . . .76 A4
Bath BA2 . . . . .101 D4
Bleadon BS24 . . . . .122 B8
Bristol BS5 . . . . .65 A7
Clevedon BS21 . . . . .57 F3
Long Ashton BS41 . . . . .62 B2
Midsomer Norton BA3 . . . .138 F8
Portishead BS20 . . . . .44 D4
Hillside St BS4 . . . . .64 A4
Hillside View
Midsomer Norton
BA3 . . . . .133 A3
Peasedown St John
BA2 . . . . .134 C8
Hillside W BS24 . . . . .105 F2
Hill St
Bristol BS1 . . . . .142 C2
Bristol, Kingswood BS15 . . .65 F8
Bristol, St George BS5 . . . . .64 F8
Bristol, Windmill Hill BS3 . . .63 F4
Hilltop Gdns
Bristol, St George BS5 . . . . .65 A7
Bristol, Upper Soundwell
BS16 . . . . .51 D2
Hilltop Rd BS16 . . . . .51 D2
Hilltop View BS5 . . . . .65 A7
Hillview
Midsomer Norton
BA3 . . . . .138 E7
Timsbury BA2 . . . . .116 B1
Hill View
Bristol, Blackhorse
BS16 . . . . .52 A8
Bristol BS8 . . . . .142 B2
Bristol, Filton BS34 . . . . . . .36 A3
Bristol, Henleaze BS9 . . . . .49 C6
Bristol, Upper Soundwell
BS16 . . . . .51 D2
Farrington Gurney
BS39 . . . . .132 B3
Marksbury BA2 . . . . .99 B1
Priston BA2 . . . . .117 A5
Hillview Ave BS21 . . . . .57 F2
Hill View Cl BS30 . . . . .66 C4
Hill View Ct
Bristol BS16 . . . . .51 C5
Weston-S-M BS22 . . . . . . .105 D8
Hill View Cwn Pk BS40 . . . .77 B1
Hillview Gdns BS40 . . . . . . .94 C8
Hill View Ho **2** BS15 . . . . .51 C1

Hill View Park Homes
BS22 . . . . .105 D8
Hillview Rd
Loxton BS26 . . . . .123 C4
Pucklechurch BS16 . . . . . . .53 C5
Hill View Rd
Bath BA1 . . . . .85 B2
Bristol BS13 . . . . .79 A8
Weston-S-M BS23 . . . . . . .105 A7
Hillyfield Rd BS13 . . . . .79 A6
Hillyfields BS25 . . . . .125 B8
Hillyfields Way BS25 . . . . .125 A8
Hilton Ct **3** BS5 . . . . .64 B8
Hinckley Cl BS22 . . . . .89 C4
Hind Pitts BS25 . . . . .125 F7
HINTON 54 D6
Hinton BS24 . . . . .105 A2
HINTON BLEWETT 130 F6
HINTON CHARTERHOUSE
. . . . .119 E1
Hinton Cl
Bath BA2 . . . . .100 F6
Saltford BS31 . . . . .82 E3
Hinton Dr BS30 . . . . .66 C6
Hinton Hill BA2 . . . . .119 A1
Hinton La **13** BS8 . . . . .62 F6
Hinton Rd
Bristol, Fishponds
BS16 . . . . .51 A4
Bristol, Lower Easton
BS5 . . . . .50 C1
Hinton Villas BA2 . . . . .119 E1
Hippisley Dr BS26 . . . . . . .125 D2
Hiscocks Dr BA2 . . . . .101 E4
Hitchen Cl SN14 . . . . .69 F8
Hither Bath Bridge
BS4 . . . . .64 C1
Hither Gn BS21 . . . . .57 H2
Hither Green Ind Est
BS21 . . . . .57 H2
Hither Mead BS36 . . . . .38 B6
Hoare's La BA1 . . . . .140 B3
Hobart Rd BS23 . . . . .104 D3
Hobbiton Rd BS22 . . . . .89 A4
Hobbs Ct **1** BS48 . . . . .59 F2
Hobbs La
Barrow Gurney BS48 . . . . . .77 E3
Bristol BS30 . . . . .52 B1
Hobb's La BS1 . . . . .142 C2
HOBB'S WALL 115 E5
Hobhouse Cl BS9 . . . . .49 C7
Hobwell La BS41 . . . . .62 C2
Hockeys La BS16 . . . . .51 A4
Hockley Ct BA1 . . . . .84 E4
Hoddon La BS16 . . . . .53 D5
Hodshill BA2 . . . . .118 F6
Hoecroft BA3 . . . . .138 D2
Hoecroft Gdns BA3 . . . . . .138 D3
Hogarth Mews BS22 . . . . . .89 A3
Hogarth Wlk
Bristol BS7 . . . . .50 C7
Weston-S-M BS22 . . . . .89 A3
Hogues Wlk BS13 . . . . .79 B4
Holbeach Way BS14 . . . . . . .80 A2
Holbrook Cres BS13 . . . . . .79 D4
HOLBROOK COMMON 67 B8
Holbrook Cres BS13 . . . . . .79 D4
Holbrook La BS30 . . . . .67 B8
Holburne Mus of Art*
BA2 . . . . .102 B7
HOLCOMBE 139 D1
Holcombe BS14 . . . . .80 A5
Holcombe Cl BA2 . . . . .85 F1
Holcombe Gn BA1 . . . . .84 B2
Holcombe Gr BS31 . . . . .81 D5
Holcombe La BA2 . . . . .85 F1
Holcombe Vale BA2 . . . . . . .85 F1
Holdenhurst Rd BS15 . . . . . .51 C1
Holders Wlk BS41 . . . . .77 F8
Holford Cl BS48 . . . . .59 E1
Holford Ct BS14 . . . . .80 B5
Holland Rd
Bath BA1 . . . . .85 B1
Clevedon BS21 . . . . .57 D1
Holland St BS23 . . . . .105 A8
Hollidge Gdns **3** BS3 . . . . .63 D4
Hollies La BA1 . . . . .86 A6
Hollies The
Bristol BS15 . . . . .65 E6
Midsomer Norton BA3 . . . .133 A1
Hollis Ave BS20 . . . . .45 C3
Hollis Cl BS41 . . . . .78 A8
Hollis Cres BS20 . . . . .45 C3
Hollis Gdns SN14 . . . . .31 E4
Hollister's Dr BS13 . . . . . . .79 D4
Holloway BA2 . . . . .141 B1
Holloway Hill SN14 . . . . . . .56 F7
Holloway Rd BS35 . . . . .22 C4
HOLLOW BROOK 112 C8
Hollowbrook La BS39,
BS40 . . . . .113 D6
Hollow La BS22 . . . . .88 F3
Hollow Marsh La BA3,
BS39 . . . . .131 B4
Hollowmead BS49 . . . . .91 E8
Hollowmead Cl BS49 . . . . . .91 F8
Hollow Rd
Almondsbury BS32 . . . . . . .24 A4
Bristol BS15 . . . . .65 E6
Shipham BS25 . . . . .125 F8
Hollow The
Bath BA2 . . . . .101 B4
Dunkerton BA2 . . . . .117 D4
Marshfield SN14 . . . . .69 E6
Holly Brook BS14 . . . . .80 E5
Hollybrook Pk BS15 . . . . . . .51 B2
Hollybush Cl
Acton Turville GL9 . . . . .43 A6

Hollybush Cl continued
Winsley BA15 . . . . .120 E7
Hollybush La
Bristol BS9 . . . . .48 E5
Bristol BS9 . . . . .48 F4
Holly Cl
Alveston BS35 . . . . .14 F4
Bristol BS5 . . . . .51 A2
Nailsea BS48 . . . . .60 A3
Pucklechurch BS16 . . . . . . .53 C5
Weston-S-M BS22 . . . . .89 A1
Holly Cres BS15 . . . . .51 E1
Holly Ct BS2 . . . . .142 C4
Holly Dr
Bath BA2 . . . . .118 D8
Colerne SN14 . . . . .70 F6
Holly Gn BS15 . . . . .52 A1
Holly Gr BS16 . . . . .51 C3
Hollyguest Rd BS15 . . . . . . .65 E6
Holly Hill BS37 . . . . .26 E3
Holly Hill Rd BS15 . . . . .51 F1
Holly Ho BS11 . . . . .34 C2
Holly La BS21 . . . . .57 H6
Hollyleigh Ave BS34 . . . . . .35 F2
Holly Lodge Cl BS5 . . . . . . .51 A2
Holly Lodge Rd BS5 . . . . . . .51 A2
Hollyman Wlk **5** BS21 . . . .57 H3
Hollymead La BS9 . . . . .48 E4
Hollyridge BS14 . . . . .80 C6
Holly Ridge BS20 . . . . .45 A5
Holly Wlk
Keynsham BS31 . . . . .81 D4
Radstock BA3 . . . . .133 E1
Hollywood La BS10,
BS35 . . . . .35 A7
Hollywood Rd BS4 . . . . .64 D2
Holmdale Rd BS34 . . . . .36 C3
Holmes Cl BS9 . . . . .49 B5
Holmesdale Rd BS3 . . . . . . .63 E3
Holmes Gr BS9 . . . . .49 B5
Holmes Hill Rd BS5 . . . . . . .64 F8
Holmes St BS5 . . . . .64 B6
Holm La BS35 . . . . .13 B2
Holmlea BS20 . . . . .45 F5
Holmoak Rd BS31 . . . . .81 C4
Holm Rd BS24 . . . . .105 E2
Holms Rd BS23 . . . . .105 A5
Holmwood BS15 . . . . .65 C5
Holmwood Cl BS36 . . . . . . .37 D6
Holmwood Gdns BS9 . . . . . .49 B8
Holroyd Ho BS3 . . . . .63 D3
Holsom Cl BS14 . . . . .80 F6
Holsom Rd BS14 . . . . .80 F6
Holst Gdns BS4 . . . . .79 D7
Holton Rd BS7 . . . . .50 A6
Holtsdown La BA1 . . . . .85 F7
Holwell Cl BS39 . . . . .132 E4
Holybrook Trad Est
BS15 . . . . .51 B2
Holy Cross RC Prim Sch
BS3 . . . . .63 C4
Holy Family RC Prim Sch
BS34 . . . . .36 B8
Holymead Inf Sch BS4 . . . .64 D2
Holymead Jun Sch
BS4 . . . . .64 D2
Holyrood Cl BS34 . . . . .36 D4
Holy Trinity Prim Sch
BS32 . . . . .24 C2
Holy Well Cl BS4 . . . . .64 E6
Homeapple Hill BS30 . . . . . .66 F6
Homeavon Ho BS31 . . . . . . .81 F5
Home Cl
Bristol BS10 . . . . .35 E2
Wrington BS40 . . . . .92 E3
Home Farm Cl BA2 . . . . . .134 B7
Home Farm Ct BS22 . . . . . .89 C3
Home Farm Rd BS8 . . . . . . .62 B8
Home Farm Way BS35 . . . . .23 A1
Homefield
Congresbury BS49 . . . . .91 E3
Locking BS24 . . . . .106 A5
Thornbury BS35 . . . . .15 D8
Timsbury BA2 . . . . .116 C2
Yate BS37 . . . . .27 E3
Homefield Cl
Locking BS24 . . . . .106 A5
Saltford BS31 . . . . .82 E3
Wincanton BS25 . . . . .107 F1
Home Field Cl BS16 . . . . . . .52 B6
Homefield Dr BS16 . . . . . . .51 A5
Homefield Ind Est
BS24 . . . . .106 A5
Homefield Rd
Pucklechurch BS16 . . . . . . .53 B5
Saltford BS31 . . . . .82 F3
Homeground
Bristol BS16 . . . . .52 B6
Clevedon BS21 . . . . .57 H2
Home Ground
Bristol, Eastfield BS9 . . . . .49 B7
Bristol, Shirehampton
BS11 . . . . .47 D7
Homelea Pk E BA1 . . . . . . .101 A7
Homelea Pk W BA1 . . . . . .101 A7
Homeleaze Rd BS10 . . . . . .35 D3
Homemead BA2 . . . . .100 A8
Home Mead
Bristol, Cadbury Heath
BS30 . . . . .66 A4
Bristol, Filwood Park
BS4 . . . . .79 E7
Homemead Dr BS4 . . . . . . .64 D1
Home Orch
Chew Stoke BS40 . . . . . . .112 D8
Yate BS37 . . . . .27 D2
Homestead BS20 . . . . .44 E3
Homestead Cl BS36 . . . . . . .38 D7

Homestead Gdns BS16....51 B8
Homestead Rd BS34......36 A3
Homestead The
Clevedon BS21............57 E3
Keynsham BS31............81 F2
Homestead Way
BS25..................125 A8
Honeyborne Way GL12.....18 B5
Honey Garston Cl BS13...79 B4
Honey Garston Rd
BS13.......................79 B4
HONEY HALL 108 C7
Honeyhall La BS49......108 D7
Honey Hill Rd BS15.......65 F8
Honeylands BS20.........45 C3
Honeymead BS14..........80 C6
Honeysuckle Cl BS32.....24 E2
Honey Suckle La BS16....50 E5
Honeysuckle Pl BS24....106 A8
Honey Way BS15...........65 F8
Honeywick Cl BS3..........63 C2
Honister Ho BS34.........36 A8
Honiton 9 BS22............89 A2
Honiton Rd
Bristol BS16...............51 A3
Clevedon BS21..............57 G1
HOOK 116 D2
Hook Hill BA2...........116 D2
Hook La BA3, BS39.......130 E4
Hooks Batch BS40.......110 C4
Hooper Rd BS14...........80 D5
Hoover's La BS36, BS37....26 C2
Hopechapel Hill 11
BS8........................62 F6
Hope Cote Lo BA2.......102 C1
Hope Cotts BS21..........73 B2
Hope Ct BS1..............142 B1
Hope Rd
Bristol BS3................63 C2
Yate BS37..................27 A2
Hope Sq BS8...............62 F6
Hope Terr BA3...........133 B1
Hopetoun Rd BS2..........49 F3
Hopewell Gdns BS11......47 F7
HOPEWELL HILL 51 D1
Hopkin Cl BS35............15 D7
Hopkins Ct 13 BS6.........49 B1
Hopkins St BS23.........104 E8
Hopland Cl BS30...........66 B3
Hopp's Rd BS15...........65 D7
Horesham Gr BS13.......79 C5
HORFIELD 49 F6
Horfield CE Prim Sch
BS10.......................49 D7
Horfield Ct BS7............49 E4
Horfield Rd BS2.........143 A4
Horley Rd BS2.............50 A2
Hornbeam Ho 5 BS16.....51 C6
Hornbeams The BS16.....37 B1
Hornbeam Wlk BS31......81 C3
Horne Cl BA3.............138 F1
Horn's La BS26...........125 B2
HORSECASTLE 74 A2
Horsecastle Cl BS49......74 A1
Horsecastle Farm Rd
BS49.......................74 A1
Horsecombe Brow
BA2......................102 A1
Horsecombe Gr BA2....102 A1
Horsecombe Vale
BA2......................102 A1
Horsecroft Gdns BS30....66 A6
Horsefair The BS1.......143 B3
Horse La BS35..............8 D5
Horseleaze La BS25....108 D1
Horsepool La BS30........67 F8
Horsepool Rd BS13.......78 E3
Horse Race La BS8.......61 A6
Horseshoe Ct BS36.......38 D7
Horseshoe Dr BS9.........48 C4
Horseshoe La BS37.......28 B1
Horseshoe Wlk BA2.....102 B5
Horse St BS37.............28 C1
Horse World* BS14.......80 D3
Horsford Rd GL12.........11 B5
Horstmann Cl 2 BA1....101 B7
Hortham La BS32.........24 E5
HORTON 29 B6
Horton CE Prim Sch
BS37.......................29 C5
Horton Ct* BS37..........29 D7
Horton Hill BS37..........29 C5
Horton Ho BA2...........141 C4
Horton Rd
Chipping Sodbury BS37.....28 C2
Chipping Sodbury, Little
Sodbury End BS37.......28 D4
Horton St BS2...........143 C3
Horwood Ct 3 BS30......66 A4
Horwood La GL12.........18 B4
Horwood Rd BS48........59 F1
Hosey Wlk BS13..........79 A5
Host St BS1..............143 A3
Hot Bath St 9 BA1......141 B2
Hottom Gdns BS7.........50 A7
Hot Water La BS15.......52 A3
Hotwell Hts BS8........142 A2
Hotwell Rd BS8..........142 B1
HOTWELLS 142 A1
Hotwells Ho BS8........142 A2
Hotwells Prim Sch BS8....62 F6
Houlgate Way BS26.....125 B1
Houlton St BS2..........143 C4
Hounds Cl BS37...........28 B1
Hounds Rd BS37..........28 B1
HOUNSLEY BATCH.......95 A3
Howard Ave BS5..........64 E8
Howard Cl BS31...........82 D3
Howard Rd
Bristol, Southville BS3......63 C4
Bristol, Staple Hill BS16....51 D4
Bristol, Westbury Park
BS6........................49 B4
Thornbury BS35.............8 C2
Howard St BS5............50 E1
Howard Wlk BS30.........66 D7
Howecroft Ct BS9.........48 E4
Howecroft Gdns BS9......48 E4
Howells Mead BS16.......52 B7
Howes Cl BS30............66 A6
Howett Rd 16 BS5.........64 C7
Howgrove Hill La BS40....94 C2
How Hill BA2.............101 A6
Howitt Way 1 BS24......105 F7
HOWLEY 5 E1
Howsmoor La
Bristol, Lyde Green
BS16.......................52 C8
Bristol, New England
BS16.......................52 B8
Hoylake BS37..............39 E8
Hoylake Dr BS30..........66 B6
Huckford La BS36........38 A4
Huckford Rd BS36........37 E5
Huckley Way BS32........36 F6
Hudds Hill Gdns 9
BS5.........................64 F8
Hudd's Hill Rd BS5.......64 F8
Hudd's Vale Rd BS5......64 E8
Hudson Cl BS37...........39 F8
Hughenden Rd
Bristol, Clifton BS8........49 A2
Bristol, Horfield BS7.......49 E5
Weston-S-M BS23........105 A8
Hughes Gdns BS7.........50 A8
Huish Ct BA3............134 B2
Hulbert Cl BS4............65 A2
Hulse Rd BS4..............64 D1
Humberstan Wlk BS11....47 E8
Humber Way BS11........33 D5
Humphry Davy Way 6
BS8........................62 F5
Humphrys Barton BS4....64 F5
Hungerford Cl BS4........80 E8
Hungerford Cres BS4.....64 E1
Hungerford Gdns BS4.....80 E8
Hungerford Rd
Bath BA1..................101 C7
Bristol BS4.................80 E8
Hungerford Terr BA2....118 D1
Hungerford Wlk BS4......64 E1
Hung Rd BS11.............47 E5
HUNSTRETE 98 D2
Hunstrete Rd BA2.......115 F7
Hunters Cl BS15..........65 C5
Hunters Dr BS15..........51 F1
Hunters Mead GL9........20 A2
Hunters Rd BS15.........65 C5
Hunters Rd E BS15........65 C4
Hunters Rest Miniature
Rlwy* BS39...............115 A5
Hunter's Way BS34.......36 B3
HUNTINGFORD 10 F8
Huntingham Rd BS13.....78 F4
Huntley Gr BS48..........60 A1
Hunts Ground Rd BS34....36 F4
Hunts La BS7...............49 E6
Hunt's La BS49............91 E8
Hurle Cres BS8............49 B1
Hurle Rd BS8..............49 B1
Hurlingham Rd BS7.......49 F2
Hurn La BS31..............82 A3
Hurn Rd BS21..............57 H2
Hursley Hill
Bristol BS14, BS39.........97 D8
Whitchurch BS14..........80 D1
Hursley La BS14..........80 E1
Hurston Rd BS4...........79 D7
Hurst Rd
Bristol BS4.................79 F8
Weston-S-M BS23........105 A6
Hurst Wlk BS4.............79 F8
Hurstwood Rd BS16.......51 D5
HUTTON 105 E2
Hutton CE Prim Sch
BS24......................105 E2
Hutton Cl
Bristol BS9.................48 E7
Keynsham BS31............82 A2
Hutton Hill BS24.........105 F2
Hutton Moor La BS22,
BS24......................105 C6
Hutton Moor Pk BS24....105 C6
Hutton Moor Rd BS22....105 C7
Hutton Moor Rdbt
BS22......................105 C7
Huyton Rd BS5............50 E3
Hyatts Wood Rd BS48....76 E1
Hyde Apartments BS6.....49 C3
Hyde Ave BS35..............8 B3
Hyde's La SN14............69 A6
Hydes The BS31...........81 F6
Hyde The BS21............73 C8
Hyland Gr BS9.............48 F8
HYSTFIELD 3 B5

I

ICELTON 89 C8
Ida Rd 2 BS5..............64 C8
Iddesleigh Rd BS6........49 B3
Idstone Rd BS16...........51 B4
Idwal Cl BA2..............134 C8
Iford Cl BS31...............82 E3
Iford Fields BA15........120 E2
Iford Hill BA15...........120 E2
Iford La BA2, BA15......120 C3
Ilchester Cres BS13.......63 B1
Ilchester Rd BS13.........79 B8
Iles Cl BS15................65 D4
Ilex Ave BS21..............57 G2
Ilex Cl BS13................78 F6
Ilex La BS25..............107 F1
Ilminster BS24...........105 A2
Ilminster Ave BS4........79 F8
Ilminster Avenue Prim Sch
BS4.........................80 A8
Ilminster Cl
Clevedon BS21.............57 G2
Nailsea BS48..............75 D8
Ilsyn Gr BS14..............80 D7
Imber Court Cl BS14......80 B8
Imperial Arc 11 BS3......63 D4
Imperial Pk BS13..........79 C6
Imperial Rd
Bristol BS14...............80 C8
8 Bristol, Clifton BS6......49 B1
Imperial Wlk BS14........64 B1
Inchalloch 18 BA1.........85 A1
Inclosures The 5
BS22......................105 F8
INGLESBATCH 117 C8
Ingleside Rd BS15........51 C1
Inglestone Rd GL12.......18 B5
Ingleton Dr BS22..........89 A4
Ingmire Rd BS5............50 B3
INGST 13 C4
Ingst Hill BS35............13 B3
Ingst Rd BS35..............13 D4
Inkerman Cl BS7..........49 E7
Inman Ho BA1............141 C4
INMAN'S BATCH 95 A5
Inn Cotts BS11.............48 A7
Inner Down The BS32.....14 D3
Inner Elm Terr BA3......133 C1
Innicks Cl BS40..........111 D1
Innocks Est GL11............5 D4
Innox Gdns BS13..........79 A5
Innox Gr BA2.............100 F2
Innox La BA1...............85 B5
Innox Rd BA2.............101 B5
Inns Court Ave BS4.......79 D7
Inns Court Dr BS4........79 D6
Inns Court Gn BS4........79 D7
Instow 7 BS22.............89 A2
Instow Rd BS4.............79 E8
Instow Wlk BS4...........79 E8
International Helicopter
Mus* BS24...............105 E5
International Trad Est
BS11........................33 B2
Interplex 16 BS32.........24 C3
Inverness Rd BA2........101 C6
IO Ctr BS11.................33 F5
Ipswich Dr BS4............64 E6
Irby Rd BS3................63 A3
Irena Rd BS16.............50 F3
Ireton Rd BS3..............63 B3
IRON ACTON 26 D4
Iron Acton CE Prim Sch
BS37........................26 E4
Iron Acton Way BS37.....27 B3
Ironchurch Rd BS11.......33 C5
Iron Hogg La GL12..........9 C3
Ironmould La
Bristol BS4.................65 A1
Keynsham BS31............81 A8
Irving Cl
Bristol BS16................51 E4
Clevedon BS21.............57 H3
Irving Ho BS1............142 C3
ISF Rd BS11................33 C3
Island Gdns BS16..........50 C4
Island The BA3...........133 A1
Island Trad Pk BS11.......33 C1
Isle Of Rhé GL11.............5 C5
Isleys Ct BS30.............65 F3
Islington Rd BS3...........63 C4
Ison Hill Rd BS10.........34 D3
ITCHINGTON 15 F2
Itchington Rd
Alveston BS35, GL12.......15 F4
Tytherington GL12.........16 B4
Ivo Peters Rd BA2.......141 A2
Ivor Rd BS5................64 C8
Ivy Ave BA2..............101 C4
Ivy Bank Pk BA2.........101 F2
Ivybridge 8 BS22..........89 A2
Ivy Cl BS48.................59 D1
Ivy Ct BS20.................44 F5
Ivy Gr BA2................101 C4
Ivy House Cotts BS29....106 D7
Ivy La
Bristol BS16................51 A3
Weston-S-M BS24........106 A8
Ivy Lo 4 BS9...............49 A7
Ivy Pl BA2................101 C4
Ivy Terr BS37...............39 B4
Ivywell Rd BS9.............48 E3
Ivy Wlk
Banwell BS29.............106 E4
Midsomer Norton BA3.....139 B8
IWOOD 92 A3
Iwood La BS40.............92 A2

J

Jack Knight Ho BS7.......49 F5
Jack Price Cl BS13........79 C3
Jackson Cl BS35...........22 D7
Jacob Ct BS2.............143 C3
Jacobs Bldg The BS8....142 B3
Jacob's Ct BS1...........142 C2
Jacobs Mdw BS20..........45 F4
Jacob St
Bristol BS2................143 B3
Bristol BS2................143 C3
Jacob's Wells Rd BS8....142 B2
Jaguar Ho 3 BA1.........141 B3
Jamaica St BS2...........143 B4
James Cl BS16.............51 E4
James Rd BS16.............51 E3
James St W BA1..........141 B2
James St
Bristol, Baptist Mills
BS2.........................50 A2
Bristol BS5................143 C4
Jane St BS5.................64 B7
Jarrets Rd BS10............35 D2
Jarvis St BS5...............64 B6
Jasmine Cl BS22...........89 A1
Jasmine Ct 8 BS23.......104 E8
Jasmine Gr BS11...........34 C2
Jasmine La BS49...........74 F2
Jasmine Way BS24.........89 A1
Jasper St BS3...............63 B3
Jays The GL12..............16 B6
Jay View BS23............105 A5
Jean Rd BS4.................64 E2
JEFFERIES HILL 65 C5
Jefferies Hill Bottom
BS15........................65 B5
Jeffery Ct BS30.............66 B6
Jeffreys Ct 9 BS16........50 E3
Jekyll Cl BS16..............50 E8
Jellicoe Ave BS16..........50 E8
Jellicoe Ct BS22............88 E4
Jena Ct BS31................82 D3
Jenner Cl BS37.............40 D8
Jennings Ct 1 BS3.........63 A4
Jersey Ave BS4.............64 F4
Jesmond Rd
Clevedon BS21.............57 E3
Weston-S-M BS22..........89 C4
Jesse Hughes Ct BA1......85 C2
Jessop Cres BS10..........35 A1
Jessop Ct BS1.............143 B2
Jessop Underpass BS3....62 F4
Jews La
Bath BA2..................101 C6
Churchill BS25...........108 F4
Jim O'Neil Ho BS11........47 D7
Jinty La BS16...............52 B2
Jobbins Cl BS37............40 A8
Jocelin Dr BS22............88 F4
Jocelyn Rd BS7.............49 F7
Jockey La BS5..............65 A7
John Cabot City Tech Coll
BS15........................65 C7
John Cabot Ct BS1.......142 A1
John Carr's Terr BS8....142 B2
John Cozens Ho 6
BS2........................143 C3
John James Ct BS7.........50 B7
John Repton Gdns
BS10........................35 B2
John Slessor Ct BA1.....141 B4
Johnson Dr BS30...........65 F5
Johnson Rd BS16...........52 C5
Johnsons La BS5............50 D1
Johnsons Rd
Bristol BS5.................50 C1
1 Bristol, Moorfields
BS5.........................64 C8
John St
Bath BA1..................141 B3
Bristol, Baptist Mills BS2....50 A2
Bristol BS1................143 A3
Bristol, Two Mile Hill
BS15........................65 C8
Johnstone St BA2........141 C2
John Wesley Ct 10
BS16........................51 D5
John Wesley Rd BS5.......65 B6
John Wesleys Chapel*
BS1........................143 B3
Jones Cl BS49...............74 A1
Jonny Ball La BS2.......143 A3
Jordan Wlk BS32...........36 D8
Jorrocks Ind Est BS37.....39 C4
Joyce Cl BS7................50 A8
Joy Hill BS8.................62 F6
Jubilee Cres BS16..........52 A6
Jubilee Ct
Bristol BS4.................64 D4
Weston-S-M BS23........104 F8
Jubilee Dr
Failand BS8.................61 B4
Thornbury BS35.............8 D1
Jubilee Gdns BS37.........28 A2
Jubilee Ho BS34............36 C8
Jubilee La
Churchill BS40...........109 A6
Cromhall GL12..............17 B7
Jubilee Path BS22..........88 C1
Jubilee Pl
Bristol BS1................143 A1
Bristol, Woodstock BS15.....65 F7
Clevedon BS21.............57 F1
Jubilee Rd
Axbridge BS26...........125 C2
Bristol, Baptist Mills BS2....50 A1
Bristol, Crew's Hole BS5....64 F7
Bristol, Staple Hill BS15.....51 E3
Bristol, Upper Knowle
BS4.........................64 C2
Radstock BA3.............133 D1
Weston-S-M BS23........104 E7
Jubilee St BS2............143 C2
Jubilee Terr BS39........132 E6
Jubilee Way
Avonmouth BS11...........33 B2
Weston-S-M BS22..........89 C3
Julian Cl BS9................48 E3
Julian Ct BS9................48 E3
Julian Rd
Bath BA1..................141 B3
Bristol BS9.................48 E3
Julier Ho BA1.............141 C4
Julius Cl BS16..............52 C6
Julius Rd BS7...............49 D3
Junction Ave BA2.........141 A1
Junction Rd
Bath BA2..................141 A1
Bristol BS4.................64 C4
Junction Way BS15,
BS16........................52 B3
Juniper Ct 2 BS5...........50 C2
Juniper Pl BS22............88 F4
Juniper Way BS34..........37 A7
Jupiter Rd BS34............35 E7
Justice Ave BS31...........82 E3
Justice Rd BS16............51 A3
Jutland Rd BS11............33 B1

K

Karelean Ct BS10..........35 D3
Karen Cl BS48..............76 A4
Karen Dr BS48..............76 A5
Kathdene Gdns BS7.......49 F3
Katherine Cl GL12..........11 A5
Katherine Lady Berkeley's
Sch GL12...................11 F6
Kaynton Mead BA1.......101 B7
Keats Ct BS7................50 A8
Keats Ho 4 BS23.........104 F4
Keats Rd BA3.............139 C8
Keble Ave BS13............78 F5
Keeds La BS41..............61 F1
Keedwell Hill BS41........61 F1
Keel Cl BS5.................64 F6
Keel's Hill BA2...........134 C8
Keene's Way BS21.........57 E2
Keen's Gr BS35.............22 C7
Keepers La BS7.............49 F3
Keep The
Bristol BS30................66 D5
Weston-S-M BS22..........89 A3
Keg Store The BS1.......143 B2
Keinton Wlk BS10.........35 A2
Kelbra Cres BS36..........38 B6
Kellaway Ave BS7..........49 D5
Kellaway Cres BS9.........49 D6
Kellaway Ct BS6............49 D5
Kellways BS48..............76 A4
Kelso Pl BA1..............101 D7
Kelso Villa BA1...........101 D7
KELSTON 83 C3
Kelston Cl
Saltford BS31..............82 D4
Yate BS37...................39 D7
Kelston Gdns
Bristol BS10................49 D8
Weston-S-M BS22..........89 B5
Kelston Gr BS15............65 E6
Kelston Rd
Bath BA1....................83 E1
Bristol BS10................49 D8
Keynsham BS31............81 D5
Weston-S-M BS22..........89 B5
Kelston View BA2.........101 A5
Kelston Wlk BS16..........51 C4
Kelting Gr BS21............57 H2
Kemble Cl
Bristol BS15................65 E6
Nailsea BS48...............60 A1
Kemble Gdns BS11........47 F5
Kemble Ho BS34...........23 F1
Kemperleye Way BS32....36 D7
Kempe's Cl BS41...........62 A2
Kempe Way BS24.........105 E7
Kempthorne La BA2.....101 E1
Kempton Cl
2 Bristol BS16..............37 F1
Thornbury BS35.............8 B3
Kencot Wlk BS13...........79 B3
Kendall Gdns BS16........51 D4
Kendall Rd BS16............51 D4
Kendal Rd BS7..............50 A7
KENDLESHIRE 38 A4
Kendon Dr BS10............49 D7
Kendon Way BS10..........49 D8
Kenilworth BS37............39 F8
Kenilworth Cl BS31........81 D4
Kenilworth Ct BA1.......102 B8
Kenilworth Dr BS30.......66 B2
Kenilworth Rd BS6.........49 C1
Kenmare Rd BS4............63 E1
Kenmeade Cl BS25.......125 E8
Kenmore Cres BS7.........35 E1
Kenmore Dr BS7............35 E1
Kenmore Gr BS7............35 E1
KENN 73 F7
Kennard Cl BS15...........65 C7
Kennard Rd BS15...........65 C8
Kennard Rise BS15.........65 C8
Kennaway Rd BS21.........57 G2
Kenn Bsns Pk BS21........73 E8
Kenn Cl BS23.............105 A5
Kenn Ct BS4.................79 E7
Kennedy Ho BS37..........27 F1
Kennedy Way BS37........27 F1
Kennel Dr GL9..............30 E2

Kennel La BS26..........123 E3
Kennel Lodge Rd BS3....62 E4
Kenn Est BS21..........73 E5
Kenneth Rd BS4.........64 D2
Kennet Pk BA2..........85 E1
Kennet Rd BS31.........82 A4
Kennet Way **4** BS35..15 D8
Kennford **6** BS22....88 F2
Kennington Ave
  Bristol, Bishopston BS7....49 F4
  3 Bristol, Two Mile Hill
  BS15..................51 D1
Kennington Rd BA1......101 B7
Kennion Rd BS5.........65 A7
Kennmoor Cl BS30.......66 A6
Kenn Moor Dr BS21......57 G1
KENN MOOR GATE.........74 F4
Kennmoor Rd BS21.......74 A6
Kenn Moor Rd BS49......74 B1
Kenn Rd
  Bristol BS5............65 A7
  Clevedon BS21.........73 F6
Kenn St BS21...........73 F7
Kensal Ave BS3.........63 E3
Kensal Rd BS3..........63 E3
Kensington BS24........105 E7
Kensington Apartments
  BS6...................49 C3
Kensington Cl BS35.....8 B2
Kensington Ct
  Bath BA1..............85 B2
  Bristol BS8...........142 A3
Kensington Gdns BA1....85 B1
Kensington Ho **6** BS5..65 A8
KENSINGTON PARK........64 C3
Kensington Park Rd
  BS4...................64 C2
Kensington Pk **12** BS5..50 A1
Kensington Pl
  Bath BA1..............85 B1
  Bristol BS8...........142 A3
Kensington Rd
  Bristol, Redland BS6...49 C1
  3 Bristol, St George
  BS5...................65 A8
  7 Bristol, Staple Hill
  BS16..................51 D4
  Weston-S-M BS23.......104 F5
Kent Ave BS37..........27 F3
Kent Cl BS34...........36 D4
Kent Mews BS16.........50 E7
Kenton Ho BS34.........23 F1
Kenton Mews BS9........49 C5
Kent Rd
  Bristol BS7...........49 E4
  Congresbury BS49......91 D5
Kents Gn BS15..........51 E2
Kentshare La BS40......95 B6
Kent St
  Bristol BS3...........63 C3
  Cheddar BS27..........126 B1
Kent Way BS22..........89 B4
Kenwood Cl BS15........51 F1
Keppel Cl BS31.........82 D2
Kerry Rd BS4...........63 E1
Kersteman Rd BS6.......49 C3
Kestrel Cl
  Bristol BS34..........35 E8
  Chipping Sodbury BS37..39 F8
  Thornbury BS35........8 D2
Kestrel Dr
  Pucklechurch BS16.....53 C4
  Weston-S-M BS22.......88 E1
Keswick Wlk BS10.......35 C2
Ketch Rd BS3...........63 F3
Kewhaven Bglws BS22....88 B4
Kew Rd BS23............87 E1
Kewside BS22...........88 B4
KEWSTOKE...............88 B4
Kewstoke Prim Sch
  BS22..................88 B3
Kewstoke Rd
  Bath BA2..............102 A2
  Bristol BS9...........48 E4
  Weston-S-M BS22.......88 C3
Kew Wlk BS4............80 C8
Keyes Path BS22........88 F4
KEYNSHAM...............81 E7
Keynsham By-Pass
  BS31..................81 E7
Keynsham Hosp BS31.....81 F4
Keynsham Prim Sch
  BS31..................81 D5
Keynsham Rd BS30,
  BS31..................82 A8
Keynsham Sta BS31......81 F6
Keys Ave BS7...........49 F7
Kidney Hill BS37.......39 A3
Kielder Dr BS22........88 F3
Kilbirnie Rd BS14......80 A3
Kilburn Ct **17** BS5..64 B8
Kilburn St **19** BS5..64 B8
Kildare BA2............102 B7
Kildare Rd BS4.........63 D1
Kilkenny La BA2........118 B8
Kilkenny Pl BS20.......45 C6
Killcott Rd GL12.......19 E8
KILLING'S KNAP.........139 B4
KILMERSDON.............140 B5
Kilmersdon CE Prim Sch
  BA3...................140 A6
Kilmersdon Rd
  Bristol BS13..........79 B4
  Radstock BA3..........139 E8

Kilminster Cl BS34.....36 D7
Kilminster Rd BS11.....47 D7
Kiln Cl BS15...........51 B2
Kiln Ct BS5............64 B8
Kilnhurst Cl BS30......65 F2
Kiln Pk BS23...........105 A6
Kilve BS24.............105 A2
Kilvert Cl BS4.........64 D5
Kimberley Ave BS16.....51 C5
Kimberley Cl BS16......51 F7
Kimberley Cres BS16....51 C5
Kimberley Rd
  Bristol, Fishponds
  BS16..................51 C5
  Bristol, Kingswood BS15...51 D1
  Clevedon BS21.........57 E2
Kinber Cl BA1..........84 A3
Kinema Ho BS4..........64 C4
King Alfred Way
  BA15..................120 D7
Kingcott Mill Farm Cvns
  BS48..................77 B8
King Dick's La **7** BS5..64 F8
KINGDOWN...............94 D5
Kingdown Rd BS40.......94 C5
King Edmund Com Sch
  BS37..................27 E1
King Edward Cl BS14....80 A6
King Edward Rd BA2.....101 D5
King Edward's Pre-Prep
  Sch BA1...............101 C8
King Edward's Sch
  BA2...................102 C7
Kingfisher Cl
  Bristol BS32..........24 E2
  Thornbury BS35........8 D2
Kingfisher Dr
  Bristol BS16..........50 E6
  Midsomer Norton BA3...139 B8
Kingfisher Rd
  Chipping Sodbury BS37...40 A8
  Portishead BS20.......46 A6
  Weston-S-M BS22.......105 F8
King George's Rd
  Bath BA2..............101 C6
  Bristol BS13..........78 F5
King George V Pl
  BS1...................143 A2
King John's Hunting Lo*
  BS26..................125 C2
King John's Rd BS15....51 B2
King La
  Clutton BS39..........114 F4
  Horton BS37...........29 A7
King Rd
  Bristol BS4...........64 C1
  Churchill BS49........108 E6
King Road Ave BS11.....33 B2
Kingrove Cres BS37.....40 C8
Kingrove La BS37.......40 C7
Kings Ave BS15.........65 B4
King's Ave BS6, BS7....49 C4
Kings Chase BS15.......65 D8
Kingscote BS37.........39 D6
Kingscote Pk BS5.......65 B6
Kingscourt Cl BS14.....80 A4
Kings Court Prim Sch
  BS37..................39 E8
Kings Croft BS41.......61 E1
Kings Ct
  Bath BA1..............141 B2
  Bristol BS1...........143 A2
  Bristol, Little Stoke BS34...36 C6
  Bristol, St Pauls BS1...143 B4
  Bristol, Southville BS3...63 C4
  2 Bristol, Withywood
  BS13..................78 F4
  6 Nailsea BS48....59 E2
KINGSDOWN
  Bathford...............86 F3
  Bristol................143 A4
Kingsdown Gr SN13......86 F3
Kingsdown Par BS6......143 A4
Kingsdown View **18**..85 A1
Kings Dr
  Bristol, Hanham BS15...65 B4
  Bristol, Stoke Gifford
  BS34..................37 A4
King's Dr BS7..........49 C4
Kingsfield BA2.........101 C3
Kingsfield La
  Bristol, Longwell Green
  BS15..................65 E5
  Bristol, Mount Hill BS30...65 E4
Kingsfield Rdbt BS15...65 E5
Kings Fields BS37......27 A8
Kingsfield Sch BS15....66 A8
King's Forest Prim Sch
  BS15..................51 F2
Kingsgate Ct BS37......39 E8
KINGSGATE PARK.........39 E8
King's Head La BS13....78 F7
Kingshill BS48.........59 C2
Kingshill CE Prim Sch
  BS48..................59 D3
Kingshill Gdns BS48....59 C1
Kingshill Ho BS4.......64 B1
Kingshill La BS40......112 C4
Kingshill Rd BS4.......64 B1
Kingsholme Ct BS23.....87 E1
Kingsholme Rd BS15.....51 D1
Kingsholm Rd BS10......49 D8
King's La
  Clevedon BS21.........57 F5
  6 Weston-S-M BS23..104 E8
Kingsland Cl **1** BS2..64 A6

Kingsland Rd BS2.......64 A6
Kingsland Road Bridge **3**
  BS2...................64 A6
Kingsland Trad Est
  Bristol BS2...........143 C3
  Bristol, Newton BS2...64 A7
Kingsleigh Cl BS15.....65 F7
Kingsleigh Gdns BS15...65 F7
Kingsleigh Pk BS15.....65 F7
Kingsley Ho
  Bristol BS2...........143 C2
  Bristol, Westbury on Trym
  BS9...................49 A8
Kingsley Pl **1** BS3..63 C4
Kingsley Rd
  Bristol, Lower Easton
  BS5...................50 C1
  Bristol, Montpelier BS6...49 D2
  Clevedon BS21.........57 F2
  Radstock BA3..........133 C1
  Weston-S-M BS23.......104 F3
Kingsmarsh Ho **3** BS5..64 B7
KINGSMEAD..............141 A2
Kingsmead BS48.........59 C2
Kingsmead Ct **12** BA1..141 B2
Kingsmead N BA1........141 B2
Kingsmead Rd BS5.......51 A1
Kingsmead Sq BA1.......141 B2
Kingsmead St BA1.......141 B2
Kingsmead W BA1........141 B2
Kingsmill Wlk BS5......51 A1
Kingsmill BS9..........48 D5
Kings Oak Mdw BS39.....114 E2
King's Parade Ave **1**
  BS8...................49 B1
King's Parade Mews
  BS8...................49 A1
Kings Park Ave BS2.....64 C6
King Sq BS2............143 A4
King Square Ave BS2....143 A4
Kings Quarter Apartments
  14 BS2............143 A4
Kings Rd BS40..........92 D1
King's Rd
  Bristol BS8...........142 A3
  Bristol, Kensington Park
  BS4...................64 C3
  Clevedon BS21.........57 F5
  Portishead BS20.......44 F4
Kings Sq BS30..........82 D8
King St
  Avonmouth BS11........33 A1
  Bristol BS1...........143 A2
  Bristol, Lower Easton
  BS5...................50 C1
  Bristol, St George BS15...65 B8
Kingston Ave
  Clevedon BS21.........57 G3
  Saltford BS31.........82 C3
Kingston Bldgs **5**
  BA1...................141 C2
Kingston Cl BS16.......52 A7
Kingston Dr
  Bristol BS16..........52 A7
  Nailsea BS48..........75 C8
Kingston La BS40.......94 F8
Kingston Mead BS40.....94 F7
Kingston Rd
  Bath BA1..............141 C2
  Bristol BS3...........63 C4
KINGSTON SEYMOUR.......73 C2
Kingston Way BS48......75 C8
Kingstree St BS4.......64 A4
KINGSWAY...............101 C3
Kingsway
  Bath BA2..............101 C3
  Bristol, Little Stoke BS34...36 C6
  Bristol, St George BS5...65 B7
  Portishead BS20.......44 F4
Kingsway Ave BS15......65 B8
Kingsway Cres BS15.....65 C8
Kingsway Pk BS30.......66 B6
Kingsway Sh Prec BS5...65 B7
Kingswear **3** BS22..89 A2
Kingswear Rd BS3.......63 D2
Kings Weston Ave
  BS11..................47 E8
Kingsweston Down Nature
  Res* BS9, BS11........34 C1
Kings Weston La
  Avonmouth BS11........33 E3
  Bristol BS11..........48 A8
Kings Weston Rd BS11,
  BS10..................34 C1
Kings Wlk BS13.........78 F7
KINGSWOOD
  Bristol................65 E8
  Wotton-under-Edge.....11 E4
Kingswood Abbey
  Gatehouse* GL12.......11 F5
Kingswood Douglas Ind
  Est BS15..............65 D7
Kingswood Foundation Est
  BS15..................65 C7
Kingswood Heritage
  Mus* BS30.............66 B6
Kingswood Hts BS15.....51 D1
Kingswood Ind Est
  BS30..................65 F4
Kingswood Prep Sch
  BA1...................84 E1
Kingswood Rd GL12......11 F5
Kingswood Sch BA1......84 E2

Kingswood Trad Est
  BS15..................51 D1
KINGTON................7 E1
Kington La BS35........7 E1
Kington Rd BS35........7 E3
Kingwell View BS39.....115 D2
King William Ave
  BS1...................143 A2
King William St BS3....63 B4
Kinsale Rd BS14........80 C7
Kinsale Wlk BS4........63 E1
Kinvara Rd BS4.........79 E8
Kipling Ave BA2........101 F4
Kipling Rd
  Bristol BS7...........36 B1
  Radstock BA3..........133 C1
  Weston-S-M BS23.......105 A3
Kirkby Rd BS11.........34 A1
Kirkstone Gdns BS10....35 C2
Kirkstone Ho BS34......36 A8
Kirtlington Rd BS5.....50 B3
Kite Hay Cl BS16.......50 E5
Kites Cl BS32..........24 C2
Kite Wlk **3** BS22...105 E8
Kitley Hill BA3........133 C4
Knapp La GL12..........10 B3
Knapp Rd BS35..........8 C2
Knapps Cl BS25.........124 F8
Knapps Dr BS25.........124 F8
Knapps La BS5..........50 E2
Knapp The BS37.........27 F5
Kneller Cl BS11........48 A8
Knight Cl BS22.........89 A5
KNIGHTCOTT.............106 F3
Knightcott BS29........106 F3
Knightcott Gdns BS29...106 F3
Knightcott Ind Est
  BS29..................106 E3
Knightcott Pk BS29.....107 A3
Knightcott Rd
  Abbots Leigh BS8......61 F8
  Banwell BS29..........106 F3
Knighton Rd BS10.......35 E1
Knightsbridge Pk BS13..79 E4
Knights Cl BS9.........49 B6
Knightstone Cl
  Axbridge BS26.........125 C1
  Peasedown St John
  BA2...................134 B8
Knightstone Cswy
  BS23..................104 C8
Knightstone Ct
  Bristol BS5...........50 D2
  Clevedon BS21.........57 F1
  Weston-S-M BS23.......87 D1
Knightstone Gdns BS23..64 B2
Knightstone Ho BS23....104 E6
Knightstone Ho
  1 Bristol BS2.....143 A4
  Weston-S-M BS23.......104 D8
Knightstone Lo BS6.....49 D1
Knightstone Mount
  BS5...................65 A6
Knightstone Pk **4**
  BS23..................104 E5
Knightstone Pl
  Bath BA1..............84 B1
  Bristol BS15..........65 B2
  7 Weston-S-M BS22..88 F2
Knightstone Rd BS23....104 C8
Knightstone Rise **5**
  BS5...................64 F8
Knightstone Sq BS14....80 C5
Knightstone Wlk BS22...142 C4
Knightwood Rd BS34.....36 F5
Knobsbury Hill BA3.....140 D6
Knobsbury La BA3.......140 C6
Knole Cl BS32..........23 F4
Knole Ct BS10..........35 A3
Knole La BS10..........35 B3
Knole Pk BS32..........23 F3
Knoll Ct BS9...........48 D3
Knoll Hill BS9.........48 D3
Knoll The BS20.........45 D7
Knovill Cl BS11........34 B2
KNOWLE................63 F3
KNOWLE PARK...........64 A1
Knowle Park Jun Sch
  BS4...................64 A1
Knowle Rd BS2..........63 F3
Knowles Rd BS21........57 E2
Knowsley Rd BS16.......50 E3
Kyght Cl BS15..........66 A8
Kylross Ave BS14.......80 B5
Kynges Mill Cl BS16....51 A7
Kyngstone Ct **10** BS16..50 E3
Kyrle Gdns BA1.........85 F3

L

Labbott The BS31.......81 E5
Laburnum Cl BA3........138 F8
Laburnum Ct BS23.......105 B7
Laburnum Gr
  Bristol BS16..........51 B4
  Midsomer Norton BA3...138 F8
Laburnum Rd
  Bristol BS15..........65 C5
  Weston-S-M BS23.......105 B7
Laburnum Terr BA1......85 F3
Laburnum Wlk BS31......81 C3
Lacey Rd BS14..........80 F6
Lacock Dr BS30.........65 F5
Ladd Cl BS15...........65 F7
Ladden Mead BS37.......27 D4
Ladies Mile BS8........48 F1

Ladman Gr BS14.........80 E6
Ladman Rd BS14.........80 E5
Ladycroft **4** BS21..57 C1
Ladye Bay BS21.........57 F7
Ladye Wake BS22........88 F4
Ladymead BS20..........45 F5
Ladymeade BS48........76 A7
Ladymead Ho BA1........141 C3
Ladymead La BS40.......108 F5
Ladysmith Rd BS6.......49 B4
Ladywell Rd BA1........92 D2
Laggan Gdns BA1........84 E1
Laggan Ho BA1..........84 E1
Lakemead Gdns **3**
  BS13..................78 F4
Lakemead Gr BS13.......78 F6
Lake Rd
  Bristol BS10..........49 C8
  Portishead BS20.......45 D7
Lakeside BS16..........50 E3
Lakeside Cl BS40.......111 D5
Lakeside Ct BS24.......89 B1
Lake View BS16.........50 F3
Lake View Rd BS5.......64 D8
Lakewood Cres BS10.....49 B8
Lakewood Rd BS10.......49 B8
La Maison BS5..........51 A2
Lambert Pl BA4.........79 D6
Lamb Hill BS5..........64 E8
Lambley Rd BS5.........64 E8
Lambourn Cl BS3........63 D3
Lambourne Way BS20.....45 F5
Lambourn Rd BS31.......82 A4
Lambretta Scooter Mus*
  BS23..................104 E8
Lambridge **6** BA1...85 C1
LAMBRIDGE..............85 C1
Lambridge **6** BA1...85 C1
Lambridge Bldgs **1**
  BA1...................85 C1
Lambridge Grange **6**
  BA1...................85 C2
Lambridge Mews **5**
  BA1...................85 C1
Lambridge Pl BA1.......85 C1
Lambridge St BA1.......85 C1
Lambrook Rd BS16.......51 A4
Lamb St BS2............143 C3
Lamington Cl BS13......78 F6
Lamont Ho **7** BA1...85 C1
Lamord Gate BS34.......36 E5
Lampard's Bldgs BA1....141 B4
Lampeter Rd BS9........49 A7
Lamplea Rd BS21........73 D2
Lampton Ave BS13......79 E3
Lampton Gr BS13........79 E3
Lampton Rd BS41.......61 F1
Lanaway Rd BS16........51 B6
Lancashire Rd BS7.....49 E3
Lancaster Cl BS34......36 D4
Lancaster House Sch
  BS23..................104 F3
Lancaster Rd
  Bristol BS2...........50 A2
  Yate BS37.............27 E3
Lancaster St **10** BS5..64 C7
Lancelot Rd BS16.......50 E8
Landemann Cir BS23....87 E1
Landemann Path **2**
  BS23..................104 E8
Landmark Ct BS1.......142 C1
Landrail Wlk BS16......50 F6
Landsdown View BA1.....84 B2
Landseer Ave BS7.......50 B7
Landseer Cl BS22.......88 F3
Landseer Rd BA2........101 B4
Land The BS36..........38 C7
Lanercost Rd BS10......35 C2
Lanesborough Rise
  BS14..................80 D6
Lanes Dairy BS34.......36 A3
Lanes End BS4..........64 C1
Lane The BS35..........22 F2
Laneys Dro BS24........105 E5
Langdale Ct BS34.......36 A8
Langdale Rd BS16.......50 F4
Langdon Rd BA2........101 B4
Langdown Ct BS14......80 E5
Langfield Cl BS10......34 E3
Langford Court Cotts
  BS40..................109 E5
Langford La BS40.......109 E5
Langford Rd
  Bristol BS13..........78 F8
  Lower Langford BS40...109 C6
Langfords La BS39......132 C8
Langford's La BS39.....115 D1
Langford Way BS15......65 E7
Langham Pl BA11.......137 F1
Langham Rd BS4.........64 B2
Langhill Ave BS4.......79 D7
Langley Cres BS3.......62 E1
Langley Mow BS16.......52 B7
Langleys Cotts BA3.....138 B8
Langley's La BA3,
  BS39..................132 C1
Langport Gdns BS48.....75 E8
Langport Rd BS23.......104 E5
LANGRIDGE.............84 E7
Langridge La BA1.......84 D8
Langsdown Ho **7** BS2..49 F2
Langton Court Rd BS4...64 D5
Langton Court Sch BS4..64 D4
Langton Ct **11** BS16..50 E3
Langton Ho **9** BS2...143 C3
Langton Pk BS3.........63 C4
Langton Way BS4........64 F6

LANSDOWN
Bath 84 E1
Upper Langridge 84 B6
Lansdown BS37 39 E8
Lansdown Cl BS15 51 D2
Lansdown Cres
2 Bath BA1 84 F1
Timsbury BA2 116 C2
Lansdown Ct BS23 104 F8
Lansdowne BS16 37 C1
Lansdowne Ct 8 BS5 64 A8
Lansdown Gdns BS22 89 B5
Lansdown Gr BA1 141 B4
Lansdown Grove Ct BA1 141 B4
Lansdown Grove Lo BA1 141 B4
Lansdown Ho
Bath BA1 84 F1
Bristol BS15 51 D2
Lansdown Hts BA1 84 F1
Lansdown La
Bath BA1 84 B4
Upton Cheyney BS30 67 C1
Lansdown Mans BA1 141 B4
Lansdown Mews 9 BA1 141 B3
Lansdown Pk BA1 84 E3
Lansdown Pl
Bristol BS8 142 A3
High Littleton BS39 115 D1
Lansdown Pl E BA1 141 B4
Lansdown Pl W 1 BA1 84 F1
Lansdown Rd
Bath BA1 84 E2
Bristol BS8 142 A3
Bristol, Kingswood BS15 51 D2
Bristol, Redland BS6 49 C1
6 Bristol, Upper Easton BS5 64 B8
Pucklechurch BS16 53 C6
Saltford BS31 82 E3
Lansdown Terr BS6 49 D5
Lansdown View
Bath BA2 101 C5
Bristol BS15 65 F8
Faulkland BA3 135 D1
Timsbury BA2 116 C2
Tunley BA2 117 B4
Lanthony Cl BS24 106 A8
Lapdown La GL9 41 D1
Laphams Ct 11 BS30 65 F4
Lapwing Cl BS32 24 D2
Lapwing Gdns
Bristol BS16 50 F6
Weston-S-M BS22 88 F1
Larch Cl
Churchill BS40 109 A5
Nailsea BS48 60 A2
Larch Ct BA3 139 D8
Larches The BS22 89 A3
Larchgrove Cres BS22 88 F1
Larchgrove Wlk BS22 88 F1
Larch Rd
Bristol BS15 51 E3
Colerne SN14 70 F6
Larch Way BS34 35 E7
Larchwood Ct BA3 134 A3
Lark Cl BA3 139 B8
Larkfield BS36 38 D7
LARKHALL 85 C2
Larkhall Pl BA1 85 C2
Larkhall Terr BA1 85 C2
Larkhill Rd BS24 106 B6
Lark Pl BA1 101 D7
Lark Rd BS22 88 F1
Lark Rise BS37 27 F4
Larks Field BS16 50 E5
Lark's La BS37 26 B7
Larksleaze Rd BS30 65 F2
Larkspur Cl BS35 8 D1
Lasbury Gr BS13 79 C5
Latchmoor Ho BS13 79 A8
Late Broads BA15 120 D7
Latimer Cl BS4 64 E4
LATTERIDGE 26 B6
Latteridge La
Latteridge BS37 26 A7
Tytherington BS35 15 F1
Latteridge Rd BS37 26 D4
Latton Rd BS7 49 F8
Launceston Ave BS15 65 B5
Launceston Rd BS15 51 B1
Laura Pl BA2 141 C3
Laurel Dr
Colerne SN14 70 F6
Nailsea BS48 59 F2
Paulton BS39 132 E5
Weston-S-M BS23 104 E2
Laurel Gdns
Timsbury BA2 116 B1
Yatton BS49 74 B1
Laurel Ho BS25 125 A8
Laurel St BS15 65 D8
Laurels The
Bristol, Catbrain BS10 35 A6
Bristol, Mangotsfield BS16 52 A6
Churchill BS25 108 F4
Weston-S-M BS23 104 E2
Westwood BA15 120 F3
Laurel Terr BS49 74 B1
Laurie Cres BS9 49 D6
Laurie Lee Ct 3 BS30 66 A5
Lavender Cl
Thornbury BS35 8 D1
Weston-S-M BS22 89 A5
Lavender Ct BS5 50 F1
Lavender Way BS32 36 F7
Lavenham Rd BS37 27 B2
Lavers Cl BS15 65 E6
Lavington Cl BS21 57 D1
Lavington Rd BS5 65 B6
Lawford Ave BS34 36 C6
Lawfords Gate BS2 143 C3
Lawfords Gate Ho 17 BS2 143 C3
Lawford St BS2 143 C3
Lawn Ave BS16 51 B5
Lawn Rd BS16 51 B5
Lawnside BS48 76 B5
Lawns Rd BS37 27 F2
Lawns The
Bristol BS11 47 E7
Weston-S-M BS22 89 B3
Yatton BS49 74 A1
Lawnwood Ind Units 14 BS5 64 B8
Lawnwood Rd 15 BS5 64 B8
Lawrence Ave BS5 50 B1
Lawrence Cl
Bristol BS15 52 A2
Weston-S-M BS22 88 E2
Lawrence Dr BS37 27 B2
Lawrence Gr BS9 49 B5
Lawrence Hill BS5 64 B7
Lawrence Hill Ind Pk BS5 64 B8
Lawrence Hill Rdbt BS5 64 A7
Lawrence Hill Sta BS5 64 B7
Lawrence Mews BS22 88 E2
Lawrence Rd
Weston-S-M BS22 88 E2
Wrington BS40 92 E2
LAWRENCE WESTON 34 A1
Lawrence Weston Rd
Avonmouth BS11 33 F4
Bristol BS11 34 A2
Laws Dr BS24 105 F7
Lawson Cl BS31 82 C2
Laxey Rd BS7 49 F7
Laxton Cl BS35 14 A3
Laxton Dr GL12 11 F4
Laxton Way BA2 134 D7
Lays Dr BS31 81 C5
Lays Farm Bsns Ctr BS31 81 C4
Lays Farm Trad Est BS31 81 C4
Lays La BS40 110 D4
Leach Cl BS21 57 F1
Lea Croft BS13 79 A4
Leading Edge The BS8 142 B2
Leafy Way BS24 106 B4
Lea Grove Rd BS21 57 E4
Leaholme Gdns BS14 80 A3
Leaman Cl BS37 28 B1
Leap Vale BS16 52 A8
Leap Valley Cres BS16 52 A8
Lear Cl BS30 66 B5
Leawood Ct 3 BS23 87 C1
Leaze La BS40 127 E8
Leaze The
Radstock BA3 139 D8
Yate BS37 27 D2
Leda Ave BS14 80 A7
Ledbury Rd BS16 51 C4
Leechpool Way BS37 27 E5
Lee Cl BS34 35 F8
Leedham Rd BS24 106 C5
Leeming Way BS11 47 C8
Lees Ct BS15 51 E1
Lees Hill BS15 51 E2
Leeside BS20 45 C5
Lees La BS30 66 D5
Leewood Rd BS23 87 F1
Leg La BS40 110 B3
Leicester Sq BS16 51 D3
Leicester St 6 BS3 63 D4
Leicester Wlk BS4 64 F5
Leigh Cl BA1 85 A2
Leigh Court Bsns Ctr BS8 48 A2
Leigh Ct BS9 48 D3
Leigh La
Cold Ashton BA1 69 B3
Westerleigh BS37 39 B1
Leigh Rd BS8 142 B4
Leigh St BS3 63 A4
Leighton Cres BS24 122 A8
Leighton Rd
Bath BA1 84 A3
Bristol, Southville BS3 63 B4
Bristol, Upper Knowle BS4 64 B2
Leigh View Rd BS20 45 E7
Leighwood Dr BS48 59 B1
LEIGH WOODS 62 D8
Leigh Woods Forest Walks* BS8 48 C1
Leinster Ave BS4 79 D8
Leisure Rd BS15 65 E5
Lemon La BS2 143 C4
Lena Ave 3 BS5 50 C1
Lena St BS5 50 C1
Lennox Way BS11 33 B1
Lenover Gdns BS13 79 B4
Leonard La BS1 143 A3
Leonard Rd BS5 64 D7
Leonards Ave BS5 50 C1
Leopold Bldgs BA1 141 C4
Leopold Rd BS6 49 E2
Les Brown Ct BS2 143 C2
Lescren Way BS11 33 D1
Leslie Rise BA15 120 F3
Lester Dr BS22 89 A3
Lewington Rd BS16 51 C4
Lewins Mead BS1 143 A3
Lewin St 9 BS5 64 D7
Lewis Cl
Bristol, Emerson's Green BS16 52 C5
Bristol, North Common BS30 66 D5
Lewisham Gr BS23 105 A8
Lewis Rd BS13 79 A8
Lewis St BS2 64 B5
Lewton La BS36 37 E7
LEYHILL 10 B4
Ley La BS35 13 F3
Leyland Wlk BS13 78 F4
Leys The BS21 57 D1
Leyton Villas BS6 49 B2
Liberty Gdns BS1 142 C1
Liberty Ind Pk BS3 63 A1
Liberty La BS40 110 E2
Lichfield Rd BS4 64 E6
Lilac Cl BS10 35 C1
Lilac Ct BS31 81 C4
Lilac Terr BA3 133 C2
Lilac Way BS22 89 A5
Lilian Terr BS39 132 E5
Lillian St 5 BS5 64 C8
Lillington Cl BA3 134 B2
Lillington Rd BA3 134 B2
Lilliput Ave BS37 40 A8
Lilliput Ct BS37 40 B8
Lillypool Cheese & Cider Farm* BS25 125 F6
Lilstock Ave BS7 49 F4
Lilton Wlk BS13 63 A1
Lilymead Ave BS4 64 A3
Lime Ave GL9 42 B8
Limebreach Wood BS48 59 D3
Limeburn Hill BS40 95 E5
Lime Cl
Bristol BS10 35 B3
Locking BS24 106 B4
Weston-S-M BS22 89 A1
Lime Croft BS37 27 F4
Lime Ct BS31 81 C4
Lime Gr
Alveston BS35 14 F4
Bath BA2 102 B6
Lime Grove Gdns BA2 102 B6
Lime Kiln Cl BS34 36 D3
Lime Kiln Gdns BS32 24 D2
Limekiln La BA2 102 F4
Lime Kiln La BS21 57 F3
Limekiln Rd BS37, GL12 17 C2
Lime Kiln Rd BS1 142 B2
Limekilns Cl BS31 81 F5
Lime Rd
Bristol, Hanham BS15 65 A5
Bristol, Southville BS3 63 B4
Limerick Rd BS6 49 C2
Limes The
Badminton GL9 30 E2
Bristol BS16 37 B1
Lime Terr BA3 133 D1
Lime Tree Gr BS20 47 D3
Lime Trees Rd BS9 49 D6
LIMPLEY STOKE 120 A6
Limpley Stoke Rd BA15 120 D6
Lincoln Cl BS31 81 C4
Lincoln Ct BS16 50 D6
Lincoln St BS5 64 B7
Lincombe Ave BS16 51 D6
Lincombe Rd
Bristol BS16 51 C6
Radstock BA3 139 D8
Lincott View BA2 134 C8
Linden Ave BS23 105 B8
Linden Cl
Bristol BS14 80 E6
Bristol, Mayfield Park BS16 51 A2
Colerne SN14 70 F6
Radstock BA3 139 E8
Winterbourne BS36 37 E6
Linden Ct BS21 57 F4
Linden Dr BS32 36 E8
Linden Gdns BA1 101 D8
Linden Grange BS6 49 C3
Linden Ho BS16 50 C5
Linden Quarter 13 BS3 63 C3
Linden Rd
Bristol BS6 49 B4
Clevedon BS21 57 F4
Lindens The BS22 88 E4
Lindisfarne Cl BA15 120 E6
Lindon Ct 4 BS15 51 B1
Lindon Ho BS4 64 E3
Lindrea St 3 BS3 63 B3
Lindsay Rd BS7 50 A4
Lindsey Cl BS20 44 F4
Linemere Cl BS48 76 D6
Lines Way BS14 80 C3
Lingfield Pk BS16 37 F2
Link La
Burrington BS40 109 F3
Monkton Farleigh BA15 103 F8
Linkmead BA3 138 F2
Link Rd
Bristol BS34 36 B3
Nailsea BS48 59 F2
Portishead BS20 45 C5
Yate BS37 27 F1
Link Sch The BA2 118 E8
Links Ct BS23 104 D4
Linkside BS21 57 G6
Links Rd BS23 104 C2
Linley Cl BA2 101 A5
Linleys The BA1 101 C7
Linne Ho BA2 101 A5
Linnell Cl BS7 50 B6
Linnet Cl
Bristol BS34 35 E8
Weston-S-M BS22 88 E1
Linnet Gdns BS20 45 F6
Linnet Way BA3 139 B8
Lintern Cres BS30 66 B6
Lintham Dr BS15 65 F6
Linton's Wlk BS14 80 A7
Lion Cl BS48 59 D2
Lipgate Pl BS20 45 D3
Lippiat Hill BA3 135 C3
Lippiatt La
Shipham BS25 125 F8
Timsbury BA2 116 B3
LIPYEATE 139 E1
Lisburn Rd BS4 63 E1
Lisle Rd BS22 89 B4
Lister Gr BA15 120 F3
Litfield Pl BS8 62 F7
Litfield Rd BS8 62 F8
Litt Hill BA3 130 F2
Little Ann St BS2, BS5 143 C4
LITTLE BADMINTON 30 E5
Little Birch Croft BS14 80 A3
Little Bishop St BS2 143 B4
LITTLE BRISTOL 11 B3
Little Bristol Cl GL12 11 B4
Little Bristol La GL12 11 B4
Littlebrook BS39 132 E6
Little Caroline Pl 4 BS8 62 F5
Littlecross Ho BS3 63 B4
Littledean BS37 39 E7
Little Dowles BS30 66 A4
Littlefields Ave BS29 107 B3
Littlefields Rd BS29 107 B3
Littlefields Rise BS29 107 B3
Little George St
Bristol BS2 143 C4
Weston-S-M BS23 104 E7
Little Green La BS35 22 A7
Little Halt BS20 44 E4
Little Ham BS21 73 C8
Little Hayes BS16 51 B6
Little Headley Cl BS13 79 B7
Little King St BS1 143 A2
Little La BA2 116 A6
Little Mdw BS34 37 A6
Little Mead BS11 34 B1
Little Mead Cl BS24 105 E3
Little Meadow End BS48 75 E8
Little Mead Prim Sch BS10 35 C2
Little Orch BS23 104 D1
Little Paradise BS3 63 D3
Little Parr Cl BS16 50 C5
Little Paul St BS2 142 C4
LITTLE SODBURY 29 B3
LITTLE SODBURY END 28 E4
Little Stanhope St BA1 141 A2
LITTLE STOKE 36 D7
Little Stoke La BS34 36 D6
Little Stoke Prim Sch BS34 36 D6
Little Stoke Rd BS9 48 E4
Little Thatch Cl BS14 80 C6
LITTLETON 95 C4
Littleton Ct BS34 23 F1
LITTLETON DREW 43 E5
Littleton Drew La GL9 43 A6
Littleton La
Wellow BA2 135 C7
Winford BS40 95 D5
Littleton Mills BS40 95 D4
Littleton Rd BS3 63 D2
Littleton St 4 BS5 50 C1
LITTLETON-UPON-SEVERN 13 E8
Little Withey Mead BS9 48 F5
Littlewood Cl BS14 80 B3
Littlewood La BS49 75 C2
LITTON 130 F2
Litton BS24 105 A2
Livingstone Mews 11 BS3 63 C3
Livingstone Rd BA2 101 D5
Livingstone Terr BA2 141 A1
Llanarth Villas 3 BS6 49 D1
Llewellyn Ct BS9 49 A8
Llewellyn Way BS22 89 B3
Lockemor Rd BS13 79 F4
Lockes Paddock BS22 89 C3
Lock Gdns BS13 78 E7
LOCKING 106 A4
Locking Farm Ind Est BS24 106 A5
Locking Head Dro
Locking BS24 105 F5
Locking BS24 106 A6
Weston-S-M BS24 106 A8
Locking Moor Rd
Locking BS24 106 B5
Weston-S-M BS22 105 D8
Locking Parklands BS24 106 B5
Locking Prim Sch BS24 106 B4
Locking Rd BS22, BS23 105 B7
Locking Road Bsns Pk BS23 105 A7
Lockingwell Rd BS31 81 D5
LOCKLEAZE 50 C7
Lockleaze Prim Sch BS7 50 B6
Lockleaze Rd BS7 50 A6
Lock's Acre BS35 15 B5
LOCKSBROOK 101 B6
Locksbrook Ct 8 BA1 101 B6
Locksbrook Pl 6 BA1 101 C7
Locksbrook Rd
Bath BA1 101 C6
Weston-S-M BS22 89 B5
Locksbrook Trad Est 7 BA1 101 B6
Lockside BS20 45 E7
Lockside Sq BS20 45 E7
Lock's La BS37 25 E4
Lodge Causeway Trad Ctr BS16 50 F3
Lodge Cl BS49 91 B8
Lodge Cswy BS16 51 A3
Lodge Ct BS9 48 E4
Lodge Dr
Bristol BS30 66 C2
Long Ashton BS41 62 B2
Weston-S-M BS23 88 A1
Lodge Gdns BA2 101 D1
Lodge Hill BS15 51 C2
Lodge La BS48 60 B2
Lodge Pl BS1 142 C3
Lodge Rd
Bristol BS15 51 C1
Wick BS30 53 B1
Yate BS37 27 A3
Lodgeside Ave BS15 51 C1
Lodgeside Gdns BS15 51 C1
Lodge St BS1 142 C3
Lodges The BA3 138 D1
Lodge The BS40 92 E2
Lodge Wlk BS16 51 D6
Lodore Rd BS16 50 F3
LODWAY 47 B5
Lodway BS20 47 C4
Lodway Cl BS20 47 C5
Lodway Gdns BS20 47 C4
Lodway Rd BS4 64 C2
Logan Rd BS7 49 D3
Logus Ct 14 BS30 65 F4
Lombard St BS3 63 D4
Lombardy Cl 5 BS22 105 E8
Lomond Rd BS7 35 F1
Londonderry Farm BS30 82 A8
London Rd
Bath BA1 141 C4
Bristol, St Pauls BS2 49 F1
Bristol, Warmley BS30 66 D7
Wick BS30 67 E6
London Rd E BA1 86 A3
London Rd W BA1 85 E2
London Sq BS20 45 E7
London St
Bath BA1 141 C4
Bristol BS15 65 D8
Longacre BS21 73 B8
Long Acre BA1 141 C4
Long Acre Ho BA1 141 C4
Long Acre Rd BS14 80 A3
Long Acres Cl BS9 48 D7
LONG ASHTON 62 A1
Long Ashton Bsns Pk BS41 62 B1
Long Ashton Rd BS41 62 B2
Long Ave BS21 57 D2
Long Barnaby BA3 133 A2
Long Beach Rd BS30 66 B3
Longbottom BS25 126 A6
Longbrook Trad Est BS3 62 E3
Long Cl
Bristol, Fishponds BS16 51 C6
Bristol, Little Stoke BS32 36 E6
Long Croft BS37 27 D4
Longcross GL12 10 B1
LONG CROSS 94 D7
Long Cross
Bristol, Lawrence Weston BS11 34 B2
Bristol, Shirehampton BS11 47 F8
Felton BS40 94 D7
Longden Rd BS16 51 F6
Longdown Dr BS22 89 B4
Long Eaton Dr BS14 80 B7
Longfellow Ave BA2 101 F4
Longfellow Rd BA3 139 C8
Longfield Rd BS7 49 E3
Longford BS37 39 C8
Longford Ave BS10 49 D8
Long Fox Manor BS4 65 A1
Long Handstones BS30 66 A4
Long Hay Cl BA2 101 B5
LONGHOUSE 117 D5
Long La
Backwell BS48 76 C2
Felton BS40 94 B5
Wrington BS40 93 B2
Longlands Ho 13 BS5 64 C7

Long Lease SN14 . . . . .43 C1
Longleat Cl BS9 . . . . .49 C5
Longleaze Gdns BS24 . . . . .105 F3
Long Mdw BS16 . . . . .50 D6
Long Mead BS37 . . . . .27 E5
Longmead Ave BS7 . . . . .49 D5
Longmead Cl BA2 . . . . .136 F4
Longmead Croft BS13 . . . . . .78 F4
Longmeadow Rd BS31 . . . . .81 C4
Longmead Rd BS16 . . . . .38 B1
Longmoor Ct BS3 . . . . .63 A2
Longmoor Rd BS3 . . . . .63 A2
Longney Pl BS34 . . . . .23 F1
Long Rd BS16 . . . . .52 A5
Longreach BS31 . . . . .82 C4
Longreach Gr BS14 . . . . .80 D6
Longridge Way BS24 . . . . .105 F7
Long Row BS1 . . . . .143 B2
Longs Dr BS37 . . . . .27 C2
Longs View GL12 . . . . .11 A5
Long-Thorn BS48 . . . . .75 F6
Longthorne Pl BA2 . . . . . . .101 F2
Long Thorn La BS40 . . . . . .111 E7
Longton Grove Rd **3**
 BS23 .104 E8
Longton Ind Est BS23 . . . .104 F6
Long Valley Rd BA2 . . . . . .100 F5
Longvernal BA3 . . . . .132 F1
Longvernal Prim Sch
 BA3 . . . . .132 F1
Longway Ave BS13,
 BS14 . . . . .79 F4
LONGWELL GREEN 65 E3
Longwell Green Prim Sch
 BS30 . . . . .65 F3
Longwell Green Trad Pk
 BS30 . . . . .65 E4
Longwell Rd BS30 . . . . .65 F3
Longwood BS4 . . . . .65 A2
Longwood Ho BS8 . . . . .61 D4
Longwood La BS8,
 BS41 . . . . .61 F4
Lons Ct BS30 . . . . .66 C1
Lonsdale Ave BS23 . . . . . .104 F4
Lonsdale Bsns Ctr
 BS15 . . . . .51 C2
Lorain Wlk BS10 . . . . .34 F2
Lorne Rd BA2 . . . . .101 D6
Lorton Cl BS10 . . . . .35 B1
Lorton Rd BS10 . . . . .35 B1
Lotts' Ave BS48 . . . . .76 B5
Lotus Ct BS22 . . . . .88 C1
Loughman Cl **2** BS15 . . . .65 E8
Louisa St BS2 . . . . .143 C2
Louise Ave BS16 . . . . .52 A5
Love La
 Chipping Sodbury BS37 . . . .40 A8
 Yate BS37 . . . . .28 A4
Lovelinch Gdns BS41 . . . . . .61 F1
Lovell Ave BS30 . . . . .66 D4
Lovell Dr BS39 . . . . .113 C4
Lovell's Hill BS15 . . . . .65 B5
Lovells Mill BS39 . . . . .113 D4
Lovells The BS20 . . . . .47 B4
Loveridge Ct BS36 . . . . .38 B7
Loveringe Cl BS10 . . . . .34 F4
Lovers La BA3, BS39 . . . . .133 A5
Lovers' Wlk BS23 . . . . .104 D8
Loves Hill BA2 . . . . .116 A1
Love's La BA2 . . . . .115 F6
Lowbourne BS14 . . . . .79 F6
LOWER ALMONDSBURY

 . . . . .24 A6

Lower Ashley Rd
 Bristol, Baptist Mills BS2,
 BS5 . . . . .50 A1
 13 Bristol, St Pauls BS2 . . .49 F1
Lower Batch BS40 . . . . .96 B3
Lower Borough Walls
 BA1 . . . . .141 C2
Lower Bristol Rd
 Bath BA2 . . . . .101 B6
 Clutton BS39 . . . . .114 F4
Lower Burlington Rd
 BS20 . . . . .45 E7
Lower Camden Pl
 BA1 . . . . .141 C4
LOWER CANADA 105 F2
Lower Castle St BS1 . . . . .143 B3
Lower Chapel La BS36 . . . . .38 C7
Lower Chapel Rd BS15 . . . .65 C5
Lower Cheltenham Pl
 BS6 . . . . .49 F1
Lower Church La BS2 . . . .143 A3
Lower Church Rd
 BS23 .104 D8
LOWER CLAVERHAM 74 F2
Lower Claverham BS49 . . .74 F3
Lower Clifton Hill
 BS8 . . . . .142 B2
Lower Cock Rd BS15 . . . . . .65 F7
Lower College St
 BS1 . . . . .142 C2
Lower Conham Vale
 BS15 . . . . .65 A5
Lower Court Rd BS32 . . . . .24 A5
Lower Down Rd BS20 . . . . .45 B5
Lower East Hayes
 BA1 . . . . .102 B8
LOWER EASTON 50 D2
LOWER FAILAND 61 A8
Lower Fallow Cl BS14 . . . .79 F3
Lower Farm La BA2 . . . . . .100 B7
Lower Gay St BS2 . . . . .143 A4
Lower Grove Rd BS16 . . . . .50 F4

Lower Guinea St BS1 . . . .143 A1
LOWER HAMSWELL 68 C3
Lower Hanham Rd
 BS15 . . . . .65 C6
LOWER HAZEL 14 F3
Lower Hedgemead Rd
 BA1 . . . . .141 C4
Lower High St BS11 . . . . . . .47 D7
Lower Ho BS34 . . . . .36 A3
Lower House Cres
 BS34 . . . . .36 B4
Lowerhouse La GL11 . . . . . . .5 D5
Lower Kewstoke Rd
 BS22 . . . . .88 E3
LOWER KILCOTT 20 A7
Lower Kingsdown Rd
 SN13 . . . . .86 F3
Lower Knole La BS10 . . . . . .35 A3
LOWER KNOWLE 63 E1
Lower Knowles Rd
 BS21 . . . . .57 E2
Lower Lamb St BS1 . . . . . .142 C2
LOWER LANGFORD 109 C5
Lower Linden Rd BS21 . . . .57 F3
Lower Maudlin St
 BS1 . . . . .143 A3
Lower Moor Rd BS37 . . . . .27 E4
LOWER MORTON 8 C4
Lower Northend BA1 . . . . . .85 F5
Lower Norton La
 Weston-S-M BS22 . . . . .88 E4
 Weston-S-M, Norton
 BS22 . . . . .88 C4
Lower Oldfield Pk
 BA2 . . . . .141 A1
Lower Parade Ground Rd
 BS24 .106 C5
Lower Park Row BS1 . . . . .143 A3
LOWER PEASEDOWN

 . . . . .134 B8

Lower Queen's Rd
 BS21 . . . . .57 F3
Lower Rd BS39 . . . . .130 E6
Lower Redland Mews **2**
 BS6 . . . . .49 B2
Lower Redland Rd BS6 . . .49 B2
Lower Sidney St BS3 . . . . .63 A4
LOWER SOUNDWELL 51 F2
Lower St SN14 . . . . .54 D4
Lower Station Rd
 6 Bristol, Ridgeway
 BS16 . . . . .51 A4
 Bristol, Staple Hill BS16 . . .51 C4
Lower Stoke BA2 . . . . .120 A8
LOWER STONE 3 C1
Lower Stone Cl BS36 . . . . . .38 C7
LOWER STRODE 112 A8
Lower Strode Rd BS40 . . .112 A7
Lower Strode Rd BS21 . . . .73 A7
LOWER SWAINSWICK 85 C3
Lower Thirlmere Rd
 BS34 . . . . .36 A8
Lower Tockington Rd
 BS32 . . . . .14 B1
LOWER WESTON 101 C7
Lower Whitelands
 BA3 . . . . .134 B3
LOWER WICK 4 E6
LOWER WRITHLINGTON

 . . . . .134 C3

Lowlis Cl BS10 . . . . .34 F3
Lowther Rd BS10 . . . . .35 C2
Loxley Gdns BA1 . . . . .101 C4
LOXTON 123 C4
Loxton Dr BA2 . . . . .101 B6
Loxton Rd BS23 . . . . .104 F2
Loxton Sq BS14 . . . . .80 A6
Lucas Cl BS4 . . . . .64 D1
Luccombe Hill BS6 . . . . . . .49 B2
LUCKINGTON 31 F4
Luckington Com Sch
 SN14 . . . . .31 E5
Luckington Court Gdns*
 SN14 . . . . .32 A4
Luckington Cross
 BA11 .140 B2
Luckington Rd
 Acton Turville GL9 . . . . .43 A7
 Bristol BS7 . . . . .49 E8
Lucklands Rd BA1 . . . . .84 C1
Luckley Ave BS13 . . . . .79 D5
Luckwell Prim Sch
 BS3 . . . . .63 A3
Luckwell Rd BS3 . . . . .63 B3
Lucky La BS3 . . . . .63 D4
Ludlow Cl
 Bristol, St Pauls BS2 . . . . . .49 F1
 Bristol, Willsbridge BS30 . . .66 B2
 Keynsham BS31 . . . . .81 D5
Ludlow Ct BS30 . . . . .66 B1
Ludlow Rd BS7 . . . . .50 A7
Ludwell Cl BS36 . . . . .37 D5
Ludwells Orch BS39 . . . . .132 E5
Luggard's Cross BS21 . . . . .59 C4
Luke's Cl BA3 . . . . .133 F3
Lullington Rd BS4 . . . . .64 B2
LULSGATE BOTTOM 94 A8
Lulsgate Rd BS13 . . . . .79 A8
Lulworth Cres BS16 . . . . . . .51 F8
Lulworth Rd BS31 . . . . .81 E4
Lundy Gate BS20 . . . . .45 F6
Lunty Mead BS48 . . . . .75 F6
Lurgan Wlk BS4 . . . . .63 D1
Lutyens Cl BS14 . . . . .80 B8
Luvers La BS40 . . . . .110 D1
Lux Furlong BS9 . . . . .48 B7
Luxton St BS5 . . . . .64 B8

Lwr Station App Rd
 BS1 . . . . .143 C1
Lychgate Pk BS24 . . . . . . .106 A4
Lydbrook Cl BS37 . . . . .39 D8
Lyddieth Ct BA15 . . . . .120 E7
Lyddington Rd BS7 . . . . .49 F8
Lyddon Rd BS22 . . . . .89 B3
Lyde Cl BA2 . . . . .136 E5
Lyde Gn BA2 . . . . .136 E5
LYDE GREEN 52 E8
Lyde Green Rdbt BS16 . . .52 B8
Lydford Wlk BS3 . . . . .63 C2
Lydiard Croft BS15 . . . . .65 C4
Lydney Rd
 Bristol, Southmead
 BS10 . . . . .35 D1
 Bristol, Staple Hill BS16 . . .51 E4
Lydstep Terr BS3 . . . . .63 C4
LYE CROSS 93 C1
Lye Cross Rd BS40 . . . . .93 C1
Lyefield Rd BS22 . . . . .88 E4
LYE HOLE 93 E2
Lye Hole La BS40 . . . . .93 D2
Lye Mead BS40 . . . . .95 A6
Lyes The BS49 . . . . .91 D3
Lyme Gdns BA1 . . . . .101 B7
Lyme Rd BA1 . . . . .101 B7
Lymore Ave BA2 . . . . .101 C5
Lymore Gdns BA2 . . . . . . .101 C5
Lymore Terr BA2 . . . . .101 C4
LYMPSHAM 122 B1
Lympsham CE Fst Sch
 BS24 .122 B1
Lympsham Gn BA2 . . . . . .118 D8
Lympsham Rd BS24 . . . . .122 B1
Lynbrook BS41 . . . . .61 F1
Lynbrook La BA2 . . . . .101 F3
Lynch Cl BS22 . . . . .88 F3
Lynch Cres BS25 . . . . .124 F7
Lynch Hill BA3 . . . . .133 A5
Lynch Rd BS40 . . . . .109 A5
Lynchmead BS25 . . . . .125 A7
Lynch The BS25 . . . . .124 F7
Lyncombe Hall BA2 . . . . .102 A4
LYNCOMBE HILL 102 A4
Lyncombe Hill BA2 . . . . . .141 C1
LYNCOMBE VALE 102 A3
Lyncombe Vale BA2 . . . . .102 A4
Lyncombe Vale Rd
 BA2 . . . . .102 A4
Lyncombe Wlk BS16 . . . . .51 B2
Lyndale Ave BS9 . . . . .48 D5
Lyndale Rd
 Bristol BS5 . . . . .64 D8
 Yate BS37 . . . . .27 D1
Lynde Cl BS13 . . . . .79 B4
Lyndhurst Rd
 Bath BA2 . . . . .101 C6
 Bristol BS9 . . . . .48 F7
 Keynsham BS31 . . . . .81 F3
 Midsomer Norton BA3 . . . .139 B8
 Weston-S-M BS23 . . . . . . .104 E4
Lyndhurst Terr BA1 . . . . . .141 C4
Lynfield Pk BA1 . . . . .84 C1
Lynmouth Cl BS22 . . . . .89 A2
Lynmouth Rd **1** BS2 . . . .50 A2
Lynn Rd BS16 . . . . .50 D5
Lynton **1** BS15 . . . . .66 A8
Lynton Cl BS20 . . . . .45 E4
Lynton Pl **2** BS5 . . . . .64 C8
Lynton Rd
 Bristol BS3 . . . . .63 D2
 Midsomer Norton BA3 . . . .139 B8
Lynton Way BS16 . . . . .37 B1
Lynwood Cl BA3 . . . . .139 A8
Lynwood Rd BS3 . . . . .63 B2
Lynx Cres BS24 . . . . .105 B2
Lyons Court Rd BS14 . . . . .80 D7
Lyons Ct BS23 . . . . .104 F7
Lyppiatt Rd BS5 . . . . .64 D8
Lyppincourt Rd BS10 . . . . .35 A3
Lypstone Cl BS24 . . . . .106 A8
Lysander Rd BS10,
 BS34 . . . . .35 C6
Lysander Wlk BS34 . . . . . . .36 E5
Lytchet Dr BS16 . . . . .51 F8
Lytes Cary Rd BS31 . . . . . . .82 A3
Lytham Ho BS4 . . . . .64 D1
Lytham Rd BS4 . . . . .64 D1
Lytton Gdns BA2 . . . . .101 B4
Lytton Gr
 Bristol BS7 . . . . .50 A8
 Keynsham BS31 . . . . .82 A3
Lyveden Gdns BS13 . . . . . .79 B5
Lyvedon Way BS41 . . . . . . .62 B1

M

Mabberley Cl BS16 . . . . . . .52 C5
McAdam Way BS1 . . . . .62 F5
Macaulay Bldgs BA2 . . . .102 C4
Macauley Rd BS7 . . . . .50 A8
McCrae Rd BS24 . . . . .106 B5
Macdonald Wlk **3**
 BS15 . . . . .65 D8
Macey's Rd BS13 . . . . .79 D3
Macfarlane Chase
 BS23 .105 A5
Machin Cl BS10 . . . . .34 F3
Machin Gdns BS10 . . . . . . .35 A3
Machin Rd BS10 . . . . .35 A3
Macies The BA1 . . . . .84 B3
Mackie Ave BS34 . . . . .36 B2
Mackie Gr BS34 . . . . .36 B2
Mackie Rd BS34 . . . . .36 B2
Mackley La BA2 . . . . .136 E3
McLaren Rd BS11 . . . . .33 B1
Macleod Cl BS21 . . . . .57 C2

Macquarie Farm Cl
 BS49 . . . . .74 A1
Macrae Ct BS15 . . . . .65 E8
Macrae Rd BS20 . . . . .47 E4
Madam La
 Weston-S-M BS22 . . . . .88 F2
 Weston-S-M BS22 . . . . .89 A3
 Weston-S-M BS22 . . . . .89 A4
Madam's Paddock
 BS40 . . . . .96 B3
Madeira Ct BS23 . . . . .104 C8
Madeira Rd
 Clevedon BS21 . . . . .57 F3
 Weston-S-M BS23 . . . . .87 C1
Madeline Rd BS16 . . . . .50 F2
Madison Cl BS37 . . . . .27 D2
Maesbury BS15 . . . . .65 E6
Maesbury Rd BS31 . . . . .82 A2
Maesknoll La BS14,
 BS39 . . . . .97 B8
Maesknoll Rd BS4 . . . . .64 A2
Magdalena Ct BS1 . . . . . . .143 B1
Magdalen Ave BA2 . . . . . .141 B1
Magdalene Pl BS2 . . . . .49 F1
Magdalene Rd BA3 . . . . . .134 C2
Magdalen Rd BA2 . . . . . . .141 B1
Magdalen Way BS22 . . . . .89 A3
Magellan Cl BS22 . . . . .88 F4
Maggs Cl BS10 . . . . .35 C3
Maggs Folly BS39 . . . . . . .115 D2
Maggs Hill BA2 . . . . .116 B2
Maggs La
 Bristol BS5 . . . . .50 E2
 Whitchurch BS14 . . . . .80 C4
Magnolia Ave BS22 . . . . . . .89 A1
Magnolia Cl BS22 . . . . .105 E2
Magnolia Grange BS22 . . .88 F1
Magnolia Rd BA3 . . . . .133 E1
Magpie Bottom La
 Bristol, Kingswood
 BS15 . . . . .65 C6
 Bristol, St George BS5 . . . . .65 B6
Magpie Cl BS22 . . . . .105 E8
MAIDEN HEAD 78 F1
Maidenhead Rd BS13 . . . .79 D3
Maiden Way BS11 . . . . .47 C8
Maidstone Gr BS24 . . . . . .105 A1
Maidstone St BS3 . . . . .63 F3
Main Dr BS10 . . . . .34 E1
MAINES BATCH 92 E3
Main Rd
 Bristol BS16 . . . . .52 D5
 Brockley BS49 . . . . .75 D2
 Flax Bourton BS48 . . . . .76 F7
 Hutton BS24 . . . . .105 E2
Main St BS39 . . . . .132 A4
Main View BS36 . . . . .38 D7
Maisemore BS37 . . . . .39 E8
Maisemore Ave BS34 . . . .24 B1
Makin Cl BS30 . . . . .66 C5
Malago Rd BS3 . . . . .63 D3
Malago Vale Trad Est
 BS3 . . . . .63 D3
Malago Wlk BS13 . . . . .78 E4
Malden Mead BS14 . . . . . .80 A5
Maldowers La **2** BS5 . . .65 A8
Malin Par BS20 . . . . .45 F6
Mallard Cl
 Bristol BS32 . . . . .24 D2
 Bristol, Crofts End BS5 . . . .50 F1
 Chipping Sodbury BS37 . . .40 A8
Mallard Wlk **7** BS22 . . .105 E8
Mallow Cl
 Clevedon BS21 . . . . .57 G2
 Thornbury BS35 . . . . .8 D2
Mall The
 Bath BA1 . . . . .141 C2
 Bristol, Clifton BS8 . . . . .62 F7
 Mall The BS34 . . . . .36 D6
Malmains Dr BS16 . . . . . . .37 B1
Malmesbury Cl
 Bristol, Bishopston
 BS6 . . . . .49 C4
 Bristol, Longwell Green
 BS30 . . . . .65 F5
Malmesbury Ct BA3 . . . . .139 C6
Malvern Bldgs BA1 . . . . . . .85 A2
Malvern Ct BS5 . . . . .64 F7
Malvern Dr
 Bristol BS30 . . . . .66 C5
 Thornbury BS35 . . . . .15 D8
Malvern Rd
 Bristol, Crew's Hole
 BS5 . . . . .64 F7
 Bristol, Kensington Park
 BS4 . . . . .64 D3
 Weston-S-M BS23 . . . . . . .104 E5
Malvern Terr **3** BA1 . . . .85 A1
Malvern Villas **2** BA1 . . .85 A1
Manchester Cotts
 BS23 . . . . .88 E3
Mancroft Ave BS11 . . . . . . .47 F7
Mandy Mdws BA3 . . . . . . .132 F1
MANGOTSFIELD 52 A6
Mangotsfield CE Prim Sch
 BS16 . . . . .52 B6
Mangotsfield Rd BS16 . . .52 A5
Mangotsfield Sch
 BS16 . . . . .52 B6
MANIARDS GREEN 2 C2
Manilla Cres BS23 . . . . .87 C1
Manilla Pl BS23 . . . . .87 C1
Manilla Rd BS8 . . . . .142 A3

Manmoor La BS21 . . . . .58 A1
Manorbrook Prim Sch
 BS35 . . . . .8 C2
Manor Cl
 Easton-in-G BS20 . . . . .47 A4
 Farrington Gurney
 BS39 .132 A3
 Frampton Cotterell BS36 . . .38 C6
 Portishead BS20 . . . . .45 A5
 Tockington BS32 . . . . .14 C1
 Wellow BA2 . . . . .118 D1
Manor Cl The BS8 . . . . .62 A8
Manor Coalpit Heath CE
 Prim Sch The BS36 . . . . . . .38 D6
Manor Copse Rd BA3 . . .134 C2
Manor Cotts GL11 . . . . .5 F5
Manor Court Dr BS7 . . . . .49 E7
Manor Ct
 Backwell BS48 . . . . .76 A5
 Bristol, Fishponds BS16 . . .50 E4
 9 Bristol, Upper Easton
 BS5 . . . . .50 B1
 Locking BS24 . . . . .106 B4
 Weston-S-M BS23 . . . . . . .105 A8
Manor Dr BA1 . . . . .86 C2
Manor Farm
 Aust BS35 . . . . .13 B7
 Bristol BS32 . . . . .36 D8
Manor Farm BS24 . . . . .88 E5
Manor Farm Cl BS24 . . . .105 B2
Manor Farm Cres
 BS32 . . . . .36 D8
 Weston-S-M BS24 . . . . . . .105 B2
Manor Gardens Ho
 BS16 . . . . .50 F5
Manor Gdns
 Farnborough BA2 . . . . .115 F6
 Farrington Gurney
 BS39 .132 A3
 Locking BS24 . . . . .106 A4
 Weston-S-M BS22 . . . . .88 B4
Manor Gr
 Bristol BS34 . . . . .24 B2
 Bristol, Mangotsfield
 BS16 . . . . .52 A4
Manor Grange BS24 . . . . .122 B7
Manor Ho
 6 Bristol, Lower Easton
 BS5 . . . . .50 B1
 Bristol, Tyndall's Park
 BS2 . . . . .142 C3
Manor La
 Abbots Leigh BS8 . . . . .61 F8
 Charfield GL12 . . . . .11 A4
 Winterbourne BS36 . . . . . . .37 A1
Manor Park Cl BA3 . . . . . .134 C2
Manor Pk
 Bath BA1 . . . . .101 B8
 Bristol BS6 . . . . .49 B3
 Radstock BA3 . . . . .134 C2
 Tockington BS32 . . . . .14 C1
 Weston-S-M BS23 . . . . . . .104 E1
Manor Pl
 Bristol, Frenchay BS16 . . . .37 C1
 Bristol, Stoke Gifford
 BS34 . . . . .37 A4
Manor Rd
 Abbots Leigh BS8 . . . . .61 F7
 Bath BA1 . . . . .84 C1
 Bristol, Bishopston BS7 . . .49 E4
 Bristol, Bishopsworth
 BS13 . . . . .79 A6
 Bristol, Fishponds BS16 . . .51 A5
 Bristol, Mangotsfield
 BS16 . . . . .52 A4
 Rangeworthy BS37 . . . . . . .27 A7
 Saltford BS31 . . . . .82 C2
 Weston-S-M BS23 . . . . . . .105 A8
 Wick BS30 . . . . .67 C5
Manor Terr BA3 . . . . .134 C2
Manor Valley BS23 . . . . . . .88 A1
Manor Villas BA1 . . . . .84 C1
Manor Way
 Chipping Sodbury BS37 . . .28 C2
 Failand BS8 . . . . .61 C4
Manor Wlk BS35 . . . . .8 B3
Mansbrook Ho **3**
 BA3 . . . . .133 A1
Mansel Cl BS31 . . . . .82 C3
Mansfield Ave BS23 . . . . .105 B8
Mansfield St BS3 . . . . .105 B8
Mansfield St BS3 . . . . .63 C2
Manston Cl BS14 . . . . .80 C7
Manvers St BA1 . . . . .141 C1
Manworthy Rd BS4 . . . . . . .64 D3
Manx Rd BS7 . . . . .49 F8
Maple Ave
 Bristol BS16 . . . . .51 C3
 Thornbury BS35 . . . . .8 C1
Maple Cl
 Bristol, Little Stoke BS34 . .36 D7
 Bristol, Oldland BS30 . . . . .66 B4
 Weston-S-M BS23 . . . . . . .105 A8
Maple Ct
 Bristol BS9 . . . . .48 F8
 5 Bristol BS15 . . . . .51 D1
 6 Weston-S-M BS23 . . . .87 C1
Maple Dr BA3 . . . . .133 E1
Maple Gdns BA2 . . . . .101 E4
Maple Gr BA2 . . . . .101 E4
Maple Ho **3** BS2 . . . . . . .143 A4
Maple Leaf Ct BS8 . . . . . . .142 A3
Mapleleaze BS4 . . . . .64 D3
Maplemeade BS7 . . . . .49 C4
Maple Rd
 Bristol, Horfield BS7 . . . . . .49 F5

Maple Rd *continued*
Bristol, St Anne's BS4 64 D5
Mapleridge La BS37 28 D7
Maple Rise BA3 134 B2
Maples The BS48 59 C1
Maplestone Rd BS14 80 A3
Maple Wlk
Keynsham BS31 81 D4
Pucklechurch BS16 53 C5
Mapstone Cl BS16 37 B3
Marbeck Rd BS10 35 B1
Marchfields Way BS23 105 A5
Marconi Cl BS23 105 B7
Marconi Rd BS20 44 F5
Mardale Cl BS10 35 C2
Marden Rd BS31 82 A4
Mardon Rd BS4 64 D6
Mardyke Ferry Rd BS1 142 B1
Margaret Rd 4 BS13 78 F4
Margaret's Bldgs BA1 141 B3
Margaret's Hill BA1 141 C4
Margate St BS3 63 F3
Marguerite Rd BS13 78 F7
Marigold Wlk BS3 63 A2
Marina Gdns BS16 50 E3
Marindrin Dr BS22 89 B4
Marine Hill BS21 57 E5
Marine Par
Clevedon BS21 57 E4
Pill BS20 47 C5
Weston-S-M BS23 87 B1
Weston-S-M BS23 104 D6
Mariners Cl BS48 76 A6
Mariner's Cl BS22 88 D1
Mariners Dr
Backwell BS48 76 A6
Bristol BS9 48 D4
Mariners' Path BS9 48 E3
Mariner's Way BS20 47 C5
Marion Rd BS15 65 B3
Marion Wlk BS5 65 A7
Marissal Cl BS10 34 E3
Marissal Rd BS10 34 E3
Mariston Way BS30 66 C6
Maritime Heritage Ctr* BS1 142 B1
Marjoram Pl BS32 36 F7
Marjoram Way BS20 45 F5
Market Ave BS22 89 C3
Market Gate BS2 143 C3
Market Ind Est BS49 74 B1
Market La BS23 104 D8
Market Pl
Marshfield SN14 70 A8
Radstock BA3 133 F2
Winford BS40 94 F7
Marketside BS2 64 B4
Market Sq BS16 51 C3
Mark La BS1 142 C2
Marklands BS9 48 E3
MARKSBURY 99 B1
Marksbury CE Prim Sch BA2 99 B2
Marksbury Rd BS3 63 D2
Marlborough Ave 13 BS16 50 E3
Marlborough Bldgs BA1 141 A3
Marlborough Dr
Bristol BS16 37 B1
Weston-S-M BS22 89 B2
Marlborough Flats 8 BS2 143 A4
Marlborough Hill BS2 143 A4
Marlborough Hill Pl BS2 143 A4
Marlborough Ho 15 BS2 143 A4
Marlborough La BA1 141 A3
Marlborough St
Bath BA1 141 A4
Bristol BS2 143 A4
Bristol, Eastville BS5 50 E3
Marlepit Gr BS13 78 F6
Marle Pits 1 BS48 76 A6
Marlfield Wlk BS13 78 E7
Marling Rd BS5 64 F8
Marlowe Ho 3 BS23 104 F4
Marlwood Dr BS10 35 A3
Marlwood Sch BS32 14 F5
Marmaduke St BS3 63 F3
Marmion Cres BS10 34 F3
Marne Cl BS14 80 D5
Marron Cl BS26 125 C2
Marsden Rd BA2 101 B3
Marshacre La BS35 13 F6
Marshall Ho 1 BS16 50 F4
Marshall Wlk BS4 79 D7
Marsham Way BS30 65 F4
Marsh Cl BS36 37 E5
MARSH COMMON 22 E4
Marsh Common Rd BS35 22 E3
MARSHFIELD 69 E8
Marshfield CE Prim Sch SN14 70 B8
Marshfield La BS30 67 D1
Marshfield Pk BS16 51 C8
Marshfield Rd
Bristol, Frenchay BS16 51 C8
Bristol, Hillfields BS16 51 C4
Tormarton GL9 41 E1
Marshfield Way BA1 85 A1
Marsh La
Bristol, Ashton Vale BS3 63 B2
Bristol, Barton Hill BS5 64 C6
Burton SN14, GL9 43 C4
Easton-in-G BS20 47 A4
Farrington Gurney BS39 132 A3
Portbury BS20 46 F6
Temple Cloud BS39 115 A1
Marsh Lane Ind Est BS20 46 F7
Marsh Rd
Bristol BS3 62 F3
Rode BA11 137 F1
Yatton BS49 91 B8
Marsh St
Avonmouth BS11 47 C8
Bristol BS1 143 A2
Marshwall La BS32 23 E6
Marson Rd BS21 57 F3
Marston Rd BS4 64 B3
Martcombe Rd BS20 47 C2
Martha's Orch BS13 78 E7
Martin Cl BS34 35 E8
Martin Ct 12 BS16 50 E3
Martindale Ct BS22 105 D8
Martindale Rd BS22 105 D8
Martingale Rd BS4 64 D4
Martins Cl BS15 65 C5
Martins Gr BS22 88 E2
Martin's Rd BS15 65 C5
Martin St 2 BS3 63 B3
Martins The BS20 46 A6
Martock BS24 104 F2
Martock Cres BS3 63 C1
Martock Rd
Bristol BS3 63 C2
Keynsham BS31 82 A3
Martor Ind Est SN14 56 A2
Mart The 6 BS23 104 E7
Marwood Rd BS4 79 E8
Marybush La BS2 143 B3
Mary Carpenter Pl 15 BS2 49 F1
Mary Ct BS5 64 D8
Mary Elton Prim Sch BS21 57 D1
Marygold Leaze BS30 66 A4
Mary Seacole Ct 8 BS2 50 A2
Mary St BS5 64 D8
Mascot Rd BS3 63 D3
Masefield Ho BS23 105 A4
Masefield Way BS7 50 A6
Maskelyne Ave BS10 49 D7
Masons View BS36 37 F7
Matchells Cl BS4 64 E6
Materman Rd BS14 80 E5
Matford Cl
Bristol BS10 35 D4
Winterbourne BS36 37 E5
Matford La GL13 3 F4
Matthews Cl BS14 80 F6
Matthew's Rd 17 BS5 64 C7
Maules La BS16 36 F2
Maunsell Rd
Bristol BS11 34 B2
Weston-S-M BS24 105 E7
Maurice Rd BS6 49 E2
Mautravers Cl BS32 36 D7
Mawdeley Ho 11 BS3 63 C4
Max Mill La BS25 124 C8
Maxse Rd BS4 64 B2
Maybank Rd BS37 27 D1
Maybec Gdns BS5 65 A6
Maybourne BS4 65 A2
Maybrick Rd BA2 101 D5
Maycliffe Pk BS6 49 F2
Mayfair Ave BS48 59 F1
Mayfield Ave
Bristol BS16 51 A2
Weston-S-M BS22 88 E1
Mayfield Ct BS16 51 A3
MAYFIELD PARK 51 A2
Mayfield Pk BS16 51 A2
Mayfield Pk N BS16 51 A2
Mayfield Pk S BS16 51 A2
Mayfield Rd BA2 101 D5
Mayfields BS31 81 E5
Mayflower Gdns BS48 60 A2
May Gr GL12 11 B5
Maynard Cl
Bristol BS13 79 C5
4 Clevedon BS21 57 H3
Maynard Rd BS13 79 C5
Maynard Terr BS39 114 F3
Mayors Bldgs BS16 51 B5
May Park Prim Sch BS5 50 C2
Maypole Cl
Clutton BS39 114 E3
Hawkesbury Upton GL9 20 A2
Maypole Ct 1 BS15 65 B5
Mays Cl BS36 38 D7
Maysfield Cl BS20 45 D3
Maysgreen La BS24 90 B3
MAYSHILL 26 E1
May's La BS24 90 C3
Maysmead La BS40 109 C6
May St BS15 51 C1
Maytree Ave BS13 79 B7
Maytree Cl BS13 79 B7
May Tree Cl BS48 59 C1
May Tree Rd BA3 133 E1
Maytrees BS5 50 C2
May Tree Wlk BS31 81 C3
Mayville Ave BS34 36 A3
Maywood Ave 3 BS16 51 B4
Maywood Cres BS16 51 B4
Maywood Rd BS16 51 C4
Maze St BS5 64 B6
Mead Cl
Bath BA2 101 E3
Bristol BS11 47 E6
Mead Ct BS36 37 E6
Mead Ct Bsns Pk BS35 15 B8
Meade Ho BA2 101 A5
Meadgate BS16 52 B7
MEADGATE EAST 116 E2
MEADGATE WEST 116 D2
Mead La
Blagdon BS40 110 E3
Ingst BS35 13 D2
Saltford BS31 82 F4
Sandford BS25 107 E4
Meadlands BA2 100 B7
Meadowbank BS22 88 F3
Meadowbrook Prim Sch BS32 36 E8
Meadow Cl
Backwell BS48 76 B6
Bristol BS16 51 F7
Farrington Gurney BS39 132 A3
Nailsea BS48 59 E3
Meadow Court Dr BS30 66 C3
Meadowcroft BS16 52 A8
Meadow Croft BS24 105 B2
Meadow Ct BA1 101 A7
Meadow Dr
Bath BA2 118 D8
Locking BS24 106 B4
Portishead BS20 44 F1
Meadow Gdns BA1 84 A1
Meadow Gr BS11 47 D7
Meadow La BA2 85 D1
Meadowland BS49 74 A1
Meadowland Rd BS10 34 E4
Meadowlands BS22 89 C2
Meadow Mead
Frampton Cotterell BS36 38 B8
Yate BS37 27 E5
Meadow Pk BA1 86 B3
Meadow Pl BS22 89 D3
Meadow Rd
Chipping Sodbury BS37 28 A1
Clevedon BS21 57 G3
Leyhill GL12 10 B4
Paulton BS39 132 F4
Meadows Cl BS20 44 F5
Meadows End BS25 108 D4
Meadowside 2 BS35 15 D8
Meadowside Dr BS14 80 A3
Meadows Prim Sch The BS30 82 D8
Meadow St
Avonmouth BS11 33 A1
Axbridge BS26 125 C2
Weston-S-M BS23 104 E7
Meadows The
Bristol BS15 65 D4
Luckington SN14 31 F4
Meadowsweet Ave BS34 36 B3
Meadow Vale BS5 51 A1
Meadow View
Frampton Cotterell BS36 38 D7
Radstock BA3 134 A1
Meadow View Cl BA1 101 A8
Meadow Villas 14 BS23 104 E8
Meadow Way BS32 36 E7
Mead Rd
Bristol BS34 36 F5
Chipping Sodbury BS37 28 C1
Portishead BS20 45 C2
Mead Rise BS3 63 F4
Mead St BS4 143 C1
Meads The
Bristol BS16 51 F7
Burton SN14 43 B3
Mead Terr BS40 110 E2
Mead The
Alveston BS35 15 A5
Bristol BS34 36 B4
Clutton BS39 114 E3
Dundry BS41 78 D2
Farmborough BA2 116 A6
Paulton BS39 132 D5
Shipham BS25 125 E8
Stratton-on-t-F BA3 138 F2
Timsbury BA2 116 C3
Winsley BA15 120 E7
Mead Vale BS22 105 E8
Mead Vale Com Prim Sch BS22 88 E1
Meadway
Bristol BS9 48 C6
Farmborough BA2 116 A6
Temple Cloud BS39 114 E1
Mead Way BS35 15 B7
Meadway Ave BS48 59 D2
Mearcombe La BS24 122 F6
Meardon Rd BS14 80 E6
Meare BS24 104 F2
Meare Rd BA2 102 A2
MEARNS 115 E2
Mede Cl BS1 143 B1
Media Ho BS8 142 B3
Medical Ave BS2, BS8 142 C3
Medina Cl BS35 15 C7
Medway Cl BS31 82 A3
Medway Ct BS35 15 D8
Medway Dr
Frampton Cotterell BS36 38 B7
Keynsham BS31 82 A3
Meere Bank BS11 34 B1
Meetinghouse La BS49 75 A1
Meg Thatcher's Gdns BS5 65 B7
Meg Thatchers Gn BS5 65 B7
Melbourne Dr BS37 28 C1
Melbourne Rd BS7 49 D4
Melbourne Terr 2 BS21 57 F2
Melbury Rd BS4 64 A2
Melcombe Ct BA2 101 D4
Melcombe Rd BA2 101 D4
Melita Rd BS6 49 E3
Mellent Ave BS13 79 C3
Mells Cl BS31 82 A2
Mells La BA3 134 B1
Melrose Ave
Bristol BS8 142 B4
Yate BS37 28 A2
Melrose Cl BS37 28 A2
Melrose Gr BA2 101 B3
Melrose Pl BS8 142 B4
Melrose Terr BA1 85 A2
Melton Cres BS7 50 A7
Melville Rd BS6 49 B1
Melville Terr BS3 63 C3
Melvin Sq BS4 63 E1
Memorial Cl BS15 65 B4
Memorial Rd
Bristol BS15 65 B4
Wrington BS40 92 E2
Memorial Stadium (Bristol Rovers FC)* BS7 49 F6
Mendip Ave BS22 88 F2
Mendip Cl
Axbridge BS26 125 D2
Keynsham BS31 81 D5
3 Nailsea BS48 59 E1
Paulton BS39 132 E4
Yatton BS49 91 B7
Mendip Cres BS16 52 A8
Mendip Ct BS16 36 E1
Mendip Edge BS24 121 F8
Mendip Fields BA3 138 C2
Mendip Gdns
Bath BA2 118 D8
Yatton BS49 91 B7
Mendip Green Fst Sch BS22 88 E1
Mendip Lo BS25 125 A8
Mendip Rd
Bristol BS3 63 D3
Locking BS24 106 D4
Portishead BS20 45 B5
Weston-S-M BS23 105 A7
Yatton BS49 91 B7
Mendip Rise BS24 106 B4
Mendip View BS30 67 C7
Mendip View Ave BS16 51 A3
Mendip View Bsns Pk BS24 90 C5
Mendip Villas
Cheddar BS27 126 A1
Compton Martin BS40 128 F7
Mendip Way BA3 133 F3
Menhyr Gr BS10 35 B3
Menlea BS40 110 D3
Mercer Ct BS14 80 B8
Merchants Almshouses BS1 143 A2
Merchants Ct BS8 142 A1
Merchants Quay BS1 143 A1
Merchants Rd
Bristol BS8 142 A3
Bristol, Hotwells BS8 142 A1
Merchants Row BS1 142 C1
Merchant St BS1 143 B3
Merchants The SN14 31 E4
Merchants Trad Pk BS2 64 C6
Mercia Dr BS2 50 A2
Mercier Cl BS37 27 F2
Meredith Ct BS1 142 A1
Merfield Rd BS4 64 B2
Meriden BA1 101 D8
Meridian Pl BS8 142 B3
Meridian Rd BS6 49 C1
Meridian Vale BS8 142 B3
Meriet Ave BS13 79 B4
Merioneth St BS3 63 F3
Meriton St BS2 64 B5
Merlin Cl
Bristol BS9 48 F8
1 Weston-S-M BS22 105 E8
Merlin Ct BS10 49 B7
Merlin Pk BS20 45 A4
Merlin Rd BS10, BS34 35 C6
Merlin Ridge BS16 53 C4
Merlin Way BS37 39 F8
Merrett Ct BS7 50 B6
Merrick Ct BS1 143 A1
Merrick Fields BA3 138 C4
Merrimans Rd BS11 47 D8
Merryfield Rd BS24 106 B6
Merryholes La BS12 14 D3
Merryweather Cl BS32 36 D8
Merryweathers BS4 64 E2
Merrywood Cl 5 BS3 63 C4
Merrywood Ct BS4 64 B2
Merrywood Rd BS3 63 C4
Merstham Rd 13 BS2 50 A2
Merton Dr BS24 106 A8
Merton Rd BS7 49 E5
Mervyn Rd BS7 49 E4
Meryl Ct BS6 49 B1
Metford Gr BS6 49 B3
Metford Pl BS6 49 C3
Metford Rd BS6 49 C3
Methwyn Cl BS22 105 C7
Metropolitan The BS1 143 B1
Mews The BA1 101 A8
Mewswell Dr BS27 126 B1
Mezellion Pl 14 BA1 85 B1
Michaels Mead BA1 84 B2
Middle Ave BS1 143 A2
Middledown Rd SN14 55 C1
Middleford Ho BS13 79 C4
Middle La
Bath BA1 85 B1
Kingston Seymour BS21 72 F4
Middlemead BA3 138 F3
Middlepiece La BA2, BS31 99 B7
Middle Rd BS15 51 F3
Middle St BS40 129 F4
Middle Stoke BA2 120 A6
Middleton Rd BS11 47 F8
Middlewood Cl BA2 101 C2
Middle Yeo Gn BS48 59 D3
MIDFORD 119 C6
Midford BS24 104 F2
Midford Hill BA2 119 C5
Midford La BA2 119 E7
Midford Rd BA2 119 B7
Midhaven Rise BS22 88 E4
Midland Bridge Rd BA1, BA2 141 A2
Midland Mews BS2 143 C3
Midland Rd
Bath BA1 101 D7
Bristol BS2 143 C3
Bristol, Staple Hill BS16 51 D4
Midland Road Bsns Pk BS16 51 D4
Midland St BS2 143 C2
Midland Terr BS16 50 F3
Midland Way BS35 15 C7
Midland Way Bsns Pk BS35 15 B8
Midsomer Ent Pk BA3 133 C2
MIDSOMER NORTON 133 B3
Midsomer Norton Prim Sch BA3 133 B1
Midsomer Norton S* BA3 139 A8
Midsummer Bldgs BA1 85 B2
Milburn Rd BS23 104 F7
Milbury Gdns BS22 88 C2
Mildred St BS5 64 C7
Miles Cl BS20 47 E3
Miles Ct
Bristol, Cadbury Heath BS30 65 F4
Bristol, Clifton BS8 49 A1
Miles Rd BS8 49 A1
Miles's Bldgs BA1 141 B3
Miles St BA2 141 C1
Milestone Ct BS22 89 D2
Mile Wlk BS14 80 A6
Milford Ave BS30 67 B7
Milford St BS3 63 C4
Milk St BA1 141 B2
Millard Cl BS10 35 D2
Millards Ct BA3 133 B3
Millards Hill BA3 133 B3
Millard's Hill BA3 133 C3
Millar Ho BS8 142 A3
Mill Ave BS1 143 A2
Millbank Cl BS4 64 E3
Millbook Ct 3 BS6 49 E1
Millbourn Cl BA15 120 D7
Millbrook Ave BS4 64 F3
Millbrook Cl BS30 66 C6
Millbrook Ct BA2 141 C1
Millbrook Pl BA2 141 C1
Millbrook Rd BS37 27 B2
Mill Cl
Frampton Cotterell BS36 38 C7
Portbury BS20 46 D2
Mill Cotts BS31 82 F2
Mill Cres BS37 39 B4
Millcross BS21 73 C8
Mill Ct 1 BA3 133 A1
Millennium Cl BS36 38 D7
Millennium Prom BS1 142 C1
Miller Cl BS23 104 F8
Millers Cl BS20 47 C4
Millers Ct BS21 73 E8
Millers Dr BS30 66 D5
Millers Rise BS22 89 A4
Miller Wlk BA2 85 F1
Millfield
Midsomer Norton BA3 138 F8
Thornbury BS35 8 C2
Millfield Dr BS30 66 C6
Millground Rd BS13 78 F5
Millgrove St N BS2 143 A4
Mill Hill BA2 118 E1
Mill Ho
11 Bristol, Baptist Mills BS5 50 A1
Bristol BS1 143 A2

Millier Rd BS49 . . . . 92 B8
Milliman Cl BS13 . . . . 79 C5
Mill La
  Bathampton BA2 . . . . 85 F2
  3 Bath BA2 . . . . 101 B6
  Bitton BS30 . . . . 82 E8
  Bristol, Southville BS3 . . . . 63 D4
  Bristol, Warmley BS30 . . . . 66 C5
  Butcombe BS40 . . . . 111 A8
  Chew Stoke BS40 . . . . 112 D8
  Chipping Sodbury BS37 . . . . . . 40 E6
  Compton Martin BS40 . . . . . . 129 A7
  Congresbury BS49 . . . . 91 D4
  Doynton BS30 . . . . 53 F1
  Falfield GL12 . . . . 9 F7
  Frampton Cotterell BS36 . . . . 26 B1
  Monkton Combe BA2 . . . . . . 119 E8
  Portbury BS20 . . . . 46 E3
  Priston BA2 . . . . 117 A7
  Timsbury BA2 . . . . 116 B1
  Tockington BS32 . . . . 14 B1
  Upton Cheyney BS30 . . . . 66 F1
  Wrington BS40 . . . . 109 F8
Mill Leg BS49 . . . . 91 D4
Millmead Ho BS13 . . . . 79 C4
Millmead Rd BA2 . . . . 101 C5
Millpill Cl BS9 . . . . 48 D5
Millpond Prim Sch
  BS5 . . . . 50 A1
Millpond St **10** BS5 . . . . 50 A1
Millpool Ct BS10 . . . . 49 B8
Mill Rd
  Radstock BA3 . . . . 134 B2
  Winterbourne BS36 . . . . 37 D4
Mill Road Ind Est BA3 . . . . . 134 B3
Mill Steps BS36 . . . . 37 E4
Mill Stream Cl BS26 . . . . 125 C1
Millward Gr BS16 . . . . 51 C4
Millward Terr BS39 . . . . 132 E6
Milner Gn BS30 . . . . 66 A5
Milner Rd BS7 . . . . 49 F5
Milsom Pl BA1 . . . . 141 B3
Milsom St
  Bath BA1 . . . . 141 B3
  Bristol BS5 . . . . 64 A8
MILTON 88 C2
Milton Ave
  Bath BA2 . . . . 101 F4
  Weston-S-M BS23 . . . . 105 A8
Milton Brow BS22 . . . . 88 B2
Milton Cl
  Nailsea BS48 . . . . 59 E3
  Yate BS37 . . . . 27 D2
Milton Ct BS23 . . . . 105 A8
Milton Gn BS22 . . . . 88 C1
Milton Hill BS22 . . . . 88 B2
Milton Park Prim Sch
  BS22 . . . . 88 C1
Milton Park Rd BS22 . . . . 88 C1
Milton Pk **1** BS5 . . . . 64 C7
Milton Rd
  Bristol BS7 . . . . 49 E6
  Radstock BA3 . . . . 133 C1
  Weston-S-M BS22,
  BS23 . . . . 105 B8
  Yate BS37 . . . . 27 D2
Milton Rise BS22 . . . . 88 C1
Miltons Cl BS13 . . . . 79 D4
Milverton BS22 . . . . 104 F2
Milverton Gdns BS6 . . . . 49 F2
Milward Rd BS31 . . . . 81 E6
Mina Rd BS2 . . . . 50 A2
Minehead Rd BS4 . . . . 63 F1
Miners Cl BS41 . . . . 61 F2
Minerva Ct BA2 . . . . 141 C3
Minerva Gdns BA2 . . . . 101 C4
Minsmere Rd BS31 . . . . 82 A4
Minster Cl BS37 . . . . 39 D7
Minster Way BA2 . . . . 102 C8
Minton Cl BS14 . . . . 80 B5
Minto Rd BS2 . . . . 50 A2
Minto Road Ind Ctr **9**
  BS2 . . . . 50 A2
Mission Rd BS37 . . . . 27 B4
Mitchell La BS1 . . . . 143 B2
Mitchell Wlk BS30 . . . . 66 D7
Mitford-Slade Ct BS49 . . . . 91 C7
Mivart St BS5 . . . . 50 C1
Mizzymead Cl **1** BS48 . . . . . . 59 D1
Mizzymead Rd BS48 . . . . 59 E1
Mizzymead Rise BS48 . . . . 59 E1
Modecombe Gr BS10 . . . . 34 F3
Mogg St BS2 . . . . 50 A2
Molesworth Cl BS13 . . . . 79 A4
Molesworth Dr BS13 . . . . 79 A4
Molly Cl BS39 . . . . 131 E8
Monarch Ct BS16 . . . . 38 A1
Monarch Ho **11** BS3 . . . . 63 B3
Monger Cotts BS39 . . . . 132 F4
Monger La
  Midsomer Norton
  BA3 . . . . 133 A3
  Paulton BS39 . . . . 133 A4
Monica Wills Ho **18**
  BS3 . . . . 63 C3
Monk Rd BS7 . . . . 49 D4
Monks Ave BS15 . . . . 65 B8
Monksdale Rd BA2 . . . . 101 D4
Monks Hill BS22 . . . . 88 B3
Monks Ho **3** BS37 . . . . 39 D7
Monk's Park Ave BS7 . . . . 49 E8
Monks Park Sch BS7 . . . . 49 E8
Monks Park Way BS7 . . . . 49 E8
Monkton Ave BS24 . . . . 105 A2

MONKTON COMBE 102 F1
Monkton Combe Jun Sch
  BA2 . . . . 102 C1
Monkton Combe Jun Sch
(Pre-Prep) BA2 . . . . 102 C1
Monkton Combe Sch
  BA2 . . . . 102 E1
MONKTON FARLEIGH
  . . . . 103 F7
Monkton Rd BS15 . . . . 65 B5
Monmouth Cl BS20 . . . . 44 F4
Monmouth Ct
  Bath BA1 . . . . 141 A2
  Pill BS20 . . . . 47 C5
Monmouth Hill BS32 . . . . 23 E4
Monmouth Paddock
  BA2 . . . . 136 C5
Monmouth Pl BA1 . . . . 141 B2
Monmouth Rd
  Bristol BS7 . . . . 49 D4
  Keynsham BS31 . . . . 81 D5
  Pill BS20 . . . . 47 C5
Monmouth St
  Bath BA1 . . . . 141 B2
  Bristol BS3 . . . . 63 F3
Monsdale Cl BS10 . . . . 35 A3
Monsdale Dr BS10 . . . . 35 A2
Montacute Cir 4
  BS22 . . . . 105 F8
Montague Cl BS34 . . . . 36 E5
Montague Ct 4 BS2 . . . . 143 A4
Montague Flats 6
  BS2 . . . . 143 A4
Montague Hill BS2 . . . . 143 A4
Montague Hill S 5
  BS2 . . . . 143 A4
Montague Ho 4 BA1 . . . . 85 C1
Montague Pl BS6 . . . . 143 A4
Montague Rd
  Saltford BS31 . . . . 82 D2
  Shoscombe BA2 . . . . 134 E5
Montague St BS1 . . . . 143 A4
Montepelier BS23 . . . . 104 F8
Montgomery St BS3 . . . . 63 F3
MONTPELIER 49 E2
Montpelier Central 1
  BS6 . . . . 49 E1
Montpelier Ct BS6 . . . . 49 E2
Montpelier E BS23 . . . . 87 F1
Montpelier Sta BS6 . . . . 49 E1
Montreal Ave BS7 . . . . 50 A8
Montreaux Ct **9** BS16 . . . . 51 D3
Montreaux Ho **2** BS5 . . . . 65 A7
Montrose Ave BS6 . . . . 49 C1
Montrose Cotts BA1 . . . . 84 C1
Montrose Dr BS30 . . . . 66 B6
Montrose Pk BS4 . . . . 64 D2
Montroy Cl BS9 . . . . 49 C6
Montsurs Cl BA3 . . . . 138 D3
Mont The 2 BS6 . . . . 49 E1
Moon St BS2 . . . . 143 B4
Moor Croft Dr BS30 . . . . 65 F3
Moor Croft Rd BS24 . . . . 105 E3
Mordell Cl BS37 . . . . 27 D1
MOOREND 37 E2
Moorend Farm Ave
  BS11 . . . . 33 E5
Moorend Gdns BS11 . . . . 47 F7
Moorend Rd BS16 . . . . 37 D3
Moor End Spout BS48 . . . . 59 D2
Moorfield Rd BS48 . . . . 76 A6
MOORFIELDS 64 C8
Moorfields Cl BA2 . . . . 101 D3
Moorfields Ct BS48 . . . . 59 D2
Moorfields Dr BA2 . . . . 101 D4
Moorfields Ho
  Bristol BS5 . . . . 64 C7
  Nailsea BS48 . . . . 59 D2
Moorfields Rd
  Bath BA2 . . . . 101 D4
  Nailsea BS48 . . . . 59 D2
Moor Gn BS26 . . . . 125 C1
Moor Gr BS11 . . . . 48 A8
Moorgrove Ho BS9 . . . . 48 C7
Moorham Rd BS25 . . . . 108 A1
Moorhill St **17** BS5 . . . . 50 B1
Moor House Cvn Pk
  BS10 . . . . 34 A4
Moorhouse La BS10 . . . . 34 B4
Moorings The
  Bath BA2 . . . . 102 B6
  Pill BS20 . . . . 47 C4
Moor La
  Backwell BS48 . . . . 75 F6
  Clapton in G BS20 . . . . 45 E1
  Clevedon BS21 . . . . 57 G2
  Clevedon BS21 . . . . 58 A2
  Hutton BS24 . . . . 105 D3
  Tickenham BS21 . . . . 58 F4
  Tockington BS32 . . . . 24 A8
  Walton in g BS21 . . . . 58 C6
  Weston-S-M BS24 . . . . 105 F7
Moorland Cotts BS26 . . . . 124 F2
Moorland Pk BS24 . . . . 90 E5
Moorland Rd
  Bath BA2 . . . . 101 D5
  Weston-S-M BS23 . . . . 104 E4
  Yate BS37 . . . . 27 D1
MOORLANDS 101 D3
Moorlands BS48 . . . . 59 D2
Moorlands Inf Sch
  BA2 . . . . 101 D4
Moorlands Jun Sch
  BA2 . . . . 101 D3
Moorlands Rd
  Bristol, Mayfield Park
  BS16 . . . . 51 A2
  Bristol, Ridgeway BS16 . . . . . . 50 F3

Moorland St BS26 . . . . 125 C1
Moorlands The BA2 . . . . 101 D3
Moorlay Cres BS40 . . . . 94 F8
MOORLEDGE 96 E1
Moorledge La BS39,
  BS40 . . . . 113 F7
Moorledge Rd BS40 . . . . 96 B1
Moorpark Ave BS37 . . . . 27 D1
Moor Pk BS21 . . . . 57 G2
Moor Rd
  Banwell BS29 . . . . 107 B5
  Yatton BS49 . . . . 74 B2
Moorsfield BS39 . . . . 114 F3
Moorside Ave 74 B1
Moorside Ct BS21 . . . . 57 G2
Moorside Villas BS21 . . . . 57 G2
MOORSLADE 3 D1
Moorslade La GL12 . . . . 3 D1
Moravian Ct **4** BS15 . . . . 65 D8
Moravian Rd BS15 . . . . 65 D8
Moravian Rd Bsns Pk
  BS15 . . . . 65 D8
Morden Wlk BS14 . . . . 80 D7
Moreton Cl BS14 . . . . 80 A4
Moreton La BS40 . . . . 112 E2
Moreton Mans **5** BS23 . . . . . . 87 C1
Morford St BA1 . . . . 141 B4
Morgan Cl
  Saltford BS31 . . . . 82 D2
  Weston-S-M BS22 . . . . 106 B8
Morgan Pl BS48 . . . . 77 B8
Morgans Bldgs BS20 . . . . 59 F8
Morgans Hill Cl BS48 . . . . 75 D8
Morgan's La BS40 . . . . 129 F2
Morgan St BS2 . . . . 49 F1
Morgan Way BA2 . . . . 134 E7
Morley Ave BS16 . . . . 52 A4
Morley Cl
  Bristol, Little Stoke
  BS34 . . . . 36 C7
  Bristol, Staple Hill BS16 . . . . . 51 D4
Morley Rd
  Bristol, Southville BS3 . . . . 63 C4
  Bristol, Staple Hill BS16 . . . . . 51 D3
Morley Sq BS7 . . . . 49 E4
Morley St
  Bristol, Baptist Mills
  BS2 . . . . 49 F1
  Bristol, Russell Town
  BS5 . . . . 64 B7
Morley Terr
  1 Bath BA2 . . . . 101 D6
  3 Bristol BS15 . . . . 51 D1
  Radstock BA3 . . . . 134 A3
Mornington Rd **14** BS8 . . . . . . 49 A2
Morpeth Rd BS4 . . . . 79 D8
Morris Cl BA1 . . . . 86 B3
Morris La BA1 . . . . 86 B3
Morris Rd BS7 . . . . 50 A5
Morse Rd BS5 . . . . 64 C7
Morston Ct BS22 . . . . 105 C7
Mortimer Cl BA1 . . . . 84 B2
Mortimer Rd
  Bristol BS8 . . . . 142 A3
  Bristol, Filton BS34 . . . . 36 B2
MORTON 8 D3
Morton Mill BS35 . . . . 8 C3
Morton St
  Bristol BS5 . . . . 64 B7
  Thornbury BS35 . . . . 8 C4
Morton Way BS35 . . . . 8 D1
Moseley Gr BS23 . . . . 104 E2
Motorway Distribution Ctr
  BS11 . . . . 33 C2
Mountain Ash BA1 . . . . 84 D1
MOUNTAIN BOWER 8 A3
Mountain Mews 5
  BS5 . . . . 65 A7
Mountain's La BA2 . . . . 115 E6
Mountain Wood BA1 . . . . 86 C2
Mountbatten Cl
  Weston-S-M BS22 . . . . 88 E4
  Yate BS37 . . . . 27 D3
Mount Beacon BA1 . . . . 85 A1
Mount Beacon Pl 3
  BA1 . . . . 85 A1
Mount Cl BS36 . . . . 37 F8
Mount Cres BS36 . . . . 37 E5
Monteney's La GL12 . . . . 18 D7
Mount Gdns BS15 . . . . 65 C6
Mount Gr BA2 . . . . 101 B3
Mount Haviland BA1 . . . . 84 B3
MOUNT HILL 65 E6
Mount Hill Rd BS15 . . . . 65 D6
Mount Pleasant
  Bath BA2 . . . . 102 D1
  Hallen BS10 . . . . 34 C4
  Pill BS20 . . . . 47 D4
  Radstock BA3 . . . . 134 B2
Mount Pleasant Terr
  BS3 . . . . 63 C4
Mount Rd
  Bath BA1 . . . . 141 B4
  Bath, Southdown BA2 . . . . . . 101 B3
Mount The BS49 . . . . 91 C8
Mount View
  Bath, Beacon Hill BA1 . . . . 85 A1
  Bath, Southdown BA2 . . . . . . 101 B3
Mow Barton
  Bristol BS13 . . . . 78 F6
  Yate BS37 . . . . 27 D2
Mowbray Rd BS14 . . . . 80 C7
Mowcroft Rd BS13 . . . . 79 D4
Moxham Dr BS13 . . . . 79 C4
Muddy La BS22 . . . . 89 A8
Mud La BS49 . . . . 91 E7
Muirfield
  Bristol BS30 . . . . 66 A3

Muirfield *continued*
  Yate BS37 . . . . 39 E8
Mulberry Ave BS20 . . . . 45 E5
Mulberry Cl
  Backwell BS48 . . . . 76 A6
  1 Bristol BS15 . . . . 65 E8
  Portishead BS20 . . . . 45 F5
  Weston-S-M BS22 . . . . 89 A1
Mulberry Ct BS4 . . . . 64 D4
Mulberry Dr BS15 . . . . 51 F1
Mulberry Gdns 10
  BS16 . . . . 51 D3
Mulberry La BS24 . . . . 122 C6
Mulberry Mews BA1 . . . . 84 C1
Mulberry Rd BS49 . . . . 91 E3
Mulberry Wlk BS9 . . . . 48 C8
Mule St GL13 . . . . 4 A3
Muller Ave BS7 . . . . 49 F4
Muller Rd BS5, BS7 . . . . 50 B3
Mulready Cl BS7 . . . . 50 C6
Mumbles Hill BS35 . . . . 14 E7
Mumbleys La
  Thornbury, Alveston Down
  BS35 . . . . 14 E6
  Thornbury, Kington BS35 . . . . 14 E8
Munscroft Ct BS23 . . . . 104 F8
Murdock Sq BS7 . . . . 49 F7
Murford Ave BS13 . . . . 79 B4
Murford Wlk BS13 . . . . 79 B4
Murhill BA2 . . . . 120 C6
Murray St **9** BS3 . . . . 63 C4
Musgrove Cl BS11 . . . . 34 C2
Mus of Bath at Work*
  BA1 . . . . 141 B4
Mus of Costume*
  BA1 . . . . 141 B3
Mus of East Asian Art*
  BA1 . . . . 141 B3
Myrtleberry Mead
  BS22 . . . . 89 A5
Myrtle Ct BS3 . . . . 63 B4
Myrtle Dr BS11 . . . . 47 E5
Myrtle Gdns BS49 . . . . 91 C8
Myrtle Hill BS20 . . . . 47 C5
Myrtle Rd BS2 . . . . 142 C4
Myrtle St BS3 . . . . 63 B3
Myrtles The BS24 . . . . 105 D2
Myrtle Tree Cres BS22 . . . . 88 A6

N

Nags Head Hill BS5 . . . . 65 A7
NAILSEA 59 E3
Nailsea & Backwell Sta
  BS48 . . . . 75 F7
Nailsea Cl BS13 . . . . 79 A7
Nailsea Moor La BS48 . . . . 74 F7
Nailsea Park Cl BS48 . . . . 59 F2
Nailsea Pk BS48 . . . . 59 F2
Nailsea Sch BS48 . . . . 59 E1
Nailsea Wall BS21 . . . . 74 C8
Nailsea Wall La BS48 . . . . 74 E7
NAILWELL 117 D6
Naishcombe Hill BS30 . . . . 67 C7
Naishes Ave BA2 . . . . 134 D7
Naish Farm BA3 . . . . 138 D3
Naish Hill BS20 . . . . 45 F1
Naish Ho BA2 . . . . 101 A6
Naish La BS48 . . . . 77 D3
Naish's Cross BA3 . . . . 138 D3
Naite The BS35 . . . . 7 D6
Nanny Hurn's La
  BS39 . . . . 114 A1
Napier Ct BS1 . . . . 142 B1
Napier Ho BS6 . . . . 49 B2
Napier Miles Rd BS11 . . . . 48 A8
Napier Rd
  Avonmouth BS11 . . . . 33 B1
  Bath BA1 . . . . 84 A3
  Bristol, Baptist Mills BS5 . . . . . 50 B2
  Bristol, Redland BS6 . . . . 49 B2
Napier Sq BS11 . . . . 33 A1
Napier St BS5 . . . . 64 B6
Narroways Rd BS2 . . . . 50 A3
Narrow La BS16 . . . . 51 E4
Narrow Plain BS2 . . . . 143 B2
Narrow Quay BS1 . . . . 143 A2
Naseby Wlk BS5 . . . . 50 F1
Nash Cl BS31 . . . . 82 A5
Nash Dr BS7 . . . . 50 C7
Nates La BS40 . . . . 92 F1
Naunton Way BS22 . . . . 88 B2
Neads Dr BS30 . . . . 66 C5
Neale Way BS11 . . . . 33 C1
Neate Ct BS34 . . . . 36 C8
Neath Rd BS5 . . . . 64 D8
Nelson Bldgs BA1 . . . . 141 C4
Nelson Ct BS22 . . . . 88 E4
Nelson Ho
  Bath BA1 . . . . 141 A3
  6 Bristol BS1 . . . . 143 A3
  3 Bristol, Staple Hill
  BS16 . . . . 51 D5
Nelson Pl BA1 . . . . 141 C4
Nelson Pl E BA1 . . . . 141 C4
Nelson Pl W BA1 . . . . 141 A2
Nelson Rd
  Bristol BS16 . . . . 51 D5
  4 Bristol, Staple Hill
  BS16 . . . . 51 D4
Nelson St
  Bristol, Ashton Vale
  BS3 . . . . 63 A2
  Bristol BS1 . . . . 143 A3
Nelson Villas BA1 . . . . 141 A2

Nempnett St BS40 . . . . 111 D5
NEMPNETT THRUBWELL
  . . . . 111 D5
Neston Wlk BS4 . . . . 79 F8
NETHAM 64 D6
Netham Ct **22** BS5 . . . . 64 D7
Netham Gdns **21** BS5 . . . . 64 D7
Netham Park Ind Est
  BS5 . . . . 64 D6
Netham Rd BS5 . . . . 64 D6
Netham View Ind Pk **20**
  BS5 . . . . 64 D7
Netherdale Cvn Site
  BS25 . . . . 125 B6
Netherton Wood La
  BS48 . . . . 75 A6
Netherways BS21 . . . . 57 D1
Nettlestone Cl BS10 . . . . 34 E4
NETTLETON GREEN 43 B1
Nettleton Rd SN14 . . . . 43 B2
Nevalan Dr BS5 . . . . 65 A6
Neva Rd BS23 . . . . 104 E6
Neville Rd BS15 . . . . 51 E2
Nevil Rd BS7 . . . . 49 E4
Newark St BA1 . . . . 141 C1
New Bldgs
  Bristol BS16 . . . . 50 F4
  Peasedown St John
  BA2 . . . . 134 B8
New Bond St BA1 . . . . 141 C2
New Bond Street Pl
  BA1 . . . . 141 C2
Newbourne Rd BS22 . . . . 105 C8
Newbrick Rd BS34 . . . . 37 A5
NEWBRIDGE 101 B8
Newbridge Cl BS4 . . . . 64 D5
Newbridge Ct BA1 . . . . 101 B7
Newbridge Gdns BA1 . . . . 101 A8
Newbridge Hill BA1 . . . . 101 B7
Newbridge Ho BS9 . . . . 48 C4
Newbridge Prim Sch
  BA1 . . . . 101 B7
Newbridge Rd
  Bath BA1, BA2 . . . . 101 B7
  Bristol BS4 . . . . 64 E6
Newbridge Trad Est
  BS4 . . . . 64 D5
New Bristol Rd BS22 . . . . 89 A2
New Brunswick Ave
  BS5 . . . . 65 B7
NEWBURY 140 B1
Newbury Rd BS7 . . . . 50 A7
New Charlotte St BS3 . . . . 63 D4
New Charlton Way
  BS10 . . . . 35 A6
NEW CHELTENHAM 51 F1
New Cheltenham Rd
  BS15 . . . . 51 E1
New Church Rd BS23 . . . . 104 D2
Newclose La BS40 . . . . 112 D1
Newcombe Dr BS9 . . . . 48 C4
Newcombe La BS25 . . . . 125 B7
Newcombe Rd BS9 . . . . 48 F7
New Cut Bow BS21 . . . . 73 A6
Newditch La BS40 . . . . 77 C1
NEW ENGLAND 52 B7
Newent Ave BS15 . . . . 65 B7
Newfields BS40 . . . . 127 C8
New Fosseway Rd
  BS14 . . . . 80 B6
New Fosseway Sch
  BS14 . . . . 80 B6
Newfoundland Rd
  6 Bristol, Baptist Mills
  BS2 . . . . 50 A1
  Bristol BS2 . . . . 143 C4
Newfoundland St
  BS2 . . . . 143 C4
Newfoundland Way
  Bristol BS2 . . . . 143 C4
  Portishead BS20 . . . . 45 E6
Newgate BS1 . . . . 143 B3
Newhaven Pl BS20 . . . . 44 E4
Newhaven Rd BS20 . . . . 44 D4
New John St **17** BS3 . . . . 63 C2
New Kings Ct BS7 . . . . 49 C4
New Kingsley Rd BS2 . . . . 143 C2
New King St BA1 . . . . 141 B2
New La BS35 . . . . 15 C5
Newland Dr BS13 . . . . 79 A4
Newland Ho BA1 . . . . 84 F1
Newland Hts **12** BS2 . . . . 49 F2
Newland Rd
  Bristol BS13 . . . . 79 A3
  Weston-S-M BS23 . . . . 104 F6
Newlands Ave BS36 . . . . 38 C2
Newlands Cl BS20 . . . . 45 C5
Newlands Gn BS21 . . . . 57 G3
Newlands Hill BS20 . . . . 45 C4
Newlands Rd BS31 . . . . 81 D4
Newlands The BS16 . . . . 51 B2
Newland Wlk BS13 . . . . 79 A4
NEWLEAZE 36 B2
Newleaze BS34 . . . . 36 A2
New Leaze BS32 . . . . 24 C2
Newleaze Ho BS34 . . . . 36 B2
Newlyn Ave BS9 . . . . 48 D5
Newlyn Way BS37 . . . . 27 F1
Newlyn Wlk BS4 . . . . 64 B1
Newman Cl BS37 . . . . 39 B4
Newmans La BA2 . . . . 116 B7
Newmarket Ave 11
  BS1 . . . . 143 A3
New Mdws BS14 . . . . 80 A5
New Mills La GL12 . . . . 19 E1
Newnham Cl BS14 . . . . 80 D7
Newnham Pl BS34 . . . . 23 F1

New Oak Prim Sch
BS14......................80 A7
New Orchard St BA1.....141 C2
New Park Ho BS21......57 F5
NEW PASSAGE 12 A1
New Passage Rd BS35 ...12 A1
New Pit Cotts BA2.....116 F1
Newpit La BS30............6 F2
NEWPORT 4 B8
Newport Cl
  Clevedon BS21........57 E2
  Portishead BS20......44 F4
Newport Rd BS20......47 C5
Newport St BS3........63 E3
Newquay Rd
  Bristol BS4...........63 F1
  Bristol BS4...........79 F8
New Queen St
  Bristol, St George
  BS15...............65 B8
  Bristol, Windmill Hill BS3...63 E4
New Rd
  Banwell BS29.......106 E4
  Bathford BA1........86 D2
  Bristol, Filton BS34...35 F3
  Bristol, Harry Stoke
  BS34...............36 D3
  Churchill BS25......108 F4
  Clevedon BS21.......57 F2
  Freshford BA2......120 B5
  High Littleton BS39 ...115 C3
  Kilmersdon BA3.....140 E4
  Kingswood GL12 ......11 F6
  North Nibley GL11......5 E4
  Olveston BS35........14 A2
  Pensford BS39.......97 D3
  Pill BS20.............47 C4
  Rangeworthy BS37....27 A8
  Rangeworthy, Hall End
  BS37...............17 C1
  Redhill BS40........94 A4
  Shipham BS25.......108 E1
  Tytherington GL12....16 C6
New Rock Ind Est
  BA3...............138 D2
Newry Wlk BS4........63 E1
New Sandringham Ho 8
  BS7...............49 D2
New Siblands Sch BS35....8 D1
Newsome Ave BS4.....47 C4
New St
  Bath BA1...........141 B2
  Bristol BS2.........143 C3
  Charfield GL12.......11 A6
New Stadium Rd BS5....50 B2
New Station Rd BS16....51 D5
New Station Way BS16...51 A4
New Street Flats 4
  BS2...............143 C3
New Thomas St BS2 ...143 C2
NEWTON
  Bristol............64 A7
  Thornbury............8 D6
Newton Cl
  Bristol BS15.........52 A1
  West Harptree BS40 ...129 E6
Newton Dr BS30........66 A5
Newton Gn BS48.......75 C8
Newton Rd
  Bath BA2...........100 F6
  Bristol BS30.........66 A5
  Weston-S-M BS23....104 E6
NEWTON ST LOE 100 D6
Newton's Rd
  Weston-S-M BS22.....88 E3
  Weston-S-M BS22.....88 E4
Newton St BS5.......64 A8
NEWTOWN 124 D2
Newtown GL12 ....11 A5
NEW TOWN
  Bishop Sutton 113 D7
  Hinton Charterhouse ...136 F8
  Paulton 132 D6
Newtown Chapel
  BS39..............132 D5
New Tyning La BS37 ...29 C4
New Walls BS22.......62 A4
New Wlk BS15........65 B5
Niblett Cl BS15.......55 F6
Niblett's Hill BS5.....65 A6
NIBLEY 27 A1
Nibley Bsns Pk BS37 ...27 A1
NIBLEY GREEN 5 C5
Nibley La BS37.......26 F3
Nibley Rd BS11.......47 E5
Nicholas La BS5.......65 A6
Nicholas Rd BS5......50 B1
Nicholas St BS3......63 E4
Nicholettes BS30......66 D5
Nicholls Ct BS36......37 E7
Nicholls La BS36......37 E6
Nichol's Rd BS20......44 F5
Nigel Pk BS11.......47 E7
Nightingale Cl
  Bristol BS4..........64 E6
  Frampton Cotterell BS36...38 A6
  Thornbury BS35........8 D2
  Weston-S-M BS22.....88 E1
Nightingale Ct
  Bristol BS4..........64 E6
  Weston-S-M BS22.....88 E1
Nightingale Gdns
  BS48..............59 D2
Nightingale La BS36 ...38 A8
Nightingale Rise BS20 ...44 F3
Nightingale Way BA3 ...139 B8
Nile St BA1.........141 A2
Nine Tree Hill 16 BS1 ...49 E1

Ninth Ave BS7.........36 B1
Nippors Way BS24 .....124 F8
Nithsdale Rd BS23....104 E4
Nixon Trad Units
  BS24..............105 A3
No 1 Royal Cres Mus*
  BA1...............141 B3
Noah's Ark Zoo Farm*
  BS48..............60 B6
Noble Ave BS30.......66 C4
Nomis Pk BS49........91 E2
Nordrach La BS40....128 D5
Nore Gdns BS20......45 C6
Nore Park Dr BS20.....44 F5
Nore Rd BS20........45 A6
Norfolk Ave
  Bristol BS2.........143 B4
  Bristol, Montpelier BS6...49 C2
Norfolk Bldgs BA1....141 A2
Norfolk Cres BA1....141 A2
Norfolk Gr BS31......81 C4
Norfolk Hts 10 BS2 ...143 B4
Norfolk Pl BS3.......63 C3
Norfolk Rd
  Portishead BS20......45 A4
  Weston-S-M BS23....104 F5
Norland Rd BS8.......62 F8
Norley La GL9........41 D2
Norley Rd BS7........49 F7
Normanby Rd 20 BS5 ...50 B1
Norman Gr BS15.......51 D2
Norman Rd
  Bristol, Baptist Mills
  BS2...............50 A2
  Bristol, Warmley BS30...66 B8
  Saltford BS31........82 E3
Norman's Cotts BS36 ...37 D7
Normans The BA1.....85 F1
Normans Way BS20 ....46 E7
Normanton Rd 16 BS8 ...49 A2
Norrisville Rd 8 BS6 ...49 E1
Northampton Bldgs
  BA1...............141 B4
Northampton Ho BS48 ...60 D3
Northampton St BA1 ...141 B4
Northanger Ct 5
  BA2...............141 C3
Northavon Bsns Ctr
  BS37..............27 C3
North Chew Terr BS40 ...96 B3
North Cnr 8 BS3......63 B3
NORTH COMMON 66 D6
North Contemporis
  BS8...............142 A3
NORTH CORNER 25 F1
Northcote Ho BS8 ....142 A3
Northcote Rd
  Bristol, Clifton BS8 ....48 F1
  Bristol, Crew's Hole BS5...64 E7
  Bristol, Mangotsfield
  BS16..............51 F6
North Croft BS9......50 B1
North Croft BS30.....66 D4
North Ct BS32........24 D3
North Devon Rd BS16...51 A5
North Down Cl BS25...125 F8
North Down La BS25...125 F8
North Dro BS48........59 A2
North East Rd BS35....8 C2
NORTHEND 114 E5
North End
  Luckington SN14.....31 E5
  Midsomer Norton BA3...133 B2
NORTH END 73 F3
Northend Ave BS15....51 D2
Northend Gdns BS15...51 D2
Northend Rd BS15....51 E1
North End Rd BS49....73 F3
Northern Way BS21...57 H3
NORTHFIELD 134 B1
Northfield
  Radstock BA3.......134 A3
  Timsbury BA2......116 C3
  Winsley BA15.......120 F7
  Yate BS37...........39 D8
Northfield Ave BS15...65 D5
Northfield Ho
  Bath BA1...........84 F1
  10 Bristol BS3.......63 C4
Northfield La SN14....55 F1
Northfield Rd
  Bristol BS5..........65 B7
  Portishead BS20......44 E3
Northfields BA1......84 F1
Northfields Cl BA1....84 F1
Northgate St BA1....141 C2
North Gr BS20........47 C4
North Green St 12 BS8 ...62 F6
North Hills Cl BS24 ...105 B2
North La
  Bath BA2...........102 D5
  Nailsea BS48........59 A8
  2 Weston-S-M BS23 ...104 E7
Northleach Wlk BS11...47 F5
North Leaze BS41.....62 B2
Northleaze CE Prim Sch
  BS41..............62 B1
Northleigh Ave BS22...88 C1
North Mdws BS26....134 E8
Northmead Ave BA3 ...132 F2
Northmead Cl BA3....132 F2
Northmead La BS37...26 D6
Northmead Rd BA3....132 F2
NORTH NIBLEY 5 D4
North Nibley CE Prim Sch
  GL11...............5 D5

Northover Ct BS35.....22 E6
Northover Rd BS9......35 A1
North Par
  Bath BA2...........141 C2
  Yate BS37............27 E2
North Parade Bldgs 6
  BA1...............141 C2
North Parade Pas 7
  BA1...............141 C2
North Pk
  Bath BA2...........102 B6
  Park BS15...........51 E1
North Rd
  Banwell BS29.......107 A3
  Bath, Bathwick BA2...102 C6
  Bath, Combe Down BA2...102 B2
  7 Bristol BS3........63 A4
  Bristol, Montpelier BS6...49 C2
  Bristol, Stoke Gifford
  BS34..............36 F4
  Leigh Woods BS8.....62 D7
  Lympsham BS24.....122 D2
  Midsomer Norton BA3...133 A1
  Thornbury BS35........8 C2
  Timsbury BA2......116 C2
  Winterbourne BS36.....37 F7
  Yate BS37...........27 B3
  Yate, Engine Common
Northridge Bsns Ctr
  BS37..............27 C2
North Road Com Prim Sch
  BS37..............27 B4
North Side Rd BS48....93 F8
North Somerset Mus*
  BS23..............104 E8
North St
  Bristol BS1..........143 A2
  Bristol, Downend BS16...51 E5
  Bristol, Oldland Common
  BS30..............66 C4
  Bristol, Southville BS3...63 B3
  Nailsea BS48........59 B1
  Norton St Philip BA2...136 E4
  Weston-S-M BS23....104 E8
  Wickwar GL12........18 A6
NORTH STOKE 83 C6
North Stoke La BS30...83 B8
Northumberland Bldgs 1
  BA1...............141 B2
Northumberland Pl 9
  BA1...............141 C2
Northumberland Rd
  BS6...............49 D2
Northumbria Dr BS9 ...49 B4
North View
  Bristol BS6..........49 A4
  Bristol, Mangotsfield
  BS16..............51 E5
  Midsomer Norton BA3...133 B2
  Radstock BA3.......133 F1
North View Cl BA2....101 B5
North View Dr BS29...107 A2
NORTHVILLE 36 A1
Northville Rd BS7.....36 A1
North Way
  Bath BA2...........101 A5
  Bristol BS34.........36 B4
  Midsomer Norton BA3...133 A1
NORTH WESTON 45 C2
NORTH WICK 12 E2
North Wick BS39......96 D8
Northwick Gdns BS39...113 D4
Northwick Rd
  Bristol BS7..........49 F8
  Chew Magna BS39, BS41...96 D7
NORTH WIDCOMBE 113 B1
North Wlk BS37.......27 E1
Northwoods Wlk BS10...35 D3
North Worle Sh Ctr
  BS22..............89 B2
NORTON 88 D4
Norton Cl
  Bristol BS15.........65 F7
  Chew Magna BS40....96 B8
Norton Grange BA2 ...136 E5
NORTON HAWKFIELD ...96 F6
NORTON HILL 139 B7
Norton Hill Sch BA3 ...139 B8
Norton Ho
  7 Bristol BS1.......143 B1
  Bristol, Patchway BS34 ...23 F1
Norton La
  Chew Magna BS39,
  BS40..............96 D5
  Wellow BA2.........136 B7
  Weston-S-M BS24.....88 C4
  Whitchurch BS14......80 C2
NORTON MALREWARD
  ....97 B7
Norton Radstock Coll
  BA3..............133 F2
Norton Rd BS4.......64 A3
NORTON ST PHILIP ...136 F4
Norton St Philip CE Fst
  Sch BA2...........136 E4
NORTON'S WOOD 58 C5
Nortons Wood La
  BS21..............58 A5
Norwich Dr BS4......64 E6
Norwood Ave BA2....126 F7
Norwood Farm* BA2...136 A5
Norwood Gr BS20.....44 F5
Notgrove Cl BS22.....88 B2
Nottingham Rd BS7...49 E3
Nottingham St BS3...63 F3

Nova Scotia Pl BS1....142 A1
Nova Way BS11.......33 B1
Novers Cres BS4......79 C8
Novers Hill BS4.......79 C8
Novers Hill Trad Est
  BS3...............63 C1
Novers La BS4........79 D8
NOVERS PARK 79 D8
Novers Park Cl BS4....63 C1
Novers Park Dr BS4....79 C8
Novers Park Rd BS4....79 D8
Novers Rd BS4........79 C8
Nowhere La BS48......60 A1
Nugent Hill BS6......49 D1
Nunney Cl BS31.......82 A2
NUPDOWN 2 A4
Nupdown Rd BS35......1 E5
Nurseries The GL12 ...16 B5
Nursery Gdns BS10....35 A3
Nursery Rise BA3.....138 E4
Nursery The BS3......63 B3
Nutfield Gr BS34......36 B1
Nutgrove Ave BS3.....63 E3
Nutgrove La BS40.....96 A4
Nuthatch Dr BS16.....50 F6
Nuthatch Gdns BS16...51 A6
Nutwell Rd BS22......88 E2
Nutwell Sq BS22......88 E2
NYE 107 E8
Nye Dro BS24........107 E8
Nye Rd BS25........107 F5
Nympsfield BS15......51 E2

O

Oak Ave BA2.........101 C3
Oak Cl
  Bristol BS34.........36 D7
  Yate BS37............27 D3
Oak Ct
  Bristol BS14.........80 A5
  Weston-S-M BS23....89 C3
Oakdale Ave BS16.....51 D8
Oakdale Cl BS16......51 E8
Oakdale Ct BS16......51 D7
Oakdale Gdns BS22...88 F2
Oakdale Rd
  Bristol BS16.........80 A8
  Bristol, Downend BS16...51 D8
Oakdale Wlk BS16....51 E7
Oakdene Ave BS5.....50 D3
Oak Dr BS20.........45 B4
Oakenhill Rd BS4.....64 E2
Oakenhill Wlk BS4....64 E2
Oakes La GL9........42 B5
Oakfield Cl BA1......101 D8
Oakfield Gr BS8.....142 B4
Oakfield Mans BS8 ...142 B4
Oakfield Pl BS8......142 B4
Oakfield Rd
  Bristol BS8..........142 B4
  Bristol, Kingswood BS15...65 D7
  Keynsham BS31......81 F2
Oakford Ave BS23....104 F8
Oakford La
  Batheaston SN14.....86 A8
  Marshfield SN14......70 B2
Oak Gr BS20.........47 C5
Oakhanger Dr BS11....34 B1
Oakhill BS24........105 A2
Oakhill Ave BS30......66 C2
Oakhill Cl BS48.......60 B1
Oakhill La BS10.......34 C4
Oakhill Rd BA2.......101 F2
Oak Ho BS13.........79 D4
Oakhurst Rd BS9......48 F5
Oakland Dr BS24......105 A4
Oakland Rd
  Bristol, Crew's Hole
  BS5...............64 E8
  6 Bristol, Redland BS6 ...49 B1
Oaklands
  Clevedon BS21........57 E4
  Paulton BS39.......132 E4
  Temple Cloud BS39...114 E1
Oaklands Cl BS16.....52 B5
Oaklands Dr
  Almondsbury BS32.....24 A4
  Bristol, Frenchay BS16 ...51 A7
  Bristol, Oldland Common
  BS30..............66 C2
Oaklands Rd BS16.....52 A5
Oakleaze BS36........38 D7
Oakleaze Rd BS35......8 B1
Oakleigh Ave BS5.....50 D1
Oakleigh Cl BS48.....76 B5
Oakleigh Gdns BS30...66 C2
Oakley
  Bath BA2...........102 E5
  Clevedon BS21........73 B8
Oakley Rd BS7........49 F5
Oak Lo BS37.........39 D8
Oakmeade Pk BS4.....64 B2
Oak Rd
  Bristol BS7..........49 E5
  Colerne SN14........70 F5
  Winscombe BS25....125 A8
Oakridge Cl
  Bristol BS15.........66 A7
  Winscombe BS25....125 B7
Oakridge La BS25....125 C6
Oaksey Gr BS48......141 B8

Oaks The
  Bristol BS7..........49 E4
  Nailsea BS48........60 A2
  Winford BS40........94 F7
Oak Terr BA3........133 D1
Oak Tree Ave BS16....53 B4
Oak Tree Cl BS15.....65 C3
Oaktree Cres BS32.....24 C2
Oaktree Ct BS11......47 E7
Oaktree Gdns BS13...78 E5
Oaktree Pk BS24.....105 E5
Oaktree Pk BS22......89 C3
Oak Tree Wlk BS31....81 D3
Oakwood Ave BS9.....49 C6
Oakwood Gdns BS36...38 E7
Oakwood Pk BS16.....51 A3
Oakwood Rd BS9......49 B6
Oatfield BS48.........76 F1
Oatlands Ave BS14....80 A6
Oatley Ho BS9........49 A5
Oban Rd BS7.........49 F5
Oberon Ave BS5......50 E2
Observatory Field
  BS25..............125 B8
Observatory The BS22...88 D3
ODD DOWN 101 D2
Odeon Bldgs BS23....104 E7
Odins Rd BA2.......101 D1
Okebourne Cl BS10....35 B4
Okebourne Rd BS10....35 B4
Okeford Ho BS9......48 F7
Old Acre Rd BS14......80 A4
Old Ashley Hill BS6....49 F2
Old Aust Rd BS32.....24 C5
Old Banwell Rd BS24...106 B4
Old Barn La BS40......94 A5
Old Barrow Hill BS11...47 D7
Old Bond St 4 BA1....141 B2
Old Bread St BS2.....143 C2
Old Brewery The BS20...47 C4
Old Brewhouse The
  BA1...............84 B2
Oldbridge Rd BS14....80 C3
Old Bristol Rd
  Ridge BS40.........129 A3
  Weston-S-M BS22.....89 A2
Oldbury Chase BS30....66 A2
Oldbury Court Dr BS16....51 B6
Oldbury Court Prim Sch
  BS16..............51 C7
Oldbury Court Rd
  BS16..............51 A5
Oldbury La
  Thornbury BS35.......8 B4
  Wick BS30...........67 D5
OLDBURY NAITE 7 E7
OLDBURY-ON-SEVERN
  ....7 C6
Oldbury-on-Severn Prim
  Sch BS35............7 B5
Old Butchers Yd
  BS26..............125 C2
Old Chapel BA1......141 C4
Old Chapel La BS48...74 F7
Old Chelsea La BS8....61 C4
Old Church St BS30....66 D7
Old Church Rd
  Axbridge BS26.....125 C1
  Clevedon BS21........57 E3
  Nailsea BS48........75 D8
  Weston-S-M BS23....104 D2
Old Coach Rd BS26....124 E2
Old Dairy Ct BS21.....57 G3
Old Dairy The BA2....101 D4
OLD DOWN 14 D4
Old Down Hill BS32....14 B2
Old Down Rd GL9......42 C8
Old Drill Hall The
  BS2...............143 C3
Old England Way BA2...134 E8
Old Farm La BS5......65 B6
Old Ferry Rd BA2.....101 C6
Oldfield BS21.........57 G1
Oldfield Girls Sch BA1 ...83 F1
Oldfield La BA2......101 E4
OLDFIELD PARK 101 E4
Oldfield Park Inf Sch
  BA2..............101 D6
Oldfield Park Jun Sch
  BA2..............101 C4
Oldfield Park Sta
  BA2..............101 D6
Oldfield Pl BS8......62 F5
Oldfield Rd
  Bath BA2...........141 A1
  Bristol BS8.........142 A1
Oldfields La BS35......25 D7
Old Forge The BA2....117 B4
Old Forge Way BA2....134 E8
Old Fosse Rd BA2....101 C1
Old Frome Rd BA2....118 C8
Old Gloucester Rd
  Alveston BS35........15 B5
  Bristol, Stoke Gifford
  BS16..............37 B4
  Hambrook BS16.......37 D7
  North Corner BS36....25 D3
  Thornbury BS35........9 B2
Old Hill
  Winford BS40........94 D6
  Wrington BS40........92 F3
Old House The BA2....120 C5
Old Hundred La GL9....41 D2

Old Junction Rd BS23...105 B5
Old King St BA1 ....141 B3
Old King Street Ct
 BS1.....................143 B3
Old La
 Bristol BS16...........52 C6
 Farmborough BA2 .....116 A6
 Nailsea BS21...........59 C4
OLDLAND 66 A3
OLDLAND COMMON ...66 D3
Oldland Common Sta*
 BS30...................66 C3
Oldlands Ave BS36.....38 C6
Old Malthouse The
 BS2....................143 C4
Old Manor Cl GL12 ....11 A5
Old Market Rdbt BS2 ..143 C3
Old Market St BS2 ....143 C3
Oldmead Wlk BS13 ....78 E7
Old Midford Rd BA2 ...119 B7
Old Millard's Hill BA3...133 B3
Old Mill Cl BS37.......39 B4
Old Mill Rd BS20 ......45 D5
OLD MILLS 132 D3
Old Mills Ind Est
 BS39..................132 E2
Old Mills La BS39......132 D3
Old Mill Way BS24 ....106 A8
OLDMIXON 105 B1
Oldmixon Cres BS24...105 A3
Oldmixon Prim Sch
 BS24...................105 A2
Oldmixon Rd BS24.....105 B1
Old Mixon Rd BS24....105 C1
Old Newbridge Hill
 BA1....................101 A8
Old Orch BA1..........141 C3
Old Orchard St BA1....141 C2
Old Park Hill BS2......142 C3
Old Park Rd
 Bristol BS11...........47 D7
 Clevedon BS21.........57 G4
Old Pit Rd BA3 ....139 C8
Old Pit Terr BA3 ....133 E4
Old Pk BS2 ....142 C3
Old Police Sta The
 BS4....................64 A3
Old Pooles Yd BS4.....64 E2
Old Post Office La
 BS23..................104 D8
Old Priory Rd BS20....47 B4
Old Quarry BA2........101 D2
Old Quarry Rd BS11....47 E7
Old Quarry Rise BS11..47 E7
Old Rd
 Pensford BS39.........97 E3
 Radstock BA3 ....134 C1
Old Rectory Rd GL12 ..11 B4
Old School Cl BS25....108 F4
Old School Ct SN14 ...70 A8
Old School Hill BA2....118 F7
Old School Ho BS4 ....64 B2
Old School Ho The
 BA1....................141 B4
Old School House The
 BS2....................143 C4
Old School La BS24....122 C6
Old Smiths Yd BS15....65 D5
Old Sneed Ave BS9....48 D4
Old Sneed Cotts BS9...48 E4
Old Sneed Pk BS9 .....48 D4
Old Sneed Rd BS9.....48 D4
OLD SODBURY 41 B8
Old Sodbury CE Prim Sch
 BS37..................41 B8
Old Station Cl BS40...92 D1
Old Station Rd BS40...57 G3
Old Tannery The [20]
 BS2....................143 C3
Old Tarnwell BS39.....97 B2
Old Tk BA2 ....119 F7
Old Vicarage Ct BS14 ..80 C4
Old Vicarage Gn BS31..81 E6
Old Vicarage Pl BS8 ...49 A1
Old Vicarage The
 Bristol BS13...........78 F6
 Bristol, Montpelier BS6...49 E1
Oldville Ave BS21......57 F2
Old Walcot Sch The
 BA1....................141 C3
Old Wall BS24 ....121 D5
Old Water Gdns The
 BS40..................110 E2
Old Wells Rd BA2......101 F3
Old Wesleyan Chapel The
 BS30...................66 B5
Old Weston Rd
 Congresbury BS49.....91 B5
 Flax Bourton BS48....77 B8
Oldwood La BS37......27 B8
Old Work Ho The BS55..64 E8
Olive Gdns BS35.......14 F4
Oliver Brooks Rd BA3...138 E7
OLVESTON 14 B3
Olveston CE Prim Sch
 BS35...................14 A3
Olveston Rd BS7.......49 E5
Olympus Cl BS34 ......36 D6
Olympus Rd BS34......35 D7
Onega Ctr BA1 ....141 A3
Onega Terr BA1........141 A3
Oolite Dr BA2 ....101 D1
Oolite Rd BA2 ....101 D1
Oram Ct BS30 ....65 F4

ORANGE END 19 C4
Orange Gr BA1 ....141 C2
Orange St BS2.........143 C4
Orchard Ave
 Bristol BS1............142 C2
 Midsomer Norton BA3...132 F1
 Portishead BS21......58 E4
 Thornbury BS35........8 D1
Orchard Bvd BS30 .....66 B4
Orchard Cl
 Banwell BS29..........107 B3
 Bishop Sutton BS39...113 C3
 Bristol, Kingswood BS15...65 E8
 Bristol, Westbury on T
  BS9..................48 F5
 Charfield GL12.........11 A5
 Congresbury BS49.....91 D4
 Felton BS40............94 C8
 Flax Bourton BS48....77 A8
 Keynsham BS31........81 D6
 Locking BS24..........105 F4
 Portishead BS20......45 D5
 Weston-S-M, Kewstoke
  BS22................88 B2
 Weston-S-M, Worle
  BS22................88 B2
 Westwood BA15.......120 F3
 Winterbourne BS36....37 E5
 Wrington BS40.........92 E2
 Yate BS37.............27 F2
Orchard Cotts
 [18] Bristol BS16......51 D5
 Keynsham BS31........81 B2
 Timsbury BA2..........116 F1
Orchard Cres BS11.....47 D7
Orchard Ct
 Bristol BS9............48 C3
 Bristol, Filton BS34...36 A2
 [18] Bristol, Pile Marsh
  BS5..................64 D7
 Claverham BS49.......74 F1
 Yate BS37.............27 B3
Orchard Dr
 Aust BS35.............13 A7
 Bristol BS13...........79 A6
 Sandford BS25........108 A4
Orchard End BS40.....129 F4
Orchard Gate BS32....24 C2
Orchard Gdns
 Bristol BS15...........65 E8
 Paulton BS39.........132 E6
Orchard Grange BS35...8 B2
Orchard Ho
 BS23..................64 F8
 Weston-S-M BS22.....88 F2
Orchard La BS1........142 C2
Orchard Lea
 [6] Alveston BS35.....15 A5
 Pill BS20...............47 D4
Orchard Lo BA2........102 F8
Orchard Pk BS14 ......80 D4
Orchard Pl [1] BS23...104 E7
Orchard Rd
 Axbridge BS26.........125 C1
 Backwell BS48.........76 A6
 Bristol, Ashley Down BS7...49 E4
 Bristol, Crew's Hole BS5...64 F8
 Bristol, Kingswood BS15...65 E8
 Clevedon BS21.........57 F2
 Frampton Cotterell BS36...38 D7
 Hutton BS24...........105 E2
 Long Ashton BS41.....61 F1
 Nailsea BS48..........59 D1
 Paulton BS39.........132 E6
 Pucklechurch BS16....53 B5
Orchard Rise BS35.....14 A3
Orchard Sq BS5........64 D7
Orchard St
 Bristol BS1............142 C2
 Weston-S-M BS23.....104 E8
Orchards The
 Bristol, Kingswood
  BS15................65 F7
 Bristol, Shirehampton
  BS11................47 E6
Orchard Terr [5] BA2..101 B6
Orchard The
 Banwell BS29..........107 A3
 Bath, Combe Down BA2...102 B1
 Bath, Newbridge BA1...101 A7
 Bristol BS34...........36 F5
 Corston BA2..........100 B8
 Frampton Cotterell BS36...38 C8
 Freshford BA2........120 C5
 Locking BS24..........106 A5
 Pensford BS39.........97 E4
 Pill BS20...............47 C4
 Tytherington GL12....116 B5
 Upper Stanton Drew
  BS39................97 A2
Orchard Vale
 Bristol BS15...........65 F7
 Midsomer Norton BA3...132 F1
Orchard Way BA2......134 D7
Orchard Wlk
 Churchill BS25........108 E4
 Kingswood GL12.......11 F4
Orchid Dr BA2 ....101 C1
Oriel Gdns BA1........85 C2
Oriel Gr BA2 ....101 B4
Orion Dr BS34 ....36 D6
Orland Way BS30......66 C3
Orlebar Gdns BS11....34 B2
Ormerod Rd BS9 ......48 E5
Ormonds Cl BS32......24 E1
Ormsley Cl BS34.......36 C8
Orpen Gdns BS7.......50 B5

Orpen Pk BS32........24 B3
Orpheus Ave BS34 ....36 D6
Orwell Dr BS31........82 A4
Orwell St BS3 ....63 E3
Osborne Ave
 Bristol BS7............49 F3
 Weston-S-M BS23.....104 F7
Osborne Cl BS34 ......36 D4
Osborne Rd
 Bath BA1..............101 B7
 Bristol, Clifton BS8...49 A1
 Bristol, Southville BS3...63 C4
 Severn Beach BS35...22 A7
 Weston-S-M BS23.....104 F7
Osborne Terr [16] BS3...63 B2
Osborne Villas BS2....142 C4
Osborne Wallis Ho
 BS8....................142 A1
Osmond Rd [2] BS24...105 F7
Osprey Cl BS14........79 D5
Osprey Gdns BS22.....88 F1
Osprey Pk BS35........8 D3
Osprey Rd [15] BS5....64 C7
Ostlings La BA1........86 B2
Otago Terr [5] BA1....85 C2
Ottawa Rd BS23.......104 F3
Otterford Cl BS14......80 B5
Otter Rd [8] BS21......57 G1
Ottrells Mead BS32....24 C3
Our Lady of Lourdes RC
 Prim Sch BS15........65 E7
Our Lady of the Rosary RC
 Prim Sch BS11........48 A8
OVAL THE 101 C4
Oval The BA2..........101 C4
OVER 23 D2
Overdale
 Clandown BA3........133 E5
 Peasedown St John
  BA2.................116 F3
Overhill BS20..........47 D4
Over La BS35 ....23 D2
Overndale Rd BS16 ....51 C6
Overndale Sch BS37...41 A7
Overnhill Rd BS16......51 D5
Overnhurst Ct [2] BS16...51 D5
Overstables La BS21...57 F3
Overton [5] BS4........64 D1
Overton Rd BS6.......49 E2
Owen Dr BS8..........61 B4
Owen Gr BS9...........49 B5
Owen Henry Ho BS2...50 A6
Owen St [2] BS5.......64 B8
Owls Head Rd BS15...65 E6
Oxbarton St BS34......36 F5
Oxenham Ct BS5......64 D8
Oxen Leaze BS32......24 E2
Oxford Pl
 Bath BA2..............102 C2
 [2] Bristol, Clifton BS8...62 F6
 [14] Bristol, Upper Easton
  BS5..................50 B1
Oxford Rd BS3.........104 D7
Oxford Row BA1.......141 B3
Oxford Sq BS24........106 B6
Oxford St
 Bristol BS2............143 C2
 [7] Bristol, Redfield BS5...64 C7
 Bristol, The Dings BS2...64 A4
 Bristol, Tyndall's Park BS2,
  BS6.................142 C4
 Bristol, Windmill Hill BS3...63 F4
 Weston-S-M BS23.....104 D7
Oxhouse Gdns BS10...34 E3
Oxhouse Ind Est BS22...89 A5
Oxhouse La
 Failand BS8...........61 B6
 Winford BS40.........94 D6
Oxleaze BS13..........79 D4
Oxleaze La BS41.......78 E3
Oxney Pl BA2..........134 C7
Ozenhay BS39.........130 E6
Ozleworth BS15........66 A8

P

Pack Horse La BA2....118 F7
Pacquet Ho BS20......47 D5
Paddock Cl
 Bristol, Emerson's Green
  BS16................52 C6
Paddock Gdn BS14....79 F4
Paddock Gdns BS35...15 A5
Paddock Pk BS22......89 B2
Paddocks The
 Bath BA2..............102 B1
 Thornbury BS35.......38 A1
 Sandford BS25........108 C4
 Thornbury BS35........8 D1
 Weston-S-M BS23.....104 D2
Paddock The
 Banwell BS29..........107 A3
 Clevedon BS21........57 F2
 Corston BA2..........100 B7
 Portishead BS20......45 D4
Paddock Woods BA2...102 D2
Padfield Cl BA2........101 B5
Padleigh Hill BA2......101 B2
Padmore Ct [7] BS5...64 D7
Pagans Hill BS40......95 D2
Page Ct BS16..........51 F4
Page Rd BS16.........51 F4
Page's Ct BS49........91 C8

Pages Mead BS11......47 C8
Painswick Ave BS34 ...36 B8
Painswick Dr BS37.....27 E1
Paintworks BS4 ....64 B4
Palace Yard Mews
 BA1...................141 B2
Palmdale Cl BS30......66 A3
Palmer Ave BS35......22 C3
Palmer Row [7] BS23...104 E8
Palmers Cl BS30.......66 A6
Palmer's Elm BS24....90 B4
Palmers La BA2........117 B3
Palmers Leaze BS34...37 A6
Palmer St BS23........104 E8
Palmerston Rd BS6....49 C4
Palmerston St BS3.....63 C3
Palmer's Way BS24...105 D2
Palmyra Rd BS3.......63 B2
Pamela Ho [9] BS16...51 D5
Panoramic The BS1....142 C3
Pantile The [18] BS3...63 C3
Parade Ct BS5.........50 F2
Parade The
 [1] Bath BA2.........101 B6
 Bristol, Bishopsworth
  BS13................79 A6
 Bristol, Shirehampton
  BS11................47 E6
 Chipping Sodbury BS37...28 A1
Paradise Row BS39....98 A6
Paragon Ct [13] BS23...87 C1
Paragon Rd BS23......87 C1
Paragon Sch The
 BA2...................102 A3
Paragon The
 Bath BA1..............141 C3
 Bristol BS8............62 F6
Parbrook Ct BS14.....80 B5
Parfitt's Hill [8] BS5...64 F6
Parish Brook Rd BS48...59 B2
Parish The BS3........142 B1
Park Ave
 Bath BA2..............141 B1
 Bristol BS32...........24 A2
 Bristol, Eastville BS5...50 D3
 Bristol, Rose Green BS5...64 E8
 Bristol, Windmill Hill BS3...63 E3
 Frampton Cotterell BS36...38 B6
 Winterbourne BS36....37 F2
 Yatton BS49...........74 B1
Park Batch BS40.......110 F3
Park Cl
 Bristol, Cadbury Heath
  BS30................66 B5
 Bristol, Kingswood BS15...65 E7
 Keynsham BS31........81 D5
 Paulton BS39.........132 D5
Park Cnr BS39.........132 D6
PARK CORNER 120 A4
Park Cres
 Bristol, Cadbury Heath
  BS30................66 B5
 Bristol, Frenchay BS16...37 C1
 Bristol, Rose Green BS5...64 E8
Park Ct [5] BS23......104 E5
Park End BS25.........108 E8
Park End BS29.........106 E4
Parkers Ave BS30......67 C7
Parkers Barton BS5....64 A4
Parker's Cl BS16.......35 E4
Parker St [5] BS3......63 B3
Parkes Rd BS24........106 C5
Park Farm Bsns Pk
 BS40...................94 B7
Park Farm Ct [19] BS30...65 F4
Park Farm Village Gn
 BS36...................38 B6
PARKFIELD 53 A7
Parkfield BS26.........125 D1
Parkfield Ave BS5......64 D7
Parkfield Gdns BS39...113 D3
Parkfield Rank BS16...53 A7
Parkfield Rd BS16.....53 A6
Park Gdns BA1........101 D8
Park Gr BS9...........49 C5
Park Hill BS11.........47 F6
Park Ho BA2 ....101 E4
Parkhouse La BS31....81 C2
Parkhurst Ave [4] BS16...51 B4
Parkhurst Rd BS23....105 A7
Park La
 Bath BA1..............101 D7
 Blagdon BS40.........110 F3
 Bristol BS2............142 C3
 Faulkland BA3.........135 B1
 Frampton Cotterell BS36...38 B6
 North Nibley GL11.....5 E7
Parklands
 Bristol BS8............142 A4
 Bristol, Kingswood BS15...65 E8
 High Littleton BS39...115 D2
Parklands Ave BS22...89 A4
Parklands Rd BS3.....62 E4
Park Lawn Ct BS34....23 E1
Park Leaze BS34......36 B8
Park Pl
 Bath BA1..............141 A4
 Bristol, Kingsdown BS8...142 B3
 Bristol, Victoria Park
  BS2.................142 C3
 Weston-S-M BS23.....104 D8
Park Rd
 Bath BA1..............101 B7

Park Rd continued
 Bristol BS3............142 B1
 Bristol, Cadbury Heath
  BS30................66 B5
 Bristol, Kingswood BS15...65 D8
 Bristol, Northville BS7...36 A1
 Bristol, Shirehampton
  BS11................47 F6
 Bristol, Staple Hill BS16...51 E5
 Bristol, Stapleton BS16...50 D5
 Clevedon BS21........57 F4
 Congresbury BS49.....91 E3
 Keynsham BS31........81 E4
 Leyhill GL12...........10 B4
 Paulton BS39.........132 D5
 Thornbury BS35........8 B2
Park Row
 Bristol BS1............142 C3
 Frampton Cotterell BS36...38 A8
Parkside Ave BS36.....37 E6
Parkside Gdns BS5....50 B4
Park St
 Bath BA1..............141 A4
 Bristol BS1............142 C3
 Bristol BS4............64 A4
 Bristol, Crew's Hole BS5...64 F8
 Bristol, Totterdown BS4...64 A3
 Hawkesbury Upton GL9...20 A2
 Iron Acton BS37.......26 C3
Parkstone Ave BS7....49 F6
Park Street Ave BS1...142 C3
Park Street Mews
 BA1...................141 A4
Park The
 Bristol BS32...........24 C3
 Bristol, Frenchay BS16...37 B1
 Bristol, Kingswood BS15...65 E8
 Bristol, Willsbridge BS30...66 B1
 Keynsham BS31........81 E6
 Portishead BS20......45 F5
 Yatton BS49...........74 B1
Park View
 Bath BA1..............101 D6
 Bristol, Kingswood BS15...65 E7
 Bristol, Southville BS3...63 C4
 Yate BS37.............39 E8
Park View Ave BS35...8 C2
Park View Ct BS16....51 E5
Park View Terr BS5....64 E8
Park Villas BS23.......104 D8
Parkwall Cres BS30....65 F4
Parkwall Prim Sch
 BS30...................66 A4
Parkwall Rd BS30......66 A4
Parkway
 Bristol BS34...........37 A4
 Timsbury BA2.........116 E2
Park Way
 Bristol BS30...........66 B5
 Midsomer Norton BA3...139 A8
Park Way BS22.........89 B1
Parkway La BS39......36 A4
Parkway Trad Est [16]
 BS2....................49 F2
Park Wlk BS20.........47 D4
Park Wood Cl BS14....79 F4
Parliament St BS4.....64 A4
Parnall Cres BS37.....27 C2
Parnall Rd BS16.......51 A3
Parnall Road Ind Est
 BS16...................51 A3
Parnell Rd
 Bristol BS16...........50 E7
 Clevedon BS21........57 F3
Parry Cl BA2...........101 B4
Parry's Cl BS9.........48 E5
Parrys Gr BS9.........48 E5
Parry's La BS9.........48 F5
Parslow Barton [4] BS5...65 A7
Parsonage Cl BS40....94 F6
Parsonage Ct BS20...45 D4
Parsonage La
 Axbridge BS26........125 E2
 Bath BA1..............141 B2
 Chilcompton BA3.....138 C4
 Pensford BS39........97 D6
 Winford BS40.........94 F6
Parsonage Rd BS41....62 C2
Parsons Ave BS34.....36 F5
Parsons Gn
 Clevedon BS21........73 C8
 Weston-S-M BS22.....89 A3
Parsons Mead BS48...75 F7
Parsons Paddock BS14...80 A7
Parson Street Prim Sch
 BS3....................63 C2
Parson Street Sta BS3...63 B2
Parsons Way BS25....124 C6
Parsons Wlk BS30.....66 D7
Partis Coll BA1.........101 A8
Partis Way BA1.........101 A8
Partition St BS1........142 C2
Partridge Cl
 Weston-S-M BS22.....88 F1
 Yate BS37.............27 F4
Partridge Dr BS16.....51 C6
Partridge Rd BS16.....53 C4
Passage Leaze BS11...47 D6
Passage Rd
 Aust BS35.............12 F2
 Bristol, Brentry BS10...34 F3
 Bristol, Westbury on Trym
  BS9.................34 F1
Passage Road Brentry Hill
 BS9, BS10............35 A2
Passage St BS2........143 B2

Pastures Ave BS22 . . . . 89 C3
Pastures The BA15 . . . . 120 E3
Patch Croft BS21 . . . . 73 C8
Patch Ct BS16 . . . . 52 A8
Patch Elm La BS37 . . . . 26 F7
Patch La BS37 . . . . 27 A8
PATCHWAY 24 B2
Patchway Brook BS32 . . 24 C2
Patchway CE Prim Sch BS34 . . . . 24 C1
Patchway Com Coll BS32 . . . . 24 B1
Patchway Sta BS34 . . . . 36 C6
Patchway Trad Est BS34 . . . . 35 E7
Patterson Ho 8 BS1 . . . . 143 B1
Paul Alan Ho 21 BS5 . . . . 64 C7
Paulman Gdns BS41 . . . . 77 F8
Paulmont Rise BS39 . . . . 114 C1
Paul's Cswy BS49 . . . . . . 91 D4
Paul St BS2 . . . . 142 C4
Paulto' Hill BA3, BS39 . . 133 B6
PAULTON 132 F5
Paulton Dr BS7 . . . . 49 C4
Paulton Inf Sch BS39 . . . 132 E5
Paulton Jun Sch BS39 . . . . 132 E5
Paulton La BA2, BA3 . . 133 D7
Paulton Meml Hospl BS39 . . . . 132 F4
Paulton Rd
  Farrington Gurney BS39 . . . . 132 B4
  Hallatrow BS39 . . . . 132 B7
  Midsomer Norton BA3 . . 132 F1
Paultow Ave BS3 . . . . 63 E3
Paultow Rd BS3 . . . . 63 E3
Paulwood Rd BS39 . . . . 114 E1
Pavey Cl BS13 . . . . 79 C4
Pavey Rd BS13 . . . . 79 C4
Pavilions The BS4 . . . . . . 64 C1
Pawlett BS24 . . . . 105 A2
Pawlett Rd BS13 . . . . 79 C3
Pawlett Wlk BS13 . . . . . . 79 C3
Paxton BS16 . . . . 50 E8
Paybridge Rd BS13 . . . . . 78 F4
Payne Dr BS5 . . . . 64 B7
Payne Rd BS24 . . . . 105 D2
Paynes Ho 17 BS23 . . . . 104 E8
Paynes Orchard Pk BS10 . . . . 35 D5
Peache Ct BS16 . . . . 51 E6
Peache Rd BS16 . . . . 51 F6
Peacocks La BS15 . . . . . . 65 C7
Pearces Hill BS16 . . . . . . 51 B7
Pearl St BS3 . . . . 63 B3
Pearsall Rd BS30 . . . . 65 E2
Pearse Cl BS22 . . . . 89 B5
Peart Cl BS13 . . . . 78 E5
Peart Dr BS13 . . . . 78 E4
Pear Tree Ave BS41 . . . . . 77 E8
Peartree Cl BS13 . . . . 79 A4
Peartree Field BS20 . . . . . 59 F5
Peartree Gdns BS24 . . . 122 C6
Pear Tree Hey BS37 . . . . . 25 E5
Pear Tree Ind Est BS40 . . . . 109 C4
Peartree La
  Bristol, Lower Soundwell BS15 . . . . 51 F2
  Bristol, St George BS5 . . . 65 B6
Pear Tree Rd BS32 . . . . . . 24 C2
PEASEDOWN ST JOHN 134 C8
Peasedown St John Prim Sch BA2 . . . . 134 C7
Pedder Rd BS21 . . . . 57 F1
Peelers Ct 3 BS26 . . . . 125 C1
Peel St BS5 . . . . 143 C4
Pegasus Lo BS13 . . . . . . 104 D5
Pegasus Pk BS34 . . . . 36 C6
Peg Hill BS37 . . . . 27 F4
Pelican Cl BS22 . . . . 105 E8
Pemberton Ct BS16 . . . . . 51 C5
Pembery Rd BS3 . . . . 63 B3
Pembroke Ave BS11 . . . . . 47 E6
Pembroke Ct BS21 . . . . . . 57 E4
Pembroke Gate BS8 . . . . . 49 A1
Pembroke Gr BS8 . . . . . . 142 A3
Pembroke Lo 1 BS23 . . . 87 C1
Pembroke Mans BS8 . . . . 142 A3
Pembroke Pl BS8 . . . . . . 142 A1
Pembroke Rd
  Bristol BS8 . . . . 142 A4
  Bristol, Kingswood BS15 . . 51 C1
  Bristol, Shirehampton BS11 . . . . 47 E6
  Bristol, Southville BS3 . . . 63 C4
  Portishead BS20 . . . . 44 E4
  Weston-S-M BS23 . . . . . 104 F4
Pembroke St BS2 . . . . . . 143 B4
Pembroke Vale BS8 . . . . 142 A4
Pembroke Way BS15 . . . . 65 F7
Penarth Dr BS22 . . . . . . 105 A1
Pendennis Ave BS16 . . . . 51 D4
Pendennis Ho 5 BS16 . . . 51 D5
Pendennis Pk
  Bristol, Brislington BS4 . . 64 D1
  1 Bristol, Staple Hill BS16 . . . . 51 B5
Pendennis Rd BS16 . . . . . 51 D5
Pendle Ct BS25 . . . . 125 A7
Pendlesham Gdns BS23 . . . . 88 A1
Pendock Cl BS30 . . . . 66 C1
Pendock Ct BS16 . . . . 52 B7

Pendock Rd
  Bristol BS16 . . . . 51 C6
  Winterbourne BS36 . . . . . 37 E5
Penfield Ct BS2 . . . . 50 A2
Penfield Rd BS2 . . . . 50 A2
Penlea Ct BS11 . . . . 47 D7
Pennard BS24 . . . . 105 A2
Pennard Ct
  Bath BA2 . . . . 101 A6
  Bristol BS14 . . . . 80 B5
Pennard Gn BA2 . . . . . . 101 A6
Penn Cl BS26 . . . . 125 C1
Penn Dr BS16 . . . . 37 C1
Penn La BA6 . . . . 101 A8
Penngrove BS30 . . . . 66 A3
Penn Hill Rd BA1 . . . . . . 84 A1
Pennine Gdns BS23 . . . . . 88 A1
Pennine Rd BS30 . . . . 66 C4
Pennings The BS26 . . . . 125 C2
Pennlea BS13 . . . . 79 C7
Penn Lea Ct BA1 . . . . . . 101 B8
Penn Lea Rd BA1 . . . . . . 101 B8
Pennon Rise BS1 . . . . . . 142 C1
Penn St BS1 . . . . 143 B3
Penns The BS21 . . . . 57 G2
PENNSYLVANIA 68 F7
Penn Way BS26 . . . . 125 C1
Pennycress BS22 . . . . . . 105 D7
Pennyquick BA2 . . . . . . 100 D6
Pennyquick View BA2 . . 100 F6
Pennyroyal Gr BS16 . . . . . 50 E4
Pennywell Ct 3 BS5 . . . 64 A8
Pennywell Est 3 BS21 . . 57 F2
Pennywell Rd BS2, BS5 . . 64 A8
Pen Park Rd BS10 . . . . . . 35 D2
Penpole Ave BS11 . . . . . . 47 E6
Penpole Cl BS11 . . . . 47 D7
Penpole La BS11 . . . . 47 E7
Penpole Pk BS11 . . . . 47 E7
Penpole Pl BS11 . . . . 47 E6
Penrice Cl BS22 . . . . 88 F4
Penrith Gdns BS10 . . . . . 49 D8
Penrose BS14 . . . . 79 F7
Penrose Dr BS34 . . . . 36 D7
Pensford Ct BS14 . . . . 80 D5
Pensfield Pk BS10 . . . . . . 35 D4
Pensford Hill BS39 . . . . . . 97 D5
Pensford La BS39 . . . . 97 A3
Pensford Old La BS39 . . . 97 E3
Pensford Prim Sch BS39 . . . . 97 D4
Pentagon The BS9 . . . . . . 48 B5
Penthouse Hill BA1 . . . . . 85 F3
Pentire Ave BS13 . . . . 79 A6
Pentland Ave BS35 . . . . . . 15 E8
Peppershells La BS39 . . . 98 C6
Pepys Ct BS31 . . . . 82 D2
Pera Pl BA1 . . . . 141 C4
Pera Rd BA1 . . . . 141 C4
Percival Rd BS8 . . . . 62 F8
Percival Terr BS39 . . . . . 131 F4
Percy St 1 BA1 . . . . 141 A1
Percy St 2 BS3 . . . . 63 D4
Percy Walker Ct BS16 . . . 51 C6
Peregrine Cl BS22 . . . . . . 88 F1
Perfect View BA1 . . . . 85 A1
Perrett Ho 22 BS2 . . . . . 143 C3
Perretts Ct BS1 . . . . 142 C1
Perrett Way BS20 . . . . 47 E4
Perrin Cl BS39 . . . . 131 E8
Perrings The BS48 . . . . . . 75 E8
Perrinpit Rd BS36 . . . . . . 25 E2
Perrott Rd BS15 . . . . 52 A1
Perry Cl BS36 . . . . 37 D4
Perry Court Inf Sch BS14 . . . . 80 A6
Perry Court Jun Sch BS14 . . . . 80 A6
Perrycroft Ave BS13 . . . . . 79 A6
Perrycroft Rd BS13 . . . . . 79 A6
Perrymans Cl
  Bristol BS16 . . . . 51 A6
  Doynton BS30 . . . . 68 A8
PERRYMEAD 102 B3
Perrymead
  Bath BA2 . . . . 102 B3
  Weston-S-M BS22 . . . . . . 89 B5
Perrymead Ct BA2 . . . . . 102 B4
Perrymead Pl BA2 . . . . . 102 B4
Perry Rd
  Bristol BS1 . . . . 143 A3
  Long Ashton BS41 . . . . . . 61 F1
Perrys Lea BS32 . . . . 24 D2
Pesley Cl BS13 . . . . 79 A4
Petercole Dr BS13 . . . . . . 79 A6
Peterside BS39 . . . . 131 E8
Peterson Sq BS13 . . . . . . 79 C3
Peter's Terr BS5 . . . . 64 B7
Petersway Gdns BS5 . . . . 65 A6
Petherbridge Way BS7 . . . 50 A5
Petherton Cl BS15 . . . . . . 65 E7
Petherton Gdns BS14 . . . 80 B7
Petherton Rd BS14 . . . . . 80 B7
Pethick Ho BS4 . . . . 79 D7
Peto Garden at Iford Manor The* BA15 . . . . 120 E3
Peto Gr BA15 . . . . 120 F3
Pettigrove Gdns BS15 . . . 65 E7
Pettigrove Rd BS15 . . . . . 65 E6
PETTY FRANCE 30 A7
Pevensey Wlk BS4 . . . . . . 79 D7
Peverell Cl BS10 . . . . 34 F3
Peverell Dr BS10 . . . . 34 F3
Philippa Cl BS14 . . . . 80 A7
Philips Ho 2 BS2 . . . . . 143 B4

Philip St
  Bristol, St Philip's Marsh BS2 . . . . 64 B5
  Bristol, Windmill Hill BS3 . . . . 63 D4
Phillips Rd BS23 . . . . . . 105 A6
Phillis Hill BS39 . . . . 132 F4
Phippen St 1 BS1 . . . . 143 B1
Phipps Barton BS15 . . . . 65 B8
Phipps St BS3 . . . . 63 B4
Phoenix Bsns Pk BS3 . . . 63 A2
Phoenix Gr BS6 . . . . 49 C5
Phoenix Ho
  Bath BA1 . . . . 141 B4
  Bristol BS5 . . . . 64 B6
Phoenix Way BS20 . . . . . . 45 F6
Piccadilly Pl BA1 . . . . . . 102 B8
Pickedmoor La BS35 . . . . . 7 F5
Pickwick Rd BA1 . . . . 85 A2
Picton La BS6 . . . . 49 E1
Picton Mews 6 BS6 . . . . 49 E1
Picton St BS6 . . . . 49 E1
Pier Cl BS20 . . . . 45 E7
Pier Rd BS20 . . . . 45 E7
Pierrepont Pl 9 BA1 . . . 141 C2
Pierrepont St BA1 . . . . . 141 C2
Pigeon House Dr BS13 . . 79 D4
Pigeon La BS40 . . . . 93 D1
Pigott Ave BS13 . . . . 79 A4
Pilemarsh BS5 . . . . 64 D7
PILE MARSH 64 D7
Pilgrims Way
  Avonmouth BS11 . . . . 47 C1
  Bristol BS11 . . . . 51 D8
  Chew Stoke BS40 . . . . . 112 D8
  Weston-S-M BS22 . . . . . . 88 E3
Pilgrims Wharf BS4 . . . . . 64 E7
Pilkington Cl BS34 . . . . . 36 C2
PILL 47 C4
Pillingers Gdns BS6 . . . . . 49 B2
Pillingers Rd BS15 . . . . . 65 C7
Pill Ho
  Abbots Leigh BS8 . . . . . . 47 F1
  Pill BS20 . . . . 47 E2
Pill St BS20 . . . . 47 D4
Pill Way BS21 . . . . 57 D2
PILNING 22 D7
Pilning Prim Sch BS35 . . 22 C8
Pilning Sta BS35 . . . . 23 C8
Pimms La BS22 . . . . 88 B3
Pimm's La BS22 . . . . 88 B2
Pimpernel Mead BS32 . . 36 E7
Pinchay La BS40 . . . . 95 A5
Pinckney Gn BA15 . . . . . 103 E5
Pincots La GL12 . . . . 18 B3
Pine Cl
  Thornbury BS35 . . . . 8 C1
  Weston-S-M BS22 . . . . . . 88 D2
Pinecroft
  Bristol BS14 . . . . 79 F7
  Portishead BS20 . . . . 44 F6
Pine Ct
  Chew Magna BS40 . . . . . . 96 B3
  Keynsham BS31 . . . . 81 C4
  Radstock BA3 . . . . 134 A2
Pinefield BS9 . . . . 49 B7
Pine Gr BS7 . . . . 36 A1
Pine Grove Pl BS7 . . . . . . 49 D3
Pine Hill BS22 . . . . 88 D2
Pine Lea BS24 . . . . 122 B6
Pine Rd BS10 . . . . 35 B3
Pine Ridge Cl BS9 . . . . . . 48 C4
Pines Cl BA3 . . . . 138 D3
Pines Rd BS30 . . . . 66 C1
Pines The
  Bristol, Lower Soundwell BS15 . . . . 52 A3
  Bristol, Sneyd Park BS9 . . 48 D3
Pines Way
  Bath BA2 . . . . 141 A2
  Radstock BA3 . . . . 134 A2
Pines Way Ind Est BA2 . . . . 141 A2
Pinetree Rd BS24 . . . . . . 106 D4
Pine Wlk BA3 . . . . 133 E1
Pinewood BS15 . . . . 51 F1
Pinewood Ave BA3 . . . . . 132 F1
Pinewood Cl BS9 . . . . 49 B7
Pinewood Gr BA3 . . . . . . 132 F1
Pinewood Rd BA3 . . . . . 132 F1
Pinewood Way SN14 . . . . 70 F7
Pinhay Rd BS13 . . . . 79 B6
Pinkers Mead BS16 . . . . . 52 C6
Pinkhams Twist BS14 . . . 80 A5
Pinnell Gr BS16 . . . . 52 C7
Pioneer Ave BA2 . . . . . . 101 F1
Pioneer Pk BS4 . . . . 64 C5
Pipehouse BA2 . . . . 119 E4
Pipehouse La BA2 . . . . . 119 E4
Pipe La 3 BS1 . . . . 142 C2
Piper Rd BS37 . . . . 27 E3
Pippin Ct 2 BA2 . . . . . . 134 D7
Pippin Cl 4 BS20 . . . . . 65 F4
Pippins The BS20 . . . . 45 F5
Pitchcombe BS37 . . . . 39 C7
Pitchcombe Gdns BS9 . . 48 D7
Pitching The BA3 . . . . . . 138 D5
Pitch La BS6 . . . . 49 D1
Pitch & Pay La BS9 . . . . . 48 E3
Pitch & Pay Pk BS9 . . . . . 48 E3
Pitfour Terr BA2 . . . . 116 B2
Pithay Ct BS1 . . . . 143 A3
Pithay The
  Bristol BS1 . . . . 143 A3
  Paulton BS39 . . . . 132 E6

Pit La
  Backwell BS48 . . . . 76 A4
  Ubley BS40 . . . . 111 F5
Pitlochry Cl BS7 . . . . 35 F1
Pitman Ct BA1 . . . . 85 C2
Pitman Ho BA2 . . . . 101 D4
Pitman Rd BS23 . . . . 104 E6
Pit Rd BA3 . . . . 133 B1
PITT COURT 5 F5
Pitt Rd BS7 . . . . 49 E5
Pittville Cl BS35 . . . . 8 C3
Pitville Pl 16 BS6 . . . . . 49 B1
Pitway Cl BS39 . . . . 131 F4
Pitway La BS39 . . . . 131 E4
Pixash Bsns Ctr BS31 . . . 82 B5
Pixash La BS31 . . . . 82 C5
Pixash Works BS31 . . . . . 82 C5
Pizey Ave BS21 . . . . 57 D2
Pizey Ave Ind Est BS21 . . 57 E2
Pizey Cl BS21 . . . . 57 D2
Plain The
  Norton St Philip BA2 . . . 136 E4
  Thornbury BS35 . . . . 8 B1
Players Cl BS16 . . . . 37 B3
Playford Gdns BS11 . . . . . 47 E8
Plaza The BS2 . . . . 143 C2
Pleasant Ho 4 BS16 . . . 51 D5
Pleasant Pl BA1 . . . . 86 D2
Pleasant Rd BS16 . . . . . . 51 D5
Pleshey Cl BS22 . . . . 88 D2
Plimsoll Ho
  5 Bristol BS1 . . . . 143 B1
  Bristol, Woolcott Park BS6 . . . . 49 B1
Ploughed Paddock BS48 . . . . 59 D1
Plover Cl
  Weston-S-M BS22 . . . . . . 88 F1
  Yate BS37 . . . . 27 C2
Plovers Rise BA3 . . . . . . 134 A3
Plowright Ho 8 BS15 . . . 65 B5
Plumers Cl 2 BS21 . . . . 57 C1
Plumley Cres BS24 . . . . . 106 A4
Plumley Ct BS23 . . . . . . 104 D4
Plumptre Cl BS39 . . . . . . 132 E5
Plumpton Ct BS16 . . . . . . 37 F1
Plumtree Cl BS39 . . . . . . 132 E5
Plum Tree Rd BS22 . . . . 105 E8
Plunder St BS49 . . . . 92 B7
Podgers Dr BA1 . . . . 84 B2
Podium The BA1 . . . . . . 141 C2
Poets' Cl BS5 . . . . 64 D8
Poets Cnr BA3 . . . . 139 C8
Polar Gdns SN14 . . . . 31 E4
Polden Cl BS48 . . . . 59 E1
Polden Ho BS3 . . . . 63 D3
Polden Rd
  Portishead BS20 . . . . 45 B5
  Weston-S-M BS23 . . . . . 104 F8
Polestar Way BS24 . . . . . 106 A8
Pollard Rd BS22 . . . . 105 E8
Polly Barnes Cl 6 BS15 . . . . 65 B5
Polly Barnes Hill BS15 . . 65 B5
Polygon Rd BS8 . . . . 142 A2
Polygon The
  Avonmouth BS11 . . . . 33 D1
  16 Bristol BS8 . . . . . . 62 F6
Pomfrett Gdns BS14 . . . . 80 E5
Pomphrey Hill BS16 . . . . 52 C4
Pond Cotts BA3 . . . . 135 D2
Pond Mead BS20 . . . . 47 D4
Ponsford Rd BS4 . . . . 64 B1
Ponting Cl BS5 . . . . 51 A1
Pool Cnr BS32 . . . . 14 B2
Poole Court Dr BS37 . . . . 27 E2
Poole Ho BA2 . . . . 100 F5
Poole St BS11 . . . . 47 B8
Pooles Wharf BS8 . . . . . 142 A1
Pooles Wharf Ct BS8 . . . 142 A1
Pool Farm BS37 . . . . 39 D5
Pool Ho BS34 . . . . 36 A8
Pool La BS40 . . . . 93 A2
Pool Rd BS15 . . . . 51 E3
Poor Hill BA2 . . . . 115 F6
Pope's Wlk BA2 . . . . 102 B3
Poplar Ave BS9 . . . . 48 D6
Poplar Cl
  Bath BA2 . . . . 101 D4
  Bristol BS30 . . . . 66 C6
Poplar Dr BS16 . . . . 53 B5
Poplar Fields BS36 . . . . . 38 D6
Poplar Gardens Ho 3 BS15 . . . . 65 E8
Poplar La GL12 . . . . 18 B4
Poplar Pl
  Bristol BS16 . . . . 51 A3
  17 Weston-S-M BS23 . . 104 E8
Poplar Rd
  Bath BA2 . . . . 118 D8
  Bristol, Hanham BS15 . . . 65 A5
  Bristol, Highridge BS13 . . 78 F7
  Bristol, North Common BS30 . . . . 66 D6
  Bristol, Speedwell BS5 . . . 50 F1
Poplar Rdbt BS11 . . . . . . 33 C1
Poplars The
  Easton-in-G BS20 . . . . . . 47 B4
  Weston-S-M BS22 . . . . . . 89 A1
Poplar Terr BS15 . . . . 65 E8
Poplar Way SN14 . . . . 70 F5
Poplar Way E BS11 . . . . . 33 F4
Poplar Way W BS11 . . . . . 33 D6

Poplar Wlk BS24 . . . . . . 105 E5
Pople's La BA11 . . . . 140 F1
Pople Wlk BS7 . . . . 49 F3
Poppy Cl BS22 . . . . 89 A5
Poppy Mead BS32 . . . . . . 36 E7
Porlock Cl
  3 Clevedon BS21 . . . . . 57 G1
  Weston-S-M BS23 . . . . . 104 F2
Porlock Gdns BS48 . . . . . 59 E1
Porlock Rd
  Bath BA2 . . . . 102 A1
  Bristol BS3 . . . . 63 D3
Portal Rd BS24 . . . . 106 D4
PORTBURY 46 E3
Portbury Comm BS20 . . . 45 E4
Portbury Gr BS11 . . . . . . 47 D6
Portbury Hundred The BS20 . . . . 46 C4
Portbury La BS20 . . . . 60 E7
Portbury Way BS20 . . . . . 46 E5
Portbury Wlk BS11 . . . . . 47 D6
Port Elizabeth Ho BS10 . . . . 35 B1
PORTISHEAD 45 B4
Portishead Bsns Pk BS20 . . . . 46 C4
Portishead Lo BS20 . . . . . 45 D6
Portishead Office Pk BS20 . . . . 45 E5
Portishead Prim sch BS20 . . . . 45 E5
Portishead Rd BS22 . . . . 89 B4
Portishead Way BS3 . . . . 62 E3
Portland Cl BS48 . . . . 59 D1
Portland Ct
  Bristol BS1 . . . . 142 B1
  Bristol, Upper Soundwell BS16 . . . . 51 D3
Portland Dr BS20 . . . . 45 E4
Portland Lofts 5 BS2 . . 143 B4
Portland Mans 9 BS2 . . 143 B4
Portland Pl
  Bath BA1 . . . . 141 B4
  Bristol BS16 . . . . 51 D3
Portland Rd BA1 . . . . . . 141 B4
Portland Sq BS2 . . . . 143 B4
Portland St
  Bristol, Clifton BS8 . . . . . 62 F7
  Bristol, Staple Hill BS16 . . 51 D3
Portland Terr BA1 . . . . . 141 B4
Portmeade Dro BS26 . . . 125 C1
Portmeirion Cl BS14 . . . . 80 B5
Port Side Ct 5 BS5 . . . . 64 F6
Port View BS20 . . . . 47 C5
Portview Rd BS11 . . . . . . 47 B8
Portwall La BS1 . . . . 143 B1
Portwall La E 10 BS1 . . 143 B1
Portway
  Bristol BS8 . . . . 48 C3
  Bristol, Shirehampton BS11 . . . . 47 C6
Portway Com Sch BS11 . . . . 47 E6
Portway La BS37 . . . . 28 E2
Portway Rdbt BS37 . . . . . 28 E2
Post Office La
  Blagdon BS40 . . . . 110 D3
  Flax Bourton BS48 . . . . . 76 F7
Post Office Rd BS24 . . . . 106 C5
Poston Way BA15 . . . . . . 120 E2
POTTERS HILL 77 B1
Potterswood BS15 . . . . . . 65 D7
Pottery Cl BS23 . . . . 105 A6
Potts Cl BA1 . . . . 85 F3
Pound Dr BS16 . . . . 50 F5
Pound La
  Bristol BS16 . . . . 50 F4
  Nailsea BS48 . . . . 59 D3
Pound Mead BS40 . . . . . . 94 C8
Pound Mill Bsns Ctr BS35 . . . . 5 F5
Pound Rd BS15 . . . . 51 F2
Pound The
  Almondsbury BS32 . . . . . 24 A5
  Oldbury-on-S BS35 . . . . . . 7 B6
  Redhill BS40 . . . . 93 D3
Pountney Dr 2 BS5 . . . . 64 B8
Powel Ct BS30 . . . . 53 L1
Powells Acres BS21 . . . . . 57 G3
Powis Cl BS22 . . . . 88 F2
Powlett Ct BA2 . . . . 102 C7
Powlett Rd BA2 . . . . 102 B8
Pow's Hill BA3 . . . . 133 D5
Pow's Orch BA3 . . . . 133 A1
Poynting Cl BA2 . . . . . . 101 F1
Poyntz Ct BS30 . . . . 65 D7
Poyntz Rd BS4 . . . . 79 F8
Praters La 2 BS16 . . . . . 51 D4
Preacher Cl BS5 . . . . 65 B6
Preanes Gn BS22 . . . . . . 89 A3
Precinct The BS20 . . . . . . 45 E5
Preddy's La BS5 . . . . 65 A6
Prescot Cl BS22 . . . . 88 B2
Prescott BS37 . . . . 39 D8
Press Moor Dr BS30 . . . . 66 A5
Prestbury BS37 . . . . 39 D8
Preston Wlk BS4 . . . . 79 F8
Prestwick Cl BS4 . . . . 64 D1
Pretoria Rd BS34 . . . . 35 F8
Prewett St BS1 . . . . 143 B1
Priddy Cl BA2 . . . . 101 B5
Priddy Ct BS14 . . . . 80 B5
Priddy Dr BS14 . . . . 80 B5

Priests Way BS22 .... **88** D2
Priestwood Cl BS10 .... **35** A3
Primrose Cl
 Bristol BS32 .... 24 C2
 Bristol, St George BS15 ... **65** C8
Primrose Dr BS35 .... 8 D2
PRIMROSE HILL **84** D1
Primrose Hill BA1 .... **84** D1
Primrose La
 Bristol BS15 .... 51 C1
 Midsomer Norton BA3 .... **133** B1
Primrose Terr BS15 .... 51 C1
Princes Bldgs BA1 .... **141** B3
Prince's Bldgs **13** BS8 ... 62 F6
Princes Ct BS30 .... 65 F4
Princes' La BS8 .... 62 F6
Princes' Pl BS7 .... **49** E3
Prince's Rd BS21 .... 57 F3
Princess Cl BS31 .... 81 E4
Princess Gdns BS16 .... 50 D6
Princess Row BS2 .... 143 A4
Princess St
 Bristol, Newton BS2 .... 64 A7
 Bristol, Windmill Hill BS3... 63 E4
Princes St BA1 .... 141 B2
Prince's St
 Bristol BS2 .... 143 C4
 Clandown BA3 .... 133 E5
Princess Victoria St
 BS8 .... 62 F6
Prince St BS1 .... 143 A1
Prinknash Cl **13** BS37 ... 39 D7
Prior Park Bldgs BA2 ...... 102 B5
Prior Park Coll BA2 .... 102 C2
Prior Park Cotts BA2 .... 141 C1
Prior Park Gdns BA2 .... 102 B5
Prior Park Landscape
 Gdn* BA2 .... 102 C2
Prior Rd BA2 .... 102 B4
Priors Hill BA1 .... 116 A2
Prior's Hill **12** BS6 .... 49 D1
Priors Lea BS37 .... 27 E1
Priory Ave BS9 .... 49 A7
Priory Cl
 Bath BA2 .... 102 B2
 Midsomer Norton BA3 ..... 133 A1
 Priory Com Sch BS22 ...... 89 B3
Priory Court Rd BS9 .... 49 A7
Priory Ct
 Bristol, Hanham BS15 ..... 65 C3
 Bristol, Upper Knowle
  BS4 .... 64 B2
Priory Dene BS9 .... 49 A7
Priory Farm Trad Est
 BS20 .... 46 D3
Priory Gdns
 Bristol, Horfield BS7 ...... 49 F8
 Bristol, Shirehampton
  BS11 .... 47 D7
 Easton-in-G BS20 .... 47 B4
Priory Mews BS23 .... 105 B7
Priory Rd
 Bristol BS8 .... 142 C4
 Bristol, Shirehampton
  BS11 .... 47 D6
 Bristol, Upper Knowle
  BS4 .... 64 B2
 Easton-in-G BS20 .... 47 B4
 Keynsham BS31 .... 81 E7
 Portbury BS20 .... 46 D3
 Weston-S-M BS23 .... 105 A7
Priory Wlk BS20 .... 46 D3
PRISTON 117 B5
Priston Cl BS22 .... 89 B5
Priston La BA2, BA3 .... 117 A5
Priston Rd BA2 .... 117 D6
Pritchard St BS2 .... 143 B4
Privet Dr BS13 .... 79 C5
Probyn Cl BS16 .... 51 A7
Pro-Cathedral BS8 .... 142 B3
Proctor Cl BS4 .... 64 D1
Proctor Ho BS1 .... 143 B1
Promenade The BS7 .... 49 D2
Prospect Ave BS15 .... 51 B1
Prospect Cl
 Easter Compton BS35 ...... 23 A2
 Frampton Cotterell BS36.. 37 F8
 Winterbourne BS36 .... 37 E4
Prospect Cres BS15 .... 51 F2
Prospect Gdns BA1 .... 85 F5
Prospect Ho BS22 .... 88 E3
Prospect La BS36 .... 37 F8
Prospect Pl
 Bath, Beacon Hill BA1 ..... 85 A1
 Bathford BA1 .... 86 D2
 Bath, Weston BA1 .... 84 C2
 1 Bristol, Montpelier
  BS6 .... 49 D2
 Bristol, Moorfields BS5 ... 64 C8
 Weston-S-M BS23 .... 104 E8
Prospect Rd
 Bath BA2 .... 102 C4
 Severn Beach BS35 .... 22 A5
Prospect Terr **5** BS3 .... 63 C3
Protheroes Ho BS1 .... 142 C2
Proud Cross BS40 .... 129 E4
Providence La BA1 .... 61 F2
Providence Pl BS2 .... 143 C2
PROVIDENCE PLACE 132 F1
Providence Rise BS41 ..... 61 F2
Providence View BS41 .... 62 A1
Prowse Cl BS35 .... 8 C1
Prowse's La BS26 .... 125 A1
Prudham St **7** BS5 ...... 50 C1
PUBLOW 97 F5

Publow La BS39 .... **97** E5
PUCKLECHURCH 53 A5
Pucklechurch CE Prim Sch
 BS16 .... 53 C6
Pucklechurch Trad Est
 BS16 .... 53 B4
Pudding Pie La BS40 ..... 109 A5
Pudding Pie La BS40 ..... 109 A6
Puffin Cl BS22 .... 105 D8
PULLENS GREEN 7 C5
Pullin Ct BS30 .... 66 D4
Pulis Gn **3** BS35 .... 8 B1
Pulteney Ave BA2 .... 102 B6
Pulteney Bridge BA2 ..... 141 C2
Pulteney Gdns BA2 .... 102 B6
Pulteney Gr BA2 .... 102 B6
Pulteney Mews BA2 .... 102 B7
Pulteney Rd BA2 .... 102 B6
Pulteney Terr BA2 .... 102 B6
Pump La
 Bathford BA1 .... 86 B2
 Bristol BS1 .... 143 B1
 Redhill BS40 .... 93 D2
 Tockington BS32 .... 14 D4
Purcell Wlk BS4 .... 79 D7
Purdown Rd BS7 .... 49 F5
Purdue Cl BS22 .... 89 B3
Purdy Ct BS16 .... 51 A4
Purlewent Dr BA1 .... 84 C1
PURN 122 A7
Purn La BS24 .... 122 A8
Purn Rd BS24 .... 121 F8
Purn Way BS24 .... 122 B7
Pursey Dr BS32 .... 36 F6
Purton Cl BS15 .... 65 E6
Purton Rd BS7 .... 49 D2
Purving Row BS24 .... 122 C1
Purving Row La BS24 .... 122 C1
Puttingthorpe Dr
 BS22 .... 105 C7
Puxley Cl BS14 .... 80 E6
PUXTON 90 D3
Puxton La BS24 .... 90 D3
Puxton Moor La BS24 .... 90 E2
Puxton Rd BS24 .... 90 C2
Pye Cnr BS25 .... 108 D4
PYE CORNER 37 D3
Pye Croft BS32 .... 24 E3
Pyecroft Ave BS9 .... 49 C7
Pyghtell The SN14 .... 31 E5
Pylewell La BS25 .... 108 D1
Pylle Hill Cres BS3 .... 63 F4
Pyne Point BS21 .... 57 E3
Pynne Cl BS14 .... 80 F5
Pynne Rd BS14 .... 80 F5
Pyracantha Wlk BS14 .... 80 A6

Q

QEH Theatre* BS8 .... 142 B3
Quadrangle The BS37 .... 39 C4
Quadrant BS32 .... 24 B3
Quadrant E BS16 .... 51 C3
Quadrant The BS32 .... 24 A3
Quadrant The BS6 .... 49 B3
Quadrant W BS16 .... 51 C3
Quadrilles The BS35 ...... 22 A6
Quaker Ct **1** BS8 .... 8 B1
Quaker La BS35 .... 8 B1
Quaker's Cl BS16 .... 51 D8
Quaker's Friars BS1 ..... 143 B3
Quaker's Rd BS16 .... 51 E8
Quantock Cl BS30 .... 66 C5
Quantock Cl BS16 .... 36 E1
Quantock Rd
 Bristol BS3 .... 63 D3
 Portishead BS20 .... 45 B5
 Weston-S-M BS23 .... 104 E4
Quantocks BA2 .... 102 A1
Quarries The BS32 .... 24 C6
Quarrington Rd BS7 ...... 49 F5
Quarry Barton BS16 ...... 37 C4
Quarry Cl
 Bath BA2 .... 101 F1
 Limpley Stoke BA2 .... 120 D6
Quarry Hay BS40 .... 112 D8
Quarry La
 Bristol BS11 .... 34 C1
 Winterbourne BS36 .... 37 E4
Quarrymans Ct BA2 ...... 102 B1
Quarry Mead BS35 .... 14 F5
Quarry Rd
 Alveston BS35 .... 14 F5
 Bath BA2 .... 102 D6
 Bristol BS8 .... 49 A2
 Bristol, Frenchay BS16 ... 51 C7
 Bristol, Kingswood BS15 . 65 E6
 Chipping Sodbury BS37 .. 28 A1
 Portishead BS20 .... 45 C4
 Sandford BS25 .... 108 A2
Quarry Rock Gdns
 BA2 .... 102 D5
Quarry Stps **8** BS8 ..... 49 A2
Quarry The BS11 .... 34 C1
Quarry Vale Cotts
 BA2 .... 102 B1
Quarry Way
 Bristol, Emerson's Green
  BS16 .... 38 A1
 Bristol, Fishponds BS16 .. 50 E5
 Nailsea BS48 .... 59 D3
Quays Ave BS20 .... 45 E5
Quayside La **4** BS5 ..... 64 F6
Quay St BS1 .... 143 A3
Quays The BS1 .... 142 C1

Quebec BA2 .... 101 A6
Quedgeley BS37 .... 39 C8
Queen Ann Rd BS5 .... 64 B6
Queen Charlotte St
 BS1 .... 143 A2
QUEEN CHARLTON 81 B3
Queen Charlton La
 BS14 .... 80 D2
Queen Elizabeth's Hospital
 Sch BS8 .... 142 B3
Queen Quay BS1 .... 143 A2
Queens Apartments
 BS8 .... 142 C3
Queen's Ave
 Bristol BS8 .... 142 B3
 Portishead BS20 .... 45 C5
Queenscote BS20 .... 45 F5
Queens Ct BS31 .... 81 E5
Queen's Ct BS8 .... 142 B3
Queensdale Cres BS4 .... 64 A1
Queens Down Ct BS4 .... 64 C3
Queensdown Gdns
 BS4 .... 64 C2
Queens Down Gdns
 BS4 .... 64 C3
Queens Dr BS15 .... 65 B4
Queen's Dr
 Bath BA2 .... 102 A2
 Bristol BS7 .... 49 C5
Queens Gate BS9 .... 48 D5
Queenshill Rd BS4 .... 64 A1
Queensholm Ave BS16 ... 37 E1
Queensholm Cl BS16 .... 37 E1
Queensholm Cres
 BS16 .... 37 E1
Queensholm Dr BS16 .... 37 E1
Queens Mans BS8 .... 142 B3
Queens Par BS1 .... 142 C2
Queen's Par BA1 .... 141 B3
Queen's Parade Pl
 BA1 .... 141 B3
Queens Pl BA2 .... 102 B5
Queen Sq
 Bath BA1 .... 141 B2
 Bristol BS1 .... 143 A2
 Saltford BS31 .... 82 F3
Queen Square Ave **10**
 BS1 .... 143 A2
Queen Square Ho
 BS1 .... 143 A2
Queen Square Pl BA1 ... 141 B3
Queens Rd
 Banwell BS29 .... 107 A3
 Bristol BS4 .... 64 C2
 Keynsham BS31 .... 81 D4
 Nailsea BS48 .... 59 D1
 Portishead BS20 .... 44 E4
Queen's Rd
 Bristol, Ashley Down
  BS7 .... 49 F5
 Bristol, Bishopsworth BS13,
  BS41 .... 78 F4
 Bristol BS8 .... 142 B3
 Bristol, Cadbury Heath
  BS30 .... 66 B4
 Bristol, Crew's Hole BS5 . 64 F7
 Pucklechurch BS16 .... 53 B5
 Radstock BA3 .... 134 B2
 Weston-S-M BS23 .... 87 D1
Queen St
 Avonmouth BS11 .... 33 A1
 Bath BA1 .... 141 B2
 Bristol BS2 .... 143 B3
 Bristol, Eastville BS5 ..... 50 D3
 Bristol, St George BS15 .. 65 B8
Queensway
 Bristol BS34 .... 36 D6
 Weston-S-M BS22 .... 88 F4
Queens Way BS20 .... 44 E4
Queensway The BS22 .... 89 B2
Queens Wlk BS35 .... 8 B3
Queen Victoria Rd BS6 ... 49 A4
Queen Victoria St BS2 ... 64 A6
Quickthorn Cl BS14 ...... 80 A6
Quiet St BA1 .... 141 B2
Quilter Gr BS4 .... 79 D7

R

Raby Mews BA2 .... 102 B7
Raby Pl BA2 .... 102 B7
Rackfield Pl BA2 .... 101 B6
Rackham Cl BS7 .... 50 B6
Rackhay BS1 .... 143 A2
Rackley La BS26 .... 124 B2
Rackvernal Ct BA3 ...... 133 B1
Rackvernal Rd BA3 ..... 133 B1
RADFORD 133 C8
Radford Hill
 Camerton BA2, BA3 ...... 133 C7
 Timsbury BA2 .... 116 C1
Radley Rd BS16 .... 51 B4
Radnor Bsns Ctr BS7 ... 49 E5
Radnor Rd
 Bristol, Horfield BS7 ..... 49 E5
 Bristol, Westbury on Trym
  BS9 .... 49 B5
RADSTOCK 133 E1
Radstock Mus* BA3 ..... 133 F2
Radstock Rd BA3 .... 133 C2
Raeburn Rd BS5 .... 65 B6
Rag La BA3 .... 134 D5
Rag La GL12 .... 17 D5
Raglan Cl BA3 .... 138 C4
Ragland La BA1 .... 85 A2

Ragland St BA1 .... **85** A2
Raglan La
 Bristol BS5 .... 65 A7
 Winford BS40 .... 94 E7
Raglan Pl
 Bristol BS7 .... 49 D3
 Thornbury BS35 .... 15 B8
 12 Weston-S-M BS23 . 87 C1
Raglan Rd BS7 .... 49 D3
Raglan Terr BA1 .... 85 A2
Raglan Villas BA1 .... 85 A1
Raglan Wlk BS31 .... 81 D4
Railton Jones Cl BS34 .. 36 E3
Railway Arches BS2 ..... 143 C2
Railway Cotts BS37 ...... 40 E8
Railway La BA2 .... 118 D1
Railway Pl BA1 .... 141 C1
Railway St BA1 .... 141 C1
Railway Terr
 Bristol BS16 .... 51 C4
 Shoscombe BA2 .... 134 E4
Railway View Pl BA3 .... 133 B2
Rainham Ct BA2 .... 87 C1
Rainham Ct **8** BS23 ... 87 C1
Rains Batch BS40 .... 127 E6
Raleigh Cl BS31 .... 82 D2
Raleigh Ct **3** BS23 ... 104 E5
Raleigh Rd BS3 .... 63 B4
Raleigh Rise BS20 .... 45 B5
Ralph Allen Dr BA2 ..... 102 B2
Ralph Allen Sch BA2 ... 102 E2
Ralph Rd BS7 .... 49 F4
RAM HILL 38 D4
Ram Hill BS36 .... 38 D4
Ram Hill Bsns Pk BS36.. 38 D5
Ramsay Cl BS22 .... 88 E4
Ramscombe La BA1 ..... 85 F6
Ramsey Rd BS7 .... 49 F4
Ranchways BS20 .... 44 F4
Randall Cl BS15 .... 51 F2
Randall Rd BS8 .... 142 B2
Randolph Ave
 Bristol BS13 .... 79 B5
 Yate BS37 .... 27 D4
Randolph Cl BS13 .... 79 B5
Rangers Wlk BS15 .... 65 C4
RANGEWORTHY 27 B8
Rangeworthy CE Prim Sch
 BS37 .... 27 C7
Rankers La BS39 .... 98 C5
Rannoch Rd BS7 .... 35 F1
Ranscombe Ave BS22 .. 88 D2
Ransford BS21 .... 57 D1
Raphael Ct BS1 .... 143 B1
Ratcliffe Dr BS34 .... 36 E5
Rathbone Cl BS36 .... 38 C5
Raven Cl BS22 .... 88 E3
Raven Ct BS9 .... 48 F8
Ravendale Dr BS30 ...... 66 B2
Ravenglass Cres BS10 .. 35 D2
Ravenhill Ave BS3 .... 63 F2
Ravenhill Rd BS3 .... 63 F3
Ravenscourt Rd BS34 ... 36 B7
Ravenswood BS30 .... 66 B3
Ravenswood Rd BS6 .... 49 C1
Ravenswood Sch BS48 . 59 D3
Rawlins Ave BS22 .... 89 A5
Rawnsley Ho **13** BS5 . 50 A1
Rayens Cl BS41 .... 61 F1
Rayens Cross Rd BS41 . 61 F1
Rayleigh Rd BS9 .... 48 E7
Raymend Rd BS3 .... 63 E3
Raymend Wlk BS3 .... 63 E2
Raymill BS4 .... 65 A2
Raymore Ho BS16 .... 51 F4
Raynes Rd BS3 .... 63 A3
Raynham Rd BS22 ...... 104 F8
Raysfield Inf Sch BS37 . 39 F8
Raysfield Jun Sch
 BS37 .... 39 F8
Reading Cl BS15 .... 65 B8
Rearing Unit The BS35 .. 7 E7
Rector's Way BS23 ...... 104 F4
Rectory Cl
 Farmborough BA2 .... 116 A6
 Wraxall BS48 .... 60 A2
 Yate BS37 .... 27 F3
Rectory Dr BS49 .... 91 C7
Rectory Gdns BS10 ..... 34 E2
Rectory La
 Bleadon BS24 .... 122 C6
 Bristol BS34 .... 36 A3
 Compton Martin BS40 .. 129 B6
 Cromhall GL12 .... 17 A8
 Timsbury BA2 .... 116 B2
Rectory Rd
 Easton-in-G BS20 .... 47 B3
 Frampton Cotterell BS36. 38 A8
Rectory Way
 Lympsham BS24 .... 121 F2
 Yatton BS49 .... 91 C7
Recurium Lo BS26 ...... 125 B2
Redacre BS40 .... 93 D3
Redcar Ct BS16 .... 37 F1
Redcatch Rd BS4 .... 63 F2
Redcliff Backs BS1 ..... 143 B2
Redcliff Cres BS3 .... 63 F4
REDCLIFFE BAY 44 E4
Redcliffe Cl BS20 .... 44 E3
Redcliffe Par E BS1 .... 143 A1
Redcliffe Par W BS1 ... 143 A1
Redcliffe Way BS1 ..... 143 B1
Redcliff Hill BS1 .... 143 B1
Redcliff Mead La BS1 .. 143 B1
Redcliff St BS1 .... 143 B2
Redcroft BS40 .... 93 D3

Redcross Mews **14**
 BS2 .... 143 C3
Redcross St BS2 .... 143 C3
Redding Pit La BS40 .... 94 E4
Reddings The
 Bristol BS15 .... 51 F2
 Compton Martin BS40 .. 129 B7
REDFIELD 64 C7
Redfield Edge Prim Sch
 BS30 .... 66 D4
Redfield Gr BA3 .... 139 A8
Redfield Hill BS30 ...... 66 E3
Redfield Rd
 Bristol BS34 .... 36 B7
 Midsomer Norton BA3 .. 139 A8
Redford Cres BS13 ...... 78 F3
Redford La BS16 .... 53 D4
Redford Wlk BS13 .... 78 F3
Redham La BS35 .... 22 F8
REDHILL 93 D3
Red Hill
 Peasedown St John
  BA2 .... 116 C1
 Redhill BS40 .... 93 D2
Redhill Cl BS16 .... 50 E3
Redhill Dr BS16 .... 50 E3
Redhill Farm Bsns Pk
 BS35 .... 13 F6
Redhill La BS35 .... 13 E6
Red House La
 Almondsbury BS32 .... 24 A4
 Bristol BS9 .... 48 E6
REDLAND 49 C3
Redland Ave BS20 .... 46 F6
Redland Court Rd BS6 .. 49 C2
Redland Gr BS6 .... 49 C2
Redland Green Rd BS6 . 49 C3
Redland High Sch BS6 . 49 C2
Redland Hill BS6 .... 49 B2
Redland Pk
 Bath BA2 .... 100 F6
 Bristol BS6 .... 49 B2
Redland Rd BS6 .... 49 C2
Redland Sta BS6 .... 49 C2
Redlands Terr BA3 ..... 138 F8
Redland Terr **8** BS6 .. 49 C2
Red Lodge Bsns Pk
 BS24 .... 89 D1
Red Lodge The* BS8 .. 142 C3
Redlynch La BS31 .... 81 D2
Red Maids Jun Sch The
 BS9 .... 49 A6
Red Maids Sch The
 BS9 .... 49 A6
Redpoll Dr BS20 .... 46 A6
RED POST 134 B7
Red Post Ct BA2 .... 134 B7
Red Rd TA8 .... 121 A2
Redshard La BS40 ..... 109 B7
Redshelf Wlk BS10 ..... 35 C3
REDWICK 22 B8
Redwick Cl BS11 .... 34 C2
Redwick Crossroads
 BS35 .... 22 C7
Redwick Gdns BS35 .... 22 C7
Redwick & Northwick CE
 Prim Sch BS35 .... 12 D2
Redwick Rd
 Pilning BS35 .... 22 C8
 Redwick BS35 .... 22 B8
Redwing Dr BS22 .... 88 D2
Redwing Gdns BS16 ... 50 E6
Redwood Cl
 Bristol BS30 .... 66 A3
 Nailsea BS48 .... 60 A2
 Radstock BA3 .... 139 E8
Redwood Ho BS13 ...... 79 D3
Redwood La BS48 ...... 77 C2
Redwoods The BS31 ... 81 D6
Reed Cl BS10 .... 49 D6
Reed Ct BS30 .... 65 F3
Reedley Rd BS9 .... 48 F5
Reedling Cl BS16 .... 50 E6
Reed's Row GL12 .... 19 D7
Reed Way BS22 .... 89 C3
Regency Dr BS4 .... 65 A2
Regent Apartments
 BS6 .... 49 C3
Regent Rd BS3 .... 63 E4
Regents Cl BS35 .... 8 B2
Regents St BS8 .... 142 A2
Regent St
 Bristol, Kingswood
  BS15 .... 65 D8
 Weston-S-M BS23 .... 104 E7
Regents The BS31 ...... 81 F6
REGIL 94 F2
Regil La BS40 .... 95 A6
Regil Rd BS40 .... 94 F3
Regina The BA1 .... 141 B3
Remenham Dr BS9 ..... 49 B5
Remenham Pk BS9 .... 49 B5
Rendcomb Cl BS22 .... 88 B2
Rendle Ho BS16 .... 51 F4
Rene Rd **12** BS5 ..... 50 B1
Rennison Ct BS23 ..... 104 E4
Repton Hall BS10 ...... 35 B2
Repton Rd BS4 .... 64 D3
Retford Ho BA2 .... 102 E5
Retort Rd BS11 .... 33 C3
Retreat The
 Radstock BA3 .... 134 E3
 Weston-S-M BS23 ...... 87 C1
Reubens Ct BS22 .... 88 F3
Reubins The BS5 .... 64 A8
Reynolds Cl BS31 ...... 82 A5
Reynold's Wlk BS7 .... 50 A7
Rhode Cl BS31 .... 82 A3

Rhodyate BS40 110 D2
Rhodyate Hill BS49 91 F6
Rhodyate La BS49 92 A7
Rhodyate The BS29 107 C1
Rhyne Terr BS23 104 D2
Rhyne View BS48 59 B1
Ribblesdale BS35 15 D8
Richards Cl BS22 89 B4
Richeson Cl BS10 34 F2
Richeson Wlk BS10 34 F2
Richmond Apartments
BS6 49 C3
Richmond Ave
Bristol, Montpelier BS6 49 F2
Bristol, Stoke Gifford
BS34 36 E5
Richmond Cl
Bath BA1 84 F1
Keynsham BS31 81 D4
Portishead BS20 45 E5
Richmond Ct
Bristol BS34 23 F1
7 Bristol, Clifton BS8 49 A2
2 Bristol, Windmill Hill
BS3 63 F4
Richmond Dale 6 BS8 49 A2
Richmond Gn BS48 59 F1
Richmond Hill
Bath BA1 84 F1
Bristol BS8 142 B3
Richmond Hill Ave
BS8 142 B3
Richmond Hts
Bath BA1 84 F2
Bristol BS8 142 B3
Richmond La
Bath BA1 84 F1
Bristol BS8 142 A3
Richmond Mews BS8 142 A3
Richmond Park Rd
BS8 142 A3
Richmond Pl BA1 84 F1
Richmond Rd
Bath BA1 84 F1
Bristol, Mangotsfield
BS16 52 A5
Bristol, Montpelier BS6 49 E1
Bristol, Pile Marsh BS5 64 E7
Richmond St
Bristol BS3 63 F4
Weston-S-M BS23 104 D7
Richmond Terr
Avonmouth BS11 33 B1
Bristol BS8 142 A3
Ricketts La BS22 89 A2
RICKFORD 110 B3
Rickford Cotts BS40 110 B4
Rickford La BS40 110 A3
Rickford Rd BS48 59 F1
Rickford Rise BS40 110 A3
Ricklands The BS40 95 A6
Rickyard Rd BS40 92 E2
Ride The BS15 52 A2
RIDGE 129 C5
Ridge Cl BS20 45 A4
Ridge Cres BS40 129 E6
Ridge Green Cl BA2 118 D8
Ridgehill BS9 49 C6
Ridge Jun Sch The
BS37 27 F2
Ridge La BS40 129 D5
Ridgemeade BS14 80 B4
Ridgemount Gdns
BS14 80 B5
Ridge The
Bristol, Hengrove BS14 80 C5
Bristol, Shirehampton
BS11 47 E7
Frampton Cotterell BS36 38 C7
Yatton BS49 91 B8
Ridgeview BS41 62 B2
Ridgeview Ho BS20 45 E3
RIDGEWAY 50 F3
Ridgeway
Frampton Cotterell
BS36 38 D7
Nailsea BS48 59 C1
Yate BS37 28 A2
Ridgeway Ave BS23 104 E6
Ridgeway Cl BS40 129 E6
Ridgeway Ct
Bristol BS14 80 C5
Bristol, Henbury BS10 35 A1
Ridgeway Gdns BS14 80 C5
Ridgeway Ind Ctr BS5 50 E2
Ridgeway La BS14 80 B5
Ridgeway Par BS5 50 E3
Ridgeway Rd
Bristol BS16 50 F3
Long Ashton BS41 62 A2
Ridgeway The
Bristol BS10 35 A1
Weston-S-M BS22 88 B2
Ridgewood BS9 48 D3
Riding Barn Hill BS30 67 A6
Ridingleaze BS11 34 A1
Ridings Cl BS37 28 D1
Ridings High Sch The
BS36 37 D6
Ridings Rd BS36 38 C6
Ridings The
Bristol BS13 78 E4
Frampton Cotterell BS36 38 C6
Ridley Ave BS15, BS16 52 B3
Ringspit La BS14, BS39 97 E8
Ringswell SN14 70 A7
Ringswell Gdns BA1 85 B1
Ringwell BA2 136 E4
Ringwell La BA2 136 E4
Ringwood Cres BS10 35 D1
Ringwood Gr BS23 88 A1
Ringwood Rd BA2 101 C5
Ripley Rd BS5 51 A1
Ripon Ct BS16 37 F2
Ripon Rd BS4 64 E6
Rippleside BS20 45 C5
Rippleside Rd BS21 57 G5
Ripple The BS21 59 D4
Risdale Rd BS3 62 F1
Risedale Ho BS15 65 D5
Risedale Rd BS25 125 A8
Rivendell BS22 89 A4
Rivergate BS1 143 C2
Riverland Dr BS13 78 F5
Riverleaze
Bristol BS9 48 C5
Portishead BS20 44 F6
River Mead
Clevedon BS21 73 D8
Yate BS37 27 C3
River Pl BA2 101 B6
River Rd
Chipping Sodbury BS37 28 A1
Portbury BS20 46 F8
RIVERSIDE 138 F7
Riverside BS24, BS29 107 B5
Riverside Bsns Pk
Bath BA2 141 B1
Bristol BS4 64 D6
Riverside Cl
Bristol BS11 47 F5
Clevedon BS21 57 D1
Midsomer Norton BA3 138 F7
Weston-S-M BS22 89 C3
Riverside Cotts
Bristol BS15 65 B1
Radstock BA3 134 A2
Riverside Ct
Bath BA2 141 B1
2 Bristol BS4 64 F6
Riverside Dr BS16 51 C7
Riverside Gdns
Bath BA1 141 B2
Midsomer Norton BA3 138 F7
Riverside Mews BS4 64 F6
Riverside Pk BS35 21 F6
Riverside Rd
Bath BA2 141 B2
Midsomer Norton BA3 138 F7
Riverside Stps BS4 64 E7
Riverside Way BS15 65 C3
Riverside Wlk
6 Bristol BS5 64 F6
Midsomer Norton BA3 138 F7
Rivers Rd BA1 141 C4
Rivers St BA1 141 B3
Rivers Street Mews
BA1 141 B3
River St BS2 143 C3
River Street Pl 5
BA1 141 B3
River Terr BS31 81 F5
River View BS16 50 E5
Riverway BS48 59 F3
River Wlk BS22 89 D2
Riverwood Ho BS16 37 C1
Riverwood Rd BS16 37 C1
Riviera Cres BS16 51 E4
Riviera Way BS34 37 A4
Roach's La GL9 30 D2
Road Hill
Batheaston SN13 86 E8
Colerne SN14 70 D1
Road Two BS10 22 A3
Roath Rd BS20 45 D5
Robbins Cl
Bristol BS32 36 F6
Marshfield SN14 69 F8
Robbins Ct BS16 52 B6
Robel Ave BS36 38 A8
Robert Ct
Bristol BS16 52 B7
Leigh Woods BS8 62 D7
Robertson Dr BS4 64 F6
Robertson Rd BS5 50 C2
Robert St
Bristol, Baptist Mills
BS5 50 B2
16 Bristol, Russell Town
BS5 64 B7
Robin Cl
Bristol, Brentry BS10 35 B2
Bristol BS14 80 D6
Midsomer Norton BA3 139 B8
Weston-S-M BS22 105 E8
Robin Dr BS24 105 E2
Robinia Wlk BS14 80 A7
Robin La BS21 57 F5
Robinson Cl BS48 76 A5
Robinson Dr BS5 64 A8
Robinson Way BS48 76 A5
Robin Way BS37 40 A7
Rob-Lynne Ct BS25 124 F8
Rochester Cl BS24 105 A1
Rochester Rd BS4 64 F5
Rochfort Ct BA1 102 B8
Rock Ave BS48 59 C2
Rock Cl BS4 64 E2
Rock Cotts BS20 47 E4
Rockeries Dr BS25 124 F8
Rockhall Cotts BA2 102 B1
Rock Hall Cotts BA2 102 B1
Rockhall Ho
Bath BA2 102 B1
10 Weston-S-M BS23 87 C1
Rockhall La BA2 102 B1
ROCKHAMPTON 8 E7
Rockhill Est BS31 81 F4
Rock Ho BS10 35 C3
Rockingham Gdns
BS11 48 A8
Rockingham Gr BS23 88 A1
Rockingham Rdbt
BS11 33 D6
Rock La
Bath BA2 102 B1
Bristol BS34 36 F4
Rockland Gr BS16 50 D5
Rockland Rd BS16 51 D7
Rockleaze
Bristol BS9 48 E2
9 Thornbury BS35 8 B1
Rockleaze Ave BS9 48 E3
Rockleaze Ct BS9 48 E3
Rockleaze Mans 12
BS23 87 C1
Rockleaze Rd BS9 48 E3
Rockliffe Ave BA2 102 B8
Rockliffe Rd BA2 102 B8
Rock Rd
Chilcompton BA3 138 D2
Keynsham BS31 81 E5
Midsomer Norton BA3 133 B2
Wick BS30 67 D8
Yatton BS49 91 C7
Rockside Ave BS16 51 F8
Rockside Dr BS9 49 C6
Rockside Gdns
Bristol BS16 51 F8
Frampton Cotterell BS36 38 C8
Rocks La BS40 77 E1
Rock St BS35 15 B8
Rockstowes Way BS10 35 D3
Rock The BS4 64 E3
Rockwell Ave BS11 34 B1
Rockwood Ho BS37 28 A4
Rodborough BS37 39 C7
Rodborough Way BS15 66 A7
Rodbourne Rd BS10 49 E6
RODE 137 F1
Rode Hill BA11 137 E1
Rodford Prim Sch
BS37 39 D7
Rodfords Mead BS14 80 A7
Rodford Way BS37 39 D7
Rodmead Wlk BS13 79 A4
Rodmoor Rd BS20 45 D6
Rodney BS24 105 A2
Rodney Ave BS15 65 A8
Rodney Cres BS34 36 A4
Rodney Ho BA2 101 A6
Rodney Pl BS8 142 A3
Rodney Rd
Backwell BS48 76 A6
Bristol BS15 65 A8
Saltford BS31 82 E2
Rodney Wlk BS15 51 A1
Rodway Ct BS16 52 A5
Rodway Hill BS16 52 B3
Rodway Hill Rd BS16 52 A4
Rodway Rd
Bristol BS34 36 A8
Bristol, Mangotsfield
BS16 52 A5
Bristol, Patchway BS34 35 F7
Rodway View BS15 51 F3
Roebuck Cl BS22 89 B4
Roegate Dr BS4 64 E6
Roegate Ho BS5 51 A1
Rogers Cl
Bristol BS30 66 B5
Clutton BS39 114 E3
Rogers Ct BS37 28 C1
Rogers Wlk BS30 66 D7
Rokeby Ave BS6 49 C1
ROLSTONE 89 F2
Roman Baths & Pump
Room The* BA1 141 C2
Roman Farm Ct BS11 34 C2
Roman Farm Rd BS4 79 E7
Roman Ho BA1 141 C4
Roman Rd
Bath BA1 141 C3
Bleadon BS24 122 C8
Bristol BS5 50 B1
Sandford BS25 107 F4
Roman Way
Bristol BS9 48 C4
Paulton BS39 132 C6
Peasedown St John
BA2 134 E7
Roman Wlk
Bristol, Kensington Park
BS4 64 C3
Bristol, Stoke Gifford
BS34 36 E5
Romney Ave BS7 50 B6
Romo Ct BS16 51 C4
Ronald Rd BS16 50 F6
Ronaldson BS30 66 C2
Ronayne Wlk BS16 51 C6
Ron Jones Ho 3 BS1 143 B4
Rookery Cl BS22 88 E3
Rookery La
Pilning BS35 23 A6
Pucklechurch BS30,
SN14 53 F4
Rookery Rd BS4 64 A3
Rookery Way BS14 79 F4
Rooksbridge Wlk BA2 101 B5
Roper's La BS40 92 E3
Rope Walk Ho 23 BS2 143 C3
Rope Wlk BS48 76 A5
Rosary Rdbt The BS16 52 D7
Rosary The BS16 52 D7
Rose Acre BS10 35 A3
Rosebay Mead BS16 50 E5
Roseberry Pk BS5 64 D8
Roseberry Pl BA2 101 C6
Roseberry Rd
Bath BA2 101 C6
Bristol BS5 64 C7
Rosebery Ave BS2 50 A1
Rosebery Ct 7 BS2 50 A1
Rosebery Terr BS8 142 B2
Rose Cl BS36 37 E4
Rose Cotts BS22 89 C2
Rosedale Ave BS23 105 A7
Rosedale Rd BS16 51 C3
Rose Gdns BS22 89 B4
ROSE GREEN 50 E1
Rose Green Cl BS5 50 E2
Rose Green Rd BS5 50 D2
Rose Hill BA1 85 C3
Rose La BS36 38 D6
Roseland Cl BA1 85 C3
Roselarge Gdns BS10 35 A2
Rosemary Cl BS32 36 F7
Rosemary Cres BS20 45 F5
Rosemary La
Bristol BS5 50 C2
Freshford BA2 120 B4
Rose Mead BS7 50 A7
Rose Meare Gdns
BS13 78 E7
Rosemont Terr BS8 142 A2
Rosemount Ct BS15 65 B8
Rosemount La BA2 102 B4
Rosemount Rd BS48 77 B8
Rosenberg Ho 6 BA1 141 B2
Rose Oak Dr BS36 38 D7
Rose Oak Gdns BS36 38 D7
Rose Oak La BS36 38 D7
Rose Rd BS5 64 E7
Rosery Cl BS9 49 A8
Rosery The BS16 51 C3
Rose Terr
Bath BA2 102 C2
Bristol BS8 142 B3
Rose Tree Ho BS16 51 F4
Rosevear BS2 64 A7
Roseville Ave BS30 66 A2
Rosewarn Cl BA2 101 A4
Rosewell Ct BA1 141 B2
Rose Wlk BS16 51 C3
Rosewood Ave BS35 14 F5
Roshni Gar E 16 BS5 50 B1
Roshni Gar W 15 BS5 50 B1
Rosling Rd BS7 49 E6
Roslyn Ave BS22 88 C1
Roslyn Rd BS6 49 C1
Rossall Ave BS34 36 C6
Rossall Rd BS4 64 D3
Ross Cl BS37 28 B1
Rossendale Cl BS22 88 F3
Rossiter Grange 5
BS13 78 F4
Rossiter Rd BA2 141 C1
Rossiter's La BS5 65 A6
Rossiter Wood Ct BS11 34 B2
Rosslyn Cl 1 BA1 101 B7
Rosslyn Rd BA1 101 B7
Rosslyn Way BS35 8 C3
ROTCOMBE 115 D2
Rotcombe La BS39 115 D2
Rotcombe Vale BS39 115 D2
Rounceval St BS37 28 A1
Roundhill Gr BA2 101 B3
Roundhill Pk BA2 101 A4
Roundmoor Cl BS31 82 D3
Roundmoor Gdns
BS14 80 D7
Round Oak Rd BS27 126 A1
Roundways BS36 38 D6
Rousham Rd BS5 50 A3
Rowacres
Bath BA2 101 B3
Bristol BS14 79 F6
Rowan Cl
Bristol BS16 51 A2
Nailsea BS48 60 A2
Rowan Ct
10 Bristol BS5 64 B7
Radstock BA3 133 E1
Yate BS37 27 C3
Rowan Ho BS13 79 D4
Rowan Pl BS24 89 B1
Rowans The
Bristol BS16 37 B1
Portishead BS20 45 B4
Rowan Tree Ho BS16 51 F4
Rowan Way
Bristol BS15 65 B3
Churchill BS40 109 A5
Rowan Wlk BS31 81 C4
ROWBERROW 109 A1
Rowberrow BS14 79 F7
Rowberrow La BS25 125 F8
Rowberrow Way BS48 59 E1
Rowland Ave BS16 50 D4
Rowlands Cl BA1 86 B2
Rowlandson Gdns BS7 50 B6
Rowley St BS3 63 C3
Rownham Cl BS3 62 E4
Rownham Ct BS8 142 A1
Rownham Hill BS8 62 E6
Rownham Mead BS8 142 A1
Row Of Ashes La BS40 93 F4
Rows The BS22 88 E2
Row The BS35 13 A7
Roxburgh BS8 62 F8
Royal Albert Rd BS6 49 A4
Royal Ave BA1 141 B3
Royal Cl BS10 34 D3
Royal Cres* BA1 141 A3
Royal Cres BS23 104 D8
Royal Ct BS23 104 D4
Royal Fort Rd BS2,
BS8 142 C3
Royal High Sch
Bath BA1 141 B4
Bath, Lansdown BA1 84 F2
Royal National Hospl for
Rheumatic Diseases
BA1 141 B2
Royal Par
Bristol BS8 142 B3
Weston-S-M BS23 104 D8
Royal Park Mews
BS8 142 A3
Royal Pk BS8 142 A3
Royal Portbury Dock Rd
BS20 46 E5
Royal Prom BS8 142 B3
Royal Rd BS16 52 A6
Royal Sands BS23 104 D4
Royal United Hospl
BA1 101 B8
Royal Victoria Pk BS10 35 B2
Royal West of England
Acad* BS8 142 B3
Royal York Cres BS8 62 F6
Royal York Ho 7 BS8 142 A2
Royal York Mews 6
BS8 142 A2
Royal York Villas BS8 142 A2
Royate Hill BS5 50 D2
Roycroft Rd BS34 36 B2
Roy King Gdns BS30 66 C6
Royston Lo BS23 104 D6
Royston Wlk BS10 35 D2
Rozel Ho 14 BS23 87 C1
Rozel Rd BS7 49 E5
Rubens Cl BS31 82 A5
Ruby St BS3 63 B3
Ruckley Ford BA3 135 A2
Ruddymead BS21 57 F2
Rudford Cl BS34 24 B1
Rudge Cl BS15 51 F2
RUDGEWAY 14 F1
Rudgeway Pk BS35 14 F1
Rudgeway Rd BS39 132 E4
Rudgewood Cl BS13 79 D4
Rudgleigh Ave BS20 47 C4
Rudgleigh Rd BS20 47 C4
Rudhall Gn BS22 89 B3
Rudhall Gr BS10 49 E7
Rudmore Pk BA1 101 A7
Rudthorpe Rd BS7 49 E5
Ruett La BS39 132 B4
Ruffet Rd BS36 38 B4
Rugby Rd BS4 64 D3
Runnymead Ave BS4 64 D2
Runnymede BS15 51 E1
Runswick Rd BS4 64 C3
Rupert Ho BS2 142 C4
Rupert St
Bristol BS1 143 A3
Bristol, Redfield BS5 64 C7
Rusham BS13 78 F4
Rush Cl BS32 24 D2
Rushgrove Gdns
BS39 113 C4
RUSH HILL 101 B2
Rush Hill
Bath BA2 101 C2
Farrington Gurney
BS39 131 F3
Rushmead La SN14 55 F2
Rushmoor BS21 57 C1
Rushmoor Gr BS48 76 A5
Rushmoor La BS48 76 A5
Rushton Dr BS36 38 D7
Rushway BS40 109 F4
Rushy BS30 66 A4
Rushy Way BS16 38 A1
Ruskin Gr BS7 50 A8
Ruskin Ho BS34 36 A8
Ruskin Rd BA3 133 C1
Russell Ave BS15 65 E7
Russell Cl BS40 95 A6
Russell Gr BS6 49 C5
Russell Rd
Bristol, Chester Park
BS16 51 B2
Bristol, Westbury Park
BS6 49 B4
Clevedon BS21 57 E3
Locking BS24 106 C6
Russell St BA1 141 B3
RUSSELL TOWN 64 B7
Russell Town Ave BS5 64 B8
Russell Town Ind Pk 18
BS5 64 C7
Russet Cl BS35 14 A3
Russet Ct GL12 11 F4
Russets The BS20 45 F4
Russett Cl BS48 76 B6
Russett Gr BS48 75 C8
Russet Way BA2 134 D7
Russ La BS21 73 E4
Russ St BS2 143 C2
Rustic Pk BS35 22 A6
Rutherford Cl BS30 66 A3
Ruthven Rd BS4 79 E8
Rutland Ave BS30 66 A2
Rutland Cl BS22 105 C8

Rutland Rd BS7.....49 E3
Rydal Ave BS24.....106 A4
Rydal Ho BS34.....36 A8
Rydal Rd BS23.....104 F4
Ryde Rd BS4.....64 B2
Rye Cl BS13.....78 E6
Ryecroft Ave BS22.....88 E2
Ryecroft Ct BS36.....38 C7
Ryecroft Rd BS36.....38 C8
Ryecroft Rise BS41.....64 B3
Ryedown La BS30.....66 D2
Ryland Pl 1 BS2.....50 A2
Rylestone Cl BS36.....37 F8
Rylestone Gr BS9.....48 F5
Rysdale Rd BS9.....48 F6

S

Sabin Cl BA2.....101 B3
Sabrina Way BS9.....48 C4
Saco Ho
11 Bath BA1.....141 B2
Bristol BS1.....143 B2
Sacred Heart Prep Sch
BS40.....96 A3
Sadbury Cl BS22.....89 B4
Saddlers Ct BS15.....51 D1
Sadlier Cl BS11.....48 A8
Saffron Ct BA1.....141 C4
Saffron Ho 10 BS23.....104 E8
Saffrons The 7 BS22.....89 B4
Sage Cl BS20.....44 E4
Sages Mead BS32.....36 E8
St Agnes Ave BS4.....63 F2
St Agnes Ct BS48.....60 A1
St Agnes Gdns BS4.....63 F2
St Agnes Wlk BS4.....63 F2
St Aidan's Cl BS5.....65 B6
St Aidan's Rd BS5.....65 B6
St Alban's Rd BS6.....49 B4
St Aldams Dr BS16.....53 B5
St Aldwyn's Cl BS7.....49 F8
St Andrews
Bristol BS30.....66 B6
Yate BS37.....27 F1
St Andrew's CE Jun Sch
BS49.....91 C4
St Andrew's CE Prim Sch
BA1.....141 B4
St Andrew's CE Prim Sch
GL12.....10 A1
St Andrews Cl
Nailsea BS48.....60 A1
Weston-S-M BS22.....88 F3
St Andrew's Cl BS49.....91 C4
St Andrew's Dr BS21.....57 C2
St Andrews Gate Rdbt
BS11.....33 B2
Saint Andrews Mews
BS6.....49 E3
St Andrew's Par 1
BS23.....104 F4
St Andrews Rd BS48.....76 B5
St Andrew's Rd
Avonmouth BS11.....33 B1
Bristol BS6.....49 E2
St Andrews Road Sta
BS11.....33 B4
St Andrew's Terr BA1.....141 B3
St Andrews Trad Est
BS11.....33 C2
ST ANNE'S.....64 E5
St Anne's Ave BS31.....81 D6
St Anne's CE Prim Sch
BS30.....66 C3
St Anne's CE Prim Sch
BS24.....90 B5
St Annes Cl 7 BS5.....64 F6
St Annes Cl BS30.....66 B4
St Annes Ct BS4.....64 D5
St Annes Ct BS5.....81 D6
St Annes Dr BS30.....66 C2
St Anne's Dr
Frampton Cotterell
BS36.....38 C5
Wick BS30.....67 B7
St Anne's Inf Sch BS4.....64 D5
St Anne's Jun Sch BS4.....64 D5
ST ANNE'S PARK.....64 E6
St Anne's Park Prim Sch
BS4.....64 E5
St Anne's Park Rd BS4.....64 E6
St Anne's Rd
Bristol, St Anne's Park
BS4.....64 D6
Bristol, St George BS5.....65 B6
St Anne's Terr BS4.....64 E5
St Ann's Pl BA1.....141 B2
St Ann's Way BA2.....102 C6
St Anthony's Cl BA3.....133 A2
St Anthony's Dr BS30.....67 B7
St Aubin's Ave BS4.....64 F3
St Aubyn's Ave BS4.....104 D2
St Augustines of
Canterbury RC Sch
BS16.....51 F7
St Augustine's Par
BS1.....143 A2
St Augustine's Pl 1
BS1.....143 A2
St Austell Cl BS48.....76 A8
St Austell Rd BS22.....105 B8
St Barnabas CE Prim Sch
Bristol, Montpelier BS6.....49 F1

St Barnabas CE Prim Sch
continued
Bristol, North Common
BS30.....66 C6
Portishead BS20.....45 B5
St Barnabas Cl
Bristol, Lower Knowle
BS4.....63 F1
Bristol, Warmley BS30.....66 C7
Midsomer Norton BA3.....133 B3
St Barnabas Ho BS30.....66 C7
St Bartholomew's Rd
BS7.....49 E2
St Bede's RC Coll BS11.....34 B2
St Bede's Rd BS15.....51 D2
St Benedict's RC Prim Sch
BA3.....139 C7
St Bernadette RC Prim
Sch BS14.....80 B6
St Bernadette RC Prim Sch
BS14.....80 B6
St Bernard's RC Prim Sch
BS11.....47 E6
St Bernard's Rd BS11.....47 E6
St Bonaventure's RC Prim
Sch BS7.....49 D4
St Brelades Gr BS4.....64 F5
St Brendans Rdbt
BS11.....33 C1
St Brendan's Sixth Form
Coll BS4.....65 A1
St Brendan's Way BS11.....33 B1
St Brenda's Ct BS48.....142 A3
St Briavels Dr BS37.....39 D8
St Bridges Cl BS22.....88 A6
St Bridges Ct BS22.....88 A6
St Cadoc Ho BS31.....81 F5
ST CATHERINE.....69 F1
St Catherine's Cl BA2.....102 C6
St Catherines Ct BS4.....64 A2
St Catherine's Hosp 11
BA1.....141 C2
St Catherine's Ind Est
BS3.....63 D3
St Catherine's Mead
BS20.....47 D3
St Catherines Pl 7
BS3.....63 D4
St Catherine's Terr
BS3.....63 D3
St Chad's Ave BA3.....133 A1
St Chad's Gn BA3.....139 A8
St Charles Cl BA3.....133 A2
St Christophers Cl
BA2.....102 C8
St Christopher's Ct
BS21.....57 E5
St Christopher's Sch
BS6.....49 B4
St Clements Ct
Bath BA1.....84 C1
Bristol, St Pauls BS2.....143 C4
5 Bristol, Upper Soundwell
BS16.....51 D3
Clevedon BS21.....57 E4
Keynsham BS31.....81 E4
2 Weston-S-M BS22.....89 A2
St Clements Rd BS31.....81 F4
St David's Ave BS30.....66 B5
St David's Cl BS22.....88 B2
St David's Cres BS4.....64 F6
St David's Ct BS21.....73 E8
St Davids Mews BS1.....142 C2
St Dunstans Cl BS31.....81 E6
St Dunstan's Rd BS3.....63 C2
St Edward's Rd BS8.....142 B2
St Edyth's Rd BS9.....48 C6
SS Peter & Paul RC Cath*
BS8.....142 A4
SS Peter & Paul RC Prim
Sch BS8.....142 C4
St Fagans Cl BS30.....66 B2
St Francis Dr
Wick BS30.....67 B7
Winterbourne BS36.....37 F6
St Francis RC Prim Sch
BS48.....59 F1
St Francis Rd
6 Bristol BS3.....63 A4
Keynsham BS31.....81 D6
St Gabriel's Bsns Pk 3
BS5.....64 B8
St Gabriel's Rd BS5.....64 B8
ST GEORGE.....65 A7
St George CE Prim Sch
BS1.....142 B2
ST GEORGES.....89 D3
St George's* BS1.....142 C2
St Georges Ho 10 BS5.....64 F6
St Georges Bldgs
BA1.....141 A3
St George's Hill
Bath BA2.....102 D8
Easton-in-G BS20.....47 A3
St Georges Ho BS5.....64 E8
St George's Ho BS8.....142 B2
St George's Hts 12
BS5.....64 D7
St Georges Ind Est
BS11.....33 B3
St Georges Pl BA1.....141 A3
St Georges Prim Sch
BS22.....89 C3
St Georges Rd BS1.....142 C2
St George's Rd
Keynsham BS31.....81 D6
Portbury BS20.....46 E7
St Giles Barton GL12.....19 D8

St Gregory's RC Sch
BA2.....118 D8
St Gregory's Rd BS7.....49 F8
St Helena Rd BS6.....49 B4
St Helens CE Prim Sch
BS35.....15 A4
St Helens Dr
Bristol BS30.....66 C2
Wick BS30.....67 C7
St Helen's Wlk BS5.....51 A1
St Helier Ave BS4.....64 F3
St Hilary Cl BS9.....48 D5
St Ivel Way BS30.....66 C6
St Ives Cl BS48.....60 A1
St Ives Rd BS23.....105 A5
St James BS24.....105 E7
St James' Barton BS1.....143 B4
St James' Cl BS35.....8 C3
St James' Ct BS32.....24 C3
St James Pl BS32.....52 A5
St James's Cl BS8.....49 B1
St James's Par BA1.....141 B2
St James's Pk BA1.....141 B4
St James's Sq BA1.....141 A4
St James's St
Bath BA1.....141 B4
Bristol BS16.....52 A5
St James St BS2.....104 D7
St John's BA1.....101 B8
St John's Ave BS21.....57 F3
St John's Bridge 5
BS1.....143 A3
St John's CE Prim Sch
BS8.....49 A2
St John's CE Prim Sch
BS31.....81 E5
St John's CE Prim Sch
BA3.....133 A1
St John's Cl
Peasedown St John
BA2.....134 B7
Weston-S-M BS23.....87 D1
St John's Cres
Bristol BS3.....63 E2
Midsomer Norton BA3.....133 A2
St Johns Ct
Axbridge BS26.....125 B2
Bath BA2.....141 C3
Bristol, Bedminster BS3.....63 D2
Bristol BS16.....51 A3
Keynsham BS31.....81 E6
St John's Ho BS5.....64 D8
St John's La BS3.....63 E2
St John's Mead CE Prim
Sch BS37.....28 B1
St John's Pl BA1.....141 B2
St John's RC Prim Sch
BA2.....102 B6
St Johns Rd BS16.....116 B1
St John's Rd
Backwell BS48.....76 B5
Bath BA2.....141 C3
Bath, Lower Weston
BA1.....101 C7
Bristol, Bedminster BS3.....63 C3
Bristol, Clifton BS8.....49 A1
Bristol, Southville BS3.....63 D4
Clevedon BS21.....57 F3
St Johns St 4 BS5.....63 D3
St John's St BS3.....63 C3
St John St 2 BS35.....8 B1
St Johns Way BS37.....28 C2
St John the Evangelist CE
Prim Sch BS21.....57 E1
St Joseph's RC Prim Sch
Bristol BS16.....51 B3
Portishead BS20.....45 D3
St Joseph's Rd
Bristol BS10.....35 B3
Weston-S-M BS23.....87 E1
St Judes Ho 21 BS2.....143 C3
St Jude's Terr BS22.....88 C1
St Julian's CE Prim Sch
BA2.....118 E1
St Julian's Rd BA2.....134 F5
St Katharine's CE Prim
Sch BS40.....94 A7
St Katherine's Sch
BS20.....47 E3
St Kenya Ct BS31.....81 F5
St Keyna Ct BS31.....81 F5
St Keyna Rd BS31.....81 E5
St Kilda's Rd BA2.....101 D5
St Ladoc Rd BS31.....81 D6
St Laud Cl BS9.....48 D5
St Leonard's Rd
Bristol, Horfield BS7.....49 E5
Bristol, Lower Easton
BS5.....50 C2
St Loe Cl BS14.....79 F3
St Lucia Cl BS7.....49 E7
St Lucia Cres BS7.....49 E7
St Lukes Cl BS16.....52 C7
St Luke's Cres BS3.....63 F4
St Luke's Ct BS3.....63 E4
St Luke's Gdns BS4.....64 E4
St Luke's Mews BS4.....64 E2
St Luke's Rd
Bath BA2.....101 F3
Bristol BS3.....63 F4
Midsomer Norton BA3.....132 F2
St Luke St 1 BS5.....64 B7
St Margarets Cl BS48.....76 A5
St Margaret's Cl BS31.....81 D6
St Margaret's Dr BS9.....49 C5

St Margaret's La BS48.....76 A5
St Margaret's Terr
BS23.....104 D8
St Mark's Ave 1 BS5.....50 B1
St Mark's CE Sch BA1.....85 B2
St Marks Church Ho 4
BS5.....50 B1
St Marks Cl BS31.....81 E6
St Mark's Ecumenical CE/
Methodist Prim Sch
BS22.....88 F4
St Marks Gdns BA2.....141 C1
St Mark's Gr 8 BS5.....50 B1
St Mark's Ho 13 BS5.....50 B1
St Mark's Rd
Bath BA2.....141 C1
Bristol BS5.....50 B1
Midsomer Norton BA3.....133 A2
Weston-S-M BS22.....89 A3
St Mark's Terr 11 BS5.....50 B1
St Martins BS21.....57 E5
St Martin's CE Jun Sch
BS22.....88 D2
St Martins Cl BS4.....64 A1
St Martins Ct BS22.....88 E3
St Martin's Ct BA2.....101 E1
St Martin's Garden Prim
Sch BA2.....101 D1
St Martin's Gdns BS4.....64 B1
St Martins Hospl BA2.....101 E1
St Martins Ind Pk BS11.....33 F5
St Martin's La SN14.....69 F8
St Martin's Pk SN14.....69 F8
St Martin's Rd BS4.....64 B2
St Martin's Wlk BS4.....64 B1
St Mary CE Prim Sch
BA3.....133 A1
St Mary Redcliffe CE Prim
Sch BS3.....63 E4
St Mary Redcliffe &
Temple Sch BS1.....143 B1
St Mary's Bldgs BA2.....141 B1
St Mary's CE Prim Sch
Portbury BS20.....46 E3
Radstock BA3.....134 C1
Thornbury BS35.....8 A2
St Mary's CE Prim Sch
Timsbury BA2.....116 C3
Yate BS37.....27 E2
St Marys Cl
Bristol BS30.....66 B5
Hutton BS24.....105 D2
St Mary's Cl
Bath BA2.....102 B6
Timsbury BA2.....116 B2
St Mary's Ct BS24.....105 A1
St Mary's Gdns BS40.....109 B5
St Mary's Gr BS48.....75 C8
St Mary's Hospl BS8.....142 B3
St Mary's Park Rd
BS20.....45 C4
St Mary's Pk BS48.....75 C8
St Mary's Prim Sch
BS20.....46 E3
St Marys RC Prim Sch
BS34.....37 A7
St Mary's RC Prim Sch
BA1.....84 B1
St Mary's Rd
Bristol BS11.....47 D7
Hutton BS24.....105 D2
Leigh Woods BS8.....62 D6
Portishead BS20.....45 C4
St Marys Rise BA3.....134 C2
St Mary's St BS26.....125 C2
St Mary St BS35.....15 B8
St Marys Way 6 BS35.....8 B1
St Mary's Way BS37.....27 F2
St Mary's Wlk BS11.....47 D6
St Matthew's Ave 11
BS6.....49 D1
St Matthew's Cl BS23.....87 D1
St Matthews Hall 20
BS5.....64 C7
St Matthew's Pl BA2.....102 B5
St Matthew's Rd BS6.....143 A4
St Matthias & Dr Bell's CE
Prim Sch BS16.....51 A4
St Matthias Ho BS2.....143 B3
St Matthias Pk BS2.....143 B3
St Michael on the Mount
CE Prim Sch BS2.....142 C3
St Michael's Ave
Clevedon BS21.....57 F1
Weston-S-M BS22.....89 A3
St Michael's CE Jun Sch
BA2.....101 A6
St Michaels CE Prim Sch
BS36.....37 E6
St Michael's CE Prim Sch
BS34.....36 E5
St Michael's Cl BS7.....49 E7
St Michael's Ct BS36.....37 E7
St Michael's Ct BS15.....65 B8
St Michael's Ct BA2.....119 E8
St Michael's Hill BS2.....142 C4
St Michael's Hospl
BS2.....142 C4
St Michael's Pk BS2.....142 C4
St Michael's Rd BA1.....141 B2
St Michaels Rd BA2.....101 A5
St Michael's Rd BA2.....101 A5
St Monica Ct BS9.....49 A5
St Nicholas Almshouses 7
BS1.....143 A2
St Nicholas' CE Prim Sch
BA3.....134 A2

St Nicholas Chantry CE
Prim Sch BS21.....57 G3
St Nicholas Cl BA15.....120 D7
St Nicholas Ct BA2.....85 F1
St Nicholas of Tolentine
RC Prim Sch BS5.....64 A8
St Nicholas Pk 10 BS5.....50 B1
St Nicholas Rd
Bristol BS2.....143 C4
Weston-S-M BS23.....104 D2
Whitchurch BS14.....80 C4
St Nicholas' Rd BS2.....49 F1
St Nicholas St BS1.....143 A2
St Nicholas Way BS48.....75 D2
St Oswald's Ct BS13.....79 A8
St Oswald's Ct BS6.....49 B3
St Oswald's Rd BS6.....49 B3
St Patricks Ct BS31.....81 E5
St Patrick's Ct BA2.....102 B6
St PAULS.....64 C4
St Pauls Ho 13 BS3.....63 D4
St Pauls Pl
Bath BA1.....141 B2
Midsomer Norton BA3.....133 A2
St Paul's Rd
Bristol BS8.....142 B4
2 Bristol, Southville
BS3.....63 D4
Weston-S-M BS23.....104 E5
St Paul's St BS2.....143 B4
St Peter's Ave BS23.....87 D1
St Peter's CE Prim Sch
BS20.....45 C4
St Peter's Cres BS36.....38 B8
St Peters Ct 12 BS3.....63 D4
St Peter's Ho BS8.....142 B2
St Peters Lo BS20.....45 D4
St Peter's Rd BS20.....45 D4
St Peters Rd BS30.....66 A8
St Peter's Rise BS13.....79 B7
St Peter's Terr 6
BA2.....101 B6
St Peter's Wlk 3 BS9.....49 B6
St Philips Central BS2.....64 A5
St Philip's CE Prim Sch
BA2.....101 D2
St Philips Cswy BS2.....64 B5
ST PHILIP'S MARSH.....64 B5
St Philips Rd BS2.....143 C3
St Philips Trad Pk BS2.....64 B4
St Phillips Rd BS2.....64 A4
St Pias X RC Prim Sch
BS13.....79 A5
St Pierre Dr BS30.....66 B6
St Ronan's Ave BS6.....49 C2
St Saviour's CE Inf Sch
BA1.....85 B2
St Saviour's CE Jun Sch
BA1.....85 B2
St Saviours Ho BS4.....63 F2
St Saviour's Rd BA1.....85 C2
St Saviour's Rise BS30.....66 B3
St Saviour's Terr 10
BA1.....85 B1
St Saviours Way 4
BA1.....85 C1
St Stephen's Ave 3
BS1.....143 A2
St Stephens Bsns Ctr
BS30.....66 C5
St Stephen's CE Jun Sch
BS15.....51 D2
St Stephen's CE Prim Sch
BA1.....84 F1
St Stephens Cl
Bristol, Brentry BS10.....35 C2
Bristol, Upper Soundwell
BS16.....51 E3
St Stephen's Cl BA1.....84 F1
St Stephen's Ct 1 BA1.....141 B4
St Stephen's Pl BA1.....141 B4
St Stephen's Rd
Bath BA1.....141 B4
Bristol BS16.....51 D2
St Stephen's St BS1.....143 A2
St Swithin's Pl BA1.....141 C4
St Swithin's Yd BA2.....141 C3
St Teresa's RC Prim Sch
BS16.....35 E5
St Thomas Pl BS1.....143 B2
St Thomas Rd BA3.....133 B2
St Thomas St E BS1.....143 B2
St Thomas St BS1.....143 B2
St Ursula's High Sch
BS9.....49 A6
St Vigor & St John CE
Prim Sch BA3.....138 C3
St Vincent's Hill 1
BS6.....49 A2
St Vincents Rd BS8.....142 A2
St Vincents Trad Est
BS2.....64 C6
Saint Way BS34.....37 A4
St Werburgh's Pk BS2.....50 A2
St Werburgh's Prim Sch
BS2.....50 A2
St Werburgh's Rd BS2.....49 F2
St Whytes Rd BS4.....79 C8
St Winifreds Dr BA2.....102 D2
St Wulfstans Ave BS10.....49 A8
Salcombe Gdns BS22.....89 A2
Salcombe Rd BS4.....64 A1
Salem Rd BS36.....37 F7

Salisbury Ave BS15 . . . . **65** B8
Salisbury Dr BS16 . . . . **51** E6
Salisbury Gdns BS16 . . . . . **51** E5
Salisbury Pk BS16 . . . . **51** E6
Salisbury Rd
  Bath BA1 . . . . **85** B2
  Bristol, Mangotsfield
  BS16 . . . . **51** E6
  Bristol, Redland BS6 . . . . **49** D2
  Bristol, St Anne's BS4 . . . **64** D5
  Paulton BS39 . . . . **132** F4
  Weston-S-M BS22 . . . . **88** C1
Salisbury St
  Bristol, The Marsh BS5 . . **64** E7
  Bristol, Russell Town
  BS5 . . . . **64** B6
Salisbury Terr BS23 . . . . . **104** D7
Sallybarn Cl BS30 . . . . **65** E2
Sally Hill BS20 . . . . **45** F2
Sally In The Wood BA1,
  BA15 . . . . **103** D6
Sally Lunn's Kitchen Mus*
  BA1 . . . . **141** C2
Sallysmead Cl BS13 . . . . . . **79** B4
Sallys Way BS36 . . . . **37** F7
Salmon Cl BS35 . . . . **22** A6
Salmons Way BS16 . . . . **52** B8
SALTFORD **82** D2
Saltford CE Prim Sch
  BS31 . . . . **82** E3
Saltford Cl BS4 . . . . **64** D1
Salthouse Ct BS21 . . . . **57** D2
Salthouse Farm Pk
  BS35 . . . . **22** A7
Salthouse Rd BS21 . . . . **57** D2
Salthrop Rd BS7 . . . . **49** E4
Saltings Cl BS21 . . . . **57** D2
Saltmarsh Dr BS11 . . . . **34** A1
Saltwell Ave BS14 . . . . **80** C5
Salway Cl BS40 . . . . **92** E3
Sambourne La BS20 . . . . . . **47** C4
Samian Way BS34 . . . . **36** E5
Sampson House Bsns Pk
  BS34 . . . . **34** D7
Sampsons Rd BS13 . . . . **79** D4
Samuel St BS5 . . . . **64** C8
Samuel White Rd BS15 . . . **65** A4
Samuel White's Inf Sch
  BS15 . . . . **65** C4
Samuel Wright Cl
  BS30 . . . . **66** D5
San Andreas BS34 . . . . **35** E6
Sanctuary Gdns BS9 . . . . . **48** D3
Sanctuary The BS11 . . . . . . **47** E4
Sandbach Rd BS4 . . . . **64** D4
Sandbed Rd BS2 . . . . **50** A2
Sandburrows Rd BS13 . . . . **78** F6
Sandburrows Wlk
  BS13 . . . . **78** F6
Sandcroft BS14 . . . . **79** F6
Sandcroft Ave BS23 . . . . . **104** D2
Sand Farm La BS22 . . . . . . **88** A6
SANDFORD **108** A3
Sandford Cl **2** BS21 . . . . . **57** D1
Sandford Prim Sch
  BS25 . . . . **108** B4
Sandford Rd
  Bristol BS8 . . . . **142** A1
  Weston-S-M BS23 . . . . . . **105** A4
  Winscombe BS25 . . . . **107** F1
Sandgate Rd BS4 . . . . **64** D3
Sand Hill BS4 . . . . **64** C4
Sandholme Cl BS16 . . . . . . **51** D8
Sandholme Rd BS4 . . . . **64** D4
Sandhurst BS37 . . . . **39** D8
Sandhurst Cl BS34 . . . . **24** B1
Sandhurst Rd BS4 . . . . **64** D4
Sandling Ave BS7 . . . . **50** A7
Sandmead Rd BS25 . . . . . **108** A4
Sandown Cl BS16 . . . . **37** F1
Sandown Rd
  Bristol, Filton BS34 . . . . . **36** C3
  Bristol, Kensington Park
  BS4 . . . . **64** D4
Sandpiper Dr BS22 . . . . **88** F1
Sandpits La GL9 . . . . **20** A2
Sand Rd BS22 . . . . **88** B5
Sandringham Ave
  BS16 . . . . **51** E8
Sandringham Ct **2**
  BS23 . . . . **104** F5
Sandringham Pk BS16 . . . . **51** E8
Sandringham Rd
  Bristol, Kensington Park
  BS4 . . . . **64** D4
  Bristol, Longwell Green
  BS30 . . . . **65** F2
  Bristol, Stoke Gifford
  BS34 . . . . **36** D4
  1 Weston-S-M BS23 . . . **104** F5
Sands Hill SN14 . . . . **54** E3
Sands La BS36 . . . . **25** F1
Sandstone Rise BS36 . . . . . **37** E4
Sandwich Rd BS4 . . . . **64** D4
Sandy Cl BS32 . . . . **36** E4
Sandy La
  Aust BS35 . . . . **13** A7
  Aust BS35 . . . . **13** A7
  Bristol BS5 . . . . **50** C3
  Easton-in-G BS8 . . . . **61** A8
  Failand BS8 . . . . **61** C7
  Stanton Drew BS39,
  BS40 . . . . **96** E3
Sandyleaze BS9 . . . . **48** E7
Sandy Lo BS37 . . . . **39** E8
Sandy Park Rd BS4 . . . . **64** C3
Sarabeth Dr BA2 . . . . **117** A4

Saracen St BA1 . . . . **141** C3
Saracens The BS7 . . . . **49** E5
Sarah St BS5 . . . . **64** B7
Sargent St BS3 . . . . **63** E4
Sarum Cl BS16 . . . . **52** C6
Sarum Cres BS10 . . . . **35** C1
Sassoon Ct BS30 . . . . **66** D5
Satchfield Cl BS10 . . . . **34** F2
Satchfield Cres BS10 . . . . . **34** F2
Satellite Bsns Pk BS5 . . . . **64** D6
Sates Way BS9 . . . . **49** C6
Saunders Rd BS16 . . . . **51** E4
Saunton Wlk BS4 . . . . **79** E8
Savages Wood BS32 . . . . . . **36** E8
Savages Wood Rd
  BS32 . . . . **36** D8
Savernake Rd BS22 . . . . . . **88** F3
Saville Cres BS22 . . . . **105** C8
Saville Gate Cl BS9 . . . . . . **48** F4
Saville Mews BS6 . . . . **143** A4
Saville Pl BS8 . . . . **142** A2
Saville Rd
  Bristol BS9 . . . . **48** F3
  Weston-S-M BS22 . . . . . . **105** C8
Saville Row BS1 . . . . **141** B3
Savoy Rd BS4 . . . . **64** D4
Savoy The BS11 . . . . **47** E6
Saw Cl BA1 . . . . **141** B2
Sawmill Gdns BA3 . . . . . . **138** D3
Saw Mill La **5** BS35 . . . . . . **8** B1
Sawyers Cl
  Chilcompton BA3 . . . . . . **138** D3
  Wraxall BS48 . . . . **60** A2
Sawyers St BS21 . . . . **57** G3
Saxby Cl
  Clevedon BS21 . . . . **57** D1
  Weston-S-M BS22 . . . . **89** B4
Saxon Ct
  Axbridge BS26 . . . . **125** C1
  Weston-S-M BS22 . . . . **89** D3
Saxon Rd
  Bristol BS2 . . . . **50** A2
  Weston-S-M BS22 . . . . . . **105** C8
Saxon St BS40 . . . . **109** D6
Saxon Way
  Bristol BS32 . . . . **24** C1
  Peasedown St John
  BA2 . . . . **134** E8
  Winsley BA15 . . . . **120** F7
Says La BS40 . . . . **109** B4
Say Wlk BS30 . . . . **66** D7
SBI Ctr BS15 . . . . **65** B5
Scafell Cl BS23 . . . . **88** A1
Scandrett Cl BS10 . . . . **34** F3
Scantleberry Cl BS16 . . . . **51** D8
Scaurs The BS22 . . . . **88** F2
School Cl
  Banwell BS29 . . . . **107** B3
  Bristol BS14 . . . . **79** F4
  Bristol, Eastville BS5 . . . . **50** D2
  Bristol, Patchway BS34 . . **36** C8
  Hillesley GL12 . . . . **19** E8
School Ct BS34 . . . . **37** A5
School La
  Badminton GL9 . . . . **30** E2
  Barrow Gurney BS48 . . . . **77** D5
  Batheaston BA1 . . . . **85** F4
  2 Bristol BS16 . . . . **50** E5
  Chew Stoke BS40 . . . . . . **112** D8
  Farrington Gurney
  BS39 . . . . **132** A4
  Felton BS48 . . . . **94** A8
  Kilmersdon BA3 . . . . **140** A6
  Rowberrow BS25 . . . . . . **109** A1
  Wick St L BS22 . . . . **89** B7
School of Christ the King
  RC Prim Sch BS4 . . . . **79** E8
School Rd
  Bristol, Brook Hill BS4 . . **64** E3
  Bristol BS15 . . . . **65** C8
  Bristol, Cadbury Heath
  BS30 . . . . **66** A4
  Bristol, Oldland Common
  BS30 . . . . **66** A4
  Bristol, Totterdown BS4 . . **64** A3
  Frampton Cotterell BS36 . **38** A8
  Wrington BS40 . . . . **92** E2
School View BS48 . . . . **60** A1
School Way BS35 . . . . **22** A6
School Wlk
  Bristol BS5 . . . . **50** D1
  Yate BS37 . . . . **27** C2
Scobell Rise BS39 . . . . . . **115** D2
Scop The BS32 . . . . **24** B5
Score La BS40 . . . . **110** E2
Score The BS40 . . . . **110** E3
Scotch Horn Cl BS48 . . . . . **59** F2
Scotch Horn Way **5**
  BS48 . . . . **59** F2
Scot Elm Dr BS24 . . . . **89** D1
Scot La BS40 . . . . **99** F8
Scotland La BS4, BS14 . . . . **81** A7
Scott Cl
  BS16 . . . . **51** A4
Scott Lawrence Cl
  BS16 . . . . **51** A7
Scott Rd BS23 . . . . **105** A4
Scott Way BS37 . . . . **39** F8
Scott Wlk BS30 . . . . **66** D7
Scumbrum La BS39 . . . . . **115** C2
Sea Bank Rd BS20 . . . . **32** E1
Seabrook Rd BS22 . . . . **88** D1
Seagry Cl BS10 . . . . **35** C1
SEA MILLS **48** B6
Sea Mills Inf Sch BS9 . . . . **48** C7
Sea Mills Jun Sch BS9 . . . . **48** B5
Sea Mills La BS9 . . . . **48** C5

Sea Mills Sta BS9 . . . . **48** B4
SeaQuarium* BS23 . . . . . **104** D6
Searle Court Ave **64** E4
Searle Cres BS23 . . . . **105** A6
Seaton Cl BA2 . . . . **57** G2
Seaton Dr BA2 . . . . **63** D1
Seaton Rd BS5 . . . . **50** C1
Seavale Mews BS21 . . . . . . **57** E4
Seavale Rd BS21 . . . . **57** E4
Seaview Rd
  Portishead, Redcliffe Bay
  BS20 . . . . **44** F4
  Portishead, West Hill
  BS20 . . . . **44** F6
Seawalls BS9 . . . . **48** D2
Seawalls Rd BS9 . . . . **48** D2
Second Ave
  Bath BA2 . . . . **101** D5
  Bristol BS14 . . . . **80** B7
  Radstock BA3 . . . . **139** C7
Second Way BS11 . . . . **33** D1
Seddon Rd **4** BS2 . . . . **50** A3
Sedgefield Gdns BS16 . . . . **37** F1
Sedgemoor Cl BS48 . . . . . . **75** E8
Sedgemoor Rd
  Bath BA2 . . . . **101** F2
  Weston-S-M BS23 . . . . **87** F1
Sedgwick Ho BS11 . . . . **47** E7
Sefton Park Jun & Inf
  Schs BS7 . . . . **49** F3
Sefton Park Rd BS7 . . . . . . **49** F3
Sefton Sq BS24 . . . . **106** A8
Selborne Rd BS7 . . . . **49** F5
Selbourne Cl BA1 . . . . **101** A8
Selbourne Rd BS23 . . . . . . **104** E4
Selbrooke Cres BS16 . . . . . **51** C6
Selby Rd BS5 . . . . **50** F1
Selden Rd BS14 . . . . **80** E5
Selkirk Rd BS15 . . . . **51** C1
Selley Wlk BS13 . . . . **79** A5
Selway Ct BA2 . . . . **102** B2
Selwood Cl BS22 . . . . **105** C7
Selworthy Cl BS31 . . . . **81** D5
Selworthy Gdns **4**
  BS48 . . . . **59** E1
Selworthy Ho BA2 . . . . . . **101** F2
Selworthy Rd
  Bristol BS4 . . . . **64** B2
  Weston-S-M BS23 . . . . . . **105** A4
Selworthy Terr BA2 . . . . . **101** F2
Seneca Pl **1** BS5 . . . . **64** D7
Seneca St BS5 . . . . **64** D7
Septimus Bldgs BS14 . . . . **79** D5
Serbert Cl BS20 . . . . **45** E5
Serbert Rd BS20 . . . . **45** E5
Serbert Way BS20 . . . . **45** E5
Sercombe Pk BS21 . . . . **57** G1
Serlo Ct BS22 . . . . **89** A4
Serridge La BS36 . . . . **38** D4
Seven Acres La BA1 . . . . . . **85** F5
Seven Acres The **3**
  BS24 . . . . **105** F7
Seven Dials BA1 . . . . **141** B2
Seventh Ave
  Bristol BS14 . . . . **80** A7
  Bristol, Filton BS7 . . . . . . **36** B1
Seven Acres BS23 . . . . **104** E5
SEVERN BEACH **22** A6
Severn Beach Prim Sch
  BS35 . . . . **22** A6
Severn Beach Sta
  BS35 . . . . **22** A6
Severn Bridges Visitor
  Ctr* BS35 . . . . **21** F8
Severn Cl GL12 . . . . **11** A4
Severn Dr BS35 . . . . **8** B2
Severn Grange BS10 . . . . . **34** D3
Severn Ho BS10 . . . . **34** D3
Severn La GL13 . . . . **2** E8
Severnleigh Gdns BS9 . . . . **48** F3
Severnleigh Ho BS9 . . . . . . **48** F3
Severnmeade BS20 . . . . . . **44** F5
Severn Rd
  Bristol BS11 . . . . **33** C4
  Bristol BS11 . . . . **47** D6
  Hallen BS10 . . . . **34** A7
  Pill BS20 . . . . **47** C5
  Portishead BS20 . . . . **45** C5
  Severn Beach BS35 . . . . . **21** F3
  Weston-S-M BS23 . . . . . . **104** C5
Severnside Trad Est
  BS11 . . . . **33** C5
Severn View BS10 . . . . **34** C1
Severn View Ind Pk
  BS10 . . . . **21** F3
Severn View Rd BS35 . . . . . **8** C2
Severn Way
  Bristol BS34 . . . . **23** F1
  Keynsham BS31 . . . . **82** A5
Severnwood Gdns
  BS35 . . . . **22** A5
Sevier Rd BS26 . . . . **123** C3
Sevier St BS2 . . . . **49** F2
Seville Ct BS20 . . . . **45** E7
Seville Rd BS20 . . . . **45** E7
Seward Terr BA3 . . . . **134** C2
Sewell Ho BS25 . . . . **125** A8
Seymour Ave BS7 . . . . **49** E4
Seymour Rd
  4 Bath BA1 . . . . **85** A1
  Bristol, Ashley Down BS7 . **49** F4
  Bristol, Kingswood BS15 . **51** C1
  Bristol, Staple Hill BS16 . **51** E4

Seymour Rd *continued*
  Bristol, Upper Easton
  BS5 . . . . **50** A1
Seyton Wlk BS34 . . . . **36** E5
Shackel Hendy Mews
  BS16 . . . . **52** B5
Shackleton Ave BS37 . . . . . **39** F8
Shadow Wlk BS24 . . . . **106** C3
Shadwell Rd BS7 . . . . **49** D3
Shaftesbury Ave
  2 Bath BA1 . . . . **101** C7
  Bristol BS6 . . . . **49** E1
Shaftesbury Cl BS48 . . . . . **75** D8
Shaftesbury Crusade
  BS2 . . . . **64** A6
Shaftesbury Mews **7**
  BA2 . . . . **101** D5
Shaftesbury Rd
  Bath BA2 . . . . **101** D5
  Weston-S-M BS23 . . . . . . **105** B8
Shaftesbury Terr
  2 Bristol BS5 . . . . **64** D7
  Radstock BA3 . . . . **134** A3
Shaft Rd
  Monkton Combe BA2 . . . **102** E1
  Severn Beach BS35 . . . . . **22** A8
Shakespeare Ave
  2 Bath BA2 . . . . **101** F4
  Bristol BS7 . . . . **50** A8
Shakespeare Ct BS23 . . . . **104** F2
Shakespeare Rd BA3 . . . . **133** C1
Shaldon Rd BS7 . . . . **50** A4
Shallowbrooks La
  SN14 . . . . **31** F8
Shallows The BS31 . . . . **82** F3
Sham Castle La BA2 . . . . . **102** C7
Shamrock Rd BS5 . . . . **50** D3
Shanklin Dr BS34 . . . . **36** B3
Shannon Ct BS35 . . . . **15** D8
Shannon Wlk BS20 . . . . . . **45** F6
Shapcott Cl BS14 . . . . **64** B1
Shaplands BS9 . . . . **48** F4
Sharland Ct BS9 . . . . **48** E3
Sharland Gr BS13 . . . . **79** C4
SHARPSTONE **120** A4
Shaw Cl
  Bristol BS16 . . . . **52** B3
  3 Bristol, Upper Easton
  BS5 . . . . **64** B8
Shaw Gdns BS14 . . . . **80** A8
Shaws Way BA2 . . . . **100** F5
Shaymoor La BS35 . . . . **23** A4
Shearmore Cl BS7 . . . . **50** A7
Shearwater Ct BS16 . . . . . . **50** F6
Sheene Ct Ind Est **12**
  BS3 . . . . **63** C3
Sheene Rd BS3 . . . . **63** C3
Sheene Way BS3 . . . . **63** C3
Sheepfair La SN14 . . . . **69** F8
Sheephouse Cvn Pk
  BS20 . . . . **46** E7
Sheeps Croft BS13 . . . . **79** A5
Sheepway BS20 . . . . **46** B5
Sheepway La BS20 . . . . **46** C5
Sheepwood Cl BS10 . . . . . . **35** A2
Sheepwood Rd BS10 . . . . . **35** A2
Shelling Sch BS35 . . . . **8** B2
Sheldare Barton BS5 . . . . . **65** B8
Sheldon Cl BS21 . . . . **57** H2
Sheldrake Dr BS16 . . . . **50** E6
Shellard Rd BS34 . . . . **36** A2
Shellards La BS35 . . . . **15** E2
Shellards Rd BS30 . . . . **65** F3
Shelley Ave BS21 . . . . **57** F2
Shelley Cl BS5 . . . . **64** F8
Shelley Ho BS34 . . . . **24** A1
Shelley Rd
  Bath BA2 . . . . **101** F4
  Radstock BA3 . . . . **133** C1
  Weston-S-M BS23 . . . . . . **105** A4
Shelley Way BS7 . . . . **50** A8
Shellmor Ave BS34 . . . . **24** B1
Shellmor Cl **1** BS32 . . . . . **24** B1
Shepherds Cl
  Bristol BS16 . . . . **51** E5
  Chipping Sodbury BS37 . . **40** F3
Shepherds Wlk
  3 Bristol BS22 . . . . **89** C2
Shepherds Wlk
  Bristol BS32 . . . . **36** D8
Sheppard Rd BS16 . . . . **51** C6
Sheppards Gdns BA1 . . . . . **84** B1
Sheppards Wlk BA3 . . . . . **138** D3
SHEPPERDINE **1** D3
Shepperdine Rd BS35 . . . . . **1** D2
Sheppy's Mill BS49 . . . . . . **91** D5
Shepton BS24 . . . . **105** A2
Shepton Wlk BS3 . . . . **63** C2
SHERBORNE **130** D3
Sherbourne Ave BS32 . . . . **36** E7
Sherbourne Cl BS15 . . . . . . **51** F2
Sherbourne's Brake
  BS32 . . . . **36** E6
Sherbourne St BS5 . . . . **64** C7
Sheridan Rd
  Bath BA2 . . . . **101** A8
  Bristol BS7 . . . . **50** A8
Sheridan Way BS30 . . . . . . **66** A2
Sherrings The BS34 . . . . . . **36** B8
Sherrymans Way BS13 . . . . **79** B8
Sherston Cl
  Bristol BS16 . . . . **51** B5
  Nailsea BS48 . . . . **60** A1
Sherston Rd
  Bristol BS7 . . . . **49** E8
  Luckington SN14 . . . . **31** F5

Sa'

Sherwell Rd P
Sherwood Cl D . . .
Sherwood Cres BS22 . . . . . .
Sherwood Rd
  Bristol BS15 . . . . **51** B1
  Keynsham BS31 . . . . **81** E5
Shetland Rd BS10 . . . . **35** D1
Shetland Way BS48 . . . . . . **60** A1
Shickle Gr BA2 . . . . **101** D1
Shield Ct BS15 . . . . **65** D5
Shield Ret Ctr BS34 . . . . . . **36** A3
Shield Road Prim Sch
  BS7 . . . . **36** A1
Shields Ave BS7 . . . . **36** A1
Shiels Dr BS32 . . . . **36** D7
Shilton Cl BS15 . . . . **65** F7
Shimsey Cl **2** BS16 . . . . . . **51** C6
Shiners Elms BS49 . . . . **91** B8
SHIPHAM **125** F7
Shipham CE Fst Sch
  BS25 . . . . **125** E8
Shipham Cl
  Bristol BS14 . . . . **80** B5
  Nailsea BS48 . . . . **75** F8
Shipham La BS25 . . . . **108** B1
Shipham Rd BS27 . . . . **126** A3
Ship La BS1 . . . . **143** B1
SHIPLATE **122** F6
Shiplate Rd BS24 . . . . **122** E6
Shipley Mow BS16 . . . . **52** B6
Shipley Rd BS9 . . . . **49** A8
Shipman Ct BS16 . . . . **51** F4
Shire Gdns BS11 . . . . **47** D8
SHIREHAMPTON **47** E7
Shirehampton Prim Sch
  BS11 . . . . **47** D6
Shirehampton Rd BS9 . . . . **48** C6
Shirehampton Sta
  BS11 . . . . **47** D5
Shire Hill SN14 . . . . **56** A7
Shire Way BS37 . . . . **39** C6
Shirref Ct **3** BS16 . . . . **49** B1
SHOCKERWICK **86** E5
Shockerwick La BA1 . . . . . **86** D4
Shophouse Rd BA2 . . . . . **101** B5
Shop La GL9 . . . . **30** E2
Shopland Ho **8** BS21 . . . . **57** E2
Shoreditch BS40 . . . . **112** C7
Shorland Ho BS8 . . . . **49** A1
Shorthill Rd BS37 . . . . **39** C4
Short La
  Litton BA3 . . . . **130** F2
  Long Ashton BS41 . . . . . . **62** A2
Shortlands Rd BS11 . . . . . . **34** A1
Short St BS2 . . . . **64** A5
Short Way
  Failand BS8 . . . . **61** B4
  Thornbury BS35 . . . . **15** B7
SHORTWOOD **52** E4
Shortwood Hill BS16 . . . . . **52** E4
Shortwood Rd
  Bristol BS13 . . . . **79** E3
  Pucklechurch BS16 . . . . . . **53** E4
Shortwood View BS15 . . . . **65** F8
Shortwood Wlk BS13 . . . . . **79** E3
SHOSCOMBE **134** E6
Shoscombe CE Prim Sch
  BA2 . . . . **134** F5
SHOSCOMBE VALE **134** F5
Showering Cl BS14 . . . . **80** D5
Showering Rd BS14 . . . . . . **80** D5
Shrewsbury Bow
  BS24 . . . . **106** A8
Shrubbery Ave BS23 . . . . . **87** D1
Shrubbery Cotts **4**
  BS6 . . . . **49** B2
Shrubbery Ct **6** BS16 . . . . **51** D5
Shrubbery Rd
  Bristol BS16 . . . . **51** D5
  Weston-S-M BS23 . . . . **87** D1
Shrubbery Terr **11**
  BS23 . . . . **87** C1
Shrubbery Wlk BS23 . . . . . **87** D1
Shrubbery Wlk W
  BS23 . . . . **87** C1
Shums Ct **3** BA1 . . . . **141** C2
Shuter Rd BS13 . . . . **78** E5
Sibland BS35 . . . . **15** D8
Sibland Cl **3** BS35 . . . . **15** D8
Sibland Rd BS35 . . . . **15** D8
Sibland Way BS35 . . . . **15** D8
SIDCOT **125** C7
Sidcot BS4 . . . . **64** D2
Sidcot Dr BS25 . . . . **125** A7
Sidcot La BS25 . . . . **125** C8
Sidcot Jun Sch BS25 . . . . **125** C8
Sidcot Sch BS25 . . . . **125** B7
Sideland Cl BS14 . . . . **80** E6
Sidelands Rd BS16 . . . . **51** C6
Sidelings The BS40 . . . . . **128** D8
Sidings The
  Bristol, Lower Soundwell
  BS16 . . . . **52** A6
  Bristol, Newleaze BS34 . . **36** C2
  Charfield GL12 . . . . **11** B5
Sidmouth Cl BS35 . . . . **63** D1
Sidmouth Gdns BS3 . . . . . . **63** D2
Sidmouth Rd BS3 . . . . **63** E2
Sidney Hill Cottage Homes
  BS25 . . . . **108** E4
Signal Rd BS16 . . . . **51** F4
Silbury Rd BS3 . . . . **62** E2
Silbury Rise BS31 . . . . **82** A2
Silcox Rd BS13 . . . . **79** C4
Silklands Gr BS9 . . . . **48** C5

Silverberry Rd BS22 . . . . . . 89 A1
Silver Birch Cl BS34 . . . . . 36 D7
Silvercombe 1 BS23 . . . . 104 E5
Silver Ct BS48 . . . . 59 C2
Silverhill Brake BS35 . . . . 14 E1
Silverhill Rd BS10 . . . . . . 34 E4
Silverhill Sch BS36 . . . . . . 37 E7
Silverlow Rd BS48 . . . . . . 59 D2
Silver Mead BS41 . . . . 91 D2
Silver Moor La BS29 . . . 106 F7
Silver St
  Bristol BS1 . . . . 143 A3
  Chew Magna BS40 . . . . . 96 B3
  Congresbury BS49 . . . . . 91 D2
  Holcombe BA3 . . . . 139 C1
  Kilmersdon BA3 . . . . . . 140 B5
  Midsomer Norton BA3 . . 139 A7
  Nailsea BS48 . . . . 59 D2
  Portishead BS20 . . . . 44 F1
  7 Thornbury BS35 . . . . . . 8 B1
  Wrington BS40 . . . . 92 E2
Silverstone Way BS49 . . . 91 D3
Silverthorne La BS2 . . . . . 64 A6
Silverthorne Wharf
  BS2 . . . . 64 B6
Silverton Ct BS4 . . . . 63 F1
Simmonds Bldgs BS16 . . . 37 C3
Simmonds View BS34 . . . . 36 F5
Simons Cl BS22 . . . . 89 A2
Simon's Cl BS39 . . . . 132 F5
Simons Mews 3
  BS23 . . . . 104 F7
Sinclair Ho
  Bristol BS8 . . . . 142 A2
  Bristol, Filton BS34 . . . . 36 A2
Singapore Rd BS23 . . . . . 104 E3
SINGLE HILL 135 A5
Single Hill BA2 . . . . 134 F5
SION HILL 84 E1
Sion Hill
  Bath BA1 . . . . 84 E1
  Bristol BS8 . . . . 62 F7
Sion Hill Pl BA1 . . . . 84 E1
Sion Pl
  Bath BA2 . . . . 102 B6
  Bristol BS8 . . . . 62 F7
Sion Rd
  Bath BA1 . . . . 84 E1
  Bristol BS3 . . . . 63 C3
Sir Bernard Lovell Sch
  BS30 . . . . 66 C4
Sir Bernard Lovell Sch
  (annexe) BS30 . . . . 66 D5
Sir Bevil Grenville's Mon*
  BA1 . . . . 68 A1
Sir John's La
  Bristol BS7 . . . . 50 B5
  Bristol, Eastville BS5 . . . 50 B4
Siskin Cl BS20 . . . . 44 E4
Siskin Wlk BS22 . . . . 105 F8
SISTON 52 F3
Siston Cl BS15 . . . . 52 A2
Siston Comm
  Bristol BS15 . . . . 52 A2
  Bristol BS30 . . . . 52 B1
Siston Ctr The BS15 . . . . . 52 B1
Siston Hill BS30 . . . . 52 B1
Siston Hill Rdbt BS15 . . . . 52 B2
Siston La BS30 . . . . 52 F2
Siston Pk BS15 . . . . 52 A2
Sixpence BS39 . . . . 115 D2
Six Streams BA1 . . . . 84 B2
Sixth Ave
  Bristol BS14 . . . . 80 A7
  Bristol, Filton BS7 . . . . . 36 B1
Sixty Acres Cl BS8 . . . . . . 61 B4
Six Ways BS21 . . . . 52 F4
Skinner's Hill BA2 . . . . . 133 F7
Skinners La BS25 . . . . . . 108 F4
Skippon Ct BS15 . . . . 65 E5
Skylark Ave BS21 . . . . 44 B1
Skypark Rd BS3 . . . . 63 C3
Sladacre La BS40 . . . . . . 110 E2
Sladebrook Ave BA2 . . . 101 C1
Sladebrook Ct BA2 . . . . 101 C1
Sladebrook Rd BA2 . . . . 101 B4
Slade La
  Barrow Gurney BS48 . . . . 77 C4
  Lympsham BS24 . . . . . . 122 B1
Slade Rd BS20 . . . . 45 D5
Slades Ct 2 BS48 . . . . 76 A6
Slad The BS35 . . . . 15 F6
Slate La BS14, BS39 . . . . 98 B7
Sleep La BS14 . . . . 80 D3
Slimbridge Cl BS37 . . . . . 39 F7
Sloan St BS5 . . . . 64 D8
Sloe Cl BS22 . . . . 105 D8
Slough La SN14 . . . . 68 F5
Slymbridge Ave BS10 . . . . 35 A3
Smallbrook La BS39 . . . . . 98 B6
Smallcombe Cl BA3 . . . . 133 E5
Smallcombe Rd BA3 . . . . 133 E4
Slade Down End
  BS25 . . . . 107 F2
Small La BS16 . . . . 50 E5
Small St
  Bristol BS1 . . . . 143 A3
  Bristol, St Philip's Marsh
  BS2 . . . . 64 A5
Smallway BS49 . . . . 91 D5
Smallwood View BA3 . . . 138 E7
Smarts Gn BS37 . . . . 40 C8
SMART'S GREEN 40 D8
Smeaton Rd BS1 . . . . 62 F5

SMITHAM HILL 129 D2
Smithcourt Dr BS34 . . . . . 36 D6
Smithmead BS13 . . . . 79 B5
Smiths Ct BS34 . . . . 36 A8
Smith's Forge Ind Est
  BS16 . . . . 73 F3
Smoke La BS11 . . . . 33 D6
Smythe Croft BS14 . . . . . 80 A3
Smyth Ho BS8 . . . . 62 E6
Smyth Rd BS3 . . . . 63 A3
Smyths Cl BS11 . . . . 33 A1
Smyth Terr 9 BS3 . . . . . . 63 C4
SNEYD PARK 48 D3
Sneyd Park Ho BS9 . . . . . 48 D3
Snowberry Cl
  Bristol BS32 . . . . 36 E8
  Weston-S-M BS22 . . . . . 89 A1
Snowberry Wlk BS5 . . . . . 50 E1
Snowdon Cl BS16 . . . . . . 50 F4
Snowdon Ho BS16 . . . . . 50 F5
Snowdon Rd BS16 . . . . . 50 F4
Snowdon Vale BS23 . . . . . 88 A1
Snowdrop Cl BS22 . . . . . . 89 A5
Snow Hill BA1 . . . . 85 A1
Snow Hill Ho BA1 . . . . . 141 C4
Soapers La BS35 . . . . 15 B8
Soaphouse Ind Est
  BS5 . . . . 64 E8
Sodbury Rd
  Acton Turville GL9 . . . . . 42 F7
  Wickwar GL12 . . . . 18 A4
Solent Way BS35 . . . . 15 D7
Solon Ct BS13 . . . . 78 F5
Solsbury Cl BA1 . . . . 85 F3
Solsbury La BA1 . . . . 85 F4
Solsbury View 18 BA1 . . . 85 A2
Solsbury Way BA1 . . . . . . 85 A2
Somer Ave BA3 . . . . 132 F2
Somerby Cl BS32 . . . . 36 D7
Somer Ct BA3 . . . . 133 B1
SOMERDALE 81 E7
Somerdale Ave
  Bath BA2 . . . . 101 D2
  Bristol BS4 . . . . 64 A1
  Weston-S-M BS22 . . . . 105 C8
Somerdale Cl BS22 . . . . 105 C8
Somerdale Rd BS31 . . . . . 81 F7
Somerdale Rd N BS30,
  BS31 . . . . 81 F8
Somerdale View BA2 . . . 101 C2
Somerford Cl BS10 . . . . . 34 F1
Somer Ho 2 BA1 . . . . . . 133 A1
Somer Lea BA3 . . . . 138 D5
Somer Rd BA3 . . . . 63 C1
Somermead BS3 . . . . 132 F2
Somerset Ave
  Weston-S-M BS22,
  BS24 . . . . 106 A8
  Yate BS37 . . . . 27 F3
Somerset Cl GL12 . . . . . . 11 F4
Somerset Cres BS34 . . . . 36 F5
Somerset & Dorset Joint
  Rly* BA3 . . . . 116 B2
Somerset Ho
  Bath BA2 . . . . 101 D3
  12 Bristol BS2 . . . . 143 C3
  Portishead BS20 . . . . 45 D4
Somerset La BA1 . . . . 84 E1
Somerset Mews
  Portishead BS20 . . . . 45 D4
  Weston-S-M BS23 . . . . 104 F6
Somerset Pl BA1 . . . . 84 E1
Somerset Rd
  Bristol BS4 . . . . 64 B3
  Clevedon BS21 . . . . 57 G3
  Portishead BS20 . . . . 44 F5
Somerset Sq
  Bristol BS1 . . . . 143 B1
  4 Nailsea BS48 . . . . 59 E2
Somerset St
  Bath BA1 . . . . 141 C1
  Bristol BS1 . . . . 143 B1
  Bristol, Kingsdown BS2 . 143 A4
Somerset Terr BS3 . . . . . 63 D3
Somerset Way BS39 . . . . 132 E6
Somerton BS24 . . . . 105 A2
Somerton Cl BS15 . . . . . . 65 E7
Somerton Rd
  Bristol BS7 . . . . 49 E6
  Clevedon BS21 . . . . 57 G1
Somervale Rd BA3 . . . . . 133 E2
Somervale Sch BA3 . . . . 133 A1
Somerville Cl BS31 . . . . . 82 E2
Somerville Ct BS10 . . . . . 49 A8
Somerville Rd BS7 . . . . . 49 E3
Somerville Rd E 1
  BS6 . . . . 49 F3
Soper Gdns BS4 . . . . 79 D7
Sophia Gdns BS22 . . . . . 89 B4
Sopworth Rd SN14 . . . . . 31 E5
Sorrel Cl BS35 . . . . 8 D2
Soundwell Rd BS15,
  BS16 . . . . 51 D2
Southampton Gdns
  BS7 . . . . 49 F5
Southampton Mews
  BS7 . . . . 49 F5
South Ave
  Bath BA2 . . . . 101 D5
  Portishead BS20 . . . . 45 D6
  Yate BS37 . . . . 27 B1
Southbourne Gdns
  BS5 . . . . 85 B1
Southbourne Mans
  BA2 . . . . 141 C2
Southbow Ho 2 BS3 . . . . 63 A3

South Bristol Bsns Pk
  BS3 . . . . 79 E7
South Bristol Ret Pk
  BS3 . . . . 63 A3
South Bristol Trad Pk
  BS3 . . . . 63 A3
South Combe BS24 . . . . 122 B6
Southcot Pl BA2 . . . . . . 141 C1
South Croft
  Bristol BS9 . . . . 49 C7
  Winscombe BS25 . . . . . 107 F2
South Ct BS32 . . . . 24 D3
South Dene BS9 . . . . 48 E3
SOUTHDOWN 101 B4
Southdown Ave BA2 . . . 101 B3
Southdown Com Inf Sch
  BA2 . . . . 101 B3
Southdown Jun Sch
  BA2 . . . . 101 B3
Southdown Rd
  Bristol BA2 . . . . 101 B4
  Bristol BS9 . . . . 48 F8
SOUTHEND 5 E3
Southend Ho GL12 . . . . . 18 A5
Southend Rd BS23 . . . . . 104 E5
Southernhay
  Bristol BS8 . . . . 142 B2
  Bristol, Staple Hill BS16 . . 51 D4
Southernhay Ave BS8 . . . 142 B2
Southernhay Cres
  BS8 . . . . 142 B2
Southern Way BS21 . . . . . 57 E1
Southey Ave BS15 . . . . . . 51 E1
Southey Ct BS15 . . . . 51 E1
Southey St BS2 . . . . 49 F2
SOUTHFIELD 134 A2
Southfield
  Norton St Philip BA2 . . . 136 F4
  Radstock BA3 . . . . 134 A2
Southfield Cl
  Nailsea BS48 . . . . 59 E3
  Weston-S-M BS23 . . . . 104 D2
Southfield Ct BS9 . . . . . . 49 A7
Southfield Rd
  Bristol, Cotham BS6 . . . 49 D1
  Bristol, Westbury on Trym
  BS9 . . . . 49 A7
  Nailsea BS48 . . . . 59 F3
Southfield Rd Trad Est
  BS48 . . . . 59 F3
Southfield Way BS37 . . . . 28 A4
Southgate BA1 . . . . 141 C2
Southgate Sh Ctr
  BA1 . . . . 141 C2
South Gloucestershire
  Central Teaching Unit
  BS16 . . . . 52 A4
South Gr
  Bristol BS6 . . . . 49 C5
  Pill BS20 . . . . 47 C4
South Green St 5 BS8 . . . 62 F6
South Hayes BS5 . . . . 50 B4
South Hill BS25 . . . . 107 F2
Southlands
  Bath BA1 . . . . 84 B1
  Bristol, Clifton BS8 . . . . 49 A1
  Bristol, Knowle Park BS4 . . 64 A1
  Tytherington GL12 . . . . . 16 B4
Southlands Dr BA2 . . . . . 116 B2
Southlands Way BS49 . . . 91 E5
South Lawn BS24 . . . . . 105 F4
South Lawn Cl BS24 . . . 105 F4
South Lea Rd BA1 . . . . . 101 A8
Southleaze BS25 . . . . . . 125 A6
Southleigh BS25 . . . . . . 124 F8
Southleigh Mews
  BS8 . . . . 142 B4
Southleigh Rd BS8 . . . . . 142 B4
South Liberty La
  Bristol BS3 . . . . 63 A1
  2 Bristol BS3 . . . . 63 B2
South Mdws BS40 . . . . . . 92 E2
SOUTHMEAD 35 D1
Southmead BS25 . . . . . . 125 A8
Southmead Hospl
  BS10 . . . . 49 E8
Southmead Rd
  Bristol BS10, BS34 . . . . 35 E1
  Weston-S-M BS22 . . . . 105 B7
Southmead Way BS10 . . . 49 D8
Southover Cl BS9 . . . . . . 49 A8
Southover Rd BS39 . . . . 115 D1
South Par
  Bath BA2 . . . . 141 C2
  Chew Magna BS40 . . . . . 96 B3
  Weston-S-M BS23 . . . . 104 D8
  Yate BS37 . . . . 27 E1
South Parade Cotts
  BA2 . . . . 102 C1
South Parade Mans
  BS8 . . . . 142 B4
South Rd
  7 Bristol, Bedminster
  BS3 . . . . 63 C3
  Bristol, Kingswood BS15 . . 65 D8
  Bristol, Redland BS6 . . . 49 C2
  Lympsham BS24 . . . . . . 122 B1
  Midsomer Norton BA3 . . 133 B1
  Portishead BS20 . . . . 45 D4
  Timsbury BA2 . . . . 116 B2
  Weston-S-M BS23 . . . . . 87 C1
  Woodhouse Down BS32 . . 24 F4
South Rock Ind Est
  BA3 . . . . 138 D1

Southsea Rd BS34 . . . . . . 36 A8
Southside BS23 . . . . 104 E8
Southside Cl BS9 . . . . 91 E5
Southside Cl BS9 . . . . 48 B8
Southside Cres BS22 . . . . 88 A4
South St
  Bristol BS3 . . . . 63 B3
  Stratton-on-t-F BA3 . . . 138 F2
SOUTHSTOKE 118 E7
Southstoke La BA2 . . . . . 118 F8
Southstoke Rd BA2 . . . . 101 F1
South Street Prim Sch
  BS3 . . . . 63 B3
South Terr
  6 Bristol BS6 . . . . 49 B2
  Weston-S-M BS23 . . . . 104 D8
SOUTH TWERTON 101 C5
South View
  Bristol BS16 . . . . 51 E5
  Clandown BA3 . . . . 133 E5
  Frampton Cotterell BS36 . . 38 B7
  Monkton Combe BA2 . . 102 E1
  Paulton BS39 . . . . 132 E6
  Portishead BS20 . . . . 45 D7
  Timsbury BA2 . . . . 116 B2
South View Bsns Pk
  BS16 . . . . 51 F5
Southview Cl BS24 . . . . . 105 E2
South View Cres BS36 . . . 38 D6
South View Pl BA3 . . . . . 133 B2
South View Rd BA2 . . . . 101 D6
South View Rise BS36 . . . 38 D6
South View Terr BS49 . . . 74 F1
SOUTHVILLE 63 C4
Southville Prim Sch
  BS3 . . . . 63 C4
Southville Rd
  Bristol BS3 . . . . 63 C4
  Weston-S-M BS23 . . . . 104 E4
Southville Terr BA2 . . . . 102 B4
Southway Cl BS21 . . . . . . 57 F1
Southway Dr BS15 . . . . . 66 D5
Southwell St BS2 . . . . . . 142 C4
SOUTH WIDCOMBE 130 C6
South Wlk BS37 . . . . 27 E1
Southwood Ave BS9 . . . . 48 C8
Southwood Dr BS9 . . . . . 48 B8
Southwood Dr E BS9 . . . 48 C8
Sovereign Sh Ctr
  BS23 . . . . 104 D8
Spalding Cl BS7 . . . . 50 A3
Spaniorum View BS35 . . . 22 F2
Spar Rd
  Avonmouth BS11 . . . . . . 33 D4
  Yate BS37 . . . . 27 D2
Spartley Dr BS13 . . . . 78 F6
Spartley Wlk BS13 . . . . . . 78 F6
Specklemead BS39 . . . . . 132 D5
SPEEDWELL 51 A2
Speedwell Ave 6 BS5 . . . 64 D7
Speedwell Cl BS35 . . . . . . 8 D2
Speedwell Ind Est 1
  BS21 . . . . 57 E2
Speedwell Rd BS5,
  BS15 . . . . 51 A1
Speedwell Tech Coll
  BS15 . . . . 51 A1
Spencer Dr
  Midsomer Norton
  BA3 . . . . 133 A2
  Weston-S-M BS22 . . . . . 89 B3
Spencer Ho 6 BS1 . . . . . 143 B1
Spencers Belle Vue
  BA1 . . . . 141 B4
Spencers Ct BS35 . . . . . . 15 B5
Spencers Cl BS35 . . . . . 138 E8
Spey Cl BS35 . . . . 15 C8
Spey Ct BS35 . . . . 15 C8
SPIKE ISLAND 142 B1
Spike Island Artspace*
  BS1 . . . . 142 A1
Spindleberry Gr BS48 . . . 60 A2
Spinners End BS22 . . . . . 89 B4
Spinney Croft BS13 . . . . . 78 F5
Spinney Rd BS24 . . . . . . 106 D4
Spinney The
  Bristol BS32 . . . . 36 E7
  Frampton Cotterell BS36 . . 38 B7
  Portishead BS20 . . . . 45 C4
  Weston-S-M BS22 . . . . 104 F1
Spires View 4 BS16 . . . . 50 E5
Spratts Bridge BS40 . . . . 96 A3
Sprigg Dr BS20 . . . . 44 F1
Spring Cres BA2 . . . . . . 141 C2
Springfield
  Norton St Philip BA2 . . 136 E4
  Peasedown St John
  BA2 . . . . 134 C7
  1 Thornbury BS35 . . . . 15 D8
Springfield Ave
  Bristol, Horfield BS7 . . . 49 F5
  Bristol, Mangotsfield
  BS16 . . . . 52 A7
  Bristol, Shirehampton
  BS11 . . . . 47 D6
  Weston-S-M BS22 . . . . . 88 D1
Springfield Bldgs
  Midsomer Norton
  BS39 . . . . 132 D2
  Radstock BA3 . . . . 134 A3
Springfield Cl
  Bath BA2 . . . . 101 B5
  Bristol BS16 . . . . 52 A7
  Cross BS26 . . . . 124 F2
Springfield Cotts BS30 . . 83 A8
Springfield Cres BA3 . . . 134 A3
Springfield Gdns
  BS29 . . . . 107 A3

Springfield Gr BS6 . . . . . . 49 C5
Springfield Ho
  Bristol BS6 . . . . 142 C4
  Portishead BS20 . . . . 45 C4
Springfield Hts BA3 . . . . 133 E4
Springfield Lawns
  BS11 . . . . 47 D6
Springfield Pl
  Bath BA1 . . . . 84 F1
  Clandown BA3 . . . . 133 E4
Springfield Rd
  Bristol, Cotham BS6 . . . 49 D1
  Bristol, Mangotsfield
  BS16 . . . . 52 A7
  Pill BS20 . . . . 47 C4
  Portishead BS20 . . . . 45 B5
Springfields BS34 . . . . . . 36 A2
Springfort BS9 . . . . 48 F3
Spring Gardens Rd
  BA2 . . . . 141 C2
Spring Gdns
  Bath BA2 . . . . 141 C2
  Bristol BS4 . . . . 64 A1
Spring Ground Rd
  BS39 . . . . 132 E5
Spring Hill
  Bristol BS2 . . . . 143 A4
  Bristol, Upper Soundwell
  BS15 . . . . 51 E2
  Weston-S-M BS22 . . . . . 88 D2
Springhill Cl BS39 . . . . . 132 C6
Spring Hill Dr BS22 . . . . . 88 E1
Spring La 2 BS35 . . . . . . 15 C8
Spring La
  Bath BA1 . . . . 85 B2
  Dundry BS41 . . . . 79 A1
Springleaze
  Bristol, Knowle Park
  BS4 . . . . 64 A1
  Bristol, Mangotsfield
  BS16 . . . . 52 A7
Spring Rise BS20 . . . . 45 C3
Spring St BS3 . . . . 63 E4
Spring Street Pl BS3 . . . . 63 E4
Spring Terr BS22 . . . . 88 C2
Spring Vale BA1 . . . . 85 B2
Spring Valley BS22 . . . . . 88 C2
Springville Cl BS30 . . . . . 66 A3
Springwater Pk Trad Est
  BS5 . . . . 64 E7
Springwood Dr BS10 . . . . 34 D3
Spring Wood Gdns
  BS4 . . . . 105 A3
Spruce Way
  Bath BA2 . . . . 118 E8
  Bristol BS34 . . . . 35 F7
  Weston-S-M BS22 . . . . 105 E8
Square The
  Alveston BS35 . . . . 15 A4
  Axbridge BS26 . . . . 125 C2
  Banwell BS29 . . . . 107 B3
  Bath BA2 . . . . 141 B1
  Bristol BS1 . . . . 143 C2
  Bristol, Knowle Park BS4 . . 64 A1
  Bristol, Staple Hill BS16 . . 51 E4
  Shipham BS25 . . . . 124 C1
  Temple Cloud BS39 . . . 114 E1
  Timsbury BA2 . . . . 116 B2
  Wellow BA2 . . . . 118 D1
  Winscombe BS25 . . . . . 124 E6
Squire La BS40 . . . . 111 C1
Squires Ct BS30 . . . . 65 F4
Squires Leaze BS35 . . . . . 8 D2
Stabbins Cl BS22 . . . . . . 89 B5
Stables The BA3 . . . . . . 141 A5
Stable Yd BA2 . . . . 101 D6
Stable Yd The GL9 . . . . . . 30 B7
Stackpool Rd BS3 . . . . . . 63 C4
Staddlestones BA3 . . . . 138 F7
Stadium Rd BS6 . . . . 49 C5
Stafford Cres BS35 . . . . . . 8 B1
Stafford Pl BS23 . . . . . . 104 E8
Stafford Rd
  Bristol BS2 . . . . 50 A2
  Portishead BS20 . . . . 45 E4
  Weston-S-M BS23 . . . . 104 F7
Staffords Ct BS30 . . . . . . 66 A6
Stafford St BS3 . . . . 63 D4
Stainer Cl BS4 . . . . 79 D7
Stalcombe La BA2 . . . . . . 99 B4
Stall St BA1 . . . . 141 C2
Stambrook Pk BA1 . . . . . 86 A5
Stanbridge Cl BS16 . . . . . 51 F6
Stanbridge Prim Sch
  BS16 . . . . 51 F6
Stanbridge Rd BS16 . . . . 51 F6
Stanbury Ave BS16 . . . . . 51 C5
Stanbury Rd BS3 . . . . 63 E3
Stancombe La BS48 . . . . 76 E7
Standfast Rd BS10 . . . . . . 34 F3
Standish Ave BS34 . . . . . 24 C1
Standish Cl BS10 . . . . 34 F1
Standon Way BS10 . . . . . 35 C2
Stane Way BS11 . . . . 47 C7
Stanfield Cl BS7 . . . . 50 C6
Stanford Cl BS36 . . . . 37 F8
Stanford Pl BS4 . . . . 79 D7
Stanhope Pl BA1 . . . . . . 141 A2
Stanhope Rd
  Bristol BS30 . . . . 65 F2
  Weston-S-M BS23 . . . . 104 E3
Stanhope St BS2 . . . . 64 C5
Stanier Rd
  Bath BA2 . . . . 141 A2
  Bristol BS15, BS16 . . . . 52 B3

Stanley Ave
Bristol, Bishopston BS7....49 E3
Bristol, Filton BS34 ......36 B2
Stanley Chase BS5.......50 E2
Stanley Cres BS34.......36 B2
Stanley Ct BA3 ....133 B2
Stanley Gdns BS30.......66 B4
Stanley Gr BS23.........104 F7
Stanley Hill BS4 ....44 A4
Stanley Mead BS32 ......24 E2
Stanley Park Rd BS16....51 E3
Stanley Pk BS5 ....50 C1
Stanley Rd
Bristol, Cotham BS6 ....49 C1
Bristol, Warmley BS5......66 C7
☑ Weston-S-M BS23.......104 F7
Stanley Rd W BA2 ....101 D5
Stanley St N ☑ BS3.......63 C3
Stanley St S BS3..........63 C2
Stanley St ☑ BS3 ✗......63 C3
Stanley Terr
Bristol BS3.................63 C2
Radstock BA3..............134 A3
Stanley Villas ☑ BA1....85 A1
Stanshalls Cl BS40.......94 C8
Stanshalls Dr BS40.......94 C8
Stanshalls La BS40.......94 C8
Stanshaw Cl BS16.........51 A7
Stanshawe Cres BS37.....27 E1
Stanshawes Court Dr
BS37......................39 E8
Stanshawes Dr BS37......27 D1
Stanshaw Rd BS16.........51 A7
Stanshaws Cl BS32.......24 C2
Stanton Cl BS15 ....51 F1
STANTON DREW 96 F2
Stanton Drew Prim Sch
BS39......................97 A2
Stanton Drew Stone
Circles* BS39.............97 A3
Stanton La BS39..........97 D4
STANTON PRIOR 99 E2
Stanton Rd
Bristol BS10................35 E2
Chew Magna BS40.........96 B3
STANTON WICK 114 D8
Stanton Wick La BS39....97 B1
Stanway BS30 ....66 C1
Stanway Cl BA2 ....101 D1
Staple Gr BS31 ....81 D5
Staple Grove Cres BS5...66 B7
STAPLE HILL 51 E4
Staple Hill Prim Sch
BS16......................51 D4
Staple Hill Rd BS16......51 B4
Staples Cl BS21..........57 G1
Staples Gn BS22..........89 B3
Staples Hill BA2.........120 C4
Staples Rd BS37..........27 D2
STAPLETON 50 D4
Stapleton Cl BS16........50 D5
Stapleton Rd
Bristol, Baptist Mills
BS5......................50 B1
Bristol, Eastville BS5.....50 C1
Stapleton Road Sta
BS5......................50 B1
STAR 108 D1
Star Ave BS34 ....37 A4
Star Barn Rd BS34........37 E7
Starcross Rd BS22........89 A2
Star La
Bristol BS16................50 F3
Pill BS20 ....47 D4
Starling Cl BS22.........105 E8
Starrs Cl BS26..........125 B2
STARVEALL 20 D4
Starveall Ct BS5 ....51 A1
Station App
Pensford BS39..............97 D5
Weston-S-M BS23..........104 E7
Station Ave ☑ BS16.......51 A4
Station Ave S ☑ BS16....51 A4
Station Cl
Backwell BS48..............75 F7
Bristol BS15................66 C8
Chipping Sodbury BS37....40 D8
Congresbury BS49..........91 C4
Station Ct BS5............64 E8
Station La BS7...........50 A4
Station Lo ☑ BS23......104 E7
Station Mead BA3........138 D3
Station Rd
Acton Turville GL9.........42 F8
Axbridge BS26.............125 C2
Backwell BS48.............76 A6
Bath BA1..................101 C7
Blagdon BS40.............110 E3
Bristol, Ashley Down BS7..49 F4
Bristol, Filton BS34.......36 A3
Bristol, Fishponds BS16...51 A4
Bristol, Henbury BS10.....34 F4
Bristol, Montpelier BS6....49 E2
Bristol, Newleaze BS34....36 C2
Bristol, Patchway BS34....36 C7
Bristol, Shirehampton
BS11......................47 D5
Bristol, Shirehampton
BS11......................47 E6
Bristol, Staple Hill BS15...51 F3
Bristol, Upper Knowle
BS4......................64 D2
Bristol, Warmley BS30.....66 C6
Charfield GL12...............11 B5
Clevedon BS21............57 G3
Clutton BS39...............114 F3
Congresbury BS49.........91 C4
Flax Bourton BS48.........77 A8

Station Rd *continued*
Frampton Cotterell BS36...38 C5
Freshford BA2.............120 C5
Iron Acton BS37............26 D3
Keynsham BS31............81 E6
Midsomer Norton BA3....133 B2
Nailsea BS48...............59 F2
Pill BS20...................47 C4
Pilning BS35................22 F4
Portbury BS20..............46 D3
Portishead BS20............45 D6
Sandford BS25.............107 F4
Severn Beach BS35.........22 A6
Wellow BA2................118 D1
Weston-S-M BS23.........104 E7
Weston-S-M, St Georges
BS22.....................89 D2
Weston-S-M, Worle
BS22.....................88 F2
Wickwar GL12...............18 B7
Winterbourne BS36.........37 E4
Wrington BS40.............92 D2
Yate BS37..................27 C2
Yatton BS49................74 B1
Station Road Bsns Ctr
BS15......................52 A3
Station Road Link
BS15......................52 A2
Station Road Workshops
BS15......................52 A3
Station Yd BS36 ....37 D4
Staunton Fields BS14.....80 C4
Staunton La BS14.........80 D3
Staunton Way BS14.......80 D4
Staveley Cres BS10.......35 C2
Staverton Cl BS32........24 C1
Staverton Way BS15......66 A7
Stavordale Gr BS14.......80 B6
Staynes Cres BS15........65 E8
Steam Mills BA3.........138 F8
Steanbridge BS32.........36 D6
Stean Bridge Rd BS32....36 E6
Steel Ct BS30..............65 F3
Steel Mills BS31..........81 F4
STEEP HOLM 104 B2
Steevens Ho (Almshouses)
☑ BS2....................143 C3
Stella Gr BS3 ....63 A2
Stephens Dr BS30.........65 F5
Stephen St BS5............64 C8
Stepney Rd BS5 ....50 C1
Stepney Wlk BS5 ....50 C1
Stepping Stones The
BS4......................64 E6
Sterncourt Rd BS16.......51 A7
Stevens Cres BS3..........63 F4
Stevens La BS24.........122 C1
Stevens Wlk BS32.........36 D8
Steway La BA1............86 B6
Stibbs Ct BS30............65 F4
Stibbs Hill BS5............65 A7
Stickland BS21...........57 E1
STIDCOT 16 E6
Stidcote La GL12 ....16 E5
Stidcot La GL12...........16 D5
Stile Acres BS11 ....34 A1
Stilemead La BS40.........94 D1
Stileway Bsns Pk BS21...73 B8
Stillhouse La BS3.........63 D4
Stillingfleet Rd BS13......79 C5
Stillman Cl BS13..........78 E4
Stinchcombe BS37.........27 E1
Stirling Cl BS37............27 D4
Stirling Rd BS4............64 C3
Stirling Way BS31.........81 E4
Stirtingale Ave BA2......101 C3
Stirtingale Rd BA2.......101 C3
Stitchings La BA2........117 D7
Stitchings Shord La
BS39......................113 C4
STOCK 109 B8
Stock Hill BS35.............7 C1
Stockhill Cl BA3.........138 C3
Stockhill Rd BA3.........138 C2
Stock La BS40............109 A7
Stockmead BS40.........109 B5
Stockton Cl
Bristol BS14................79 F4
Bristol, Oldland BS30.....66 B3
Stock Way N BS48.........59 F2
Stock Way S BS48.........59 E2
Stockwell Ave BS16.......52 A6
Stockwell Cl BS16.........51 F7
Stockwell Dr BS16.........52 A6
STOCKWOOD 80 E5
Stockwood Chambers
BS5......................64 C7
Stockwood Cres BS4......63 F2
Stockwood Green Prim
Sch BS14..................80 A4
Stockwood Hill BS31......81 C7
Stockwood La
Bristol BS14................80 E5
Keynsham BS14, BS31....81 B7
Stockwood Rd BS4........64 F5
Stockwood Vale BS31.....81 C6
Stodelgh Cl BS22..........89 B3
STOKE BISHOP 48 C5
Stoke Bishop CE Prim Sch
BS9......................48 D5
Stoke Bridge Ave
BS34......................36 D6
Stoke Cotts BS9 ....48 E4
Stokefield Cl BS35..........8 B1
STOKE GIFFORD 36 F4
Stoke Gr BS9 ....48 E6

Stoke Hamlet BS9 ....48 F6
Stoke Hill
Bristol BS9.................48 E3
Chew Stoke BS40.........112 D7
Stoke La
Bristol, Broomhill BS16....50 E7
Bristol, Patchway BS34....36 C8
Bristol, Westbury on T
BS9......................48 F6
Stokeleigh Wlk BS9........48 C5
Stoke Lodge Prim Sch
BS34......................36 C8
Stoke Mdws BS32.........24 D1
Stokemead BS34...........36 C8
Stoke Mead BA2.........119 F7
Stoke Paddock Rd
BS9......................48 D6
Stoke Park Rd BS9........48 F4
Stoke Park Rd S BS9......48 E3
Stoke Rd
Bristol BS8, BS9............48 F3
Portishead BS20............45 D5
Stokes Croft BS1.........143 B4
Stokes Ct ☑ BS30 ....66 A4
Stoke View BS3............36 A3
Stoke View Bsns Pk ☑
BS16.....................50 F4
Stoke View Rd BS16.......50 F3
STONE 3 E4
Stoneable Rd BA3.........134 A3
Stoneage La BA2.........117 B1
STON EASTON 131 E1
Stoneberry Rd BS14.......80 B3
STONEBRIDGE 107 A4
Stonebridge BS21.........57 F1
Stonebridge Pk BS5.......50 E2
Stonebridge Rd BS23....104 F4
Stonechat Gdns BS16.....50 E6
Stonechat Gn BS20........46 A6
Stone Cl BS36.............37 E4
STONE-EDGE BATCH 59 D4
Stonehenge La BS48.......59 E4
Stonehill BS15.............65 E4
STONE HILL 65 E4
Stonehill Ctr BS30.........65 E4
Stonehill Farm BS15.......65 E4
Stonehouse Cl BA2.......102 B2
Stonehouse La BA2.......102 B2
Stone House Mews
BS37......................28 B1
Stone La BS36.............37 F3
Stoneleigh BS40...........96 B3
Stoneleigh Cres BS4......64 A2
Stoneleigh Ct BA1.........84 E3
Stoneleigh Dr BS30........65 F5
Stoneleigh Ho BS8.......142 B3
Stoneleigh Rd BS4........64 A2
Stoneleigh Wlk BS4.......64 A2
Stone Monolith BS34......35 E6
Stone's Cross BA3........133 B2
Stones Ct BS6.............49 B2
Stonewell Dr BS49.........91 D3
Stonewell Gr BS49.........91 D3
Stonewell La BS49.........91 D3
Stonewell Park Rd
BS49......................91 D3
Stone with Woodford CE
Prim Sch GL13.............3 E4
Stoneyard La BA3........130 D2
Stoneyfield Cl BS20.......47 B5
Stoneyfields BS20.........47 B4
Stoney Littleton Long
Barrow* BA2.............135 C7
Stoney Steep BS48........60 A5
Stoney Stile Rd BS15......15 A5
STONY LITTLETON 135 B6
Stores Rd BS11............33 C4
Stormont Cl BS23.........104 F3
Stormont Ct BS24.........105 E7
Stothard Rd BS7...........50 B7
Stottbury Rd BS7..........50 A6
Stoulton Gr BS10..........35 A3
Stourden Cl BS16..........51 A7
Stourton Dr BS30..........65 F4
Stover Rd BS37............27 B2
Stover Trad Est BS37......27 B2
Stowborough Cotts
BA2......................134 C7
Stowell Hill Rd GL12......16 B6
STOWEY 113 F4
Stowey Bottom BS39.....113 E5
Stowey Crossroads
BS39......................113 F5
Stowey Pk BS49...........91 D7
Stowey Rd BS39..........113 F2
Stowey Rd BS49...........91 C8
Stow Hill Rd GL12.........16 B6
Stowick Gdns BS11........34 C2
Stradbrook Ave BS5.......65 B7
Stradling Ave BS23......104 F5
Stradling Rd BS11.........34 C2
Stradlings Yd BS2........142 C4
Straightmead BA3.........130 F1
Straight St BS2...........143 C2
Straits Par BS16...........51 B5
Stratford Cl BS14..........79 F3
Stratford Ct BS9............48 F8
Stratford La BS40.........112 E1
Strathearn Dr BS10........35 B2
Strathmore Rd BS7........49 F5
Stratton Cl BS34...........36 C7
STRATTON-ON-THE-
FOSSE 138 F1
Stratton Pl BS30...........65 F2
Stratton Rd BS31..........82 E3
Strawberry Cl BS48.......59 D1

Strawberry Field
BS26.....................125 D2
Strawberry Gdns BS48....75 D8
Strawberry Hill BS21......57 H4
Strawberry La
Bristol BS5.................64 E7
Dundry BS13, BS41.........78 E3
Strawbridge Rd ☑ BS5....64 B7
Stream Cl BS10............35 D3
Streamcross BS49.........74 D1
Streamleaze
Chew Magna BS40..........96 B3
Thornbury BS35............15 C8
Streamleaze Ct BS35.....15 B8
Streamside
Chew Magna BS40..........96 B3
☑ Clevedon BS21..........57 H3
Stream Side BS16.........51 F6
Streamside Rd BS37.......28 A1
Streamside Wlk BS4.......64 E3
Street The BS16............37 B2
STREET END 110 E2
Street End La BS40.......110 D2
Street The
Acton Turville GL9..........42 F6
Alveston BS35...............15 B5
Bishop Sutton BS39.......113 D4
Burton SN14................43 B4
Chew Stoke BS40.........112 D8
Chilcompton BA3.........138 D5
Compton Martin BS40....129 B7
Farmborough BA2.........115 F6
Luckington SN14............31 E4
North Nibley GL11...........5 D8
Olveston BS35...............14 A3
Radstock BA3.............133 F2
Stowey BS39...............113 F4
Ubley BS40................111 D1
Winford BS40...............94 F1
Stretford Ave BS5.........64 D8
Stretford Rd BS5..........64 D8
Stride Cl BS35.............22 A6
STRODE 111 E7
Strode Comm BS35.........15 F5
Strode Gdns BS35..........14 F5
Strode Rd BS21............57 E2
Strode Way BS21..........57 E1
Stroud Rd
Bristol, Patchway BS34.....35 F8
Bristol, Shirehampton
BS11......................47 E5
Petty France BS37..........30 B7
Stroud Way BS24.........105 E7
Stuart Ho BS23............104 E4
Stuart Pl BA2..............101 D6
Stuart Rd BS23...........105 A5
Stuart St BS5..............64 C7
Studland Ct BS9...........49 B6
Sturdon Rd BS3............63 A3
Sturmer Cl BS37...........27 E4
Sturmey Way BS20........47 D4
Sturminster Cl BS14.......80 D6
Sturminster Lo BS14......80 D5
Sturminster Rd BS14......80 D6
Suffolk Ho BA1...........101 C8
Sulis Manor Rd BA2......118 D8
Sullivan Cl BS4............79 D6
Sumerlin Dr BS21..........57 H3
Summer Ct BS8...........142 B3
Summerfield BS22..........89 A3
Summerfield Rd BA1.......85 A1
Summerfield Terr BA1.....85 A1
Summer Ground Dr
BS13......................79 A5
Summerhayes BS30........66 D5
Summer Hill BS4...........64 A4
Summerhill Jun & Inf Schs
BS4......................64 E8
Summerhill Rd
Bath BA1...................84 D1
Bristol BS5.................64 E8
Summerhill Terr BS5.......64 E7
Summerhouse BS21........59 D4
Summer House Way
BS30......................66 B7
Summerlands
Banwell BS29..............106 E5
Burton SN14................43 F3
Monkton Combe BA2.....119 D8
Weston-S-M BS22, BS24...89 B1
Weston-S-M BS23
BS24.....................106 C8
Summer La N BS22.........89 A2
Summer La BS24..........105 D7
Summerlands Rd
BS23......................105 B8
Summer Lane Park Homes
BS29......................106 D8
Summerlays Cl BA2.......102 B6
Summerlays Pl BA2.......102 B6
Summerlea BA2...........117 A5
Summerleaze
Bristol BS16................51 C3
Keynsham BS31............81 E7
Summers Dr BS30..........54 A1
Summers Mead BS37......27 E4
Summers Rd ☑ BS2.......50 A1
Summer St ☑ BS3.........63 C4
Summers Terr ☑ BS2......50 A1
SUNDAYSHILL 9 C8
Sundays Hill BS32.........24 A4
Sundayshill La GL12........9 D7
Sunderland Pl BS8.......142 B3

Sta–Syc **175**

Sunderland St ☑
BA2......................141 C3
Sundridge Pk BS37........39 E8
Sunfield Rd BS24.........105 E3
Sunningdale
Bristol BS8.................142 B4
Yate BS37..................39 E8
Sunningdale Cl BS48......60 A1
Sunningdale Dr BS30......66 B6
Sunningdale Rd BS22......88 F3
Sunnybank
☑ Bath BA2...............102 B4
Bristol BS16................51 E6
Westerleigh BS37..........39 A3
Sunny Bank
Bristol BS15.................51 B1
Wick BS30..................67 B7
Sunnybank Ct BS24........89 B1
Sunnybank Way BS24......89 B1
Sunnydene BS4............64 D4
Sunny Hill BS9.............48 C7
Sunnyhill Dr BS11.........47 E6
Sunnyhill Ho E BS11......47 F6
Sunnyhill Ho W BS11......47 F6
Sunnymead
Bristol BS9.................66 D6
Bristol BS4................81 F3
Midsomer Norton BA3....132 F2
Stratton-on-t-F BA3......138 F2
Sunnymede Rd BS48.......59 D3
Sunny Mount BA3.........133 B2
Sunnyside
Bristol BS9.................48 E5
Clutton BS39...............115 A4
Farrington Gurney
BS39......................132 B3
Frampton Cotterell BS36...38 B8
Sunnyside Cres BS21......57 F3
Sunnyside Farm Trad Est
BS20......................47 C2
Sunnyside Gdns BA2.....116 B2
Sunnyside La
Hambrook BS16............37 C2
Yate BS37..................27 C1
Sunnyside Rd
Clevedon BS21..............57 F3
Weston-S-M BS23.........104 E5
Sunnyside Rd N BS23....104 E6
Sunnyside View BA2.....134 C7
Sunnyvale
Camerton BA2.............133 D4
Clevedon BS21..............57 D1
Sunnyvale Dr BS30........66 B3
Sunny Wlk BS15............51 B1
Sunridge BS16.............51 D6
Sunridge Cl BA3.........138 F3
Sunridge Pk BA3.........138 F8
Sunrise Gr BS4.............64 D4
Sunset Cl BA2.............134 C7
Surrey Rd BS7..............49 E3
Surrey St BS2.............143 B4
Sussex Pl
Bath BA2...................141 C1
Bristol BS2.................49 F1
Sussex St BS2.............64 A6
Sutcliffe Ho BA1.........102 B8
Sutherland Ave
Bristol BS16.................51 E7
Yate BS37..................27 C4
Sutherland Dr BS24......105 D2
Sutherland Pl ☑ BS8......49 A2
Sutton Ave BS4............64 D4
Sutton Cl BS22...........105 E8
Sutton Ct BS39...........113 F5
Sutton Hill Rd BS39......113 D4
Sutton La BS40.............93 F1
Sutton Pk BS39...........113 D4
Sutton St BA2.............102 B7
SUTTON WICK 114 A1
Swainswick BS14...........79 F6
Swainswick CE Prim Sch
BA1.......................85 B5
Swainswick Gdns BA1.....85 C3
Swainswick La BA1.........85 D4
Swaish Dr ☑ BS30........66 A4
Swallow Cl BA3...........139 B8
Swallow Ct BS14..........80 A5
Swallow Dr BS34..........35 C8
Swallow Gdns BS22......105 E8
Swallow Pk BS35...........8 D3
Swallows Ct BS34..........36 E4
Swallow St BA1...........141 C2
Swallows The BS22.......105 D7
Swan Cl BS22.............105 E8
Swancombe
Blagdon BS40..............110 E2
Clapton in G BS20..........59 E8
Swane Rd BS14............80 F6
Swan Field BS37...........27 F2
Swan La BS36..............37 C8
Swanley La GL13............4 B5
Swanmoor Cres BS10......35 A4
Sweetgrass Rd BS24......106 A8
Sweets Cl BS15............51 E2
Sweets Rd BS15...........51 E2
Swift Cl BS22...............88 F1
SWINEFORD 83 A7
Swinhay La GL12...........11 B8
Swiss Dr BS3...............62 F2
Swiss Rd
Bristol BS3.................62 F1
Weston-S-M BS23.........104 F1
Sycamore Cl
Bristol, Hanham BS15......65 B3
Bristol, Whitehall BS5......50 E1

Sycamore Cl *continued*
Locking BS24 105 E5
Nailsea BS48 59 E2
Shipham BS25 125 E8
Weston-S-M BS23 105 A8
Sycamore Ct BS7 49 E3
Sycamore Dr
Bristol BS34 35 F7
Thornbury BS35 8 C1
Sycamore Ho 6 BS16 51 C6
Sycamore Rd BA3 134 B2
Sycamores BS23 87 E1
Sydenham Bldgs BA2 141 A2
Sydenham Hill BS6 49 D1
Sydenham La BS6 49 E1
Sydenham Pl 15 BS6 49 E1
Sydenham Rd
Bath BA2 141 A2
Bristol, Cotham BS6 49 E1
Bristol, Totterdown BS4 64 A3
Sydenham Terr BA2 102 C1
Sydenham Way BS15 65 C3
Sydney Bldgs BA2 102 B6
Sydney Ho BA2 102 B7
Sydney Mews BA2 102 B7
Sydney Pl BA2 102 B7
Sydney Rd BA2 102 B7
Sydney Row BS1 142 B1
Sydney Wharf BA2 102 B7
Sylvan Way BS9 48 B7
Sylvia Ave BS3 63 F3
Symes Ave BS13 79 C4
Symes Pk BA1 84 A2
Symington Rd BS16 51 B5
Syston View BS15 66 A8
Syston Way BS15 51 D1

T

Tabernacle Rd BS15 65 C6
Tackley Rd BS5 50 B3
TADWICK 68 E1
Tadwick La BA1 85 A6
Tailor's Ct 9 BS1 143 A3
Talbot Ave BS15 51 C1
Talbot Ct BS4 64 B2
Talbot Rd BS4 64 C2
TALBOT'S END 10 C1
Talgarth Rd BS7 49 F4
Tallis Gr BS4 79 D6
Tamar Cl BS35 15 D7
Tamar Dr BS31 82 A4
Tamar Rd
Bristol BS2 64 C6
Weston-S-M BS22 89 A2
Tamblyn Cl BA3 134 A3
Tamsin Ct BS31 81 F5
Tamworth Rd BS31 81 E4
Tanhouse La BS37 27 D7
Tankard's Cl BS8 142 C3
Tanner Cl BS30 65 F5
Tanner Ct BS30 65 F5
Tanners Ct
Bristol, Frenchay BS16 37 B1
4 Bristol, Two Mile Hill BS15 51 C1
Thornbury BS35 15 B8
Tanners La SN14 69 F8
Tanners Wlk
Bath BA2 100 F5
Marshfield SN14 69 F8
Tanorth Cl BS14 80 A3
Tanorth Rd BS14 79 F3
Tansy La BS20 45 F5
Tanyard The BS30 66 B2
Tapsters BS30 66 A4
Tara Cl BS36 25 F1
Tarn Ho BS34 36 A8
Tarnock Ave BS14 80 A7
Tarnwell BS39 97 A2
Tarragon Pl BS32 36 F7
Taunton Rd BS22 89 B4
Taunton Wlk BS7 50 A7
Taveners Wlk BS48 59 F3
Taverner Cl BS4 79 D7
Taverners Cl 6 BS23 104 F4
TAVERN SCOTT 95 D1
Tavistock Rd
Bristol BS4 63 F1
Weston-S-M BS22 89 A2
Tavistock Wlk BS4 63 F1
Tawny Way BS22 105 F8
Taylor Cl BS15 65 F8
Taylor Ct BS22 89 B4
Taylor Gdns BS13 78 F4
Taylors Bank 10 BS1 143 A3
Tayman Cl BS10 49 E6
Tayman Ridge BS30 82 D8
Taynton Cl BS30 66 C2
Teal Cl
Bristol BS32 24 D2
Weston-S-M BS22 88 F1
Teal Way BS20 45 F6
Teasel Mead BS32 36 E7
Teasel Wlk BS22 105 D7
Teddington Cl BA2 101 C4
Teesdale Cl BS22 105 D8
Teewell Ave BS16 51 E4
Teewell Cl BS16 51 E4
Teewell Ct BS16 51 E4
Teewell Hill BS16 51 E4
Teignmouth Rd
Bristol BS4 63 F1
Clevedon BS21 57 G3
Telephone Ave BS1 143 A2
Telford Ho
Bath BA2 101 D3
Leigh Woods BS8 62 E7
Telford Wlk BS5 51 A1
TELLISFORD 137 E4
Tellisford La BA2 136 F4
Templar Rd BS37 27 E3
Templars Ct 1 BS22 105 D7
Templars Way BS25 125 E7
Temple Back BS1 143 B2
Temple Back E BS1 143 C2
Temple Bridge Bsns Pk BS39 131 F7
Temple Church* BS1 143 B2
Temple Circus Giratory BS1 143 B1
TEMPLE CLOUD 114 E1
Temple Ct BS31 81 E5
Temple Gate BS1 143 B1
Temple Gate District Ctr BS3 63 F4
Temple Inn La BS39 114 E1
Templeland Rd BS13 78 F5
Temple Rose St BS1 143 B2
Temple St
Bristol, Bedminster BS3 63 B2
Bristol BS1 143 B2
Keynsham BS31 81 F5
Temple Trad Est BS2 64 C5
Temple Way BS2 143 B2
Temple Way Underpass BS2 143 C3
Tenby Rd BS31 81 D4
Tenby St BS5 64 B7
Tennessee Gr BS6 49 C5
Tennis Court Ave BS39 132 D5
Tenniscourt Rd BS15 52 A1
Tennis Court Rd BS39 132 D5
Tennis Rd BS4 64 A2
Tennyson Ave BS21 57 D2
Tennyson Cl BS31 81 F6
Tennyson Rd
Bath BA1 101 D7
Bristol BS7 49 E5
Weston-S-M BS23 105 A3
Tenterk Cl BS24 122 B6
Tenth Ave BS7 36 B1
Tereslake Gn BS10 35 D4
Terrace The BS25 125 E7
Terrace Wlk BA1 141 C2
Terrell Gdns 14 BS5 64 D7
Terrell St BS2 143 A4
Terris Ct BS34 36 E4
Terry Hill BA3 140 D8
Terry Ho BS1 142 C3
Tetbury Cl BS34 36 C7
Tetbury Gdns BS48 60 A1
Tetbury Rd BS15 65 B8
Teviot Rd BS31 82 A4
Tewkesbury Rd 12 BS2 50 A2
Tewther Rd BS13 79 D3
Teyfant Com Sch BS13 79 E4
Teyfant Rd BS13 79 E4
Teyfant Wlk BS13 79 E4
Thackeray BS7 50 A8
Thackeray Ave BS21 57 G4
Thackeray Ho BS23 105 A5
Thackeray Rd BS21 57 G4
Thames Cl GL12 11 A4
Thames Ho 9 BS35 15 C8
Thanet Rd BS3 63 B2
Thatcher Cl BS20 45 D4
Thatchers Cl BS5 65 B7
Theatre Royal*
Bath BA1 141 B2
Bristol BS1 143 A2
THE GIBB 43 F3
THE KNAPP 8 F3
There-and-Back-Again La BS1 142 C3
Theresa Ave BS7 49 E4
Thermae Bath Spa* BA1 141 B2
Theynes Croft BS41 62 B1
Thicket Ave BS16 51 C3
THICKET MEAD 132 F3
Thicket Mead BA3 133 A2
Thicket Rd BS16 51 C4
Thicket Wlk BS35 8 C1
Thiery Rd BS4 64 C2
Thingwall Pk BS16 50 E3
Third Ave
Bath BA2 101 D5
Bristol BS14 80 B7
Bristol, Filton BS7 36 A1
Radstock BA3 139 D7
Third Way BS11 33 C2
Thirlmere Ct BS30 66 D6
Thirlmere Rd
Bristol BS34 36 A8
Weston-S-M BS23 105 A4
Thistle St 1 BS3 63 B3
Thomas Ave BS16 52 B8
Thomas Cl BS29 107 A3
Thomas Ct BS1 143 B2
Thomas La BS1 143 B2
Thomas Lane Apartments BS1 143 B2
Thomas Pring Wlk 1 BS5 51 A1
Thomas St N 13 BS2 49 D1
Thomas St
Bath BA1 141 C4
Bristol BS2 143 B4
Thomas St *continued*
8 Bristol, Russell Town BS5 64 B7
Bristol, St Pauls BS2 49 F1
Thomas Way BS16 50 E7
Thompson Rd BS14 80 E6
Thomson Rd 7 BS5 64 B8
Thornbank Pl BA2 141 A1
THORNBURY 8 E2
Thornbury Dr BS23 104 D2
Thornbury Hospl BS35 8 C1
Thornbury Ind Est BS35 15 B7
Thornbury Mus* BS35 15 B8
Thornbury Office Pk BS35 15 B8
Thornbury Rd
Alveston BS35 15 A5
Weston-S-M BS23 104 C2
Thorn Cl
Weston-S-M BS22 89 B2
Yate BS37 27 D1
Thorndale BS8 142 A4
Thorndale Cl BS22 105 D8
Thorndale Mews BS8 142 A4
Thornhayes Cl BS36 38 A8
Thornhills The BS16 51 B6
Thornleigh Rd BS7 49 E5
Thornmead Gr BS10 35 A2
Thorns Farm BS37 27 E1
Thornycroft Cl BS7 50 B7
Thorpe Lo 10 BS6 49 D1
Three Brooks La BS32 36 E8
Three Oaks Cl BS16 51 C4
Three Queens' La BS1 143 B2
Threeways Sch Summerfield Site BA1 84 D1
Three Wells Rd BS13 78 F4
Thrissell St BS5 64 A8
Throgmorton Rd BS4 79 F8
Thrubwell La BS40 94 B4
Thrush Cl 4 BS22 105 E8
Thurlestone BS14 80 A6
Thurlow Rd BS5 50 C2
Thurston's Barton BS5 50 E1
Thyme Cl BS20 45 F5
Tibberton BS15 66 A8
Tibbott Rd BS14 80 D5
Tibbott Wlk BS14 80 D5
Tichborne Rd
Bristol BS5 64 C7
Weston-S-M BS23 87 E1
TICKENHAM 58 F4
Tickenham CE Prim Sch BS21 58 F4
Tickenham Hill BS48 59 E4
Tickenham Rd BS21 58 A4
Tide Gr BS11 48 A8
Tidenham Way BS34 23 F1
Tiffany Ct BS1 143 B1
Tiledown BS39 114 E1
Tiledown Cl BS39 114 F1
Tilley Cl
Farmborough BA2 116 A5
Keynsham BS31 82 A2
Tilley La BA2 116 A5
Tilling Rd BS10 49 E7
Tilling Wlk BS10 49 E7
Tilting Rd BS35 8 B2
Timber Dene BS16 50 D4
Timberscombe Wlk BS14 80 C5
Timbers The BA3 139 B7
TIMSBURY 116 B1
TIMSBURY BOTTOM 116 A1
Timsbury Rd
Bristol BS3 63 E2
Farmborough BA2 116 B5
High Littleton BS39 115 D1
Timsbury Village Workshops BA2 115 F3
Timsbury Wlk BS3 63 E2
Timsbury Workshop Est BA2 115 F3
Tindell Ct 12 BS30 65 F4
Tinker's La
Compton Martin BS40 129 B7
Kilmersdon BA11 140 B1
Tintagel Cl BS31 81 D4
Tintern Ave BS5 64 D8
Tintern Cl BS30 65 F6
Tippetts Rd BS15 65 D6
Tirley Ho BS34 23 F1
Tirley Way BS22 88 B2
Titan Barrow BA1 86 C2
Tiverton Gdns BS22 89 A2
Tiverton Rd 2 BS21 57 G1
Tiverton Wlk BS16 51 A2
Tivoli Ho BS23 104 E8
Tivoli La BS23 104 E8
Tobias Gdns BS37 27 D1
TOCKINGTON 14 C1
Tockington Gn BS32 14 B2
Tockington La BS32 24 A7
Tockington Manor Sch BS32 14 C2
Tockington Park La BS32 24 E8
Toddington Cl BS37 39 D8
Toghill La BS30 68 A8
Tolland BS24 105 A2
Toll Bridge Rd BA1 85 E3
Toll Down Way SN14 43 A3
Toll House Ct 5 BS3 63 A4
Toll Rd BS23 121 F8
Tone Rd BS21 57 F1
Top Rd BS25 125 F7
Tor Cl BS22 89 A2
TORMARTON 41 E2
Tormarton Cres BS10 34 F4
Tormarton Intc BS37 41 B1
Tormarton Rd
Acton Turville GL9 42 E6
Marshfield, East End SN14 70 A8
Marshfield SN14 56 A4
Tormynton Rd BS22 88 E3
Toronto Rd BS7 50 A8
Torpoint Rd BS3 63 D2
Torrance Cl BS30 66 D6
Torridge Rd BS31 82 A4
Torrington Ave BS4 79 F8
Torrington Cres BS22 89 A3
TORTWORTH 10 C7
TORTWORTH GREEN 10 C5
Tortworth Prim Sch GL12 10 C7
Tortworth Rd BS7 49 E5
Torwood House Sch BS6 49 A3
Totnes Cl BS22 89 A2
Totshill Dr BS13 79 E4
Totshill Gr BS13 79 E4
Tottenham Pl BS8 142 B3
TOTTERDOWN 64 A4
Totterdown Bridge Ind Est BS2 64 A4
Totterdown La BS24 105 A1
Totterdown Rd BS23 104 F4
TOTTEROAK 28 F5
Touching End La SN14 69 F8
Touchstone Ave BS34 36 F5
Tovey Cl BS22 88 E4
TOWERHEAD 107 D4
Towerhead Rd BS29 107 D3
Tower Hill
Bristol BS2 143 B3
Locking BS24 106 D4
Tower House La BS48 60 A4
Tower La
Bristol BS1 143 A3
Bristol, Cadbury Heath BS30 66 B6
Towerleaze BS9 48 D3
Tower Rd
Bristol BS15 51 C1
Portishead BS20 45 A4
Tower Rd N BS30 66 B7
Tower Rd S BS30 66 B5
Tower St BS1 143 B2
Tower The
Bristol BS1 143 B2
Bristol, Redland BS6 49 C3
Tower Wlk BS23 87 D1
Town Barton BA2 136 F4
Town End BA2 136 F4
Townsend
Almondsbury BS32 23 F4
East Harptree BS40 130 A5
TOWNS END 132 E4
Townsend Cl BS14 80 F5
Townsend La BS32 24 A5
Townsend Rd BS14 80 F5
Townshend Rd BS22 89 B5
TOWNWELL 10 B2
Townwell GL12 10 B2
Tozers Hill BS4 64 C2
Tracy Cl BS14 79 F7
Trafalgar Ct BS23 104 E7
Trafalgar Rd BA1 84 B1
Trafalgar Terr 3 BS3 63 B2
Tralee Wlk BS4 63 D1
Tramshed The BA1 141 C3
Tramway Rd BS4 64 C3
Tranmere Ave BS10 35 A4
Tranmere Gr BS10 35 A3
Transom Ho BS1 143 B2
Tranton La GL13 2 C4
Tratman Wlk BS10 34 F3
Travers Cl BS4 79 D6
Travers Wlk BS34 36 F5
Trawden Cl BS23 88 A1
Tredegar Rd BS16 51 B3
Treefield Pl 5 BS2 50 A2
Treefield Rd BS21 57 F2
Tree Leaze BS37 27 F2
Treetops Cvn Pk BS16 51 A8
Tregarth Rd BS3 62 F1
Trelawn Cl BS22 89 D2
Trelawney Ave BS5 64 D8
Trelawney Pk BS4 64 D3
Trelawney Rd BS6 49 C1
Trelissick Gdns 3 BS22 105 F8
Trellick Wlk BS16 50 E8
Tremes Cl SN14 69 F8
Tremlett Mews 3 BS22 89 B4
Trenchard Rd
Locking BS24 106 D4
Saltford BS31 82 D3
Trenchard St BS1 142 C3
Trench La BS32 24 E2
Trendlewood Pk BS16 50 E5
Trendlewood Way BS48 60 A1
Trenleigh Dr BS22 89 A2
Trent Dr BS35 15 D7
Trent Gr BS31 82 A4
Trentham Cl 7 BS2 50 A2
Trescothick Cl BS31 81 E6
Trescothick Dr BS30 66 D4
Tresham Cl BS32 24 D2
Trevanna Rd BS3 62 F1
Trevelyan Rd BS23 104 F7
Trevelyan Wlk
Bristol, Henbury BS10 34 F3
Bristol, Stoke Gifford BS34 37 A5
Treverdowe Wlk BS10 34 D3
Trevethin Cl BS15 65 D7
Trevisa Gr BS10 35 C4
Trewartha Cl BS23 104 F8
Trewartha Pk BS23 104 F8
Trewint Gdns BS4 79 F8
Triangle Ct 2 BA2 101 D5
Triangle Ctr The BS21 57 F3
Triangle E BA2 101 D5
Triangle N BA2 101 D5
Triangle S BS8 142 B3
Triangle The
Clevedon BS21 57 F3
Paulton BS39 132 E6
Portishead BS20 45 B5
Wrington BS40 92 D2
Triangle Villas 1 BA2 101 D5
Triangle W
Bath BA2 101 D5
Bristol BS8 142 B3
Trident Cl BS16 38 A1
Trim Bridge 3 BA1 141 B2
Trim St BA1 141 B2
Trinder Rd BS20 47 B4
Trinity CE Prim Sch GL9 43 A6
Trinity Cl BA1 141 B2
Trinity Coll BS9 48 E4
Trinity Ct
5 Bristol BS15 65 E8
Bristol, Horfield BS7 49 E5
Nailsea BS48 59 C1
Trinity Mews 15 BS2 143 C3
Trinity Pl
3 Bristol BS8 142 A2
4 Weston-S-M BS23 87 C1
Trinity Rd
Bath BA2 102 B2
Bristol BS2 64 A7
Nailsea BS48 59 D1
Weston-S-M BS23 87 C1
Trinity St
Bath BA1 141 B2
Bristol BS2 64 A7
Trinity Wlk
Bristol BS2 143 C3
Bristol, Newton BS2 64 A7
Trin Mills BS1 143 A1
Tripps Cnr BS49 91 D7
Tripps Row BS41 62 A1
Troon BS37 39 E8
Troon Dr BS30 66 B6
Troopers' Hill Rd BS5 65 A7
Trossachs Dr BA2 102 D8
Trowbridge Rd BS10 35 C1
Trowbridge Wlk BS10 35 C1
Trubodys Yd BS30 66 E7
Trubshaw Cl BS7 49 F6
Trumpet La BS5 65 B7
Truro Rd
Bristol BS3 63 B3
Nailsea BS48 60 A1
Trym Bank BS9 48 D7
Trym Cross Rd BS9 48 C5
Trymleaze BS9 48 C5
Trym Rd BS9 49 A7
Trym Side BS9 48 C5
Trymwood Cl BS10 34 F2
Trymwood Par BS9 48 D6
T T Trad Est BS37 28 C1
Tucker's La BS40 128 E8
Tucker St BS2 143 C3
Tuckett Ho BS16 51 C7
Tuckett La BS16 51 C7
TUCKING MILL 119 D8
Tucking Mill Cotts BA2 119 D7
Tuckingmill La BS39 98 E5
Tuckmill BS21 57 D1
Tudor Cl BS30 66 C3
Tudor Rd
Bristol, Hanham BS15 65 C5
Bristol, Lower Easton BS5 50 C1
Bristol, St Pauls BS2 49 F1
2 Portishead BS20 45 E4
Weston-S-M BS22 89 A4
Tuffley Rd BS10 49 C8
Tufton Ave BS11 48 A8
Tugela Rd BS13 78 F7
Tuggy's La BA2 119 E1
Tunbridge Cl BS40 96 B2
Tunbridge Rd BS40 96 B2
Tunbridge Way BS16 52 A8
TUNLEY 117 B3
Tunley Hill BA2 116 E2
Tunley Rd BA2, BA3 117 D5
Tunnel La BA3 138 F5
Tunstall Cl BS9 48 E4
TURLEIGH 120 F6
Turley Rd BS5 50 D1
Turnberry
Bristol BS30 66 B6
Yate BS37 39 E8
Turnberry Wlk 3 BS4 64 D1
Turnbridge Cl BS10 35 D4
Turnbridge Rd BS10 35 C3
Turnbury Ave BS48 60 A1
Turnbury Cl BS22 88 F3
Turner Cl BS31 82 A5
Turner Ct BS22 88 F3
Turner Dr BS37 27 B1

Tur–Wal 177

Turner Gdns BS7 50 B6
Turners Ct 9 BS30 65 F4
Turner's Twr BA3 135 A1
Turner Way BS21 57 D1
Turner Wlk BS30 66 D7
Turnpike Cl BS37 27 E2
Turnpike Gate GL12 18 B6
Turnpike Rd
Cross BS26 124 E1
Shipham BS25 125 E8
Turtlegate Ave BS13 78 E4
Turtlegate Wlk BS13 78 E4
Turville Dr BS7 50 A6
Tuscany Ho BS6 49 A3
Tutton Way BS21 57 F1
Tuttors Hill BS27 126 C1
Tweed Cl BS35 15 C8
Tweed Rd BS21 57 E1
Tweed Rd Ind Est 2 BS21 57 E1
Tweeny La BS30 66 D6
Twenty Acres Rd BS10 35 B2
TWERTON 101 A5
Twerton Farm Cl 2 BA2 101 B6
Twerton Inf Sch BA2 101 A5
Twickenham Rd BS6 49 C5
Twinhoe La BA2 118 E2
Twinnell Ho 5 BS5 64 A8
Two Acres Cvn Pk BS21 44 B2
Two Acres Rd BS14 80 A7
Two Mile Ct BS15 65 C8
TWO MILE HILL 51 C1
Two Mile Hill Jun & Inf Schs BS15 65 C8
Twomile Hill Rd BS15 65 B8
Two Stones La BS37 40 C8
Two Trees BS40 127 E8
Twynings The BS15 51 E2
Tybalt Way BS34 36 E5
Tydeman Rd BS20 45 F5
Tyler Cl BS15 65 E5
Tyler Gn 2 BS22 89 B4
Tylers Farm BS37 27 F4
Tyler's La BS16 51 D5
Tyler St BS2 64 A6
Tylers Way BS37 27 F5
Tyndale Ave
Bristol BS16 51 A4
Yate BS37 27 D3
Tyndale Ct GL11 5 E4
Tyndale Ct 7 BS6 49 B1
Tyndale Mon The* GL11 5 E4
Tyndale Rd BS15 51 E2
Tyndale View BS35 15 B8
Tyndall Ave BS8 142 C4
Tyndall Ho 5 BS2 143 C3
Tyndall Rd BS5 64 B8
Tyndalls Ct BS8 142 C4
Tyndalls Ho BS8 142 C4
TYNDALL'S PARK 142 C4
Tyndalls Park Mews BS2 142 C4
Tyndall's Park Rd BS8 142 C4
Tyndalls Way BS10 49 E8
Tyne Gr BS20 45 F6
Tyne Ho 8 BS35 15 C8
Tyne Rd BS7 49 D3
Tyne St BS2 50 A2
TYNING
Radstock 134 B3
Timsbury 116 A2
Tyning Cl
Bristol BS14 80 A7
Yate BS37 27 E2
Tyning End BA2 102 B5
Tyning Hill BA3 134 B3
Tyning La BA1 85 B1
Tyning Pl BA2 102 C2
Tyning Rd
Bathampton BA2 85 F2
Bath BA2 102 C2
Bristol BS3 63 F3
Peasedown St John BA2 134 D7
Saltford BS31 82 E2
Winsley BA15 120 E7
Tynings BS39 114 D3
Tynings Mews BS23 104 E4
Tynings Sch The BS16 51 E4
Tynings The
Clevedon BS21 57 C1
Portishead BS20 44 F1
Tynings Way
Clutton BS39 114 E3
Westwood BA15 120 F3
Tyning Terr
14 Bath BA1 85 A1
18 Bath BA1 85 B1
Tyning The
Bath BA2 102 B5
Freshford BA2 120 B4
Tynte Ave BS13 79 E3
Tyntesfield* BS48 60 F4
Tyntesfield Rd BS13 79 A8
Tyrone Wlk BS4 79 E8
Tyrrel Way BS34 36 E5
Tythe Ct SN14 70 A8
TYTHERINGTON 16 C5
Tytherington Rd BS35 16 A6

U

UBLEY 111 E1
Ubley CE Prim Sch BS40 111 D1
Ubley Dro BS40 128 B7
UBLEY SIDELING 128 D8
UDLEY 92 C4
Ullswater Cl
Bristol BS30 66 D6
Weston-S-M BS23 105 A4
Yate BS37 27 E3
Ullswater Dr BA1 85 A2
Ullswater Rd BS10 35 C1
Uncombe Cl BS48 76 D7
Underbanks BS20 47 D4
Underdown Ho BS1 143 A1
Underhill Ave BA3 132 F2
Underhill Dr BS23 104 D1
Underhill La BA3 132 F2
Underhill Rd GL12 11 A5
Under Knoll BA2 134 E8
Under La BS40 93 D1
Underleaf Way BA2 134 D7
Undertown BS40 129 A7
Undertown La BS40 129 A7
Underwood Ave BS22 88 B1
Underwood Cl BS35 15 A4
Underwood End BS25 108 A4
Underwood Rd BS20 45 C3
Unicorn Bsns Pk BS4 64 D5
Unicorn Pk BS4 64 D5
Union Pas BA1 141 C2
Union Pl BS23 104 D7
Union Rd 2 BS2 64 A6
Union St
Bath BA1 141 C2
Bristol BS1 143 B3
Nailsea BS48 59 C1
Weston-S-M BS23 104 D7
Unite Ho BS1 142 C2
Unity Ct BS31 82 A5
Unity Rd BS31 82 A6
Unity St
Bristol, Brandon Hill BS1 142 C2
Bristol BS2 143 C3
Bristol, Kingswood BS15 65 C8
University Cl BS9 48 F4
University Rd BS8 142 C3
University Wlk BS8 142 C3
Univ of Bath BA2 102 E5
Univ of Bristol BS8 142 C3
Univ of Bristol Botanic Gdns* BS9 48 F4
Univ of Bristol Dorothy Hodgkin Bldg BS1 143 A4
Univ of Bristol Langford House Sch of Veterinary Science BS40 109 B6
Univ of the West of England BS3 62 E4
Univ of the West of England Faculty of Health & Social Care BS16 50 E5
Univ of the West of England Frenchay Campus BS16 36 E1
Univ of the West of England, St Matthias Campus BS16 51 A5
UPHILL 104 C2
Uphill Ct BS23 104 D2
Uphill Dr BA1 85 B2
Uphill Farm Cvn Pk BS23 104 E1
Uphill Prim Sch BS23 104 D2
Uphill Rd BS7 49 F5
Uphill Rd N BS23 104 D4
Uphill Rd S BS23 104 D2
Uphill Way BS23 104 D1
Upjohn Cres BS13 79 D3
Uplands Cl BA2 119 F7
Uplands Dr BS31 82 F2
Uplands Rd
Bristol BS16 51 D3
Saltford BS31 82 F2
Uplands The BS48 75 C8
Upper Bath Rd BS35 15 B8
Upper Belgrave Rd BS8 49 A2
Upper Belmont Rd BS7 49 E3
Upper Berkeley Pl BS8 142 B3
Upper Bloomfield Rd BA2 101 D1
Upper Borough Walls BA1 141 C2
Upper Bristol Rd
Bath BA1 101 D7
Clutton BS39 114 D3
Weston-S-M BS22 88 B1
Upper Byron Pl BS8 142 B3
Upper Camden Pl BA1 141 C4
UPPER CANADA 106 A1
Upper Chapel La BS36 38 C7
Upper Cheltenham Pl BS6 49 E1
Upper Church La
Bristol BS2 142 C3
Hutton BS24 105 D2
Upper Church Rd BS23 87 D1
Upper Church St BA1 141 B3
Upper Conham Vale BS15 65 A5
Upper Cranbrook Rd BS6 49 B4
Upper East Hayes BA1 85 B1
UPPER EASTON 64 B8
UPPER EASTVILLE 50 E3
Upper Farm Cl BA2 136 F4
Upper Furlong BA2 116 B3
Upper Green La BS40 111 B7
Upper Hedgemead Rd BA1 141 B4
UPPER HILL 2 E5
Upper Horfield Prim Sch BS7 50 A8
Upper Kewstoke Rd BS23 87 B1
UPPER KILCOTT 20 C5
UPPER KNOWLE 64 B2
Upper Lambridge St BA1 85 C2
UPPER LANGFORD 109 C3
UPPER LANGRIDGE 84 B7
Upper Lansdown Mews BA1 84 F1
UPPER LITTLETON 95 C6
Upper Maudlin St BS2 143 A3
Upper Merryfield BA3 139 E1
UPPER MORTON 8 E4
Upper Mount Pleasant BA2 120 A4
Upper Myrtle Hill BS20 47 C4
Upper New Rd BS27 126 A1
Upper Oldfield Pk BA2 141 A1
Upper Perry Hill BS3 63 C4
Upper Pitching BA3 138 D5
UPPER RADFORD 133 B8
Upper Rd BS39 130 E6
Upper Sandhurst Rd BS4 64 D4
UPPER SOUNDWELL 51 D3
Upper St
Bristol BS4 64 A4
Dyrham SN14 54 D4
Upper Stanton BS39 97 A2
UPPER STANTON DREW 97 B2
Upper Station Rd BS16 51 D4
Upper Stone Cl BS36 38 C7
Upper Strode BS40 111 F7
UPPER SWAINSWICK 85 B5
Upper Sydney St BS3 63 B3
Upper Terr BS11 34 B1
Upper Tockington Rd BS32 14 A2
Upper Town La BS40 94 C8
Upper Wells St BS1 142 C3
UPPER WESTON 84 A3
UPPER WESTWOOD 120 E4
UPPER WICK 5 A6
UPPER WRAXALL 56 E2
Upper York St BS2 143 B4
Upton BS24 105 A2
UPTON CHEYNEY 83 B8
Upton Cotts BS41 95 F8
Upton La BS41 96 A8
Upton Rd BS3 63 B4
Urchinwood La BS49 91 F4
Urfords Dr 1 BS16 51 C6
Usk Ct 5 BS35 15 C8

V

Valda Rd BS22 88 C2
Vale Cres BS22 89 C2
Vale Ct BS8 142 A4
Vale End BS48 59 D1
Vale Foundry La BS3 62 F2
Vale La BS3 79 C8
Vale Mill Way BS24 105 F8
Valentine Cl BS14 80 B5
Valerian Cl BS11 47 F6
Vale St BS4 64 A4
Vale The BS16 52 F6
Valetta Cl BS23 104 F3
Vale View BA3 134 A2
Vale View Pl 16 BA1 85 B1
Vale View Terr BA1 85 F3
Valley Cl 6 BS48 59 E2
Valley Ct BS20 44 E3
Valley Gdns
Bristol BS16 51 F8
Nailsea BS48 59 E2
Valley Rd
Bristol, Bedminster Down BS13 79 A8
Bristol, Mangotsfield BS16 52 A5
Bristol, Warmley BS30 66 D6
Clevedon BS21 57 H5
Leigh Woods BS8 62 C7
Portishead BS20 45 A2
Valley View
Chilcompton BA3 138 D3
Clutton BS39 114 E3
Valley View Cl BA1 85 B3
Valley View Rd
Bath BA1 85 C3
Paulton BS39 132 E6
Valley Way Rd BS48 59 E3
Valley Wlk BA3 133 B2
Valls The BS32 36 F6
Valma Rocks BS5 65 A6
Vanbrugh La BS16 50 E7
Van Diemen's La BA1 84 F2
Vandyck Ave BS31 81 F6
Vane St BA2 102 B7
Vantage Office Pk BS34 37 A6
Varsity Way BS24 106 B6
Vassall Ct BS16 51 B5
Vassall Rd BS16 51 B5
Vattingstone Ho BS35 14 F5
Vattingstone La BS35 14 F5
Vaughan Cl BS10 34 F3
Vauxhall Terr 3 BS3 63 A4
Vayre Cl BS37 28 C1
Veale The BS24 122 C6
Vee La BS40 94 D8
Vellore La BA2 102 C7
Venns Gate BS27 126 A1
Ventnor Ave 1 BS5 64 F8
Ventnor Rd
Bristol, Filton BS34 36 B3
Bristol, St George BS5 50 F1
Venton Ct 5 BS15 65 B5
Venture The BS4 63 E1
Venue The BS10 35 C6
Venus La BS39 114 E3
Venus St BS49 91 E2
Vera Rd BS16 50 F2
Verbena Way BS22 89 A1
Vereland Rd BS24 105 E3
Verlands BS49 91 E5
Vernals La GL12 11 C8
Vernham Gr BA2 101 C1
Vernhamwood Cl BA2 101 C1
Vernon Cl BS31 82 D3
Vernon La BS26 124 B3
Vernon Pk BA2 101 C6
Vernon St 5 BS2 63 F4
Vernon Terr BA2 101 C6
Vernslade BA1 84 A2
Verrier Rd BS5 64 C7
Verwood Dr BS30 66 C2
Vian End BS22 88 F4
Vicarage Cl BS22 89 A3
Vicarage Cotts 12 BS16 51 D5
Vicarage Ct
Bristol, Jefferies Hill BS15 65 B5
19 Bristol, Russell Town BS5 64 C7
Vicarage Gdns BA2 134 B7
Vicarage La
Barrow Gurney BS48 77 C6
Compton Bishop BS26 124 B3
Compton Dando BS39 98 D6
Hillesley GL12 19 D8
Norton St Philip BA2 136 E4
Olveston BS35 14 B3
Vicarage Rd
Bristol, Bishopsworth BS13 79 A6
Bristol, Hanham BS15 65 B5
Bristol, Moorfields BS5 64 C8
Bristol, Southville BS3 63 B4
Frampton Cotterell BS36 38 C6
Leigh Woods BS8 62 D6
Pilning BS35 22 C7
Vicars Cl BS16 51 B4
Victor Ho BS34 36 C7
Victoria Art Gall The* BA2 141 C2
Victoria Ave BS5 64 C7
Victoria Bldgs BA2 101 D6
Victoria Bridge Ct BA1 141 A3
Victoria Bridge Rd BA1, BA2 141 A2
Victoria Cl
Bath BA2 101 C5
Portishead BS20 45 D5
Thornbury BS35 8 B3
Victoria Cotts BA2 118 F7
Victoria Cres BS35 22 A6
Victoria Ct
7 Bristol, Cotham BS6 49 D1
Bristol, Redland BS6 49 A3
Clevedon BS21 57 E3
Portishead BS20 45 D5
Victoria Gdns
Batheaston BA1 85 F3
8 Bristol BS6 49 D1
Victoria Gr BS3 63 E4
Victoria Ho
Bath BA1 101 D8
Keynsham BS31 81 F4
Victoria Jubilee Homes BS40 109 C6
Victoria Lo BS22 88 E2
Victoria Par BS5 64 C8
VICTORIA PARK 142 B3
Victoria Park Bsns Ctr BA1 101 D7
Victoria Park Com Inf Sch BS3 63 E3
Victoria Park Com Jun Sch BS3 63 E3
Victoria Park Ct BS3 63 F3
Victoria Pk
Bristol, Fishponds BS16 51 A5
Bristol, Kingswood BS15 51 D1
Weston-S-M BS23 87 D1
Victoria Pl
Bath, Combe Down BA2 102 C1
2 Bath, Lambridge BA1 85 C1
Bristol BS3 63 C3
Paulton BS39 132 D5
Victoria Pl *continued*
Weston-S-M BS23 104 D8
Victoria Quadrant BS23 104 E8
Victoria Rd
Avonmouth BS11 47 B7
4 Bath BA2 101 D6
Bristol, Hanham BS15 65 C5
Bristol, St Philip's Marsh BS2 64 A5
Bristol, Warmley BS30 66 D5
Clevedon BS21 57 E3
Saltford BS31 82 D3
Victoria Rooms* BS8 142 B3
Victoria Sq
Bristol BS8 142 A3
Portishead BS20 45 D5
Weston-S-M BS23 104 D7
Victoria St
Bristol BS1 143 B2
Bristol, Staple Hill BS16 51 D5
Victoria Terr
Bath BA2 101 D6
15 Bristol, Clifton BS8 62 F6
Bristol, St Philip's Marsh BS2 64 B5
Paulton BS39 132 E6
Victoria Wlk BS6 49 D1
Victor Rd BS3 63 C3
Victor St
9 Bristol, Russell Town BS5 64 B6
Bristol, St Philip's Marsh BS2 64 A4
Vigor Rd BS13 79 B5
Village Cl BS37 27 D1
Village Farm BS35 14 A6
Village The BS16 52 C7
Villa Rosa 16 BS23 87 C1
Villice La BS40 129 A7
Villiers Rd BS5 50 B1
Vilner La BS35 15 B7
Vimpany Cl BS10 34 F3
Vimpennys La BS35 22 E1
Vincent Cl BS11 34 C2
Vincent Ct 2 BS16 51 D3
Vine Gdns BS22 89 A2
Viner's La GL9 43 B5
Vinery The BS25 125 A7
Vineyard La GL12 11 F5
Vineyards BA1 141 C3
Vining Wlk 4 BS5 64 B8
VINNEY GREEN 52 A7
Vinney La BS37 28 F8
Vinny Ave BS16 52 A7
Vintery Leys BS9 49 B7
Virginia Cl BS37 28 A1
Vivian St BS3 63 D3
Vivien Ave BA3 133 A2
Vowell Cl BS13 79 B4
Vowles Cl BS48 60 A3
Voyager Cl BS34 37 A4
Vulcan Ho BA2 141 C3
Vynes Cl BS48 60 A1
Vynes Ind Est BS48 60 A3
Vynes Way BS48 60 A1
Vyvyan Rd BS8 142 A3
Vyvyan Terr BS8 142 A3

W

Wadehurst Ind Pk BS2 64 A7
Wade Rd BS37 27 A3
Wades Rd BS34 36 B3
Wade St BS2 143 C3
Wadham Dr BS16 37 B1
Wadham Gr BS16 52 B5
Wadham St BS23 104 D8
Wagtail Gdns BS22 105 E8
Wainbridge Cres BS35 22 D7
Wainbrook Dr BS5 50 D2
Wains Cl 3 BS21 57 E2
Wainwright Cl 5 BS22 89 B4
Waits Cl BS29 106 F3
Wakedean Gdns BS49 74 A1
Wakeford Rd 1 BS16 52 A7
Wakeford Way BS30 66 D7
Wakehurst Gdns BS24 105 E7
Walcot Bldgs
Bath BA1 102 B8
Bath BA1 141 C4
Walcot Ct BA1 141 C4
Walcot Gate BA1 141 C4
Walcot Ho BA1 141 C4
Walcot Par BA1 141 C4
Walcot St BA1 141 C3
Walcot Terr BA1 141 C4
Waldegrave Rd BA1 84 E1
Waldegrave Terr BA3 134 A3
Walden Rd BS31 82 A4
Walford Ave BS22 89 C3
Walker Cl
Bristol, Downend BS16 52 A7
Bristol, Upper Easton BS5 64 B8
Walker Ct BS16 51 F5
Walkers Dr BS24 105 F7
Walker St BS2 142 C4
Walker Way BS35 15 B7
Walk Mill La GL12 11 F4
Walk The GL12 11 F5
WALLACE 129 E3
Wallace La BS40 129 E3

Wallace Rd BA1 . . . . .85 B1
Wallcroft Ho BS6 . . . . .49 A3
Wallenge Cl BS39 . . . . .132 F6
Wallenge Dr BS39 . . . . . . .132 F6
Walley La BA4 . . . . .113 B7
Wallingford Rd BS4 . . . . . . .79 D7
Walliscote Ave BS9 . . . . . . .49 C6
Walliscote Grove Rd **11**
BS23 . . . . .104 E7
Walliscote Prim Sch
BS23 . . . . .104 E7
Walliscote Rd
Bristol BS9 . . . . .49 C6
Weston-S-M BS23 . . . . . . .104 D6
Walliscote Rd S BS23 . . . .104 D4
Walls Est BS2 . . . . .49 F3
WALL MEAD 116 C4
Wallscourt Rd BS34 . . . . . . .36 B2
Wallscourt Rd S BS34 . . . . .36 B1
Wallsend La SN14 . . . . .55 C5
Wally Court Rd BS40 . . . . .112 E8
Walmsley Terr **4** BA1 . . . .85 B1
Walnut Ave BS37 . . . . .28 A2
Walnut Bldgs BA3 . . . . . . .134 A3
Walnut Cl
Axbridge BS26 . . . . .125 B1
Bristol BS15 . . . . .51 F1
Easton-in-G BS20 . . . . .47 A3
Frampton Cotterell BS36 . . .38 C6
Keynsham BS31 . . . . .81 C4
Nailsea BS48 . . . . .75 E8
Thornbury BS35 . . . . .8 D1
Weston-S-M BS24 . . . . . . .105 B2
Walnut Cres BS15 . . . . .65 F8
Walnut Dr
Bath BA2 . . . . .101 E4
Colerne SN14 . . . . .70 F6
Walnut La BS15 . . . . .66 A8
Walnut Tree Cl
Almondsbury BS32 . . . . .24 A5
Ubley BS40 . . . . .111 D1
Walnut Tree Ct BS49 . . . . . .91 D4
Walnut Wlk
Bristol BS13 . . . . .79 A6
Keynsham BS31 . . . . .81 C4
Walsh Ave BS14 . . . . .80 A7
Walsh Cl BS24 . . . . .105 B2
Walshe Ave BS37 . . . . .28 C1
Walsingham Rd BS6 . . . . . .49 E2
Walter St BS3 . . . . .63 A4
Walton BA2 . . . . .101 A6
Walton Ave BS4 . . . . .64 D5
Walton Bay House Park
Homes BS21 . . . . .44 B1
Walton Cl
Bristol BS30 . . . . .66 C1
Keynsham BS31 . . . . .81 D4
Walton Cross BS40 . . . . . . .94 F8
Walton Cross BS21 . . . . . . .58 B7
Walton Heath BS37 . . . . . . .27 F1
WALTON IN GORDANO
. . . . .58 B7
Walton Rd
Bristol BS11 . . . . .47 D6
Clevedon BS21 . . . . .57 H4
Walton Rise BS9 . . . . .49 A7
WALTON ST MARY 57 G5
Walton St
Bristol BS5 . . . . .50 B1
Portishead BS21 . . . . .44 A1
Walton in g BS21 . . . . .58 A1
Walwyn Cl BA2 . . . . .101 A6
Walwyn Gdns BS13 . . . . . . .79 C3
Wansbeck Rd BS31 . . . . . . .82 A4
Wansbrough Rd BS22 . . . . .89 B4
Wanscow Wlk BS9 . . . . . . .49 B6
Wansdyke Bsns Ctr
BA2 . . . . .101 D4
Wansdyke Ct BS14 . . . . . . .80 B5
Wansdyke Prim Sch
BS14 . . . . .79 F4
Wansdyke Rd BA2 . . . . . . .101 D1
Wansdyke Workshops
Keynsham BS31 . . . . .82 A6
Peasedown St John
BA2 . . . . .134 D6
WAPLEY 39 E4
Wapley Hill BS37 . . . . .39 E4
Wapley Rank BS37 . . . . . . .39 D5
Wapley Rd BS37 . . . . .40 B3
Wapping Rd BS1 . . . . .143 A1
Warden Rd BS3 . . . . .63 C4
Wardour Rd BS4 . . . . .79 D8
Ware Ct BS36 . . . . .37 D5
Wareham Cl BS48 . . . . .59 D1
Warend Hill GL11 . . . . .5 F6
Waring Ho BS1 . . . . .143 A1
WARLEIGH 103 C6
Warleigh Dr BA1 . . . . .86 A3
Warleigh La BA1 . . . . .103 C5
Warleigh Manor BA1 . . . . .103 C5
Warleys La BS24 . . . . .89 C1
Warman Cl BS14 . . . . .80 F6
Warman Rd BS14 . . . . .80 F6
Warmington Rd BS14 . . . . .80 C8
Warminster Rd
Bristol BS2 . . . . .50 A2
Claverton BA2, BA3 . . . . . .103 B5
WARMLEY 66 B7
WARMLEY HILL 65 E8
Warmley Park Sch
BS30 . . . . .66 B7
WARMLEY TOWER 66 B6

Warne Pk BS23 . . . . .105 A6
Warner Cl
Bristol BS15 . . . . .65 F6
Cleeve BS49 . . . . .92 A7
Warne Rd BS23 . . . . .105 A6
Warns The BS30 . . . . .66 A4
Warren Cl
Bristol BS32 . . . . .24 D3
Hutton BS24 . . . . .105 D2
Warren Croft GL11 . . . . .5 E4
Warren Gdns BS14 . . . . . . .80 F5
Warren La BA1 . . . . .77 E8
Warren Rd BS34 . . . . .36 B3
Warren's Cl BS27 . . . . .126 B1
Warrens Hill BS27 . . . . . . .126 B1
Warrens Hill Rd BS27 . . . .126 D4
Warren Way BS37 . . . . .27 E3
Warrilow Cl BS22 . . . . .89 B5
Warrington Rd BS4 . . . . . . .64 D2
Warry Cl BS48 . . . . .60 B2
Warth La BS22 . . . . .89 A8
Warwick Ave **7** BS5 . . . . .50 B1
Warwick Cl
Bristol BS30 . . . . .66 B2
Weston-S-M BS22 . . . . . . .105 C8
Warwick Gdns BS39 . . . . .114 D3
Warwick Pl BS35 . . . . .8 A1
Warwick Rd
Bath BA1 . . . . .101 B7
Bristol, Baptist Mills BS5 . . .50 B1
Bristol, Redland BS6 . . . . . .49 B1
Keynsham BS31 . . . . .81 D4
Washingpool Hill BS35 . . . .14 C1
Washingpool Hill Rd
BS32 . . . . .14 C1
Washingpool La BS11 . . . . .33 F7
Washing Pound La
Bristol BS14 . . . . .80 B5
Nailsea BS48 . . . . .59 B4
Washington Ave BS5 . . . . . .50 C1
Washpool La BA2 . . . . .100 F2
Watch Elm Cl BS32 . . . . . . .36 E6
Watch House Pl BS20 . . . . .45 E7
Watch House Rd BS20 . . . . .47 D4
Watchill Ave BS13 . . . . .78 F6
Watchill Cl BS13 . . . . .78 F6
Watcombe Cl BS22 . . . . . . .88 E1
Waterbridge Rd BS13 . . . . .78 F4
Watercress Cl BS48 . . . . . . .60 B2
Watercress Rd BS2 . . . . . . .49 F3
Waterdale Cl BS9 . . . . .49 C7
Waterdale Gdns BS9 . . . . . .49 C7
Waterford Cl BS35 . . . . . . .15 D8
Waterford Pk BA3 . . . . . . .133 E1
Waterford Rd BS9 . . . . .49 B6
Waterfront Ho BA2 . . . . . .141 B1
Waterhouse La BS9 . . . . . .119 F8
Water La
Bristol BS31 . . . . .143 B2
Bristol, Hanham Green
BS15 . . . . .65 B2
Bristol, Upper Knowle
BS4 . . . . .64 D2
Bristol, Windmill Hill BS3 . . .63 F3
Paulton BA3, BS39 . . . . . . .133 A4
Pill BS20 . . . . .47 C4
Waterloo Bldgs **4**
BA2 . . . . .101 B6
Waterloo Ho BS20 . . . . .47 D5
Waterloo Pl **10** BS2 . . . .143 C3
Waterloo Rd
Bristol BS2 . . . . .143 C3
Radstock BA3 . . . . .134 A2
Waterloo St
Bristol BS2 . . . . .143 C3
10 Bristol, Clifton BS8 . .62 F7
Weston-S-M BS23 . . . . . . .104 E8
Watermead Cl **13** BA1 . .141 B2
Watermill Cl GL12 . . . . .9 E7
Watermore Gdns BS36 . . . .38 C7
Waters Edge BS20 . . . . .45 E7
Watershed Media Ctr*
BS1 . . . . .143 A2
WATERSIDE 133 E1
Waterside Cres BA3 . . . . . .133 D1
Waterside Dr BS32 . . . . . . .24 A1
Waterside La BS32 . . . . . . .140 A6
Waterside Rd BA3 . . . . . . .133 D1
Waterside Way BA3 . . . . . .139 D8
Water's La BS9 . . . . .49 A7
Waters Rd BS15 . . . . .65 C8
Water St BS40 . . . . .129 F4
Watery La
Bath BA2 . . . . .101 A6
Doynton BS30 . . . . .68 A8
Nailsea BS48 . . . . .59 B2
Stratton-on-t-F BA3 . . . . . .139 A3
Winford BS40 . . . . .95 B4
Wathen Rd BS6 . . . . .49 F3
Watkins Yd BS9 . . . . .49 A8
WATLEY'S END 37 F7
Watley's End Rd BS36 . . . . .37 F7
Watling Way BS11 . . . . .47 D2
Watson Ave BS4 . . . . .64 D4
Watson's Rd BS30 . . . . .66 B5
Watters Cl BS36 . . . . .38 D6
Wavell Cl BS37 . . . . .27 D3
Waveney Rd BS31 . . . . .82 A3
Wavering Down Rise
BS26 . . . . .125 A3
Waverley Ho BS1 . . . . .142 C1
Waverley Rd
Backwell BS48 . . . . .76 A7
Bristol, Cotham BS6 . . . . . .49 B1
Bristol, Shirehampton
BS11 . . . . .47 E6

Waverley Rd continued
Weston-S-M BS23 . . . . . . .104 F7
Wayford Cl BS31 . . . . .82 B2
Waverley St **9** BS5 . . . . . .50 A1
Waverly Ct BS41 . . . . .91 D3
Wayacre Dro BS24 . . . . . . .121 E6
Waycroft Prim Sch
BS14 . . . . .80 E5
Wayfield Gdns BA1 . . . . . . .85 F4
Wayford Cl BS31 . . . . .82 A3
Wayland Ct **7** BS16 . . . . .51 A4
Wayland Rd BS22 . . . . .88 E3
Wayleaze
Frampton Cotterell
BS36 . . . . .38 D7
Wapley BS37 . . . . .39 F3
Wayside BS22 . . . . .88 D2
Wayside Cl BS36 . . . . .38 B7
Wayside Dr BS21 . . . . .57 G5
WAY WICK 89 C1
WCA Ho BS1 . . . . .143 A2
Weal Terr BA1 . . . . .84 B2
Weal The BA1 . . . . .84 C2
Weare Ct BS1 . . . . .142 A1
Weatherley Dr BS20 . . . . . .44 F3
Weatherly Ave BA2 . . . . . .101 D2
Weavers Cl GL12 . . . . .11 F4
Weavers Orch BS32 . . . . . .24 D3
WEBBINGTON 123 E4
Webbington Rd BS26 . . . .124 C3
Webbs Heath BS30 . . . . . . .66 E8
WEBB'S HEATH 66 E8
Webbs Mead BS40 . . . . . .112 D8
Webb St BS5 . . . . .64 A8
Webbs Wood BS32 . . . . . . .36 F7
Webbs Wood Rd BS32 . . . .36 F7
Wedgewood Rd BS16 . . . . .37 D1
Wedgwood Cl BS14 . . . . . . .80 B5
Wedgwood Rd BA2 . . . . . .101 A5
Wedlock Way BS3 . . . . .62 F3
Wedmore Cl
Bath BA2 . . . . .101 A3
Bristol BS15 . . . . .65 F7
Wedmore Pk BA2 . . . . .101 A3
Wedmore Rd
Clevedon BS21 . . . . .57 D1
Nailsea BS48 . . . . .75 E8
Saltford BS31 . . . . .82 D4
Wedmore Vale BS3 . . . . . . .63 E2
Weedon Cl **6** BS2 . . . . . .50 A2
Weekesley La BA2 . . . . . . .116 D1
Weetwood Rd BS49 . . . . . . .91 E5
Weight Rd **2** BS5 . . . . . .64 C7
Weind The BS22 . . . . .88 D2
Weir La
Abbots Leigh BS8 . . . . .61 F5
Marshfield SN14 . . . . .69 F8
Weir Rd BS49 . . . . .91 E3
Welland Rd BS31 . . . . .81 F4
Wellard Cl **1** BS22 . . . . .89 B4
Well Cl
Long Ashton BS41 . . . . .62 B1
Weston-S-M BS24 . . . . . . .105 B2
Winscombe BS25 . . . . .125 A8
Wellesley Prim Sch
BS37 . . . . .39 D6
Wellgarth Ct BS4 . . . . .64 A2
Wellgarth Rd BS4 . . . . .64 A2
Wellgarth Wlk BS4 . . . . . . .64 A2
Well House Cl BS9 . . . . .48 E3
Wellington Ave BS6 . . . . . .49 E1
Wellington Bldgs BA1 . . . . .84 F2
Wellington Cres BS7 . . . . . .49 E6
Wellington Ct
11 Bristol BS6 . . . . .49 E1
Clevedon BS21 . . . . .57 E5
Wellington Dr
Bristol BS9 . . . . .49 D6
Weston-S-M BS22 . . . . . . .89 A3
Wellington Hill BS7 . . . . . . .49 E6
Wellington Hill W BS9 . . . . .49 D7
Wellington La BS6 . . . . .49 E1
Wellington Mews
BS11 . . . . .47 D5
Wellington Pk BS8 . . . . .49 A2
Wellington Pl
Bristol BS16 . . . . .37 B1
Weston-S-M BS23 . . . . . . .104 D7
Wellington Rd
Bristol BS2 . . . . .143 C4
Bristol, Kingswood BS15 . . .51 D2
Yate BS37 . . . . .27 E3
Wellington Terr
20 Bristol BS8 . . . . .62 F6
Clevedon BS21 . . . . .57 F5
Wellington Wlk BS10 . . . . . .49 C7
Well La
Badminton GL9 . . . . .30 E5
Banwell BS29 . . . . .106 E3
Yatton BS49 . . . . .91 C8
WELLOW 118 D3
Wellow Brook Ct BA3 . . . .133 B3
Wellow Brook Mdw
BA3 . . . . .133 B2
Wellow La
Hinton Charterhouse
BA2 . . . . .119 D1
Norton St Philip BA2 . . . . .136 D5
Peasedown St John
BA2 . . . . .134 C6
Shoscombe BA2 . . . . .134 C6
Wellow Mead BA2 . . . . . . .134 B7
Wellow Rd BA2 . . . . .135 B8
Wellow Tyning BA3 . . . . . .134 D7
Well Pk BS49 . . . . .91 E4
Wells Cl
Bristol BS14 . . . . .80 C5

Wells Cl continued
Nailsea BS48 . . . . .60 B1
Wellsea Gr BS23 . . . . .105 B7
Wells Rd
Bath BA2 . . . . .141 B1
Bristol, Hengrove BS14 . . . .80 C7
Bristol, Upper Knowle
BS4 . . . . .64 B2
Chilcompton BA3 . . . . .138 F4
Clevedon BS21 . . . . .57 F1
Corston BA2 . . . . .100 B7
Dundry BS40, BS41 . . . . . . .95 F7
Hallatrow BS39 . . . . .132 B7
Norton St Philip BA2,
BA3 . . . . .136 C3
Radstock BA3 . . . . .133 C2
Wells Sq BA3 . . . . .133 D1
Wells St BS3 . . . . .63 A4
Wellstead Ave BS37 . . . . . .27 D1
Wellsway **1** BA2 . . . . . .101 F3
Wellsway Cl BA2 . . . . .101 D1
Wellsway Pk BA2 . . . . .118 D8
Wellsway Rd BS31 . . . . . . .81 F3
Wellsway Sch BS31 . . . . . .82 A5
Well The BS9 . . . . .48 E3
Welsford Ave BS16 . . . . . . .50 D4
Welsford Rd BS16 . . . . .50 C4
Welsh Back BS1 . . . . .143 A2
WELTON 133 B2
Welton Gr BA3 . . . . .133 B3
WELTON HOLLOW 133 D2
Welton Prim Sch BA3 . . . .133 C2
Welton Rd BA3 . . . . .133 C2
Welton Vale BA3 . . . . .133 B2
Welton Wlk BS15 . . . . .51 C2
Wemberham Cres
BS49 . . . . .74 A1
Wemberham La BS49 . . . . .90 E8
Wenmore Cl BS16 . . . . .37 D1
Wentforth Dr **2** BS15 . . .51 C2
Wentwood Dr BS24 . . . . . .105 A1
Wentworth
Bristol BS30 . . . . .66 A6
Yate BS37 . . . . .27 E1
Wentworth Cl BS22 . . . . . .89 A3
Wentworth Rd BS7 . . . . . . .49 D3
Wescott Gr BS11 . . . . .34 C2
Wesley Ave
Bristol BS15 . . . . .65 D5
Radstock BA3 . . . . .133 C1
Wesley Cl
6 Bristol, Upper Soundwell
BS16 . . . . .51 D3
Bristol, Whitehall BS5 . . . . .50 D1
Wesley Ct BS22 . . . . .104 F8
Wesley Dr BS22 . . . . .89 A3
Wesley Hill BS15 . . . . .51 D1
Wesley La BS30 . . . . .66 B5
Wesley Pl BS8 . . . . .49 A2
Wesley Rd
Bristol BS7 . . . . .49 E4
Radstock BA3 . . . . .133 D1
Wesley St BS3 . . . . .63 C3
Wesley Theological Coll
BS10 . . . . .34 F1
Wessex Ave BS7 . . . . .49 F7
Wessex Ct BS7 . . . . .49 F7
Wessex Ho BS2 . . . . .143 C3
Wessex Rd BS24 . . . . .105 B2
Westacre Cl BS10 . . . . .35 A2
West Ave BA2 . . . . .101 C5
Westaway Cl BS49 . . . . . . .91 C7
Westaway Pk BS49 . . . . . . .91 D7
Westbourne Ave
Clevedon BS21 . . . . .57 D2
Keynsham BS31 . . . . .81 E5
Westbourne Cl **2**
BS16 . . . . .52 A7
Westbourne Cres
BS21 . . . . .57 D2
Westbourne Ct BS5 . . . . . . .64 B8
Westbourne Gr **15** BS3 . .63 C3
Westbourne Ho BA2 . . . . .141 C2
Westbourne Pl BS8 . . . . . .142 B3
Westbourne Rd
Bristol, Downend BS16 . . . .51 F8
8 Bristol, Upper Easton
BS5 . . . . .64 B8
Westbourne Terr BS16 . . . .51 B7
West Broadway BS9 . . . . . .49 D6
Westbrooke Ct BS1 . . . . . .142 A1
Westbrook Pk BA1 . . . . .84 A2
Westbrook Rd
Bristol BS4 . . . . .80 D8
Weston-S-M BS22 . . . . . . .88 D8
Westbury Court Rd
BS9 . . . . .49 A7
Westbury Cres BS23 . . . . .104 F2
Westbury Ct BS9 . . . . .49 A7
Westbury Hill BS9 . . . . .49 A7
Westbury La BS9 . . . . .48 C7
Westbury Mews **6**
BS9 . . . . .49 A7
WESTBURY ON TRYM 48 F7
Westbury-on-Trym CE
Prim Sch BS9 . . . . .49 A8
WESTBURY PARK 49 A3
Westbury Park Prim Sch
BS6 . . . . .49 B3
Westbury Pk BS6 . . . . .49 A4
Westbury Rd BS6 . . . . .49 A4
Westbury Terr BA2 . . . . . . .117 C5
Westbury View BA2 . . . . . .134 E8
West Cl BA2 . . . . .101 A3
West Coombe BS9 . . . . .48 D6
West Country Water Pk*
BS36 . . . . .24 F2

West Croft
Blagdon BS40 . . . . .110 E2
Bristol BS9 . . . . .49 C7
Clevedon BS21 . . . . .57 D2
West Ct BS20 . . . . .45 C4
West Dene BS9 . . . . .48 D5
West Dundry La BS41 . . . . .78 E2
WESTEND 7 B6
WEST END 110 E3
West End
Bristol BS3 . . . . .142 C1
Bristol, Kingsdown BS2 . . .143 A4
WEST END
Clevedon 57 D2
Nailsea 74 F7
West End BS35 . . . . .7 C6
WEST END 17 E5
West End Farm Cvn Pk
BS24 . . . . .105 C4
Westend La BS35 . . . . .7 B6
West End La BS48 . . . . .75 A8
Westend Rd GL12 . . . . .17 C5
West End Trad Est
BS48 . . . . .59 B1
Westering Cl BS16 . . . . .52 A5
WESTERLEIGH 39 B4
Westerleigh Bsns Pk
BS37 . . . . .27 B1
Westerleigh Cl BS16 . . . . . .51 F7
WESTERLEIGH HILL 39 D3
Westerleigh Rd
Bath BA2 . . . . .102 B1
Bristol BS16 . . . . .51 F6
Clevedon BS21 . . . . .57 D2
Henfield BS36 . . . . .38 D2
Pucklechurch BS16 . . . . . . .53 C7
Westerleigh Rd BS36, BS37 .39 B5
Yate BS37 . . . . .39 C8
Western Approach
Distribution Pk BS35 . . . . .22 C4
Western Ave BS36 . . . . .26 A1
Western Ct
Bristol BS34 . . . . .37 A4
Clevedon BS21 . . . . .57 F3
Western Dr BS14 . . . . .79 F6
Western Grange BS34 . . . . .36 A3
Western La BS40 . . . . .129 C3
Western Rd BS7 . . . . .49 E6
Westex Ho BS23 . . . . .105 B5
WESTFIELD 139 C8
Westfield BS21 . . . . .73 D8
Westfield Cl
Backwell BS48 . . . . .76 A6
Bath BA2 . . . . .101 E3
Bristol BS15 . . . . .65 D5
Keynsham BS31 . . . . .81 C5
Weston-S-M BS23 . . . . . . .104 D2
Westfield Cres BS29 . . . . .107 A3
Westfield Dr BS48 . . . . .76 A6
Westfield Ho
Bath BA2 . . . . .101 E3
Stoke Bishop BS9 . . . . .48 F5
Westfield Ind & Trad Est
BA3 . . . . .139 C7
Westfield La BS34 . . . . .36 E3
Westfield Pk
Bath BA1 . . . . .101 A7
Bristol BS6 . . . . .49 B1
Westfield Pk S BA1 . . . . . .101 A7
Westfield Pl BS8 . . . . .62 F7
Westfield Prim Sch
BA3 . . . . .139 C8
Westfield Rd
Backwell BS48 . . . . .76 A6
Banwell BS29 . . . . .107 A3
Bristol BS9 . . . . .49 A8
Weston-S-M BS23 . . . . . . .104 D2
Westfield Terr BA3 . . . . . . .133 D1
Westfield Way BS32 . . . . . .24 D2
West Garston BS29 . . . . . .107 A3
Westgate BS1 . . . . .142 B1
Westgate Bldgs BA1 . . . . .141 B2
Westgate St BA1 . . . . .141 B2
West Gr BS6 . . . . .49 F1
Westhall Rd BA1 . . . . .101 D7
WEST HARPTREE 129 E6
West Harptree Rd
BS40 . . . . .129 F5
Westhaven Cl BS48 . . . . . . .76 A6
Westhaven Sch BS23 . . . . .104 D2
West Hay Rd BS40 . . . . . . .92 C3
WEST HEWISH 90 F5
WEST HILL 60 A5
West Hill BS48 . . . . .60 A5
WEST HILL 45 A5
West Hill BS20 . . . . .45 C6
West Hill Ct BS20 . . . . .45 C6
WEST HILL GARDENS
. . . . .133 C1
West Hill Gdns
Radstock BA3 . . . . .133 C1
Radstock BA3 . . . . .133 C1
West Hill Rd BA3 . . . . .133 D1
WEST KINGTON 56 F7
West Leaze BS48 . . . . .94 C8
Westland Ave BS30 . . . . . . .66 C6
Westland Distribution Pk
BS24 . . . . .105 A3
West Lea Rd BA1 . . . . .84 A1
West Leaze Pl BS32 . . . . . .36 E6
Westleigh Cl
Bristol BS10 . . . . .35 D1
Yate BS37 . . . . .27 C1
Westleigh Ct BS37 . . . . .27 C1
Westleigh Inf Sch
BS48 . . . . .76 A6
Westleigh Pk BS14 . . . . . . .80 B8

Westleigh Rd BS10 ....35 D1
West Links BS23........ 104 D2
West Links Cl BS22 ....88 B3
West Littleton Rd
Marshfield SN14 ....69 F8
West Littleton SN14 ....55 E2
West Mall BS8...........62 F7
Westmarch Way BS22.....89 A4
Westmarsh BS35...........7 B5
Westmarsh La BS35.........7 B5
Westmead BA3 .... 138 D3
Westmead Gdns BA1........84 A2
Westmead Ho BS11 ....33 B1
Westmead Rd BS5 ....65 B7
Westminster Cl 1 BS9......49 A7
Westminster Rd BS5......64 D8
Westmoreland Dr
BA2 .... 141 A2
Westmoreland Rd
Bath BA2 .... 141 A1
Bristol BS6..............49 B3
Westmoreland St
BA2 .... 141 A2
Westmoreland Station Rd
BA2 .... 141 A1
Westmorland Ho BS6 .....49 A3
Westmorland Terr
BS37.....................41 D7
WESTON 84 B1
Weston All Saints CE Prim
Sch BA1 ....84 A2
Weston Ave 4 BS5 ....64 D7
Weston Bsns Pk BS24....105 E5
Weston Cl BS9 ....48 C7
Weston Coll
Nailsea BS48.............59 E2
Weston-S-M BS23 .... 104 D8
Weston Coll Univ Campus
BS23..................104 F2
Weston Coll (Westcliff)
BS23....................87 B1
Weston Cres BS7 ....49 E6
Weston Ct BS24 ....105 B3
Weston Dro BS20..........58 F8
Weston Euro Pk BS24....105 B4
Weston Express Bsns Pk
BS22.................. 105 C6
Weston Farm La BA1 .....84 C2
Weston Gateway Tourist
Pk BS24 ....89 C1
Weston General Hospl
BS23..................104 E2
Westonia BS22 ....88 E2
Westonian Ct BS9 ....48 C4
Weston Ind Est BS24.....105 B2
WESTON IN GORDANO
.........................44 F1
Weston La
Bath BA1 .... 101 C8
Christon BS26 .... 123 C7
Weston Lo
Bath BA1 ....84 A2
Weston-S-M BS23 .... 104 D8
Weston Lock Ret BA2.... 101 C6
Weston Milton Sta
BS22.................. 105 C7
Weston Miniature Rly*
BS23 .... 104 D5
WESTON PARK 84 C1
Weston Park Ct BA1 ......84 D1
Weston Park Prim Sch
BS11....................47 F8
Weston Pk BA1............84 C1
Weston Pk E BA1 ....84 D1
Weston Pk W BA1 ....84 C1
Weston Rd
Bath BA1 .... 101 D8
Brean TA8 .... 121 A5
Congresbury BS49.........91 B5
Failand BS8 ....61 C3
Long Ashton BS41..........77 D8
Weston Ret Pk BS23.... 105 A6
Westons Brake BS16.......38 A1
Westons Hill Dr BS16......38 A1
WESTON-SUPER-MARE
.......................104 B8
Weston-Super-Mare Sta
BS23...................104 E7
Westons Way BS15 ....65 F7
Weston Way BS24 ....105 F2
Weston Wood Rd BS20.....45 C3
Westover Cl BS9...........34 F1
Westover Dr BS9 ....35 A1
Westover Gdns BS9........48 F8
Westover Rd
Bristol BS9...............35 A1
Bristol BS9...............48 F8
Westover Rise BS9.........35 A1
West Par BS9..............48 C7
West Park Rd BS16 ....51 E5
West Pk BS8 ....142 B4
West Point Row BS32.....24 C3
Westpoint Trad Est
BS15....................65 D7
West Priory Cl BS9 ....49 A7
West Rd
Lympsham BS24 ....122 B1
Midsomer Norton BA3.... 133 A3
Yatton BS49..............91 B7
West Ridge BS36 ....38 C7
West Rocke Ave BS9......48 D6
West Rolstone Rd
BS24....................90 A1
West Shrubbery 5
BS6.....................49 B2
West St
Axbridge BS26...........125 B2
Banwell BS29............107 B3
West St *continued*
Bristol, Bedminster BS3 ....63 C3
Bristol BS2............. 143 C3
2 Bristol, Kingswood
BS15...................65 D8
Bristol, Oldland Common
BS30....................66 C4
Tytherington GL12.........16 B5
Weston-S-M BS23 .... 104 D8
West Terr BA2 .... 137 C1
WEST TOWN
Backwell 75 F5
Ubley 111 B6
West Town Ave BS4 ....64 D1
West Town Dr 2 BS4 .....64 D1
West Town Gr BS4 ....80 D8
West Town La BS4,
BS14....................64 D1
West Town Lane Prim Sch
BS4.....................64 C1
West Town Pk BS4 ....64 D1
West Town Rd
Backwell BS48............76 A5
Bristol BS11..............47 C7
West Tyning BA2..........99 B1
Westview BS39 .... 132 C5
West View
Alveston BS35 ....14 F4
Bristol BS16..............52 A6
Westview Orch BA2......120 B5
West View Rd
Batheaston BA1...........86 A3
Bristol BS3...............63 B3
Keynsham BS31...........81 E5
Westward BS41............62 B2
Westward Cl BS40 ....92 D2
Westward Dr BS20.........47 C4
Westward Gdns BS41 .....62 B2
Westward Rd BS13.........78 F7
Westway BS48............59 E2
West Way
Bristol BS10, BS34 ....35 E4
Clevedon BS21............57 E3
Westway Farm BS39 .... 113 C3
WEST WICK 89 C1
West Wick BS24 ....89 C1
West Wick Rdbt BS22,
BS24...................106 B8
West Wlk BS37 ....27 E1
WESTWOOD 120 E3
Westwood BA2 ....102 E6
Westwood Ave BS39 ..... 115 C2
Westwood Cl 2 BS22 .....88 F2
Westwood Cres BS4 ......64 D5
Westwood Rd BS4 ....80 D8
Westwoods BA1 ....86 B3
Westwood-with-Iford
Prim Sch BA15.........120 F3
Wetherby Ct BS16 ....37 F1
Wetherby Gr 1 BS16 .....37 F1
Wetherell Pl BS8 ....142 B3
Wetlands La BS20 ....45 C3
Wexford Rd BS4 ....79 D8
Weymouth Ct BA1 ....102 B8
Weymouth Rd BS3.........63 D2
Weymouth St BA1 ....102 B8
Wharfedale BS35 ....15 D8
Wharf La BS20 ....46 B5
Wharf Rd 8 BS16 ....50 F4
Wharfside BS24 ....121 E3
Wharnecliffe Cl BS14 .....80 B5
Wharnecliffe Gdns
BS14....................80 B5
Whartons 8 BS4 ....64 D1
Whatley Ct 9 BS8.........49 B1
Whatley Rd BS8 ....49 B1
Wheatfield Dr
Bristol BS32..............24 D1
Weston-S-M BS22 ....89 A5
Wheatfield Prim Sch
BS32....................24 D1
Wheathill Cl BS31 ....81 D5
Wheelers Cl BA3 .... 133 D2
Wheelers Dr BA3 .... 133 C2
WHEELER'S HILL 133 C2
Wheelers Patch BS16......52 B5
Wheelers Rd BA3........ 133 D2
Whinchat Gdns BS16......50 F6
Whippington Ct BS1.....143 B3
Whistle Rd BS16..........52 B2
Whistley La BS40 ....129 F6
Whitby Rd BS4 ....64 C4
WHITCHURCH 80 D4
Whitchurch District Ctr
BS14....................80 A5
Whitchurch La
Bristol, Bishopsworth
BS13...................79 B5
Bristol BS14..............79 E5
Bristol, Hartcliffe BS13 .....79 C5
Dundry BS41 ....79 C1
Whitchurch Prim Sch
BS14....................80 C4
Whitchurch Rd BS13......79 A6
Whitebeam Ct BS5 ....64 E8
Whitebeam Ho 7
BS16....................51 C6
Whitebrook La BA2...... 134 A8
Whitecroft Way BS15 .....66 A7
WHITE CROSS
Bishop Sutton 113 E1
Hallatrow................131 F6
Whitecross Ave BS14 .....80 C6
White Cross Gate
BS39...................131 F6
Whitecross La BS29..... 107 A4
Whitecross Rd
East Harptree BS40.......129 F4
Whitecross Rd *continued*
Weston-S-M BS23 ....104 E6
Whitefield Ave
Bristol, Hanham BS15 ......65 D5
Bristol, Speedwell BS5 .....51 A1
Whitefield Cl
Batheaston BA1...........86 B4
7 Bristol BS16............51 D3
Whitefield Fishponds Com
Sch BS16 ....50 F4
Whitefield Rd BS5 ....51 A2
Whitefields BS37 ....28 C1
Whitegate Cl BS24.......122 B6
Whitegates BS36 ....37 D6
WHITEHALL 50 D1
Whitehall Ave BS5........50 E1
Whitehall Gdns BS5 ......50 D1
Whitehall Prim Sch
BS5.....................50 D1
Whitehall Rd BS5.........64 C8
Whitehall Trad Est 4
BS5.....................64 C8
WHITE HILL 134 F6
White Hill BA2 ....134 F6
Whitehorn Vale BS10......35 C3
White Horse Rd BA15....120 E7
White House Bsns Ctr The
BS15....................65 D7
Whitehouse Ctr (PRU)
BS13....................79 C5
Whitehouse La
Bristol BS3...............63 D4
Litton BA3 .... 130 D3
Pilning BS35 ....22 C7
Wraxall BS48.............60 A6
White House La BS26.... 123 A3
Whitehouse Pl BS3 ....63 E4
Whitehouse Rd BS49......91 F8
Whitehouse St BS3 ....63 E4
Whiteladies Rd BS8.......142 B4
Whitelands Hill BA3 .....134 B3
Whiteleaze BS10..........49 C8
White Lodge Pk BS20.....45 D6
White Lodge Rd BS16.....51 F4
Whitemead Ho 3 BS3 ....63 A3
Whitemore Ct BA1........86 A4
Whiteoak Way BS48 ......75 D8
White Ox Mead La
BA2...................117 F1
White Ox-mead La
BA2...................134 E8
White Post BA3 ....139 B6
Whitesfield Ct BS48.......59 D2
Whitesfield Rd BS48 ......59 D1
WHITESHILL 37 D3
Whiteshill BS16...........37 D3
Whites Hill BS5...........65 A6
White St BS5........... 143 C4
White Tree Rbdt BS6......49 A4
White Tree Rd BS9........49 B4
Whitewall La BS35.........8 F1
WHITEWAY
Bath................... 101 A4
Bristol 51 A1
Whiteway Cl
Bristol, St Anne's Park
BS4....................64 E6
Bristol, St George BS5......65 A8
Whiteway Ct 1 BS5 ......65 A8
Whiteway Mews BS5.......65 A8
Whiteway Rd
Bath BA2 .... 101 A3
Bristol BS5, BS15 ....51 A1
Whitewells Rd BA1 ....85 A2
Whitewood Rd BS5 ....50 F1
WHITFIELD 9 C3
Whitfield Ho 7 BS15 .....65 D8
Whitfield Rd BS35 ....8 C2
Whiting Rd BS13 ....79 A4
Whitland Ave BS13 ....79 B5
Whitland Rd BS13 ....79 B5
WHITLEY BATTS 97 F2
Whitley Cl BS37 ....27 C3
Whitley Mead BS34.......36 E3
Whitling St BS40 ....95 A2
Whitmead Gdns BS13.....79 C4
Whitmore Ave BS4........65 A3
Whitson Ho 1 BS2 ...... 143 C3
Whitson St BS1......... 143 A4
Whitting Rd BS23........104 E4
Whittington Dr BS22.......88 D2
Whittington Rd BS16.......51 C6
Whittock Rd BS14 ....80 D6
Whittock Sq BS14 ....80 D7
Whittucks Cl BS15 ....65 D4
Whittucks Rd BS15 ....65 C4
Whitwell Rd BS14 ....80 B8
Whytes Cl BS9............49 A8
WICK 67 D6
Wick CE Prim Sch
BS30....................67 B6
Wick Cres BS4............64 D3
Wick Ct BS24.............89 B1
Wickets The
Bristol, Filton BS7 ....35 F1
Bristol, Upper Soundwell
BS15...................51 D2
Wicketts The BS7 ....35 F2
Wickfield BS21 ....57 E1
Wickham Cl BS37.........40 D8
Wickham Ct
Bristol BS16..............50 D5
Clevedon BS21............57 E3
Wickham Glen BS16 ......50 D5
Wickham Hill BS16 ....50 D5
Wickham Theatre*
BS8 .... 142 C3
Wickham View BS16 ......50 D4
Wick House Cl BS31 ......82 D3
Wick La
Lympsham BS24 ....121 E1
Peasedown St John BA2,
BA3...................116 F1
Pensford BS39.............97 D3
Upton Cheyney BS30.......67 A2
WICKLANE 117 A1
Wicklow Rd BS4..........79 E8
Wick Rd
Bishop Sutton BS39...... 113 C3
Bristol BS4...............64 D4
Lympsham BS24 .... 121 D2
Pilning BS35 ....22 C7
Wick St L BS22 ....89 B7
Wick Rdbt BS16 ....38 A2
WICK ST LAWRENCE 89 B7
WICKWAR 18 B5
Wickwar Rd
Kingswood GL12 ....11 E4
Rangeworthy BS37 ....17 B1
Yate BS37 ....28 B5
Wick Wick Cl BS16,
BS36....................38 A2
WIDCOMBE 102 C4
Widcombe BS14 ....80 A6
Widcombe CE Jun Sch
BA2...................102 B5
Widcombe Cl 3 BS5......65 A7
Widcombe Cres BA2.....102 B5
Widcombe Hill BA2..... 102 C4
Widcombe Inf Sch
BA2 ....102 B5
Widcombe Par BA2..... 141 C1
Widcombe Rise BA2.....102 B5
Widcombe Terr BA2......102 B5
Widmore Gr BS13.........79 B5
Wight Row BS20..........45 F6
Wigmore Gdns BS22......88 D2
Wigton Cres BS10 ....35 C2
Wilbye Gr BS4............79 D7
Wilcox Cl BS15 ....65 C6
Wildcountry La BS48......77 E6
Wildcroft Ho BS9..........49 B4
Wildcroft Rd BS9 ....49 B4
Wilder Ct BS2 ....143 B4
Wilder St BS2 ....143 B4
Willada Cl BS3 ....63 B2
William Daw Cl BS29 ....106 F3
William Herschel Mus*
BA1 ....141 B2
William Mason Cl 19
BS5.....................64 B7
Williams Cl BS30 ....65 F3
Williamson Rd BS7 ....49 F3
William St
Bath BA2 .... 141 C3
Bristol, Fishponds BS16 ....51 B3
8 Bristol, Moorfields
BS5....................64 C8
Bristol, Newton BS2 ....64 A6
Bristol, St Pauls BS2 ....49 F1
Bristol, Totterdown BS3.....63 F4
Bristol, Windmill Hill BS3....63 E4
Williamstowe BA2...... 102 C1
Willinton Rd BS4 ....79 F8
Willis Rd BS15............51 F2
Willmott Cres BS23.......104 F3
Willment Way BS11.......33 D1
Willmott Cl BS14 ....79 F3
Willoughby Cl
Alveston BS35 ....15 A4
Bristol BS13..............79 B7
Willoughby Rd BS7 ....49 E5
Willow Bank BS10 ....49 C7
Willow Bed Cl BS16.......51 B6
Willow Cl
Bath BA2 ....118 E8
Bristol, Patchway BS34.....35 E7
Bristol, Warmley BS30......66 D6
Charfield GL12............11 A4
Clevedon BS21............57 G3
Long Ashton BS41..........61 F1
Portishead BS20 ....45 C4
Radstock BA3 ....133 E2
Weston-S-M, St Georges
BS22...................89 D2
Weston-S-M, Uphill
BS23..................104 E2
Wick BS30...............67 B6
Willow Ct BS7 ....50 A7
Willowdown BS22 ....88 E4
Willow Dr
Bleadon BS24 .... 122 C6
Hutton BS24 .... 105 E2
Weston-S-M BS24 ....105 E5
Willowfalls The BA1 ......85 E3
Willow Gdns BS22 ....89 D2
Willow Gn BA2 .... 101 D4
Willow Gr 1 BS16 ....51 C2
Willow Ho BS13 ....79 D4
Willow Rd BS15 ....65 C3
Willow Sh Ctr The
BS16....................51 E6
Willows The
Bristol, Bradley Stoke
BS32...................36 D8
Bristol BS16..............51 E4
Bristol, Frenchay BS16 .....37 B1
Frampton Cotterell BS36....38 F7
Keynsham BS31...........81 E6
Nailsea BS48.............59 F3
Yate BS37 ....27 D2
Willow The BA3..........138 F2
Willow Way BS36 ....38 C6
Willow Wlk
Bristol BS10..............35 B3
Keynsham BS31...........81 D4
WILLSBRIDGE 66 B1
Willsbridge Hill BS30 .....66 A2
Willsbridge Ho BS30......66 A2
Willsbridge Mill*
BS30 ....66 B2
Wills Dr BS5 ....64 A8
Wills Way BS4............79 D6
Willway St BS3 ....63 D4
WILMINGTON 100 A1
Wilmot Ct BS30...........66 A6
Wilmots Way BS20........47 D4
Wilshire Ave BS15 ....65 D5
Wilson Pl BS2 .... 143 C4
Wilson St BS2 .... 143 C4
Wilton Cl BS10 ....35 C1
Wilton Ct BS23 .... 104 D7
Wilton Gdns BS23 ...... 104 D7
Wiltons BS40.............92 D2
Wiltshire Ave BS37 ....28 A3
Wiltshire Pl BS15.........51 E3
Wiltshire Way BA1........85 A2
Wilverley Ind Est BS4.....64 E1
Wimbledon Rd BS6.......49 C5
Wimblestone Rd
BS25...................107 F2
Wimborne Rd BS3 ....63 C1
Winash Cl BS14...........80 D7
Wincanton Cl
Bristol BS16..............37 F1
Nailsea BS48.............60 B1
Winchcombe Cl BS48.....76 A8
Winchcombe Gr BS11.....47 F5
Winchcombe Rd BS36 ....38 B8
Winchester Ave BS4 ......64 D3
Winchester Ct BS16.......50 E6
Winchester Rd
5 Bath BA2 .... 101 D5
Bristol BS4...............64 D3
Wincombe Trad Est
BS2.....................64 A4
Wincroft BS30............66 C4
Windcliff Cres BS11.......47 E7
Windermere Ave
BS23...................104 F4
Windermere Rd BS34 .....36 A8
Windermere Way
BS30....................66 D6
Windmill Bsns Pk
BS21....................73 E8
Windmill Cl BS3 ....63 E4
Windmill Farm Bsns Ctr
BS3.....................63 D4
WINDMILL HILL 63 E3
Windmill Hill
Bristol BS3...............63 D3
Hutton BS24 .... 106 A2
Windmill La BS10.........34 D3
Windmill Rd BS21 ....73 E8
Windrush Cl BA2 ....100 F4
Windrush Ct BS35 ....15 C8
Windrush Gn BS31........82 A4
Windrush Rd BS31........82 A4
Windscreens Ave BS2.....64 A7
Windsor Ave
Bristol BS5...............65 B6
Keynsham BS31...........81 E4
Windsor Bridge Rd BA1,
BA2 .... 101 D7
Windsor Castle BA1 .... 101 D7
Windsor Cl
Bristol BS34..............36 E4
Clevedon BS21............57 F2
Windsor Cres BS10 ....34 C4
Windsor Ct
4 Bath BA1 .... 101 C7
14 Bristol, Clifton BS8......62 F6
Bristol, Downend BS16 .....51 E7
Wick BS30...............67 C7
Windsor Dr
Nailsea BS48.............59 E2
Yate BS37 ....27 D2
Windsor Gr 20 BS5.......64 B8
Windsor Pl
5 Bath BA1 .... 101 C7
Bristol, Clifton BS8 ....62 F6
Bristol, Mangotsfield
BS16...................52 A5
Windsor Rd
Bristol, Longwell Green
BS30...................65 F2
Bristol, Montpelier BS6.....49 E2
Weston-S-M BS22 ....88 C2
Windsor Terr
Bristol, Clifton BS8 ....62 F6
Bristol, Windmill Hill BS3....63 F4
Paulton BS39............132 E5
Windsor Villas 3
BA1 .... 101 C7
Windwhistle Circ
BS23...................104 F4
Windwhistle La BS23 ....104 E3
Windwhistle Prim Sch
BS23...................104 F3
Windwhistle Rd BS23 ... 104 D3
Windyridge BS16 ....51 E4
Wineberry Cl BS5.........50 D1
Wine St
Bath BA1 .... 141 C2
Bristol BS1............. 143 A3
Winfield Rd BS30 ....66 C7
WINFORD 94 F7
Winford Bsns Pk BS40 ....95 D4
Winford CE Prim Sch
BS40....................94 F7
Winford Cl BS20 ....45 E4

Winford Ct BS6.............49 A5
Winford Gr BS13.........79 A8
Winford La BS41...........78 C1
Winford Rd BS40..........95 F3
Winford Terr BS41........78 C5
Wingard Cl BS23........104 D2
Wingard Ct BS8...........51 A5
Wingfield Rd BS3.........63 E2
Winifred's La BA1.........84 E1
Winkworth Pl 4 BS2.....49 F1
Winnowing End BS25....108 A3
Winsbury View BA2........99 B1
Winsbury Way BS32.......24 D1
WINSCOMBE 124 F7
Winscombe Dro
  Shipham BS25.........125 D6
  Winscombe BS25.......125 A5
Winscombe Hill BS25...124 F5
Winscombe Rd BS23.....105 A7
Winscombe Woodborough
  Prim Sch BS25.........125 A8
Winsford La 2 BS5......64 A8
Winsham Cl BS14.........80 B5
WINSLEY 120 D7
Winsley CE Prim Sch
  BA15....................120 F7
Winsley Hill BA2.........120 B6
Winsley Rd
  Bristol BS6..............49 D1
  Winsley BA15..........120 F7
Winsley Wlk 4 BS5......64 B6
Winstone Ct BS2........142 C3
WINTERBOURNE 37 F6
WINTERBOURNE DOWN
  ....37 F4
Winterbourne Hill
  BS36......................37 D5
Winterbourne Rd BS34...36 E6
Winterfield Cl BS39....132 E4
Winterfield Pk BS39....132 E4
Winterfield Rd BS39....132 E5
WINTERHEAD 125 D8
Winters La BS40..........93 D6
Winterstoke Cl 6 BS3...63 B2
Winterstoke Commercial
  Ctr BS23...............105 A6
Winterstoke Ctr 1
  BS3.......................63 B2
Winterstoke Ho 1
  BS3.......................63 A3
Winterstoke Rd
  Bristol BS3..............63 A2
  Weston-S-M BS23,
  BS24...................105 B4
Winterstoke Underpass
  BS8.......................62 F4
Wint Hill BS29...........107 B2
Winton St BS2.............63 F4
Wisemans Ho BS8.........64 A2
Wishford Mews BA3......133 C2
Wisley Wlk BS22.........105 F7
Wistaria Ave BS37........28 A1
Wisteria Ave BS24......105 D2
Witchell Rd BS5...........64 C7
Witch Hazel Rd BS13.....79 F3
Witcombe BS37...........39 C7
Witcombe Cl BS15........51 F1
Witham Rd BS31...........82 A3
Witherlies Rd BS16.......50 F6
Withey Cl E
  Bristol BS9..............48 F6
  Stoke Bishop BS9......48 F6
Withey Cl W BS9.........48 F5
Witheys The BS14.........80 C4
Withies La BA3...........139 A8
Withies Pk BA3..........138 F8
Withington Cl BS30.......66 C2
Withleigh Rd BS4.........64 B2
Withy Cl BS48.............59 F3
WITHYDITCH 117 C3
Withyditch La BA2.......117 C4
Withymead Rd SN14......70 A8
WITHY MILLS 133 A7
Withypool Gdns BS14.....80 B5
Withys The BS20..........47 D4
WITHYWOOD 79 A4
Withywood Com Sch
  BS13......................79 A5
Withywood Gdns 1
  BS13......................78 F4
Withywood Rd BS13......78 F4
Witney Cl BS31...........82 D3
Witney Mead BS36........38 B8
Woburn Cl BS30...........65 F5
Woburn Rd BS5...........50 B3
Wolferton Rd BS7........49 F2
Wolfridge Gdns BS10....35 A4
Wolfridge La BS10........35 A4
Wolfridge Ride BS35.....14 F4
Wolseley Rd BS7.........49 D3
Wolvershill Ind Units
  BS29.....................106 C6
Wolvershill Pk BS29....107 A3
Wolvershill Rd BS29....106 E6
WONDERSTONE 122 D6
Woodacre BS20............47 E4
Woodbine Rd BS5.........64 D8
WOODBOROUGH 125 A8
Woodborough Cres
  BS25.....................125 A8
Woodborough Ct
  BS25.....................125 A8
*borough Dr
  ....125 A8

Woodborough Hill Cotts
  BA2.....................134 C4
Woodborough La
  BA3.....................134 A4
Woodborough Rd
  Radstock BA3.........134 A3
  Winscombe BS25......124 F8
Woodborough St BS5.....50 B1
Woodbridge Rd BS4......64 A2
Woodbury La BS8.........49 A2
Woodchester
  Bristol BS15............51 E3
  Yate BS37................39 E2
Woodchester Rd BS10....49 C7
Woodcliff Ave BS22.......88 C1
Woodcliff Rd BS22........88 C1
Woodcote BS15............65 D6
Woodcote Rd BS16.......51 B3
Woodcote Wlk BS16......51 B2
Woodcroft BS39.........113 C3
Woodcroft Ave BS5.......50 D1
Woodcroft Cl BS4........64 E4
Woodcroft Rd BS4........64 E4
Wooddene BS25..........125 A8
Woodend BS15............65 D6
Woodend La BS35..........2 E1
Woodend Rd BS36........37 E5
Wood End Wlk BS9........48 C6
Woodfield Cl BS6.........49 B2
WOODFORD 4 A4
Woodford Cl BS48........60 A1
Woodford Ct 2 BS23...104 E5
Woodgrove Rd BS10......34 D2
Woodhall Cl BS16.........51 F6
WOODHILL 45 D7
Woodhill BS49.............91 E6
Woodhill Ave BS20.......45 D6
Woodhill Cl BS20..........45 D6
Wood Hill Pk BS20........45 D7
Woodhill Rd BS20........45 D6
Woodhill Views BS48.....59 F3
Woodhouse Ave BS32....24 D7
Woodhouse Cl BS32.......24 D6
WOODHOUSE DOWN 24 D7
Woodhouse Gr BS7........49 E6
Woodhouse Rd BA2.....101 A6
Woodhurst Rd BS23.....105 A7
Woodington Ct 1
  BS30.....................65 F4
Woodington Rd BS21....57 E1
Wood Kilns The BS49....74 A1
Wood La
  Axbridge BS26........125 D2
  Clapton in G BS20......59 E8
  Horton BS37.............19 A1
  Weston-S-M BS23......87 F1
Woodland Ave BS15......51 D2
Woodland Cl
  Bristol BS15............51 C1
  Failand BS8.............61 B4
Woodland Cotts BA2...120 D6
Woodland Ct
  Bristol BS9..............48 C3
  Bristol, Tyndall's Park
  BS8.....................142 C4
Woodland Glade BS21....57 G5
Woodland Gr
  Bath, Bushey Norwood
  BA2.....................102 E5
  Bath, Weston Park BA1...84 C1
  Bristol BS9..............48 D6
Woodland Pl 2 BA2....102 D5
Woodland Rd
  Bristol BS8.............142 C4
  Leyhill GL12.............10 B4
  Nailsea BS48.............59 E3
  Weston-S-M BS23.....104 D4
Woodlands
  Axbridge BS26........125 D2
  Bristol BS9..............48 E3
  Bristol, Downend BS16..51 E6
  Bristol, Patchway BS32..24 D3
  Tytherington GL12......16 B6
  Weston-S-M BS23......87 D1
Woodlands Ct
  Bristol, Patchway BS32..24 B3
  Bristol, Shirehampton
  BS11.....................47 E5
Woodlands Dr BA2.....120 B6
Woodlands La
  Bristol BS32.............24 C3
  Woodhouse Down BS32..24 E5
Woodlands Pk
  Bath BA1................85 C2
  Bristol BS32.............24 C3
Woodlands Rd
  Charfield GL12...........11 A4
  Clevedon BS21..........57 E4
  Portishead BS20........45 D8
  Tytherington GL12......16 B6
Woodlands Rise BS16....51 D6
Woodlands The BA2....116 F3
Woodland Terr
  Bristol, Kingswood
  BS15.....................65 E7
  Bristol, Redland BS6....49 B2
Woodland Way
  Bristol BS15............51 C2
  Failand BS8..............61 B4
Woodleaze BS9...........48 B6
Woodleigh BS35...........8 C1
Woodleigh Gdns BS14...80 C6
Woodmancote BS37......39 D8
Woodmancote Rd 7
  BS6.......................49 B2
Woodmans Cl BS37.......40 B8
Woodmans Rd BS37......40 C8
Woodmans Vale BS37...40 C8

Woodmarsh Cl BS14......80 A4
Woodmead Gdns BS13...79 C4
Woodmead La BS30.......54 A1
Woodmill BS49............74 A1
Woodnook The BS10.....35 C2
Woodpecker Ave BA3...139 B8
Woodpecker Cres
  BS16......................53 C4
Woodpecker Dr BS22...105 E8
Wood Rd BS15............65 D8
Woods Hill BA2..........120 A6
Woodside
  Bristol BS9..............48 D3
  Midsomer Norton BA3..132 E1
Woodside Ave BA3......105 B2
Woodside Ct BS23......105 A8
Woodside Gdns BS20....44 E5
Woodside Gr BS10........34 D3
Woodside Rd
  Bristol, Downend BS16...51 C7
  Bristol, Kingswood BS15..65 C7
  Bristol, St Anne's Park
  BS4.....................64 E6
  Clevedon BS21..........57 G5
  Frampton Cotterell BS36..38 C4
Woodspring Ave BS22....88 A3
Woodspring Cres BS22...88 A3
Woodspring Priory*
  BS22......................71 C1
Wood St
  Bath BA1................141 B2
  Bath, Beechen Cliff BA2..141 B1
  Bristol BS5...............50 B2
WOODSTOCK 65 F7
Woodstock Ave BS6......49 C1
Woodstock Cl BS15......65 F8
Woodstock Rd
  Bristol, Kingswood
  BS15.....................65 F7
  Bristol, Redland BS6....49 C2
  Weston-S-M BS22.....105 B8
  Woodstock Sch BS10...34 E2
Woodview
  Chilcompton BA3......138 E5
  2 Clevedon BS21.......57 H3
  High Littleton BS39...115 D1
  Paulton BS39...........132 C5
Woodview Cl BS11.......47 E7
Woodview Cotts BS35..132 B7
Woodview Dr BS49.......92 B8
Woodview Terr
  Bath BA2.................100 F6
  Nailsea BS48.............59 F2
  Weston-S-M BS23......105 A8
Woodward Ave BS37.....27 B1
Woodward Dr BS30.......65 F4
Woodwell Rd BS11.......47 E5
Woodyleaze Dr BS15.....65 D6
Wookey Cl BS48..........75 F8
Woolcot St BS6...........49 B2
WOOLCOTT PARK 49 B1
Wooler Rd BS23..........104 E8
WOOLLARD 98 A6
Woollard La
  Bristol BS14, BS39......98 A2
  Whitchurch BS14........80 E1
WOOLLEY 84 F5
Woolley La BA1...........85 A4
Woolley Rd BS14.........80 E5
Woolvers Way BS24....106 B6
WOOLVERTON 137 C1
Wootton Cres BS4........64 E6
Wootton Pk BS14, BS4...64 B1
Wootton Rd BS4..........64 F6
Worcester Bldgs BA1....85 B2
Worcester Cl
  Bristol BS16.............51 B2
  Peasedown St John
  BA2.....................134 D7
Worcester Cres BS8.....142 A4
Worcester Gdns BS48....75 C8
Worcester Pk BA1.........85 B2
Worcester Pl BA1.........85 B2
Worcester Rd
  Bristol BS8.............142 A4
  Bristol, Kingswood BS15..51 D1
Worcester Terr
  Bath BA1.................85 B2
  Bristol BS8.............142 A4
Wordsworth Ho BS34....36 A8
Wordsworth Rd
  Bristol BS7...............50 B7
  Clevedon BS21..........57 E2
  Weston-S-M BS23......105 A3
Workshop Rd BS11.......33 C4
Worldsend La BS37........2 E1
World's End La BS31.....82 C5
WORLE 88 F2
WORLEBURY 88 A2
Worlebury CE Fst Sch
  BS22......................88 B3
Worlebury Cl BS22.......88 B3
Worlebury Hill Rd BS22,
  BS23......................88 B2
Worlebury Park Rd
  BS22......................88 A2
Worle Com Sch BS22....88 E1
Worle Ct BS22.............88 F3
Worle Ind Est BS22.......89 B2
Worle Moor Rd BS24...105 E7
Worle Sta BS22...........89 B1
Wormcliff La SN13.......86 F3
Worrall Mews 8 BS8....49 A2
Worrall Pl 11 BS8........49 A2
Worrall Rd BS8...........49 A2
Worrel's La BS16, BS36...37 D3
Worsley St BS5............64 D7
Worthing Rd BS34........35 F8

Worthings The BS24....122 B1
Worthy Cl BS15............65 F6
Worthy Cres BS24......122 B1
Worthy La 2 BS1.........7 B3
Worthy Pl 4 BS23......104 E8
Worthy Rd BS11...........33 D7
Worthys The BS34........37 A6
Wotton Rd
  Charfield GL12............11 B5
  Iron Acton BS37..........26 F5
  Kingswood GL12.........11 F5
Wrangle Farm Gn
  BS21......................57 G2
WRANGLE THE 129 A5
Wrangle The 5 BS24...105 E7
WRAXALL 60 C3
Wraxall CE Prim Sch
  BS48......................60 B4
Wraxall Gr BS13.........79 A8
Wraxall Hill BS48........60 C3
Wraxall Rd BS30..........66 A6
Wrenbert Rd BS16........51 D5
Wren Cl
  Bristol BS16.............50 E7
  Weston-S-M BS22.....105 D8
Wren Dr BS16.............51 A6
Wright Way BS16.........50 E8
WRINGTON 92 E1
Wrington CE Prim Sch
  BS40......................92 E2
Wrington Cl BS34.........36 C7
Wrington Cres BS13......79 A7
Wrington Hill BS40.......92 F5
Wrington La BS49........91 E5
Wrington Mead BS49....91 E5
Wrington Rd BS49........91 F4
WRITHLINGTON 134 C2
Writhlington Sch BA2...134 C2
Writhlington Sch
  BA3.....................134 C1
Wroughton Dr BS13......79 D4
Wroughton Gdns BS13...79 D4
Wroxham Dr BS34........36 C8
Wyatt Ave BS13...........78 F5
Wyatt Cl BS13.............78 F5
Wyatt's Cl BS48...........59 D2
Watts View BS4...........64 E6
Wychwood BS15...........65 E6
Wyck Beck Rd BS10......35 A3
Wycliffe Rd BS9...........49 B7
Wycliffe Row 9 BS3......63 F4
Wycombe Gr BS4.........64 D2
Wye Croft Cl BS10........35 D3
Wye Ct BS35...............15 C8
Wyedale Ave BS9.........48 C7
Wykis Ct BS15.............65 E5
Wyllie Ct BS22............89 A5
Wymbush Cres BS13.....79 C5
Wymbush Gdns BS13....79 C5
Wyndam Ct BS2..........143 B4
Wyndham Cres
  Bristol BS4...............65 A3
  Easton-in-G BS20........47 B4
Wyndham Way BS20.....45 E5
Wyndham Way Ret Pk
  BS20......................45 D5
Wynstones The BS15....65 C7
Wynter Cl BS22............89 A3
Wyvern Cl BS23..........104 F7
Wyvern Com Sch
  BS23.....................104 F7
Wyvern Mews 6
  BS23.....................104 F7
Wyvern Villas BS9........49 A8

Y

Yadley Cl BS25..........125 A7
Yadley La BS25..........125 A6
Yadley Way BS25.......125 A7
Yanel La BS25............108 B5
Yanleigh Cl BS13.........78 D6
YANLEY 78 C8
Yanley La BS41, BS13...78 C7
Yarbury Way BS24.......89 B1
Yard The BS2..............50 A3
Yarrow Ct BS22...........89 A5
YATE 27 C1
Yate Her Ctr* BS37......27 E2
Yate Rd BS37..............26 F3
YATE ROCKS 27 F7
Yate Rocks BS37..........27 F7
Yate Sta BS37.............27 C2
YATTON 91 C8
Yatton CE Jun Sch
  BS49......................91 C8
Yatton Cl BS13............78 F8
Yatton Inf Sch BS49.....91 C8
Yatton Sta BS49..........74 A1
Yeaman's Ho BS1.......143 B1
Yeates Ct BS21............57 G3
Yeatman Cl BS39.......113 D4
Yelverton Rd BS4.........64 E1
Yeo Bank La BS21........72 F1
Yeo Cl BS23...............105 A5
Yeo Ct
  Clevedon BS21..........57 E2
  Congresbury BS49......91 D4
Yeo La BS41...............61 F1
Yeolands Dr BS21........57 D1
Yeomans Cl BS9..........48 D5
Yeomanside Cl BS14....80 C5
Yeomans Orch BS40.....92 E3
Yeomead BS48............59 F3
Yeomeads BS41...........61 F1
Yeo Moor BS21............57 G2

Yeo Moor Inf Sch
  BS21......................57 G2
Yeo Moor Jun Sch
  BS21......................57 G2
Yeo Valley Way BS48....60 B2
Yeoward Rd BS21.........57 G1
Yeo Way BS21.............57 D2
Yewcroft Cl BS14.........80 A4
Yewtree Batch BS40.....94 A3
Yew Tree Cl
  Bishop Sutton BS39....113 D4
  Lower Langford BS40....109 E6
  Nailsea BS48.............59 C3
Yew Tree Cotts BS40...110 E3
Yew Tree Ct BS14........80 B5
Yew Tree Dr
  Bristol BS15.............51 F3
  Weston-S-M BS22.....106 B8
Yew Tree Gdns
  Nailsea BS48.............59 C3
  Pill BS20..................47 C4
  Sandford BS25.........108 A4
Yew Tree La
  Compton Martin BS40..129 A7
  Kingston Seymour BS21..73 B1
Yew Tree Pk BS49........91 D3
Yomede Pk BA1..........101 A7
York Ave BS7...............49 F4
York Bldgs
  Bath BA1................141 B3
  Bristol BS3...............63 E4
York Cl
  Bristol, Bromley Heath
  BS16......................37 F1
  Bristol, Stoke Gifford
  BS34......................36 D4
  Weston-S-M BS22.......89 A4
  Yate BS37.................27 E4
York Ct BS2..............143 B4
York Gdns
  Bristol BS8...............62 F6
  Winterbourne BS36......37 F8
York Ho BS8..............142 A3
York Pl
  Bath BA1................102 B8
  Bristol, Brandon Hill
  BS1.....................142 C2
  Bristol, Victoria Park
  BS8.....................142 B3
York Rd
  Bristol BS2.............143 C1
  Bristol, Lower Easton
  BS5.....................50 C1
  Bristol, Montpelier BS6..49 E1
  Bristol, Staple Hill BS16..51 E4
  Bristol, Windmill Hill BS3..63 E4
York St
  Bath BA1................141 C2
  Bristol, Baptist Mills BS2..50 A2
  Bristol BS3.............143 B4
  2 Bristol, Clifton BS8...49 A2
  Bristol, Redfield BS5....64 C7
  Weston-S-M BS23......104 D7
Youngs Ct BS16...........52 B8
Youngwood La BS48.....75 D7

Z

Zetland Rd BS6...........49 D2
Zig Zag BS21..............57 F4
Zinc Rd BS11..............33 C3
Zion Hill BA3.............138 B7
Zone The 7 BS5..........65 A8

Addresses

Name and Address	Telephone	Page	Grid reference